Echoes of Eden

RABBI ARI D. KAHN

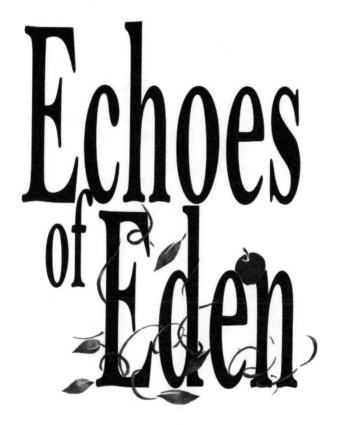

Echoes of Eden

Sefer Bereishit

ME'OREI HA'AISH • FIRE AND FLAME
INSIGHTS INTO THE WEEKLY TORAH PORTION

OU**PRESS**

gefen פן
publishing house בית הוצאה לאור
JERUSALEM • NEW YORK Est. 1981

Cover Design: S. Kim Glassman
Typesetting: David Yehoshua

ISBN: 978-965-229-499-9

3 5 7 9 8 6 4 2 1

Gefen Publishing House Ltd.
6 Hatzvi Street
Jerusalem 94386, Israel
972-2-538-0247
orders@gefenpublishing.com

Gefen Books
11 Edison Place
Springfield, NJ 07081
1-800-477-5257
orders@gefenpublishing.com

OU Press
an imprint of the Orthodox Union
11 Broadway
New York, NY 10004
www.oupress.org
oupress@ou.org

www.gefenpublishing.com

Printed in Israel   *Send for our free catalogue*

Library of Congress Cataloging-in-Publication Data

Kahn, Ari D.
Me'orei ha'Aish, fire and flame: insights into the weekly Torah portion / Ari D. Kahn.
p. cm. — (Me'orei ha'Aish fire and flame; v. 1)

ISBN 978-965-229-499-9

1. Bible. O.T. Pentateuch—Commentaries. I. Title.

BS1225.53.K338 2011   •   222'.107--dc23   •   2011022049

This volume is dedicated in honor of

Al Gindi

אברהם ניסם בן אסתר ויצחק גינדי

*May the Torah learned by those
who read it bring merit to him and his entire family.
May Al continue to lead and inspire his community
for many years to come,
in good health and happiness.*

Table of Contents

Foreword

OU Press is proud to be the co-publisher, together with Gefen Publishing House, of *Echoes of Eden*, Rabbi Ari Kahn's essays on the book of Bereishit.

Known to our sages as *Sefer Hayetzirah*, the Book of Creation, Bereishit begins with the cosmic drama of the creation of the universe. Creation, however, is not only the opening episode, but is the theme that unifies the entire book. Woven throughout are the beginnings of human civilization and culture, the initial stirrings of man's relationship with God, and the formative stages of the nascent Jewish nation. To characterize the biblical narrative as a history of beginnings, however, is to ignore its richness and the depth of its message. Our sages say, "*ma'aseh avot siman le-banim.*" The record recounted in the Torah concerning our biblical ancestors – the travail and triumph, spiritual quest and divine response, family discord and reconciliation – is possessed of a dimension far more profound than a mere retelling of the past. All of these occurrences are a *siman*, an adumbration, of the fate and destiny of the Jewish nation far in the future. The events of the book of Bereishit contain within them the seed of the future.

A similar concept is expressed by Ramban in his commentary on Parashat Bereishit. On the phrase "*asher bara Elokim la'asot,*" Ramban asks why the word "*la'asot,*" which has the connotation of the future tense, is used. Shouldn't the Torah have used the word "*ve'asa,*" which is the past tense? Shouldn't the phrase have referred to God resting from all the creative work that He *did*, rather than referring to His resting from the creative work He *will do*? Ramban answers that, in fact, contained within the six days of creation was the potential for all future history. According to Ramban, each day of creation consisted not simply of one day, but represented one thousand years, consistent with the tradition that the world was created to exist for a total of six thousand years before the advent of the messianic era. Perhaps we can understand Ramban's approach more generally and conceptually, that each day of creation represented an entire epoch, so that the six days of creation represent all of history that has occurred and that will occur until the ultimate redemption. The reason the Torah uses the word "*la'asot*" is that within the six days of creation, God created also the potential for the entire future. "*La'asot*" describes not only the past, but also the potential for the future that is embedded within the past.

Rabbi Ari Kahn, a distinguished scholar and educator, is director of Foreign Student Programs and a senior lecturer in Jewish studies at Bar-Ilan University. He received his ordination from Yeshiva University's Rabbi Isaac Elchanan Theological Seminary where he was a student of "the Rav," Rabbi Joseph Soloveitchik. Rabbi Kahn possesses his own spark of creativity, which is readily apparent in this book. Culling material and ideas from an extraordinarily wide range of sources, many of them seldom cited in the more conventional studies of *Chumash*, he has presented us with a series of strikingly original interpretive essays distinguished by their novel approach and thought-provoking conclusions. Each chapter in itself is a gem, and taken together they are a *tour de force* of innovative *parshanut*. Rabbi Kahn has rendered a great service to us all by using his creative sensibility to help unlock the potential of profound Torah knowledge contained in the book of Bereishit.

Our thanks also go to Mr. Raymond Gindi for his generous support in the publication of this edition.

Menachem Genack

General Editor
OU Press

Preface

The essays in this book are based on lectures delivered in Matan, Yeshivat Aish Hatorah, Bar Ilan University and in various *shiurim* in the community of Givat Ze'ev. Over the past few years, the dissemination of these lectures has grown, as they were recorded, transcribed and posted on various websites. Often, in my visits to Jewish communities around the world, I have been pleasantly surprised to find eager students who are familiar with my *shiurim* and have put time and effort into studying and learning the ideas that were shared in this way.

I would like to thank all of these readers and listeners for encouraging me, for asking questions that led me to sharpen and reexamine my own ideas and for being a receptive audience. The feedback and encouragement I have received has been humbling. I have little doubt that the Torah I have been privileged to teach was inspired by the merit of these students. They alone are to be credited with the special *siyatta diShmaya* granted to those who learn with the intention to teach.

This volume is the first of a projected five-part series on the five books of the Torah. Ideas that were presented in seminal form in lectures are given more in-depth treatment in print, and sources are cited. The objective is to give the reader an encompassing view of the topic. The footnotes introduce parallel and related ideas for those who wish to delve deeper, essentially turning this volume into a study guide for a richer learning experience.

Methods and ideas that I culled from my teachers have been reformulated and expressed in a manner that contemporary students can readily appreciate. The profound impact of *mori v'rabbi* Rabbi Yosef Dov Soloveitchik, זצוק״ל, should be obvious to all readers, both when he is cited and when I attempt to apply the methodology I learned at his feet.

I would like to thank Rabbi Menachem Genack and Rabbi Gil Student of the OU Press for their encouragement, and for choosing this work to be part of the exciting mission of the Orthodox Union to further impact the world with the beauty and wealth of Jewish ideas. I would also like to thank the staff at Gefen books – Ilan Greenfield, Michael Fischberger, Smadar Belilty, Tziporah Levine, Ita Olesker and Kezia Pride – who have magically and professionally turned a manuscript into a book. Thanks also to S. Kim Glassman for the artwork that turned an idea into a picture.

As with the previous works I have published, it is my profound honor to thank my parents, Rabbi Dr. Pinchas and Rivka Kahn, who have raised me to appreciate and love Torah. Their contribution can be felt throughout the book. May they enjoy many years of health and happiness and much *nachat* from all their children, grandchildren and great-grandchildren.

It is with sadness that I note that since my last book was published, my father-in-law, Moshe Chaim Linder, and my mother-in-law, Bernice Linder, have passed on to the world of truth. They took much pleasure in my writings and teachings; I know they would have taken great pleasure in this volume as well. May their souls soar to the highest echelon of heaven, and may the Torah taught here be a merit to them and their memory.

Many friends and colleagues have encouraged me to publish these essays. Special thanks go to Raymond and Elizabeth Gindi, without whose support this volume would not have come to fruition. May God grant them many years of health, happiness and success. May they have much *nachat* from their parents, children and grandchildren, and continue to be a source of inspiration.

Special thanks are also extended to our friends Mitch and Joleen Julis, who have assured that the next volume, on Sefer Shmot, will be printed. May God grant them health, happiness and success, and *nachat* from their children. May they continue to inspire us for many years to come.

I also wish to thank the Manricks family, Avraham, Sarah and their son Gavriel, who have dedicated themselves to the dissemination of my *divrei Torah*. May God answer their prayers, and grant them much health, happiness, success and *nachat* from their children.

Special thanks to Alyta Pitaru, whose constant efforts have allowed me to spend time writing. May she and her family be blessed with much health, happiness and *nachat*.

The process of turning *Torah Shebe'al Peh* into *Torah Shebikhtav* is not an easy one. My writing was honed by the editing and sharp eye of my wife, Naomi. This volume is truly a joint effort; her skill and sensitivity are manifest in literally every line of this book. May the Torah learned from these pages be of merit to our other "joint efforts," and may God watch over and protect our children. May all the members of our family, who have been blessed in so many ways, continue to enjoy God's tremendous *hesed.* May our children all continue in the path of Torah, and may we continue to share, in health and happiness, many more years and many more volumes of Torah.

Ari Kahn

Givat Ze'ev
8 Adar Sheini 5771

Parashat Bereishit

In Search of the Serpent

As Creation unfolds, God creates a variety of species and presents them to Adam, who in turn gives them names. The curious partnership thus forged between the all-powerful and infinite God and finite man will continue to unfold until the end of time. Adam is endowed with numerous gifts; he is animated by the breath of God and is created in God's image. The power of speech that he has been given is used to give names to all the animals, indicating man's additional ability to conceptualize and categorize.

בראשית ב:יט-כ

וַיִּצֶר ה' אֱלֹקִים מִן הָאֲדָמָה כָּל חַיַּת הַשָּׂדֶה וְאֵת כָּל עוֹף הַשָּׁמַיִם וַיָּבֵא אֶל הָאָדָם לִרְאוֹת מַה יִּקְרָא לוֹ וְכֹל אֲשֶׁר יִקְרָא לוֹ הָאָדָם נֶפֶשׁ חַיָּה הוּא שְׁמוֹ: וַיִּקְרָא הָאָדָם שֵׁמוֹת לְכָל הַבְּהֵמָה וּלְעוֹף הַשָּׁמַיִם וּלְכֹל חַיַּת הַשָּׂדֶה...

God Almighty formed from the earth all animals of the field and all birds of the sky, and brought them to Adam to see what he would call them, and whatever man called the living creatures is their name. Adam gave names to all the animals and birds of heaven and animals of the field... (Bereishit 2:19–20)

But man is lonely. In a strange juxtaposition, the same verse in which Adam named the animals also states that he was alone. Apparently, Adam was seeking something, and the verse tells us what it was that he did not find: an appropriate partner.[1]

---

1. Rashi (2:20) notes that God showed him the animals, male and female; upon seeing that each species had a mate Adam sensed his own loneliness. Also see Rashi's comments on 2:18, for a theological consideration.

   רש"י, בראשית ב:כ

   ולאדם לא מצא עזר ויפל ה' אלקים תרדמה: כשהביאן הביאן לפניו כל מין ומין זכר ונקבה, אמר לכלם יש בן זוג ולי אין בן זוג, מיד ויפל.

   רש"י, בראשית ב:יח

   לא טוב היות וגו': שלא יאמרו שתי רשויות הן הקב"ה יחיד בעליונים ואין לו זוג, וזה יחיד בתחתונים ואין לו זוג.

בראשית ב:כ

‫...וּלְאָדָם לֹא מָצָא עֵזֶר כְּנֶגְדּוֹ:‬

...and the man did not find a helpmate. (Bereishit 2:20)

And yet, this comes as no surprise to the reader. God Himself notes and comments upon Adam's solitary state in the preceding verse:

בראשית ב:יח

‫וַיֹּאמֶר ה' אֱלֹקִים לֹא טוֹב הֱיוֹת הָאָדָם לְבַדּוֹ אֶעֱשֶׂה לּוֹ עֵזֶר כְּנֶגְדּוֹ:‬

God Almighty said, "It is not good that man is alone; I will make for him a helpmate." (Bereishit 2:18)

We might be tempted to describe the topic of Adam's loneliness as having been interrupted in the narrative by the naming of the animals, but this textual curiosity leads to some rather unconventional insights.[2] The reader is left with the impression that Adam may have sought a solution for his dilemma among the animals. Rashi (commenting on a later verse) reports that Adam did, in fact, seek a mate among the animals but did not find an appropriate match.[3] All of Creation was new and unexplored. Boundaries

---

2. Many of the textual oddities pointed out in this essay were noted by my teacher Rabbi Yosef Soloveitchik. See *Family Redeemed: Essays on Family Relationships*, MeOtzar HoRav Series (New York: Toras HoRav Foundation, 2000), 3–30.

3. Rashi (Bereishit 2:23), based on Talmud Bavli Yevamot 63a, says that Adam was intimate with all the animals. The Alshikh (*Torat Moshe* 2:19–20) says that this should not be taken literally; rather, Adam entertained these possibilities in his imagination and not in practice. Maharal (in *Be'er haGolah*, fifth *be'er*) also insists on a nonliteral approach to this teaching.

רש"י, בראשית פרק ב:כג

‫זאת הפעם: מלמד שבא אדם על כל בהמה וחיה ולא נתקררה דעתו בהם עד שבא על חוה.‬

תלמוד בבלי, מסכת יבמות דף סג עמוד א

‫ואמר רבי אלעזר, מאי דכתיב (שם) "זאת הפעם עצם מעצמי ובשר משבשרי", מלמד שבא אדם על כל בהמה וחיה, ולא נתקררה דעתו עד שבא על חוה.‬

ספר תורת משה, בראשית ב:יט–כ

‫והנה אמרו רבותינו ז"ל (יבמות סג.) מלמד שבא אדם על כל בהמה וחיה ולא נתקררה דעתו כו', כי הנה גם שאין הדבר כפשוטו, כי אם שבא בשפיטת שכלו.‬

ספר באר הגולה, הבאר החמישי

‫פרק הבא על יבמתו (יבמות סג.) אמר ר' אליעזר מאי דכתיב זאת הפעם עצם מעצמי מלמד שבא אדם על כל בהמה חיה ועוף ולא נתקררה דעתו עד שבא אל חוה ע"כ. ואין הפי' חלילה שבא עליהם למשכב, שהרי‬

were not yet clearly defined or fully grasped. Adam sought to classify and become familiar, to understand and empathize. Through this process, he understood what we now take for granted: the lines were solidified, the boundaries drawn. Similarities were explored, and the significance of the differences between the species was brought into focus.[4]

Aside from the "newness" of the world, there may be another factor that made this seemingly irrelevant tangent of naming the animals a necessary element in the development of the narrative. Homo sapiens clearly have much in common with the animal kingdom, though man would like to believe that the similarity is limited to certain aspects of physiology.

When man is created the Torah describes the new creature as follows:

בראשית א:כז

וַיִּבְרָא אֱלֹקִים אֶת הָאָדָם בְּצַלְמוֹ בְּצֶלֶם אֱלֹקִים בָּרָא אֹתוֹ זָכָר וּנְקֵבָה בָּרָא אֹתָם:

The Almighty created Adam in His image, in the image of the Almighty he was created, male and female they were created. (Bereishit 1:27)

Man is created in the image of the Almighty, and man is male and female. Neither of these statements is easily understood. What does it mean to be "in the image of the Almighty"? Furthermore, if Hava (Eve) is introduced later in the narrative, what does the reference at this juncture to "male and female" imply? What is it about this creation that is "male and female"?

הקב"ה כבר צוה אותו על העריות ב ויצו כמו שפרשו חכמים (סנהדרין נו:) רק פירושו מפני שהאדם הוא צורת כל המינים והוא נותן להם שלימות, וכל צורה הוא מתחבר לאשר הוא לו צורה.

4. Rabbi Pinhas Eliyahu Horowitz of Vilna (*Sefer haBrit*, part 2, chapter 12) goes so far as to say that anyone who takes this passage literally is a "fool."

ספר הברית, חלק ב מאמר יב: "דרך הקודש", פרק ה

אפס יש ויש הרבה מאמרים בדברי חז"ל אף בעניני דעלמא מה גם בכבוד ה' והבורא יתברך שאינם חייבים עליהם להפשיטם מן הנגלות והפשוטה תיכף ומיד ולאמר שלא כוונו בהם רק לאיזה סוד ושם בסתר או דבר חכמה גנוזה אשר הסתירו תחת לשונם, כמו מה שאמרו (בפרק הבא על יבמתו) בא אדם הראשון על כל בהמה וחיה ולא נתקררה דעתו עד שבא על חוה וכדומה לזה למרבה, וכל המתאמץ לקיימן כפשוטן לא די במה שנאמר עליו פתי יאמין לכל דבר אבל ראוי הוא שיאמר עליו מעקש שפתיו הוא כסיל כי משפיל כבוד חכמים מאד בזה וכסיל אדם בוזה עמו וחכמי ישראל הקדמונים במה שמתאמץ לפרש כפשוטו דברים העומדים ברומו של עולם וספוני טמוני חכמות גדולות אשר הסתירו באותן הדברים ולא כוונו לדברים החיצוניים ההם כלל.

In the second chapter, Adam is reintroduced, with some striking differences. The second chapter describes the "formation" of man, as opposed to the "creation" described in the first chapter. The two terms are far from synonymous: creation implies something totally new, ex nihilo, from nothingness. The second chapter describes the formation of man from preexisting matter:

בראשית ב:ז

וַיִּיצֶר ה' אֱלֹקִים אֶת הָאָדָם עָפָר מִן הָאֲדָמָה וַיִּפַּח בְּאַפָּיו נִשְׁמַת חַיִּים וַיְהִי הָאָדָם לְנֶפֶשׁ חַיָּה:

God Almighty formed the man [Adam] from the dust of the earth and blew in his nostrils the breath of life, and the man became a living soul. (Bereishit 2:7)

Instead of "creation from nothing," man is formed out of the earth. This form is then given a divine spirit. Man is a hybrid, composed of earthly and divine stuff.[5]

This two-stage creation described in the second chapter is perplexing. Whereas the first chapter told of a male and female, in the second chapter the female is nowhere to be found. Whereas the first chapter describes ex nihilo creation, the second chapter tells a seemingly different story, a story of formation, of shaping physical material and imbuing it with a divine breath.

It is possible to reconcile these differences with a very literal reading of the text: God did indeed create man (and woman) as He created everything else – ex nihilo. Yet unlike all the other creations, God perfected this particular one at a subsequent stage, with the additional act that separated man from the rest of creation: God took this (previously created) man and breathed into him a divine breath – gave him a soul. It is this man, this more perfect, more elevated version of the earlier creation, that is estranged from all of creation.

---

5. Eloquently described by the Baalei haTosafot, Bereishit 2:7: "The soul is from above and the body from below."

פירוש בעלי התוספות, בראשית ב:ז

ויפח באפיו נשמת חיים: ברא האדם הנשמה מן העליונים והגוף מן התחתונים.

The act of naming the animals is, in a sense, Adam's declaration of independence from the animal world. Yet the moment Adam actively engages the divine breath with which he is imbued, a spiritual void is created. Adam is no longer satisfied with an instinctual,[6] pedestrian existence. He seeks existence of a higher order; he seeks meaning. By imbuing this being with a soul, God lifted him above all the other creatures He had created – including the earlier version of man, the unelevated, soulless men and women who peopled the created universe. This new Adam is unable to find an appropriate mate within the existing framework. Adam experiences a spiritual crisis when he studies and classifies the animal world, and comes to the realization that the other humanoids are no less primitive: although they, too, are created in the image of the Almighty, and are endowed with great capabilities, they lack the "breath of God" that he has been given. They lack souls. He understands that it will be impossible for him to find a mate for himself among them. There are no others who possess a soul, and Adam is existentially, though not physically, alone.

God intervenes: Adam is presented with Hava. Though forged from his own body, the more salient aspect of their relationship is that she is – literally – Adam's soul mate. The physical unity, both in terms of their origin and the subsequent consummation of their reunion, is seen as a physical expression of their spiritual identity; they are one, and they are unique in that they possess a soul. It is one soul, divided between the male and female bodies God forms for them. The mate that God forms for Adam is, like him, shaped from pre-existing material, but endowed with so much more.

While the suggestion that there were other humanoids with whom Adam felt no spiritual or existential kinship may seem antinomian, at odds with mainstream rabbinic doctrine, we are taught that the Torah's truth exists

---

6. See *haKtav v'haKabbalah*, Bereishit 2:19.

הכתב והקבלה, בראשית ב:יט

וזהו ולאדם לא מצא עזר כנגדו, ולזה כיונו באמרם שבא אדם על כל בהמה וחיה ולא נתקררה דעתו בהם, והמכוון במקרא, אם בבעלי חיים אלו שהובאו לפניו ימצא האדם אחד מהם שראוי לקרותו בשם, נפש חיה, ר"ל בעל חי שיש לו בחירה חפשית ורצונית...כן ישאר שמו עליו, ותהיה לו לעזר כי יהיה דומה בדמה, כי גם הוא נקרא בשם נפש חיה, לבחירה חפשית ורצונית שיש לו, כמבואר (לעיל ב:ז), ויהי האדם לנפש חיה, וכאשר לא מצא בהם אחד שראוי לקרותו כן, אמר ולאדם לא מצא עזר.

on many levels, and the text of the Torah may be legitimately understood in many ways.[7] In fact there are rabbinic teachings that may only be understood in light of this suggestion.[8] As we shall see, many rabbinic authorities, including the Rambam, were of the opinion that there were "animals in human shape and form," devoid of the soul that set Adam apart, lacking that divine breath that Adam and Hava shared between them.

---

7. The rabbis say there are seventy faces to the Torah; see Bamidbar Rabbah 13:15–16. Other rabbinic sources attribute different numbers of facets or faces to the Torah. Apparently, this very teaching regarding the variety and multiplicity of layers of the Torah's meanings is, itself, subject to this same variety.

במדבר רבה פרשת נשא, פרשה יג

כשם שיין חשבונו שבעים כך יש שבעים פנים בתורה.

ויקרא רבה (מרגליות) פרשת אמור, פרשה כו

ר' יוסי ממלחייא ור' יהושע דסכנין בשם ר' לוי: תינוקות שהיו בימי דוד עד שלא טעמו טעם חטא היו יודעין לדרוש את התורה ארבעים ותשע פנים טמא וארבעים ותשע פנים טהור.

פסיקתא רבתי (איש שלום) פסקא יד – פרה

א"ר יוחנן בן פזי: שהתורה נדרשת ארבעים ותשע פנים.

8. Regarding the permissibility of interpreting verses in a manner that seems to contradict accepted rabbinic tradition – in nonlegal areas – see Ohr haHayim, Bereishit 1:1, Vayikra 19:3; the commentary of Rav Shmuel Shtarshun, *Rashash al Shabbat* 70b; Rav Yom Tov Heller, found in *Tosafot Yom Tov*, commentary to Nazir 5:5; Rav Asher Weiss, *Minhat Asher*, Sefer Devarim, page 181.

אור החיים, בראשית א:א

דע כי רשות נתונה לנו לפרש משמעות הכתובים בנתיבות העיון ויישוב הדעת הגם שקדמונו ראשונים ויישבו באופן אחר, כי שבעים פנים לתורה (במד"ר נשא יג:טז), ואין אנו מוזהרים שלא לנטות מדברי הראשונים אלא בפירושים שישתנה הדין לפיהן, ולזה תמצא שהאמוראים אין כח בהם לחלוק על התנאים במשפטי ה', אבל ביישוב הכתובים ובמשמעות מצינו להם בכמה מקומות שיפרשו באופן אחר.

אור החיים, ויקרא יט:ג

ובדרך הזה מצינו לרבותינו ז"ל שדרשו בכמה מקומות, והן אמת אם לא היה הדין יוצא מדרך זה, הייתי יכול לפרש הכתוב כדברינו שכבר הרשות נתונה לנו לפרש הכתוב, הגם שיהיה בסדר אחר משונה מדברי הראשונים כל שאין הדין משתנה.

רש"ש, תלמוד בבלי, מסכת שבת דף ע עמוד ב

גמרא ושמואל אחת שהיא הנה כו' למ"ל. הן גם לר"נ ע"כ למ"ל מדיליף מלא תבערו א"כ ס"ל לשמואל בהא כר"נ, ובדרשה דל"ת ס"ל כר"י ומה שחדש דרשה דמחלליה כו' דלא כחד אינו קושיא כיון דהדין דחילוק מלאכות אמת ומקובל יוכל אמורא להסמיכו על מקרא חדש אשר לא שערוהו התנאים כמו בפק"נ שדוחה אה"ש (ביומא פ"ה) ובפרי עץ הדר דהוא אתרוג (בסוכה לה) וכן בכ"מ ובזה לא נצטרך לדה"ת בכאן אך לכאורה סתירה למש"כ (מב"מ ס"א) דפריך שם והא תנא נאמר קאמר ופירש"י והיכי פליג אמורא אתנא כו' ע"ש אבל יל"פ דל"ק שם רק כיון דתנא יליף מגז"ש ואין אדם דן ג"ש אא"כ קבלה מרבו הל"מ א"כ ע"כ מפשטיה דקרא לא שמעינן ליה ודו"ק שם.

When Adam and Hava are introduced, it is love at first sight:

בראשית ב:כג–כד

וַיֹּאמֶר הָאָדָם זֹאת הַפַּעַם עֶצֶם מֵעֲצָמַי וּבָשָׂר מִבְּשָׂרִי לְזֹאת יִקָּרֵא אִשָּׁה כִּי מֵאִישׁ לֻקֳחָה זֹאת: עַל כֵּן יַעֲזָב אִישׁ אֶת אָבִיו וְאֶת אִמּוֹ וְדָבַק בְּאִשְׁתּוֹ וְהָיוּ לְבָשָׂר אֶחָד:

Adam said, "This time the bones are of my bones and the flesh of my flesh; this one will be called woman for she was taken from man." Therefore a man shall leave his father and mother and cling to his wife, and they shall be of one flesh.[9] (Bereishit 2:23–24)

Despite their physical and spiritual unity, Adam and Hava each possess a unique personality. Each represents a unique aspect of the soul with which they are imbued. Aside from their gender, there is a major difference between them: Adam has had experiences that Hava has not shared. Adam has already explored the animal kingdom thoroughly, and has gained insight into the differences between the species and a firm grasp of his own place within the larger framework of Creation. Adam has acquainted himself thoroughly with the world, has attempted to live as one with the

---

9. It is unclear who makes this declaration; according to the conventional understanding that Adam is the only humanoid on the planet, this would be a very curious statement for him to make, therefore some commentaries suggest that it is God who makes this declaration. See Rashi's comments. Others believe that it is the continuation of Adam's statement; see *Toldot Yitzhak*. Yet others say that it was added later when the Torah was written, but was not part of Adam's soliloquy; see Radak who cites this opinion, but settles on Adam as the speaker.

רש"י, בראשית ב:כד
על כן יעזב איש: רוח הקודש אומרת כן, לאסור על בני נח את העריות.

תולדות יצחק, בראשית ב:כד
על כן יעזב איש את אביו ואת אמו וגו': טעם על כן, לפי שאמר זאת הפעם עצם מעצמי ובשר מבשרי, אמר מאחר שאשתי בשרי היא, כל אשה היא כאלו היא אמי חוה ואני כאלו הוא אדם הראשון אם כן ראוי הוא שיעזוב את אביו ואת אמו ודבק באשתו, לפי שאשתו היא בשרו, אבל האב אינו בשר הבן, וראוי שיעזוב למי שאינו בשרו וידבק בבשרו.

רד"ק, בראשית ב:כד
על כן יעזב איש: יש מפרשים כי זה ה דברי אדם, והנכון כי אדם אמרו, ויידע כי יוליד בנים כי לכך נברא להוליד הוא ומינו בעולם כשאר ב"ח. ופשט הכתוב קרוב לתרגומו כי לא אמר שיעזב איש אביו ואמו בעבור אשתו שלא יעבדם ויכבדם כפי כחו, אלא אמר כי דין הוא כי יעזב איש את אביו ואת אמו שגדל עמהם עד שנשא אשה ויעזבם מלדור עמהם ודבק באשתו וידור עמה בבית עמה אחד.

other creatures, and has found that life shallow and unfulfilling. Hava is less experienced, more innocent. She does not share Adam's knowledge of the boundaries between the various orders of creation. Therefore, she is more easily led astray by the first slick paramour that entices her.

Adam immediately grasps the nature of their relationship, because he has seen more and experienced more. But what was Hava's reaction to meeting Adam? The text is silent. Hava does not speak, but her actions tell us more than words: Adam and Hava are joined. They are intimate, joined physically, and their union is a totally natural coming together of body and soul:

בראשית ב:כה

וַיִּהְיוּ שְׁנֵיהֶם עֲרוּמִּים הָאָדָם וְאִשְׁתּוֹ וְלֹא יִתְבֹּשָׁשׁוּ:

The two of them were naked, man and his wife, and they were not embarrassed. (Bereishit 2:25)

They knew one another, to the exclusion of everything else in creation – but they were not alone. In fact, one of the other creatures spied upon them from a distance, and he was jealous; he had designs on Hava.[10] The Serpent was a walking, talking, upright creature, capable of sophisticated communication, of manipulative speech, of advanced planning and tactical maneuvering, of posing and arguing. Although we tend to imagine the "Serpent" as a "serpent," we should keep in mind that the creature who seduced Hava

---

10. Rashi 3:1, based on Bereishit Rabbah 18:6.

רש"י, בראשית ג:א

...אלא למדך מאיזו עילה קפץ הנחש עליהם, ראה אותם ערומים ועוסקים בתשמיש לעין כל ונתאוה לה.

בראשית רבה, פרשה יח פסקה ו

והנחש היה ערום: לא היה צריך קרא לומר, אלא ויעש ה' אלקים לאדם ולאשתו וגו'. אמר ר' יהושע בן קרחה: להודיעך מאי זו חטייה קפץ עליהם אותו הרשע, מתוך שראה אותן מתעסקין בדרך ארץ ונתאוה לה. "...and they were not ashamed. Now the serpent was more subtle, etc.': Now surely Scripture should have stated, 'And the Almighty God made for Adam and his wife garments of skin' (Bereishit 3:21) [immediately after the former verse]? Said R. Yehoshua b. Korhah: It teaches you through what sin that wicked creature inveigled them – because he saw them engaged in their natural functions, he [the serpent] conceived a passion for her."

assumed its lowly, legless, slithering form only as a result of its sin.[11] At the point at which the Serpent presents himself and his seductive arguments to Hava, this "proto-serpent" had far more in common with Adam and Hava than we might care to imagine.[12] Perhaps this walking, talking Serpent is best described as a soulless humanoid. Because he, too, was created in the image of the Almighty, the Serpent possessed great capabilities of speech and reasoning, but he uses these gifts as weapons of destruction in order to satisfy his own desire.

Hava is the object of his desire, and he intends to be rid of Adam in order to have her for his own.[13] The Serpent uses cunning speech – truthful, yet deceptive – to deliver a message that seems to pass through Hava to Adam. The Serpent attacks the very idea of the limitations set forth by God:

---

11. The serpent was cursed that it would crawl on its belly (Bereishit 3:14). Rashi infers that it had legs which were amputated.

רש"י, בראשית ג:יד

על גחונך תלך: רגלים היו לו ונקצצו.

12. See Yalkut Shimoni, Yeshayahu, chapter 65, *remez* 509, where God is cited as saying to the serpent, "I created you to stand on two feet like man…but you wanted to kill him in order to marry Hava." See also Bereishit Rabbah 19:1.

ילקוט שמעוני ישעיהו, פרק סה רמז תקט

אמר ר' לוי: לעתיד לבא הכל מתרפאין, חוץ מן הנחש וגבעוני. נחש מנין ונחש עפר לחמו, גבעוני מנין והעובד העיר יעבדוהו מכל שבטיי ישראל. ור' יוסי בר' חנינא בשם ר' ירמיה בר אבא: אמר לו הקב"ה לנחש אני עשיתיך שתהא מלך על כל בהמה וחיה ואתה לא בקשת ארור אתה מכל הבהמה, אני עשיתיך שתהא מהלך <u>קוממיות כאדם</u> ולא בקשת על גחונך תלך, אני עשיתיך שתהא אוכל מאכל כאדם ולא בקשת ועפר תאכל כל ימי חייך, אתה בקשת להרוג את אדם ולישא את חוה ואיבה אשית בינך ובין האשה, הוי מה שבקשת לא נתן לו ומה שבידיך נטול הימנו, וכן אתה מוצא בקין וקרח ובלעם ודואג ואחיתופל וגחזי ואבשלום ואדוניה ועוזיה והמן מה שבקשו לא נתן להם ומה שבידם נטול מהם.

בראשית רבה, פרשה יט פסקה א

ערום מכל: ארור מכל. רבי הושעיא רבה אמר: דקרטיס היה עומד כקנה ורגלים היו לו. רבי ירמיה בן אלעזר אמר: אפיקורס היה.

"'Now the serpent was more subtle than any beast of the field': R. Hoshaya the Elder said: He stood out distinguished [erect] like a reed, and he had feet. R. Yirmiyah b. Elazar said: He was an unbeliever."

13. Rashi 3:15.

רש"י, בראשית ג:טו

ואיבה אשית: אתה לא נתכוונת אלא שימות אדם כשיאכל הוא תחלה ותשא את חוה, ולא באת לדבר אל חוה תחלה אלא לפי שהנשים קלות להתפתות ויודעות לפתות את בעליהן, לפיכך ואיבה אשית.

בראשית ג:א

וְהַנָּחָשׁ הָיָה עָרוּם מִכֹּל חַיַּת הַשָּׂדֶה אֲשֶׁר עָשָׂה ה' אֱלֹקִים וַיֹּאמֶר אֶל הָאִשָּׁה אַף
כִּי אָמַר אֱלֹקִים לֹא תֹאכְלוּ מִכֹּל עֵץ הַגָּן:

*The serpent was more devious than all the animals of the field that
were made by God Almighty, and he said to the woman, "For the
Almighty has said not to eat of every tree of the garden." (Bereishit
3:1)*

In the Serpent's mind, limits are deleterious; they run counter to his
instinctual sensibilities. In truth, God had allowed man to enjoy every tree
with the exception of the *one* tree that would bring death into the world.
It is this limit that the Serpent abhors: if man cannot have everything,
he essentially has nothing. The very fact that there is a limitation – even
one that protects man from death – drives the Serpent's desire. There
is one other limitation that haunts him, another object of his desire –
the only woman who is off-limits to him, the one and only woman
in all of creation who was married, in a ceremony performed by God
and attended by the angels. This one woman that he cannot have is the
one he lusts for.

When the Serpent has Hava's ear, he presses on with a curiously male-
oriented seduction; he speaks of power:

בראשית ג:ה

כִּי יֹדֵעַ אֱלֹקִים כִּי בְּיוֹם אֲכָלְכֶם מִמֶּנּוּ וְנִפְקְחוּ עֵינֵיכֶם וִהְיִיתֶם כֵּאלֹקִים יֹדְעֵי
טוֹב וָרָע:

*For the Almighty knows that on the day you eat from it your eyes
will be opened and you will be like a deity, knowing good and evil.
(Bereishit 3:5)*

The promise was power, but this is not what speaks to Hava. Her reaction
resonates with desire of a totally different sort:

בראשית ג:ו

וַתֵּרֶא הָאִשָּׁה כִּי טוֹב הָעֵץ לְמַאֲכָל וְכִי תַאֲוָה הוּא לָעֵינַיִם וְנֶחְמָד הָעֵץ לְהַשְׂכִּיל
וַתִּקַּח מִפִּרְיוֹ וַתֹּאכַל וַתִּתֵּן גַּם לְאִישָׁהּ עִמָּהּ וַיֹּאכַל:

*The woman saw that the tree was good to eat and lustful to the eye,
and pleasant to learn; she took of its fruit and ate, and she gave also
to her husband and he ate.* (Bereishit 3:6)

When the Serpent speaks of power,[14] Hava seems strangely indifferent;
indeed, someone interested in power would not immediately share it.[15]
Hava is enticed by the aesthetics, by the beauty. Her reaction is not greed
for power but lust for beauty and experience.

As is their wont, our sages look into the words that are said, but also learn
from the silences in the text. In the Midrash, they examine the roots of
Hava's lust by noting that one important character was absent during most
of this episode. Where was Adam? The rabbis have an interesting answer:
he was sleeping.

בראשית רבה, פרשה יט:ג

ותאמר האשה אל הנחש: והיכן היה אדם באותה שעה? אבא בר קורייה אמר:
נתעסק בדרך הארץ וישן לו.

*"And the woman said to the Serpent": Now where was Adam during
this conversation? Abba b. Koriah said: He had engaged in his
natural functions [i.e., intercourse] and then fallen asleep.* (Bereishit
Rabbah 19:3)

After they consummate their union, Adam falls into a satisfied slumber,
leaving the Serpent to work his wiles on Hava, who has been left alone,
aroused and unsatisfied. The Serpent speaks of power, but Hava responds
with lust. According to rabbinic literature, the Serpent took full advantage
of her vulnerability, and successfully seduced Hava.[16] The object of his
desire was won.

---

14. See Rabbi Yosef Soloveitchik, *Family Redeemed*, page 23.

15. Ibid., page 24.

16. See Talmud Bavli Shabbat 146a and Rashi's commentary.

מסכת שבת דף קמו עמוד א

שבשעה שבא נחש על חוה, הטיל בה זוהמא, ישראל – שעמדו על הר סיני, פסקה זוהמתן.

רש"י, מסכת שבת דף קמו עמוד א

כשבא נחש על חוה: כשנתן לה עצה לאכול מן העץ בא עליה, דכתיב (בראשית ג) הנחש השיאני לשון
נשואין.

As in so many cases, we may gain great insight into the sin by carefully examining the lessons of the punishment. Rabbi Yosef Dov Soloveitchik explained that God does not punish indiscriminately; there is always a correlation between the sin and the punishment. In fact, it would be more appropriate to say that God does not "punish" as much as provide man with the spiritual antidote to effectuate the healing *(tikkun)* that man needs to be spiritually whole, to regain spiritual equilibrium. According to Rabbi Soloveitchik, Hava's sin was an attempt to have a meaningless "fling." She knew that Adam, and no other, was her soul mate, yet she followed the enticements of her own thirst for experiential satisfaction, to satisfy her own desire for esthetic enrichment. Therefore the "punishment" that she receives involves childbirth and emotional dependence. The lesson for Hava is that relationships have consequences – in a very physical way, but also on an emotional, spiritual plane. The meaningless "hookup" is at odds with the divine will as well as with her own spiritual identity.

From Adam's punishment – to work the land and find sustenance through the sweat of his brow – we may deduce that the Serpent's message was, indeed, communicated through Hava and internalized by Adam. The promise of power won Adam over; he did, indeed, wish to be a god. Adam's punishment/*tikkun* is to do what God Himself has done until this point in Bereishit – to work, to be creative.

The Serpent is deemed unredeemable. He may no longer share man's form or stature; the Serpent becomes a serpent, forced to crawl on the earth. His form is reduced to something that no longer reflects the divine image. His body now reflects the animal element alone, devoid of any higher element. He is brought down to the most elemental level – a creature of the earth alone, a strangely phallic symbol of lust devoid of spiritual or emotional connection.

But this is not the end of the story. There was a relationship between Hava and the Serpent – a relationship that, according to a number of rabbinic sources, bore fruit. There are those among our sages who taught that one of Hava's children was not fathered by Adam, rather the father was the Serpent.[17] That child's name was Kayin (Cain):

---

17. This idea is found in many sources. See Yalkut Shimoni, Parashat Bereishit, chapter 4,

זוהר, בראשית דף כח עמוד ב

וערב רב ודאי אינון הוו זוהמא דאטיל נחש בחוה. ומההיא זוהמא נפק קין
וקטל להבל רועה צאן.

*The mixed multitude are the impurity which the serpent injected
into Hava. From this impurity came forth Kayin, who killed Hevel
[Abel] the shepherd.* (Zohar, Bereishit 28b)[18]

Many rabbinic masters insist that these mystical sources should only be
understood as a commentary on the thematic relationship between the
behavior of Kayin and the behavior of the Serpent, to explain a spiritual

---

remez 35; Pirkei d'Rebbi Eliezer (edition of M. Higger, *Horeb* 8 [1944]), chapters 21–22.

ילקוט שמעוני, פרשת בראשית פרק ד רמז לה

אלא את ה' לשעבר אדם נברא מאדמה וחוה נבראת מאדם מכאן ואילך בצלמנו כדמותנו לא איש בלא
אשה ולא אשה בלא איש ולא שניהם בלא שכינה. בא עליה רוכב הנחש ועברה את קין ואחר כך בעלה
אדם ועברה את הבל שנאמר והאדם ידע את חוה אשתו מהו ידע ידע שהיתה מעוברת וראתה את דמותו
שלא היה מן התחתונים אלא מן העליונים והבינה ואמרה קניתי איש את ה'.

פרקי דרבי אליעזר, פרק כא

ומפרי העץ אשר בתוך הגן: תני ר' זעירא: ומפרי העץ אין העץ אלא אדם שנמשל לעץ שנ' כי האדם עץ
השדה. אשר בתוך הגן אין גן אלא אשה שנמשלה לגן שנ' גן נעול אחותי כלה. ואמר הגן ולא אמר אשה
תפש לשון נקיה מה הגינה הזאת כל מה שנזרעה צמחה ומוציאה כך האשה הזאת כל מה שנזרעה הרה
ויולדת בבעילה. בא אליה רוכב נחש ועברה את קין ואחר כך בא אליה אדם ועברה את הבל שנ' והאדם
ידע את חוה אשתו מה ידע ידע שהיתה מעוברת וראה את דמותו שלא היה מן התחתונים אלא מן העליונים
ואיתנביאת ואמרה קניתי איש לה'.

פרקי דרבי אליעזר, פרק כב

ויחי אדם מאה ושלשים שנה ויולד בדמותו כצלמו, מכאן אתה למד שלא היה קין לא מזרעו ולא מדמותו
ולא כצלמו של אדם, עד שנולד שת, והיה כדמותו וכצלמו, מכאן אתה למד שלא היה קין של אדם אביו,
שנ' ויולד כדמותו כצלמו. ר' שמעון אומר: משת עלו ונתייחסו כל הדורות של צדיקים ומקין עלו ונתייחסו
כל הדורות של רשעים המורדים והפושעים שמרדו בצורם ואמרו אין אנו צריכין לטיפת גשמיך ולא ללכת
בדרכיך, שנ' ויאמרו לאל סור ממנו.

18. This idea is found in many other places in the Zoharic literature. See Zohar, Shmot
231a; Vayikra 76b; Bereishit Hashmatot 253b; Zohar Hadash Megilot, Shir haShirim 6a;
Zohar Hadash Sitrei Otiot Bereishit 15b.
Zohar, Shmot 231a: "But when Adam and his wife sinned and the Serpent had intercourse
with Hava and injected into her his venom, she bore Kayin, whose image was in part
derived from on high and in part from the venom of the unclean and low side. Hence it
was the Serpent who brought death into the world, in that it was his side that was the cause
of it. It is the way of the serpent to lie in wait to slay, and thus the one that sprang from
him followed the same course. So Scripture says: 'And it came to pass when they were
in the field, that Kayin rose up against Hevel his brother, and slew him' (Bereishit 4:8)."

dynamic and not to be understood literally.[19] Whether the Zohar explains Kayin's murderous, jealous outburst by pointing to his actual, physical father, or only to his "spiritual father" is for the reader to decide. But if these sources are read literally, many more questions arise, and our neatly organized concepts of biblical man may require revision.

As we have noted, the Rambam himself believed that there were once humanoids, devoid of the "breath of God," walking this earth:

ספר מורה נבוכים, חלק א פרק ז

ובזאת השאלה נאמר באדם: "ויחי אדם שלושים ומאת שנה, ויולד בדמותו כצלמו", וכבר קדם לך ענין "צלם אדם ודמותו" מה הוא. וכל מי שקדמו לו מן הבנים לא הגיעה אליהם הצורה האנושית באמת, אשר היא "צלם אדם ודמותו", הנאמר עליה: "בצלם אלוקים ובדמותו". אמנם שת, כאשר לימדהו והבינהו ונמצא שלם השלמות האנושי, נאמר בו: "ויולד בדמותו כצלמו". וכבר ידעת, כי כל מי שלא הגיעה לו זאת הצורה, אשר בארנו ענינה, **הוא אינו איש, אבל בהמה על צורת איש ותבניתו, אבל יש לו יכולת על מיני ההזק וחידוש הרעות, מה שאין כן לשאר בעלי החיים**. כי השכל והמחשבה שהיו מוכנים להגיע השלמות אשר לא הגיע, ישתמש בהם במיני התחבולות המביאות לרע והולד הנזקים, כאילו הוא דבר ידמה לאדם או יחקהו. וכן היו בני אדם הקודמים לשת; ואמרו במדרש: "כל אותן מאה ושלושים שנה שהיה אדם נזוף בהן היה מוליד רוחות" – רצונם לומר: "שדים"; וכאשר רצהו האלוה, הוליד "בדמותו כצלמו" – והוא אמרו: "ויחי אדם שלושים ומאת שנה ויולד בדמותו כצלמו":

Those sons of Adam who were born before that time were not human in the true sense of the word. They did not possess "the form of the Almighty." With reference to Shet [Seth] who had been instructed, enlightened and brought to human perfection, it could rightly be said, "he [Adam] begat a son in his likeness, in his form." It is acknowledged that a man who does not possess this "form" (the nature of which has just been explained) **is not human, but a mere animal in human shape and form. Yet such a creature has the**

---

19. See Ramban, *Torat ha'Adam*, section 123.

ספר תורת האדם להרמב״ן, אות קכג שער הגמול

וכן אמר שהיה סמאל רוכב על הנחש, ואמרו שהיה עץ החיים צווח כשנגעה בו חוה אל תבואני רגל גאוה ויד רשעים אל תנידני, <u>הנה עשה בכאן הכל משל ורמז</u>....

power to cause harm and injury, a power that does not belong to other creatures. *For those gifts of intelligence and judgment with which he has been endowed for the purpose of acquiring perfection, but which he has failed to apply to their proper aim, are used by him for wicked and mischievous ends; he begets evil things, as though he merely resembled man, or simulated his outward appearance. Such was the condition of those sons of Adam who preceded Shet. In reference to this subject the Midrash says: "During the 130 years when Adam was under rebuke he begat spirits," i.e., demons; when, however, he was again restored to divine favor "he begat in his likeness, in his form." This is the meaning of the passage, "Adam lived one hundred thirty years, and he begat in his likeness, in his form"* (Bereishit 5:3). (Guide for the Perplexed 1:7)[20]

This "animal with human form" is a creature without the more perfected essence given to Adam and Hava, and even they, after their sin, did not pass down this soul to their offspring automatically. None of their descendants before Shet rose above the human form to achieve a more elevated existence, and many, many offspring of these soulless beings populated the earth. The description of the generation of the flood describes these powerful, humanoid brutes.

בראשית ו:א–ב

וַיְהִי כִּי הֵחֵל הָאָדָם לָרֹב עַל פְּנֵי הָאֲדָמָה וּבָנוֹת יֻלְּדוּ לָהֶם: וַיִּרְאוּ בְנֵי הָאֱלֹהִים אֶת בְּנוֹת הָאָדָם כִּי טֹבֹת הֵנָּה וַיִּקְחוּ לָהֶם נָשִׁים מִכֹּל אֲשֶׁר בָּחָרוּ:

And when man began to multiply on the face of the earth, and daughters were born to them, the sons of the powerful [or, those created in the form of the Almighty] saw that the daughters of men were attractive, and they took whatever women they chose. (Bereishit 6:1–2)

---

20. Emphasis added. All emphases throughout the book, in both Hebrew and English, are my own.

We sense two different classes or species: man – Adam and his children; and the powerful brutes who, like the Serpent, desired these women and "took them" by force.

When the flood came, all these "animals in human form," devoid of souls but formed in the divine image and graced with the power of speech, were wiped out. The world was cleansed[21] of them all – but for one exception, and herein lies the story of the family of Noah…[22]

---

21. See Rabbi Meir ibn Gabbai, *Avodat haKodesh*, part 4, chapter 14.

ספר עבודת הקודש, חלק ד פרק יד

ובמדרש רות הנעלם, (דף פג עמוד א) כד נפקו תולדין לעלמא מאדם וחוה מההוא זוהמא נפקו והכי שמענא מרבותי ואינון שמעו עד פומא דאליהו ז"ל דאמר הכי מאי דכתיב והאדם ידע את חוה אשתו ותהר ותלד את קין וגו'? והאדם דא אדם קדמאה דכד אתא נחש על חוה אטיל בה זוהמא וקין מההוא עסטורא דההוא זוהמא נפק. מה דרכו של נחש להרוג ולהמית הכי נמי קין מיד נעשה הורג כד"א כי משרש נחש יצא צפע, משרש נחש דא נחש הקדמוני, יצא צפע זה קין שיצא משרשו ועיקרו של נחש, ופריו שרף מעופף שנעשה הורג כשרף לחש למכתו מעופף כפול כבר נענש הנחש כפול במינו. ואי תימא דהא מההוא זוהמא נפק ואת אמרת והאדם ידע את חוה אשתו ותהר ותלד את קין ודאי מאדם הוה ולא מההוא זוהמא. אלא ההוא נחש הטיל זוהמא בחוה וההוא זוהמא דאשתאיב בה הוה מכשכשא במעהא ולא הוה ליה גופא לאתכללא ביה ולנפקא ההוא רוחא לעלמא. כיון שבא אדם הראשון אתער ההוא זוהמא בההוא זרע דהוה במעהא ואתכלל ביה ועבד גופא לההוא רוחא בישא ונפק לעלמא בדיוקנא סומקא שניא מכל שאר בני אדם דהוו אבתריה. ועוד דההוא זרעא דאטיל אדם למעבד גופא מההוא סטרא בישא הוה ואתתקף ההוא רוחא בישא ואיגלים ביה לעלמא, כיון דחמת חוה אמרה קניתי איש את ה' עם ה'. וכד איתי קרבנא מההוא סטרא בישא אייתי דכתיב ויהי מקץ ימים ולא כתיב מקץ ימין עד כאן.

הנה בארו כי קין בא מהזוהמא שהטיל רוכב נחש בחוה שבא עליה ממש. וכן דרשו ז"ל הנחש השיאני עשה בה מעשה אישות.... ולזה בא מסומן בסימן הרוח ההוא וקטרג על אחיו **והרגו וכל תולדותיו היו מהצד ההוא הטמא והקשה ולזה נמחו כלם במבול לא נשאר מזרע קין כי אם נעמה אשת נח לסוד נעלם**. ובבראשית רבה זה ספר תולדת אדם אלו תולדות ואין הראשונים תולדות ומה הן אלהות.

22. See below, "Parashat Noah: Na'amah."

Clothing of Light

In the aftermath of man's sin in Eden, Adam and Hava find themselves exposed, vulnerable, humiliated – naked.

בראשית ג:ז

וַתִּפָּקַחְנָה עֵינֵי שְׁנֵיהֶם וַיֵּדְעוּ כִּי עֵירֻמִּם הֵם...

And the eyes of them both were opened, and they knew[1] that they were naked...[2] (Bereishit 3:7)

In a feeble attempt to cover themselves they take fig leaves and fashion a primitive covering.

בראשית ג:ז

...וַיִּתְפְּרוּ עֲלֵה תְאֵנָה וַיַּעֲשׂוּ לָהֶם חֲגֹרֹת:

...And they sewed fig leaves together, and made themselves belts [possibly loincloths]. (Bereishit 3:7)

Their purpose was to cover up their nakedness. The choice of fig leaves has caused at least one rabbinic tradition to identify the Tree of Knowledge with the fig tree:[3] in a frantic attempt to cover up, they chose the material closest at hand.

Subsequently – after the investigation, trial, sentencing and punishment, we find the conclusion of the saga, and again their attire is addressed:

---

1. Presumably this "knowledge" was accrued by virtue of eating from the "Tree of Knowledge of Good and Evil."

2. While the verse seems unequivocal, two possibilities exist: only now they became aware of their nakedness, or alternatively (an admittedly more difficult reading) only now they *became* naked.

3. Talmud Brakhot 40a.

תלמוד בבלי, מסכת ברכות דף מ עמוד א

רבי נחמיה אומר: תאנה היתה, שבדבר שנתקלקלו בו נתקנו שנאמר ויתפרו עלה תאנה.

בראשית ג:כא

וַיַּעַשׂ ה' אֱלֹקִים לְאָדָם וּלְאִשְׁתּוֹ כָּתְנוֹת עוֹר וַיַּלְבִּשֵׁם:

And the Almighty God made for Adam and for his wife coats of skin, and clothed them. (Bereishit 3:21)

The difference is striking: Adam and Hava found flimsy fig leaves and fashioned a loincloth of sorts, whereas God provides fine leather coats to protect and provide shelter from the elements. While man only managed to cover up, God provided man with clothing. While man simply didn't want to be stark naked in public, God chose to act with kindness. Despite the sin and the resultant alienation, God acts with care and tenderness: He clothes them, He protects them; He takes care of wayward, sinful man.

We exist in a world of clothing and costumes, and it all began with a fig leaf. It was only by virtue of the bite taken from a mysterious, dangerous, deadly fruit that an awareness of nakedness was born. But what was the nature of this nakedness? Was it physical or spiritual? Was the awareness of their nakedness the result of a spiritual shift, of a metamorphosis that occurred in the aftermath of sin? Or was man altered in a more physical fashion?

We would have expected that sin would cause a spiritual reaction – but we see that Adam and Hava respond on the physical level. They cover up their bodies, which had become vulnerable; they become embarrassed, humiliated. But what of their souls? Did they seek spiritual cover? How does one cover up a tainted soul? Surely the soul was impacted, damaged and tainted by their sin. What was the reaction?

When discussing this point Rabbi Soloveitchik[4] introduced the following verse:

ישעיהו סא:י

שׂוֹשׂ אָשִׂישׂ בַּה' תָּגֵל נַפְשִׁי בֵּאלֹקַי כִּי הִלְבִּישַׁנִי בִּגְדֵי יֶשַׁע מְעִיל צְדָקָה יְעָטָנִי כֶּחָתָן יְכַהֵן פְּאֵר וְכַכַּלָּה תַּעְדֶּה כֵלֶיהָ:

---

4. Y.D. Soloveitchik, *Yemei Zikaron*, trans. Moshe Krone (Jerusalem: Orot Aliner Library, World Zionist Organization Department for Torah Education and Culture in the Diaspora, 1986), page 203.

I greatly rejoice in the Almighty, my soul rejoices in my God, for He has clothed me in the clothing of salvation, He has wrapped me in a robe of victory, like a bridegroom adorned with a turban and a bride bedecked with her finery. (Yeshayahu 61:10)

When Adam and Hava sin, they lose the clothing of salvation. The result is the loss of divine protection and the sense of proximity and intimacy with God, the feeling of a child wrapped in the embrace of a loving mother. It is then that they feel naked. Their response is to cover their bodies; apparently, they were oblivious to the damage done to their souls. In place of the "clothing of salvation" that had dissipated, they cover themselves, but God provides them with new clothing.

In partaking of the forbidden fruit, Adam and Hava succumb to their animal instincts, acting with no regard for their spiritual identity and seeking only immediate gratification. The spiritual consequences follow immediately: God clothes them in animal skins or leather, and this is no arbitrary choice. A metamorphosis has taken place; their new clothing reflects their diminished status. They have taken a step backward, closer to the animals.

What was the precise nature of this leather clothing?[5] Various traditions suggest different materials. Rashi[6] cites a tradition that it was warm, soft rabbit fur. The Targum Pseudo-Yonatan[7] says the leather came from

---

5. See the comments of the Ohr haHayim on Vayikra 19:26 regarding *orlah* – the commandment not to eat the fruits of a tree until it is three years old. This law is a *tikun* for Adam eating from the Tree of Knowledge too soon. The Zohar teaches that the Tree of Knowledge of Good and Evil was, in fact, a grape vine. Adam should have waited until nightfall of his first day of life – Friday night –and only then partaken of the fruit of the vine. This is the mystical explanation of the passage in the Talmud that says that Adam was "*mosheikh 'orlato*": Adam was born physically and spiritually perfect and therefore was born circumcised – but he pulled the foreskin back as if to "undo" his circumcision. This is a physical expression of Adam's breaking a covenant with God. After this breach, Adam receives "clothing of skin." Likewise, Hava was cursed with painful loss of virginity – which is also related to being covered with skin.

6. Rashi, Bereishit 3:21.

רש"י, בראשית ג:כא

ויש אומרים דבר הבא מן העור, כגון צמר הארנבים שהוא רך וחם ועשה להם כתנות ממנו.

7. Perhaps the snake shed its skin. Also found in Pirkei d'Rebbi Eliezer, chapter 20; see comments of the Rekanati to Bereishit 3:21.

something near at hand, from something found at the scene of their crime: God gave them garments of snake skin, as if to say: *The result of succumbing to the serpent's seduction is your nakedness, and now you will be wrapped in a fitting symbol of your treachery.*[8]

A third tradition may be found in the Midrash:

בראשית רבה, פרשה כ פסקה יב

ויעש ה' אלקים לאדם ולאשתו כתנות עור וילבישם: בתורתו של ר"מ מצאו כתוב "כתנות אור"; אלו בגדי אדם הראשון שהן דומים לפיגם (לפנס), רחבים מלמטה וצרין מלמעלה.

"And the Almighty God made for Adam and for his wife coats of skin, and clothed them": In R. Meir's Torah it was found written, "Garments of light (ohr)": this refers to Adam's garments, which were like a torch [shedding radiance], broad at the bottom and narrow at the top. (Bereishit Rabbah 20:12)

This comment is curious. Although the text of the Torah reads *'or* – עור, meaning *skin* or *leather*, the Midrash relates a tradition or commentary Rabbi Meir recorded in the margin[9] that rendered the word *ohr* – אור, meaning light. Why would God make clothing of light for them?

Rabbeinu Bahya admits that the *pshat* – the straightforward level of understanding the Torah – is that God made for wayward man "dignified clothing." However, according to Rabbeinu Bahya's understanding of the Midrash, this was clothing of light, referring specifically to primordial light, the light that was God's first act of creation, the light that predated the sun and moon. Rabbeinu Bahya explains that just as any clothing reflects the designer, this clothing, provided by God, must surely reflect the Divine. It was God's intention that the man He created live forever. Had he not eaten from the forbidden tree, man would have been immortal, like the angels.

---

8. The Hebrew word for clothing, בגד (*beged*), has the connotation of rebellion.

9. See *Torah Temimah*, Bereishit 3:31.

תורה תמימה הערות, בראשית ג הערה לא

ובמ"ר כאן איתא, בתורתו של ר' מאיר מצאו כתוב כתנות אור באל"ף, וכתבו המפרשים בתורתו של ר"מ – בחדושי תורה שלו, אבל לדעתי אין הלשון בתורתו מכוון לפי' זה, ויותר נראה לפרש שהי' מדרכו של ר"מ לעשות רמזים וחדושים קצרים בצדי הגליון מהספר שלמד בו.

Eating from the tree caused death, loss of immortality, but the new clothing was somehow angelic, possessing an element of what was lost.[10] By way of reference, Rabbeinu Bahya suggests that these garments are similar to what enveloped Moshe on Mount Sinai.[11] When Moshe descends from the mountain for the second time, the Torah describes the scene in singular detail:

שמות לד:כט–ל

וַיְהִי בְּרֶדֶת מֹשֶׁה מֵהַר סִינַי וּשְׁנֵי לֻחֹת הָעֵדֻת בְּיַד מֹשֶׁה בְּרִדְתּוֹ מִן הָהָר וּמֹשֶׁה לֹא יָדַע כִּי קָרַן[12] עוֹר פָּנָיו בְּדַבְּרוֹ אִתּוֹ: וַיַּרְא אַהֲרֹן וְכָל בְּנֵי יִשְׂרָאֵל אֶת מֹשֶׁה וְהִנֵּה קָרַן עוֹר פָּנָיו וַיִּירְאוּ מִגֶּשֶׁת אֵלָיו:

When Moshe came down from Mount Sinai with the two Tablets of the Testimony in his hands, he was not aware that his face was

---

10. Rabbeinu Bahya, Bereishit 3:21.

רבינו בחיי, בראשית ג:כא

וע"ד המדרש כתנות עור בתורתו של רבי מאיר היה כתוב כתנות אור והכוונה שהלבישם הקב"ה מיני מעלות ומאורות מן האור העליון שהיו בגן עדן כעין משה שזכה להן בהר. וממעלת המלביש תוכל ללמוד מעלת הלבוש כי הכוונה בהם לחיות לעולמים ולהיותם כמלאכי השרת.

11. Moshe remained on the mountain for forty days and nights; he neither ate nor drank during that time, achieving a demi-angelic status. See Avot d'Rabbi Natan, chapter 1.

אבות דרבי נתן פרק א

א"ר נתן: מפני מה נתעכב משה כל ששת ימים ולא שרה עליו דבור? בשביל שימרק מכל אכילה ושתיה שהיה במעיו עד שעה שנתקדש ויהא כמלאכי השרת.

12. קָרַן is a verb, translated as "glowed" or "radiated." The translation of this word as a verb is unmistakable, especially in combination with the two words that follow, קָרַן עוֹר פָּנָיו, "the skin of his face glowed." It is hard to understand how anyone could mistake the verb *karan* for the noun *keren* and claim that Moshe sprouted horns while he was up on the mountain, receiving the Torah. And yet, as is well known, various works of art have spread this misinterpretation, which is most likely based on a mistranslation of the text by Jerome in the Vulgate. On the other hand, a certain comment by Rashi in his commentary to Havakuk suggests that the light that Moshe radiated looked like rays of sun:

חבקוק ג:ד

וְנֹגַהּ כָּאוֹר תִּהְיֶה קַרְנַיִם מִיָּדוֹ לוֹ וְשָׁם חֶבְיוֹן עֻזֹּה:

"His splendor was like the sunrise; rays flashed from his hand, and there his power was hidden" (Havakuk 3:4).

רש"י, חבקוק ג:ד

כאור תהיה: כאור המיוחד של שבעת ימי בראשית היה וכן ת"י. קרנים: לשון מאור. כשהוא נוקב וזורח דרך הנקב נראה כמין קרנים בולטין וכן (שמות לד) כי קרן עור פניו.

This may offer some support for the artists' renditions of Moshe's "horns."

radiant because he had spoken with God. And Aharon and all the Israelites saw that Moshe's face was radiant, and they were afraid to come near him. (Shmot 34:29–30)

Here it clearly states that the skin on Moshe's face glowed: *'or* is spelled with an *ayin*.[13]

Rabbeinu Bahya is apparently suggesting that at times the words *'or* – "skin" (with an *ayin*) and *ohr* – "light" (with an *alef*) can be connected. This is the significance of Moshe's glowing skin.[14]

According to rabbinic tradition, when the Jews stood at Sinai and declared *na'aseh v'nishma*, "We will do and we will listen," each received two crowns; when they sinned with the Golden Calf, they lost those precious crowns. These hundreds of thousands of crowns all came to Moshe, causing him to radiate an incredible glow:

תלמוד בבלי, מסכת שבת דף פח עמוד א

דרש רבי סימלאי, בשעה שהקדימו ישראל "נעשה" ל"נשמע", באו ששים רבוא של מלאכי השרת. לכל אחד ואחד מישראל קשרו לו שתי כתרים, אחד כנגד "נעשה", ואחד כנגד "נשמע". וכיון שחטאו ישראל, ירדו מאה ועשרים רבוא מלאכי חבלה ופרקום.... אמר רב יוחנן, וכולן – זכה משה ונטלן.

R. Simlai lectured: When the Israelites gave precedence to "we will do" over "we will listen," six hundred thousand ministering angels came and set two crowns upon each Israelite, one as a reward for "we will do," and the other as a reward for "we will listen." But as soon as Israel sinned, one million two hundred thousand angels of

---

13. Despite the unequivocal status of the Torah text being written with an *ayin*, a surprisingly large number of commentators cite the text with an *alef*. I do not believe this indicates textual intrigue or doubt. Rather, I attribute it to peoples' minds playing tricks on them, and for some reason they remember – or think they remember – the text stating that Moshe's face shone (like light).

14. When Moshe descends from the mountain it is not the first time that his glow is hinted at. Commenting on the words "When she saw that he was a fine child" (Shmot 2:2), Rashi comments: "'He was fine': when he was born the house filled with light."

רש"י, שמות ב:ב

כי טוב הוא: כשנולד נתמלא הבית כולו אורה.

Moshe's glow is already discernable at his birth.

*destruction descended and removed them.... R. Yohanan observed:
And Moshe was privileged and received them all.* (Talmud Bavli
Shabbat 88a)

According to Rashi[15] the source of Moshe's glow was the concentration
of the crowns of all of Israel. The Zohar[16] reports a tradition that Adam
and Hava originally were endowed with divine primordial light, and
when they sinned, this light disappeared. When the Jewish people stood
at Sinai the light returned to each person as crowns of light. When the
Jews subsequently sinned, the crowns were forfeited, with all the light
going to Moshe. In other words, Moshe became the sole custodian of this
primordial light.[17]

---

15. See Rashi's comments on Talmud Bavli Shabbat 88a.

רש"י, מסכת שבת דף פח עמוד א

שני כתרים: מזיו שכינה.

ומשה יקח: אותו עדי, לשון אחר את האהל, לשון בהלו נרו (איוב כט) והוא היה קירון עור פניו.

16. Zohar, Bereishit 36b (*The Soncino Zohar* [New York: The Soncino Press, 1984], Judaica
    Press CD-ROM): "R. Hiya says: 'Their eyes were opened to the evil of the world, which
    they had not known hitherto. Then they knew that they were naked, since they had lost
    the celestial lustre which had formerly enveloped them, and of which they were now
    divested. 'And they sewed fig leaves': They strove to cover themselves with the [delusive]
    images from the tree of which they had eaten, the so-called "'leaves of the tree.' 'And
    they made themselves belts': R. Yose said: When they obtained knowledge of this world
    and attached themselves to it, they observed that it was governed by those 'leaves of the
    tree.' They therefore sought in them a stronghold in this world, and so made themselves
    acquainted with all kinds of magical arts, in order to gird themselves with weapons of
    those leaves of the tree, for the purpose of self-protection. R. Yehudah said: In this way
    three came up for judgment and were found guilty, and the terrestrial world was cursed
    and dislodged from its estate on account of the defilement of the serpent, until Israel
    stood before Mount Sinai.
    "Afterwards God clothed Adam and Hava in garments soothing to the skin, as it is
    written, 'He made them coats of skin (*'or*).' At first they had had coats of light (*ohr*),
    which procured them the service of the highest of the high, for the celestial angels used
    to come to enjoy that light; so it is written, 'You have made him but little lower than the
    angels, and crowned him with glory and honor' (Tehillim 8:6). Now after their sins they
    had only coats of skin (*'or*), good for the body but not for the soul."

17. *Shnei Luhot haBrit*, Tractate Pesakhim, drush no. 4.

ספר השל"ה הקדוש, מסכת פסחים, דרוש רביעי (ט)

וכמו אדם תכלית בריאותו היתה להיות כתנות אור ב'א' כאשר הארכתי בדרשות אחרות, כן משה רבינו

ע"ה קרן אור פניו. ולא כתיב נקרן דהוה משמע עתה, רק קרן כתיב כבר. והענין כי בעת מתן תורה היה

Rabbi Meir's succinct comment teaches that the clothing that God gave to Man was made of this same primordial light. Rav Yitzhak Luria (the Ari or Ari"zal),[18] citing the Zohar, also refers to this primordial material: Adam and Hava originally were imbued with supernal light. When they sinned, they lost this luster, and became naked. This is the meaning of Rabbi Meir's marginal note: God covered them with skin – but previously He had covered them with light.

The brilliance of both the method and content of Rabbi Meir's marginal comment should not be overlooked. We may gain greater appreciation for both the form and content of this teaching if we consider a second instance, reported in the Midrash, of a note in the margin of Rabbi Meir's book: God considers what He has created, and it is very good:

בראשית רבה, פרשה ט פסקה ה
בתורתו של רבי מאיר מצאו כתוב, והנה טוב מאד והנה טוב מות.

In the copy of R. Meir's Torah was found written: "'and behold, it was very (me'od) good': and behold, death (mot) was good." (Bereishit Rabbah 9:5)

In what may seem an expression of some fatalistic philosophy, Rabbi Meir adds a marginal comment, playing off the similar sounds of *me'od* and *mot*: "very good" and "death." The "goodness" of death is difficult for man to comprehend, although it may be no more difficult than the relationship

---

ראוי להיות תכלית הבריאה וכל האדם בכתנות אור, וזהו העדיים והעטרות וכתרים שנתנו להם בחורב, רק כאשר קילקלו בעגל ויתנצלו בני ישראל את עדיים, דהיינו קירון אור. ובמקום שהיו ראויין להיות כבני עליון, אכן כאדם סליק להו דהיינו אדם קדמאי. אכן משה רבינו ע"ה נשאר לו הקירון אור, כי מהיכי תיתי שינטל ממנו, כן מוכח בזוהר.

18. *Sefer haLikutim*, Parashat Bereishit, chapter 3.

ספר הליקוטים, פרשת בראשית פרק ג
ויעש ה' אלקים לאדם ולאשתו כתנות עור וילבישם: כבר ידעת מ"ש חז"ל בתורתו של ר' מאיר מצאו כתוב כתנות אור. וסוד הענין הוא, כי אדה"ר קודם שחטא היה לו זיהרא עילאה, שהיה מלובש מלבוש רוחני שהוא אור, בסוד הזיהרא עילאה שהיתה לו, כמו שידעת מדרוש שורשי הנשמות, וכיון שחטא, אותה הזיהרא נסתלקה ממנו, כנודע מס"ה פ' בראשית דף ל"ו ריש ע"ב, וז"ל, ותפקחנה עיני שניהם וגו', וידעו כי ערומים הם, דאבדו זיהרא עילאה דהוה חפי עלייהו, ואסתלק מנייהו, ואשתארו ערומים מיניה. ואותה זיהרא היתה יושבת בין החומות של ג"ע שלש מאות שנה, ואח"כ ניתנה לחנוך, כמו שידעת מדרוש שרשי הנשמות, וע"ש. ואחר שחטא אדה"ר, נהפכו הכותנות מאור לעור, והפנימיות שבהם שהוא האור לקחו חנוך ואליהו ז"ל, כנוד' מדרוש שרשי הנשמות וע"ש.

between light and skin. Both of these comments by Rabbi Meir, while at first inexplicable, stem from his unique perspective. A passage in the Talmud that provides some biographical information about Rabbi Meir can shed some light on these comments.

תלמוד בבלי, מסכת עירובין דף יג עמוד א

והאמר רב יהודה אמר שמואל משום רבי מאיר: כשהייתי לומד אצל רבי
עקיבא הייתי מטיל קנקנתום לתוך הדיו ולא אמר לי דבר. וכשבאתי אצל רבי
ישמעאל אמר לי: בני, מה מלאכתך? אמרתי לו: לבלר אני. אמר לי: בני, הוי
זהיר במלאכתך שמלאכתך מלאכת שמים היא, שמא אתה מחסר אות אחת
או מייתר אות אחת – נמצאת מחריב את כל העולם כולו.

*Did not Rav Yehudah in fact state that Shmuel stated in the name
of R. Meir: When I was studying under R. Akiva I used to put
vitriol into my ink and he told me nothing [against it], but when
I subsequently came to R. Yishmael the latter said to me, "My son,
what is your occupation?" I told him, "I am a scribe," and he said to
me, "Be meticulous in your work, for your occupation is a sacred one;
should you omit or add one single letter, you would thereby destroy
the entire universe." (Talmud Bavli Eruvin 13a)*

Rabbi Meir made his living as a scribe. He understood the importance of every letter of text. He knew that leaving out a single letter could have dire consequences. The thought of changing a word probably never crossed his mind, so he wrote comments in the margins, indicating deeper levels of understanding and meaning. His colleagues, however, did not always understand him.

תלמוד בבלי, מסכת עירובין דף יג עמוד ב

אמר רבי אחא בר חנינא: גלוי וידוע לפני מי שאמר והיה העולם שאין בדורו
של רבי מאיר כמותו, ומפני מה לא קבעו הלכה כמותו – שלא יכלו חביריו
לעמוד על סוף דעתו. שהוא אומר על טמא טהור ומראה לו פנים, על טהור
טמא ומראה לו פנים.

תנא: לא רבי מאיר שמו אלא רבי נהוראי שמו, ולמה נקרא שמו רבי מאיר –
שהוא מאיר עיני חכמים בהלכה. ולא נהוראי שמו אלא רבי נחמיה שמו, ואמרי
לה רבי אלעזר בן ערך שמו, ולמה נקרא שמו נהוראי – שמנהיר עיני חכמים
בהלכה. אמר רבי: האי דמחדדנא מחבראי – דחזיתיה לרבי מאיר מאחוריה,

ואילו חזיתיה מקמיה – הוה מחדדנא טפי. דכתיב, (ישעיהו ל) "והיו עיניך
ראות את מוריך."

R. Aha b. Hanina said: It is revealed and known before Him Who spoke and the world came into existence,[19] that in the generation of R. Meir there was none equal to him; then why was the halakhah not fixed in accordance with his views? Because his colleagues could not fathom the depths of his mind; for he would declare the ritually unclean to be clean and supply plausible proof, and the ritually clean to be unclean and also supply plausible proof.

One taught: His name was not R. Meir but R. Nehorai. Then why was he called R. Meir? Because he enlightened (hei'ir) the sages in the halakhah. His name in fact was not even Nehorai but R. Nehemiah or, as others say, R. Elazar b. Arakh. Then why was he called Nehorai? Because he enlightened (manhir) the sages in the halakhah.

Rebbi[20] declared: The only reason why I am sharper than my colleagues is that I saw the back[21] of R. Meir, but had I had a front view of him I would have been sharper still, for it is written in Scripture: "Your eyes shall see your teacher" (Yeshayahu 30:20).
(Talmud Bavli Eruvin 13b)

We learn several things from this passage: Rabbi Meir was unparalleled in his generation. Despite this, the law was not established according to his opinion, because his colleagues did not understand his dazzling brilliance. We also learn that his name *Meir* means light.[22]

---

19. This is a common form of reference to God, Who spoke the words "Let there be light" and created the universe.

20. It is significant that the Mishnah, compiled by Rabbi Yehudah haNasi (also known as "Rebbi"), is heavily based on the notes that Rabbi Meir (the scribe or notetaker) took of Rabbi Akiva's lectures. See Sanhedrin 86a.

21. This is reminiscent of the Torah's description of Moshe seeing the back (as it were) of God – which is often cited as the cause of Moshe's glowing face. See Shmot Rabbah 47:6.

22. *Be'er Mayim Hayim*, Parashat Bereishit, chapter 3.

ספר באר מים חיים, פרשת בראשית, פרק ג

ונחזור לענין ר' מאיר אשר בתורתו נעשה עור פניו אורה ממש ועל כן אמרו (עירובין יג עמוד ב) שהיה
מאיר פני חכמים בהלכה. פירוש בשעה שהיה עוסק בהלכה והיה מבהיק זיו אור פניו על החכמים אשר

Meir, who was full of light, sees in our passage in Bereishit "light" instead of "skin," and in the second instance, *death* instead of "good." His vocation may have been more than incidental in leading up to the brilliant but radical insights he had to the Torah and halakhah.

In order to better understand Rabbi Meir's teachings, let us follow the path of this primordial light once it left Adam and Hava. The Ari"zal taught:

ספר הליקוטים, פרשת בראשית פרק ג

ואחר שחטא אדם הראשון, נהפכו הכותנות מאור לעור, והפנימיות שבהם שהוא האור לקחו חנוך ואליהו ז"ל, כנודע מדרוש שרשי הנשמות ועיין שם. והחיצוניות שהוא העור, לקחו נמרוד והדומים לו.

After Adam sinned his clothing turned from light (ohr) to skin ('or), and the inner aspect, which is the light, was taken by Hanokh and Eliyahu, as we learn from the Midrash.... And the external aspect was inherited by Nimrod and those of his ilk. (Sefer haLikutim, Parashat Bereishit, chapter 3)

The primordial light lost by Adam and Hava was inherited by Hanokh and Eliyahu. The common denominator between Hanokh and Eliyahu[23] is that

---

היו אתו עד שגם הם קלטו האור על פניהם ומאורו היה מאיר גם פני חכמים, ועל כן א"ר (עירובין יג עמוד ב) האי דמחדדנא מחבראי דחזיתיה לר' מאיר מאחוריה ואלמלי חזיתיה מקמאי הויא מחדדנא טפי וכו' עד כאן.

23. The Midrash compares Hanokh and Eliyahu — specifically regarding their disappearance:

בראשית רבה, פרשה כה פסקה א

ויתהלך חנוך את האלקים ואיננו כי לקח אותו אלקים: ...אפיקורסים שאלו לרבי אבהו אמרו לו אין אנו מוצאין מיתה לחנוך אמר להם אמרו לו למה נאמרה כאן לקיחה ונאמרה להלן (מלכים ב ב) כי היום ה' לוקח את אדונך מעל ראשך. אמר להם אם ללקיחה אתם דורשים נאמר כאן לקיחה ונאמר להלן (יחזקאל כד) הנני לוקח ממך את מחמד עיניך. א"ר תנחומא יפה השיבו רבי אבהו. מטרונה שאלה את ר' יוסי אמרה לו אין אנו מוצאין מיתה בחנוך א"ל אלו נאמר (בראשית ה) ויתהלך חנוך את האלקים ושתק הייתי אומר כדבריך כשהוא אומר כי לקח אותו אלקים ואיננו כי לקח אותו אלקים בעולם הזה כי לקח אותו אלקים.

"And Hanokh walked with God, and he was not; for God took him' (5:24): ...Some sectarians asked R. Abbahu, 'We do not find that Hanokh died?' 'How so?' inquired he. "'Taking' is employed here, and also in connection with Eliyahu,' said they. 'If you stress the word "taking,"' he answered, 'then "taking" is employed here, while in Yehezkel it is said, 'Behold, I take away from you the desire of your eyes,' etc. (Yehezkel 24:16). R. Tanhuma observed: He answered them well. A matron asked R. Yose, 'Do we not find death stated of Hanokh?' Said he to her, 'Had it said, "and Hanokh walked with God,"'

although both were born as normal, mortal humans, each achieved the elevated, immortal status of angels,[24] and they live forever. The ascension of Eliyahu in a fiery chariot[25] is better known, as are his occasional visitations (at each Pesach seder and at circumcision ceremonies); Hanokh's ascension is far less explicit in the text. When the Torah deviates from standard practice and does not tell of his death, our sages elaborate:

בראשית ה:כד

וַיִּתְהַלֵּךְ חֲנוֹךְ אֶת הָאֱלֹקִים וְאֵינֶנּוּ כִּי לָקַח אֹתוֹ אֱלֹקִים:

And Hanokh walked with God; and he was no more, for God took him. (Bereishit 5:24)

The Targum Pseudo-Yonatan explains:

תרגום יונתן, בראשית ה:כד

ופלח חנוך בקושטא קדם ה' והא ליתוהי עם דיירי ארעא ארום אתנגיד וסליק לרקיעא במימר קדם ה' וקרא שמיה מיטטרון ספרא רבא.

כתר יונתן, בראשית ה:כד

ויעבוד חנוך באמת לפני ה' והנה איננו עם תושבי הארץ כי נלקח ועלה לרקיע במאמר לפני ה' ויקרא שמו מיטטרון הסופר הגדול.

And Hanokh walked in righteousness before God, and he ceased to exist with the dwellers of Earth. He ascended to heaven in front of God and he was given the name Metatron the Great Scribe. (Targum Pseudo-Yonatan Bereishit 5:24)

Hanokh, inheritor of the primordial light, became the immortal Metatron the Great Scribe, tasked with chronicling the words and deeds of mankind

---

and nothing more, I would have agreed with you, but the verse reads, "and he was no more for God had taken him'" [it means that] he was no longer in this world, for God had taken him." (Bereishit Rabbah 25:1)

24. See Reuven Margoliot, *Malakhei Elyon* (Jerusalem: Mosad Harav Kook, 1978), page 154, note 26.

25. II Melakhim 2:11: "And it came to pass, as they still went on, and talked, that, behold, there appeared a chariot of fire, and horses of fire, which parted them both asunder; and Eliyahu went up by a whirlwind into heaven."

for the divine court. The one other person described as a great scribe, "*Safra Rabba*," was Moshe, who was tasked with transmitting the word of God.[26]

Adam and Hava were supposed to live forever and be angel-like. When they sinned, they lost this quality and the primordial light that accompanied it. Hanokh and Eliyahu subsequently became angels and inherited this light. Hanokh became the Great Scribe and is now known as Metatron, the heavenly scribe. We come across him in a crucial passage in the Gemara:

תלמוד בבלי, מסכת חגיגה דף טו עמוד א

אחר קיצץ בנטיעות, עליו הכתוב אומר (קהלת ה) "אל תתן את פיך לחטיא את בשרך". מאי היא? חזא מיטטרון דאתיהבא ליה רשותא למיתב למיכתב זכוותא דישראל. אמר: גמירא דלמעלה לא הוי לא ישיבה ולא תחרות ולא עורף ולא עיפוי, שמא חס ושלום שתי רשויות הן. אפקוהו למיטטרון ומחיוהו שיתין פולסי דנורא.

> Aher *mutilated the shoots. Of him Scripture says: "Do not allow your mouth to cause your flesh to sin" (Kohelet 5:5). What does it refer to? He saw that permission was granted to Metatron to sit and write down the merits of Israel. Said he: "It is taught as a tradition that on high there is no sitting and no emulation, and no back, and no weariness. Perhaps (heaven forfend!) there are two divinities!" [Thereupon] they led Metatron forth, and punished him with sixty fiery lashes, saying to him: "Why did you not rise before him when you saw him?" Permission was [then] given to Metatron to erase the merits of* Aher. (Talmud Bavli Hagigah 15a)

The spiritual journey of four great scholars takes us, in a sense, back to the beginning – literally. They enter an orchard, or perhaps *the* orchard: *Pardes*, no less than paradise itself – or in other words, the Garden of Eden. One of the four sees an angel, Metatron the Great Scribe, sitting and recording the good deeds of Israel. *Aher* (the erstwhile sage Elisha ben Avuyah) sees him sitting at work and becomes confused. Preconceived notions of dualism[27] cause confusion between good and evil, like the fruit of the forbidden tree in Eden. *Aher* cannot reconcile what he has seen, and becomes a heretic.

---

26. See Talmud Bavli Sotah 13b.
27. See Talmud Bavli Hagigah 15a.

Despite his apostasy, *Aher* retains one famous student: Rabbi Meir continues to study with his fallen master. The sages of the Talmud question how Rabbi Meir could continue his association with such a man, and state[28] that Rabbi Meir was uniquely capable of separating the wheat from the chaff – he knew how to distinguish between good and evil. Rabbi Meir alone was not blinded by the knowledge of the forbidden tree. He did not suffer from its confusion of good and evil.

Rabbi Meir is a *sofer*, a scribe, as were Moshe and Hanokh/Metatron. It is his notes on the teachings of Rabbi Akiva, transmitted to Rebbi, which help establish the standard text of the Mishnah. He is uniquely able to separate between true and false, good and evil. Fundamentally, as a *sofer*, he is an agent of God. He facilitates the transmission of the Torah of God to this world. In this sense, as a great *sofer*, he becomes angelic. He is a messenger and transmitter of the word of God, uniquely capable of distinguishing truth from untruth.[29] Rabbi Meir sees light where others do not. As a *sofer*, he somehow reaches into heaven and pulls down the words of God and puts them on parchment, and the parchment/skin becomes holy. We should not wonder that when the text of the Torah reads *'or* (skin), Rabbi Meir reminds us, with a single word, that although a *sofer* writes on animal skin – parchment, the primordial Torah was written with light,[30] the primordial light that was lost and will one day be regained through acceptance of the Torah, by Hanokh and later by all of Israel.

Rabbi Meir had two teachers: one, as we have already seen, was Elisha ben Avuyah. The other was Rabbi Akiva. Elisha ben Avuyah became a paid informant for the Romans; he chose evil. Presumably, he lived out his days in the lap of luxury, wearing only the finest garments. Death surely came to him of natural causes, as he lay in a warm, soft bed, covered in the

---

28. Talmud Bavli Hagigah 15b.

29. "Evil" – *r'a* – is written with the same letters as "skin" (or "parchment"), *'or*. This idea is found in *'Emek haMelekh*, gate 5, chapter 42, and subsequently in the writings of Rav Tzadok haKohen of Lublin and the *Leshem*, as well as in Rabbi Natan of Breslov's *Likutei Halakhot*.

30. See Rashi, Devarim 33:2.

רש"י, דברים לג:ב
אש דת: שהיתה כתובה מאז לפניו באש שחורה על גבי אש לבנה.

finest linens. Conversely, his erstwhile colleague, Rabbi Akiva, was brutally tortured by the Romans, having the very skin peeled off his body. But what does Rabbi Meir see even in death? What he saw in Bereishit: *tov me'od / tov mot* – death itself is very good. Even when witnessing the horrific torture and death of Rabbi Akiva,[31] watching as his master's clothes and his skin are stripped from his body, Rabbi Meir still sees good – *tov*; he still sees light. Rabbi Meir is not confused by what he witnesses; he sees the good in everything,[32] because he can connect to the light[33] with which man was endowed prior to the sin, before mankind was impacted by the Tree of Knowledge of Good and Evil. Before the confusion, before the *'orlah* – the extra skin, God's goodness was in everything, everywhere. Rabbi Meir remains uniquely able to see the good in all things.[34]

In truth, Rabbi Akiva was not naked: he was clothed in the clothes of salvation. He was held tightly by the *Shekhinah* (the Divine Presence), spiritually protected like Adam and Hava before the sin, clothed in a garment of light and truth. Elisha ben Avuyah may have had the finest of furs but he was naked – devoid of salvation, spiritually cold, dark and shivering.

Living as we do in a world after the sin, we must find clothing of light to care for our vulnerable souls. In His mercy, God gave us the means to recapture the light: the words of the Torah, once written in light and now written on animal skins, banish the confusion between good and evil that defines our world. Through the words of Torah, we are able to see the goodness of God, to strip away the cloak of falsehood that obscures the lines between good and evil. Even in our world of confusion, of sin, of estrangement

---

31. Rabbi Soloveitchik makes this point. See *Yemei Zikaron*, page 205.

32. As did his teacher Rabbi Akiva (Brakhot 60b–61a) and Rabbi Akiva's teacher Nahum Ish Gamzu (see Brakhot 22a and Taanit 21a).

33. *Resisei Laylah*, section 53.

ספר רסיסי לילה, אות נג

ולעצמו לא האירה תורתו מפני ריבוי הקליפה הסובבתה. אבל רבי מאיר היה יכול להבדיל ולהפריד התוך מהקליפה כי הוא היה מלא אור כשמו שעל כן בתורתו כתוב כתנות אור באל"ף (בראשית רבה כ:יב) שגם הלבוש של עור מלא אור והוא כמו אור האבוקה שמושך אליו כל אור קטן שמתקרב לו כך היה יכול למשוך אור הפנימי שהיה באחר אליו.

34. On a halakhic level this may be challenging, and hence we are told that the law was not established according to Rabbi Meir.

from God, we are not abandoned. God clothes us in garments of light; He enables us to fulfill our ultimate destiny and to regain what was lost as a result of sin. We need only seek out the light and feel its warmth and we will, once again, be adorned in the clothing of salvation.

Parashat Noah

Na'amah

In a generation of moral decay, one man shines. Noah is righteous, perfect in his generation. From the scant biographical details reported in the verses, we know that he has three sons, but nothing is reported about his spouse, the woman behind this illustrious man.

בראשית ו:ט–י

אֵלֶּה תּוֹלְדֹת נֹחַ נֹחַ אִישׁ צַדִּיק תָּמִים הָיָה בְּדֹרֹתָיו אֶת הָאֱלֹקִים הִתְהַלֶּךְ נֹחַ:

וַיּוֹלֶד נֹחַ שְׁלֹשָׁה בָנִים אֶת שֵׁם אֶת חָם וְאֶת יָפֶת:

These are the generations of Noah: Noah was a righteous man, perfect in his generation. Noah walked with God. Noah fathered three sons: Shem, Ham, and Yafet. (Bereishit 6:9–10)

When Noah is informed of the impending disaster, of the lethal flood that will wash away most of humanity, he is also told that his immediate family will be saved.

בראשית ו:יז–יח

וַאֲנִי הִנְנִי מֵבִיא אֶת הַמַּבּוּל מַיִם עַל הָאָרֶץ לְשַׁחֵת כָּל בָּשָׂר אֲשֶׁר בּוֹ רוּחַ חַיִּים מִתַּחַת הַשָּׁמָיִם כֹּל אֲשֶׁר בָּאָרֶץ יִגְוָע: וַהֲקִמֹתִי אֶת בְּרִיתִי אִתָּךְ וּבָאתָ אֶל הַתֵּבָה אַתָּה וּבָנֶיךָ וְאִשְׁתְּךָ וּנְשֵׁי בָנֶיךָ אִתָּךְ:

And, behold, I, Myself, bring a flood of waters upon the earth, to destroy all flesh that possesses the breath of life, from under heaven, and everything that is on the earth shall die. But with you will I establish my covenant, and you shall come into the ark – you, and your sons, and your wife, and your sons' wives with you. (Bereishit 6:17–18)

The syntax of this verse is curious: rather than stating "you and your wife, your sons and their wives," the order of the relationships seems unnatural: "you and your sons, your wife and your son's wives." Rashi learns from this syntax that conjugal relations were prohibited on the ark; the men and women were segregated.[1]

Strangely, other than the fact that Noah is instructed to separate from the mother of his children while on the ark, there is nothing else in the text of the Torah about this woman.

This lacuna is filled in by the Oral Torah; tradition identifies Noah's wife by name from among the offspring listed in the genealogical roster at the end of Parashat Bereishit. And this name affords us a great deal of information and insight.

בראשית ד:כב

וְצִלָּה גַם הִוא יָלְדָה אֶת תּוּבַל קַיִן לֹטֵשׁ כָּל חֹרֵשׁ נְחֹשֶׁת וּבַרְזֶל וַאֲחוֹת תּוּבַל קַיִן נַעֲמָה:

...Tzillah also had a son, Tuval Kayin, maker of all copper and iron implements; and Tuval Kayin's sister was Naamah. (Bereishit 4:22)

רש"י, בראשית ד:כב

נעמה: היא אשתו של נח.

Naamah: This is the wife of Noah. (Rashi, Bereishit 4:22)

Noah's wife is identified as Na'amah, daughter of Lemekh and Tzillah. One might posit that tradition makes this identification in keeping with the internal logic often described as the biblical "theory of conservation of characters":[2] later in the text, a woman named Na'amah makes a significant appearance in the narrative, and the sages always attempt to avoid spreading the onomasticon of biblical characters too thin. However, the more we delve into this woman's background and life story, the more we understand the story of the flood, and the more it becomes apparent that

---

1. Rashi, Bereishit 6:18.

   רש"י, בראשית ו:יח

   אתה ובניך ואשתך: האנשים לבד והנשים לבד, מכאן שנאסרו בתשמיש המטה.

2. This idea is found many places in the Talmud and Midrash. For a full discussion see Rabbi Zvi Hirsch Chajes, *A Student's Guide to the Talmud* (New York: Feldheim Publishers, 1960), especially chapters 11 and 12, page 172 ff.

the sages did not identify Noah's wife as Na'amah in an arbitrary pastiche of biblical names and characters; Noah's wife could only be Na'amah.

Rashi makes the connection between the child born to Lemekh and Tzillah and the unnamed wife of Noah. Ironically, Noah's father was also named Lemekh. Lest one think that this is in fact the same Lemekh, we need only review the fourth chapter of Bereishit to trace Na'amah's family line back to Kayin, and the fifth chapter of Bereishit to find the family line of Noah which began with Shet. These are, in fact, distinct, independent families that merge in the union of Noah and Na'amah, whose fathers happened to have the same name. As we shall see, their genealogies are not only quite distinct, they are qualitatively different. But in order to fully understand the significance of the union of Noah and Na'amah, we must take a step back to view the larger picture.

In addition to Kayin and Shet, Adam originally had a third son, Hevel, whose death hovers over the narrative; it is the pivotal moment, the major episode, the trauma in need of healing. A replacement for Hevel must be found.

It is in this context that Na'amah's family line begins – as a postscript to the tragic murder of Hevel by his brother Kayin.

בראשית ד:יז

וַיֵּדַע קַיִן אֶת אִשְׁתּוֹ וַתַּהַר וַתֵּלֶד אֶת חֲנוֹךְ וַיְהִי בֹּנֶה עִיר וַיִּקְרָא שֵׁם הָעִיר כְּשֵׁם בְּנוֹ חֲנוֹךְ:

And Kayin was intimate with his wife; and she conceived, and bore Hanokh; and he built a city, and called the name of the city after the name of his son, Hanokh. (Bereishit 4:17)

Kayin moves on with his life; he marries and has a child named Hanokh.[3] He then builds a city, and names it after his son. Ironically, or perhaps defiantly, Kayin, who is condemned to wander the earth in punishment for the murder of Hevel, is the first person to attempt to build an urban center. The name he chooses for his son and for the city he builds, Hanokh, has a connotation of "to establish."

---

3. As with many of the names is this chapter, Hanokh also appears in chapter 5; a cursory glance at the genealogical record reveals that the two Hanokhs are not related.

Hanokh, in turn, has a descendant named Lemekh, who starts a family in an interesting fashion; he takes not one – but two wives.

וַיִּוָּלֵד לַחֲנוֹךְ אֶת עִירָד וְעִירָד יָלַד אֶת מְחוּיָאֵל וּמְחִיָּיאֵל יָלַד אֶת מְתוּשָׁאֵל וּמְתוּשָׁאֵל יָלַד אֶת לָמֶךְ: וַיִּקַּח לוֹ לֶמֶךְ שְׁתֵּי נָשִׁים שֵׁם הָאַחַת עָדָה וְשֵׁם הַשֵּׁנִית צִלָּה:

And to Hanokh was born Irad; and Irad fathered Mehuyael; and Mehuyael fathered Metushael; and Metushael fathered Lamekh. And Lemekh took for himself two wives; the name of one was Adah, and the name of the other, Tzillah. (Bereishit 4:18–19)

Rashi paints the practice of taking two wives in unmistakably negative terms: this is the behavior of the generation of the flood. One wife was wed for solely utilitarian purposes: she was to bear children and work in the household. The other wife was designated for pleasure: she would be rendered infertile by means of a birth-control potion, for the sake of maintaining her figure. This "trophy wife" would dress in beautiful clothing and eat delicacies while the other wife worked.[4] While this practice was not the main transgression of the generation of the flood, it is certainly among the morally reprehensible behaviors our sages regarded as the cause of the flood.[5] In fact, similar practices continued to draw harsh rebuke in the words of the prophets – and are tragically echoed in our own day and age. The prophets Malakhi and Yeshayahu saw this practice as an expression of immorality and disloyalty, and warned that God Himself would treat whoever was disloyal to "the wife of his youth" in kind.

---

4. Rashi, Bereishit 4:19.

רש"י, בראשית ד:יט

שתי נשים: (ב"ר) כך היה דרכן של דור המבול אחת לפריה ורביה ואחת לתשמיש. זו שהיא לתשמיש משקה כוס של עקרין כדי שתעקר ומקושטת ככלה ומאכילה מעדנים וחברתה נזופה ואבלה כאלמנה וזהו שפירש איוב (כד:כא) רועה עקרה לא תלד ואלמנה לא ייטיב כמו שמפורש באגדת חלק.

5. Rashi (Bereishit 6:13) states that the final judgment was for theft, but enumerates (in 6:11) many other sins that were characteristic of that society and contributed to the moral decay that was punished by the flood.

רש"י, בראשית ו:יג

כי מלאה הארץ חמס: לא נחתם גזר דינם אלא על הגזל.

רש"י, בראשית ו:יא

ותשחת: לשון ערוה ועבודה זרה, כמו (דברים ד) פן תשחיתון, כי השחית כל בשר וגו'. ותמלא הארץ חמס: גזל.

מלאכי ב:יד

וַאֲמַרְתֶּם עַל מָה עַל כִּי ה' הֵעִיד בֵּינְךָ וּבֵין אֵשֶׁת נְעוּרֶיךָ אֲשֶׁר אַתָּה בָּגַדְתָּה בָּהּ וְהִיא חֲבֶרְתְּךָ וְאֵשֶׁת בְּרִיתֶךָ:

And you say, "Why [do we suffer] so?" Because God has been witness between you and the wife of your youth, to whom you have been faithless, yet she is your companion, and the wife of your covenant. (Malakhi 2:14)[6]

ישעיהו נד:ו

כִּי כְאִשָּׁה עֲזוּבָה וַעֲצוּבַת רוּחַ קְרָאָךְ ה' וְאֵשֶׁת נְעוּרִים כִּי תִמָּאֵס אָמַר אֱלֹקָיִךְ:

For God has called you as a woman forsaken and grieved in spirit, but the wife of [your] youth, can she be rejected? says your God. (Yeshayahu 54:6)[7]

These verses were expounded by the sages of the Talmud, who stressed that the bonds between a young man and his bride are sacred in a way that no other union can equal:

תלמוד בבלי, מסכת סנהדרין דף כב עמוד א

אמר רבי אליעזר: כל המגרש את אשתו ראשונה – אפילו מזבח מוריד עליו דמעות, שנאמר, (מלאכי ב) "וזאת שנית תעשו כסות דמעה את מזבח ה' בכי ואנקה מאין עוד פנות אל המנחה ולקחת רצון מידכם", וכתיב, (מלאכי ב) "ואמרתם על מה על כי ה' העיד בינך ובין אשת נעוריך אשר אתה בגדתה בה והיא חברתך ואשת בריתך"....אמר רבי שמואל בר נחמן: לכל יש תמורה, חוץ מאשת נעורים, שנאמר, (ישעיהו נד) "ואשת נעורים כי תמאס".

R. Eliezer said: If ([a man] divorces his first wife, the very Altar sheds tears, as it is written: "And this further you do, you cover the Altar of God with tears, with weeping and with sighing, so much that He no longer regards your offerings, nor does He receive them with goodwill from your hand" (Malakhi 2:13). Further it is written: "Yet you say, 'Why?' Because God has been witness between you and the wife of your youth, to whom you have been faithless, yet

---

6. The relationship between husband and wife, and the rejected wife, are used here as metaphors for Israel's relationship with God and with Judaism.

7. This section of the book of Yeshayahu is the Haftarah reading for Parashat Noah.

*she is your companion and the wife of your covenant" (ibid.).... R.
Samuel b. Nahman said: All things can be replaced, except the wife
of one's youth, as it is written, "And a wife of [your] youth, can she be
rejected?" (Yeshayahu 54:6).* (Talmud Bavli Sanhedrin 22a)

The Jewish ethos abhors the rejection of the first wife. This is the case not
only when a man takes two wives, but also if he casts aside the first wife, the
older woman who has borne his children and built her life around him and
their home, in favor of a younger woman. Lemekh was the first to create the
impossible situation of "eating your cake and having it too" – one wife for
work and one wife for play. While this is not the only instance in Bereishit
in which a man takes two wives, in no other case did the man set out to do
so as a premeditated course of action. In almost every instance the arrival
of the second wife is due to infertility in the first. Other than Lemekh, the
only person who set out *a priori* to take two wives was Esav.

בראשית כו:לד

וַיְהִי עֵשָׂו בֶּן אַרְבָּעִים שָׁנָה וַיִּקַּח אִשָּׁה אֶת יְהוּדִית בַּת בְּאֵרִי הַחִתִּי וְאֶת בָּשְׂמַת
בַּת אֵילֹן הַחִתִּי:

*And Esav was forty years old when he married Judith the daughter
of Be'eri the Hittite, and Bas'mat the daughter of Elon the Hittite.*
(Bereishit 26:34)

Esav reminds us of Kayin in many ways, not the least of which is his
penchant for violence. Esav's propensity for superficial thinking, as well as
his insatiable need to dominate and possess, are the defining traits of his
character.[8] It should therefore come as no surprise that the model he chose
for his most intimate relationships is this morally reprehensible practice
introduced by Lemekh. Indeed, this must be viewed as one more in a long
list of behaviors that connect Esav with Kayin and his descendants.

Lemekh's behavior represents a corruption of the morals upon which human
society is based. The paradigm that existed up to this point is based upon
very different principles. The first chapter of Bereishit introduces male and

---

8. See my book *Explorations* (Jerusalem: Targum Press, 2000), Parashat Toldot and
Parashat Vayehi.

female with the stated purpose of procreation, while the second chapter speaks of oneness, even sexual unity, but makes no mention of procreation. Which is the "real" wife from a Torah perspective? Apparently, the answer is – both. The merger of the two images creates the unified picture of the whole woman. To divide the roles is to objectify women based on utility; this is not the ideal to which the Torah ascribes, nor the ideal toward which mankind is meant to strive. A wife, a partner, a helpmate – a soul mate – is both a mother and a lover.

Nonetheless, Lemekh takes his two wives, dissecting and rebuilding the moral underpinnings of the family unit to reflect his personal greed and egocentrism. Rashi teaches that Adah was designated to be the childbearer,[9] while Tzillah was chosen for her beauty.[10] In fulfillment of her role, Adah bears children. First, she has a child named Yaval, a name that seems to shadow *Hevel*. We are forced to consider the complexity of this situation over and over: Kayin killed Hevel, and his descendants name their children, time and time again, after the "missing" brother, the brother whom their own forefather killed.

בראשית ד:כ

וַתֵּלֶד עָדָה אֶת יָבָל הוּא הָיָה אֲבִי יֹשֵׁב אֹהֶל וּמִקְנֶה:

And Adah bore Yaval; he was the father of those who live in tents, and of those who raise flocks. (Bereishit 4:20)

Not only is his name reminiscent of Hevel, but Yaval adopts Hevel's vocation; he becomes a man of the tents and a shepherd. Adah's second son is named Yuval, a name remarkably similar to his brother Yaval and, again, reminiscent of Hevel.

---

9. See Rashi, Bereishit 4:19. Ironically, the name Adah connotes beauty, which perhaps would have made her the more natural candidate for "pleasure wife."

רש"י, בראשית ד:יט

עדה: היא של פריה ורביה ועל שם שמגונה עליו ומוסרת מאצלו (ס"א ממאכלו) עדה תרגום של סורה.

10. See Rashi, Bereishit 4:19. The literal meaning of the name Tzillah is "her shadow."

רש"י, בראשית ד:יט

צלה: היא של תשמיש על שם שיושבת תמיד בצלו דברי אגדה הם בבראשית רבה.

בראשית ד:כא

וְשֵׁם אָחִיו יוּבָל הוּא הָיָה אֲבִי כָּל תֹּפֵשׂ כִּנּוֹר וְעוּגָב:

*And his brother's name was Yuval; he was the father of all who
handle the harp and pipe. (Bereishit 4:21)*

Yuval is a musician; the merger of Adah's two sons thus produces a
musician/shepherd, stirring for the reader images of King David. Lemekh,
fifth in the line established by Kayin after his exile, seems intent on making
reparations. Not only does he kill Kayin, he names his children after Kayin's
victim, a man who never had children of his own. Lemekh's children are,
in some way, replacements for Hevel.

And yet, while the names Lemekh gives his children seem to indicate an
attempt to replace Hevel, Lemekh's *modus operandi* is very Kayin-like.[11]

בראשית ד:כג–כד

וַיֹּאמֶר לֶמֶךְ לְנָשָׁיו עָדָה וְצִלָּה שְׁמַעַן קוֹלִי נְשֵׁי לֶמֶךְ הַאְזֵנָּה אִמְרָתִי כִּי אִישׁ הָרַגְתִּי
לְפִצְעִי וְיֶלֶד לְחַבֻּרָתִי: כִּי שִׁבְעָתַיִם יֻקַּם קָיִן וְלֶמֶךְ שִׁבְעִים וְשִׁבְעָה:

*And Lemekh said to his wives: "Adah and Tzillah, hear my voice; you
wives of Lemekh, listen to my speech; for I have slain a man[12] for
wounding me, and a young man for hurting me. If Kayin shall be*

---

11. See Rashi, Bereishit 4:1, which is based on Bereishit Rabbah 22:2.

רש"י, בראשית ד:א

את קין את אחיו את הבל: ג' אתים ריבוים הם מלמד שתאומה נולדה עם קין, ועם הבל נולדו שתים, לכך
נאמר ותוסף (ב"ר).

בראשית רבה, פרשה כב פסקה ב

אר"א בן עזריה: ג' פלאים נעשו באותו היום בו ביום נבראו בו ביום שמשו בו ביום הוציאו תולדות. א"ל
רבי יהושע בן קרחה: עלו למטה שנים וירדו שבעה קין ותאומתו והבל ושתי תאומותיו.
R. Elazar b. Azaryah said: Three wonders were performed on that day: on that very day
they were created, on that very day they cohabited, and on that very day they produced
offspring. R. Yehoshua b. Korhah said: Only two entered the bed, and seven left it: Kayin
and his twin sister, Hevel and his two twin sisters.

12. While the verse is inexplicit as to the identity of the victim of Lemekh, tradition tells us
that it is Kayin. See Rashi, Bereishit 4:23.

רש"י, בראשית ד:כג

שמעןן קולי: שהיו פורשות ממנו מתשמיש לפי שהרג את קין ואת תובל קין בנו, שהיה למך סומא ותובל
קין מושכו, וראה את קין ונדמה לו כחיה ואמר לאביו למשוך בקשת, והרגו. וכיון שידע שהוא קין זקנו,
הכה כף אל כף וספק את בנו ביניהם והרגו, והיו נשיו פורשות ממנו והוא מפייסן.

avenged sevenfold, truly Lemekh seventy and sevenfold." (Bereishit 4:23–24)

Lemekh is not only a descendant of Kayin in terms of genealogy or genetics; his behavior indicates that he is a follower of Kayin, behaviorally and perhaps philosophically. Lemekh is the second person in history to commit murder; the victim is none other than the first person in history to have committed murder – Kayin himself! Lemekh draws the parallel between them, expressing to his wives his own inner sense that his fate will parallel that of Kayin.

Yet despite Lemekh's best plans, Tzillah, the "trophy wife," also bears children:[13] first a son named Tuval-Kayin, a name that seems to conjure up not only Hevel, but a merger with Kayin. This son of Tzillah worked with metals:

בראשית ד:כב

וְצִלָּה גַם הִוא יָלְדָה אֶת תּוּבַל קַיִן לֹטֵשׁ כָּל חֹרֵשׁ נְחֹשֶׁת וּבַרְזֶל...

And Tzillah, she also bore Tuval-Kayin, forger of every sharp instrument in bronze and iron... (Bereishit 4:22)

Here again, we are told of Tuval-Kayin's choice of vocation. We cannot but wonder what it was that attracted Tuval-Kayin to this particular line of work; was it in imitation of Kayin's vocation as a farmer that Tuval-Kayin produced plowshares and farming implements, or in imitation of the homicidal tendencies of Kayin and his own father Lemekh that he perfected the manufacture of weapons? It is not difficult to imagine either scenario, or even a third possibility: could he have convinced others that the sharp instruments he was producing were intended for peaceful, domestic use – when in fact he fully intended to fall into step with his murderous ancestors when the opportunity presented itself?[14]

---

13. See Da'at Zekeinim miBaalei haTosafot, 4:19.

דעת זקנים מבעלי התוספות, בראשית ד:יט

ופי' דצלה היתה אותה של תשמיש. וקשיא לי דהא כתיב אח"כ וצלה גם היא ילדה. וי"ל דלהכי כתיב גם כלומר אף צלה שנבחרה לתשמיש ילדה ולא הועיל לה כוס של עיקרין.

14. See Rashi, Bereishit 4:22.

רש"י, בראשית ד:כב

תובל קין: תובל אומנתו של קין. תובל לשון תבלין תיבל והתקין אומנתו של קין לעשות כלי זיין לרוצחים.

It seems only in passing that we are told that Tuval-Kayin had a sister, Na'amah.

וְצִלָּה גַם הִוא יָלְדָה אֶת תּוּבַל קַיִן לֹטֵשׁ כָּל חֹרֵשׁ נְחֹשֶׁת וּבַרְזֶל וַאֲחוֹת תּוּבַל קַיִן נַעֲמָה:

And Tzillah, she also bore Tuval-Kayin, forger of every sharp instrument in bronze and iron; and Tuval-Kayin's sister was Na'amah. (Bereishit 4:22)

Na'amah was not "incidentally" the sister of Tuval-Kayin. She was the final link in a chain that began with Kayin and is traced through Lemekh, who bestowed upon his children the legacy of Hevel. This very Na'amah will facilitate the merger of the genealogical lines: a descendant of Kayin, a stand-in for Hevel, she marries Noah, a descendant of Shet – himself a replacement for Hevel:

וַיֵּדַע אָדָם עוֹד אֶת אִשְׁתּוֹ וַתֵּלֶד בֵּן וַתִּקְרָא אֶת שְׁמוֹ שֵׁת כִּי שָׁת לִי אֱלֹקִים זֶרַע אַחֵר תַּחַת הֶבֶל כִּי הֲרָגוֹ קָיִן: וּלְשֵׁת גַּם הוּא יֻלַּד בֵּן וַיִּקְרָא אֶת שְׁמוֹ אֱנוֹשׁ אָז הוּחַל לִקְרֹא בְּשֵׁם ה':

And Adam was intimate with his wife again; and she bore a son, and called his name Shet, "For God has appointed me another seed instead of Hevel, whom Kayin slew." And as for Shet, he also bore a son; and he called his name Enosh; then men began to call upon the Almighty God by name. (Bereishit 4:25–26)

Noah preserves the line of Shet, the elevated son of Adam and Hava who was uniquely endowed with the breath of the Divine. For better or worse, Kayin's family line is also preserved, through Na'amah. Even after the great flood that purges the world of sin and restores purity and equilibrium, Na'amah carries the line of Kayin into the world.[15] Na'amah, the wife of Noah, survives; the line of Kayin lives on.

---

15. The Maharal (*Gur Aryeh* 4:19) suggests that the descendants of Kayin hesitated to have children because they knew this line should be wiped out as punishment for Kayin's sin.

Why must this be so? Does this line deserve preservation? Is the line of Kayin redeemable? The crux of this question centers on Na'amah, and the answers offered by our sages vary. Some claim that she was a worthy mate for Noah; she, as he, was righteous.[16] Others identify Na'amah as a demonic figure[17] who was guilty of causing even the angels to fall.[18] This tradition of "fallen angels" is associated with the enigmatic "*bnei elohim*" and the equally mysterious "*Nefilim*" who appear at the very end of Parashat Bereishit, as part of the backdrop to the generation of the flood:

בראשית ו:א–ב, ד

וַיְהִי כִּי הֵחֵל הָאָדָם לָרֹב עַל פְּנֵי הָאֲדָמָה וּבָנוֹת יֻלְּדוּ לָהֶם: וַיִּרְאוּ בְנֵי הָאֱלֹהִים אֶת בְּנוֹת הָאָדָם כִּי טֹבֹת הֵנָּה וַיִּקְחוּ לָהֶם נָשִׁים מִכֹּל אֲשֶׁר בָּחָרוּ:...הַנְּפִלִים הָיוּ בָאָרֶץ בַּיָּמִים הָהֵם וְגַם אַחֲרֵי כֵן אֲשֶׁר יָבֹאוּ בְּנֵי הָאֱלֹהִים אֶל בְּנוֹת הָאָדָם וְיָלְדוּ לָהֶם הֵמָּה הַגִּבֹּרִים אֲשֶׁר מֵעוֹלָם אַנְשֵׁי הַשֵּׁם:

And when man began to multiply on the face of the earth, and daughters were born to them, the sons of the powerful saw that the

---

ספר גור אריה, בראשית ד:יט

מפני שכל העניין מדבר איך היו פורשין נשי למך מן למך בשביל שהיו יראים מפני עונש קין (רש"י שם), והוצרך לפייס אותם. והשתא לא קשה למה נכתב זה כאן, כי נכתב איך היה גדול עונש קין עד שהיו נשי למך פורשין ממנו בשביל יראת העונש. ועוד דבא לאשמועינן שכל זרע של קין נמחה, שהרי יראים היו מלהוליד, ובלאו הכי לא היינו יודעים שנענש זרעו של קין.

16. Bereishit Rabbah 23:3.

בראשית רבה, פרשה כג פסקה ג

ואחות תובל קין נעמה: א"ר אבא בר כהנא: נעמה אשתו של נח היתה. למה היו קורין אותה נעמה? שהיו מעשיה נעימים. ורבנן אמרי: נעמה אחרת היתה. ולמה היו קורין אותה נעמה? שהיתה מנעמת בתוף לעבודת כוכבים.

"'And the sister of Tuval-Kayin was Na'amah': R. Abba b. Kahana said: 'Na'amah was Noah's wife; and why was she called Na'amah? Because her deeds were pleasing (*ne'imim*).' The rabbis said: 'Na'amah was a woman of a different stamp, for the name denotes that she sang (*man'emet*) to the timbrel in honor of idolatry.'"

17. See Zohar, Vayikra 76b.

18. Both sides are quoted in the Midrash haNe'elam:

מדרש הנעלם פרשת בראשית, מאמר קין והבל ושת

א"ר יצחק: מאי דכתיב, ואחות תובל קין נעמה? אלא א"ר יצחק, צדקת היתה, ונעימה במעשיה. ר' אבהו אמר: פשוטו של מקרא מורה על שהיתה חכמה במלאכת הברזל, כמו אחיה תובל קין. משמע דכתיב, הוא היה אבי כל חרש נחשת וברזל, ואחות תובל קין נעמה, הוא הוציא אומנות זו, ואחותו עמו. הה"ד, ואחות תובל קין נעמה, שהיתה בקיאה כמותו, וא"ו דואחות מוסיף על העניין של מעלה. רבי בא אמר: אמן של שדים היתה, והולידה אותם. דהא אימא דאשמדאי, מלכא דשידי, נעמה שמה. ר' יצחק בשם ר' יוחנן אמר: על שם יופיה נקראת כך, וממנה יצאו אותן דכתיב כי טובות הנה, במראה וביופי.

daughters of men were attractive, and they took whatever women
they chose.... There were Nefilim on the earth in those days, and also
after that, when the sons of the powerful ones took the daughters of
men, and they bore their children; the same became mighty men of
old, men of renown. (Bereishit 6:1–2, 4)

This passage seems to outline the existence of various strata of society –
even strata of humanity: the sons of the powerful, the daughters of man,
the even-more-obscure Nefilim. We have suggested the possibility that
the "sons of the powerful" are "prehistoric" soulless humanoids, offspring
of Adam and Hava who did not possess the breath of the Divine that
distinguished Adam, Hava and their son Shet.[19] This line, then, would
include Kayin; it is preserved through Na'amah.[20]

Is Na'amah a demon-like temptress, or a fitting spouse for the great
tzaddik, the most righteous man of the generation? We should recall that
Noah's wife entered the ark with the other women, and Rashi noted that
this indicates the abstinence that would be practiced on the boat. If this
is Na'amah, the conclusion is startling, the contrast stark: This woman is
the daughter of Tzillah, the "trophy wife" taken by Lemekh solely for the
purpose of hedonistic pleasure. Here she stands, as the waters begin to
cover the earth, the leader of the women who have been chosen to bring
about the historic reconciliation, the rebirth of creation – through the
observance of abstinence and the preservation of holiness on the ark. Seen
in this light, Na'amah is anything but a brazen seductress.

As the flood narrative unfolds, so many details of the story begin to take
on different hues when viewed from the perspective of Na'amah's personal

---

19. See above, "In Search of the Serpent."
20. This does not help us understand the Nefilim, which literally means "the fallen ones."
    See Talmud Bavli Yoma 67b:

    תלמוד בבלי, מסכת יומא דף סז עמוד ב
    תנא דבי רבי ישמעאל: עזאזל – שמכפר על מעשה עוזא ועזאל.

    Rashi explains that these were destructive angels, products of the seduction of Na'amah.
    For more on these angels see Rav Reuven Margoliot, *Malakhei Elyon*, page 273ff; Zohar,
    Bereishit 23a. Also see Rashi, Talmud Bavli Yoma 67b, and Midrash Aggadah (Buber)
    Bereishit, chapter 4, which states that the angels were tempted by Na'amah's beauty, but
    she rebuffed their advances.

history: All of the creatures board the ark in pairs, in what may now be seen as a polemic against Lemekh's bigamy and the corruption and egocentricity of that entire generation. And yet, the order of the day, the way that Creation will be preserved and redeemed, is not through the sexuality of these pairs but through their abstinence. The family unit on the ark that is entrusted with preserving all of creation will work together with common purpose, as helpmates, as soul mates. They will assist Noah in his role of caretaker for all the species – the shepherd for all of Creation, as it were. Only when the descendants of Kayin and of Shet join together to assume the vocation left vacant by Hevel's death can humanity be redeemed. When Noah later reverts to the role of Kayin – planting a vineyard and turning his back on the role of shepherd, he is humiliated and his descendants are cursed. The role of Hevel brings salvation; the role of Kayin brings ignominy.

We may now view Ham's outrageous behavior as a throwback to the preflood generation,[21] or as a reemergence of the "Kayin genes" that Ham inherited through Na'amah. In fact, throughout the book of Bereishit, the men who use sexual conquest as a means of domination, and abuse power and sexuality in a volatile mix, are all descendants of Ham: Par'oh, [22] Avimelekh, the men of Sodom[23] are all descendants of Ham. Lemekh, too, was such a man, but he was no trendsetter; Rashi stresses that Lemekh's behavior was prototypical of that generation: the moral bankruptcy of a world in which women were objectified and valued only for their utility, coupled with a ruthless, violent struggle for power, paved the way for destruction.

As we read the story of Ham's violation of Noah in the aftermath of the flood, as we trace this same streak of violence and sexuality from the Serpent,[24] through Kayin, to Ham, and through the generations of Ham's

21. See *Ma'arekhet ha'Elokut*, chapter 13.

ספר מערכת האלקות, פרק שלושה עשר

גם נשארו לקיום העולם אחר דור המבול שהיתה כמו בריאה חדשה שבעה.... אמנם לא רצה השם ית' להאביד מביתו של נח הצדיק ומזרעו כלום בזכותו לא קדם המבול ולא אחר המבול. אמנם קלקל חם ונתקלקל זרעו.

22. Bereishit 12:15.

23. Bereishit 10:19, 13:13.

24. See above, "In Search of the Serpent."

descendants, a certain fatalism seeps in. Was it really necessary to preserve the line of Kayin, to keep this streak alive and send it out into the world after the flood? Once again, the answer lies with Na'amah. Here is the child of Lemekh and Tzillah, the product of an unholy union, born in hedonism and selfishness, heir to the dubious legacy of violence passed down from Kayin. And yet, Na'amah was a righteous woman. She was a worthy mate for the son of Shet, a worthy progenitor for the new world that would arise after the flood. In fact, Na'amah is held up as a shining example of the efficacy of *teshuvah* (repentance): Rav Tzadok haKohen points to Na'amah as proof that Kayin's *teshuvah* was real; no descendents of the stature of Na'amah and Avraham could have been possible otherwise. *Teshuvah* is an absolute; it is always possible and always effective.[25] Without the possibility of *teshuvah*, our continued existence is impossible.

Our failures are always attributable to others – background and social pressures, genetics and upbringing. We learn from Na'amah that despite the violent, oppressive nature of the surrounding society, despite the extremely challenging family history, despite the genetic and genealogical challenges with which we are born, we are all capable of making choices for our own lives. Although the line of the Serpent, of Kayin, lives on within each of us,[26] God does not despair of our capacity to rise above, to connect with the divine breath with which He has endowed each and every one of us. And if He believes in us, can we believe any less?

---

25. *Pri Tzaddik*, Parashat Vayeilekh and Shabbat Teshuvah, section 8.

ספר פרי צדיק פרשת וילך ושבת תשובה, אות ח

וכן מצינו בקין שבאמת הועיל תשובתו דאיתא (בר"ר פ' כ"ג) נעמה אשתו של נח היתה ויצא ממנה כל העולם ואברהם אבינו ע"ה וכל אומה הישראלית. וכן בשורש נשמות איתא מהאר"י הקדוש דמחצה משורש קין ומחצה משורש הבל.

26. See *Ma'arekhet ha'Elokut*, chapter 13.

ספר מערכת האלקות, פרק שלושה עשר

גם נשארו לקיום העולם אחר דור המבול כמו בריאה חדשה שבעה. נח ושלושה בניו וג' נשי בניו. ואולי נשארה נעמה אשת נח שהיתה עודפת על מספר הז' מזרע קין בעבור שלא רצה השם ית' למחו' לגמרי שמם מאות' שהיו ראשונים בבריאה....

The Raven – Nevermore?

"Prophet!" said I, "thing of evil! – prophet still, if bird or devil! –
Whether Tempter sent, or whether tempest tossed thee here ashore,
Desolate yet all undaunted, on this desert land enchanted –
On this home by horror haunted – tell me truly, I implore –
Is there – is there balm in Gilead – tell me – tell me, I implore!"
Quoth the Raven, "Nevermore."

From "The Raven," by Edgar Allan Poe[1]

In the aftermath of the destruction, as Noah floats along on his ark, the waters have become eerily still, and a strange silence has replaced the angry, deadly storm. Now the Torah reports that Noah and all of creation have been remembered:

בראשית ח:א

וַיִּזְכֹּר אֱלֹקִים אֶת נֹחַ וְאֵת כָּל הַחַיָּה וְאֶת כָּל הַבְּהֵמָה אֲשֶׁר אִתּוֹ בַּתֵּבָה וַיַּעֲבֵר
אֱלֹקִים רוּחַ עַל הָאָרֶץ וַיָּשֹׁכּוּ הַמָּיִם:

But the Almighty remembered Noah and all the wild animals and the livestock that were with him in the ark, and the Almighty sent a wind over the earth, and the waters receded. (Bereishit 8:1)

The name of God utilized in this section is Elokim. The connotation of this name is "God of Judgment,"[2] as opposed to "God of Mercy." We might have thought that a "harsh and angry God" punished humankind and brought all of creation to the brink of extinction, and then a kind (albeit perhaps fickle) God changed His mind, but the Torah informs us that now that judgment has been meted out, Elokim, this very same aspect of Judgment,

---

1. First published on January 29, 1845, in the *New York Evening Mirror*.

2. See Shmot 20:1 and Rashi's comments, as well as Rashi's comments on Tehillim 58:12. Occasionally the word *elohim* refers to a human judge. See Exodus 22:28. This name denotes "possessing power," hence our use of the name "Almighty" in translation.

remembers Noah. At the end of forty days Noah opens the window and sends forth a raven:

בראשית ח:ו–ז

וַיְהִי מִקֵּץ אַרְבָּעִים יוֹם וַיִּפְתַּח נֹחַ אֶת חַלּוֹן הַתֵּבָה אֲשֶׁר עָשָׂה: וַיְשַׁלַּח אֶת הָעֹרֵב

וַיֵּצֵא יָצוֹא וָשׁוֹב עַד יְבֹשֶׁת הַמַּיִם מֵעַל הָאָרֶץ:

After forty days Noah opened the window he had made in the ark and sent out a raven, and it kept flying back and forth until the water had dried up from the earth. (Bereishit 8:6–7)

The raven suffers from a negative reputation, associated in both rabbinic and general Western literature with demonic forces.[3] In the unforgettable words of Edgar Allan Poe, quoted above:

"Prophet!" said I, "thing of evil! – prophet still, if bird or devil![4]

While we can leave it to scholars of American poetry to reveal Poe's sources of information and attitude, the negativity toward the raven apparently goes all the way back to chapter 8 of Bereishit. But why the antagonism? What dastardly deed did the raven commit to deserve this reputation? Compare the raven to the dove, which is regarded as a loving, faithful, loyal harbinger of peace. The contrast is stark – as stark as black verses white. While in fact the raven is dark and the dove is white, can the Torah actually ascribe such significance to pigmentation? Let us continue the story and see what happens with the dove.

בראשית ח:ח–יב

וַיְשַׁלַּח אֶת הַיּוֹנָה מֵאִתּוֹ לִרְאוֹת הֲקַלּוּ הַמַּיִם מֵעַל פְּנֵי הָאֲדָמָה: וְלֹא מָצְאָה הַיּוֹנָה

מָנוֹחַ לְכַף רַגְלָהּ וַתָּשָׁב אֵלָיו אֶל הַתֵּבָה כִּי מַיִם עַל פְּנֵי כָל הָאָרֶץ וַיִּשְׁלַח יָדוֹ

וַיִּקָּחֶהָ וַיָּבֵא אֹתָהּ אֵלָיו אֶל הַתֵּבָה: וַיָּחֶל עוֹד שִׁבְעַת יָמִים אֲחֵרִים וַיֹּסֶף שַׁלַּח אֶת

הַיּוֹנָה מִן הַתֵּבָה: וַתָּבֹא אֵלָיו הַיּוֹנָה לְעֵת עֶרֶב וְהִנֵּה עָלֵה זַיִת טָרָף בְּפִיהָ וַיֵּדַע נֹחַ

---

3.   The *Be'er Mayim Hayim* points out that the word raven in Hebrew is spelled *ayin resh bet*, the same letters which spell *b'ra* in reverse, which means "in evil":

ספר באר מים חיים פרשת נח, פרק ח

ואולם הנה כבר כתבנו אשר העורב לא נשלח כלל בשליחות כי אם שלחו מן התיבה שלא יהיה עמו עבור

שראה אותו ברע, אותיות ערב.

4.   See note 1, above.

כִּי קַלּוּ הַמַּיִם מֵעַל הָאָרֶץ: וַיִּיָחֶל עוֹד שִׁבְעַת יָמִים אֲחֵרִים וַיְשַׁלַּח אֶת הַיּוֹנָה וְלֹא
יָסְפָה שׁוּב אֵלָיו עוֹד:

Then he sent out a dove to see if the water had receded from the
surface of the ground. But the dove could find no place to set its feet
because there was water over all the surface of the earth, so it returned
to Noah in the ark. He reached out his hand and took the dove and
brought it back to himself in the ark. He waited seven more days and
again sent out the dove from the ark. When the dove returned to him
in the evening, there in its beak was a freshly plucked olive leaf! Then
Noah knew that the water had receded from the earth. He waited
seven more days and sent the dove out again, but this time it did not
return to him. (Bereishit 8:8–12)

A careful reading of the verses brings several problems to light: While the
objective of the dove's mission is clearly stated, "to see if the water had
receded," the text does not reveal the motivation for sending the raven.
While the juxtaposition of the two birds might suggest a common mission,
the lack of explanation for the raven's mission is nonetheless striking. This
leads to additional questions about the raven: We don't know why specifically
the raven was chosen or if the mission was successful or aborted. Was
this Noah's idea, or was he commanded to send the raven out? Did Noah
perhaps seek permission or approval for his initiative? The text is silent.

When we compare the two verses that describe the sending of the raven and
dove respectively, we notice a second difference: When Noah sends the dove,
the word used is *mei'ito* – מֵאִתּוֹ: literally rendered, he sent the dove "from
himself" (an idiom that is difficult to translate). The reader is left with the
impression that Noah had a close relationship with this dove – perhaps it was
his personal pet. This sort of modifier is entirely absent in the case of the raven.

The dove's mission was successfully completed when it returned with the
olive branch in its beak, creating the enduring image of peace. But what of
the raven? Why was it sent and how did it fare? The Hizkuni suggests an
ominous mandate for the raven:

חזקוני, בראשית ח:ז
וישלח את הערב: לפי שדרכו לאכול נבלות ואם קלו המים ימצא מתי מבול
מושלכים על פני שפת המים.

> *"And he sent out a raven": Because its nature is to eat carcasses, and*
> *if the water had subsided, it would find corpses strewn on the shore.*
> (Hizkuni, Bereishit 8:7)

In contrast to the olive branch in the mouth of the dove, eternal symbol
of peace, we have a vivid image of the predatory, carnivorous raven
descending upon corpses, perhaps even mutilating one to bring something
back to Noah. The image persists despite the raven's failure to even leave
the immediate vicinity of the ark, much less bring back any flesh. While the
Hizkuni's explanation may be the correct reading of the text and of Noah's
motivation for sending the raven, we are still baffled as to why this is not
stated explicitly – namely that the raven was also sent to see if the water
had subsided. This, coupled with the other outstanding textual oddity –
the dove described as having been sent "from him" – leaves us searching
for the deeper meaning of the narrative. Rabbi Naftali Tzvi Yehudah
Berlin (the Netziv) in his Torah commentary *Ha'amek Davar*[5] raises some
important questions: Why were the raven and dove singled out? There are
many birds that fly farther and better then these two. Furthermore, who
gave Noah permission to release these birds prior to the time when all the
other inhabitants of the ark would be released? The Netziv theorizes that
these two birds were not of the "two by two" brought to the ark, rather they
were Noah's pets. With this suggestion, the Netziv solves one problem, but
exchanges it for another: while we may now know why Noah was permitted
to send these birds, we don't know how he was allowed to bring them to
the ark in the first place.

The Ohr haHayim also questions why the raven was sent, but rejects the
suggestion that it was in order to check the water level – the Torah surely
would have stated this, as it does subsequently regarding the dove's mission.
Rather, in keeping with a Talmudic tradition,[6] the Ohr haHayim reveals

---

5. *Ha'amek Davar*, Bereishit 8:7.

העמק דבר, בראשית ח:ז

את העורב: יש להתבונן למה שלח שני עופות הללו, דוקא עורב ויונה. והלא יש הרבה עופות שפורחים
טוב יותר מהם. והתו מאין הי' רשות לנח להוציאם מן התבה לפני זמן היציאה לכולם. ע"כ היה נראה לפי
הפשט דעורב ויונה הללו לא היו מן הזוגות שנכנסו להחיות זרע בדבר ה'. אלא בשביל שהי' נח לפני מי
המבול כאחד מן השרים שמנהגם הי' גם אז לגדל עורבים ויונים.

6. Talmud Bavli Sanhedrin 108b.

why the raven was sent: because Noah didn't want it around. The Talmud suggests that the raven was cast out because it broke protocol and had relations on the ark. While the dove was sent on a reconnaissance mission, the raven was simply expelled. The raven, for his part, refused to leave.

The Talmud recounts that the raven lodges a complaint: he accuses Noah of acting with cruelty and prejudice, for his expulsion would result in the extinction of the species.[7] In fact, that is just one of many accusations the raven puts forth:

תלמוד בבלי, מסכת סנהדרין דף קח עמוד ב

וישלח את הערב, אמר ריש לקיש: תשובה ניצחת השיבו עורב לנח, אמר לו:
רבך שונאני ואתה שנאתני. רבך שונאני – מן הטהורין שבעה, מן הטמאים
שנים. ואתה שנאתני – שאתה מניח ממין שבעה ושולח ממין שנים, אם פוגע
בי שר חמה או שר צנה לא נמצא עולם חסר בריה אחת?

"And he sent forth a raven": Resh Lakish said: The raven gave Noah a triumphant retort. It said to him, "Your Master hates me, and you hate me. Your Master hates me – [since He commanded] seven [pairs to be taken] of the clean [creatures], but only two of the unclean. You hate me – seeing that you leave the species of which there are seven, and send one of which there are only two. Should the angel of heat or of cold smite me, would not the world be short of one kind?" (Talmud Bavli Sanhedrin 108b)

The Talmud describes the raven as having a winning argument. He accuses both Noah and God of hating him: God had shown an obvious preference for other species, commanding Noah to preserve seven of each. And surely it would have been more prudent for Noah to send a bird from one of the species of which more than two of a kind had been on board the ark.

בראשית רבה, פרשה לג סימן ה

ויהי מקץ ארבעים יום ויפתח נח: הדא מסייעא לההוא דא"ר אבא בר כהנא:
חלון.
וישלח את העורב: הה"ד (תהלים קה) "שלח חשך ויחשיך".

---

7. In his commentary to Sanhedrin 108, The *Ben Y'hoyada* points out that once the raven had relations, a new generation of raven was now on the way, and there was no danger of extinction.

ויצא יצא ושוב: ר' יודן בשם ר' יודה ב"ר סימון: התחיל משיבו תשובות. א"ל,
מכל בהמה חיה ועוף שיש כאן אין אתה משלח אלא לי! א"ל, מה צורך לעולם
בך? לא לאכילה לא לקרבן.

_"And it came to pass at the end of forty days, that Noah opened the
halon [window] of the ark": This supports the view of R. Abba b.
Kahana that it was a window [trapdoor]._

_"And he sent forth a raven": Thus it is written, "He sent darkness, and
it was dark" (Tehilim 105:28)._

_"And it went forth to and fro (yatzo va'shov)": R. Yudan said in the
name of R. Yudah b. R. Simon: It began arguing with him: "Of all
the birds that you have here you send none but me!" "What need
then has the world of you?" he retorted. "For food? For a sacrifice?"[8]_
(Bereishit Rabbah 33:5)

Perhaps Noah sees the world through utilitarian eyes: either something
can be used or it has no value. If a raven can't be eaten and can't be used as
an offering, the world simply doesn't need it.

Then the raven goes even further and hurls a bizarre accusation:

תלמוד בבלי, מסכת סנהדרין דף קח עמוד ב

או שמא לאשתי אתה צריך? אמר לו: רשע: במותר לי נאסר לי – בנאסר לי לא
כל שכן. ומנלן דנאסרו – דכתיב, (בראשית ו) "ובאת אל התבה אתה ובניך
ואשתך ונשי בניך אתך", וכתיב, (בראשית ח) "צא מן התבה אתה ואשתך
ובניך ונשי בניך אתך", ואמר רבי יוחנן: מיכן אמרו שנאסרו בתשמיש המטה.

_"Or perhaps you desire my mate!" "You evil one!" he exclaimed. "Even
that which is [usually] permitted me has [now] been forbidden; how
much more so that which is [always] forbidden me!" And whence do
we know that they were forbidden? From the verse, "And you shall
enter into the ark, you, and your sons, and your wife, and the wives
of your sons with you," while further on it is written, "Go forth from
the ark, you, and your wife, and your sons, and your sons' wives
with you." Whereon R. Yohanan observed: From this we deduce that
cohabitation had been forbidden._ (Talmud Bavli Sanhedrin 108b)

---

8. Apparently Noah is not troubled by the potential extinction of the raven.

The raven accuses Noah of fancying his spouse; Noah honors the accusation with a response, proving the raven's charge outrageous: if, while on the ark, he has maintained abstinence from his own wife, how much more so would he avoid intimacy with the raven's spouse, who is always off limits! What could have made the raven construe the situation in this manner? The Talmud portrays this as a case of projection. The raven was one of three who broke boundaries on the ark and engaged in illicit sexual behavior:

תלמוד בבלי, מסכת סנהדרין דף קח עמוד ב

תנו רבנן: שלשה שמשו בתיבה, וכולם לקו: כלב, ועורב, וחם. כלב – נקשר, עורב – רק, חם – לקה בעורו.

Our rabbis taught: Three copulated in the ark, and they were all punished: the dog, the raven, and Ham. The dog was doomed to be tied, the raven expectorates [his seed into his mate's mouth]. And Ham was smitten in his skin. (Talmud Bavli Sanhedrin 108b)

Noah's perspective of the raven is negative, but of the three transgressors, surely the one who bore the most responsibility was Ham – though some commentators suggest that only after seeing the raven engaging in this behavior did Ham "heat up"[9] and follow suit. While Noah doesn't have much use for the raven, seeing him as dark and devoid of utility, he also may not have much use for his son Ham, whose outrageous and immoral behavior in the following verses leads Noah to cast a dire curse upon one of Ham's sons.[10] In citing Ham's punishment by affliction of the skin, the analogy between Ham and the raven is drawn on more than one level, and we return to the theme of pigment. Later in the narrative we are also told that one of Ham's children is Kush – meaning *black*.

As a result of the raven's immoral behavior, Noah sees it as a symbol of the darkness and cruelty that surround him and that have led to the massive, nearly total destruction of the world and its inhabitants.[11] The Torah

---

9. The name *Ham* means hot. See comments of Rav Shimshon Raphael Hirsch to this section.

10. See 9:24–26.

11. See Rav Tzadok haKohen, *Kometz haMinhah*, part 2, section 24, where sources are cited stating that the raven hates its own offspring.

teaches that God's kindness was held in abeyance during the flood, while the attribute of Elokim[12] reigned. But from Noah's perspective, it appears that God has simply abandoned the world.[13] For his first overture in the postdiluvian world Noah sends forth a symbol of cruelty and darkness. Only later does he explore the possibility of kindness, loyalty and peace, sending the white dove, which represents God's mercy and kindness. The dove's character is reflected even in in its name, as the Hebrew word *yonah* is composed of three of the four letters of the Divine Name that denotes omnipresence. Noah rejects the raven, casts it away and identifies with the dove that he sends "*mei'ito*" – of or from himself.

There is, however, someone who does not concur with Noah's judgment and attitude toward the raven: God, the creator of this dark, maligned creature.

בראשית רבה, פרשה לג פסקה ה

רבי ברכיה בשם רבי אבא בר כהנא אמר: אמר לו הקב"ה, "קבלו, שעתיד העולם להצטרך לו". אמר לו, "אימתי?" אמר לו, "'עד יבשת המים מעל הארץ'. עתיד צדיק אחד לעמוד ולייבש את העולם ואני מצריכו לו", הה"ד (מלכים א, יז) "והעורבים מביאים לו לחם ובשר בבקר ולחם ובשר בערב."

R. Berekhyah said in R. Abba b. Kahana's name: The Holy One, blessed be He, said to him [Noah], "Take it back, because the world

---

ספר קומץ המנחה, חלק ב אות כד

והעורב שונא בנו כמו שאמרו בכתובות (מט ע"ב) ובשאר דוכתי הוא כמו שאמרו ז"ל (בבא בתרא טז ע"א) הוא שטן הוא יצר הרע הוא מלאך המות ורשעים תרדף רעה. ולכך הקדים נח שליחות העורב לעולם מן היונה כמו שקדם עשו ליעקב כי לעולם הקליפה קדמה לפרי.

12. The issue of the use of the different names of God, used as an intellectual battering ram by certain students of biblical criticism, sheds much light on bibilical study when properly understood, particularly when studying Bereishit and Noah. If one keeps in mind that the Torah always uses YHVH in connection with offerings, some insight may be achieved. The commandment to bring certain animals to the ark "two by two," simply to insure survival of the species, is ordered by Elokim – a name associated with nature. The command to bring ritually pure animals onto the ark seven by seven, to facilitate the bringing of offerings after the flood, is commanded by YHVH. The two names are merged in 9:26–27.

13. See Zohar Hadash, Bereishit 38b.

זוהר חדש, בראשית דף לח עמוד ב

אלא א"ר חייא למה שלח את העורב? דא"ר חייא מצטער הוה נח טפי על אובדא דעלמא. אמר רבש"ע ידעתי כי אתה רחום ואתה לא רחמת על עולמך ונהפך רחמנותך לאכזרות אתה לא רחמת על בניך יצא זה שאינו מרחם על בניו ונהפך להם לאכזרי ולפיכך שלח את העורב רמז הוא דקא רמז.

*will need it in the future." "When?" he asked. "'When the waters dry
off from on the earth' (Bereishit 8:7) – a righteous man will arise
and dry up the world, and will cause him to have need of them [the
ravens]," as it is written, "And the ravens brought him bread and
meat..." (I Melakhim 17:6). (Bereishit Rabbah 33:5)*

This midrash refers to an episode that we may consider an inverse of the
flood – a time of drought. The raven comes into its own, as it were, and
rises to the occasion.

מלכים א, יז:א–ו

וַיֹּאמֶר אֵלִיָּהוּ הַתִּשְׁבִּי מִתֹּשָׁבֵי גִלְעָד אֶל אַחְאָב חַי ה' אֱלֹקֵי יִשְׂרָאֵל אֲשֶׁר עָמַדְתִּי
לְפָנָיו אִם יִהְיֶה הַשָּׁנִים הָאֵלֶּה טַל וּמָטָר כִּי אִם לְפִי דְבָרִי: וַיְהִי דְבַר ה' אֵלָיו
לֵאמֹר: לֵךְ מִזֶּה וּפָנִיתָ לְּךָ קֵדְמָה וְנִסְתַּרְתָּ בְּנַחַל כְּרִית אֲשֶׁר עַל פְּנֵי הַיַּרְדֵּן: וְהָיָה
מֵהַנַּחַל תִּשְׁתֶּה וְאֶת הָעֹרְבִים צִוִּיתִי לְכַלְכֶּלְךָ שָׁם: וַיֵּלֶךְ וַיַּעַשׂ כִּדְבַר ה' וַיֵּלֶךְ וַיֵּשֶׁב
בְּנַחַל כְּרִית אֲשֶׁר עַל פְּנֵי הַיַּרְדֵּן: וְהָעֹרְבִים מְבִיאִים לוֹ לֶחֶם וּבָשָׂר בַּבֹּקֶר וְלֶחֶם
וּבָשָׂר בָּעֶרֶב...

*Now Eliyahu the Tishbite, a resident of Gilead, said to Ahav, "By the
God of Israel (YHVH) whom I serve, there will be neither dew nor
rain in the next few years except at my word." Then the word of God
came to Eliyahu: "Leave here, turn eastward and hide in the Krit
Ravine, east of the Jordan. You will drink from the brook, and I have
ordered the ravens to feed you there." So he did what God had told
him. He went to the Krit Ravine, east of the Jordan, and stayed there.
The ravens brought him bread and meat in the morning and bread
and meat in the evening...* (I Melakhim 17:1–6)

God's answer to Noah is, "I have a plan for the raven. He will be needed
in the future." The name of the raven in Hebrew, *'orev*, does not mean
"black"; it comes from the root word meaning "mixture."[14] While Noah

---

14. The raven represents the mixture or confusion of good and evil that is the result of
eating from the Tree of Knowledge. See comments of *Noam Elimelekh* to Parashat Ki
Tavo.

ספר נועם אלימלך, פרשת כי תבא

וזהו דמצינו באליהו הנביא ז"ל וישב בנחל כרית והעורבים מביאים לו לחם. ולכאורה למה בחר ה'
בעורבים שהם אכזרים על בניהם שהם יביאו לו לחם ועל פי דברינו הנ"ל כך פירושו וישב בנחל שהיה

may treat the raven as black,[15] especially when compared to the fair dove, whose name and nature possess a hint of the Divine, the raven is apparently far more complex – reflecting the mixture of good and bad, a representation of post-Eden reality. Noah chooses to reject and expel the raven. He does not accept the merger of good and evil. He sees his own survival as testimony to the eradication of evil and the triumph of good. God sees things differently.

There is another book that grapples with this same tension: should an imperfect society be saved or eradicated? The prophet who chooses to see the world in black and white is none other than the prophet named Yonah, the Hebrew word for dove.

יונה א:א–ד

וַיְהִי דְּבַר ה' אֶל יוֹנָה בֶן אֲמִתַּי לֵאמֹר: קוּם לֵךְ אֶל נִינְוֵה הָעִיר הַגְּדוֹלָה וּקְרָא עָלֶיהָ כִּי עָלְתָה רָעָתָם לְפָנָי: וַיָּקָם יוֹנָה לִבְרֹחַ תַּרְשִׁישָׁה מִלִּפְנֵי ה' וַיֵּרֶד יָפוֹ וַיִּמְצָא אֳנִיָּה בָּאָה תַרְשִׁישׁ וַיִּתֵּן שְׂכָרָהּ וַיֵּרֶד בָּהּ לָבוֹא עִמָּהֶם תַּרְשִׁישָׁה מִלִּפְנֵי ה': וה' הֵטִיל רוּחַ גְּדוֹלָה אֶל הַיָּם וַיְהִי סַעַר גָּדוֹל בַּיָּם וְהָאֳנִיָּה חִשְּׁבָה לְהִשָּׁבֵר:

The word of God came to Yonah son of Amittai: "Go to the great city of Nineveh and preach against it, because its wickedness has come up before me." But Yonah ran away from God and headed for Tarshish. He went down to Jaffa, where he found a ship bound for that port. After paying the fare, he went aboard and sailed for Tarshish to flee

---

ממשיך השפעות מנחל העליון. ודרכי העורבים הם הקליפות לטרוף טרף ההשפעות אלא העובד ד' מאהבה גם הם ישלימו ויסכימו עמו לבלתי יגעו בהשפעה וזהו רמז שהעורבים הביאו לו לחם רוצה לומר שגם הקליפות הסכימו עמו...

...או יאמר בדרך הרמז וישלח הרמז את העורב ויצא יצוא ושוב. על דרך שפירש הרב הגלאנטי ז"ל (והבאתיו למעלה ב קץ כל בשר) את מאמר חז"ל (ברכות נ"ט.) הקב"ה מוריד שתי דמעות לים הגדול על דרך משל שבא אחד ומרד כנגדו והמלך מתכעס על ידי זה ועל ידי זה יכאב ח"ו לב המלך בעת כעסו, מה עושה לוקח איש הלזה ושולח אותו למקום המשפט שיגמרו דינו שם והם עושים המשפט להשיב גמולו בראשו, ועל ידי זה נדחה מלב המלך כל בחינת הכעס וכאיבת לב כיון ששולחו לקבל משפטו. וכן הרשע המורד נגד מלך מלכי המלכים הקב"ה הוא מערב רע בטוב וטוב ברע והוא נקרא דמע מלשון מלשני עירול כמו שאמרו (גיטין נ"ב ע"ב) המטמא והמדמע וכו', וכדי שלא יהיה פגם במדות העליונות מוריד אותן הדמעות לים הגדול מקום הצדק והמשפט שיחרץ שם משפטו וישולם לו שכרו משלם, וכסא המלוכה נקי, עד כאן דבריו. והנה כשזכה נח לפתוח פתח המ"ם להאיר באורה על יושבי הארץ, ירא לנפשו פן אולי יחטאו עוד בני האדם ויערבו רע בטוב וטוב ברע ויהיה פגם במדות העליונות חלילה, אשר על כן ביקש רחמים על זה, ופעל זאת. וישלח את העורב כלומר זה הדמע והעירוב רע בטוב וטוב ברע יצוא ויצא ושוב כלומר לצאת ממדות העליונות אל מדות התחתונות אשר הם בבחינת יצוא ושוב...

15. It is important to note that black is not a primary color – but rather a lack of color.

*from God. Then God sent a great wind on the sea, and such a violent
storm arose that the ship threatened to break apart.* (Yonah 1:1–4)

The name of God used here indicates compassion. Yonah runs away from
God's compassion; he thinks that he would prefer pure justice.

יונה ד:א–ג

וַיֵּרַע אֶל יוֹנָה רָעָה גְדוֹלָה וַיִּחַר לוֹ: וַיִּתְפַּלֵּל אֶל ה' וַיֹּאמַר אָנָּה ה' הֲלוֹא זֶה דְבָרִי
עַד הֱיוֹתִי עַל אַדְמָתִי עַל כֵּן קִדַּמְתִּי לִבְרֹחַ תַּרְשִׁישָׁה כִּי יָדַעְתִּי כִּי אַתָּה אֵל חַנּוּן
וְרַחוּם אֶרֶךְ אַפַּיִם וְרַב חֶסֶד וְנִחָם עַל הָרָעָה: וְעַתָּה ה' קַח נָא אֶת נַפְשִׁי מִמֶּנִּי כִּי
טוֹב מוֹתִי מֵחַיָּי:

*But Yonah was greatly displeased and became angry. He prayed to
God: "O God, is this not what I said when I was still in my own land?
That is why I was so quick to flee to Tarshish. I knew that you are
a gracious and compassionate God, slow to anger and abounding
in love, a God who relents from sending calamity. Now, O God,
take away my life, for it is better for me to die than to live."* (Yonah
4:1–3)

In order to fully appreciate the irony, we must take a closer look at the
other main protagonists in the book of Yonah, namely the inhabitants of
the city of Ninveh. What is their lineage – from which dark place did they
emerge?

בראשית י:ח–יב

וְכוּשׁ יָלַד אֶת נִמְרֹד הוּא הֵחֵל לִהְיוֹת גִּבֹּר בָּאָרֶץ: הוּא הָיָה גִבֹּר צַיִד לִפְנֵי ה' עַל כֵּן
יֵאָמַר כְּנִמְרֹד גִּבּוֹר צַיִד לִפְנֵי ה': וַתְּהִי רֵאשִׁית מַמְלַכְתּוֹ בָּבֶל וְאֶרֶךְ וְאַכַּד וְכַלְנֵה
בְּאֶרֶץ שִׁנְעָר: מִן הָאָרֶץ הַהִוא יָצָא אַשּׁוּר וַיִּבֶן אֶת נִינְוֵה וְאֶת רְחֹבֹת עִיר וְאֶת
כָּלַח: וְאֶת רֶסֶן בֵּין נִינְוֵה וּבֵין כָּלַח הִוא הָעִיר הַגְּדֹלָה:

*Kush [the son of Ham] was the father of Nimrod, who grew to be a
mighty warrior on the earth. He was a mighty hunter before God; that
is why it is said, "Like Nimrod, a mighty hunter before God." The first
centers of his kingdom were Babylon, Erekh, Akkad and Khalneh, in
Shinar. From that land he went to Assyria, where he built Nineveh,
Rehovot Ir, Kalah, and Resen, which is between Nineveh and Kalah;
that is the great city.* (Bereishit 10:8–12)

The city of Ninveh is built and populated by descendants of Ham, his son Kush and his grandson Nimrod[16] – quite an unholy trinity of forebears. Such a city should certainly be destroyed; what justification could possibly exist for its salvation? This seems to be Yonah's perspective. The rebellious prophet tries to escape God's call to judgment; he boards a seagoing ship, just as Noah did all those years before. Now Ninveh, which is thematically connected with the raven, has as its adversary Yonah – the thematic continuation of Noah and the dove. Yonah, like Noah, sees the world as black and white, while the city of Ninveh represents the raven – the *'orev* – the combination of good and evil. When Yonah looks at Ninveh – its past, present and future – he sees evil. God sees the more complex reality, the confusion of good and evil represented in the figure and personality of the raven.

How appropriate that the symbol of God's covenant with Noah, and through him with all of humanity, is the many-colored rainbow. The world is not black and white, it is multicolored, and each color melts into the next. Good is merged with evil, and evil with good. The very existence of the world in the aftermath of the deluge is a testament to the merciful God, and the symbol of His covenant is a spectacular mosaic of color. Even when the world seems foreboding, dark and evil, we must learn from God and not from Noah or Yonah: we must look more carefully and learn to distinguish between the elements of the mixture. Good may be found amongst the evil, and things that don't look completely good are not necessarily completely bad. That is the lesson taught by the raven.

---

16. According to tradition, it was Nimrod who threw Avraham into the fiery furnace. See Bereishit Rabbah 38:13.

Parashat Lekh Lekha

Love and Fear

Parashat Lekh Lekha begins in what seems to be the middle – the middle of Avraham's life, the middle of some ongoing dialogue or relationship between Avraham and God, the middle of a paradigm shift, the middle of Terah's failed voyage to Canaan. The gap in the biographical information leaves us at a loss to understand why Avraham has been chosen.[1] This dearth of detail becomes even more curious when we compare it to the previous week's parashah. Despite everything we don't know about Noah, at a very minimum we are told that he was a righteous man who walked with God. He was set apart from his generation by a certain moral uniqueness. What do we know about Avraham? Avraham was introduced at the end of Parashat Noah in almost laconic terms: Terah, son of Nahor, takes Lot, his grandson by his deceased son, as well as Avram, one of his two surviving sons, and Avram's wife Sarai, and sets out for Canaan. He makes it as far as Haran, and the narrative stops there. We know nothing of the moral fiber of this family, no personal details about any of the characters. In fact, the commentaries suggest that Terah's son Nahor was only a half-brother to Avraham and Haran, and that Sarai was actually a sister to Lot and Milkah.[2] In short, the opening statement of our present parashah takes us by surprise:

בראשית יב:א–ד

וַיֹּאמֶר ה' אֶל אַבְרָם לֶךְ לְךָ מֵאַרְצְךָ וּמִמּוֹלַדְתְּךָ וּמִבֵּית אָבִיךָ אֶל הָאָרֶץ אֲשֶׁר אַרְאֶךָּ: וְאֶעֶשְׂךָ לְגוֹי גָּדוֹל וַאֲבָרֶכְךָ וַאֲגַדְּלָה שְׁמֶךָ וֶהְיֵה בְּרָכָה: וַאֲבָרְכָה מְבָרְכֶיךָ וּמְקַלֶּלְךָ אָאֹר וְנִבְרְכוּ בְךָ כֹּל מִשְׁפְּחֹת הָאֲדָמָה:

---

1. Regarding the Midrashic material describing Avraham's early life see *Explorations. Parashat Lekh Lekha.*

2. See Rashi, Bereishit 20:12.

רש"י, בראשית כ:יב

אחותי בת אבי היא: ובת אב מותרת לבן נח שאין אבות לעוע"א. וכדי לאמת דבריו השיבו כן. וא"ת והלא בת אחיו היתה – בני בנים הרי הן כבנים והרי היא בתו של תרח. וכן הוא אומר ללוט כי אנשים אחים אנחנו.

אך לא בת אמי: הרן מאם אחרת היה.

*And God said to Avram, "Go forth from your land and your birthplace
and from the house of your father to the land that I will show you;
and I will make you into a great nation and I will bless you and I
will make your name great and you will be a blessing. And I will
bless those who bless you, and whoever curses you I will curse, and
all the nations of the earth shall be blessed through you." (Bereishit
12:1–4)*

Avram merits direct communication, intimate personal involvement
with God. He is given a direct commandment, and promised almost
unimaginable reward. We have no inkling as to the events that precipitate
this commandment.

If the text of our parashah leaves us with questions, we may turn to the
haftarah reading chosen by our sages to fill in the gaps. Yet here, too, there
is a dearth of detail. The haftarah reading for this portion is a section taken
from the book of Yeshayahu, 40:26 through 41:16. This reading speaks, in
general, about the nature of the people of Israel as God's chosen nation.
There is only one reference to Avraham in the section:

ישעיהו מא:ח

וְאַתָּה יִשְׂרָאֵל עַבְדִּי יַעֲקֹב אֲשֶׁר בְּחַרְתִּיךָ זֶרַע אַבְרָהָם אֹהֲבִי:

*You are Yisrael, my servant Yaakov whom I have chosen, descendants
of Avraham who loved Me. (Yeshayahu 41:8)*

We are left to surmise from this verse that the "chosenness" of the people
of Israel is a result of the chosenness of Yaakov, which is a result of
Avraham's love of God. Clearly, this is a central tenet of our faith, a pillar
of our national identity; where, then, can we find Avraham's love of God in
the text of the Torah? Rashi analyzes the text of the haftarah for clues:

רש"י, ישעיהו מא:ח

זרע אברהם אוהבי: שלא הכירני מתוך תוכחה ולימוד אבותיו אלא מתוך
אהבה.

*"Descendants of Avraham who loved Me": For he did not come to
know Me through words of rebuke or from what he was taught by his
forebears, but out of love. (Rashi, Yeshayahu 41:8)*

Avraham finds God not through fear or rebuke, nor through the teachings of his father, but through love. Avraham comes to a unique and solitary understanding of God, Creator and Sustainer of the Universe, as the source and essence of love. As this parashah unfolds, each episode of Avraham's life story must be seen through the prism of Avraham's discovery of God.

Other commentaries expand Rashi's comment in order to bring into focus the details of Avraham's life.

ספר השל"ה הקדוש, פרשת וירא תורה אור (ג)

ומדת החסד הוא סוד האהבה כמו שיתבאר לקמן, ומאחר שזכה אברהם אבינו למדת החסד נכנס לאהבה, אשר על זה נאמר "אברהם אוהבי".

And the attribute of hesed *is the mystery of love, as we shall see; and once Avraham merited the attribute of* hesed *he entered this love, and in this regard the verse refers to "Avraham who loved Me."*
(Shlah HaKadosh on Bereishit, Parashat Vayeira Torah Ohr, 3)

The love that Avraham discovers, the attribute of God as a loving and sustaining Creator, is manifest in God's attribute of *Hesed*, and this becomes the defining attribute of Avraham's relationship with God and with his fellow men for the rest of his life.

Other commentaries interpret this verse differently, with an ear to the echoes of the word *ahavah* as it appears later in the Torah. First, the Ramban's discussion of *ahavat Hashem* (love of God), as it appears in his commentary on the Ten Commandments:

רמב"ן, שמות כ:ו

לאהבי ולשומרי מצותי: ...לאהביו – הם המוסרים נפשם עליו, כי המודים בשם הנכבד ובאלקותו לבדו ויכפרו בכל אלוה נכר ולא יעבדו אותם עם סכנת נפשם, יקראו אוהביו, כי זו היא האהבה שנתחייבנו בה בנפשותינו, כמו שאמר (דברים ו) "ואהבת את ה' אלקיך בכל לבבך ובכל נפשך" – שתמסור נפשך וחייך באהבתו, שלא תחליפנו באל אחר, ולא תשתף עמו אל נכר. ולכך נאמר באברהם (ישעיהו מא) "זרע אברהם אוהבי", שנתן נפשו שלא יעבוד ע"ז באור כשדים. ושאר הצדיקים יקראו שומרי מצותיו. ורבים פירשו (עי' רמב"ם בפירוש משנה סנהדרין ריש פרק י) כי "אוהביו" – העובדים מאהבה שלא על מנת לקבל פרס, כמו שהזכירו חכמים [בספרי, דברים יא:יג].

"And I [God] will do hesed *to those who love Me and to those who safeguard My commandments":* ... *Those who love God are they who forfeit their souls for Him, those who know and recognize God's singularity and sovereignty and reject any foreign power or deity, even if doing so puts them in mortal danger – they are called* ohavei Hashem *(lovers of God), for this is the love that is required of us by the verse "And you shall love the Almighty your God with all of your heart and with all of your soul" (Devarim 6:5). You are required to forfeit your soul and your life for His love, that you must not exchange love of God for any other god, nor accept any other deity along with Him. In this regard Avraham is called "Avraham who loved Me" (Yeshayahu 41:8) because he forfeited his life rather than worship other gods in Ur Kasdim. Other righteous people are called "those who safeguard His commandments." And other authorities have pointed out in many instances (see Rambam's Commentary on the Mishnah, Sanhedrin, beginning of chapter 10) that "those who love Me" refers to those who serve God motivated only by love and not in the hope of receiving any reward [see Sifri, Devarim 11:13].* (Ramban, Shmot 20:6)

The Ramban equates love of God with uncompromising monotheism. The Jew is commanded to love God "with all your heart and all your soul," even to the point of martyrdom. This is the sort of love of God that Avraham had: his belief in the singularity and uniqueness of God was so absolute and exclusive that he was prepared to die rather than worship the pagan gods of Ur Kasdim. Ramban here refers to an incident that does not appear in the text of the Torah but which has become so ingrained in our collective consciousness that it is an axiom of our faith: Avraham was cast into the fiery furnace when he espoused monotheism and refused to renounce his belief in the oneness of God.

The Ramban continues his analysis of the concept of *ahavat Hashem* (love of God), and his conclusion gives us pause:

רמב"ן, שמות כ:ו

ומצאתי במכילתא (כאן): "לאוהבי" – זה אברהם וכיוצא בו. "ולשומרי מצותי" – אלו הנביאים והזקנים. רבי נתן אומר, "לאוהבי ולשומרי מצותי" – אלו שהם יושבים בארץ ישראל ונותנין נפשם על המצות: מה לך יוצא ליהרג?

עַל שִׂמְלָתִי אֶת בְּנִי; מַה לְךָ יוֹצֵא לִישָׂרֵף? עַל שֶׁקָרָאתִי בַתוֹרָה; מַה לְךָ יוֹצֵא
לִיצָלֵב? עַל שֶׁאָכַלְתִּי אֶת הַמַּצָּה; ...וְת"ק שֶׁאָמַר זֶה אַבְרָהָם וְאֵלּוּ הַנְּבִיאִים, אֵינוֹ
נָכוֹן שֶׁיֹּאמַר שֶׁהָיוּ הַנְּבִיאִים עוֹשִׂים עַל מְנָת לְקַבֵּל פְּרָס, אֲבָל יֵשׁ בָּזֶה סוֹד, אָמַר
שֶׁאַבְרָהָם מָסַר נַפְשׁוֹ בְּאַהֲבָה, כָּעִנְיָן שֶׁכָּתוּב "חֶסֶד לְאַבְרָהָם", וּשְׁאָר הַנְּבִיאִים
בִּגְבוּרָה וְהֵן בֶּן זֶה.

And I found in the Mekhilta on this verse: "To those who love Me" refers to Avraham and his kind; "To those who safeguard My commandments" refers to the prophets and the elders. Rabbi Natan says: "To those who love Me and those who safeguard My commandments" – this refers to those who dwell in the Land of Israel and martyr themselves: "Why are you being taken out to be killed?" "Because I circumcised my son." "Why are you to be burned at the stake?" "Because I studied Torah." "Why are you to be crucified?" "Because I ate matzah [on Pesach]".... And those who intimate that the first part of the verse refers to Avraham, and the second part to the prophets [intimating that the latter sought reward for their service of God] are incorrect. Herein lies a mystery: Avraham forfeited his soul out of ahavah, *whereas the others were motivated by* gevurah. (Ramban, Shmot 20:6)

Avraham was motivated by love – not by justice, not by truth, nor by any other attribute through which God relates to the world. The prophets and other righteous martyrs were motivated by these other aspects of God's uniqueness; Avraham alone related to God purely through *ahavah*.

Elsewhere, the Ramban extrapolates from this unique relationship between Avraham and God:

רמב"ן, דברים ז:ז

...וַיִּבְחַר בָּכֶם מִכָּל הָעַמִּים, שֶׁתִּהְיוּ אַתֶּם סְגֻלָּה וְנַחֲלָה לוֹ, כִּי הַבְּחִירָה בְּכָל
מָקוֹם בְּרִירָה מִן הָאֲחֵרִים. וְאָמַר הַטַּעַם: "כִּי מֵאַהֲבַת ה' אֶתְכֶם" בָּחַר בָּכֶם,
שֶׁרָאָה אֶתְכֶם רְאוּיִים לְהִתְאַהֵב לְפָנָיו וְנִבְחָרִים לְאַהֲבָה יוֹתֵר מִכָּל הָעַמִּים. וְלֹא
הִזְכִּיר בָּזֶה טַעַם מִן הַבְּחִירָה, כִּי הַנִּבְחָר לְאוֹהֵב הַיָּדוּעַ לִסְבּוֹל אֶת אוֹהֲבוֹ בְּכָל
הַבָּא עָלָיו מִמֶּנּוּ, וְיִשְׂרָאֵל רְאוּיִים לְכָךְ מִכָּל עָם....

...And He chose you from all the nations to be uniquely beloved and to be his portion, because in all cases choice is a differentiation from others. And He stated the reason: "Because of God's love for

*you He chose you," for He saw that you are worthy of being loved
and preferred you for this love more than all other nations. And He
gave no reason for this choice, because the one chosen for love is
most capable of suffering anything that may befall him because of
that love. And Israel are more capable of suffering than all the other
nations....* (Ramban, Devarim 7:7)

Just as Avraham was chosen because he was willing to go into the furnace
for his belief, the Jewish people are chosen by God because they are more
capable than others to suffer for their love and their belief. Avraham's love
of God manifests itself in his willingness to go into the furnace, and this
creates the chosenness. Over the ages, Avraham's descendants have proven
again and again that they are willing to suffer for their love of God, to die
for their belief.

Other commentaries see the manifestation of Avraham's *ahavat Hashem*
not in martyrdom but in the conduct of his life: Avraham spent his life
spreading the belief in one God, not because he was a seeker of truth but
because his love of God was so great that he could not keep it pent up in the
boundaries of his own heart. In fact, the Rambam formulates this type of
ahavat Hashem as the third in his list of positive commandments by which
each and every Jew is obligated:

ספר המצות להרמב״ם, מצות עשה, מצוה ג

מצוה ג: **היא שצונו לאהבו יתעלה**.... וכבר אמרו שמצוה זו כוללת גם כן
שנדרש ונקרא האנשים כלם לעבודתו ית׳ ולהאמין בו, וזה כשתאהב אדם
תשים לבך עליו ותשבחהו ותבקש האנשים לאהב אותו. וזה על צד המשל; כן
כשתאהב האל באמת כמה שהגיעה לך מהשגת אמיתתו הנה אתה בלי ספק
תדרש ותקרא הכופרים והסכלים לידיעת האמת אשר ידעת אותה. ולשון
ספרי: ״״ואהבת את ה״ – אהבהו על הבריות כאברהם אביך, שנאמר, ׳ואת
הנפש אשר עשו בחרן׳״. ר״ל כמו שאברהם בעבור שהיה אוהב השם – כמו
שהעיד הכתוב ״אברהם אוהבי״ – שהיה גם כן לגודל השגתו דרש האנשים
אל האמונה מחוזק אהבתו, כן אתה אהוב אותו עד שתדרש האנשים אליו.

*The third positive commandment: **The Transcendent One has
commanded that we love Him.**... And our sages have already taught
that this commandment includes that we teach and call out to all
other men to serve Him and to believe in Him, just as when you love
another person you will constantly have him in mind and praise him*

to others, and seek to make others love him. This is analogous to love of God, for a person who truly loves God will attempt to enlighten others insofar as his own grasp of God has enlightened him, and he will surely try to persuade the nonbelievers and the unenlightened to see the truth as he has seen it. So it is written in the Sifri, "'And you shall love the Almighty your God' – make him beloved upon others as did Avraham your forefather, as it is written, 'and the souls they made in Haran.'" In other words, just as Avraham, because of his love of God – as scripture testifies, "Avraham who loved Me" – sought to influence others because of the great understanding that he achieved, and because of his love of God called out to others to believe, so you should love God and thus bring others close to Him. (Rambam, Sefer Hamitzvot, Positive Commandment 3)

Avraham ohavi is reflected in Avraham's desire to teach the world about God, and the "souls they made in Haran" who went along on this epic journey were the intellectual and spiritual beneficiaries of Avraham's love of God. *Ahavat Hashem* poured from Avraham like a stream, washing over all those who came in contact with him. The huge influence Avraham had over the people of his generation is the manifestation of Avraham's love, and this is the Avraham we meet as Parashat Lekh Lekha begins.

בראשית כא:לג

וַיִּטַּע אֶשֶׁל בִּבְאֵר שָׁבַע וַיִּקְרָא שָׁם בְּשֵׁם ה' אֵל עוֹלָם:

And he planted an eshel *(orchard) in Be'er Sheva and he called there in the name of the Eternal God.* (Bereishit 21:33)

רש"י, בראשית כא:לג

אשל: רב ושמואל. חד אמר פרדס להביא ממנו פירות לאורחים בסעודה. וחד אמר פונדק לאכסניא ובו כל מיני פירות....

ויקרא שם וגו': על ידי אותו אשל נקרא שמו של הקב"ה אלוה לכל העולם. לאחר שאוכלים ושותים, אמר להם "ברכו למי שאכלתם משלו. סבורים אתם שמשלי אכלתם? משל מי שאמר והיה העולם אכלתם."

An eshel: *Rav and Shmuel disagree: One said, this refers to an orchard. [Avraham] planted an orchard in order to bring fruits to the guests at his table. The other said that this refers to an inn: [Avraham] opened an inn and guesthouse to offer passersby all types of fruit....*

*"And he called, etc.": Through the agency of this eshel the Holy One's
name was known as Master of the Entire Universe, for after they
would eat and drink [Avraham] would say to them, "Bless the One
whose food you have eaten. Do you think that you have eaten food
that belongs to me? You have eaten the food of He who spoke and
created the world."* (Rashi, Bereishit 21:33)

Kabbalistic sources interpret Avraham's acts of *hesed* in a similar vein:

ספר מערכת האלקות, פרק אחד עשר

והכוונה שיחסו המדות האלה לאבות הוא מפני שאברהם רצה לדמות לקונו
במדת חסד שרצה לגמול חסד עם אנשי דורו כדי להמשיכם לעבודת השם
ית' ולכוונה הזאת קרבם אל ביתו והאכילם והשקם והמשיך את לבם לעבודת
השם ית'. וזה היה גמר חסד שעשה להם.... ומפני שגם היא נקראת אהבה
אמר הכתוב (ישעיהו מא) "זרע אברהם אוהבי"…. ואמר בבהיר, "אמר חסד
לפני הב"ה, 'רבוש"ע! כל ימי היות אברהם בעולם לא הוצרכתי אני לעשות
מלאכתי כי אברהם היה עומד שם במקומי'".

*The reason various divine attributes are associated with the
forefathers is because Avraham wished to resemble his Creator in
the attribute of hesed. He wanted to perform acts of kindness for the
people of his generation in order to draw them to worship God. With
this intention he brought them to his home and gave them food and
drink and drew their hearts to the service of God. This is absolute
hesed that he did for them.... And because this attribute is also
called love, he was called "Avraham who loved me." ...And the Sefer
HaBahir relates that the attribute of Hesed said to the Holy One,
blessed be He, "Master of the Universe, all the days that Avraham
lived there was no need for me to perform my task, for Avraham
stood there in my place."* (Sefer Ma'arekhet haElokut, chapter 11)

The conduct and purpose of Avraham's life in Haran are built around
acts of *hesed*, but this *hesed* is of one piece with Avraham's love of God.
Avraham acts as a messenger of God, carrying out the will of God to bring
hesed into the world. He builds his home and concentrates all of his efforts
in order to invite guests in and share with them an appreciation for the
God of *Hesed*. Avraham's love of God is so great that he cannot keep it to

himself, and the enlightenment he shares with his guests – not the food or drink he offers them – is the greatest *hesed* of all.

The Rambam, and the Netziv after him, describe *ahavat Hashem* in terms that may be most accessible to students of modern philosophy:

רמב"ם, משנה תורה, הלכות תשובה, פרק י הלכה ב

העובד מאהבה עוסק בתורה ובמצות והולך בנתיבות החכמה לא מפני דבר בעולם ולא מפני יראת הרעה ולא כדי לירש הטובה אלא עושה האמת מפני שהוא אמת וסוף הטובה לבא בגללה. ומעלה זו היא מעלה גדולה מאד ואין כל חכם זוכה לה. והיא מעלת אברהם אבינו, שקראו הקב"ה אוהבו לפי שלא עבד אלא מאהבה. והיא המעלה שצונו בה הקב"ה על ידי משה, שנאמר, "ואהבת את ה' אלקיך". ובזמן שיאהוב אדם את ה' אהבה הראויה מיד יעשה כל המצות מאהבה.

One who serves God out of love engages in Torah and mitzvot and walks the paths of wisdom, not because of any worldly concern and not out of fear of the evil that may befall him, and not to inherit the benefits that will result, rather he acts according to the truth because it is truth, and in the end good will result because of it. This is a very high level and not all wise men achieve it. This is the level of Forefather Avraham, of whom God said "who loved Me," for he served God only out of love. This is the level that God commanded us through Moshe, for it says "You shall love the Almighty your God." And when a person loves God with the appropriate type of love, he will immediately fulfill all the commandments out of love. (Rambam, Mishneh Torah, Laws of Repentance, 10:2)

Avraham was the first, the prototypical seeker of truth. He sought out truth, and found that God, in His *hesed*, is the source of truth. He therefore sought to emulate God, not in the hope of any reward or advantage, but because he loved truth. This, according to the Rambam, is the highest level of service of God: to fulfill commandments and to live truth because it is truth.

The Netziv traces this train of thought in other episodes in the parashah:

העמק דבר, בראשית יד:כג

ורק מאהבה הנני עובד, "זרע אברהם אוהבי", דבאותו מעשה הראה אברהם שעובד מאהבה ולא משום גמול. והיה בזה דברו למלך סדום, דאחר שאינו

מבקש שכר מהקב"ה, ממילא "אם אקח מכל אשר לך" – האיך אקבל ממך
שכר.

And only out of love do I serve, [as it says,] "descendants of Avraham
who loved Me," for by acting thus, Avraham demonstrated that he served
only out of love and not for any reward. So it was in his words to the king
of Sodom, for he did not seek any reward from the Holy One Blessed be
He. "If I take anything that is yours" – If I seek no reward from God, I
certainly seek no reward from you. (Ha'amek Davar, Bereishit 14:23)

When Avraham declines the reward offered to him by the king of Sodom, it
is not because the money is tainted, or because Avraham hopes to receive a
much greater reward from God. Avraham seeks no reward for doing what
is right, for championing justice. He acts as he does simply because it is
truth; he acts purely out of *ahavat Hashem*.

And yet, although this school of thought seems to present an extremely intellectual approach, equating *ahavat Hashem* with the search for truth, in
this same passage the Rambam describes *ahavat Hashem* in distinctly emotional terms: *ahavat Hashem* is an all-consuming emotional state that mo-
tivates and animates. It is lovesickness for God's proximity, intimacy, favor.

This leads us to an underlying question that remains unanswered: Is
Avraham's discovery of God an expression or an outgrowth of Avraham's
own particular personality? Is he able to relate to God as a God of Love
because he himself is a person imbued with this outlook? Or does Avraham
become the person most identified with loving others because of his
discovery of God and his desire to emulate and relate to God? This question
becomes most poignant when we consider the *'akeidah*, the ultimate test
of Avraham's *hesed*. It is with this test that the Torah throws a spotlight on
the entire question of Avraham's personality, his relationship with God,
and the very essence of God's *hesed*. Our dilemma is concentrated on the
words of the angel who intervenes at the last moment and stops Avraham
from sacrificing his son Yitzhak:

בראשית כב:יא–יב

וַיִּקְרָא אֵלָיו מַלְאַךְ ה' מִן הַשָּׁמַיִם וַיֹּאמֶר אַבְרָהָם אַבְרָהָם וַיֹּאמֶר הִנֵּנִי: וַיֹּאמֶר
אַל תִּשְׁלַח יָדְךָ אֶל הַנַּעַר וְאַל תַּעַשׂ לוֹ מְאוּמָה כִּי עַתָּה יָדַעְתִּי כִּי יְרֵא אֱלֹקִים
אַתָּה וְלֹא חָשַׂכְתָּ אֶת בִּנְךָ אֶת יְחִידְךָ מִמֶּנִּי:

And an angel of God called out to him from heaven and said,
"Avraham, Avraham!" And he said, "I am here." And he said, "Do not
put your hand to the boy and do not do anything to him, for now I
know that you are God-fearing, for you did not deny me your only
son." (Bereishit 22:11–12)

Avraham relates to God as the source of all *hesed*. How, then, does he
respond to the commandment to sacrifice his son, the object of all his
hopes and prayers, the culmination of one hundred years of waiting? At
no point does Avraham argue, as he did on behalf of the people of Sodom.
At no instant does he doubt God's *hesed*; at no time does he invoke justice.
How are we to understand this?

Our first response seems to be supported by the text itself: Avraham
responded with fear. Avraham's love of God was tested by fear of God, and
he passed the test: the angel declared that Avraham had proven that he was
God-fearing. In light of everything we have seen, this answer is somehow
unsatisfying. Can it be that Avraham, whose entire relationship with God
was one of love, responded with fear? Surely, his legacy is *ahavat Hashem*,
not *yirat Hashem*.

The Recanati offers a solution:

פירוש הרקאנאטי על התורה, פרשת וירא

כי עתה ידעתי כי ירא אלקים אתה: יש לשאול כי ידענו כי אברהם היה אוהב,
שנאמר, (ישעיהו מא) "זרע אברהם אוהבי". ואיך לא שבחו במעלתו הגדולה
שהיא מצד החסד, רק שבחו במדת היראה? כי ידענו כי כל מה שעשה אברהם
אבינו ע"ה עשה מאהבה, ויש הבדל בין האוהב ליָרא כיתרון האור מן החושך.
ועל כן יש לך לדעת מאמר בעלי הקבלה כי היראה היא על שני דרכים: יראה
פנימית ויראה חיצונית. היראה חיצונה היא למטה מן האהבה והפנימית היא
למעלה מן האהבה. כיצד? יראה חיצונה היא סוד כל הירא לעבור על מצות
המלך פן יענש ויתפש במאמר המלך. יראה פנימית בהיות האדם משיג מעלת
הבורא יתעלה ורוב התענוגים והעושר והכבוד אשר בהיכלו בהגיע אדם
לידיעת מעלה זו יפחד ויבהל ויאמר שמא אינני ראוי לעמוד בהיכל המלך.

"Now I know that you are God-fearing": This raises a question, for
we know that Avraham was God loving, as it says "descendants of
Avraham who loved me." How did he [the angel] not praise him for
his great attribute of hesed, and instead only praise his yirah? We

know that everything that Avraham did, he did out of ahavah, *and the superiority of* ahavah *over* yirah *is like the superiority of light over darkness. Thus, we should take note of the kabbalistic teaching that there are two types of* yirah *– internal and external. External* yirah *is inferior to* ahavah *but internal* yirah *is greatly superior to* ahavah. *How is this so? External* yirah *is the secret of all those who fear transgressing the word of the King, for fear that they will be caught and punished. Internal* yirah *stems from comprehension of the true stature of the Creator.... When a person reaches this understanding, he becomes afraid that he is unworthy to stand in the presence of the King.* (Recanati on the Torah, Parashat Vayeira)

The *'akeidah* is not a test designed to break Avraham's natural inclination to *hesed*. Out of love of God, Avraham proceeds: even the *'akeidah* is *ahavah* because *ahavah* is doing truth because it is truth. What is the definition of truth? Whatever God says it is. God is truth, and His commandment is truth. Sacrificing Yitzhak is thus truth, a manifestation of love and not of fear. Avraham's *ahavat Hashem* brings him to the level that the Recanati describes as "internal *yirah*": Avraham does not want to cause any estrangement between himself and God; he fears causing God any disappointment. Avraham is full of love, both for God and for his own son Yitzhak. When God forces him to choose between these two loves, Avraham chooses the love of God, which necessarily assumes, and subsumes, all other love.

Ultimately, God does not force Avraham to consummate this choice, and the heavenly voice commands Avraham to desist. This, too, is seen by our sages as a test: Avraham does not fear punishment; he fears that he will be unworthy of God's presence. He is almost overcome by his desire to consummate his choice, to act upon his *ahavat Hashem*. His most concerted effort is in pulling back, stopping short of sacrifice. He overcomes his dread of separation from God; he forces himself to obey the commandment to desist, to override his inclination to give everything he has.

Avraham, motivated by his great love of God, dedicated his life to emulating God through *hesed*, and started a relationship that is replicated by his descendants to this very day. Our challenge is to emulate Avraham by finding our own love of God. We hope and pray that martyrdom will not be required of us, and that instead we can manifest our love of God through acts of *hesed*, through sharing our knowledge of God with others, by calling all of humanity to serve God – with love.

The Universal and the Particular

It begins with a word, a command – or perhaps a test:

בראשית יב:א–ג

וַיֹּאמֶר ה' אֶל אַבְרָם לֶךְ לְךָ מֵאַרְצְךָ וּמִמּוֹלַדְתְּךָ וּמִבֵּית אָבִיךָ אֶל הָאָרֶץ אֲשֶׁר
אַרְאֶךָּ: וְאֶעֶשְׂךָ לְגוֹי גָּדוֹל וַאֲבָרֶכְךָ וַאֲגַדְּלָה שְׁמֶךָ וֶהְיֵה בְּרָכָה: וַאֲבָרְכָה מְבָרְכֶיךָ
וּמְקַלֶּלְךָ אָאֹר וְנִבְרְכוּ בְךָ כֹּל מִשְׁפְּחֹת הָאֲדָמָה:

*And God said to Avram, "Go forth from your land and your birthplace
and from the house of your father to the land that I will show you;
and I will make you into a great nation and I will bless you and I
will make your name great, and you will be a blessing. And I will
bless those who bless you, and whoever curses you I will curse; and
all the nations of the earth shall be blessed through you." (Bereishit
12:1–3)*

According to at least one rabbinic source, contained in this verse are two
tests:[1]

אבות דרבי נתן, פרק לג

עשר נסיונות נתנסה אברהם אבינו לפני הקב"ה, ובכולן נמצא שלם. ואלו
הן: שנים בלך לך, ב' בשתי בניו, ב' בשתי נשיו, אחד עם המלכים ואחד בין
הבתרים, אחד באור כשדים ואחד בברית מילה.

*Our forefather Avraham was tested in ten ways before God, and he
completed each test to perfection. And these are [the tests]: two at the
time he was bidden to leave Haran, two with his two sons, two with his
two wives, one in the wars of the kings, one at the covenant "between
the pieces" [Bereishit 15:1–21], one in Ur Kasdim [where, according
to a tradition, he had been thrown into a furnace from whence he*

---

1. Though there is a consensus in rabbinic thought that Avraham was tested ten times,
   there is no consensus as to what the ten tests were.

emerged unharmed] and one in the covenant of circumcision. (Avot d'Rebbi Natan, chapter 33)

Upon contemplation, we might ask a simple question: why was leaving his hometown a test? Avraham was not exactly the most popular character back home; in fact the opposite seems true. He was vilified, persecuted, attacked and almost killed – until he was miraculously saved from a fiery furnace. Why would leaving such a place be considered a "test"? When we continue our reading of the next two verses, the "test" seems mitigated by a bounty of blessings: "And I will make you into a great nation and I will bless you and I will make your name great, and you will be a blessing. And I will bless those who bless you, and whoever curses you I will curse; and all the nations of the earth shall be blessed through you." This certainly doesn't sound like a challenge; in fact, it sounds as if Avraham has "hit the jackpot"! The promises are of incredible proportions. Where is the test?

A more careful reading of these verses reveals an almost untenable tension, which may be the key to understanding the angst that Avraham experiences in fulfilling the divine imperative. Verse 2 is a blessing that introduces a new entity, a new concept that from this point on becomes the focus of the biblical narrative: the nation, specifically "the Nation of Israel."

The joyous, nearly incredible news that a nation will emerge from the loins of Avraham is tempered by the knowledge that a certain tension will always surround this nation. The rest of humanity will never be indifferent; the nation of Avraham's children will never be "pareve" in the eyes of the world. They will always elicit some sort of reaction from others, always serve either as a source of blessing or a curse for others.

Furthermore, the blessing bestowed on Avraham may be seen as limiting: it is particular in nature, it is directed exclusively to those who will become known as the Jewish people. In Avraham's eyes, universal dreams may be challenged by particular nationalistic aspirations. Whereas Avraham has seen himself as a citizen of the world on a mission to help elevate all of mankind, his mission now becomes linked exclusively with this new entity, "the Children of Avraham."

At this juncture, what are Avraham's aspirations? Is his dream to start his own nation, or does he wish to impact the people of his hometown? Has his initial failure dissuaded him from continuing his original mission, or does he still dream of local success?

Avraham makes his journey to Israel but he doesn't come alone. His partner Sarah (Sarai) accompanies him, as does Lot, his heir apparent. In addition, we are told of another group who follow their leader:

בראשית יב:ה

וַיִּקַּח אַבְרָם אֶת שָׂרַי אִשְׁתּוֹ וְאֶת לוֹט בֶּן אָחִיו וְאֶת כָּל רְכוּשָׁם אֲשֶׁר רָכָשׁוּ וְאֶת הַנֶּפֶשׁ אֲשֶׁר עָשׂוּ בְחָרָן וַיֵּצְאוּ לָלֶכֶת אַרְצָה כְּנַעַן וַיָּבֹאוּ אַרְצָה כְּנָעַן:

And Avram took his wife Sarai, his nephew Lot, all the possessions they had accumulated and the people they had made[2] [acquired] in Haran, and they set out for the land of Canaan,[3] and they arrived in the land of Canaan. (Bereishit 12:5)

Avraham has an entourage, which is not all that unusual. What is interesting is that these are not people from Ur Kasdim (Aram Naharayim), they are people collected in Haran. They are not from his hometown, but from his latest temporary abode. In his hometown he seems to have made no impact.

They arrive in Israel at a specific place, an intentional destination: their first stop in the Land is at a place called Shekhem.[4] The Ramban[5] points out that

---

2. Rashi, in his first interpretation, tells us that these were the men and women whom Avraham and Sarah (respectively) taught and "converted." However, in a second explanation – which Rashi labels *peshat*, the straightforward meaning of the text – Rashi explains that these were the people that were acquired; i.e., slaves and members of the household staff.

    רש"י, בראשית יב:ה

    אשר עשו בחרן: שהכניסן תחת כנפי השכינה אברהם מגייר את האנשים ושרה מגיירת הנשים ומעלה עליהם הכתוב כאלו עשאום (לכך כתיב אשר עשו). ופשוטו של מקרא עבדים ושפחות שקנו להם כמו (שם לא) עשה את כל הכבוד הזה (לשון קנין) (במדבר כד) וישראל עושה חיל לשון קונה וכונס.

3. Previously Avraham's father Terah started to make his way to Canaan. The Seforno (12:5) posits that both Avraham and Terah choose Canaan as their destination because it was known as a spiritual place.

    ספורנו, בראשית יב:ה

    ויצאו ללכת ארצה כנען: שהיתה מפורסמת אצלם לארץ מוכנת להתבוננות ולעבודת האל ית'.

4. Bereishit 12:6.

5. Ramban, Bereishit 12:6.

the "acts of the fathers are a sign for the children," for it is in Shekhem that nationhood will emerge. This is where Dinah is abused, and where the local residents offer the family of Israel to join destinies, to join them and form one nation. This offer is rejected, and a process is set in motion: a nation with its own unique history begins to chart its path, undertaking the long march to fulfill its particular, unique destiny. A nation, indeed – but at this point a small, vulnerable nation that rejects the benefits of assimilation into a strong, well-established local clan. This is a defining moment, a decision that crystallizes and forms the nation of Israel.

Let us take a step back. Avraham's great work in Haran, the monumental educational challenge he has undertaken, has been described by the Talmud as no less than the end of the dark ages:

תלמוד בבלי, מסכת עבודה זרה דף ט עמוד א

תנא דבי אליהו: ששת אלפים שנה הוי העולם. שני אלפים תוהו, שני אלפים תורה, שני אלפים ימות המשיח. בעונותינו שרבו יצאו מהן מה שיצאו מהן. שני אלפים תורה מאימת? אי נימא ממתן תורה, עד השתא ליכא כולי האי! דכי מעיינת בהו תרי אלפי פרטי דהאי אלפא הוא דהואי. אלא מ"ואת הנפש אשר עשו בחרן" וגמירי דאברהם בההיא שעתא בר חמשין ותרתי הוה. כמה בצרן מדתני תנא ארבע מאה וארבעים ותמניא שנין הויין כי מעיינת ביה "מהנפש אשר עשו בחרן" עד מתן תורה.

The Tanna d'Bei Eliyahu taught: The world is to exist six thousand years; the first two thousand years are to be void, the next two thousand years are the period of the Torah and the following two thousand years are the period of Mashiah *[the Messiah]. Through our many sins a number of these have already passed [and* Mashiah *is not yet here]. From when are the two thousand years of the Torah to be reckoned? Shall we say from the giving of the Torah at Sinai? In that case, you will find that there are not quite two thousand years from then till now [i.e., the year four thousand after Creation], for if you compute the years [from Creation to the giving of the Torah] you will find that they comprise two thousand and a part of the third thousand. The period is therefore to be reckoned from the time when Avraham and Sarah had gotten souls in Haran, for we have it as a tradition that Avraham was at that time fifty-two years old.*
(Talmud Bavli Avodah Zara 9a)

Biblical chronology is an important key to understanding this Gemara: Avraham was born in the year 1948 (from the creation of the world). Therefore, when he was fifty-two years old the world was precisely two thousand year old, and at this point Avraham began teaching and attempting to influence the entire world. But what was the nature of the "Torah" that Avraham taught and practiced? There is a Talmudic discussion that examines the implications of the tradition that Avraham "kept the Torah":

תלמוד בבלי, מסכת יומא דף כח עמוד ב

אמר רב: קיים אברהם אבינו כל התורה כולה, שנאמר, (בראשית כו) "עקב אשר שמע אברהם בקלי [וַיִּשְׁמֹר מִשְׁמַרְתִּי מִצְוֹתַי חֻקּוֹתַי וְתוֹרֹתָי]". אמר ליה רב שימי בר חייא לרב: ואימא שבע מצות! – הא איכא נמי מילה. – ואימא שבע מצות ומילה! – אמר ליה: אם כן מצותי ותורתי למה לי? אמר (רב) [מסורת הש"ס: רבא] ואיתימא רב אשי: קיים אברהם אבינו אפילו עירובי תבשילין, שנאמר תורתי – אחת תורה שבכתב ואחת תורה שבעל פה.

Rav said: Our father Avraham kept the whole Torah,[6] as it is said: "Because Avraham hearkened to My voice [and kept My charge, My commandments, My statutes and My laws]" (Bereishit 26:5). R. Shimi b. Hiyya said to Rav, "Say, perhaps, that this refers to the seven [Noahide] laws?" "Surely there was also that of circumcision!" "Then say that it refers to the seven laws and circumcision [and not to the whole Torah]?" "If that were so, why does Scripture say: 'My commandments and My laws'?" Raba [or R. Ashi] said, "Avraham, our father, kept even the law concerning the 'eiruv tavshilin [a

---

6. The Midrash, which takes the same basic approach, nonetheless states that Avraham did not keep Shabbat. See Bereishit Rabbah 11:7:

בראשית רבה, פרשה יא פסקה ז

ר' יוחנן בשם ר' יוסי בר חלפתא אמר: אברהם שאין כתוב בו שמירת שבת ירש את העולם במדה שנאמר (בראשית יב) קום התהלך בארץ לארכה ולרחבה וגו' אבל יעקב שכתוב בו שמירת שבת שנאמר (שם לג) ויחן את פני העיר נכנס עם דמדומי חמה וקבע תחומין מבעוד יום ירש את העולם שלא במדה שנאמר (שם כח) והיה זרעך כעפר הארץ וגו'.

"R. Yohanan said in R. Yose's name: Avraham, who is not reported to have kept the Shabbat, inherited the world in [limited] measure, as it is written, 'Arise, walk through the land in the length of it and in the breadth of it' (Bereishit 13:17). But Yaakov, of whom the keeping of the Shabbat is mentioned, as it says, 'And he rested [encamped] before the city' (ibid. 33:18), which means that he entered at twilight and set boundaries before sunset, inherited the world without measure, [as it is written,] 'And you shall spread abroad to the west, and to the east...' (ibid. 28:14)."

rabbinic ordinance involving cooking on holidays], as it is said: 'My Torahs' – one being the Written Torah, the other, the Oral Torah."
(Talmud Bavli Yoma 28b)

There are certain sources that would seem to maintain that Avraham and Sarah's spiritual lifestyle was no different from our own. On the other hand, many authorities[7] prefer to read these sources for the symbolic[8] or deeper[9] understanding,[10] rather than in a literal way. The latter approach

---

7. The Ohr haHayim (Bereishit 49:3) maintains that the forefathers only kept laws that they found useful, or more precisely would not keep laws that they found an impediment to them.

אור החיים, בראשית מט:ג

והאבות לצד חביבותם בה' וחשקם באושר עליון קיימו הכל כאומרו (לעיל כו:ה) עקב אשר שמע וגו', ואמרו ז"ל (יומא כח ע"ב) קיים אברהם אבינו אפילו עירוב תבשילין, ואת בניו הקים תחתיו להרויח תועלת המצות ועסק התורה, אבל במקום שהיו רואים תועלת דבר ההצלחה להם, כמו שתאמר יעקב כשהרגיש בהצלחתו בנשואי ב' האחיות העלים עין מרווח הנמשך מקיום המצוה ההיא, כיון שאין לו עונש אם לא יקיימנה, כל עוד שלא נתנה תורה, ומה גם אם נאמר שהיו עושים על פי הדיבור, כי האבות נביאים היו (מגילה יד) וה' אמר להם לעשות כן.

8. The *Shem mi'Shmuel* understands that Yaakov fulfilled the commandments – even if he didn't quite perform them. He explains that commandments have bodies and souls, and Avraham was attuned to the souls and therefore didn't need the "body" of the physical performance.

ספר שם משמואל, פרשת בהר, פסח שני

ובודאי גם אברהם קיים ענין תפילין אבל הי' בלבוש אחר כי באשר היו יחידים לא הוצרכה ההתאחדות ע"י המעשה, והי' לכל אחד מעשה וכלי מיוחד.

9. The *Noam Elimelekh* (Parashat Devarim) explains that Avraham achieved the spiritual perfection of someone who had performed all the commandments.

ספר נועם אלימלך, פרשת הדברים

דאיתא בגמרא קיים אברהם אבינו עליו השלום כו' אפילו עירוב תבשילין והיינו שהיה מקדש ומטהר את כל רמ"ח אבריו ושס"ה גידיו כל אבר במצוה השייך לה דכל מצוה ומצוה יש לה בפני עצמה ואברהם אבינו על ידי שהיה עובד השם יתברך מאהבה השיג את כל מצוה ומצוה בשורשה ואפילו מצוה דרבנן יש לה שורש ועיקר בדאורייתא בעולם המיוחד לה.

10. The *Degel Mahane Efraim* understands that the ultimate objective of the commandments is the understanding that there is One God, and the rejection of all pagan entities. Avraham fulfilled this purpose more perfectly than anyone; he was cognizant of this truth all his days. A similar idea is found in the *Maor va'Shemesh*.

ספר דגל מחנה אפרים, פרשת אחרי ד"ה עוד

וכל מצוה ומצוה שייך לשורש נשמות של ישראל והוא היודע ומבין זה והוא שורש השרשים ואין עוד מלבדו ולכך קיים אברהם אבינו כל התורה כולה עד שלא ניתנה (קידושין פב ע"א) כי הגיע לאמיתת אלוהות כי כל המצוות הם שער ומבוא לבא אל אמיתת אלוהות שהוא אנכי ולא יהיה לך כמו שכתבתי מזה כבר במקום אחר אך זעירין אינון שיוכלו לבא אל אמיתת אלוהות.

maintains that only after Sinai did people begin to observe the 613 commandments, but the forefathers' acute spiritual perception and close relationship with God enabled them to fulfill the *spirit* of the entire Torah, while not necessarily obeying the letter of the laws of the Torah as they became formulated at Sinai and thereafter. Thus, the *Meshekh Hokhmah* explains that when the Talmud says Avraham kept *'eiruv tavshilin*, it doesn't mean that he observed even the minutiae of halachic observance. Rather, what the Talmud means is that Avraham comprehended and fulfilled the philosophical concept that is the underpinning of this law. An *'eiruv tavshilin* enables us to cook for unexpected guests on a holiday that falls on the eve of Shabbat. This approach encapsulates the welcoming personality of Avraham, always waiting for the unexpected guest,[11] who would be fed and bidden to make a blessing. To Avraham, the spirit of the law was as natural, clear and possessed of internal "spiritual logic" as our present practice was to the rabbis who formulated it.

The first opinion in the Talmud resolves the question of Avraham's observance with a much less complicated approach: Avraham was the first monotheist. He taught monotheism and the seven Noahide laws,[12] and that was the content of his spiritual world.[13]

ספר דגל מחנה אפרים, פרשת עקב ד"ה רק

ולהם לא היה צריך התורה להכתב כלל אך מה שנכתב כל התורה הוא לדידן שאין לנו מוחין כהם ולכך הוצרך להכתב כל התורה והמצוות שעל ידם השיגו בחינת אנכי אבל האבות ידעו הנקודה אמיתית שכל התורה והמצוות תלוין בה.

ספר מאור ושמש, רמזי יום א' של סוכות ד"ה או

אמנם הצדיק אשר כבר הגיע למעלת הדביקות באין סוף ב"ה והוא קשור במחשבתו בכל עת, עיקר עבודתו הוא במחשבה כמאמרם ז"ל קיים אברהם אבינו כל התורה כולה עד שלא ניתנה, הגם שלא מצאנו שעשה בפועל מעשה המצות כהנחת תפילין ועשיית סוכה וכדומיהן, מכל מקום המשיך על עצמו פנימיות הקדושות שרומזות אליהם המעשים ההם על ידי מחשבתו הקדושה אשר היתה דבוקה באין סוף ב"ה.

11. See Ráshi's comments on Bereishit 21:33, where he explains that one of the reasons for Avraham's magnanimous hosting of guests, aside from *imitatio Dei*, was his desire to teach people to bless God and thank God.

רש"י, בראשית כא:לג

אשל: רב ושמואל. חד אמר פרדס להביא ממנו פירות לאורחים בסעודה. וחד אמר פונדק לאכסניא ובו כל מיני פירות. ומצינו לשון נטיעה באהלים שנאמר (דניאל יא) ויטע אהלי אפדנו.

ויקרא שם וגו': על ידי אותו אשל נקרא שמו של הקב"ה אלוה לכל העולם. לאחר שאוכלים ושותים אמר להם ברכו למי שאכלתם משלו סבורים אתם שמשלי אכלתם משל מי שאמר והיה העולם אכלתם (סוטה י).

All this being said, we know of one particular commandment that Avraham received and fulfilled: circumcision.

ספר תפארת שלמה על הזמנים ומועדים, חג הסוכות

איתא בגמרא (יומא כח:ב): "קיים אברהם אבינו כל התורה כולה עד שלא ניתנה". והקשו הראשונים למה לא קיים ג"כ מצות מילה תחלה. אך הנה ידוע כי אברהם אבינו ע"ה הי' מדת החסד וזה הי' מדתו, להמשיך השפעות וחסדים לכל באי עולם בלי שום גבול. והנה כל זמן שלא מל את עצמו הי' לו איזה השתתפות עם בני דורו והי' יכול להוריק עליהם ברכה וחסד והאכילם והשקם וקרבם תחת כנפי השכינה. אכן כאשר בא בברית המילה אח"כ, נתעלה ונסתלק לו למעלה מהם ויראו מגשת אליו.

If Avraham fulfilled all the commandments of the Torah, there are many who have asked why Avraham didn't perform circumcision prior to his being commanded. Prior to being circumcised Avraham had something in common with the people of his generation. He was able to reach out to them and shower them with blessings and kindness, to feed them and give them drink and to bring them close to the Shekhinah. *However once he was circumcised he was elevated to a different level, and now people were afraid to come near him....* (Tiferet Shlomo, Moadim: Sukkot)

Avraham's basic approach was inclusive. His tent was open on all sides; he placed no limits, erected no boundaries.[14] In fact, the *Meshekh Hokhmah*[15] sees this universalism as Avraham's motivation in traveling to Egypt. He went to Egypt at a time of drought, choosing Egypt not despite its reputation

---

12. The *Arvei Nahal* understands that all 613 commandments are subsumed within the seven Noahide laws.

ספר ערבי נחל, פרשת תולדות

דע, כי כל מצוה כלולה מכל התרי"ג, וא"כ בכל מצוה יש כלל ופרט כי בכח יש בה כל התרי"ג, ובפועל הוא פרטיותה לבד, ומיד שנברא האדם נצטווה בשבע מצות וקיימו אותם האבות ויתר צדיקי הדורות עד מתן תורה וכל התרי"ג כלולים בכל מצוה מהם. ואם תקשה א"כ האבות לא הוציאו הכללות מן הכח אל הפועל, דע שהוציאו והוציאו, בכח הכנעה, בכח הכנעה ר"ל שהיו דבוקים בו ית"ש והיו שׂשׂים ושׂמחים לעשׂות רצון קונם בכל מה שיצווום והיו מוכנים לזה בתכלית ההכנה בשמחה רבה.

13. See Rambam, *Mishneh Torah*, Laws of Idolatry, chapter 1.

14. According to the *Meshekh Hokhmah*, Yaakov personifies setting up boundaries to prevent assimilation. Hence Yaakov is said to have observed "even *'eiruv tehumin.*"

15. *Meshekh Hokhmah*, Bereishit 33:18.

for corruption but precisely because of its reputation as a morally corrupt society. In Avraham's worldview, if Egypt could be redeemed, the entire world would be elevated, and by a quantum leap. Avraham saw Egypt as a boundary, a spiritual and ethical border to be crossed and dismantled. This, like so much else in his biography, reflects a deep humanism. Avraham did not want to push away his wayward son Yishmael. He interceded on behalf of the inhabitants of Sodom, despite the knowledge that their beliefs and behavior contradicted everything he himself believed and practiced. A lesser man would have accepted God's judgment and anticipated the annihilation of Sodom with satisfaction, with a sense of moral superiority, perhaps even a sense of validation. These people, after all, were the living antithesis to Avraham's weltanschauung and to the message of morality and kindness he was working to spread. The destruction of Sodom would have made his job so much easier. But for Avraham, these were not evil, corrupt enemies of his faith. They were misguided people who simply had not yet found truth.

With the command to perform the *brit milah* Avraham's life would change. There would now be a boundary between him and everyone else.[16] He would

---

משך חכמה, בראשית לג:יח

והציור בזה. דבאמת כמו שלהחי די במזון מהצומח והמדבר ניזון מהחי כן נפש המשכלת מבני נכר די לו בשבע מצות אולם נפש הישראלי מקורו ממקום גבוה חלק ד' ממעל אם אין לו כל התורה בכללה ופרטה אז אינו בחיותו. כי עם הישראלי המה מעון ומכון לאלקות בעולם השפל ואין השכינה שורה אלא באלפי רבבות ישראל (יבמות סד). וזה סו"ד מה שאמרו ש"ס רבוא. (אולי צ"ל ס' רבוא אותיות. ע' זוהר חדש סוף שה"ש) המה כללות הפרצופים ולכן אברהם חפש להפיץ שיטתו ודיעותיו באלקות לכל באי עולם באשר חשב כי הוא יחידי ואח"כ ראה כי ישמעאל יצא ממנו ולכן נטע אשל להכניס כל באי עולם לברית ואמרו בריש עו"ג (דף ט) שני אלפים תורה מוהנפש אשר עשו בחרן דשעבידו לאורייתא. וגם היה זה בכוונה שהלך למצרים מקום החכמה והחרטומים לפלפל ולקרבם לשיטותיו באחדות ובתורה. לא כן יעקב ראה שמטתו שלמה (ויקרא רבה לו:ד) ובזרעו די שיהיו מעון ומרכבה לשכינה וכמו שהבטיחו וראה שה' נצב עליו ראה להיפוך כי בניו יהיו נפרדים מעמים אחרים מוגבלים בתחום ואף ללבן חותנו הניחו בטעותו וכעס על רחל שגנבה התרפים להבדילו מעו"ג כן במצרים היו יושבים בארץ גושן נפרדים מהעמים. וכן לדורות באומה אין מקבלין גרים ושלמה (יבמות כד ע"ב) שזה כהכרח או למקנא לגדולתם וזה מליצתם שאברהם קיים עירובי תבשילין (יומא כח ע"ב) להכניס אורחים ולקבל גרים תחת כנפי השכינה אבל לא קבע תחומין שמא ימנע אחד מלבוא לשמוע דיעותיו. לא כן יעקב קבע תחומין להגביל ולתחום בין עם ישראל לעמים.

16. See the comments of the *Beit haLevi*, Bereishit 17:1.

בית הלוי, בראשית יז:א

והנה איתא במדרש פרשה זו (נ"ו תרג) שאמר אברהם עד שלא מלתי היו באים הכותים ומזדווגים לי תאמר משמלתי יהיו באים ומזדווגים לי א"ל הקב"ה די שאני פטרונך. הרי מבואר כמש"כ דהמילה נותנת הבדל גדול בין ישראל לכותים והיא גורמת שנאה ביניהם והשיב לו הקב"ה די לך שאני פטרונך ולא יועילו ולא יפסידו לך לא בקרבתם ולא בשנאתם אחרי שאני אוהבך.

now be viewed even more suspiciously by his neighbors. In fact, the rabbis express their sensitivity to Avraham's conflict between universalism and nationhood as a "hesitation" on Avraham's part when he was commanded to perform circumcision.

בראשית רבה, פרשה מו פסקה ב–ג

אמר, "אם חביבה היא המילה, מפני מה לא נתנה לאדם הראשון?" אמר לו הקדוש ב"ה לאברהם, "דייך אני ואתה בעולם, ואם אין את מקבל עליך לימול דיי לעולמי עד כאן, ודייה לערלה עד כאן ודייה למילה שתהא עגומה עד כאן". אמר, "עד שלא מלתי היו באים ומזדווגים לי. תאמר משמלתי הן באין ומזדווגים לי?" אמר לו הקב"ה, "אברהם, דייך שאני אלוקך, דייך שאני פטרונך".

[Avraham] asked, "If circumcision is so precious, why was it not given to Adam?" Said the Holy One, blessed be He, to him: "Let it suffice you that I and you are in the world. If you will not undergo circumcision, it is enough for My world to have existed until now, and it is enough for the uncircumcised state to have existed until now, and it is enough for circumcision to have been forlorn until now." Said he: "Before I circumcised myself, men came and joined me [in my new faith]. Will they come and join me when I am circumcised?" "Avraham," said God to him, "let it suffice you that I am your God; let it suffice you that I am your Patron." (Bereishit Rabbah 46:2–3)

בראשית רבה, פרשה מז פסקה

אמר אברהם, "עד שלא מלתי היו העוברים והשבים באים אצלי. תאמר משמלתי אינן באים אצלי?" אמר לו הקב"ה, "עד שלא מלת היו בני אדם באים אצלך. עכשיו אני בכבודי בא ונגלה עליך". הה"ד "וירא אליו ה' באלוני ממרא".

Avraham said, "Before I became circumcised, travelers used to visit me; now that I am circumcised, perhaps they will no longer visit me?" Said the Holy One, blessed be He, to him, "Before you were circumcised, uncircumcised mortals visited you; now I in My Glory will appear to you." Hence it is written, "And God appeared to him" [Bereishit 18:1]. (Bereishit Rabbah 47:10)

Amazingly enough, here Avraham hesitates.[17] When commanded to offer up his long-awaited son, his heir, the key to the fulfillment of all that God has promised him, Avraham marches forward like a knight of faith. But here, in this test, Avraham questions: *If circumcision is so precious, why was it not given to Adam? Why isn't this a universal command? Why is this command only being given to me and my descendants?* He worries that this new status will jeopardize his mission, setting him apart from those he hopes to impact. He fears this will put an end to his stream of visitors. God's response is telling: "I will visit you, and that is truly enough. Your relationship with Me is more important; your mission is less universal and more particular than you know."

Clearly, then, the *brit milah* is a test. The challenge may be heightened by the paradoxical nature of the command that he receives:

בראשית יז:א–יד

וַיְהִי אַבְרָם בֶּן תִּשְׁעִים שָׁנָה וְתֵשַׁע שָׁנִים וַיֵּרָא ה' אֶל אַבְרָם וַיֹּאמֶר אֵלָיו אֲנִי אֵל שַׁדַּי הִתְהַלֵּךְ לְפָנַי וֶהְיֵה תָמִים: וְאֶתְּנָה בְרִיתִי בֵּינִי וּבֵינֶךָ וְאַרְבֶּה אוֹתְךָ בִּמְאֹד מְאֹד: וַיִּפֹּל אַבְרָם עַל פָּנָיו וַיְדַבֵּר אִתּוֹ אֱלֹקִים לֵאמֹר: אֲנִי הִנֵּה בְרִיתִי אִתָּךְ וְהָיִיתָ לְאַב הֲמוֹן גּוֹיִם: וְלֹא יִקָּרֵא עוֹד אֶת שִׁמְךָ אַבְרָם וְהָיָה שִׁמְךָ אַבְרָהָם כִּי אַב הֲמוֹן גּוֹיִם נְתַתִּיךָ: וְהִפְרֵתִי אֹתְךָ בִּמְאֹד מְאֹד וּנְתַתִּיךָ לְגוֹיִם וּמְלָכִים מִמְּךָ יֵצֵאוּ: וַהֲקִמֹתִי אֶת בְּרִיתִי בֵּינִי וּבֵינֶךָ וּבֵין זַרְעֲךָ אַחֲרֶיךָ לְדֹרֹתָם לִבְרִית עוֹלָם לִהְיוֹת לְךָ לֵאלֹקִים וּלְזַרְעֲךָ אַחֲרֶיךָ: וְנָתַתִּי לְךָ וּלְזַרְעֲךָ אַחֲרֶיךָ אֵת אֶרֶץ מְגֻרֶיךָ אֵת כָּל אֶרֶץ כְּנַעַן לַאֲחֻזַּת עוֹלָם וְהָיִיתִי לָהֶם לֵאלֹקִים: וַיֹּאמֶר אֱלֹקִים אֶל אַבְרָהָם וְאַתָּה אֶת בְּרִיתִי תִשְׁמֹר אַתָּה וְזַרְעֲךָ אַחֲרֶיךָ לְדֹרֹתָם: זֹאת בְּרִיתִי אֲשֶׁר תִּשְׁמְרוּ בֵּינִי וּבֵינֵיכֶם וּבֵין זַרְעֲךָ אַחֲרֶיךָ הִמּוֹל לָכֶם כָּל זָכָר: וּנְמַלְתֶּם אֵת בְּשַׂר עָרְלַתְכֶם וְהָיָה לְאוֹת בְּרִית בֵּינִי וּבֵינֵיכֶם: וּבֶן שְׁמֹנַת יָמִים יִמּוֹל לָכֶם כָּל זָכָר לְדֹרֹתֵיכֶם יְלִיד בָּיִת וּמִקְנַת כֶּסֶף מִכֹּל בֶּן נֵכָר אֲשֶׁר לֹא מִזַּרְעֲךָ הוּא: הִמּוֹל יִמּוֹל יְלִיד בֵּיתְךָ וּמִקְנַת

---

17. The Alshikh notes that because Avraham senses that others will be impacted, he hesitates; regarding the binding of Yitzhak, where only he will suffer, he does not hesitate.

ספר תורת משה, בראשית יח:ב–ג

והנה ראוי להעיר מה ראה על ככה אברהם לטעון נגד מאמרו יתברך, מי שלא פצה את פיו באמור אליו ה' קח נא את בנך את יחידך כו' לאמר לו הלא אתה אמרת כי ביצחק יקרא לך זרע, איך בציווי זה בקש טענה ליפטר, וגם מה לו ולעוברים ושבים ערביים ערלים נגד צווי יתברך.... ונבא אל הענין והוא כי בעל המאמר הוקשה לו אומרו וירא אליו ולא אמר אל אברהם. על כן אמר כי עברו דברים בין אברהם ובינו יתברך, כי אברהם בענוותנותו היה חש יותר על קיום העולם מהנוגע אל עצמו, על כן על אומרו יתברך קח נא את בנך כו' לא דבר מאומה. אך על ענין המילה להיותה דבר זר בעיני ההמון, באומרם היתכן ברא אלהים אדם שיחשוב לבעל מום עד החסיר מאשר ברא אלהים לשיהיה שלם.

כִּסְפֶּךָ וְהָיְתָה בְרִיתִי בִּבְשַׂרְכֶם לִבְרִית עוֹלָם: וְעָרֵל זָכָר אֲשֶׁר לֹא יִמּוֹל אֶת בְּשַׂר
עָרְלָתוֹ וְנִכְרְתָה הַנֶּפֶשׁ הַהִוא מֵעַמֶּיהָ אֶת בְּרִיתִי הֵפַר:

When Avram was ninety-nine years old, God appeared to him and said, "I am God Almighty; walk before me and be pure. And I will confirm My covenant between Me and you and will greatly increase your numbers." Avram fell facedown, and God said to him, "As for Me, this is My covenant with you: You will be the father of many nations. No longer will you be called Avram; your name will be Avraham, for I have made you a father of many nations. I will make you very fruitful; I will make nations of you, and kings will come from you. I will establish My covenant as an everlasting covenant between Me and you and your descendants after you for generations to come, to be your God and the God of your descendants after you. The whole land of Canaan, where you are now an alien, I will give as an everlasting possession to you and your descendants after you; and I will be their God."

Then God said to Avraham, "As for you, you must keep My covenant, you and your descendants after you for generations to come. This is My covenant with you and your descendants after you, the covenant you are to keep: Every male among you shall be circumcised. You are to undergo circumcision, and it will be the sign of the covenant between Me and you. For the generations to come every male among you who is eight days old must be circumcised, including those born in your household or bought with money from a foreigner – those who are not your offspring. Whether born in your household or bought with your money, they must be circumcised. My covenant in your flesh is to be an everlasting covenant. Any uncircumcised male, who has not been circumcised in the flesh, will be cut off from his people; he has broken My covenant." (Bereishit 17:1–14)

Avram is told that from now on his name will be Avraham, signifying that he will be a father of many nations, *av hamon goyim*. This would seem to be the ultimate universal message: not only will Avraham be a part of the larger universal existence, he will bring nations toward God. Yet in the next breath he is told to perform circumcision, which creates boundaries and will forever separate Avraham and his descendants from all others.

In one fell swoop, in one utterance, in a single covenant – the universal vision alongside the narrow, parochial, particular mission. Apparently, Avraham is confused. How can he impact the entire world when he must first perform an act that sets him apart, an act of self-mutilation that people will view as grotesque? *Hakhnasat orhim* and *'eiruv tavshilin* (welcoming guests and making accommodations to feed them on holidays and Shabbat) were much less alienating, much more easily understood.

Apparently, what Avraham still lacks is "holiness" – *kedushah* – which is literally rendered as "set apart." This separateness is a new phase for Avraham, and not one to which he would have come without God's command. This separateness may be seen as that which contradicts Avraham's innate attribute of *hesed*, the attribute through which he has served God up to this point in his life.

How is he to reconcile *hesed* with *kedushah*? How is he to be a part of the world – involved, engaged, interested, even responsible for the world – and live a life of *kedushah*, set apart, indelibly marked by "differentness"? How will he and his descendants reconcile living in a mundane world with their unique destiny and closeness to God?

The answer presents itself later on in the text, as Avraham finds himself enmeshed in his next paradoxical challenge: the *'akeidah*, the binding of Yitzhak. Here, too, logic is defeated. If Yitzhak is to be offered up, how can he effectively be the living progeny destined to carry on the family line? Avraham and Yitzhak nonetheless set out to fulfill God's command, and they bring two other people along. Our sages[18] identify them as Yishmael and Eliezer – Avraham's first son, and a man who was like a son. Rashi, citing the Midrash, tells us that as they approach the appointed place Avraham sees something that appears to him to be ethereal, but he is unsure if it is real or surreal, physical or spiritual. He sees a cloud, he sees the *Shekhinah*; he turns to question Yishmael and Eliezer, but they see only the mountain. He turns to Yitzhak, who sees the cloud, tied as if by rope to the mountain. Avraham then turns to the other two and says, "Wait here with the *hamor* (donkey)." My teacher Rabbi Soloveitchik pointed out that at times we neglect the rest of the verse:

---

18. See Rashi ad loc.

בראשית כב:ד–ה

בַּיּוֹם הַשְּׁלִישִׁי וַיִּשָּׂא אַבְרָהָם אֶת עֵינָיו וַיַּרְא אֶת הַמָּקוֹם מֵרָחֹק: וַיֹּאמֶר אַבְרָהָם אֶל נְעָרָיו שְׁבוּ לָכֶם פֹּה עִם הַחֲמוֹר וַאֲנִי וְהַנַּעַר נֵלְכָה עַד כֹּה וְנִשְׁתַּחֲוֶה וְנָשׁוּבָה אֲלֵיכֶם:

Then on the third day Avraham lifted up his eyes, and saw the place from afar. And Avraham said to his young men, "Stay here with the donkey; and I and the lad will go yonder and worship, and return to you." (Bereishit 22:4–5)

Those last words, "and return to you," cannot be ignored. Avraham encapsulates a unique religious experience in this short statement, and we should take note of every element. This awesome religious experience would not be complete until Avraham came down the mountain and shared with others his epiphany, his feelings and his enlightenment. Avraham would have the greatest impact on the two men he left behind only after parting ways, dedicating himself to the more particular religious experience at the summit, and then returning to their company. Similarly, for the Jewish people to have an impact on the world, we must first disengage, separate ourselves, and fully explore our unique relationship with God. There will be times when we must wrest ourselves away from our deep involvement, even our responsibility for the world. We must climb lofty mountains, even engage in divinely mandated, though seemingly paradoxical, behavior. But we must always remember that eventually we must come down from the mountain, re-engage, return to the people that we left at the foot of the mountain. We must find the language and establish the relationship that will allow us to share with them what we learned at the summit.

Avraham learns to resolve the tension. Both the universal and the particular are important, but they are intertwined. The way we can accomplish our universal responsibility is by first becoming separate, different – as holy as we can possibly become. Only this will enable us to fulfill our mission of *tikkun 'olam*, to enlighten, to educate, to heal and repair the world.

What is interesting is that the *nefesh asher asu b'Haran*, the people "acquired" in Haran,[19] the people attracted by a spirituality devoid of

---

19. See the *Meshekh Hokhmah*, Bereishit 21:33, and the sources he cites.

holiness, all disappeared. In fact, the prototypical outreach that Avraham was famous for, his open tent and encouraging people to bless God, is recorded *after* the circumcision was performed.

בראשית כא:לג

וַיִּטַּע אֶשֶׁל בִּבְאֵר שָׁבַע וַיִּקְרָא שָׁם בְּשֵׁם ה' אֵל עוֹלָם:

And he planted an orchard (eshel) in Be'er Sheva and he called there in the name of the Eternal God. (Bereishit 21:33)

רש"י, בראשית כא:לג

אשל: רב ושמואל. חד אמר פרדס להביא ממנו פירות לאורחים בסעודה. וחד אמר פונדק לאכסניא ובו כל מיני פירות....

ויקרא שם וגו': על ידי אותו אשל נקרא שמו של הקב"ה אלוה לכל העולם. לאחר שאוכלים ושותים, אמר להם "ברכו למי שאכלתם משלו. סבורים אתם שמשלי אכלתם? משל מי שאמר והיה העולם אכלתם."

An eshel: Rav and Shmuel disagree: One said, this refers to an orchard. [Avraham] planted an orchard in order to bring fruits to the guests at his table. The other said that this refers to an inn: [Avraham] opened an inn and guesthouse to offer passersby all types of fruit....
"And he called," etc.: Through the agency of this eshel the Holy One's name was known as Master of the Entire Universe, for after they would eat and drink [Avraham] would say to them, "Bless the One whose food you have eaten. Do you think that you have eaten food that belongs to me? You have eaten the food of He who spoke and created the world." (Rashi, Bereishit 21:33)

The house of Avraham and Sarah was open to all, yet set apart; universal and separate at one and the same time. Only now were they able to reach out to others in a way that left a permanent impression.

משך חכמה, בראשית כא:לג

ויקרא שם בשם ה' אל עולם: יתכן דהוי כמו דכתיב לעולם, דקודם שנולד יצחק ופרסם אברהם מציאות השם והשגחתו הפרטיות ואחדותו שהוא בלתי מושג אם מת הלא נשכח כל לימודיו ועיקריו וכמו שאמרו במדרש שהנפש אשר עשו בחרן חזרו לסורן, (ע' פרקי דר"א פ' כט) אולם כאשר נולד יצחק אשר הבטיח השי"ת והקימותי להיות לך לאלקים ולזרעך אחריך וכדאמרו יבמות ק: המיוחס אחריך וידע שהוא ינחיל הדיעות האמיתיות ויפרסם אלקותו לכן אמר שהוא עכשיו אל לעולם ולא יופסק ידיעתו יתברך לדור דור והבן.

Our world, then, is not so different from that of Avraham and Sarah after all. The world still lacks holiness. By observing the commandments, both those we understand and those that seem to us paradoxical, we add holiness to our lives. We set ourselves on a higher rung, as it were. And as holiness accrues, we will find our spiritual, ethical and social abilities exponentially increased, and thus our ability to effect change and fix a broken world.

Parashat Vayeira

The Purpose of the 'Akeidah

וַיְהִי אַחַר הַדְּבָרִים הָאֵלֶּה וְהָאֱלֹקִים נִסָּה אֶת אַבְרָהָם וַיֹּאמֶר אֵלָיו אַבְרָהָם
וַיֹּאמֶר הִנֵּנִי: וַיֹּאמֶר קַח נָא אֶת בִּנְךָ אֶת יְחִידְךָ אֲשֶׁר אָהַבְתָּ אֶת יִצְחָק וְלֶךְ לְךָ אֶל
אֶרֶץ הַמֹּרִיָּה וְהַעֲלֵהוּ שָׁם לְעֹלָה עַל אַחַד הֶהָרִים אֲשֶׁר אֹמַר אֵלֶיךָ:

And it came to pass after these things that God tested Avraham, and said to him, "Avraham!" And he said, "Here I am." And He said, "Take now your son, your only son, whom you love – Yitzhak, and go to the land of Moriah; and offer him there for a burnt offering upon one of the mountains that I will tell you. (Bereishit 22:1–2)

When confronted with the divine imperative, Avraham does not flinch; he marches to the place that God told him. The word of God would be fulfilled. The Torah only tells of Avraham's actions, and the narrative gives us no sense that Avraham hesitated in any way: Avraham awakens early and sets out on his macabre mission. We are not made privy to the thoughts racing through Avraham's mind. Did this grotesque commandment cause Avraham to question the promises God had made to him, or to question his basic understanding of God as merciful and good?

Readers of the text may be far more intrigued by those thoughts than by the actions that the Torah describes. On a logical level, Avraham faced a quandary: God had previously assured him that this son, and no other, would carry on his name and his mission; the covenant forged with Avraham was to be continued through Yitzhak and his children. If Yitzhak, as yet unmarried and childless, is to be slaughtered in sacrifice, can Avraham comprehend or contend with the thought that God's words would be proven false?[1]

---

1. Rabbi Soloveitchik cited his grandfather Rav Hayim as applying one of the rules of hermeneutics in this case: When two verses contradict one another, the third, reconciling verse is sought. In this case, the third verse was the commandment of the angel who

The gnawing, haunting elements of the *'akeidah* stem from the permanence of death. If death can be temporary, if the body can be healed, reunited with the soul, then the harshest element of the *'akeidah* disappears. Can it be that Avraham's own experiences told him that the *'akeidah* was not the final act of Yitzhak's life story? Avraham himself had been thrown into a fiery furnace – apparently with his own father's blessing or acquiescence[2] – and emerged unscathed; perhaps he believed, with a conviction that few others can comprehend, that Yitzhak would live, even if he offered him as a sacrifice.

This may be related to a possible resolution that seems to elude Jewish minds: Avraham was to have killed Yitzhak, and subsequently Yitzhak would return from the dead. The idea of resurrection is certainly a Jewish idea, and is considered a basic principle of faith; nonetheless, ever since the idea was hijacked[3] by Christianity and made a central tenet of that religion, Jews seem to distance themselves from the concept, despite the fact that we confirm this principle of faith in our prayers on a thrice-daily basis.

While this may resolve some of the questions that we have regarding Avraham's mindset, it is not the scenario of choice, for the simple reason that Avraham did not, in fact, kill Yitzhak. Nonetheless, various midrashim and commentaries prefer to read Yitzhak's death into the text.

פרקי דרבי אליעזר,(היגר) - "חורב" פרק ל

ר' יהודה אומר: כיון שהגיע החרב על צוארו פרחה ויצאה נפשו של יצחק. וכיון שהשמיע קולו מבין הכרובים ואמר לו "אל תשלח ידך", נפשו חזרה לגופו וקם ועמד יצחק על רגליו וידע יצחק שכך המתים עתידים להחיות, ופתח ואמר "ברוך אתה ה' מחיה המתים".

Rav Yehudah said: When the sword reached Yitzhak's throat, his soul ascended and he died. When He made his voice heard from between

---

told Avraham to cease and desist. See Rabbi Joseph B. Soloveitchik, *Halakhic Man*, trans. Lawrence Kaplan (Philadelphia: Jewish Publication Society of America, 1983), page 143, note 5.

2. See Bereishit Rabbah 38:13, where it is reported that Terah delivered Avraham to Nimrod.

3. It is my assumption that a misreading of the *'akeidah* by early Christians is what made the crucifixion and resurrection a central part of their religion.

the keruvim *saying, "Do not raise a hand to the boy," [Yitzhak's] soul
returned to his body and Yitzhak arose and stood on his feet. Yitzhak
knew that this is how the dead would be resurrected in the future, and
he said, "Blessed are You Who resurrects the dead." (Pirkei d'Rebbi
Eliezer, chapter 30)*[4]

The scenario described in this midrash is radically different from what
we have come to visualize: Although Avraham does not actively kill him,
Yitzhak dies on the altar. His soul ascends to heaven, but is returned to
his body when the Voice of God rings out from between the *keruvim*, and
Yitzhak experiences and comprehends resurrection.

The *keruvim* are familiar to us from Bereishit: God stations a pair of
celestial protectors on the path leading back to the Garden of Eden. In our
present context, the *keruvim* function as an oracle,[5] more in line with the
description of the *keruvim* that stood in the Mishkan (Tabernacle) and
later in the Beit haMikdash in Jerusalem. In fact, this midrash apparently
has more to tell us than the alternate '*akeidah* scenario; there is, encoded
within it, a deep understanding of the function of the *keruvim* and of the
Beit haMikdash.

The '*akeidah* took place on a mountain chosen by God and shown to
Avraham, a very specific mountain called Moriah. This is the very spot
on which the Beit haMikdash was constructed generations later, the spot
upon which the Ark of the Covenant stood, shielded by the *keruvim*. Yet

---

4. The *Siftei Kohen* reports a tradition that Avraham actually severed most of Yitzhak's
   trachea and windpipe – rendering him a "kosher" offering; see *Siftei Kohen*, Bereishit
   23:2, where he cites this tradition in the name of the Zohar. The source in the Zohar
   has eluded me (and others). In fact, the *Siftei Kohen* himself did not actually find this
   passage in the written text of the Zohar; he states that he heard that such a teaching is
   recorded in the Zohar.

שפתי כהן, בראשית כג:ב

שמעתי שנמצא בזוהר שמה שלא הביא הביא יצחק עמו לפי ששחט בו אברהם רוב שנים והוליכוהו המלאכים
תיכף לגן עדן לרפאותו ונשתהה שם שלוש שנים ובירך עליו ברוך אתה ה' מחיה המתים, ולזה אמר
כשנכנס יעקב, אמר ראה ריח בני כריח שדה שהיה מכיר בו.

5. See Shmot 25:22.

שמות כה:כב

וְנוֹעַדְתִּי לְךָ שָׁם וְדִבַּרְתִּי אִתְּךָ מֵעַל הַכַּפֹּרֶת מִבֵּין שְׁנֵי הַכְּרֻבִים אֲשֶׁר עַל אֲרֹן הָעֵדֻת אֵת כָּל אֲשֶׁר אֲצַוֶּה אוֹתְךָ
אֶל בְּנֵי יִשְׂרָאֵל:

the confluence of space is not the end of the story: The sacrifice Avraham was called upon to offer was the first sacrifice in Jewish history, and it was performed on the precise spot that would later be the focal point of all sacrifice. Yitzhak is the first offering, the offering that consecrated the Altar that would stand on that very spot. The Midrashic insistence that Yitzhak died at the *'akeidah* is no mere quirk: Har haMoriah is the place of sacrifice, and Yitzhak was sacrificed.

We should note that there are other connections between Yitzhak and the Mishkan/Mikdash. The Mishkan is consecrated in the month of Nisan, even though the materials were collected and assembled months before, on the twenty-fifth of Kislev. Why the delay? The consecration of the Mishkan had to take place in Nisan, according to tradition, because Yitzhak was born in Nisan.[6]

Because the verses tell us that Yitzhak was in fact spared, we tend to analyze the episode in terms of Avraham, to delve into his thoughts and follow his actions. However, if we can entertain the possibility that Yitzhak perished – actually, or figuratively, potentially – as the Midrash suggests, we are thrust into an entirely different set of motives, considerations and thought processes. If we take the conjecture one step further, as did the Midrash, and include the resurrection, we gain insight into the inner workings of the Beit haMikdash and the sacrifices offered there: God creates man, but man sins. The result – inevitable, irrefutable – should be death.

So it was from the very first sin in the Garden of Eden: A person who turns his back on the source of all life will surely die. Yet God does not carry out the death sentence. He allows us to repent. He creates a place and an instrument of forgiveness for man to express his realization that he has

---

6. Pesikta Rabbati paragraph 6.

פסיקתא רבתי (איש שלום) פסקא ו, ותשלם כל המלאכה ד"ה דבר אחר ותשלם
מה גדלו מעשיך ה' [וגו']: מהו מאד עמקו מחשבותיך? אמר רבי חנינא: בעשרים וחמשה בכסליו נגמרה
מלאכת המשכן ועשה מקופל עד אחד בניסן, שהקימו משה אחד בניסן כמה שכתב וביום החודש הראשון
באחד לחדש תקים משכן אהל מועד (שמות מ:ב), וכל זמן שהיה מקופל היו ישראל מלמלאין על משה
לומר למה לא הוקם מיד שמא דופי אירע בו, שחשב לערב שמחת המשכן בחודש שנולד בו יצחק, שבניסן
נולד יצחק, ומניין אלא כשהמלאכים באים אצל אברהם מהו אומר לושי ועשי עגות (בראשית יח:ו) שהיה
פסח ואמרו לו שוב אשוב אליך כעת חיה והנה בן לשרה אשתך (בראשית יח). מהו כעת חיה? אמר ר'
זבדי בן לוי: סריטה סרטו לו על כותל כשתבא השמש לכאן, לא עשה אלא כיון שבא ניסן והוקם המשכן
עוד לא לימלם אדם אחר משה.

sinned and deserves to die. He is permitted to bring an offering in his place. And man, who up until that point is "as good as dead," is then reconnected with the source of all life; man is resurrected. All of the offerings brought by guilty, sinful man effectuate a type of figurative resurrection.

Yitzhak's death – or near death – represents the ability of man to return from death, to extricate himself from the limbo state between living and dead. This is what sacrifice does; this is the purpose of the Beit haMikdash. Every layer of the *'akeidah* account leads in this direction: Avraham, who represents *hesed* (kindness), offers up Yitzhak, who represents *din* (judgment). The offering is accepted: true judgment, the death sentence that is the letter of the law, is sacrificed in favor of life. *Hesed* will be the dominant trait in this place for all time. The *akeidah* is the *hanukat hamizbeiah* – the consecration of the Altar – for it establishes for all time the dynamic of the transformative and rejuvenating qualities of *hesed*, as expressed in the atonement effectuated by sacrifice.[7]

In fact, the idea of resurrection is the major element of the haftarah portion read with this parashah: in a dramatic scene, Elisha revives and resurrects a dead child.

מלכים ב, ד:לב–לז

וַיָּבֹא אֱלִישָׁע הַבַּיְתָה וְהִנֵּה הַנַּעַר מֵת מֻשְׁכָּב עַל מִטָּתוֹ: וַיָּבֹא וַיִּסְגֹּר הַדֶּלֶת בְּעַד שְׁנֵיהֶם וַיִּתְפַּלֵּל אֶל ה': וַיַּעַל וַיִּשְׁכַּב עַל הַיֶּלֶד וַיָּשֶׂם פִּיו עַל פִּיו וְעֵינָיו עַל עֵינָיו וְכַפָּיו עַל כַּפָּיו וַיִּגְהַר עָלָיו וַיָּחָם בְּשַׂר הַיָּלֶד: וַיָּשָׁב וַיֵּלֶךְ בַּבַּיִת אַחַת הֵנָּה וְאַחַת הֵנָּה וַיַּעַל וַיִּגְהַר עָלָיו וַיְזוֹרֵר הַנַּעַר עַד שֶׁבַע פְּעָמִים וַיִּפְקַח הַנַּעַר אֶת עֵינָיו: וַיִּקְרָא אֶל גֵּיחֲזִי וַיֹּאמֶר קְרָא אֶל הַשֻּׁנַמִּית הַזֹּאת וַיִּקְרָאֶהָ וַתָּבוֹא אֵלָיו וַיֹּאמֶר שְׂאִי בְנֵךְ: וַתָּבֹא וַתִּפֹּל עַל רַגְלָיו וַתִּשְׁתַּחוּ אָרְצָה וַתִּשָּׂא אֶת בְּנָהּ וַתֵּצֵא:

---

7. The consecration of the Mishkan also had a "sacrifice" – Nadav and Avihu died that day. See Vayikra 10:3 and Rashi's comments. According to mystical sources, Nadav and Avihu "returned" – their souls transmigrated. See *Explorations*, Parashat Shmini.

ויקרא י:ג

וַיֹּאמֶר מֹשֶׁה אֶל אַהֲרֹן הוּא אֲשֶׁר דִּבֶּר ד' לֵאמֹר בִּקְרֹבַי אֶקָּדֵשׁ וְעַל פְּנֵי כָל הָעָם אֶכָּבֵד וַיִּדֹּם אַהֲרֹן:

רש"י, ויקרא י:ג

הוא אשר דבר וגו': היכן דבר ונועדתי שמה לבני ישראל ונקדש בכבודי (שמות כט). אל תקרי בכבודי אלא במכובדי. אמר לו משה לאהרן אהרן אחי יודע הייתי שיתקדש הבית במיודעיו של מקום והייתי סבור או בי או בך, עכשיו רואה אני שהם גדולים ממני וממך.

And when Elisha came into the house, behold, the child was dead, and laid upon his bed. He went in, and closed the door upon the two of them, and prayed to God. And he went up, and lay upon the child, and put his mouth upon his mouth, and his eyes upon his eyes, and his hands upon his hands; and he stretched himself upon the child; and the flesh of the child became warm.[8] Then he returned, and walked in the house to and fro, and went up, and stretched himself upon him; and the child sneezed seven times, and the child opened his eyes. And he called Geihazi, and said, "Call the Shunammite." And he called her. And when she came to him, he said, "Take up your son." Then she went in, and fell at his feet, and bowed to the ground, and took up her son, and went out. (II Melakhim 4:32–37)

The background to this dramatic scene makes the connection with our parashah even more striking: As in the case of Yitzhak, this child was born to an elderly couple. The parents were informed of the birth by a messenger of God, in this case the prophet Elisha.[9] The woman's response to the news echoes Sarah's response:[10]

---

8. The Radak describes what we would call today "mouth-to-mouth" resuscitation: Even when a miracle is performed, it is preferable that it appears like a natural process.

רד"ק, מלכים ב, ד:לד

וישם פיו על פיו: כמו שפירשנו באליהו שאמר ויתמודד על הנער והכל לכוין לשון התפלה על מי שמתפלל עליו כמו שאמר ביצחק לנוכח אשתו ואפשר גם כן להנשים על הנער לחממו בחום הטבעי היוצא מפיו ומעיניו כי רוב הנסים נעשים עם מעט תחבולה מדרך העולם.

9. Many mystical sources teach that children born in miraculous circumstances are more susceptible to "harsh judgment" and death. Some examples of these "miracle children" are Yitzhak, Binyamin, Havakuk, and Yonah. See *Kometz haMinhah*, part 2, section 49.

ספר קומץ המנחה, חלק ב אות מט

ואם תאמר כולה עלי הא קריבית וכו' כי זה היה גם כן עקידת יצחק המשפט שיעקד שהוא קרוב למיתה רומז על תכלית תוקף היסורים ואחר כך יפדה ממוות מוחץ ורופא (וכן חבקוק בן השונמית שהוא בגימטריא גבורה ויראה שהיה ממדריגת יצחק כמו שמובא בזוהר (בראשית ז' ע"ב ובשלח מה.) מת וחיה שכך הוא המשפט לנפשות שממדת המשפט) ואמרו ז"ל מעשה אבות סימן לבנים והוא רמז לגלות בניו וגאולתן שכמו שעקידת יצחק כולו לה' כן הם מקבלים היסורים באהבה ועל ידי זה שבים בתשובה לה' והכל לה' וזהו הא קריבית נפשי קמך רצה לומר שהיה בעבור כבוד שמך וכנזכר לעיל.

ספר ערבי נחל, פרשת לך לך

פירש שם בנזר הקודש כי כל בן עקרה נאחז בסטרא דנוקבא, והטעם כי ולד דעלמא נאמר בו למשפחותם לבית אבותם שהולד הולך אחר אביו כי חיותו בא מחמת אביו כמ"ש ביוסף ונפשו קשורה בנפשו, משא"כ בן עקרה שהושם בה הנס וההשגחה שנתחדש בקרבה הנס ההוא ולכן חיותו בא מסטרא דנוקבא, ולכן שרה אמנו שהיתה עקרה נאמר בה ולשרה בן, והיה מסטרא דנוקבא והיה חשש שלא יהיה בן קיימא, לכן

מלכים ב, ד:י״א—י״ז

וַיְהִי הַיּוֹם וַיָּבֹא שָׁמָּה וַיָּסַר אֶל הָעֲלִיָּה וַיִּשְׁכַּב שָׁמָּה: וַיֹּאמֶר אֶל גֵּחֲזִי נַעֲרוֹ קְרָא
לַשּׁוּנַמִּית הַזֹּאת וַיִּקְרָא לָהּ וַתַּעֲמֹד לְפָנָיו: וַיֹּאמֶר לוֹ אֱמָר נָא אֵלֶיהָ הִנֵּה חָרַדְתְּ
אֵלֵינוּ אֶת כָּל הַחֲרָדָה הַזֹּאת מֶה לַעֲשׂוֹת לָךְ הֲיֵשׁ לְדַבֶּר לָךְ אֶל הַמֶּלֶךְ אוֹ אֶל שַׂר
הַצָּבָא וַתֹּאמֶר בְּתוֹךְ עַמִּי אָנֹכִי יֹשָׁבֶת: וַיֹּאמֶר וּמֶה לַעֲשׂוֹת לָהּ וַיֹּאמֶר גֵּחֲזִי אֲבָל
בֵּן אֵין לָהּ וְאִישָׁהּ זָקֵן: וַיֹּאמֶר קְרָא לָהּ וַיִּקְרָא לָהּ וַתַּעֲמֹד בַּפָּתַח: וַיֹּאמֶר לַמּוֹעֵד
הַזֶּה כָּעֵת חַיָּה אַתְּ חֹבֶקֶת בֵּן וַתֹּאמֶר אַל אֲדֹנִי אִישׁ הָאֱלֹקִים אַל תְּכַזֵּב בְּשִׁפְחָתֶךָ:
וַתַּהַר הָאִשָּׁה וַתֵּלֶד בֵּן לַמּוֹעֵד הַזֶּה כָּעֵת חַיָּה אֲשֶׁר דִּבֶּר אֵלֶיהָ אֱלִישָׁע:

*And it happened one day, [Elisha] came there, and he turned to the
chamber, and lay there. And he said to Geihazi his servant, "Call this
Shunammite." And when he had called her, she stood before him.
And he said to him, "Say now to her, 'Behold, you have been careful
to take all this trouble for us. What is to be done for you? Would you
be spoken for to the king, or to the captain of the army?'" And she
answered, "I live among my own people." And he said, "What then is
to be done for her?" And Geihazi answered, "Truly she has no child,*

הבטיח לה ה' למועד אשוב אליך כעת חיה, ר"ל שהגם שבעת הריון בהכרח יהיה בסטרא דנוקבא וברשותה
מ"מ בעת הלידה הבטיח ה' שיתגלה שם ובאור פני מלך חיים ויתקשר אז יצחק במקור החיים ויצא מתחת
רשותה לרשות אביו מסטרא דדכורא ויהיה לו חיים. ולכן נתרעמה השונמית על אלישע שלא אמר לה
ג"כ בלשון הזה למועד אשוב אליך, כי בצדיקים נאמר ותגזר אומר ויקם לך ואם יהיה הוא אצלה בעת
הלידה יהיה יכולת בידו למשוך לו חיות ממקור החיים, וע"ז השיב אלישע המלאכים שהם חיים כו' עכ"ד.

שער הים, פרשת וירא

ותהר ותלד שרה לאברהם בן וגו': הנה בכתוב הזה ראיתי, לבאר דרוש גדול, בענין בחי' אנשים שנשמותיהם
נמשכות מן הנקבה. וכמו שמצינו בענין חבקוק הנביא, בריש פרשת בשלח, וז"ל דהוה אתי מסטרא
דנוקבא, ובג"ד מותא אתקשרת לרגלוי וכו'. גם מצינו בענין יצחק, שאמרו בפרשת וירא, על והנה בן
לשרה אשתך, דהוה אתי מסטרא דנוקבא וכו'. גם מצינו בענין בנימין, דכתיב ביה (בראשית ל״ה:י״ח) ויהי
בצאת נפשה כי מתה, ותלד בן ותקרא שמו בן אוני. והנה מצינו, כי לכן מת חבקוק, והחייהו אלישע, ויצחק
נעקד, ופרחה נשמתו ממנו, כמ"ש רז"ל וצריך לדעת בחי' אלו מה עניינם.

ספר עבודת ישראל, פרשת ויצא

קראה לו בן אוני, פירוש אוני מלשון כח כמו ראשית אוני (בראשית מ״ט:ג׳) פירוש שאתה הב"ן של
כל כחי וחיותי כי לא נתקבלה תפלתי שיוסף לי בן אחר ולכן אתה הוא בן אוני כלומר כל כחי מסתלק על
ידי לידתך, ואביו קרא לו בנימין, כי בנימין הוא מעלמא דנוקבא וכמ"ש האר"י ז"ל, סוד נשמת שלשה
הצדיקים יצחק בנימין חבקוק הם משורש הדינין והם צריכים להמתקה ולתגבורת החסדים כידוע שם
מהאר"י ז"ל ולכן רצה יעקב להמתיקו בחסד וקרא לו בנימין דהיינו צירוף שמו בן ימין
כי ימין הוא החסד ונמתקו הגבורות.

10. The Pirkei d'Rebbi Eliezer, chapter 32, heightens this connection.

פרקי דרבי אליעזר (היגר) "חורב", פרק לב

אמ' לה למועד הזה כעת חיה את חובקת בן מפרי מיעיך, אמרה לה אדוני זקן מאד וחדלה ממני אורח
נשים ואי אפשר לעשות הדבר הזה אל אדוני איש האלקים אל תכזב בשפחתך.

and her husband is old." And he said, "Call her." And when he had
called her, she stood in the door. And he said, "About this season, in
the coming year, you shall embrace a son." And she said, "No, my lord,
you man of God, do not lie to your maidservant." And the woman
conceived, and bore a son at that season that Elisha had said to her,
in the following year. (II Melakhim 4:11–17)

The haftarah began with acts of kindness: Elisha helps the poor, and the
Shunammite woman and her husband go to great lengths to provide
comfortable lodging for Elisha, the "man of God." All of this parallels the
acts of kindness performed by Avraham at the start of our parashah. The
text then goes into seemingly extraneous detail regarding the amenities
prepared for Elisha's room:

מלכים ב, ד:ט–י

וַתֹּאמֶר אֶל אִישָׁהּ הִנֵּה נָא יָדַעְתִּי כִּי אִישׁ אֱלֹקִים קָדוֹשׁ הוּא עֹבֵר עָלֵינוּ תָּמִיד:
נַעֲשֶׂה נָּא עֲלִיַּת קִיר קְטַנָּה וְנָשִׂים לוֹ שָׁם מִטָּה וְשֻׁלְחָן וְכִסֵּא וּמְנוֹרָה וְהָיָה בְּבֹאוֹ
אֵלֵינוּ יָסוּר שָׁמָּה:

And she said to her husband, "Behold now, I perceive that this is a
holy man of God, who passes by us continually. Let us make a little
chamber, I beg you, on the wall; and let us set for him there a bed,
and a table, and a stool, and a lamp; and it shall be, when he comes
to us, that he shall turn in there." (II Melakhim 4:9–10)

While the objects enumerated seem ordinary, there are those who see
great symbolism in these utensils. The lamp and the table – the Menorah
and the *Shulhan* – are reminiscent of the utensils of the Beit haMikdash.
The *Reishit Hokhmah*[11] (following a teaching of the Zohar[12]) explains that

---

11. *Reishit Hokhmah, Sha'ar ha'Anavah*, chapter 3.

ספר ראשית חכמה, שער הענוה פרק שלישי

והנמשל מובן כי אנו עם ישראל כל תפלותינו ומצוותינו ותורתינו הוא להמשיך השכינה שתדור עמנו,
כמ"ש (שמות כה:ז) ועשו לי מקדש ושכנתי בתוכם, בתוכם ממש בתוך לבם, ומבואר הקדמה זו בזוהר
ותקונים ובכמה מקומות שישראל צרין צורה, וכן בזוהר (פרשת תרומה דף קלג) שמי שמתקן להקדוש
ברוך הוא מטה ושולחן כסא ומנורה הקדוש ברוך הוא יהא אושפיזיה בכל יומא, ופירש שם הענין בסוד
התפלה ע"ש. ונודע כי משכן המלך הוא לב נשבר ונדכה כמו שביארנו.

12. Zohar, Shmot 133a: "'And she said to her husband, "Behold now, I perceive that this is a

this is an attempt to emulate the essence and purpose of the Mishkan/ Beit haMikdash: to bring holiness into this world.[13] The Shunammite was attempting to build the Temple and bring holiness into her home through the acts of kindness for a holy man of God, the prophet Elisha. In turn,

---

holy man of God, who passes by us continually. Let us make a little chamber, I beg you, on the wall; and let us set for him there a bed, and a table, and a stool, and a lampstand; and it shall be, when he comes to us, that he shall turn in there'" (II Melakhim, 4:9–10): Here we have an allusion to the order of prayer: 'Behold now, I perceive' refers to the concentration of mind during prayer; 'that this is a holy man of God' refers to the supernal world which sits upon its Throne of Glory and from whence emanate all sanctifications and which sanctifies all worlds; 'who passes by us continually': with the sanctification wherewith the worlds above are nourished, he also sanctifies us here below, for there can be no completion of the sanctification above without sanctification below, as it is written: 'I shall be sanctified in the midst of the children of Israel' (Vayikra 22:32). 'Let us make a little chamber': Let us have an ordered service as a dwelling for the *Shekhinah*, which is called 'wall,' as in the verse, 'And Hizkiyah turned his face to the wall' (Yeshayahu 38:2). This dwelling place, created by our prayers and praises, consists of a bed, a table, a stool, and a menorah. By our evening prayers we provide Her (the *Shekhinah*) with a bed; by our hymns of praise and by reciting the section of the sacrifice in the morning we provide Her with a table. By the morning prayers, which are said sitting, and with the proclamation of the Divine Unity (the Shema), we provide Her with a stool; and by means of those prayers that must be said standing (Amidah) and of the Kaddish and Kedushah prayers and benedictions we provide Her with a menorah. Blessed is the man who thus endeavours daily to give hospitality to the Holy One blessed be He in this world and blessed shall he be in the world to come. For these four groups of prayers equip the *Shekhinah* with beauty, joy and luster, to greet Her Spouse with delight and ecstasy day by day, through the worship of the holy people. The bed was given to Yaakov to prepare, therefore he [composed] the evening prayer; the table was prepared by King David in the Psalms that he wrote ('You prepare a table before me' [Tehillim 23:5]); the stool was prepared by Avraham, through his close union with God, wherewith he benefited the souls of all the sons of men. The menorah was prepared by Yitzhak, who sanctified the Name of the Holy One before the eyes of the whole world, and lighted the supernal light in that sanctification. Therefore the holy people must direct its mind towards the supernal world, and prepare for the Lord of the House a bed, a table, a stool, and a menorah, in order that perfection and harmony may reign undisturbed every day, both above and below."

13. These objects may also be connected with the three commandments bestowed upon women – *Hallah*, *nidah* and lighting candles. These three elements were also found in Sarah's tent. See Rashi on Bereishit 24:67 and *Sefer haLikutim*, Shoftim, chapter 15.

רש"י, בראשית כד:סז

האהלה שרה אמו: ויביאה האהלה ונעשית דוגמת שרה אמו, כלומר והרי היא שרה אמו, שכל זמן ששרה קיימת היה נר דלוק מערב שבת לערב שבת, וברכה מצויה בעיסה, וענן קשור על האהל, ומשמתה פסקו, וכשבאת רבקה חזרו.

she is blessed with a child, granted to her in miraculous fashion – despite her husband's advanced age. When this child perishes, he is brought to the "quasi-Temple" and resurrected.

With the story told by the haftarah in mind, the parashah is cast in a somewhat different light, the various themes and events gaining different emphases. Only in the context of the haftarah do we understand that Avraham's *hesed* is not only the starting point, it is *the* point. The arrival of the long-awaited child may have seemed momentarily to be the point of the story. The tragic death of that child may have been seen as the sad end of that story. Yet the end of the story of the haftarah is the end of the Midrashic story of the 'akeidah: the resurrection of the child gives new hope when all hope was lost. This is the essence of the Beit haMikdash: to uplift man when all hope is lost, to breathe into him new hope and new life. That is why the room prepared by the Shunammite is outfitted with the very same utensils as the Temple; that is why the 'akeidah takes place on the very same spot where the Temple will one day stand. That is why the Midrash describes Yitzhak's lifeless body on the altar, as if he were killed and resurrected, for on this hallowed ground many would find their way back to God, and back to life.

ספר הליקוטים, ספר שופטים פרק טו

והנה שרה וחנה ושונמית וצרפית, כלם היו גלגול חוה. ושרה אמנו תקנה כל הג' מצות, חלה ונדה והדלקת הנר, כמ"ש רז"ל ברכה היתה מצויה בעיסתה של שרה, ונר דלוק מע"ש. ונדה, דכתיב חדל להיות לשרה אורח כנשים. ומפני שהיתה תחלת התיקון, לא נתקן כראוי. ולכך באו הג' נשים אחרים חנה ושונמית וצרפית, ותקנו הכל. חנה תקנה הנדות, דכתיב ופניה לא היו לה עוד. שונמית תקנה הנר, דכתיב ונשים לו שם כסא וכו'. וצרפית תקנה החלה, דכתיב עשי נא לי עגה קטנה וכו', ודרז"ל כי אליהו כהן היה.

Elevation

It is frightening: "Some time later God tested Avraham."

It is dramatic and haunting: "Take now your son, your only son, whom you love – Yitzhak."

It is life altering and chilling: "and go to the land of Moriah." *sacrifice*

Perhaps most of all, it is confusing: "and elevate him there as an *'olah* upon one of the mountains that I will tell you."

When we consider the *'akeidah* we must read the text carefully, without any preconceived notions, and note what it does say as well as what it does not say. Is it our imagination or is it our faulty memory? Things we think are in the text are absent, and things we don't remember suddenly "appear."

בראשית כב:א–ג

וַיְהִי אַחַר הַדְּבָרִים הָאֵלֶּה וְהָאֱלֹקִים נִסָּה אֶת אַבְרָהָם וַיֹּאמֶר אֵלָיו אַבְרָהָם
וַיֹּאמֶר הִנֵּנִי: וַיֹּאמֶר קַח נָא אֶת בִּנְךָ אֶת יְחִידְךָ אֲשֶׁר אָהַבְתָּ אֶת יִצְחָק וְלֶךְ לְךָ אֶל
אֶרֶץ הַמֹּרִיָּה וְהַעֲלֵהוּ שָׁם לְעֹלָה עַל אַחַד הֶהָרִים אֲשֶׁר אֹמַר אֵלֶיךָ: וַיַּשְׁכֵּם אַבְרָהָם
בַּבֹּקֶר וַיַּחֲבֹשׁ אֶת חֲמֹרוֹ וַיִּקַּח אֶת שְׁנֵי נְעָרָיו אִתּוֹ וְאֵת יִצְחָק בְּנוֹ וַיְבַקַּע עֲצֵי עֹלָה
וַיָּקָם וַיֵּלֶךְ אֶל הַמָּקוֹם אֲשֶׁר אָמַר לוֹ הָאֱלֹקִים:

And it came to pass after these things that God tested Avraham, and said to him, "Avraham!" And he said, "Here I am." And He said, "Take now your son, your only son, whom you love – Yitzhak, and go to the land of Moriah; and offer him there as an 'olah *upon one* ≈ *sacrifice of the mountains that I will tell you." Avraham got up early the next morning and saddled his donkey. He took with him his two servants and his son Yitzhak. He cut* 'olah *wood, and he arose and set out for the place God had told him about. (Bereishit 22:1–3)*

The first noteworthy term is "test." While we have learned that Avraham was tested ten different ways, the only instance that is explicitly called a test, and the only instance in which the nature of the test is explicit, is the *'akeidah.* This, then, is the quintessential test, the ultimate test.

107

When we continue to read the text we are left searching for something that is not there. In fact, nowhere in the entire set of instructions do we find the word that is most closely associated with this series of events: God never does command Avraham to bind Yitzhak or to tie his son in any way. Despite this, for all time this section is known as "the binding (*'akeidah*) of Yitzhak."

There is something else missing, something far more troubling: at no point in the narrative does God command Avraham to kill Yitzhak. The exact words are *v'ha'aleihu sham l'olah*, "elevate him there as an *'olah*."

Rashi comments on this verse, pointing out that God never said to slaughter Yitzhak. God did not want Yitzhak's life to be ended. He wanted Yitzhak to be "raised up," designating him as an "*'olah*." Once Yitzhak was uplifted, God commanded Avraham to take Yitzhak down.[1]

Were we to conclude from our cursory reading that God had indeed commanded Avraham to slaughter his son, we would be justifiably disturbed: elderly, saintly, loving, kind Avraham is asked to perform a grotesque and horrifying act – to kill his own son. Clearly, the episode's finale would allow us to modify our understanding: when God tells Avraham to take Yitzhak down from the altar, the larger ultimate message and lesson would be God's declaration against human sacrifice.

If God never did ask for the slaughter, why did Avraham seem to think He had? What was on Avraham's mind? Might we say that if God did not command him to slaughter Yitzhak, then Avraham should be seen as so bloodthirsty a man that he pulled a knife on his own son? Or might we say that God did command the death of Yitzhak, but subsequently He changed His mind?

Various commentaries address this problem head-on: Rabbeinu Bahya, like Rashi before him, clearly states[2] that God did not, in fact, command Avraham to slaughter Yitzhak. Rabbeinu Bahya buttresses his argument

---

1. Rashi, Bereishit 22:2.

רש"י, בראשית כב:ב

והעלהו: לא אמר לו שחטהו לפי שלא היה חפץ הקב"ה לשחטו אלא להעלהו להר לעשותו עולה ומשהעלהו אמר לו הורידהו.

2. The Baalei haTosafot make the same observation in their comments on Bereishit 22:2:

with a subtle grammatical point: had God intended Yitzhak to be an actual offering, the text should have read "*ha'aleihu 'olah*"; instead, the text reads "*ha'aleihu l'olah*," which is understood as "like on *'olah*" or "instead of an *'olah*."[3] Had God in fact commanded Avraham to sacrifice Yitzhak, it is a theological impossibility that He "changed His mind." Rabbeinu Bahya therefore draws the conclusion that Avraham, motivated by love of God, went further than God's command, and was prepared to slaughter Yitzhak.[4]

We should note that, prior to the *'akeidah*, Avraham erected numerous altars, but never brought an offering upon them.

בראשית יב:ז

וַיֵּרָא ה' אֶל אַבְרָם וַיֹּאמֶר לְזַרְעֲךָ אֶתֵּן אֶת הָאָרֶץ הַזֹּאת וַיִּבֶן שָׁם מִזְבֵּחַ לַה' הַנִּרְאֶה אֵלָיו:

God appeared to Avram and said, "To your offspring I will give this land." So he built an altar there to God who had appeared to him. (Bereishit 12:7)

In these verses, Avraham receives confirmation that indeed he has found the holy place that God had spoken of. He is granted revelation, and to

---

פירוש בעלי התוספות, בראשית כב:ב
והעלהו שם לעולה: אבל לא אמר ושחטהו שלא נתכוון המקום אלא לעלייה בלבד.

3. Rabbeinu Bahya, Bereishit 22:2.

רבינו בחיי, בראשית כב:ב
והעלהו שם לעולה: היה ראוי שיאמר והעלהו שם עולה. אבל על דרך הפשט הלמ"ד הזאת באורה במקום כלומר שתעלה אותו שם במקום עולה. וכמוהו (בראשית ו) הלבנה לאבן במקום אבן. שאם תפרש לעולה עולה ממש איך יצוה הקב"ה ואח"כ יחזור מצווייו. ואברהם מתוך תוקף האהבה הבין עולה ממש והקב"ה שבא לנסות לא כוון אלא במקום עולה.

4. *Shlah haKadosh*, Parashat Vayeira *Torah Ohr* 4.

ספר השל"ה הקדוש, פרשת וירא תורה אור (ד)
זה היה ענין קטרוג של שטן שבכל סעודה שעשה ליצחק לא הקריב קרבן, ואף בסעודה שעשה בעת בשורת יצחק שהיה כקרבן לא הקריב לפניך, אף שהקריב לשם המיוחד היה לו להיות לפניך בלי אמצעית מלאך. והשיב לו הקב"ה כבר הקריב לפני, כי ענין המילה היא קרבן, הן המילה שמל את יצחק בנו הן המילה שמל אברהם את עצמו, וקיים אדם כי יקריב, כי הקריב את עצמו. ורמז לדבר בפרשת לך לך ואברהם הקריב (בראשית יב:יא) נתקיים אחר כך ואברהם הקריב את עצמו, וכבר נודע כי המילה היא קרבן. ואמר הקב"ה להשטן כדרך שהשיב יצחק לישמעאל שהתפאר נגד יצחק על שלא עיכב למול את עצמו, באבר אחד אתה מייראני, אילו אמר ליה הקב"ה זה זבח עצמך וכו'. ואחר הדברים האלה והאלהים נסה את אברהם, פירוש אחר דבריו של ישמעאל ואחר דבריו של שטן, כי כל הפירושים הם אמת, ואלו ואלו דברי אלהים חיים כאשר יתבאר.

express his thanks he builds an altar. But quite significantly, nothing is placed upon it. In subsequent chapters Avraham builds altars on various occasions, and never puts anything on them. Instead, he "calls out to God"; he prays.

בראשית יב:ח

וַיַּעְתֵּק מִשָּׁם הָהָרָה מִקֶּדֶם לְבֵית אֵל וַיֵּט אָהֳלֹה בֵּית אֵל מִיָּם וְהָעַי מִקֶּדֶם וַיִּבֶן שָׁם מִזְבֵּחַ לַה' וַיִּקְרָא בְּשֵׁם ה':

From there he went on toward the hills east of Beit El and pitched his tent, with Beit El on the west and Ai on the east. There he built an altar to God and called on the name of God. (Bereishit 12:8)

בראשית יג:ג–ד

וַיֵּלֶךְ לְמַסָּעָיו מִנֶּגֶב וְעַד בֵּית אֵל עַד הַמָּקוֹם אֲשֶׁר הָיָה שָׁם אָהֳלֹה בַּתְּחִלָּה בֵּין בֵּית אֵל וּבֵין הָעָי: אֶל מְקוֹם הַמִּזְבֵּחַ אֲשֶׁר עָשָׂה שָׁם בָּרִאשֹׁנָה וַיִּקְרָא שָׁם אַבְרָם בְּשֵׁם ה':

From the Negev he went from place to place until he came to Beit El, to the place between Beit El and Ai where his tent had been earlier and where he had first built an altar. There Avram called on the name of God. (Bereishit 13:3–4)

If Avraham had never brought a *korban* (sacrifice) prior to the *'akeidah*, why would he assume that now God requires a sacrifice? We should note that in the *'akeidah* story an offering is eventually brought – but only after an angel intercedes.

There is another, more subtle point to consider: The name of God used in the text that commands the *'akeidah* is *Elokim*. This name is never used in the Torah in association with sacrifices:

תלמוד בבלי, מסכת מנחות דף קי עמוד א

תניא, אמר רבי שמעון בן עזאי: בוא וראה מה כתיב בפרשת קרבנות, שלא נאמר בהן לא אל ולא אלקים אלא ה', שלא ליתן פתחון פה לבעל דין לחלוק.

It was taught: R. Shimon b. Azzai said: Come and see what is written in the chapter of the sacrifices. Neither [the names] E-l nor E-lohim are found there, but only [the Tetragramaton YHVH], so as not to give sectarians any occasion to rebel. (Talmud Bavli Menahot 110a)

All of these considerations lead to the conclusion that God never intended for Avraham to kill Yitzhak – and more significantly, that Avraham was meant to understand that from the outset.

The next term that catches our attention is *"lekh lekha,"* translated as "go – for you" or "go for your sake." This is not the first usage of this phrase. As we may recall, these are very likely the first words God spoke to Avraham.

בראשית יב:א, ד

וַיֹּאמֶר ה' אֶל אַבְרָם לֶךְ לְךָ מֵאַרְצְךָ וּמִמּוֹלַדְתְּךָ וּמִבֵּית אָבִיךָ אֶל הָאָרֶץ אֲשֶׁר אַרְאֶךָּ: ...וַיֵּלֶךְ אַבְרָם כַּאֲשֶׁר דִּבֶּר אֵלָיו ה' וַיֵּלֶךְ אִתּוֹ לוֹט וְאַבְרָם בֶּן חָמֵשׁ שָׁנִים וְשִׁבְעִים שָׁנָה בְּצֵאתוֹ מֵחָרָן:

God said to Avram, "Leave your country, your birthplace and your father's household and go to the land I will show you.... So Avram went, as God had told him, and Lot went with him. Avram was seventy-five years old when he set out from Haran. (Bereishit 12:1, 4)

We should therefore expect that there be some connection – or contrast – between the two uses of the phrase *"lekh lekha."* What is it about this new mission that echoes the previous mission? In both instances, the precise location is withheld and an element of faith or trust is needed. In both cases, there is a clear commandment to do something, but in both cases information is lacking regarding the implementation of the commandment.

We should also note Avraham's zeal: Avraham does not merely accept the mission, he wakes up early in the morning and busies himself with his task with purposefulness. This is one of three instances in which the Torah records that Avraham arises early:[5] faith and enthusiasm combine to push Avraham forward, to single-mindedly fulfill his mandate.

---

5. The first recorded instance of Avraham getting up early is Bereishit 19:27–28, when Avraham arises and witnesses the cities of Sodom and Amorrah go up in smoke. The next instance is Bereishit 21:14, when Yishmael is sent away.

   בראשית יט:כז:ז

   וַיַּשְׁכֵּם אַבְרָהָם בַּבֹּקֶר אֶל הַמָּקוֹם אֲשֶׁר עָמַד שָׁם אֶת פְּנֵי ה': וַיַּשְׁקֵף עַל פְּנֵי סְדֹם וַעֲמֹרָה וְעַל כָּל פְּנֵי אֶרֶץ הַכִּכָּר וַיַּרְא וְהִנֵּה עָלָה קִיטֹר הָאָרֶץ כְּקִיטֹר הַכִּבְשָׁן:

   "Early the next morning Avraham got up and returned to the place where he had stood before God. He looked down toward Sodom and Amorrah, toward all the land of the plain, and he saw dense smoke rising from the land, like smoke from a furnace."

It may be somewhat surprising that in the case of the other *lekh lekha*, when God's first communication with Avraham is recorded, we have no reason to believe that Avraham set off immediately to fulfill God's command. The text does not say that Avraham arose early the next morning and set off on his journey. In fact, the only information we have is that Avraham was seventy-five years old when he set out. How old was he when God commanded "*lekh lekha*"? Though seemingly only tangentially related to the 'akeidah, clarifying the timing of Avraham's first journey may provide surprising insight into God's second "*lekh lekha*" command.

The Torah does not clearly state Avraham's age upon being commanded to leave his homeland, but the text offers us ancillary information as clues to constructing a timeline. When God tells Avraham, "Go forth from your land, your birthplace and your father's household," we understand "father's household" and perhaps "country," but "birthplace" is perplexing: Avraham was born in Ur Kasdim, but left his birthplace when he followed his father Terah on an aborted mission to the land of Canaan that only took Avraham as far as Haran.

בראשית יא:לא–לב

וַיִּקַּח תֶּרַח אֶת אַבְרָם בְּנוֹ וְאֶת לוֹט בֶּן הָרָן בֶּן בְּנוֹ וְאֵת שָׂרַי כַּלָּתוֹ אֵשֶׁת אַבְרָם בְּנוֹ וַיֵּצְאוּ אִתָּם מֵאוּר כַּשְׂדִּים לָלֶכֶת אַרְצָה כְּנַעַן וַיָּבֹאוּ עַד חָרָן וַיֵּשְׁבוּ שָׁם: וַיִּהְיוּ יְמֵי תֶרַח חָמֵשׁ שָׁנִים וּמָאתַיִם שָׁנָה וַיָּמָת תֶּרַח בְּחָרָן:

Terah took his son Avram, his grandson Lot son of Haran, and his daughter-in-law Sarai, the wife of his son Avram, and together they set out from Ur Kasdim to go to Canaan. They came to Haran and they settled there. Terah lived 205 years, and he died in Haran. (Bereishit 11:31–32)

It seems unequivocal that Avraham was born in Ur Kasdim,[6] and that Terah took him and other family members away from there, and the family settled in Haran. We are mystified as to why idolatrous Terah was on his way to Canaan – Israel. The Ramban[7] offers a partial solution when he

---

6. There are, however, those who debate this point; see the comments of the Ramban, below.

7. The Ramban (in his comments on Bereishit 12:1) proposes that Avraham was born in Haran, and he had subsequently traveled to Ur Kasdim.

notes that the text is inverted: the natural order would be to leave the most immediate context, his father's household, followed by the larger circle, his birthplace or hometown, and then the larger and less personal context of country. The Ramban posits that the verse is written in the inverse order, for Avraham had in fact already left his country and birthplace, along with his father and the other family members who joined this entourage, and God's commandment at this juncture is to "finish the job" and leave his father's sphere of influence as well. While this solution does explain the peculiar structure of the command, we are left none the wiser as to Terah's motivation to travel to Canaan.[8]

Later in the text, we become even more confused:

בראשית טו:ז

וַיֹּאמֶר אֵלָיו אֲנִי ה' אֲשֶׁר הוֹצֵאתִיךָ מֵאוּר כַּשְׂדִים לָתֶת לְךָ אֶת הָאָרֶץ הַזֹּאת לְרִשְׁתָּהּ:

He said to him, "I am God who brought you out of Ur Kasdim to give you this land to take possession of it." (Bereishit 15:7)

Who took Avraham out of Ur Kasdim? Was it Terah, or was it God?[9] Whose idea was this – Avraham's, Terah's, or God's? We don't know why

---

8. In a separate comment the Ramban states that the journey from Ur Kasdim to Canaan was Avraham's idea, not Terah's. See Ramban, Bereishit 11:31.

    רמב"ן, בראשית יא:לא

    ויצאו אתם מאור כשדים: בעבור כי אברם נכבד מאביו, וההולכים בעצתו ובעבורו ילכו, אמר הכתוב ויצאו אתם ואף על פי שאמר "ויקח תרח", אבל לוט ושרי בעבור אברם הלכו אתם, כי גם אחרי שנפרד אברם מאביו הלכו אתו.

9. The Netziv makes a suggestion that Terah was traveling at Avraham's request, but Avraham was a *luftmensch* – his head was in the clouds – and therefore Terah "drove" so as not to disturb Avraham's meditations about God. While this presents an idyllic description of the Avraham-Terah relationship, such a description is not supported by the text.

    העמק דבר, בראשית יא:לא

    ויקח תרח את אברם בנו וגו' ללכת ארצה כנען: אע"ג שלא הי' עוד מאמר ה' לא"א. מכ"מ כבר הי' הערה מן השמים וראה מרחוק קדושת הארץ וכמש" להלן ט"ו ז' והא דכתיב ויקח תרח וגו' אע"ג דעיקר רצון אותה יציאה הי' אברם ובעצתו מכ"מ כיון שיה' אברם שקוע ברעיונות אלקיות או חכמות ולא יכול להנהיג נסיעה הוא וביתו ע"כ נמסר הנסיעה לאביו והוא לקח את אברם וכל הכבודה על ידו.

Terah was on the way to Canaan, which is part of the reason we don't know when God spoke to Avraham and told him "*lekh lekha*."

The Ibn Ezra[10] suggests that the command of "*lekh lekha*" was given while Avraham was still in Ur Kasdim, which means that while we don't have a clear timeline, at least in this instance Avraham did not get up early the next morning and immediately obey the divine imperative. But now we understand why God asks Avraham to leave his country and birthplace – he was still there. This reading of the text leads to the conclusion that God "gets the credit" for taking Avraham out of Ur Kasdim, and Terah was a facilitator of God's will. We thus very neatly reconcile the syntax of the verses, the timeline issues and the question of motive, but we create a different problem: if God spoke to Avraham and commanded him to go to Canaan at that juncture, why did he need Terah to help him out?

Let us reframe the issue of the sequence of events. How old was Avraham when God spoke with him the first time, commanding him to leave his entire past behind and journey to an unnamed destination? A cursory reading of the text reveals that "*lekh lekha*" is the first recorded communication, and Avraham was seventy-five years old when he left on this journey. The call of "*lekh lekha*," however, is not fixed anywhere on the timeline of Avraham's life. While various rabbinic opinions mark off significant stages in Avraham's religious development, with benchmarks at three years of age, forty-eight, and again at fifty-two years of age,[11] we do not know at what point in Avraham's life he receives his first revelation, when God first confirms for Avraham his beliefs and convictions.

---

10. Ibn Ezra, Bereishit 12:1.

אבן עזרא, בראשית יב:א

השם צוה לאברהם ועודנו באור כשדים שיעזוב ארצו ומקום מולדתו גם בית אביו. והטעם שידע השם שתרח אחר שיצא ללכת אל ארץ כנען ישב בחרן. ותרח לא מת עד אחר ששים שנה שיצא אברהם מבית אביו מחרן רק הכתוב לא פירש שניו בצאתו מאור כשדים. ואחר שאמר אשר אראך – גלה לו הסוד כי כן כתוב ויצאו ללכת ארצה כנען. או יהיה טעם אראך הוא שאמר לו כי את כל הארץ אשר אתה רואה לך אתננה.

11. See below for the significance of some of these junctures on the timeline, and the seminal events that are linked to them.

Rashi actually raises the possibility that there was a direct communication from God before "*lekh lekha*." When God tells Avraham about the slavery of the Jews He speaks of four hundred years.

בראשית טו:יג

וַיֹּאמֶר לְאַבְרָם יָדֹעַ תֵּדַע כִּי גֵר יִהְיֶה זַרְעֲךָ בְּאֶרֶץ לֹא לָהֶם וַעֲבָדוּם וְעִנּוּ אֹתָם אַרְבַּע מֵאוֹת שָׁנָה:

Then God said to Avram, "Know for certain that your descendants will be strangers in a land not their own, and they will be enslaved and mistreated for four hundred years. (Bereishit 15:13)

According to accepted rabbinic chronology, the Jews were in Egypt for 210 years. Commentators who explain God's reference to four hundred years of slavery point back to the birth of Yitzhak: as any parent knows, this is when the worrying begins. When Avraham and Sarah have a child, they begin to view the world from a new perspective, considering the larger context. The child, the subject and the vehicle for their angst, provokes a heightened concern for their descendants.

To make matters more interesting, another set of figures is thrown into the mix when the story of the Exodus from Egypt is told:

שמות יב:מא

וַיְהִי מִקֵּץ שְׁלֹשִׁים שָׁנָה וְאַרְבַּע מֵאוֹת שָׁנָה וַיְהִי בְּעֶצֶם הַיּוֹם הַזֶּה יָצְאוּ כָּל צִבְאוֹת ה' מֵאֶרֶץ מִצְרָיִם:

And so, at the end of the 430 years, to the very day, all God's divisions left Egypt. (Shmot 12:41)

We see that 210 years of slavery[12] become 400 years of emotional distress, when counted from the birth of Yitzhak. But how do the 400 years become 430? Where and when are the extra 30 years? Rashi[13] explains that while we count the 400 years from the birth of Yitzhak, 30 years prior to that is

---

12. According to rabbinic tradition, of the 210 years in Egypt only 86 were years of actual slavery.

13. See Rashi, Shmot 12:40. Rashi's source is a *braita* in Seder Olam Rabbah, the definitive book on biblical chronology, chapter 1.

when God spoke to Avraham at the *Brit bein haBetarim* (the Covenant of the Split Pieces).[14] We know that Avraham was 100 years of age when Yitzhak was born, which would mean that he was seventy years old when he had this epiphany – five years prior to his arrival in the land of Canaan, and therefore prior to "*lekh lekha.*"

Rashi's reading of the text is based on a book of biblical chronology called Seder Olam Rabbah, a comprehensive, overarching timeline drawn from biblical narrative and Midrashic traditions. One of the most dramatic episodes in Avraham's life is when he is thrown into the furnace, an episode embedded in our collective memory, recorded in Midrashic and Talmudic sources but absent from the biblical text in any explicit way. However, the furnace episode may be subliminally encoded in the biblical text, within the name of Avraham's place of birth, Ur Kasdim. What was this place and why was it so named? The Targum Pseudo-Yonatan[15] translates Ur Kasdim

---

רש"י, שמות יב:מ

שלשים שנה וארבע מאות שנה: בין הכל משנולד יצחק עד עכשיו היו ארבע מאות שנה. משהיה לו זרע לאברהם נתקיים (בראשית טו:יג) כי גר יהיה זרעך, ושלשים שנה היו משנגזרה גזירת בין הבתרים עד שנולד יצחק. ואי אפשר לומר בארץ מצרים לבדה, שהרי קהת מן הבאים עם יעקב היה צא וחשוב כל שנותיו וכל שנות עמרם בנו ושמונים של משה, לא תמצאם כל כך, ועל כרחך הרבה שנים היו לקהת עד שלא ירד למצרים, והרבה משנות עמרם נבלעים בשנות קהת והרבה משמונים של משה נבלעים בשנות עמרם, הרי שלא תמצא ארבע מאות שנה לביאת מצרים, והוזקקת לומר על כרחך, שאף שאר הישיבות נקראו גרות, אפילו בחברון, שנאמר (בראשית לה:כז) אשר גר שם אברהם ויצחק, ואומר (שמות ו:ד) את ארץ מגוריהם אשר גרו בה, לפיכך אתה צריך לומר כי גר יהיה זרעך משהיה לו זרע. וכשתמנה ארבע מאות שנה משנולד יצחק, תמצא מביאתן למצרים עד יציאתן מאתים ועשר שנה, וזה אחד מן הדברים ששינו לתלמי המלך.

ברייתא דסדר עולם רבה, פרק א

אברהם אבינו ה' בשעה שנדבר עמו בין הבתרים בן ע' שנה שנאמר (שמות יב:מא) ויהי מקץ שלשים שנה וארבע מאות שנה וגו'. לאחר שנדבר עמו ירד עשה שם חמש שנים שנאמר (בראשית יב:ד) ואברהם בן חמש שנים ושבעים שנה בצאתו מחרן.

14. We should note that here Avraham does kill animals, at God's request (Bereishit 15:9–10). However, subsequent to this covenant all the altars that Avraham builds remain empty – devoid of flesh and blood – until the *'akeidah.*

15. Targum Pseudo-Yonatan, Bereishit 15:7.

תרגום יונתן, בראשית טו:ז

ואמר ליה אנא ה' דאפיקתך מאתון נורא דכשדאי למתן לך ית ארעא הדא למירתה.

כתר יונתן, בראשית טו:ז

ויאמר לו אני ה' שהוצאתיך מכבשן האש של כשדים לתת לך את הארץ הזאת לרשתה.

as "the furnace of fire in Kasdim." Thus, when God speaks to Avraham at the *Brit bein haBetarim* and says "I am God, who brought you out of Ur Kasdim" (Bereishit 15:7), what God is really saying is "I am the One who saved you from the fiery furnace." This reading forces us to conclude that the *Brit bein haBetarim* preceded "*lekh lekha.*"

According to the Seder Olam Rabbah, Avraham was at the tower of Bavel and was forty-eight years old at the time of the *Brit bein haBetarim*. The Torah tells us of the use of furnaces to forge the bricks used to build the tower,[16] and it is into one of these furnaces that the nefarious Nimrod threw Avraham, who had rejected the idolatrous overtones of Nimrod's rule. It was from that furnace that Avraham was saved.

Nimrod and his followers become known as the "generation of the dispersion." Can Terah's sudden departure for Canaan be understood in this context? Did he quit Ur Kasdim out of a nascent sense of Zionism, or was his move part of the general atmosphere in that generation? Did Terah, like others of his time, get some sort of divine inspiration that told him it was time to move on, or did he recognize and seek out some inherent spirituality in Canaan?

The Netziv concurs with Rashi and follows the same chronology, positing that the *Brit bein haBetarim* transpired when Avraham was seventy years old. The Netziv then proceeds to describe the *Brit bein haBetarim* as more of a dreamlike experience, an "awakening" or "enlightenment," rather than a full-fledged prophetic experience.[17] God whispered into Avraham's heart and told him that he should leave Ur Kasdim and head to Israel. Perhaps

---

Also see the comments of the Rosh on the Torah and *haKtav v'haKabbalah*.

הכתב והקבלה, בראשית טו:ז

מאור כשדים: היותר נכון מ"ש הרא"ש שאין המקום נקרא אור כשדים, אבל פי' אש כשדים, כמו שלישית באור תבעיר (יחזקאל ה:ב) וכן אור לו בציון ותנור (ישעיה לא:ט), ואמר קרא וימת הרן באור כשדים כלומר מת בעיר מולדתו ארם נהרים ע"י האש ששרפוהו הכשדים, וכמו שספרו לנו רבותינו (ערש"י).

16. Bereishit 11:3.

בראשית יא:ג

וַיֹּאמְרוּ אִישׁ אֶל רֵעֵהוּ הָבָה נִלְבְּנָה לְבֵנִים וְנִשְׂרְפָה לִשְׂרֵפָה וַתְּהִי לָהֶם הַלְּבֵנָה לְאָבֶן וְהַחֵמָר הָיָה לָהֶם לַחֹמֶר:
"They said to each other, 'Come, let us make bricks and bake them thoroughly.' They used brick instead of stone, and clay for mortar."

17. *Ha'amek Davar*, Bereishit 15:7.

Avraham was not the only one to experience such an "awakening"; perhaps Terah did as well.

The Ramban's line of thought is of a similar vein:[18] Avraham built an altar upon arriving in Israel, because only then did he receive actual prophecy, as opposed to the dreams, or *ruah hakodesh*, he had experienced up to that point. The *Kli Yakar*[19] reminds us of the more general principle that outside the Land of Israel prophecy may be all but impossible.

We have seen, then, that according to both the Ramban and the Netziv, "*lekh lekha*" was not a clear prophetic command but rather a "feeling," or intuition. This would explain why Avraham did not "pick up and go" early the next morning. Terah's journey may also be the result of a similar awakening. We might even dare to say that God spread this type of feeling among all of humanity, but only Avraham was willing to take up the challenge. This is reminiscent of the Midrashic[20] insight regarding receiving the Torah: God called out to many nations but only the Jews accepted the Torah.

Terah never completes the journey. Though he and Avraham ostensibly travel the same path, we do not find a description similar to the relationship

---

העמק דבר, בראשית טו:ז

ויאמר אליו: רש"י בפ' בא כ' דברית בה"ב נאמר שלשים שנה קודם שנולד יצחק ומיישב ומושב ב"י אשר ישבו במצרים שלשים שנה וארבע מאות שנה.... ונ"ל שגם בסדר עולם אין הכוונה שהי' הדבור כמשמעו אלא בהיותו בן שבעים שנה הי' לו הערה וקול דודי ית' דופק על לבו לצאת מאור כשדים ומשם לא"י. והרה"ז מפורש בישעיהו מ"א מי העיר ממזרח וגו' ומשום שאז עלה ברצון כל ענין בה"ב. אבל לא הי' שום דבור מפורש עד שהגיע לבן חמש ושבעים והגיע דבור הראשון לזרעך אתן את הארץ הזאת. ובמלחמת המלכים בא דבור של הקב"ה בשלימות בשעה שעלה במחשבת א"א שהוא צדקה בלי טעם.

18. See Ramban, *Bereishit* 12:7.

רמב"ן, בראשית יב:ז

וטעם לה' הנראה אליו, כי הודה לשם הנכבד וזבח לו זבח תודה על שנראה אליו, כי עד הנה לא נראה אליו השם ולא נתודע אליו במראה ולא במחזה, אבל נאמר לו "לך לך מארצך" בחלום הלילה או ברוח הקדש.

19. *Kli Yakar*, *Bereishit* 12:7; the Netziv concurs.

כלי יקר, בראשית יב:ז

וירא ה' אל אברם: מה שלא נראה אליו ה' מיד כשאמר לו לך לך מארצך, לפי שאז היה עדיין בחו"ל כדעת הראב"ע ובחו"ל אין שכינתו ית' נגלה וראיה מיונה, (מכילתא בא יב:ד) וא"כ לא נראה אליו שם ה' במראה כי אם קול דברים לבד היה שומע וע"כ לא בנה שם מזבח, רק לה' הנראה אליו. אבל בעוד שלא היה נראה אליו לא רצה לבנות מזבח במקום שאין השכינה שורה. וזה"ש במשה (שמות ד:א) כי יאמרו לא נראה אליך ה'. כי אין דרכו להתראות בחו"ל ובזה יכחישו לומר שגם קול לא שמעת.

20. Sifri, 343.

between father and son that characterizes the *'akeidah*, "and the two of them went together." Instead, we get the feeling that Avraham and Terah took the same trip – separately, as opposed to Avraham and Yitzhak traveling together on the way to the *'akeidah*.

בראשית כב:ו–ח

...וַיֵּלְכוּ שְׁנֵיהֶם יַחְדָּו: וַיֹּאמֶר יִצְחָק אֶל אַבְרָהָם אָבִיו וַיֹּאמֶר אָבִי וַיֹּאמֶר הִנֶּנִּי בְנִי
וַיֹּאמֶר הִנֵּה הָאֵשׁ וְהָעֵצִים וְאַיֵּה הַשֶּׂה לְעֹלָה: וַיֹּאמֶר אַבְרָהָם אֱלֹקִים יִרְאֶה לּוֹ
הַשֶּׂה לְעֹלָה בְּנִי וַיֵּלְכוּ שְׁנֵיהֶם יַחְדָּו:

...the two of them went on together. Yitzhak said to his father Avraham, "Father?"
[Avraham] replied, "Here I am, my son."
"The fire and wood are here," Yitzhak said, "but where is the lamb for the 'olah?"
Avraham said, "God will provide the lamb for the 'olah, my son." And the two of them went on together. (Bereishit 22:6–8)

They walk together, two people sharing one mission. If there is a binding, it is between Avraham and Yitzhak. With the words *"ha'aleihu sham l'olah,"* Avraham is commanded to elevate his son. The two will be joined, unlike Avraham and Terah.

Avraham receives the awakening, accepts the challenge, leaves his homeland and sets off on his way, destination unknown. The Ramban[21] notes that Avraham travels from place to place waiting for the right feeling, for confirmation from God that he has arrived at the intended place. He doesn't build an altar until he arrives in Israel. Now he knows and feels that he has found the place of holiness. He can build an altar, but he doesn't feel as of yet that it is the right place to put an offering on the altar; he continues his quest.[22] He has found a holy place – but it is not quite holy enough. He

---

21. Ramban, Bereishit 12:1.
22. See comments of the *Meshekh Hokhmah*, Bereishit 12:1 (the "first" *lekh lekha*): Avraham's entire sojourn in Israel was a search for holiness and for the appropriate place to serve God.

משך חכמה, בראשית יב:א

אל הארץ אשר אראך: יתכן לפרש כי צווהו לילך לארץ מקום המיועד לעבודה ולקרבנות ששם הקריבו אדה"ר ונח קרבנותיהם ושם יפרסם אלקות ויקדש שמו בשחוט בנו ויראה את הכחות הטמונים בסתר לבבו אשר מצא נאמן לפניו (נחמיה ט:ח) וזה שאמר אראך פועל שיראה את הטמון בלב אברהם

receives prophecy, revelation, but the places he has found are not quite holy enough for an offering. Finally, God tells him of a place where he can bring an *'olah*. We know the name and location of that place: Har haMoriah, the place that one day would be called Jerusalem. Avraham's quest, begun with the first *"lekh lekha"* call back in Haran, is about to reach its culmination.

Now, marching together with his son, Avraham knows he has found the right place – and so does Yitzhak. As they march together, father and son, overwhelmed by the holiness, both know that this is a place where one can be completely consumed by God. And instead of simple physical elevation – of lifting Yitzhak on top of a glorious mountain and having Yitzhak join him in the covenant that he has with God, Avraham seeks complete, permanent elevation. He thinks this is the place for a sacrifice. Indeed, he is correct: the offering would soon be revealed, and the place they found would one day be the Beit haMikdash, where so many offerings would be brought, and elevation achieved on a grand scale for all of Avraham's descendants.

The *Shlah haKadosh* suggests that in fact Avraham found the holiest place, the inner sanctum, the *Kodesh haKodashim*, citing the Midrashic tradition that the voice that calls out to Avraham comes from between the two *keruvim*. Such a voice, says the *Shlah*, could only be heard in the *Kodesh haKodashim*. There, deep in the holiest place, no sacrifices are offered, only incense. The command Avraham received was, in actuality, to enter the *Kodesh haKodashim*, to assume the role of *kohen gadol* (high priest) and to pass it on to Yitzhak.[23] The *'akeidah* thus unlocks for us an understanding of the core of the Beit haMikdash: Har haMoriah is named for *mor*, one

---

לאחרים וכמו שאמר המלאך (בראשית כב:יב) כי עתה ידעתי כו' והנה לפ"ז אברהם יתראה ויהיה הנראה לאחרים ודו"ק.

23. *Shlah haKadosh*, Parashat Vayeira, *Torah Ohr* 4.

ספר השל"ה הקדוש, פרשת וירא תורה אור (ד)

וכולהו נתקיימו בעקידת יצחק, כי אברהם עקדו וקשרו גם שם אותו לעולה בהר המוריה. ואפשר שהמזבח אשר בנה אברהם אבינו בהר המוריה היה במקום מזבח הפנימי שמקטירין הקטורת, כי הקטורת חביב מכל הקרבנות שבעולם, ולא היה קרבן חביב בעולם כיצחק עולה תמימה. וכן משמע קצת במדרש (פרקי דר"א לא) שאמר ויקרא אליו מלאך ה' מן השמים, מבין שני הכרובים יצא הקול. הרי שענין העקידה היה הכל במקום המקודש ביותר, שקרא אליו המלאך ממקום קדשי קדשים, ממילא מסתבר שנעקד על גבי מזבח הפנימי. וכן מצינו כשהוקם המשכן היה הקול נפסק ולא יצא מחוץ לאהל מועד, וזהו ענין שנקרא הר המוריה על שם הקטורת כי שם נעקד יצחק.

of the spices used to make the incense offering brought in the *Kodesh haKodashim*. The very core of the Beit haMikdash, of Har haMoriah, of the *Kodesh haKodashim* itself, is incense – and not sacrifice. This is the core of the *'akeidah* as well.[24]

If this is the message of the *'akeidah*, what is the test? If this was to be a test of Avraham and Yitzhak's relationship with one another, or of their relationship with God, they clearly passed with flying colors: Would the two walk together, clinging to one another and clinging to their faith in God? Yes. But their love of God pushed them beyond the actual command of God. If the commandment was to elevate Yitzhak, then Avraham certainly succeeded. God did not require Avraham to elevate Yitzhak in a traumatic manner. Perhaps Avraham, who entered Nimrod's fiery furnace because of his love of God, did not find it strange that at times God may require such heroic action. But Avraham should have paid closer attention to God's words: "I am the one who took you *out* of the furnace." God did not ask Avraham to sacrifice himself in this way. On the other hand, Avraham, who almost met his death in the furnace, knew of God's miracles and His salvation, knew that somehow Yitzhak, too, would survive. In the end, he was not wrong.

After the *'akeidah*, Avraham and Yitzhak had even more in common than before: both were willing to give up their lives for their love of God. They were both almost burnt offerings, and they were both elevated by that experience. Most importantly, they walked together.

---

24. Rashi, Bereishit 22:2.

רש"י, בראשית כב:ב

בהר המוריה: ורבותינו פירשו על שם שמשם הוראה יוצאה לישראל. ואונקלוס תרגמו על שם עבודת הקטורת שיש בו מור נרד ושאר בשמים.

Parashat Hayei Sarah

A Living Well

When we look at the beginning of the parashah we notice that something is missing. We are told of the death of Sarah, the tears, Avraham's eulogy. We are told in detail how Avraham deals with the details of burial. What is missing is the other major character who we would have expected to have shed at least as many tears: Yitzhak. Where was he? Why did he miss his mother's funeral? This question is articulated by Rabbeinu Bahya, who notes that Yitzhak's obligation to his beloved mother and his love for her should have at least equaled that of his father. Where were his tears? Where was his eulogy?[1]

Rabbeinu Bahya reminds us that Yitzhak had just endured his own stressful, traumatic episode. He was bound to an altar, and watched the blade's rapid descent; only heavenly intervention spared his life. Rabbeinu Bahya posits that, for fear that the tragedy of his mother's death may have been too much for him, Yitzhak was not informed of his mother's passing.[2] Rabbeinu Bahya then points out a blatant textual oddity: not only is Yitzhak missing from Sarah's funeral, his disappearance begins at an earlier juncture, in the aftermath of the 'akeidah.

---

1. See Rabbeinu Bahya, Bereishit 23:2.

רבינו בחיי, בראשית כג:ב

ונ"ל עוד כי היה הכתוב ראוי שיאמר ויבא אברהם ויצחק לספוד לשרה ולבכותה, כי בודאי ראוי היה יצחק לספוד לאמו הצדקת ולבכות עליה, שהרי החיוב בו גדול מאד יותר ממה שהוא באברהם, ועוד שהיא אהבתו אהבה יתרה שילדה אותו על דרך הפלא, והיתה נפשה קשורה בנפשו.

2. See Rabbeinu Bahya, Bereishit 23:2.

רבינו בחיי, בראשית כג:ב

אבל יתכן לומר שלא ידע יצחק באותו הפרק שמתה אמו, כי לפי שמיתתה היתה בשבילו בשמועת העקדה, על כן העלימו ממנו מיתתה ולא הגידו לו. ומן הטעם הזה לא ראינו שיזכירנו הכתוב ליצחק כלל לא במיתתה ולא בקבורתה, גם מעת שנעקד על גבי המזבח לא ראינוהו, שהרי כשהלכו אברהם ויצחק להר המוריה כתוב בחזרה (בראשית כב) וישב אברהם אל נעריו, והיה ראוי שיאמר וישובו אל הנערים, ולא הזכיר חזרת יצחק.

125

When Avraham sets out for the mountain he takes Yitzhak and two others, referred to as "*ne'arim*," young men or servants. The text tells us that they walked together:

בראשית כב:ג–ח

וַיַּשְׁכֵּם אַבְרָהָם בַּבֹּקֶר וַיַּחֲבֹשׁ אֶת חֲמֹרוֹ וַיִּקַּח אֶת שְׁנֵי נְעָרָיו אִתּוֹ וְאֵת יִצְחָק בְּנוֹ וַיְבַקַּע עֲצֵי עֹלָה וַיָּקָם וַיֵּלֶךְ אֶל הַמָּקוֹם אֲשֶׁר אָמַר לוֹ הָאֱלֹקִים: בַּיּוֹם הַשְּׁלִישִׁי וַיִּשָּׂא אַבְרָהָם אֶת עֵינָיו וַיַּרְא אֶת הַמָּקוֹם מֵרָחֹק: וַיֹּאמֶר אַבְרָהָם אֶל נְעָרָיו שְׁבוּ לָכֶם פֹּה עִם הַחֲמוֹר וַאֲנִי וְהַנַּעַר נֵלְכָה עַד כֹּה וְנִשְׁתַּחֲוֶה וְנָשׁוּבָה אֲלֵיכֶם: וַיִּקַּח אַבְרָהָם אֶת עֲצֵי הָעֹלָה וַיָּשֶׂם עַל יִצְחָק בְּנוֹ וַיִּקַּח בְּיָדוֹ אֶת הָאֵשׁ וְאֶת הַמַּאֲכֶלֶת **וַיֵּלְכוּ שְׁנֵיהֶם יַחְדָּו**: וַיֹּאמֶר יִצְחָק אֶל אַבְרָהָם אָבִיו וַיֹּאמֶר אָבִי וַיֹּאמֶר הִנֶּנִּי בְנִי וַיֹּאמֶר הִנֵּה הָאֵשׁ וְהָעֵצִים וְאַיֵּה הַשֶּׂה לְעֹלָה: וַיֹּאמֶר אַבְרָהָם אֱלֹקִים יִרְאֶה לּוֹ הַשֶּׂה לְעֹלָה בְּנִי **וַיֵּלְכוּ שְׁנֵיהֶם יַחְדָּו**:

Avraham got up early the next morning and saddled his donkey. He took with him his two servants and his son Yitzhak. He cut 'olah wood, and he arose and set out for the place God had told him about. On the third day – Avraham lifted up his eyes, and saw the place from afar. And Avraham said to his young men, "Stay here with the donkey, and I and the lad will go yonder and worship, and return to you." And Avraham took the wood of the 'olah, and placed it on Yitzhak his son, and he took in his hand the fire, and the knife; **and they went on both of them together.** *And Yitzhak said to Avraham his father, "My father," and [Avraham] said, "Here I am, my son." And he said, "Here are the fire and the wood, but where is the lamb for an 'olah?" And Avraham said, "God will provide for Himself the lamb for an 'olah, my son";* **and they went on both of them together.** (Bereishit 22:3–8)

Father and son walk together, united in love, united in their mission. However, at the end of the episode, we are told of only Avraham returning to the young men:

בראשית כב:יט

וַיָּשָׁב אַבְרָהָם אֶל נְעָרָיו וַיָּקֻמוּ וַיֵּלְכוּ יַחְדָּו אֶל בְּאֵר שָׁבַע וַיֵּשֶׁב אַבְרָהָם בִּבְאֵר שָׁבַע:

And Avraham returned to his young men, and they rose and went together to Be'er Sheva; and Avraham dwelled in Be'er Sheva. (Bereishit 22:19)

What happened to Yitzhak? It seems impossible that Avraham could have simply picked up and left without his precious son, the son born of a miraculous birth, the son whose life had just been saved by God Himself. He would not simply have forgotten him up on the mountain while he went on with his own business. Other commentaries have noticed this lacuna in the text as well. Ibn Ezra, to name one, protests:

אבן עזרא, בראשית כב:יט

וישב אברהם: ולא הזכיר יצחק כי הוא ברשותו והאומר ששחטו ועזבו ואח"כ
חיה אמר הפך הכתוב:

"Avraham returned": And it does not mention Yitzhak, since he was in [Avraham's] keep. And those who say that [Avraham] killed him and left [his body] behind, and then Yitzhak was resurrected, contradict the text. (Ibn Ezra, Bereishit 22:19)

While Ibn Ezra doesn't reveal who could have read the text in such a warped manner,[3] it is clear that Ibn Ezra, like Rabbeinu Bahya, is bothered by the "disappearance" of Yitzhak. Ibn Ezra insists that when the text says "Avraham" it really means Avraham and Yitzhak.

But the confusion only deepens when we note that Yitzhak "disappears" even before Avraham's descent from the mountain. It begins when the angel

---

3. The basic quandary created by the *'akeidah* is that on the one hand Yitzhak is the progeny through whom God has promised to fulfill His blessings, while on the other hand Yitzhak is to be killed. Rabbi Soloveitchik, quoting his grandfather, describes this as a classic case of two verses contradicting one another, and a third verse which reconciles the two. Mystical sources have insisted that Yitzhak did, in fact, die at the *'akeidah*, an idea found in various midrashim. The Ari"zal claims that Yitzhak, who would have been childless, dies, and a new soul that can father children enters his body. Thus, it was the *'akeidah* that made the fulfillment of Gods's promises to Avraham possible. Christological sources have long seen the *'akeidah* as a prototype for their claims of a different so-called execution and resurrection. What is particularly interesting is that some midrashim describe Yitzhak's carrying the wood as if he was bearing a cross. See Bereishit Rabbah 56:3 (and parallel sources) where the word *tzlovo* is used, a verb that may have the connotation of crucifixion. This should come as no surprise being that the New Testament often tried to parallel biblical scenes, making extensive use of extant Midrashic material.

בראשית רבה, פרשה נו פסקא ג
ויקח אברהם את עצי עולה: כזה שהוא טוען צלובו בכתפו.

calls out to Avraham, at the very apex of the mountain, at the most crucial moment of the *'akeidah*, telling him to cease and desist. It continues, like an odd shadow, throughout the death, burial, and mourning of Sarah. But it doesn't stop there: Yitzhak even misses his own courtship. A surrogate is sent to find a wife for him. Only when Rivkah arrives does Yitzhak, quite alive, return to the biblical narrative.

In rabbinic literature there are two basic approaches to Yitzhak's whereabouts during the textual "blackout." The first approach is that Yitzhak is busy learning[4] in yeshiva.[5] A second approach, found in other midrashim, describes Yitzhak as having died or almost died, or died in a metaphorical sense, depending on nuance. Yitzhak has temporarily retired to the Garden of Eden.

מדרש הגדול בראשית כב:יט, עמ' 360

ויצחק היכן הוא? אמר ר' אלעזר בן פדת אע"פ שלא מת יצחק, מעלה הכתוב כאילו מת ואפרו מוטל על גבי המזבח. לכך "וישב אברהם אל נעריו". ויצחק היכן הוא? אלא שהכניסו הקב"ה לגן עדן וישב שם בה שלש שנים.

And where was Yitzhak? Said R. Elazar b. Pedat: Even though Yitzhak did not die it is deemed as if he died, and his ashes are on the altar. Thus, "And Avraham returned to his young men." And where was Yitzhak? God took him to the Garden of Eden, where he remained for three years. (Midrash Hagadol, Bereishit 22:19, p. 360)

---

4. See Bereishit Rabbah 56:11, Targum Pseudo-Yonatan, Bereishit 22:19.

    בראשית רבה, פרשה נו פסקא יא

    וישב אברהם אל נעריו: ויצחק היכן הוא? רבי ברכיה בשם רבנן: דתמן שלחו אצל שם ללמוד ממנו תורה.

    תרגום יונתן, בראשית כב:יט

    ודברו מלאכי מרומא ית יצחק ואובלוהי לבי מדרשא דשם רבא והוה תמן תלת שנין ובההוא יומא תב אברהם לות עולימוי וקמו ואזלו כחדא לבירא דשבע ויתיב אברהם בבירא דשבע.

5. The Netziv (*Ha'amek Davar* 22:19) postulates that specifically now, after hearing how Avraham is to be rewarded for obeying God's command, Yitzhak decides it is time for him to learn what it is that God wants of him.

    העמק דבר, בראשית כב:יט

    וישב אברהם: ולא כתיב ויצחק. כבר ת"י שהוליכו לבית מדרשו של שם ללמוד תורה. וקרוב לומר כי באשר סיים ה' עקב אשר שמעת בקולי. התבונן כי כך רצון ה' לעסוק בדברי תורה. ואע"ג שאברהם למד עמו מ"מ לענין התבוננות בד"ת טוב שיהיה משני מקומות כדאיתא בעבודת כוכבים דף יט א.

Many midrashim see Yitzhak as having died, and Jewish liturgy abounds with references to the 'akeidah as if it had actually been performed to completion. Most likely, what we are meant to gain from this line of Midrashic discussion is this: Avraham's willingness to sacrifice what he loved most for God should be perceived on at least some level as if the offering was brought. On the other hand, Yitzhak ends up in Gan 'Eiden. We might interpret this as referring to a place of spiritual perfection. In a certain sense, both "paradise" and "yeshiva" may be seen as places where someone who has just been raised up on the altar as an 'olah might go to pursue the religious experience further.

While these explanations fill in the perceived holes of the biblical narrative, perhaps a close reading of the actual text of the Torah can also be instructive. The next time we see Yitzhak, the Torah tells us quite clearly where he has been:

בראשית כד:סב–סז

וְיִצְחָק בָּא מִבּוֹא בְּאֵר לַחַי רֹאִי וְהוּא יוֹשֵׁב בְּאֶרֶץ הַנֶּגֶב: וַיֵּצֵא יִצְחָק לָשׂוּחַ בַּשָּׂדֶה לִפְנוֹת עָרֶב וַיִּשָּׂא עֵינָיו וַיַּרְא וְהִנֵּה גְמַלִּים בָּאִים: וַתִּשָּׂא רִבְקָה אֶת עֵינֶיהָ וַתֵּרֶא אֶת יִצְחָק וַתִּפֹּל מֵעַל הַגָּמָל: וַתֹּאמֶר אֶל הָעֶבֶד מִי הָאִישׁ הַלָּזֶה הַהֹלֵךְ בַּשָּׂדֶה לִקְרָאתֵנוּ וַיֹּאמֶר הָעֶבֶד הוּא אֲדֹנִי וַתִּקַּח הַצָּעִיף וַתִּתְכָּס: וַיְסַפֵּר הָעֶבֶד לְיִצְחָק אֵת כָּל הַדְּבָרִים אֲשֶׁר עָשָׂה: וַיְבִאֶהָ יִצְחָק הָאֹהֱלָה שָׂרָה אִמּוֹ וַיִּקַּח אֶת רִבְקָה וַתְּהִי לוֹ לְאִשָּׁה וַיֶּאֱהָבֶהָ וַיִּנָּחֵם יִצְחָק אַחֲרֵי אִמּוֹ:

And Yitzhak was on his way, coming from Be'er La'hai Ro'i [literally, "Well of the Living One, my Beholder"]; and he dwells in the Negev. And Yitzhak went out to meditate in the field, at the turning of the evening, and he lifted up his eyes, and suddenly saw camels approaching. And Rivkah lifted up her eyes, and saw Yitzhak, and fell off the camel; And she said to the servant, "Who is this man who is walking in the field toward us?" and the servant said, "He is my master." And she took her scarf and covered herself. And the servant recounted to Yitzhak all the things that he had done, and Yitzhak brought her into the tent of Sarah his mother, and he took Rivkah, and she became his wife, and he loved her, and Yitzhak was comforted after [the death of] his mother. (Bereishit 24:62–67)

Yitzhak was comforted after the death of his mother; apparently, he had been mourning. But where had he been? The particular destination of his travels is instructive – Be'er La'hai Ro'i. We have heard of this place before.

Hagar gave this place its name when she ran away from her mistress Sarah. Rashi[6] notes Yitzhak's choice of destination, and finds within it an indication of the very tender relationship between Avraham and Yitzhak: Yitzhak traveled to Be'er La'hai Ro'i to fetch Hagar, Avraham's estranged wife.[7] Avraham is worried about his son, and arranges to bring an appropriate wife for him, while at the same time Yitzhak is concerned about his father's loneliness and brings him a familiar companion.

The Ramban[8] focuses on the spiritual qualities of Be'er La'hai Ro'i. Based on the language, he understands that this is a place that Yitzhak frequents.[9] This is his designated place of prayer, for this is a place of revelation. An angel appeared to Hagar here; this is a place of prophecy. Given the proximity to his home, he chooses this as his spiritual sanctuary, his refuge of solitude. The Seforno[10] even posits that Yitzhak was praying for a bride, and as he utters his prayer – the mission of his father's servant is successfully completed miles away.

---

6. Rashi, Bereishit 24:62.

רש"י, בראשית כד:סב

מבוא באר לחי ראי: שהלך להביא הגר לאברהם אביו שישאנה (ב"ר).

7. See Bereishit 16:1; Hagar is referred to as Sarah's servant in 16:3. A few verses later when she is presented to Avraham, it is as a wife. Later (this time by the angel) she is referred to, once again, as a servant of Sarah. See Bereishit 16:8.

8. Ramban, Bereishit 24:62.

רמב"ן, בראשית כד:סב

בא מבוא באר לחי ראי: יאמר כי יצחק בא עתה מבוא באר לחי ראי, ששב מבאר לחי שבא שמה. שאלו אמר "בא מבאר לחי ראי" היה נראה שהיה דר שם, ולכך הוצרך לפרש כי הוא שב לעירו מביאתו שבא אל באר לחי רואי לפי שעה, כי הוא יושב בארץ הנגב וחוזר לעירו.

ויתכן, בעבור היות "מבוא" מקור, שהיה יצחק הולך תמיד אל המקום ההוא, כי הוא למקום תפלה בעבור הראות שם המלאך, והוא יושב בארץ הנגב קרוב משם. וכן תרגם אונקלוס אתא ממיתוהי. ועל דעתו הוא באר שבע, שתרגם "בין קדש ובין שור" (לעיל כ:א), ו"בין קדש ובין ברד" (לעיל טז:יד), "רקם וחגרא". ואם כן המקום ההוא מקום אשל אברהם ראוי לתפלה. והנה יצחק בא מן הבאר ההיא אל עיר אחרת אשר היתה בדרך עירו, ויצא לפנות ערב לשוח בשדה עם רעיו ואוהביו אשר שם, ומצא את העבד ורבקה והלכו כלם יחדו אל עירו, ויביאה האהלה שרה אמו.

9. The Ramban also suggests that this place is within close proximity to Avraham's *eshel* – hence Yitzhak is praying in a place that Avraham had prayed.

10. Seforno, Bereishit 24:62.

ספורנו, בראשית כד:סב

בא מבא באר לחי ראי: להתפלל במקום שבו נשמעה תפלת שפחתו וקודם שהתפלל כבר נשלם ענינו בחרן וקרבה אשתו לבא על דרך טרם יקראו ואני אענה.

The text makes it clear that this trip to Be'er La'hai Ro'i is not an isolated visit. We find that after Avraham's death, this place becomes Yitzhak's home.

בראשית כה:יא

וַיְהִי אַחֲרֵי מוֹת אַבְרָהָם וַיְבָרֶךְ אֱלֹקִים אֶת יִצְחָק בְּנוֹ וַיֵּשֶׁב יִצְחָק עִם בְּאֵר לַחַי רֹאִי:

And it came to pass after the death of Avraham, that God blessed Yitzhak his son; and Yitzhak dwelled by Be'er La'hai Ro'i. (Bereishit 25:11)

Perhaps Yitzhak's choice of this place for his home is connected with Hagar's[11] revelation, but in a different way: perhaps within this choice we can sense some type of reconciliation between Yitzhak and Yishmael.[12]

We know little of the relationship between these two sons of Avraham. Yishmael, the firstborn, was banished soon after Yitzhak's birth, and he headed toward the desert, toward the area of Be'er La'hai Ro'i.[13] Is there more in common between Yitzhak and Yishmael than we might have thought? Is there any unity between these brothers? The answer would seem to be a resounding yes! Immediately before the choice of Yitzhak's residence is mentioned we are told that Avraham passed away, and his burial was tended to by both sons:

בראשית כה:ח-ט

וַיִּגְוַע וַיָּמָת אַבְרָהָם בְּשֵׂיבָה טוֹבָה זָקֵן וְשָׂבֵעַ וַיֵּאָסֶף אֶל עַמָּיו: וַיִּקְבְּרוּ אֹתוֹ יִצְחָק וְיִשְׁמָעֵאל בָּנָיו אֶל מְעָרַת הַמַּכְפֵּלָה אֶל שְׂדֵה עֶפְרֹן בֶּן צֹחַר הַחִתִּי אֲשֶׁר עַל פְּנֵי מַמְרֵא:

---

11. The *Kli Yakar* (Bereishit 25:1) identifies Keturah with Hagar and says that she, too, repented and began a "new life."

12. The *Be'er Mayim Hayim* says that Yishmael was sent away because he was a bad influence; he was a thief. Yet Yitzhak reaches out to him, despite his wayward behavior, because Yishmael is a monotheist.

ספר באר מים חיים, פרשת וירא כא:כ

ויהי אלהים את הנער: פירוש שמהיום והלאה לא עבד עבודה זרה ורק אלהים היה עמו ולא עבד, ולכן אמרו (בבא בתרא טז ע"ב) שעשה ישמעאל תשובה בחיי אברהם אף שרש"י ז"ל פירש להלן ויהי רובה קשת שהיה מלסטם הבריות מכל מקום עבודה זרה לא עבד והיה אלהים עמו לא אלהים אחרים, ואפשר קודם מות אברהם עשה תשובה מכל וכל והן.

13. See Bereishit 21:14–21.

And Avraham expired, and died in a good old age, aged and satisfied, and was gathered unto his people. And he was buried by Yitzhak and Yishmael his sons at the Cave of Makhpeilah, at the field of Ephron, son of Tzoar the Hittite, which [is] before Mamre. (Bereishit 25:8–9)

Yitzhak and Yishmael bury their father together, united. Perhaps Yitzhak's forays to Be'er La'hai Ro'i have paid dividends and now we have healing in the family. A family once divided has now achieved a semblance of unity. Perhaps as long as Sarah was alive, Yitzhak could not make this move, for it was his mother who had demanded the expulsion of Hagar and Yishmael. After Sarah's death Yitzhak is free to try and bring people together. With Avraham's death Yitchak goes one step further and chooses to live with Yishmael in Be'er La'hai Ro'i. Perhaps Yitzhak, being the reason for Yishmael's expulsion, feels a special responsibility to bring the family together.

This analysis may help us understand another relationship – the relationship between Yitzhak and his ne'er-do-well son Esav. Perhaps Yitzhak, as the favored son, has made a conscious decision not to expel a son from his home – whatever his shortcomings may be. He has seen the results of such expulsions, and commits himself to avoiding this type of discord in his own home; he seeks to heal rather than to divide or cause further estrangement. Some of the more puzzling descriptions of Yitzhak's relationship with this problematic son may be understood in this light. For example, when the Torah describes Yitzhak's love for Esav, the particulars make it sound strange, limited, even conditional:

בראשית כה:כח

וַיֶּאֱהַב יִצְחָק אֶת עֵשָׂו כִּי צַיִד בְּפִיו וְרִבְקָה אֹהֶבֶת אֶת יַעֲקֹב:

And Yitzhak loved Esav, for [his] hunting [is] in his mouth; and Rivkah loves Yaakov. (Bereishit 25:28)

Perhaps Yitzhak is searching for a reason – any reason – to love his son. This is not at all like the unconditional love Rivkah has for her son Yaakov. Yet Yitzhak is unwilling to give up on Esav, even though he pales in comparison to Yaakov. Yitzhak finds a task Esav is capable of, even well-suited to: Esav is the hunter. When Yitzhak gets older and wishes to bless his son, again he looks for Esav's positive attributes and asks him to bring him food.

Yaakov, dressed as Esav, enters his room. The Torah tells us that at this point Yitzhak was blind. Rashi[14] explains that this was due to the tears of the angels who cried during the *'akeidah*. Yitzhak takes a moment to enjoy the aroma of the meal, of the goats his son has brought him. Rashi[15] questions this particular pleasure, noting that few odors are as unsavory as the stench of goats. What did Yitzhak smell? Rashi's answer is surprising: it is the the aroma of paradise, the scent of *Gan 'Eiden*. This was a smell familiar to Yitzhak: he once lived there. Yitzhak pauses to recall this scent, to retrieve this sensory memory.

Two of Yitzhak's senses, then, were affected by the singular experience of the *'akeidah*. After being raised up on the altar, Yitzhak's sight is forever altered. But what is the nature of Yitzhak's perception, and what is the extent of his vision? Is he somehow damaged? Is he naive regarding his son's shortcomings, seeing less than we do – or does he perhaps see much more?

Yitzhak clearly sees differently: he sees through the prism of his *'akeidah* experience, an experience that took him directly to *Gan 'Eiden*. Eden is a place deep in the past of our collective conscience. It is also a place in the future. It represents a world perfected, and it represents a perfect world. This is how Yitzhak saw: not through the jaundiced eye that most people use as a spectrum, which diffuses the good and focuses on the bad. Yitzhak saw the world from the perspective of the Garden of Eden. He saw perfection. He saw the culmination of history, the realization of the process of redemption, the return to the perfected state of Eden. He saw the future.

---

14. Rashi, Bereishit 27:1.

רש"י, בראשית כז:א

ותכהין: בעשנן של אלו (שהיו מעשנות ומקטירות לע"א) ד"א כשנעקד ע"ג המזבח והיה אביו רוצה לשחטו באותה שעה נפתחו השמים וראו מלאכי השרת והיו בוכים וירדו דמעותיהם ונפלו על עיניו לפיכך כהו עיניו.

15. Rashi, Bereishit 27:27.

רש"י, בראשית כז:כז

וירח וגו': והלא אין ריח רע יותר משטף העזים אלא מלמד שנכנסה עמו ריח גן עדן.

Yitzhak's entire being is intertwined with this perspective, this type of sight or perception that focuses on the future.[16] Even his name, which represents the essence of his being, means "will laugh" – in the future. This is the real meaning of the midrashim that tell us that Yitzhak went from the *'akeidah* to *Gan 'Eiden*: his eyes were "fixed" at the *'akeidah*, his perception altered. Now he had perfect vision. Now he saw a perfect world. He saw the world from the vantage point of Eden.

That perspective, that perception, gave him the ability, even the courage, to approach a person like Yishmael, and to attempt to create harmony from the dissonance. Yitzhak saw that Yishmael can and will do *teshuvah*, that Yishmael can and will come to recognize that there is One God.

The *Meshekh Hokhmah*[17] describes the repentance of the descendants of Yishmael and Esav in the Messianic Age as another example of "the acts of the fathers are a sign for the children." Because of the actions of Yitzhak, Yishmael did return, as will his children. Because of the actions of Yitzhak, Esav remained close to his father, and his descendants will return to the fold in the future. Because Yitzhak was willing to live in the place that had spiritual importance to Yishmael, and by so doing to validate Yishmael's nascent monotheistic feelings, Yishmael and Yitzhak were able to coexist. What Yitzhak may or may not have been able to see was that while his action in the present was due to his perception of the future, what he saw in the future was a result of his actions in the present. Would that we could all see the world through rose-colored, "Eden" glasses.

---

16. According to the Zohar (Bereishit 114a), even God's future laughing will be related to Yitzhak:

זוהר, בראשית דף קיד עמוד א

אמר רבי יהודה, תא חזי שכך הוא, דכתיב מלך אסור ברהטים, וכתיב בתריה מה יפית ומה נעמת. ואמר רבי יהודה, באותו זמן, עתיד הקדוש ברוך הוא לשמח עולמו ולשמוח בבריותיו, שנאמר (תהלים קד:לא) ישמח יהו"ה במעשיו, ואזי יהיה שחוק בעולם, מה שאין עכשיו, דכתיב (שם קכו:ב) אז ימלא שחוק פינו וגו', הה"ד ותאמר שרה צחוק עשה לי אלהי"ם, שאזי עתידים בני אדם לומר שירה, שהוא עת שחוק.

17. *Meshekh Hokhmah*, Bereishit 15:15.

משך חכמה, בראשית טו:טו

תקבר בשיבה טובה: שיעשה תשובה ישמעאל בימיו, (בראשית רבה ל:ד) הנה מעשה אבות סימן לבנים (ע' סוטה לד וב"ר ע' ו) הוא רמז שבני ישמעאל באחרית הימים יתקרבו להאמת ויאמינו בד' אחד (רמב"ן פ' בראשית ב ס"פ ג) ויבדלו מהעו"ג כמוש"כ רבינו (בתשובה ע' הוצאת פריימן סימן שסד) וזה שביקש יצחק (מגלה ו סע"א) על עשו יוחן רשע (ישעיהו כו:י) שגם הוא יתרחק מעו"ג באחרית הימים והי' התשובה בארץ נכוחות כו' לכן בל יראה גאות ד' ויהי' עובד עו"ג עד ביום ההוא יהי' ד' אחד כו'.

Death of a King

Parashat Hayei Sarah describes Avraham in his advanced years; he is old, but blessed:

בראשית כד:א

וְאַבְרָהָם זָקֵן בָּא בַּיָּמִים וַה' בֵּרַךְ אֶת אַבְרָהָם בַּכֹּל:

And Avraham was old and advanced in years; and God blessed Avraham in every way. (Bereishit 24:1)

The portion from the Prophets read in conjunction with this parashah (the haftarah) has a very different opening description of the elderly King David:

מלכים א, א:א

וְהַמֶּלֶךְ דָּוִד זָקֵן בָּא בַּיָּמִים וַיְכַסֻּהוּ בַּבְּגָדִים וְלֹא יִחַם לוֹ:

And King David was old and advanced in years; and they covered him with clothes, but he was not warmed. (I Melakhim 1:1)

While the first words of each of these verses are almost identical (the only difference being the description of David as "king"), the similarity seems to end right there. Avraham is described as blessed in every way, despite his advanced years, while David's "golden years" seem far less idyllic. David is depicted as an elderly monarch whose body has rebelled against him; even simple body warmth eludes him.

David is old and cold, and a beautiful young woman named Avishag the Shunammite is brought to attend to him and keep him warm. She is described as a virgin, and the text attests that David was not intimate with her. Many of the details here are unclear: this seems like a very strange *modus operandi* to bring heat. Additionally, why was Avishag's physical beauty a factor? The commentaries address these and other problems in their search for a deeper understanding of the causes of King David's chill and the method used to dispel it.

The *Sefer haLikutim*[1] contrasts the ailments of David's old age with the later years of Avraham's life, raising some of the questions we have already noted. He then suggests that this was all part of a process of repentance that David needed to go through. It is more than ironic that David, who at one point in his life could have been accused of being too "hot-blooded," now suffers from a sort of cold that proves incurable. In his younger days, David took many wives; now a beautiful virgin lies next to him, yet he has no sexual contact with her. The *Sefer haLikutim* links all this to an earlier episode in David's biography: David had set his eyes on another man's wife, a woman whom he eventually married. In his later years, David experiences a chill that comes from within; the warm young woman brought to rekindle his own burning desire remains untouched. Avishag is part of David's rehabilitation.[2]

---

1. *Sefer haLikutim*, I Melakhim 1:1.

ספר הליקוטים, מלכים א פרק א

והמלך דוד זקן בא בימים ויכסוהו בבגדים ולא יחם לו: ענין מ"ש בא בימים, נדרש בזוהר בפ' ואברהם זקן בא בימים, ע"ש ותבין. ובמקום אחד בזוהר מביא, שמאותם הימים של האדם שהם מצות ומעשים טובים, נעשה מלבוש לנשמה. וענין זה המלבוש, נמצאה בפ' נח, וג'"כ בהיכלות פ' פקודי, ושם יעויין באורך.

ואמנם באלו הים, יש לשאול על השינוי הנמצא בין ביאת הימים של אברהם לשל דהע"ה, כי שם היה זקן ושבע ימים בן קע"ה שנה, ודוד בן ע' שנה בלבד. ועוד, אברהם נתברך בכל, ודוד ויכסוהו בבגדים ולא יחם לו. ועוד, להבין מה הם אלו הבגדים וכסויה. ולמה לא יחם לו, וכי הוא חסר בגדים כדי לכסותו כדי לחממו. ועוד, להבין תקנת עבדיו להביא לו נערה בתולה כדי שתחממהו, וכי חסר היה נערות או נשים, עד שבקשו בכל גבול ישראל וימצאו את אבישג, שדרך מציאה מצאוה. ועוד, להבין מלת סוכנת דנקט, ולא אמר ותהי למלך מחממת, כי כן אמר ולא יחם לו, ולמה שינה כאן ואמר סוכנת. ועוד, למה היתה בתולה ולא בעולה. ועוד להבין למה לא ידעה. וא"ת מבלתי יכולתו, כי זקן, כבר ידעת מ"ש רז"ל על ותבא בת שבע החדרה, מלמד שקנחה בי"ג מפות, וטעם רז"ל ידוע. ועוד להבין למה היתה יפה עד מאד, כי בלי זה איזו בתולה היא מחממת. וכ"ש אם לא תהיה יפה, כי טבעה חם יותר מהיפה, כי טבעו קר, כמו שידוע לבעלי הטבע. ועוד להבין סמיכות ענין אדוניה בן חגית לזה הענין, המתנשא לאמר אני אמלוך, וטעם רז"ל ידוע.

2. Ibid.

ודרך התשובה שעשה, היא מדה כנגד מדה. והיא זאת שאמרו לו עבדיו יבקשו למלך נערה בתולה טובת מראה ושכבה בחיקך ותהי למלך סוכנת, כלומר, אעפ"י שעדיין הוא בתוקפו, יכניע יצה"ר ולא יגע בה. וז"ש ותהי לו סוכנת, כלומר שיהיה עמה בצער וסכנה להכניע יצה"ר, ובזה יתוקן אותו עון. ולזה היתה בתולה, להראות העמים כי לא נגע בה, שאילו היתה בעולה מי מעיד שלא נגע בה. וע"י זה יתוקן המלבוש, וחם לאדוני המלך. ולזה לא לקח מנשיו או מנערותיו, כי לבו גס בהם, אלא זו יפה עד מאד ודרך מציאה, ואעפ"י שג"כ ושכבה בחיקך, ובחוזק התאוה היה מסוכן עמה בכל עת ובכל רגע, וזמ"ש וחם לאדוני המלך בכח התאוה, ועי"ז תקובל תשובתך מדה כנגד מדה. ולזה היה שמה אבישג השונמית, באותיות שמה יובן ענין התיקון, כי יש באותיותי, נשמ"ו הש"ג א"ב, כי בה נתקן והשיג נשמתו לצרור החיים את ה' אלקיו.

The Talmud addresses the questionable episode that lies behind this discussion, and raises several technical points to explain David's actions and exonerate him from guilt. Rather than accusing David of adultery, the Talmud concludes:

תלמוד בבלי, מסכת שבת דף נו עמוד א

אמר רבי שמואל בר נחמני אמר רבי יונתן: כל האומר דוד חטא – אינו אלא טועה, שנאמר, (שמואל א, יח) "ויהי דוד לכל דרכיו משכיל וה' עמו" וגו', אפשר חטא בא לידו ושכינה עמו?

R. Shmuel b. Nahmani said in R. Yonatan's name: Whoever says[3] that David sinned is patently mistaken, for it is said, "And David conducted himself wisely in all his ways, and God was with him." Is it possible that sin came to his hand, yet the Divine Presence was with him? (Talmud Bavli Shabbat 56a)

The Talmud seems to take the long view, to consider the sum total of David's life. Nonetheless, even those sages who defend David's innocence do so by citing legalisms and technicalities. Clearly, the entire episode of David's marriage to Batsheva involves moral grey areas, or, at the very least, a faint odor of immorality. In fact, the prophet Natan lambasts David for his behavior:

שמואל ב, יב:א–יג

וַיִּשְׁלַח ה' אֶת נָתָן אֶל דָּוִד וַיָּבֹא אֵלָיו וַיֹּאמֶר לוֹ שְׁנֵי אֲנָשִׁים הָיוּ בְּעִיר אֶחָד עָשִׁיר וְאֶחָד רָאשׁ: לְעָשִׁיר הָיָה צֹאן וּבָקָר הַרְבֵּה מְאֹד: וְלָרָשׁ אֵין כֹּל כִּי אִם כִּבְשָׂה אַחַת קְטַנָּה אֲשֶׁר קָנָה וַיְחַיֶּהָ וַתִּגְדַּל עִמּוֹ וְעִם בָּנָיו יַחְדָּו מִפִּתּוֹ תֹאכַל וּמִכֹּסוֹ תִשְׁתֶּה וּבְחֵיקוֹ תִשְׁכָּב וַתְּהִי לוֹ כְּבַת: וַיָּבֹא הֵלֶךְ לְאִישׁ הֶעָשִׁיר וַיַּחְמֹל לָקַחַת מִצֹּאנוֹ וּמִבְּקָרוֹ לַעֲשׂוֹת לָאֹרֵחַ הַבָּא לוֹ וַיִּקַּח אֶת כִּבְשַׂת הָאִישׁ הָרָאשׁ וַיַּעֲשֶׂהָ לָאִישׁ הַבָּא אֵלָיו: וַיִּחַר אַף דָּוִד בָּאִישׁ מְאֹד וַיֹּאמֶר אֶל נָתָן חַי ה' כִּי בֶן מָוֶת הָאִישׁ הָעֹשֶׂה זֹאת: וְאֶת הַכִּבְשָׂה יְשַׁלֵּם אַרְבַּעְתָּיִם עֵקֶב אֲשֶׁר עָשָׂה אֶת הַדָּבָר הַזֶּה וְעַל אֲשֶׁר לֹא חָמָל: וַיֹּאמֶר נָתָן אֶל דָּוִד אַתָּה הָאִישׁ כֹּה אָמַר ה' אֱלֹקֵי יִשְׂרָאֵל אָנֹכִי מְשַׁחְתִּיךָ לְמֶלֶךְ עַל יִשְׂרָאֵל וְאָנֹכִי הִצַּלְתִּיךָ מִיַּד שָׁאוּל: וָאֶתְּנָה לְךָ אֶת בֵּית אֲדֹנֶיךָ וְאֶת נְשֵׁי אֲדֹנֶיךָ

---

3. We may say that once David repented, as is evidenced by Scripture, he is considered a penitent, and it is deemed improper to remind a *ba'al teshuvah* of their past transgressions; thus the prohibition: one may not *say* "David sinned" – this is best left unspoken.

בְּחֵיקֶךְ וָאֶתְּנָה לְךָ אֶת בֵּית יִשְׂרָאֵל וִיהוּדָה וְאִם מְעָט וְאֹסִפָה לְךָ כָּהֵנָּה וְכָהֵנָּה:
מַדּוּעַ בָּזִיתָ אֶת דְּבַר ה' לַעֲשׂוֹת הָרַע בעינו בְּעֵינַי אֵת אוּרִיָּה הַחִתִּי הִכִּיתָ בַחֶרֶב
וְאֶת אִשְׁתּוֹ לָקַחְתָּ לְּךָ לְאִשָּׁה וְאֹתוֹ הָרַגְתָּ בְּחֶרֶב בְּנֵי עַמּוֹן: וְעַתָּה לֹא תָסוּר חֶרֶב
מִבֵּיתְךָ עַד עוֹלָם עֵקֶב כִּי בְזִתָנִי וַתִּקַּח אֶת אֵשֶׁת אוּרִיָּה הַחִתִּי לִהְיוֹת לְךָ לְאִשָּׁה:
כֹּה אָמַר ה' הִנְנִי מֵקִים עָלֶיךָ רָעָה מִבֵּיתֶךָ וְלָקַחְתִּי אֶת נָשֶׁיךָ לְעֵינֶיךָ וְנָתַתִּי לְרֵעֶיךָ
וְשָׁכַב עִם נָשֶׁיךָ לְעֵינֵי הַשֶּׁמֶשׁ הַזֹּאת: כִּי אַתָּה עָשִׂיתָ בַסָּתֶר וַאֲנִי אֶעֱשֶׂה אֶת הַדָּבָר
הַזֶּה נֶגֶד כָּל יִשְׂרָאֵל וְנֶגֶד הַשָּׁמֶשׁ:

וַיֹּאמֶר דָּוִד אֶל נָתָן חָטָאתִי לַה'.

And God sent Natan to David. And he came to him, and said to him, "There were two men in one city; the one rich, and the other poor. The rich man had very many flocks and herds; but the poor man had nothing, save one little ewe lamb, which he had bought and nourished, and it grew up together with him and with his children; it ate of his own food, and drank of his own cup, and lay in his bosom, and was to him as a daughter. And there came a traveler to the rich man, and he was unwilling to take from his own flock and of his own herd, to prepare for the traveler who came to him; but took the poor man's lamb, and prepared it for the man who came to him." And David's anger was greatly kindled against the man; and he said to Natan, "As God lives, the man who has done this thing shall surely die; And he shall restore the lamb fourfold, because he did this thing, and because he had no pity."

And Natan said to David, "You are the man. Thus said the Almighty God of Israel, 'I anointed you king over Israel, and I delivered you from the hand of Sha'ul. I gave you your master's house, and your master's wives to your bosom, and gave you the House of Israel and of Yehudah; and if that had been too little, I would have given to you many other things. Why have you despised the commandment of God, to do evil in His sight? You have killed Uriah the Hittite with the sword, and have taken his wife to be your wife, and have killed him with the sword of the Ammonites. And therefore the sword shall never depart from your house; because you have despised Me, and have taken the wife of Uriah the Hittite to be your wife.'

"Thus said God, 'Behold, I will raise up evil against you from your own house, and I will take your wives before your eyes, and give them to your neighbor, and he shall lie with your wives in the sight

of the sun. For you did it secretly; but I will do this thing before all Israel, and before the sun."

And David said to Natan, "I have sinned against God." (II Shmuel 12:1–13)

According to the *Sefer haLikutim*, as David lies beside a young, beautiful woman, his physical passions are suppressed and his soul reigns supreme, allowing him to fully repent for his earlier moral lapse.

Though the story of Avishag opens the haftarah, the haftarah's main thrust is the insurgence of Adoniyah, who attempts to usurp the kingdom while David is old but still quite alive.

מלכים א, א:ה–ו

וַאֲדֹנִיָּה בֶן חַגִּית מִתְנַשֵּׂא לֵאמֹר אֲנִי אֶמְלֹךְ וַיַּעַשׂ לוֹ רֶכֶב וּפָרָשִׁים וַחֲמִשִּׁים אִישׁ רָצִים לְפָנָיו:וְלֹא עֲצָבוֹ אָבִיו מִיָּמָיו לֵאמֹר מַדּוּעַ כָּכָה עָשִׂיתָ וְגַם הוּא טוֹב תֹּאַר מְאֹד וְאֹתוֹ יָלְדָה אַחֲרֵי אַבְשָׁלוֹם:

Then Adoniyah the son of Haggit exalted himself, saying, "I will be king"; and he set up chariots and horsemen for himself, and fifty men to run before him. And his father had not displeased him at any time by saying, "Why have you done so?" And he also was a very handsome man; and his mother bore him after Avshalom. (I Melakhim 1:5–6)

The closing editorial comment, that Adoniyah was born after Avshalom, is instructive:[4] like Adoniyah, Avshalom, too, had declared himself king. The memory of Avshalom's ill-conceived rebellion and tragic death must surely have haunted David and made him hesitant to give Adoniyah the rebuke he deserved. He could not bear to confront his rebellious son – again.

The *Sefer haLikutim* casts David's woes against a different backdrop altogether: David himself had behaved inappropriately to a king – to Sha'ul, and the various attempts at rebellion he was forced to contend with in his later years were punishment:

---

4. See II Shmuel 3:3–4.

שמואל א, כד:ד–ז

וַיֹּאמְרוּ אַנְשֵׁי דָוִד אֵלָיו הִנֵּה הַיּוֹם אֲשֶׁר אָמַר ה' אֵלֶיךָ הִנֵּה אָנֹכִי נֹתֵן אֶת אֹיִבְךָ
בְּיָדֶךָ וְעָשִׂיתָ לּוֹ כַּאֲשֶׁר יִטַב בְּעֵינֶיךָ וַיָּקָם דָּוִד וַיִּכְרֹת אֶת כְּנַף הַמְּעִיל אֲשֶׁר לְשָׁאוּל
בַּלָּט: וַיְהִי אַחֲרֵי כֵן וַיַּךְ לֵב דָּוִד אֹתוֹ עַל אֲשֶׁר כָּרַת אֶת כָּנָף אֲשֶׁר לְשָׁאוּל: וַיֹּאמֶר
לַאֲנָשָׁיו חָלִילָה לִּי מֵה' אִם אֶעֱשֶׂה אֶת הַדָּבָר הַזֶּה לַאדֹנִי לִמְשִׁיחַ ה' לִשְׁלֹחַ יָדִי
בּוֹ כִּי מְשִׁיחַ ה' הוּא: וַיְשַׁסַּע דָּוִד אֶת אֲנָשָׁיו בַּדְּבָרִים וְלֹא נְתָנָם לָקוּם אֶל שָׁאוּל
וְשָׁאוּל קָם מֵהַמְּעָרָה וַיֵּלֶךְ בַּדָּרֶךְ:

*And the men of David said to him, "This is the day of which God
said to you, 'Behold, I will deliver your enemy into your hand, that
you may do to him as you shall see fit.'" Then David arose, and cut off
the skirt of Sha'ul's robe secretly. And it came to pass afterward, that
David's heart struck him, because he had cut off Sha'ul's skirt. And he
said to his men, "God forbid that I should do this thing to my master,
God's anointed one, to stretch forth my hand against him, seeing he
is the anointed emissary of God." So David scolded his servants with
these words, and did not allow them to rise against Sha'ul. And Sha'ul
rose up from the cave, and went on his way.* (I Shmuel 24:4–7)

The Talmud clarifies the connection between these two episodes: David's
disrespect toward King Sha'ul was an act of rebellion against the symbolic
expression of Sha'ul's status, his royal clothing. In his old age, this very
same symbol betrays David: his clothing brings him no protection, no
warmth.

תלמוד בבלי, מסכת ברכות דף סב עמוד ב

ויקם דוד ויכרת את כנף המעיל אשר לשאול בלט: אמר רבי יוסי ברבי חנינא:
כל המבזה את הבגדים סוף אינו נהנה מהם, שנאמר, (מלכים א', א') "והמלך
דוד זקן בא בימים ויכסהו בבגדים ולא יחם לו".

*"Then David arose, and cut off the skirt of Sha'ul's robe secretly": R.
Yose b. R. Hanina said: Whoever treats garments contemptuously
will in the end derive no benefit from them, as it says, "Now King
David was old and advanced in years; and they covered him with
clothes, but he was not warmed."* (Talmud Bavli Brakhot 62b)

David's disrespect for the trappings of the monarchy rebounds against
him, when his son Adoniyah takes a page from David's book and outfits
himself with an entourage and declares himself heir to the throne. As

David supplanted Sha'ul, so Adoniyah begins his "reign" while David still lives and occupies the throne.[5]

Adoniyah was apparently fully aware of the power of the symbols of monarchy: although his attempted rebellion fails and Shlomo eventually becomes king, Adoniyah attempts to gain legitimacy by exploiting the very same symbols. He approaches Batsheva and asks to relay what he presents as an innocent request: he asks that Avishag the Shunammite, the beautiful young woman brought to warm his father, be given to him as a wife and "consolation prize."

מלכים א, ב:יג–יז

וַיָּבֹא אֲדֹנִיָּהוּ בֶן חַגֵּית אֶל בַּת שֶׁבַע אֵם שְׁלֹמֹה וַתֹּאמֶר הֲשָׁלוֹם בֹּאֶךָ וַיֹּאמֶר שָׁלוֹם: וַיֹּאמֶר דָּבָר לִי אֵלָיִךְ וַתֹּאמֶר דַּבֵּר: וַיֹּאמֶר אַתְּ יָדַעַתְּ כִּי לִי הָיְתָה הַמְּלוּכָה וְעָלַי שָׂמוּ כָל יִשְׂרָאֵל פְּנֵיהֶם לִמְלֹךְ וַתִּסֹּב הַמְּלוּכָה וַתְּהִי לְאָחִי כִּי מֵה' הָיְתָה לּוֹ: וְעַתָּה שְׁאֵלָה אַחַת אָנֹכִי שֹׁאֵל מֵאִתָּךְ אַל תָּשִׁבִי אֶת פָּנָי וַתֹּאמֶר אֵלָיו דַּבֵּר: וַיֹּאמֶר אִמְרִי נָא לִשְׁלֹמֹה הַמֶּלֶךְ כִּי לֹא יָשִׁיב אֶת פָּנָיִךְ וְיִתֶּן לִי אֶת אֲבִישַׁג הַשּׁוּנַמִּית לְאִשָּׁה:

And Adoniyah, son of Haggit, came to Batsheva the mother of Shlomo. And she said, "Do you come in peace?" and he said, "Peace." And he said, "May I speak with you?" and she said, "Speak." And he said, "You are aware that the kingdom was mine and all of Israel looked to me to rule, and the kingdom was taken from me and went to my brother, for it was God's decision to give it to him. And now I have one request of you; do not turn me away." And she said to him, "Speak." And he said, "Please tell King Shlomo, since he will not turn down your request, that he should give me Avishag the Shunammite for a wife." (I Melakhim 2:13–17)

Adoniyah was very clever, his plan well considered. He knew that he could never take one of King David's wives; this is clearly a symbol of succession and monarchy. Kings inherited the entire household of their predecessors, as did David himself. Instead, Adoniyah attempts to step into the grey area.

---

5. See *Sefer haLikutim*, I Melakhim 1:1.

ספר הליקוטים, מלכים א פרק א

וג"כ ע"י הצער שציער לשאול בכריתתו כנף מעילו, ונגע בכבוד המלכות, לזה כאן נצטער דוד. ואדניהו מתנשא לאמר אני אמלוך.

He asks for Avishag, who never had the status of a royal wife. Her position was far more utilitarian. Like the clothes with which David had been covered, Avishag was brought to the palace to warm him. King Shlomo, whose wisdom was legendary, sees through Adoniyah's subterfuge. He understands full well that granting this woman to Adoniyah as a wife would be tantamount to dressing his rebellious brother in the robes of the king. The plot comes full circle: David showed his disrespect for Sha'ul by defacing his royal garments; David's clothing rebelled against him, failing to provide warmth in his old age. Finally, David's son Adoniyah tries to rebel by "inheriting" the stand-in for clothing, Avishag the Shunammite – a very powerful symbol of legitimacy indeed. Clearly, Adoniyah has not abandoned his rebellious aspirations; he is put to death.[6]

This episode requires that we consider more carefully the meaning and significance of "clothing" as a concept. We recall that clothing was introduced only after man sinned in the Garden of Eden; such coverage only became necessary when man became vulnerable, weakened by sin. In fact, the word for "clothing," *beged*, signifies *begidah*, betrayal or rebellion; the very necessity for clothing is a sign of man's rebellion against God.

The catalyst and instigator of that sin in Eden was the Serpent. He was the first to cast his eyes upon a woman who was not his own spouse, to desire another man's wife. While the Serpent may have been the first, he was most surely not the last: this behavior became the perceived privilege of many powerful men throughout history, most especially rulers and kings. Rather than subjecting themselves to the will of the King of the Universe, they simply took what was not theirs. They felt that their status, the power that they amassed, was sufficient proof of the morality of their actions. In fact, this was the attitude that brought about the flood:[7]

---

6. See Yalkut Shimoni, I Melakhim, chapter 1, *remez* 166.

ילקוט שמעוני מלכים א, פרק א רמז קסו

ויבקשו נערה יפה בכל גבול ישראל וימצאו את אבישג השונמית: אמר רבי יעקב אמר רבי יוחנן אבישג מותרת לשלמה ואסורה לאדוניה, מותרת לשלמה מלך הוא ומלך משתמש בשרביטו של מלך, ואסורה לאדוניה הדיוט הוא.

7. For a discussion of this topic, see "In Search of the Serpent," above.

בראשית ו:ב–ג

וַיִּרְאוּ בְנֵי הָאֱלֹהִים אֶת בְּנוֹת הָאָדָם כִּי טֹבֹת הֵנָּה וַיִּקְחוּ לָהֶם נָשִׁים מִכֹּל אֲשֶׁר בָּחָרוּ:

And the sons of the powerful [or, those created in the form of the Almighty] saw that the daughters of men were attractive, and they took whatever women they chose. (Bereishit 6:2–3)

The flood did not put an end to this warped nexus of power and adultery: Avraham suffered repeatedly when confronted by this very same philosophy. His concerns regarding the intentions of the powerful men with whom he interacted were borne out on at least two occasions: both Par'oh and Avimelekh regarded it as their right to take Sarah, for they were kings, and in their minds, women were for the taking.

Avraham's defense against these advances seems quite strange to modern readers:

בראשית יב:יג

אִמְרִי נָא אֲחֹתִי אָתְּ לְמַעַן יִיטַב לִי בַעֲבוּרֵךְ וְחָיְתָה נַפְשִׁי בִּגְלָלֵךְ:

Say, I beg you, that you are my sister; that it may be well with me for your sake; and my soul shall live because of you. (Bereishit 12:13)

Sarah is instructed to say that she is Avraham's sister. We are not alone in finding this strategy peculiar, to say the least: numerous commentaries[8] take umbrage at Avraham's seeming willingness to save himself at the expense of his wife's well-being.[9] However, Avraham's tactic contains within it a deep understanding of the mindset of those with whom he is in conflict. His plan may actually be a statement aimed at and only fully understood by

---

8. See Ramban, Bereishit 12:10. I have previously written about this episode in my essay "Acts of the Fathers": http://www.aish.com/tp/i/moha/48932052.html

רמב"ן, בראשית יב:י

ורמז אליו כי בניו ירדו מצרים מפני הרעב לגור שם בארץ, והמצרים ירעו להם ויקחו מהם הנשים כאשר אמר (שמות א:כב) וכל הבת תחיון, והקב"ה ינקום נקמתם.

ודע כי אברהם אבינו חטא חטא גדול בשגגה שהביא אשתו הצדקת במכשול עון מפני פחדו פן יהרגוהו, והיה לו לבטוח בשם שיציל אותו ואת אשתו ואת כל אשר לו, כי יש באלהים כח לעזור ולהציל.

9. See Ohr haHayim, Bereishit 12:11–12, where he raises the same question as the Ramban and provides an answer.

the morally corrupt monarchs themselves, in the broader context of their respective societal mores.

The Torah often holds Egypt up as the representative of morally corrupt social systems. In fact, when the Torah lists all of the forbidden sexual perversions, the section is introduced with a general prohibition to shun Egyptian practices and mores:

ויקרא יח:א–ו

וַיְדַבֵּר ה' אֶל מֹשֶׁה לֵּאמֹר: דַּבֵּר אֶל בְּנֵי יִשְׂרָאֵל וְאָמַרְתָּ אֲלֵהֶם אֲנִי ה' אֱלֹקֵיכֶם: כְּמַעֲשֵׂה אֶרֶץ מִצְרַיִם אֲשֶׁר יְשַׁבְתֶּם בָּהּ לֹא תַעֲשׂוּ וּכְמַעֲשֵׂה אֶרֶץ כְּנַעַן אֲשֶׁר אֲנִי מֵבִיא אֶתְכֶם שָׁמָּה לֹא תַעֲשׂוּ וּבְחֻקֹּתֵיהֶם לֹא תֵלֵכוּ: אֶת מִשְׁפָּטַי תַּעֲשׂוּ וְאֶת חֻקֹּתַי תִּשְׁמְרוּ לָלֶכֶת בָּהֶם אֲנִי ה' אֱלֹקֵיכֶם: וּשְׁמַרְתֶּם אֶת חֻקֹּתַי וְאֶת מִשְׁפָּטַי

אור החיים, בראשית יב:יא

ויהי כאשר הקריב וגו' הנה נא ידעתי וגו': רז"ל אמרו (ב"ב טז א) להגיד צניעות שהיה ביניהם. וצריך לדעת לאיזה ענין אמר לה כן אברהם. אכן להיות כי רצה לצוות עליה לומר אחי הוא חש שתאמר שרה למה הכניסה בגדר סכנה שעל כל פנים היא מסתכנת או תמסר בעל כרחה ביד הטמאים על ידי הריגת הבעל או ברצונה ולא היה לו להביאה למקום כזה, והגם שבטוחים הצדיקים בהקב"ה אף על פי כן כלל זה בידינו שאין סומכין על הנס ומה גם לגבי בחירת האדם, וצא ולמד (קידושין לט ב) ממשנואל שאמר (ש"א טז) ושמע שאול והרגני, לזה אמר אליה הנה נא וגו' נתן התנצלות על הדבר כי עתה נודע לו ולא מקודם שאם היה יודע מה שידע עתה לא היה מביאה אל מצרים והיה הולך למקום אחר. וטעם נתינת לב לדעת לצד קרבתם לבא למצרים ראה פנים כעורות. או ידע בקרבית העיר כי המלך יקח האשה יפה היפה בנשים ונתן דעתו והכיר בה. ואומרים כי אשה יפת וגו' ולא הספיק לומר כי יפת מראה את, נתכוין לומר כי אחת היא בעולם אשה יפת מראה היא ואין דומה לה והבן.

ואל יקשה בעיניך שהלך עמה לארץ פלשתים אחר שידע כי אשה יפת מראה היא, כי ארץ פלשתים לא היו כעורות כל כך כמצרים. ולזה תמצא שלא הוצרך לצוות עליה שתאמר עליה היא אלא הוא אמר עליה אחותי היא כי לא היה בית מיחוש כאנשי מצרים שהיו בתכלית הכיעור והיא בתכלית היופי.

אור החיים, בראשית יב:יג

עוד ירצה בדקדוק עוד אומרו כפל ענין בעבורך ובגללך שהיה לו לומר ייטב לי וחיתה נפשי בגללך או בעבורך. אכן נתכוון לב' דברים הא' למען ייטבו לו בעבור אחותו טובה גשמיית. ועוד וחיתה נפשי וגו' על דרך מה שדרשו ז"ל (ברכות לא ב) אם ראה תראה שאם לא יפקידה תעשה שעל כרחך יראה לתת לה זרע ע"י שתלך ותסתר וכו' ותבדק כסוטה ונזרעה זרע. כמו כן חשב אברהם כי על ידי סתירת האשה עם האיש והיא נקיה ה' יפקדנה בבנים בדומין לו והוא אומרו וחיתה נפשי בפקודת הזרע בגללך פירוש בדברים המתגלגלים ממך על דרך מה שדרשו ז"ל (שבת קנא ב) בגלל הדבר וגו', ולזה הפסיק בתיבת בעבורך לומר כי הם ב' דברים. גם אומרו וחיתה בתוספת וא"ו לומר שהוא פרט חדש ואינו ענף ייטב לי כי הם ב' בחינות ההטבה אחד לגוף ואחד לנפש. ודבר זה הושג אצלו בסתירה שנסתרה עם אבימלך ולא בפעם הזאת עם פרעה לטעם כי שם לא היה חשד כי גירשו מארצו גילה כי לא עשה דבר. או אפשר כי באמצעות ב' פעמים נתפרסם הקול על שרה כי נסתרה ועל ידי זה נפקדה. שוב בא לידי מאמר רז"ל (ב"ר פנ"ג) וזה לשונם אמר רבי יצחק אמר הקב"ה כתיב (במדבר ה:כח) ואם לא נטמאה האשה וטהורה היא ונקתה ונזרעה זרע וזו שנכנסה לבית פרעה ולבית אבימלך ויצתה טהורה אין דין שתפקד עכ"ל, והם דברינו עצמם והבן. הרי שחיתה נפשו של אברהם בבנים בגלל שרה.

אֲשֶׁר יַעֲשֶׂה אֹתָם הָאָדָם וָחַי בָּהֶם אֲנִי ה': אִישׁ אִישׁ אֶל כָּל שְׁאֵר בְּשָׂרוֹ לֹא
תִקְרְבוּ לְגַלּוֹת עֶרְוָה אֲנִי ה':

*And God spoke to Moshe, saying, "Speak to the people of Israel,
and say to them, 'I am the Almighty your God. Do not adopt the
behaviors of the land of Egypt, where you dwelled, and do not adopt
the behaviors of the land of Canaan, where I bring you, nor shall you
walk in their ordinances. You shall do my judgments, and keep my
ordinances, to walk with them; I am the Almighty your God. You shall
therefore keep my statutes, and my judgments, which if a man does,
he shall live through them; I am God. None of you shall approach
to any who is near of kin to him, to uncover their nakedness; I am
God."* (Vayikra 18:1–6)

First and foremost among proscribed sexual behaviors is incest. The Netziv,
in his commentary *Ha'amek Davar*, stresses that the entire monarchial
system of Egypt was based on incest: as a "privilege" of monarchy, the
pharaohs married their own sisters.[10] It is in this milieu that Avraham is
forced to maneuver. When he instructs Sarah to say that she is his sister,
Avraham speaks to Par'oh in his own language, as it were, addressing him as
one monarch to another. He hopes that Par'oh will treat him as a significant
leader, and afford him the protection given to a visiting monarch.

In fact, this subtext may be the key to understanding more than the episode
of Avraham and Sarah in Egypt; this may be the crux of the entire relationship
of the haftarah to the parashah. While we see Avraham as "*avinu*," our
forefather Avraham, that is our own familial, familiar perspective. To others,
to the people with whom he came in contact during his later life, Avraham
was seen as king. The text itself gives us many "snapshots" of Avraham's

---

10. See *Ha'amek Davar*, Vayikra 18:3.

העמק דבר, ויקרא יח:ג

כמעשה וגו' לא תעשו ובחקתיהם לא תלכו: הקדים אזהרות הללו לפ' עריות באשר אדם עושה עבירה זו
בשני אופנים. א' מראש פרעות התאוה פרץ גדר חקי התורה וחקי הדעת של האדם ג"כ. אבל זה האופן
לא מיקרי הליכה אלא מעשה משום שאינו בא אלא במקרה. ב' מחקי המדינה שכך הנהיגו להתהלך
באופנים הללו. והעובר על חקי התורה אינו מצד תאוה אלא כך המנהג.גם כן הקדים הכתוב כמעשה ארץ
מצרים שראיתם רגילים לפרוץ בתאותם אתם לא תעשו כן. ותגדרו בפני התאוה
הבא במקרא.

ובחקתיהם: שחקקו מדעת גדוליהם שראוי לנהוג כך להיות אח נושא אחותו וכדומה.

interactions that indicate this status: for example, when Avraham returned
from the battle in which he vanquished the confederacy of five kings led by
his old nemesis Nimrod/Amrafel,[11] there was a move to anoint Avraham
king of the entire region:

בראשית יד:יז

וַיֵּצֵא מֶלֶךְ סְדֹם לִקְרָאתוֹ אַחֲרֵי שׁוּבוֹ מֵהַכּוֹת אֶת כְּדָרְלָעֹמֶר וְאֶת הַמְּלָכִים אֲשֶׁר
אִתּוֹ אֶל עֵמֶק שָׁוֵה הוּא עֵמֶק הַמֶּלֶךְ:

*And the king of Sodom went out to meet him after his return from
the victory over Kedorlaomer and the kings who were with him, in
the valley of Shaveh, which is the king's valley. (Bereishit 14:17)*

בראשית רבה, פרשה מג פסקה ה

רבי ברכיה ורבי חנינא בשם רבי שמואל בר נחמן: ששם השוו כל עובדי כוכבים
וקצצו ארזים ועשו בימה גדולה והושיבו אותו בתוכו למעלה והיו מקלסין
לפניו ואומרים לו "שמענו אדוני" וג', אמרו לו, "מלך את עלינו, נשיא את
עלינו, אלוה את עלינו". אמר להם, "אל יחסר העולם מלכו ואל יחסר אלוהו".

*R. Berekhyah and R. Helbo in the name of R. Shmuel b. Nahman
said: It was so called because there all peoples of the world became
unanimous, and said to Avraham, "Be king over us." But he replied,
"The world does not lack its King and its God." (Bereishit Rabbah 43:5)*

Long before, Avraham had come to fully understand that the world has a
King. He therefore had little use for the trappings of power and monarchy.
In his experience, monarchs caused war, bloodshed and the corruption
of morals. As far as he was concerned, the world had the only King it
needed. In fact, Avraham's attitude is deeply embedded in the Jewish
ethic: while Avraham was, according to the Midrash, the first to express
his reservations,[12] throughout the generations, the Jewish attitude toward
monarchy has always been ambivalent.

---

11. See Rashi, Bereishit 14:1, where Amrafel is identified with Nimrod.

רש"י, בראשית יד:א

אמרפל: הוא נמרוד שאמר לאברהם פול לתוך כבשן האש.

12. See Devarim 17:14 and commentaries.

These reservations notwithstanding, "outsiders" saw Avraham as a king, and he was often confronted with many of the issues with which kings are faced: waging war, accepting or rejecting payment or homage from peoples vanquished or rescued in war, economic management and foreign relations. In contrast to Par'oh and Avimelekh, who espoused the belief that monarchy entitles the ruler to whatever lies in his domain, Avraham remained firm in his conviction that leaders may not abuse their position.

The consequences of these opposing philosophies are perhaps seen most clearly in yet another issue of monarchy: succession. Here, then, is the connection between the parashah and the haftarah: The haftarah recounts a tale of palace intrigue surrounding the question of succession to the throne. Conversely, the parashah tells of the courtship of a wife for Avraham's son, Yitzhak – a strange courtship, conducted by proxy through Avraham's trusted aide. At face value, these are two very different stories, yet they are woven with a common thread: continuity. The new leader, the replacement for the father who is almost larger than life, is the topic. The contrast in the resolution of the problem of succession is striking: Avraham's trusted servant marches with fidelity to fulfill his master's quest to procure a proper wife for Yitzhak, thus insuring that Avraham's line will carry on. On the other hand, David's son Adoniyah takes steps to circumvent his father and become king, despite the fact that David is still alive and has expressed his choice of Shlomo to inherit the throne.

Both King David and "King" Avraham led lives in which they built and solidified great empires, both physical and spiritual. Both were willing and able to fight, when necessary, but Avraham's preferred tactic was to reach out with love. His following grew as he exposed others to the *hesed* of the God of the Universe whom he had discovered. In our present parashah, and in the haftarah reading associated with it, both Avraham and David were planning their respective departures from the stage of history, making provisions for the smooth transmission of their respective empires to their successors. It is therefore with a great deal of irony and no small measure of poetic justice that the Targum Pseudo-Yonatan identifies two of Avraham's better-known disciples/followers, Eliezer and Hagar, within this context of monarchy and succession.

Eliezer, the man whom Avraham saw as a potential heir, was in a sense "the man who would be king," the man passed over in favor of Yitzhak. According to tradition, Avraham entrusts Eliezer with the task of finding a wife for Yitzhak,[13] effectively entrusting the displaced heir with insuring the succession of the true heir. The trust that Avraham places in him is all the more impressive in this light, and the servant's scrupulous fulfillment of his master's wishes all the more significant. And yet, that is not all; according to Targum Pseudo-Yonatan, Eliezer was in fact the son of Nimrod![14] Here, then, is the son of Avraham's archenemy, the man who had tried to burn him alive in Ur Kasdim and to defeat him on the battlefield years later. Eliezer rejected his own father, turning his back on the empire that would rightfully be his own, in order to join Avraham. And when he is passed over by Avraham, when it is clear that Yitzhak will inherit the empire Avraham has built despite his own years of faithful service, Eliezer remains loyal to Avraham and everything he stands for. He faithfully seeks out the means for continuing Avraham's spiritual and physical legacy – through Yitzhak!

---

13. See, for example, Targum Pseudo-Yonatan, Bereishit 24:2.

כתר יונתן, בראשית כד:ב

ויאמר אברהם לאליעזר עבדו זקן של ביתו ששולט בכל אוצרות שלו שים עתה ידך בברית מילתי.

14. See Targum Pseudo-Yonatan, Bereishit 14:14. This teaching is based on various midrashim; see Midrash Aggadah, chapter 16; Yalkut Shimoni, Parashat Hayei Sarah, *remez* 109. Also see Pirkei d'Rebbi Eliezer, chapter 16, which is of the opinion that Eliezer was Nimrod's slave. The Hizkuni (Bereishit 15:2) identifies Eliezer as Nimrod's grandson.

כתר יונתן, בראשית יד:יד

וכאשר שמע אברם כי נשבה אחיו חימש את בחוריו שחיניך למלחמה מגידולי ביתו ולא רצו ללכת עמו ויבחר מהם את אליעזר בן נמרוד שהיה דומה בגבורתו ככולם שלש מאות ושמונה עשר וירדוף עד דן.

מדרש אגדה (בובר), בראשית פרק טז

וכן נתן **נמרוד אליעזר בנו** לאברהם, בשעה שניצל מכבשן האש.

פרקי דרבי אליעזר (היגר) "חורב", פרק טז

ומהיכן היה עבדו אלא שכיון שיצא מאור כשדים באו כל גדולי הדור ליתן לו מתנות ולקח **נמרוד עבדו אליעזר** ונתנו לו עבד עולם....

ילקוט שמעוני, פרשת חיי שרה רמז קט

אמר הקב"ה מה עשה לעבד זה שהיה חשוד אמר למלאכי השרת הכניסוהו חי בגן עדן הוא **אליעזר בן נמרוד** והוא תמיה גדולה יצחק יצא מגן עדן חי ואליעזר נכנס לגן עדן חי.

חזקוני, בראשית טו:ב

הוא דמשק אליעזר **בן בנו של נמרוד הרשע** היה.

Hagar was the female equivalent of Eliezer, so to speak. She served Sarah, and for a time it appeared that her own son would inherit Avraham's empire. The Torah identifies her as Egyptian, and the Targum Pseudo-Yonatan fills in the details of her biography: she was the daughter of Par'oh, the granddaughter of Nimrod.[15]

What did they see in Avraham? What led them to reject Nimrod and everything he stood for and cling to Avraham and his household? Avraham was a different kind of king. He did not take people by force; they followed him because of love. Nimrod was the first person in history described as a king; he amassed power in order to enable him to use force. Avraham taught the world about a different King, an ethical King of love. Nimrod's own descendants chose Avraham and his message of decency; in him, and through him, they had found a true leader and the real King.

---

15. Targum Pseudo-Yonatan, Bereishit 16:5.

כתר יונתן, בראשית טז:ה

ותאמר שרי לאברם כל עלבוני ממך שהייתי בטוחה שתעשה דיני שאני עזבתי ארץ ובית אבא ובאתי עמך
לארץ נכריה ועתה בעבור שלא הייתי יולדת שחררתי שפחתי ונתתיה בחיקיך ותרא כי הרתה ויתבזה
כבודי בפניה ועתה יתגלה לפני ה' עלבוני ויפרוס שלום ביני ובינך ותתמלא הארץ ממנו ולא נצטרך לבניה
של הגר בת פרעה בן נמרוד שהטילך לכבשן האש.

Parashat Toldot

Echoes of Eden

At the end of Parashat Hayei Sarah, Avraham's faithful servant completes his mission: he declines Lavan's extended hospitality and brings their "negotiation" to a successful conclusion. Rivkah herself has no small part in this conclusion. She is unequivocal; her choice is clear:

בראשית כד:נח

וַיִּקְרְאוּ לְרִבְקָה וַיֹּאמְרוּ אֵלֶיהָ הֲתֵלְכִי עִם הָאִישׁ הַזֶּה וַתֹּאמֶר אֵלֵךְ:

And they called for Rivkah and said to her, "Will you go with this man?" And she said, "I will go." (Bereishit 24:58)

Rivkah and her entourage set out, and Avraham's servant leads the way to his master's house. As they approach, they come upon Yitzhak, who is out in the field, immersed in prayer. When she sees him, Rivkah's reaction is powerful:

בראשית כד:סג–סד

וַיֵּצֵא יִצְחָק לָשׂוּחַ בַּשָּׂדֶה לִפְנוֹת עָרֶב וַיִּשָּׂא עֵינָיו וַיַּרְא וְהִנֵּה גְמַלִּים בָּאִים: וַתִּשָּׂא רִבְקָה אֶת עֵינֶיהָ וַתֵּרֶא אֶת יִצְחָק וַתִּפֹּל מֵעַל הַגָּמָל:

And Yitzhak went out to meditate [or, converse] in the field at the turning of the evening; and he lifted up his eyes, and suddenly saw camels approaching. And Rivkah lifted up her eyes, and when she saw Yitzhak, she fell [or, dismounted] off the camel. (Bereishit 24:63–64)

The scene is striking, dramatic – but Rivkah's reaction is open to various interpretations. When she sees Yitzhak in the field, without even knowing who he is, she either falls off or dismounts[1] from her camel.[2] While some

---

1. The Rashbam says that she had not been riding sidesaddle; therefore, out of considerations of modesty, upon meeting her husband she dismounted.

רשב״ם, בראשית כד:סד

ותפול מעל הגמל: לצניעות, לפי שהיתה רוכבת כמו איש משום ביעותא דגמלא כדמפורש בפסחים.

midrashim "blame" Yitzhak's physical beauty, others teach that Rivkah reacted as she did because she alone was able to discern Yitzhak's other-worldly characteristics. The Alshikh explains that she was in awe when she saw Yitzhak's holiness,[3] while other commentaries say that she was frightened when she saw him.[4] Still other sources point to Rivkah's innocence and inexperience as the source of panic and confusion that caused her to fall.[5] These sources seem to fit into a larger theme found in

---

2. Rashi (Bereishit 24:64) states that she was in shock when she saw Yitzhak.

רש"י, בראשית כד:סד

ותרא את יצחק: ראתה אותו הדור ותוהא מפניו.

ותפל: השמיטה עצמה לארץ, כתרגומו ואתרכינת הטתה עצמה לארץ ולא הגיעה עד הקרקע, כמו (יד) הטי נא כדך, ארכיני, (ש"ב כב:י) ויט שמים, וארכין, לשון מוטה לארץ, ודומה לו (תהלים לז:כד) כי יפול לא יוטל, כלומר אם יטה לארץ לא יגיע עד הקרקע.

3. *Torat Moshe*, Bereishit 24:64.

ספר תורת משה, בראשית כד:סד–סה

מה שהפילה עצמה מעל הגמל אפשר שנבעתה מזיו צלם אלקים שעל פניו, וחששה אולי הוא יצחק כי מי חוץ ממנו או אביו יהיו לו כן. ועל הזיו הלז ריבה האת באומרו את יצחק.

4. The Hizkuni (Bereishit 24:64) suggests that due to her tender age she was frightened, and when she saw him she thought he was a rapist or a thief. The Riva (Bereishit 24:64) says that Yitzhak looked like a zombie, and she thought he was some kind of thief.

חזקוני, בראשית כד:סד

ותרא את יצחק ותפל מעל הגמל: ראתה אותו הדור ובעל קומה ופרצוף מהלך לעבר השדות בלא דרך כי בושה והיא היתה קטנה בת שלש שנים כסבורה אנס או לסטים הוא ונתבהלה ונפלה.

פירוש הריב"א, בראשית כד:סד

ותפול מעל הגמל: לפי שראתה יצחק שהיה בא מגן עדן והיה בא כדרך שהמתים הולכים למעלה, ורש"י פי' שראתה אותו הדור ותוהה מפניו עכ"ל, וי"מ שהיא ראתה אותו יפה תואר. וי"מ הדור לשון כי בעי למהדר שהיו רגליו למעלה כמו דפרי'. **וי"מ שנתבהלה רבקה כשראהו הולך בדרך שאינו כבוש והיא היתה קטנה בת ג' שנים וכסבורה היא שתהיה גנב או לסטים.**

5. It is explained that when she fell she was wounded and bled; subsequently, when Yitzhak was intimate with Rivkah, the signs of her virginity were absent, and immediately the suspicion was focused on the servant Eliezer who accompanied Rivkah on her journey. Upon returning to the place where she fell, and finding the blood that corroborated their account of the injury, Rivkah and Eliezer were exonerated. See Midrash Aggadah Bereishit, chapter 24.

מדרש אגדה (בובר) בראשית, פרק כד

ותפל מעל הגמל: נפילה ממש, ובאותה נפילה איבדה בתוליה. הרהרה שראתה בעלה ולפיכך נפלה....

האהלה שרה אמו: שמצאה כשרה כאמו, ואמרו חז"ל כי על שרה שהיה ענן קשור על אוהלה, וכשהיתה מדלקת נירות בערב שבת, היו הנרות דולקות עד מוצאי שבת, וכן רבקה, וכסה הענן לאהל שרה, כשמתה שרה נסתלק הענן וכשבאתה רבקה חזר הענן, וכשם שהיתה שרה זהירה בשלשה מצות שהאשה חייבת בהם, נדה וחלה והדלקת הנר, כך היתה רבקה זהירה.

וינחם יצחק אחרי אמו: כל זמן שאמו של אדם בחייה אהבתו הולכת עם אמו, מתה אמו אהבתו הולכת

the Midrash which we may call "the preservation of Rivkah's innocence"[6]: rabbinic sources contain a wealth of comments and midrashim that stress the depravity of the home that Rivkah left behind, the corrupt world of Betuel and Lavan that Rivkah rejected without a moment's hesitation. In fact, as we shall see, the biographical details revealed – and concealed – in the text of the Torah may be part and parcel of this issue.

When Rivkah throws her lot in with Avraham's household, she effectively divorces herself from an immoral pagan society at the earliest possible opportunity. The Midrashic teachings regarding her home in Padan Aram leave no room for doubt: Rivkah's father Betuel was at the apex of this corrupt society; he was the most immoral person in Padan Aram.

The Midrashic description of the backdrop to Rivkah's departure addresses what is perceived as a lacuna in the text: When the servant first arrives looking for a bride for his master's son, Rivkah is identified as the daughter of Betuel,[7] and when negotiations commence Betuel and Lavan respond.[8] Nonetheless the next morning when the marriage is finalized, the father is nowhere to be found and the servant discusses the pending marriage with her brother Lavan instead.[9] In explaining this unconventional betrothal,

---

לאשתו. ויש אומרים שלא מצאה בתולה שחשד באליעזר, אמרה רבקה חלילה שלא שכב עמי אליעזר, אבל מפני הנפילה שנפלתי אבדתי בתולתי, ונקום ונלך למקום ההוא שנפלתי, ואולי יעשה ה' נס ותמצא שם דם בתולים, וכן עשו, הלכו ומצאו הדם על עץ אחד, והיתה מוכת עץ, והדם היה גבריאל שומר שלא יאכל ממנו לא עוף ולא חיה, ולפי שחשד לאליעזר על חנם, והוא עשה שליחות אברהם באמונה, זכה שיכנס לגן עדן חי.

6. Rivkah's innocence is attested to in the text of the Torah: Bereishit 24:16: "And the girl was very pretty to look upon, a virgin, and no man had known her." The language seems repetitive: if she is a virgin, why is it necessary to state that "no man had known her"? Rashi explains that women in those days would often "save" themselves for their husbands in terms of virginity, but they would nonetheless engage in other forms of sexual contact.

בראשית כד:טז
וְהַנַּעֲרָ טֹבַת מַרְאֶה מְאֹד בְּתוּלָה וְאִישׁ לֹא יְדָעָהּ וַתֵּרֶד הָעַיְנָה וַתְּמַלֵּא כַדָּהּ וַתָּעַל:

רש"י, בראשית כד:טז
בתולה: ממקום בתולים.
ואיש לא ידעה: שלא כדרכה, לפי שבנות הגוים היו משמרות מקום בתוליהן ומפקירות עצמן ממקום אחר, העיד על זו שנקיה מכל.

7. See Bereishit 24:15, 24, 27.
8. See Bereishit 24:50.
9. See Bereishit 24:55.

the Midrash is clearly not oblivious to the significance of Rivkah's father's name: Betuel – which may be translated as "the god of virginity." Betuel was surely not the first man in a position of power to invoke his "divine right" to spend the first night with every bride under his jurisdiction.[10] The elders of Padan Aram, upon hearing of Rivkah's upcoming marriage, insisted that if Betuel conducted himself thus with their daughters – they would demand no less for his daughter. They waited impatiently for the first sign of weakness, hoping to catch Betuel in his own evil net and sentence Betuel and Rivkah to death.[11] Rivkah knew very well what she was leaving behind, and she willingly, purposefully aligned herself with Avraham and all he stood for.

And then, she sees Yitzhak. Was it love at first sight? Physical infatuation? Awe at the sight of this holy man? The Midrash offers one more possible explanation for Rivkah's reaction upon first laying eyes on her betrothed: when Rivkah first saw Yitzhak, she saw prophetically that he would have an evil son, and she fell off of the camel.[12]

As Parashat Hayei Sarah draws to an end, Rivkah and Yitzhak meet, are wed, and their life together begins. The relationship between Yitzhak and

---

10. See below, Parashat Vayeishev, "*Keitz* Bavel – Zerubavel," p. 282, on the principle of *ius primæ noctis.*

11. Yalkut Shimoni, Parashat Hayei Sarah, *remez* 109.

ילקוט שמעוני, פרשת חיי שרה רמז קט

כיון שראו את הצמידים נתקבצו להרוג לאליעזר וראו שהיה נוטל ב' גמלים בב' ידיו ומעבירין את הנחל. כיון שראו כן אמרו אין אנו יכולין להרגו והניחו קערה לפניו וסם המות בתוכה ובזכות אברהם נתחלפה הקערה ואכל בתואל ממנה ומת, ואין ויושם אלא לשון סם. ומפני מה מת בתואל? שהוא היה מלך בארם נהרים וכל בתולה שתנשא בועל אותה לילה ראשונה ואח"כ חוזרת לבעלה. נתקבצו כל השרים ואמרו אם הוא עושה לבתו כשם שעשה לבנותינו מוטב ואם לאו אנו הורגים אותו ואת בתו לפיכך מת כדי שינצל אליעזר ורבקה.

12. Ibid.

ילקוט שמעוני, פרשת חיי שרה רמז קט

בשתי שעות ביום יצאו מחרן וקפצה הארץ לפניהם, ויצא יצחק לשוח בשדה: מהיכן יצא? מגן עדן. ותפול מעל הגמל: לפי שראתה ברוח הקדש שעתיד לצאת ממנו עשו הרשע נזדעזעה ונעשית מוכת עץ ויצא ממנה דם בתולים מיד אמר הקב"ה לגבריאל רד ושמור את הדם שלא יסריח ולא יהיה בו מום בא יצחק עליה ולא מצא לה בתולים חשדה מאליעזר אמר לה בתולותיך היכן הן אמרה לי כשנפלתי מן הגמל נעשיתי מוכת עץ אמר לה שקר את מדברת אלא אליעזר פגע בך ונשבעה לו שלא נגע בה הלכו ומצאו העץ צבוע דם מיד ידע יצחק שהיא טהורה אמר הקב"ה מה אעשה לעבד הזה שהיה חשוד אמר למלאכי השרת הכניסוהו חי בגן עדן הוא אליעזר בן נמרוד והוא תמיה גדולה יצחק יצא מגן עדן חי ואליעזר נכנס לגן עדן חי.

Rivkah blossoms; he loves her and she brings him solace.[13] But as Parashat Toldot begins, we learn that their happiness is incomplete:

בראשית כה:כ

וַיְהִי יִצְחָק בֶּן אַרְבָּעִים שָׁנָה בְּקַחְתּוֹ אֶת רִבְקָה בַּת בְּתוּאֵל הָאֲרַמִּי מִפַּדַּן אֲרָם אֲחוֹת לָבָן הָאֲרַמִּי לוֹ לְאִשָּׁה:

And Yitzhak was forty years old when he took Rivkah, daughter of Betuel the Aramean of Padan Aram, sister of Lavan the Aramean, for his wife. (Bereishit 25:20)

בראשית כה:כו

וְיִצְחָק בֶּן שִׁשִּׁים שָׁנָה בְּלֶדֶת אֹתָם:

...and Yitzhak was sixty years old when she bore them. (Bereishit 25:26)

Combining these two verses, we learn that the couple suffered through twenty years of infertility. At no point does the text tell us Rivkah's age when they married, nor do we know her age when she gives birth. For that matter, the Torah never gives us any information about Rivkah's age, and we do not even know at what point in the biblical narrative she died[14] or how old she was at her passing. The Seder Olam Rabbah,[15] a rabbinic

---

13. Bereishit 24:67.

בראשית כד:סז

וַיְבִאֶהָ יִצְחָק הָאֹהֱלָה שָׂרָה אִמּוֹ וַיִּקַּח אֶת רִבְקָה וַתְּהִי לוֹ לְאִשָּׁה וַיֶּאֱהָבֶהָ וַיִּנָּחֵם יִצְחָק אַחֲרֵי אִמּוֹ:

14. The Sifri says that Rivkah was 133 when she died, while according to Rashi it would seem that Rivkah was 122 years old. This eleven-year discrepancy is related to two readings in the Seder Olam; see below. For some of the calculations see Rabbi David Silverberg (http://www.vbm-torah.org/archive/salt-bereishit/06-10toledot.htm), who seems to have missed the Seder Olam.

ספרי דברים, פרשת וזאת הברכה פסקא שנז

שש זוגות ששנותיהם שוות רבקה וקהת לוי ועמרם יוסף ויהושע שמואל ושלמה משה והלל הזקן ורבן יוחנן בן זכיי ורבי עקיבא.

15. Seder Olam Rabbah, chapter 1.

סדר עולם רבה (ליינר), פרק א

אבינו יצחק היה כשנעקד על המזבח בן ל"ז שנה. ויגר אברהם בארץ פלשתים ימים רבים (בראשית כא:לד), הימים הללו מרובים על חברון שהיו עשרים וחמש שנה, והללו עשרים ושש שנה, בו בפרק נולדה רבקה, נמצא אבינו יצחק נשא את רבקה בת (י"ד) [ג'] שנה,

book devoted to biblical chronology, offers two variant accounts: in the first, Rivkah was a mere three years of age[16] at the time of her marriage[17] to Yitzhak; in the second version, she was a more palatable fourteen when wed.[18] The first account seems far less compatible with the verse's statement that she was "barren"; it would only be possible to speak of twenty years of infertility if Rivkah was, indeed, of childbearing age when they were wed, and the first twenty years of their marriage saw her prime childbearing years dwindle. Apparently, the opinion that Rivkah was separated from the house of her father at the tender age of three is part and parcel of the "preservation of innocence" theme we have discussed, taken to extremes.

As her biological clock winds down, Rivkah finds herself pregnant at last. The Torah tells us that Yitzhak's prayers are answered.

בראשית כה:כא

וַיֶּעְתַּר יִצְחָק לַה' לְנֹכַח אִשְׁתּוֹ כִּי עֲקָרָה הִוא וַיֵּעָתֶר לוֹ ה' וַתַּהַר רִבְקָה אִשְׁתּוֹ:

And Yitzhak prayed to God regarding [literally, in the presence of] his wife, because she was barren; and God responded to his prayer, and Rivkah, his wife, conceived. (Bereishit 25:21)

---

16. This may be intended to parallel her life with Avraham, who, according to some sources, discovered God at the age of three. Rivkah, with her heroic acts of hesed, seems to follow Avraham's example.

17. Rivkah's birth is reported after the *'akeidah*. According to some traditions, Yitzhak was thiry-seven at that time; therefore if he was forty at the time of marriage she would have been three. Other commentaries believe Yitzhak to have been significantly younger at the time of the *'akeidah*. In the ancient Near East, marriages at extremely young ages were common, even though consummation of the marriage would have been delayed for a significant amount of time.

18. See Da'at Zekeinim mi'Baalei haTosafot, Bereishit 25:20.

דעת זקנים מבעלי התוספות, בראשית כה:כ

ויהי יצחק בן ארבעים שנה: פירש"י שנשא יצחק את רבקה כשהיתה בת שלש שנים וקשיא דבשלהי ספרי מסיק ג' שנותיהן שוין קהת ורבקה ובן עזאי. וא"כ חיתה רבקה קל"ג שנים כמו קהת ואם לא היתה כי אם בת שלש שנים כשנשאה יצחק תמצא שחסר משנותיהם י"א שנים. כיצד? בת ג' נשאה ובת כ"ג היתה כשילדה. וא"כ כשילדה את יעקב היתה בת כ"ג ויעקב בן ס"א כשנתברך כדפירש"י בסוף הסדר הזה וי"ד שנה נטמן בבית עבר וכ' שנה שמש בבית לבן ושתי שנים נשתהה בדרך ובאותו פרק נתבשר על מיתת אמו כדפירש"י בפ' וישלח גבי אלון בכות. וא"כ לא היתה כי אם בת קכ"ב שנים. ל"נ שהיתה רבקה בת י"ד שנים כשנשאה יצחק והכי איתא בסדר עולם וכן א"ר יהודה ואז תמצא שהיתה קל"ג שנים מכוונים. ולפי זה ל"ל מה ששנינו בסדר עולם כשחזר אברהם מן העקדה נתבשר שנולדה רבקה כבר עבר י"א שנים.

As her dream is about to come true,[19] Rivkah experiences some sort of difficulty related to the pregnancy – and the feelings it evokes in her are reminiscent of Rivkah's reaction when she first sees Yitzhak. She is frightened, confused, alarmed. What is the cause of her distress? Here, too, the Midrashic material is diverse, and rabbinic commentaries offer widely divergent opinions. In a sort of parallel to the opinions on the earlier scene, some see her distress as the natural,[20] commonplace fears of any expectant mother – especially one who has waited for twenty years,[21] especially one living in an age when so many pregnancies ended in tragedy. Simply put, Rivkah experienced the discomfort and worry that accompany every normal pregnancy, and she prayed to God[22] for the health of her unborn child and for her own survival.[23] Other commentaries learn about the cause of her distress from the way in which God responds to her: He calms her fears by explaining that her pregnancy is strange and unusual because she is carrying twins.

---

19. We assume that Rivkah and Yitzhak shared a desire to have children, though the text does not record Rivkah having prayed for children – as it does in the case of Yitzhak; see below.

20. Rashbam says that indeed it was a normal pregnancy – for twins.

רשב"ם, בראשית כה:כב

ויתרוצצו הבנים בקרבה: לשון רץ לקראת רץ, שהיו רצים ומתנענעים בתוך גופה כדרך עוברים. וכן מן קם מתקוממים מן לן מתלוננים אבל מלשון רצץ עזב דלים הי' לומר וירצצו כמו בטרם יתנגפו רגליכם.

21. Ohr haHayim, Bereishit 25:22.

אור החיים, בראשית כה:כב

אכן פשט הכתוב הוא ויתרוצצו לשון ריצוץ, פירוש היו נדחקים ביותר כשיעור שיהיו מתרוצצים ולא יתקיימו במעיה וזה יורה כי הריונה אינו מתקיים, ותאמר א"כ למה זה אנכי, פירוש "זה" מורה באצבע חוזר אל ההריון, למה אנכי הרה לריק יגעתי, ותלך **לדרוש את ה' פירוש לבקש רחמים על קיום הריונה**, ולדעת דבר הסובב הפסדה כי מן השמים לא יעשה נס לשקר שתפקד בדבר שאינו מתקיים, ולעולם לא הקפידה על צער ההריון כי הצדיקים יסבלו צער גדול בעוה"ז לתכלית טוב הנצחי.

22. Ramban, Bereishit 25:22.

רמב"ן, בראשית כה:כב

ותלך לדרוש את ה': לשון רש"י, להגיד מה יהא בסופה ולא מצאתי דרישה אצל ה' רק להתפלל, כטעם דרשתי את ה' וענני (תהלים לד:ה), דרשוני וחיו (עמוס ה:ד), חי אני אם אדרש לכם (יחזקאל כ:ג).

23. According to Seforno, Rivkah was afraid that she would lose one of the fetuses and her life would then be in danger as well.

ספורנו, בראשית כה:כב

ותאמר אם כן: אחרי שהדבר כן שמתרוצצין ויש לחוש שימות אחד מהם ואסתכן אני בלידה כמנהג בלידת עובר מת. למה זה אנכי. למה זה התאו קרובי שתהיה אני אם הזרע באמרם את היי לאלפי רבבה וכן בעלי שהתפלל עלי בזה.

Still others regard Rivkah's distress as having very little to do with the normal physical and emotional stress of pregnancy, noting that she sought a spiritual remedy for her fears. Rashi explains that her distress stemmed from a strange phenomenon: when she would pass a place of idolatry the baby would stir and try to "escape"; conversely when she would pass the tents of Shem and Ever, a place of spirituality and holiness, the same struggle would ensue.[24] As far as Rivkah knew, she was carrying a single child with a "split personality." Rivkah's concerns had to do with the spiritual conflict[25] she felt within her womb;[26] therefore the knowledge that she was, in fact, carrying two fetuses, two distinct personalities, explains what she was feeling.

But can this answer allay her fears? We are forced to consider Rivkah's earlier prophetic experience: from the moment she saw Yitzhak, she knew that he would have an evil son. Now, the vision is being played out within her, causing her distress that she can address only to God.

Rivkah had removed herself from the corrupt world of Betuel, making a life in the tent of Sarah, married to the most holy man she had ever seen,

---

24. Rashi, Bereishit 25:22.

רש"י, בראשית כה:כב

ויתרוצצו: ע"כ המקרא הזה אומר דורשני שסתם מה היא רציצה זו וכתב אם כן למה זה אנכי. **רבותינו דרשוהו לשון ריצה כשהיתה עוברת על פתחי תורה של שם ועבר יעקב רץ ומפרכס לצאת, עוברת על פתחי ע"א עשו מפרכס לצאת.** ד"א מתרוצצים זה עם זה ומריבים בנחלת שני עולמות. ותאמר אם כן: גדול צער העבור.

25. See *Kol Eliyahu*, Bereishit 25:22.

ספר קול אליהו, בראשית כה:כב

ויתרוצצו הבנים בקרבה ותאמר א"כ למה זה אנכי ותלך לדרוש את ה': יש לפרש עפ"י דרך רמז על פי מה דאיתא בגמרא בכמה דוכתי (פסחים כ"ב, ב"ק מא, קידושין נ"ז, בכורות ו.), שמעון העמסוני היה דורש כל אתין שבתורה כיון שהגיע לאת ה' אלקיך תירא פירש וכו' עד שבא ר' עקיבא ודרש את ה' אלקיך תירא לרבות תלמידי חכמים, והנה רש"י ז"ל פירש כאן בשם המדרש על ה ויתרוצצו הבנים בקרבה כשהיתה עוברת על פתחי ע"ז היה עשו מפרכס לצאת, וכשהיתה עוברת על פתחי שם ועבר היה יעקב רוצה לצאת. והנה רבקה לא היתה יודעת שהם שני עוברים והיתה סוברת שהוא עובר אחד א"כ היה מקום להרהר ח"ו שיש שתי רשויות כיון שהוא עובר אחד ויש שני הפכים בנושא אחד ועל כן הרהרה ותאמר א"כ למה זה אנכי, ר"ל מה שכתוב בעשרת הדברות אנכי ה' אלקיך שהוא נגד מה שאירע לה ברציצה זו לכן ותלך לדרוש את ה' ר"ל לדרוש ה את ה' אלקיך תירא, ויאמר ה' לה שני גוים בבטנך אחד צדיק ואחד רשע, ואל יעלה על דעתך כלל שיש ח"ו שתי רשויות.

26. Rashi, Bereishit 25:22.

רש"י, בראשית כה:כב

לדרוש את ה': שיגיד לה מה תהא בסופה.

son of one of the greatest spiritual giants of all time. Yet at the first moment that she sees this great future unfold before her, when she sees Yitzhak in the field immersed in prayer, she knows that she has not fully broken away from evil. There is a thread of evil even here, and she is unable to escape it. It is surely no coincidence that in the twenty years of infertility Rivkah never availed herself of the solution adopted by Sarah, Rahel and Leah, a solution so common in the ancient world: Rivkah had maidservants who accompanied her from Padan Aram, yet she never suggested that Yitzhak father children with anyone else. Did the knowledge of this evil son yet to be born plant within her some deep-seated ambivalence about having children? Is this the reason she refrained from seeking solutions for their infertility? Is this perhaps the reason that the text never records Rivkah herself praying, asking, hoping for children?

We may say that Rivkah's entire adult life was lived under a cloud, a shadow cast by the vision of Esav that she had on the day she first saw Yitzhak. Our sages express this sense of foreboding in a variety of ways, at various junctures throughout Rivkah's life. In fact, even before Rivkah sees Yitzhak, Midrashic sources point to clues of this problematic destiny:

בראשית רבה , פרשה ס פסקה יד

ותקם רבקה ונערותיה וגו':...רבנן אמרי מה גמל זה יש בו סימן טומאה וסימן טהרה כך העמידה רבקה צדיק ורשע.

"And Rivkah and her maidservants arose":...The rabbis said: As a camel possesses one mark of uncleanness and one of cleanness, so did Rivkah give birth to one righteous and one wicked son. (Bereishit Rabbah 60:14)

Rivkah makes a clean break from the house of Betuel – or so she believes. She chooses the house of Avraham over the house of Betuel, the morality and holiness of Yitzhak over that of Lavan. But even as she turns her back on the corruption and depravity of Padan Aram, she rides away on a camel – symbol of a sort of moral bifurcation or schizophrenia: whereas kosher animals chew their cud and have split hooves, the camel has only one of these indicators of *kashrut*. The Midrash draws a parallel between this "half-and-half" purity of the camel, and Rivkah's destiny as mother of one righteous and one wicked son. The dread of this schism, symbolized by the camel on which she rode into the future and expressing her inability to completely escape the evil of her past, was what caused Rivkah to dismount or fall. She saw that evil would accompany her on her journey; the birth of Esav was inevitable.

As readers, we are left to ponder the inevitability of Esav's birth, the inescapability of evil. What is the source of this seed of evil that grows from the purest, holiest roots? How can it be that Esav is born of the union of Yitzhak and Rivkah? In a seemingly cryptic comment on the verse describing Rivkah's departure from Padan Aram, the Ari"zal transmits a teaching found in the Pirkei d'Rebbi Eliezer:[27]

ספר לקוטי תורה, פרשת חיי שרה

ותרכבנה על הגמלים: דע כי רבקה רכבה על הגמלים רמז לאותו נחש שארז"ל
שהיה כעין גמל ובא סמאל ורכב עליו לפתות את חוה...

"And they rode on the camels": Know that Rivkah riding on a camel is a hint to the serpent that our rabbis say was like a camel; and Sama'el [the Evil One, Satan] rode the camel to seduce Hava...
(Likutei Torah, Parashat Hayei Sarah)

The Ari"zal connects our present subject with a much earlier, much larger moral battle: In the Garden of Eden, the evil inclination utilizes very specific tools to seduce Hava.[28] Satan searched and found the most devious creature for this insidious task – the serpent, who, before the punishment, resembled a camel – either physically, or, more likely, in terms of the misleading symbols of purity. The results of the serpent's efforts are all too familiar to us: Adam and Hava sin, and each of the parties involved is punished in their own way. It is the punishment God metes out to Hava that many see echoed in Rivkah's distress:

---

27. Pirkei d'Rebbi Eliezer, chapter 12.

פרקי דרבי אליעזר (היגר) "חורב", פרק יב
מה עשה סמאל? לקח כת שלו וירד וראה כל הבריות שברא הב"ה בעולמו ולא מצא בהם חכם להרע
כנחש, שנ' והנחש היה ערום, והיה דמותו כמין גמל ועלה ורכב עליו.

28. Pirkei d'Rebbe Eliezer, chapter 21, states that the *rider* of the serpent violated Eve, and she became pregnant with Kayin.

פרקי דרבי אליעזר (היגר) "חורב", פרק כא
בא אליה **רוכב** נחש ועברה את קין, ואחר כך בא אליה אדם ועברה את הבל, שנ' והאדם ידע את חוה
אשתו, מה ידע ידע שהיתה מעוברת וראה את דמותו שלא מן התחתונים אלא מן העליונים.

בראשית ג:טז

אֶל הָאִשָּׁה אָמַר הַרְבָּה אַרְבֶּה עִצְּבוֹנֵךְ וְהֵרֹנֵךְ בְּעֶצֶב תֵּלְדִי בָנִים וְאֶל אִישֵׁךְ
תְּשׁוּקָתֵךְ וְהוּא יִמְשָׁל בָּךְ:

*To the woman He said, "I will greatly multiply the pain of your child
bearing; in sorrow you shall bring forth children; and your desire
shall be to your husband, and he shall rule over you."* (Bereishit 3:16)

While the physical challenges of pregnancy that Rivkah experienced
may be traced back to Hava, the connection seems to run much deeper.
The *Megaleh 'Amukot* explains that Rivkah was "the image of Hava" and
Yitzhak was "the image of Adam": Hava ate from the Tree of Knowledge of
Good and Evil, ingested the moral bifurcation or confusion that this Tree
of Death embodied. Rivkah carried within her two children, two fruits, as it
were – one good, the other evil. Her distress is far beyond the physical: she
seeks advice because she does not understand why her pregnancy should be
entangled in this confusion of good and evil, enmeshed in moral dualism.
She is married to the son of Avraham, to the man who had been offered as
an *'olah* to God. The father of her children is Yitzhak, whom she first sees
out in the field, deep in prayer – in the very place that cursed man must
labor. According to the Midrash, Yitzhak himself had just returned from
Eden.[29] There should be no evil growing from such roots.[30]

Our sages deal with this problem by pointing out that Rivkah's experience
does not precisely replicate the sin of Hava and its aftermath: whereas good
and evil are confused by sin, they are somehow distilled in the course of

---

29. Yalkut Shimoni, Parashat Hayei Sarah, *remez* 109.

ילקוט שמעוני, פרשת חיי שרה רמז קט
ויצא יצחק לשוח בשדה: מהיכן יצא מגן עדן, ותפול מעל הגמל כפי שראתה ברוח הקדש שעתיד לצאת
ממנו עשו הרשע נזדעזעה ונעשית מוכת עץ ממנה דם בתולים ויצא.

30. *Megaleh 'Amukot*, Parashat Toldot.

ספר מגלה עמוקות, פרשת תולדות
ויתרצצו הבנים בקרבה: ידוע שהיא היתה דיוקנא של חוה לתקן רוחה כמו שיצחק בא לתקן רוח של אדם
כן רבקה רוח של חוה וכמו שחוה היתה (בראשית ג) אם כל חי הולידה מעץ הדעת טוב ורע הבל מסטרא
דטוב וקין מסטרא דרע כן רבקה ראתה שאותן שני בנים הראשונים חזרו ובאו לעולם אז אמרה א"כ למה
שהרי רבקה נפלה מעל הגמל. אמרז"ל במדרש ותרכבנה על הגמלים רבנן אמרי גמל זה יש בו סימן טהרה
וסימן טמא כן רבקה העמידה ליצחק א' בן צדיק וא' בן רשע כיון שראתה רבקה את יצחק אור ג"ע
עמו ראתה סוף טומאה לצאת ממנה.

this miraculous pregnancy. The *Be'er Mayim Hayim* suggests that in utero, a clarification takes place, and good and evil are clearly divided – perhaps for the first time since before the sin.[31] This process alone would explain the turmoil Rivkah felt, even justify her discomfort. But this seems to be an insufficient answer for Rivkah; she questions why the evil should exist within her at all. God's answer is quite clear: like the birth of Kayin and Hevel after the sin, Rivkah will give birth to two sons. The fate of these two sons, of these two distinct moral entities, is conflict. These two sons are part of a process that will reverse the sin committed in Eden, and bring an end to the confusion of good and evil. Just as Rivkah rides the camel, subjugating the evil it represents, so her son Yaakov's destiny is to confront evil, to persevere, and to vanquish it. Even before his birth, he begins to fulfill that destiny – a destiny that we may find encoded within the punishment of the serpent:

בראשית ג:יד–טו

וַיֹּאמֶר ה' אֱלֹקִים אֶל הַנָּחָשׁ כִּי עָשִׂיתָ זֹּאת אָרוּר אַתָּה מִכָּל הַבְּהֵמָה וּמִכֹּל חַיַּת הַשָּׂדֶה עַל גְּחֹנְךָ תֵלֵךְ וְעָפָר תֹּאכַל כָּל יְמֵי חַיֶּיךָ: וְאֵיבָה אָשִׁית בֵּינְךָ וּבֵין הָאִשָּׁה וּבֵין זַרְעֲךָ וּבֵין זַרְעָהּ הוּא יְשׁוּפְךָ רֹאשׁ וְאַתָּה תְּשׁוּפֶנּוּ **עָקֵב**:

*And the Almighty God said to the serpent, "Because you have done this, you are cursed above all cattle, and above every beast of the field; upon your belly shall you go, and dust shall you eat all the days of your life. And I will put enmity between you and the woman, and between your offspring and her offspring; he [man] shall bruise your head, and you shall bruise his **heel** ('akev). (Bereishit 3:14–15)*

---

31. *Be'er Mayim Hayim*, Parashat Toldot, chapter 25.

ספר באר מים חיים, פרשת תולדות פרק כה

וידע אשר יצא עוד מיצחק איזה בן לא טוב וסבר אברהם שיתקן זה כי כל הכל בידי שמים וכו' וביקש דוקא אחר רבקה הצדקת כי אולי על ידי זכות יצחק וזכות רבקה לא ימצא פסולת בזרעו כמאמר חז"ל (ברכות י.) שאמר חזקיה לישעיהו הב לי ברתך אולי על ידי זכותא דידי ודידך הוין לי בנין דמעלי וכו', ואכן כל זה לא הועיל כי הן אמת אשר אפשר ביצחק לא היה עוד שום פסולת וזוהמא כי כבר יצא זוהמת אברהם בישמעאל, ומעת הגמל את יצחק אמרו חז"ל (בראשית רבה נג:י) שנגמל מיצר הרע ואחר כך נתקדש בהר המוריה, ואך רבקה אמנו מצד שהיה אביה רשע ואחיה רשע וכל משפחתה רשעים,... ונודע אומרם (בבא בתרא קי.) רוב בנים דומין וכו' וכמו שכתב הרב הקדוש בעל אור החיים זללה"ה ועל כן הוכרח לצאת ממנה עשו הרשע לשטף בטנה לשאוב כל הזוהמא והפסולת, שיצא יעקב נקי וזך מכל וכל ועל כן היה נמצא בעשו נשמות מתוקנים היטב כמו נשמות שמעיה ואבטליון ושאר גירי צדק הבאים מאתו כי זה היה מכח יצחק אבינו שהניח קדושתו בו.

The name that this son of Rivkah is given at birth is completely enveloped in his destiny. "Yaakov" reflects the struggle that Rivkah sensed was going on inside her, in which good and evil were separated, distilled or refined into two distinct forms. It is a name that reflects an ongoing struggle between good and evil which began with the Serpent and remains unresolved.

Yaakov's role is not an easy one. He confronts evil in many ways, using all the tools he can muster. At one point, he follows Rivkah's command and goes so far as to put on Esav's clothes – garments of treachery which, according to tradition, were passed down from the nefarious Nimrod, and had once belonged to Kayin, who had received them from Adam.[32] To confront evil, Yaakov dons these garments; he recreates a confusion of good and evil, fighting a wicked and devious enemy with his own sword, as it were.

No one is better equipped to fight evil than Yaakov, who was born to the task. Encapsulated within his name is an expression of his destiny; it is an expression of the identity that Yaakov maintains until the point that he struggles with evil and emerges victorious – though not unscathed. Only then does Yaakov, who attacked the heel of his nemesis and stood his ground in the face of evil, become Yisrael.[33]

From the very beginning, Rivkah's vision was perfect where Yitzhak's was clouded. Rivkah had a clear vision of the future, a firm grasp of the roles each of her sons would play. She had no illusions about Esav, nor did she have any doubt that Yaakov would have to use any means at his disposal to face evil and defeat it. God's message to her may not have given her

---

32. See Rabbeinu Bahya, Bereishit 3:21, and the footnotes by Rabbi Haim Dov Chavel in the Mosad Harav Kook edition (Jerusalem, 1977).

רבינו בחיי, בראשית ג:כא

ויעש ה' אלהים לאדם ולאשתו כתנות עור:... ודעת רז"ל שהיו לבושים הללו מצוייירין שם כל מיני עופות שבעולם, ואדם הורישם לקין, וכשנהרג קין באו לידו של נמרוד, הוא שכתוב: (בראשית י:ט) הוא היה גבור ציד וגו'. וכשהרג עשו לנמרוד נטלן עשו ממנו, והוא שכתוב: (בראשית כז:טו) "את בגדי עשו בנה הגדול החמודות", מאי "החמודות", שחמדן מנמרוד.

כתר יונתן, בראשית כז:טו

ותקח רבקה את בגדי עשו בנה הגדול חמודות שהיו מאדם הראשון וביום ההוא לא לבשם עשו ונשארו אצלה בביתה ותלבש את יעקב בנה הקטן.

33. For an extensive discussion of the significance of this name, see below, "Yaakov – or Yisrael?"

comfort, but it gave her perspective and purpose: We cannot escape evil; since the sin in Eden, evil has become internalized in us all. What we can do is live up to the destiny to which Yaakov and his descendants were born: to face up to Esav, to persevere against evil, and with God's help, defeat it.

The Voice – and Hands – of Yaakov

בראשית כה:כד–כו

וַיִּמְלְאוּ יָמֶיהָ לָלֶדֶת וְהִנֵּה תוֹמִם בְּבִטְנָהּ: וַיֵּצֵא הָרִאשׁוֹן אַדְמוֹנִי כֻּלּוֹ כְּאַדֶּרֶת
שֵׂעָר וַיִּקְרְאוּ שְׁמוֹ עֵשָׂו: וְאַחֲרֵי כֵן יָצָא אָחִיו וְיָדוֹ אֹחֶזֶת בַּעֲקֵב עֵשָׂו וַיִּקְרָא שְׁמוֹ
יַעֲקֹב וְיִצְחָק בֶּן שִׁשִּׁים שָׁנָה בְּלֶדֶת אֹתָם:

*And her days to bear were complete, and lo, twins [were] in her
womb; and the first came out all red, as hairy as a fur cloak, and
they called him Esav. And afterwards his brother came out, his hand
taking hold of Esav's heel, and he called him Yaakov; and Yitzhak
was sixty years old when they were born.* (Bereishit 25:24–26)

Two children are born, twin boys, yet despite having the same parents, they
seem so different from one another. Certain differences are implied, others
are explicit, yet it may actually be their similarity that is being hidden.
The first son born is described as "red and hairy." There is no physical
description offered of the second son. The text says only that Yaakov's
hand latched onto Esav's heel. Was Yaakov also redheaded? From the later
narrative we may conclude that Yaakov was in fact less hairy, but the lack
of symmetry seems strange.

The text continues:

בראשית כה:כז–כח

וַיִּגְדְּלוּ הַנְּעָרִים וַיְהִי עֵשָׂו אִישׁ יֹדֵעַ צַיִד אִישׁ שָׂדֶה וְיַעֲקֹב אִישׁ תָּם יֹשֵׁב אֹהָלִים:
וַיֶּאֱהַב יִצְחָק אֶת עֵשָׂו כִּי צַיִד בְּפִיו וְרִבְקָה אֹהֶבֶת אֶת יַעֲקֹב:

*And the boys grew, and Esav was a man skilled in hunting, a man of
the field; and Yaakov [was] a plain [or perfect, or innocent] man, a
dweller of tents. And Yitzhak loved Esav, for [his] hunting [is] in his
mouth; and Rivkah loves Yaakov.* (Bereishit 25:27–28)

Again we note the lack of symmetry: Esav is a hunting man, while Yaakov
is described as *ish tam*, which can be understood as a plain, simple, perfect

or complete man. The verse continues: Esav was a man of the field while Yaakov inhabited tents – not a "man of the tents" as we would have expected. But the most serious lack of symmetry refers to the affection of their parents. Esav is loved for a reason, for utility – he brings his father the hunt that he procures. Here the contrast is striking: Rivkah (simply) loves Yaakov – no reason, no explanation, no utility.

How are we to understand Yitzhak's love for Esav? Why would a spiritual giant like Yitzhak be swayed by venison? Rashi understands Esav's hunting skills in a metaphorical sense, explaining that Esav possessed a gift of "hunting with words." He would capture his victims with impressive banter. Rashi says that Yitzhak was taken in by Esav's feigned sincerity. Esav would ask his father questions that gave the impression that Esav, too, was steeped in spiritual and halakhic inquiry. Rashi paints Esav the "hunter" as a sycophant, using his slick tongue to convince his father of his noble character.

רש״י, בראשית כה:כז

יודע ציד: לצוד ולרמות את אביו בפיו ושואלו, "אבא, היאך מעשרין את המלח ואת התבן?" כסבור אביו שהוא מדקדק במצות.

"Skilled in hunting": He "hunted," and deceived his father. He asked, "Father, how does one take tithes from salt or straw?" His father believed that he [Esav] was scrupulous in his performance of commandments. (Rashi, Bereishit 25:27)

There are two types of deceitful people. The first has a fairly accurate sense of self, and fools others by not allowing them to see his true identity. The second type may be much more dangerous, for he deceives not only others, but himself as well. Which was Esav? The Midrash gives us a deeper acquaintance with Esav, by relating the events of his demise and his bizarre "burial." When Yaakov passed away, his children fulfilled his instructions and took his remains out of Egypt, back to the Land of Israel, to the Cave of Makhpeilah, where Avraham and Sarah, Yitzhak and Rivkah, and Leah were all buried. At the entrance to the cave they were accosted by Esav, who insisted that the Cave of Makhpeilah should be his burial ground, inherited by his right as the oldest son. A member of the funeral party is sent to bring the deed of sale in hopes of clarifying the issue. Meanwhile, one of Yaakov's grandchildren, Hushim[1] the son of Dan, takes sword in hand, and with a mighty blow separates Esav from his head. The head rolls away, coming to a stop inside the cave, where it lands in the bosom of Yitzhak who tightly holds onto the head of his beloved son.[2]

Esav's head did have a place in the cave, it was his hands that could not quite make it inside. This would seem to indicate that Esav's words were sincere, but he failed miserably when it came to the implementation. Tragically, he was a man unable to live up to his own ideals. When he asked his father about tithes, he meant it. Presumably, Yitzhak was capable of spotting insincerity. His suspicions were not aroused because Esav was, in fact, quite sincere.

There is, nonetheless, an aspect of deceit in the story of Yaakov and Esav – and the deceit is not perpetrated by Esav. The deception is in the hands of Yaakov, carried out according to the instructions of his mother Rivkah. When Yaakov stands before his dying father and receives the blessing Yitzhak intended for Esav, he is dressed as Esav and bears the food that his father had requested of Esav.

בראשית כז:כ–כב

וַיֹּאמֶר יִצְחָק אֶל בְּנוֹ מַה זֶּה מִהַרְתָּ לִמְצֹא בְּנִי וַיֹּאמֶר כִּי הִקְרָה ה' אֱלֹקֶיךָ לְפָנָי: וַיֹּאמֶר יִצְחָק אֶל יַעֲקֹב גְּשָׁה נָּא וַאֲמֻשְׁךָ בְּנִי הַאַתָּה זֶה בְּנִי עֵשָׂו אִם לֹא: וַיִּגַּשׁ יַעֲקֹב אֶל יִצְחָק אָבִיו וַיְמֻשֵּׁהוּ וַיֹּאמֶר הַקֹּל קוֹל יַעֲקֹב וְהַיָּדַיִם יְדֵי עֵשָׂו:

And Yitzhak said to his son, "What [is] this you have hastened to find, my son?" and he said, "That which the Almighty, your God, has caused to come before me." And Yitzhak said to Yaakov, "Come near,

---

1. Hushim is in a sense the inverse of Yitzhak: his sense of sight is intact but he is deaf, making him impervious to Esav's deceit. See below, Parashat Vayehi, "Salvation," note 14.

2. See Pirkei d'Rebbi Eliezer, chapter 38.

פרקי דרבי אליעזר (היגר) "חורב", פרק לח

וכשבאו למערת המכפלה בא עליהם עשו מהר חורב לחחרחר ריב ואמ' שלי הוא מערת המכפלה מה עשה יוסף שלח לרכוש מזלות ולירד למצרים ולעלות כתב עולם שהיה בינם לכך הלך נפתלי שהוא אילה שלוחה חושים בן דן היה פגום באזנו ובלשונו אמ' להם מפני מה אנחנו יושבין כאן הראהו באצבעו אמ' לו בשביל האיש הזה שאינו מניח אותנו לקבור את יעקב שלף את חרבו והתיז את ראשו של עשו ונכנס הראש לתוך מערת המכפלה ואת גוייתו שלח לארץ אחוזתו בהר שעיר מה עשה יצחק אחז בראשו של עשו והיה מתפלל לפני הב"ה ואמ' לפניו רבון כל העולמים יוחן רשע בל למד צדק יוחן רשע זה שלא למד כל המצות שבתורה שנ' בל למד צדק ועל ארץ ישראל ועל מערת המכפלה בעול הוא מדבר שנ' בארץ נכוחות יעול השיבתו רוח הקדש ואמרה אני אני לא יראה גאות ה' שנ' בל יראה גאות ה'.

*I pray you, and I will feel you, my son, whether you [are] he, my son
Esav, or not." And Yaakov came to Yitzhak his father, and he felt him,
and said, "The voice [is] the voice of Yaakov, and the hands [are] the
hands of Esav." (Bereishit 27:20–22)*

In what way are these the words of Yaakov? Is it the mode of speaking, the
inflection of his voice, or is it the content? Rashi[3] believes it is the content:
it would have been characteristic of Yaakov, and not of Esav, to give God
credit for having found his prey quickly. The Ramban[4] reminds us that as
twin brothers,[5] their voices may have been more similar than we might
care to imagine. It is not the voice, then, that arouses Yitzhak's suspicion,
but the content of the speech that is somehow incongruous. Clearly,
Yitzhak senses that something is amiss; why does he continue? If he was
truly troubled or unsure of the identity of the recipient of his blessing,
when faced with conflicting evidence, he should have waited until more
conclusive information could be gathered.[6]

Perhaps to understand the underlying issue we need to learn more about
the hands of Yaakov. When we first meet Yaakov, long before he finds

---

3. Rashi, Bereishit 27:22.

רש"י, בראשית כז:כב

קול יעקב: שמדבר בלשון תחנונים קום נא אבל עשו בלשון קנטוריא דבר יקום אבי.

4. Ramban, Bereishit 27:12.

רמב"ן, בראשית כז:יב

ואני תמה, איך לא פחד מהיכר הקול, וכל בני אדם נכרים בקולם, כמו שאמרו רבותינו (גיטין כג) היאך
סומא מותר באשתו, והיאך בני אדם מותרין בנשותיהן בלילה, אלא בטביעות עינא דקלא ואם סתם
בני אדם מכירין כן, מה יהיה ביצחק, החכם והנבקי להכיר בין בניו, שתהיה לו באמת טביעות בקול אולי
היו האחים האלה דומים בקולם ולכך אמרו (ב"ר סה:יט) כי הקול קול יעקב, דבריו, שמדבר בלשון רכה
ומזכיר שם שמים או שהיה משנה קולו לדבר כלשון אחיו, כי יש בבני אדם יודעים לעשות כן.

5. Rashbam (Bereishit 27:22) points out that as twins their voices would likely have
    sounded the same or similar.

רשב"ם, בראשית כז:כב

הקול קול יעקב: לפי שתאומים היו היה קולן דומות קצת זה לזה ולכך טעה יצחק בקולו מאחר שמצאו
איש שער על צוארו.

6. See the remarkable explanation of the *Beit haLevi*, who suggests that Esav, knowing
    that Yaakov might "try something," devised a plan: Esav told his father that he, Esav,
    will come and speak like Yaakov. Esav reasoned that if Yaakov came dressed as Esav, he
    would surely speak like Esav. Yaakov did, indeed, come dressed as Esav, but he spoke in
    his own voice. He spoke as Yaakov.

his voice, we see him using his hands: "And afterwards his brother came out, his hand taking hold of Esav's heel."[7] Perhaps this *in utero* scene foreshadows a later episode where again Yaakov uses his hands to wrestle with a "man"[8] identified as the heavenly protector of Esav.[9] Ironically, this *sar shel Esav* begs Yaakov to release him, for the time has come for him to use his voice - to pray.[10] Here, then, is the paradigm reversed: the hands of Yaakov and the voice of Esav!

We may say that the voice of Yaakov and the hands of Esav have been established as theological concepts: the former represents prayer and Torah while the latter represent tyranny and idolatry - rebellion against God.[11] Whereas the voice is an expression of something internal, hands

---

בית הלוי, בראשית כז:כב

הקול קול יעקב והידים ידי עשו, ולא הכירו ויברך אותו: לכאורה יש להבין כיון דההכרה של הקול היה נגד ההכרה של הידים במאי הכריע שהוא עשו וברכו. ולולא דמסתפינא היה אפשר לומר דהרי יצחק הרבה לבודקו אם הוא באמת עשו או הוא מטעה אותו. וי"ל דגם בתחילה נתיירא מזה וקודם שהלך מיצחק אמר לאביו סימן שיוודע שהוא עשו שישנה קולו כקולו של יעקב ולדבר בנחת כיעקב ולהזכיר שם שמים וזהו סימן שהוא עשו דאם יבא יעקב להטעותו הרי מסתמא ישנה הוא קולו שידמה כקול עשו. ועיין ברמב"ן שכתב על הא דאמר יעקב אולי ימושני אבי והא דלא נתיירא יותר שיכירו ע"י הקול משום דיכול לשנות כקולו של עשו. וזהו שאמר הקול קול יעקב והידים ידי עשו הרי שני הסימנים מתאימים ולא הכירו וע"כ ויברך אותו. וי"ל עוד דיעקב בשכלו הבין גם את סוד זה ומש"ה לא שינה קולו ודבר כדרכו. וזהו שאמר הכתוב בא אחיך במרמה ותרגם אונקלוס בא אחך בחוכמא, ולכאורה מרמה וחכמה הם שני עניינים, רק לפי הנ"ל הכל אחד דהמרמה הוא מה שלא עשה מרמה ודיבר כדרכו ולמרמה כזה לא יקרא מרמה רק חכמה שהבין כל זה שאין צריך לו לעשות מרמה רק דיבר כדרכו, ועשו נלכד ע"י ערמתו.

7. Bereishit 25:26.

8. Bereishit 32:25.

9. Rashi, Bereishit 32:25.

10. Rashi, Bereishit 32:27.

11. See Talmud Bavli Gittin 57b.

תלמוד בבלי, מסכת גיטין דף נז עמוד ב

הקול קול יעקב והידים ידי עשו, הקול – זה אדריינוס קיסר, שהרג באלכסנדריא של מצרים ששים רבוא על ששים רבוא כפלים כיוצאי מצרים; קול יעקב – זה אספסיינוס קיסר, שהרג בכרך ביתר ארבע מאות רבוא, ואמרי לה ארבעת אלפים רבוא – זו מלכות הרשעה, שהחריבה את בתינו, ושרפה את היכלנו, והגליתנו מארצנו. דבר אחר: הקול קול יעקב – אין לך תפלה שמועלת שאין בה מזרעו של יעקב; והידים ידי עשו – אין לך מלחמה שנוצחת שאין בה מזרעו של עשו. והיינו דא"ר אלעזר: (איוב ה) בשוט לשון תחבא – בחירחורי לשון תחבא.

"'The voice of Yaakov': this is the cry caused by the emperor Vespasian who killed in the city of Betar four hundred thousand myriads, or as some say, four thousand myriads. 'The hands are the hands of Esav': this is the government of Rome which has destroyed our House and burnt our Temple and driven us out of our land. Another explanation is

are external. Hands are a symbol of force. The strength they represent is part of the commonality that man shares with the animal kingdom, but the voice is *ruah* – air or spirit, emanating from within. Voice is what man has in common with God. It is the result of God's breath within us, which animates, gives existence and human identity.[12] That the realm of Yaakov is primarily one of "voice" should not surprise us. That the realm of Esav is primarily "hands" should also not surprise us.[13] To our dismay, the biblical text does not conveniently align itself into these neat categories. In some instances, as we have seen, Yaakov uses his hands and the spiritual power of Esav's voice is revealed.

From birth we see Esav as being more externally oriented. He is born covered with hair and he looks "complete," almost grown. He is therefore called "Esav," from the word *'asui* – formed, "completed." Of course, even a completely formed infant has much emotional, physical and spiritual growth ahead of him. Esav's outer-directed qualities may explain an obscure midrash[14] which says that of the nonkosher animals Esav resembles the pig: The pig[15] has split hooves, so outwardly it looks kosher. Only when

---

[as follows]: 'The voice is the voice of Yaakov': no prayer is effective unless the seed of Yaakov has a part in it. 'The hands are the hands of Esav': no war is successful unless the seed of Esav has a share in it. This is what R. Elazar said: 'You shall be hidden from the scourge of the tongue' (Iyov 5:21) – this means, you shall be protected from the heated contests of the tongue."

12. See Bereishit 2:7 and the translation of Onkelos: God breathes life into Man, and Man becomes a "living being." Onkelos renders this phrase as "speaking being."

בראשית ב:ז

וַיִּיצֶר ה' אֱלֹקִים אֶת הָאָדָם עָפָר מִן הָאֲדָמָה וַיִּפַּח בְּאַפָּיו נִשְׁמַת חַיִּים וַיְהִי הָאָדָם לְנֶפֶשׁ חַיָּה:

תרגום אונקלוס, בראשית ב:ז

ובְרָא ה' אלקים ית אדם עפרא מן ארעא ונפח באפוהי נשמתא דחיי והות באדם לרוח ממללא.

13. When Hushim kills Esav he does so with a sword. When Yitzhak refers to the hands of Esav he describes them as having a sword in them. See Bereishit 27:40.

בראשית כז:מ

וְעַל חַרְבְּךָ תִחְיֶה וְאֶת אָחִיךָ תַּעֲבֹד וְהָיָה כַּאֲשֶׁר תָּרִיד וּפָרַקְתָּ עֻלּוֹ מֵעַל צַוָּארֶךָ:

"And by your sword will you live, and your brother will you serve; and it will come to pass that when you rule, you will break his yoke from off your neck."

14. See Bereishit Rabbah 65:1.

15. The *Shlah haKadosh* sees Yaakov and Esav in one womb as representing the Tree of Knowledge of Good and Evil. He continues to say that according to some midrashim the pig will one day repent (the word *hazir* – Hebrew for pig – shares the root *hazar*,

you look internally and see that it doesn't chew its cud do you realize that despite outward appearances it is a nonkosher animal.[16]

When Esav and Yaakov are alone, Esav lets his guard down, showing his true inner self. When he comes in from the field famished and asks to be fed, the precise word that he uses is instructive: *hal'iteini*, "pour into my mouth."[17] Rashi explains that this verb is used to describe the feeding of a camel.[18] Like the pig, camels also possess only one of the two kosher symbols[19] (camels ruminate but do not have split hooves). Esav's self-definition is that deep inside he is good – even though externally he makes mistakes.

Despite the identification of Esav with Rome, and later Christendom, in rabbinic literature Esav is seen as a Jew – a sinful, rebellious Jew, but a Jew

---

which means "return"). The ultimate messianic vision is for evil to be elevated into good. For more on the pig's return, see my article "When Pigs Fly." An electronic copy can be found at http://www.aish.com/torahportion/moray/When_Pigs_Fly.asp.

ספר השל"ה הקדוש, פרשת חיי שרה תורה אור (ב)

וענין יצחק תיקן התפשטות עץ הדעת טוב ורע, הם יעקב ועשו נולדו תאומים. כי גם הרע יתוקן, כמו שאמרו רז"ל (תרגי"ו בראשית נ:יג) רישא דעשו מונח בעטפיה דיצחק, סוד החזרת הרע למוטב, בסוד עתיד חזיר לטהר. וישחוט הקב"ה מלאך המות, דהיינו בלע המות לנצח, וישאר מלאך.

16. See Rav Tzadok haKohen, *Kometz haMinhah*, part 2, section 62, for an expansion of this idea.

ספר קומץ המנחה, חלק ב אות סב

במעשה לעשו שאף על פי שהוא הפסולת מרחם כנזכר לעיל (אות סא) זהו מצד ההריון והנעלם אבל נגלהו היה נראה קדוש מרחם וכמו שאמרו (בראשית רבה סה:א) פושט טלפיו כחזיר וכו' שהרגל מורה על המעשה והסימן השני מעלת גרה שהוא שלימות האכילה מורה על הפנימיית.

17. Bereishit 25:30.

בראשית כה:ל

וַיֹּאמֶר עֵשָׂו אֶל יַעֲקֹב הַלְעִיטֵנִי נָא מִן הָאָדֹם הָאָדֹם הַזֶּה כִּי עָיֵף אָנֹכִי עַל כֵּן קָרָא שְׁמוֹ אֱדוֹם:

18. Rashi, Bereishit 25:30.

רש"י, בראשית כה:ל

הלעיטני: אפתח פי ושפוך הרבה לתוכה, כמו ששנינו אין אובסין את הגמל אבל מלעיטין אותו.

19. When Rivkah first sees her husband-to-be she falls off her camel: "And Rivkah lifted up her eyes, and saw Yitzhak, and she fell from the camel" (Bereishit 24:64). Rashi explains that she understood at that moment that just as the camel has one kosher sign and one nonkosher sign, she to will have one kosher son and one nonkosher one.

בראשית כד:סד

וַתִּשָּׂא רִבְקָה אֶת עֵינֶיהָ וַתֵּרֶא אֶת יִצְחָק וַתִּפֹּל מֵעַל הַגָּמָל:

בראשית רבה, פרשה ס פסקה יד

אמרי מה גמל זה יש בו סימן טומאה וסימן טהרה כך העמידה רבקה צדיק ורשע.

nonetheless.[20] He is portrayed as a person born into the best of families, who made his choices and eventually left the fold. Mystical writers draw a parallel to another character from Jewish history, a unique soul who makes the opposite journey, coming from a modest background and rising to the spiritual aristocracy of Judaism.

His name was Akiva. We are told that he didn't have *"zekhut avot"*[21] (ancestral merit) – either he or his father converted to Judaism. The Ari"zal[22] asserts that when Esav spoke to his father, it was Akiva's voice that Yitzhak heard: deep within the recesses of Esav's soul was a Rabbi Akiva trying to get out. The name Akiva is a variant form of the name Yaakov. Similarly, this is the aspect of Yaakov within Esav, the voice of Yaakov within Esav struggling to express itself.

Rabbi Akiva seems to combine many of the elements of both Yaakov and Esav. Like Yaakov, Rabbi Akiva is impoverished. After having great difficulty with his father-in-law, he marries a woman named Rahel, and her father disinherits them.[23] The Gemara describes the scene with great tenderness: Destitute, they have nothing but the straw on which they sleep.

---

20. See Talmud Bavli Kiddushin 18a.

21. See Talmud Bavli Brakhot 27b, Rashbetz in *Magen Avot*; Avot 3:13 says that Akiva's father Yosef was a convert.

22. See, for example, the *Meor Einayim*, Parashat Toldot.

ספר מאור עינים, פרשת תולדות

ואיתא בכתבי האר״י ז״ל שיצחק אהב את עשו כי ציד בפיו כי נשמת רבי עקיבא היתה מדברת מפיו כי היתה כלולה בו בבחינת ראש של עשו ותבין כל זה עם מה שכתוב למעלה כי הוא היה באמת רע גמור אך שראה יצחק שבשעת דבורו עמו היה משיג יצחק בתוכו נשמת רבי עקיבא שהוא מבחינת נשמות הקדושת שבאים לחיותו ואף שהיה יצחק אבינו ע״ה מרכבה לו יתברך ובודאי לא היה אפשר לעשו לרמותו כמו שנראה מהים אך הוא מובן עם מ״ש ומטעם זה תבין גם כן איך נתאחדו שניהם יעקב אבינו ע״ה שהיה מובחר שבאבות מרכבה להשם יתברך עם עשו שהוא רע גמור ולמה לא בראם השם יתברך שיוולדו לכל הפחות זה אחר זה בשני עבורין וגם תמוה שיהי בבטן צדקת כרבקה ואף שיהיה שניהם כאחד במקור אחד אך שרצה הבורא ברוך הוא על ידי השקפתו הגודלה שיעקב אבינו צריך דווקא לברר ממנו הניצוצות הקדושים ההם ונדע כי מי שרציף להעלות שום דבר המונח למטה צריך לשתות ולירד עד המקום ההוא למען יאחז בהדבר שרציף להעלותו לכך הוצרך שיתאחדו במקום אחד בבת אחת בקירוב גדול בכדי שיוכל לברר ממנו הקדושה המלובשת בו שהוא רע בעצם על ידי מותרות וסיגי הדין שביצחק כנודע ויתחיל לברר מיד ביצירתן על ידי התאחדותן ביחד במקור אחד וזהו ידו אוחזת בעקב עשו כי עקב הוא לשון הילוך כי כל הלוכן והנהגתן של העמים הוא על ידי הקדושה המלובשת בהן ואחז יעקב בעקב הנ״ל לברר בו כן כך בדורות הבאין מבני יעקב שהלכו בעקבותיו כמו רבי שבירר גם כן והוציא לאור נשמת אנטונינוס.

23. See Talmud Bavli Nedarim 50a:

Akiva lovingly picks stray bits of straw from Rahel's hair and says that one day he will buy her a beautiful piece of jewelry – Jerusalem of Gold. Just then, a poor man comes to the door; his wife, he says, has just given birth and they do not even have straw for a bed on which she may lie. Akiva and Rahel then share their one and only possession in a joyous act of *tzedakah* (charity): Rabbi Akiva gives tithes even from straw, providing an answer to the cynical question Esav posed to deceive his doting father. In fact, Esav's question was actually Akiva's question, or Akiva's confirmation that acts of charity are always possible, regardless of financial status or social station.[24]

When Esav comes in from the field, hungry and tired, he approaches Yaakov and offers to trade responsibilities. Esav is willing to sell the birthright for a bowl of porridge. This is not a case of someone bartering something that they regard as valueless; on the contrary, a strong emotional response is evoked: "Esav disdained the birthright" (Bereishit 25:34).

But what did the birthright mean to him? What were the privileges? What were the responsibilities that he so despised? Why did he shirk these responsibilities? There was not yet any religious or ritual distinction for the first born, no Beit haMikdash or requirement of service. There is only

---

תלמוד בבלי מסכת נדרים דף נ עמוד א

ר' עקיבא איתקדשת ליה ברתיה (דבר) [דכלבא שבוע], שמע (בר) כלבא שבוע אדרה הנאה מכל נכסיה, אזלא ואיתנסיבה ליה. בסיתוא הוה גנו בי תיבנא, הוה קא מנקיט ליה תיבנא מן מזייה, אמר לה: אי הואי לי, רמינא ליך ירושלים דדהבא. אתא אליהו אידמי להון כאנשא וקא קרי אבבא, אמר להו: הבו לי פורתא דתיבנא, דילדת אתתי ולית לי מידעם לאגונה. אמר לה ר' עקיבא לאנתתיה: חזי גברא דאפילו תיבנא לא אית ליה. אמרה ליה: זיל הוי בי רב.

"The daughter of Kalba Savua betrothed herself to R. Akiva. When her father heard thereof, he vowed that she was not to benefit from any of his property. Then she went and married him in winter. They slept on straw, and he had to pick out the straw from her hair. 'If only I could afford it,' he said to her, 'I would present you with a golden Jerusalem.' [Later] Eliyahu came to them in the guise of a mortal, and cried out at the door. 'Give me some straw, for my wife is in confinement and I have nothing for her to lie on.' 'See!' R. Akiva observed to his wife. 'There is a man who lacks even straw.' [Subsequently] she counselled him, 'Go, and become a scholar.'"

24. See the *Meor Einayim*, Parashat Toldot.

ספר מאור עינים, פרשת תולדות

ונודע כי רבי עקיבא נשא בתחילה את בת כלבא שבוע והדירו ממנו הנאה והיו שוכבין על תבן ובא אליהו ז"ל ואדמי ליה כגברא עניא ובקש מהם תבן דאמרו שאשתו ילדה וצריכה לשכב על תבן ונתן לו רבי עקיבא תבן וזהו מדה טובה מאוד וכל זה צפה והשיג יצחק אבינו ע"ה כי בשעת דבורו עמו היה אומר לו רצה לומר היה מדבר עמו אותו ניצוץ הקדוש שעתיד ליתן צדקה מתבן שהוא רמז על נשמת רבי עקיבא והבן.

one thing that Esav could have had in mind: the covenant God made with Avraham. Avraham's descendants are chosen; they will be blessed above all others. But with these great blessings comes an extended period of slavery. Four hundred years of subjugation must be endured before the blessings come to fruition. The path to Mount Sinai travels through Egypt, and the long detour will bring with it blood, sweat and tears – and a lot of hard work. That is what intimidated Esav. The man of great physical strength is out of his depth, subdued. He may well use his hands, but he does not relish hard work. Esav would not willingly submit to subjugation, would not willingly accept a role of weakness. Esav lived in the here and now, and disdained any rewards that were not immediate. Not so Yaakov and his descendants: Yaakov and his children take the longer view. They are ready and willing to suffer short-term hardship in their quest to be a part of the great destiny that God promised Avraham. Yaakov – and later, his descendants – are willing to suffer exile and subjugation. They accept their own enslavement. The hard work does not intimidate them, and they are liberated when they find their voice, the voice of Yaakov, and cry to God in prayer.

When the end of their enslavement finally arrives, as the Jews leave Egypt and approach Mount Sinai, they are accosted by the tribe of Amalek, descendants of Esav who are unhappy with the reversal of fortunes and destinies.[25] Their military attack on the Children of Israel would have made Esav proud. But things have changed: Yehoshua[26] is sent to lead the Jews, to fight back with the sword. The children of Yaakov literally fight fire with fire, taking up arms in a manner that may be more like Esav than like Yaakov. And while this scene unfolds on the battlefield, up on the mountain Moshe prays for victory. While the image of Moshe lifting his voice in prayer is one we have no trouble imagining, it is *how* Moshe prays that is striking: he lifts his hands in prayer. "And it came to pass,

---

25. When Esav came to stop the burial of Yaakov we are told he came from Horev – Sinai. Apparently, Hevron was not the only inheritance Esav wanted. He dreamed of the Torah from Sinai as well. See Pirkei d'Rebbi Eliezer, chapter 38.

פרקי דרבי אליעזר (היגר) "חורב", פרק לח

וכשבאו למערת המכפלה בא עליהם עשו מהר חורב לחחר ריב ואמ' שלי הוא מערת המכפלה מה עשה יוסף שלח לרכוש מזלות ולירד למצרים ולעלות כתב עולם שהיה בינם.

26. Yehoshua is a man of the tent. See Shmot 33:11.

when Moshe held up his hands, Israel prevailed; and when he let down his hands, Amalek prevailed" (Shmot 17:11). When the voice and the hands are completely united, Esav/Amalek can be defeated.[27] Only then can the Jews continue to Mount Sinai.[28] Only then will they "see the sounds" of the greatest revelation mankind has ever known. Once they have elevated their hands, the sounds, too, can be elevated.

Esav was willing to take the shortcut to Hevron, and the shortcut to Horev.[29] But the long, hard work that is necessary for real spiritual growth was foreign to him, even disdained by him. This is the true difference between the two brothers, and the greatness of Yaakov and his descendants.

The ultimate merger of lifting hands and prayer is the blessing of the *kohanim*. Hands are lifted in peace, not in war; in love rather than in anger. Ironically, the name Esav has the same numerical value as *shalom*, peace (376). While Esav may have the voice of Yaakov within him, his hands

---

27. This idea can be found in the Mabit, *Beit Elokim, Sha'ar haTefilah* chapter 18.

ספר בית אלקים, שער התפילה פרק שמנה עשר

תפלת משה על עמלק, (שמות יז) והיה כאשר ירים משה ידו וגבר ישראל וגו', במכילתא וכי ידיו של משה מגברות את ישראל או ידיו שוברות את עמלק, אלא כ"ז שהיה משה מגביה את ידיו למעלה היו ישראל מסתכלין בו ומאמינים במי שפקד את משה לעשות כן והמקום עושה להם נסים וגבורות. בהיות נכלל בברכת עשו והיה הוא כאשר תריד ופרקת עולו מעל צואריך, המתין והשגיח עמלק בעת שירפה ידיהם מן התורה ואז נלחם עמם, ולכך הוצרך משה לומר ליהושע בחר לנו אנשים גבורים יראי חטא להלחם עם עמלק, כ"א לא ילחמו עמו בכח גדול וביד חזקה, לא יוכלו לו בתפלה מצד שרפו ידיהם מן התורה, (ב"ר פ' סה) ובזמן שהקול קול יעקב אז הידים ידי עשו, ונזדרז משה רבינו בשני הדברים בתפלה ובגבורת מלחמה, והיתה תפלתו מוכיחה בעשותם מלחמ' לא שתספיק התפלה למחות זרע עמלק בלי מלחמה, ולזה הוצרך להרים ידיו כדי שיגברו ישראל, דרך רמז שיהיו ידיהם רמות על עמלק בנצחון המלחמה, וכשהיו ישראל מכוונים לבם לשמים בהרמת ידי משה היה הא-ל יתברך עושה להם נס, גם כי רפו ידיהם מן התורה ברפידים שינצחו, וכשהיה מניח ידיו וגבר עמלק, וידי משה כבדים, כלומר מצד חטאת ישראל שרפו ידיהם מן התורה, וגם כי ברכת עשו היתה ועל חרבך תחיה, היו ידיו כבדות לנצוח מלחמת עמלק בחרב ובמלחמה, עד שלקחו אבן ושמו תחתיו וישב עליה בתמיכתם, והיו ידי אמונה עד בא השמש, וחולשתו של משה גרם חולשה לנצחון המלחמה שלא נכרת זרעו של עמלק אלא שהחליש אותם יהושע.

28. See Rav Tzadok haKohen, *Divrei Sofrim*, section 36.

ספר דברי סופרים, אות לו

וזה נקרא קול כמו כמו שנאמר (בראשית כ"ז כ"ב) הקול קול יעקב ונאמר (דברים ל"ג ז') שמע ה' קול יהודה, והן הקולות דמתן תורה הנשמעות מתון האש, דיצחק הוא האש המוליד הקול ויעקב הוא הקול עצמו שמטתו שלימה שהוא כלל הכנסת ישראל שהם עצמות התורה דאמת ליעקב הדבוק באלקים חיים, וחי לעולם כמו שאמרו (תענית ה' ע"ב) דלא מת כי אכל מעץ החיים ואין עץ החיים אלא תורה כמו שמובא בתנא דבי אליהו רבא (פרק א') שנאמר (משלי ג' י"ח) עץ חיים היא וגו' והוא עצם התורה:

29. The name *Hevron* has as its root the letters *het bet resh* – which spells *haver*, friend. Horev has as its root *het resh bet*, which spells *herev*, sword.

were the hands of Esav. Esav could ask questions that would convince even Yitzhak of his sincerity. He knew how to talk, but not how to unite his speech with his actions. He was only "kosher" on the outside. In the end, his head – and only his head – gained entry to the Cave of Makhpeilah. The rest of Esav was excluded.

Parashat Vayeitzei

The Place – *haMakom*

Yaakov takes leave of his parents and begins his journey. As the sun sets he settles for the night, in a place not immediately identified by name:

בראשית כח:י–יא

וַיֵּצֵא יַעֲקֹב מִבְּאֵר שָׁבַע וַיֵּלֶךְ חָרָנָה: וַיִּפְגַּע **בַּמָּקוֹם** וַיָּלֶן שָׁם כִּי בָא הַשֶּׁמֶשׁ וַיִּקַּח מֵאַבְנֵי **הַמָּקוֹם** וַיָּשֶׂם מְרַאֲשֹׁתָיו וַיִּשְׁכַּב **בַּמָּקוֹם** הַהוּא:

*And Yaakov left Be'er Sheva, and went toward Haran. And he arrived at **the place**, and remained there all night, because the sun had set; and he took of the stones of **the place**, and put them beneath his head, and lay down in **that place**.* (Bereishit 28:10–11)

It is here that Yaakov has an epiphany. He sees a ladder reaching to heaven upon which angels are ascending and descending. When he awakes, Yaakov speaks about this place:

בראשית כח:טז–יז

וַיִּיקַץ יַעֲקֹב מִשְּׁנָתוֹ וַיֹּאמֶר אָכֵן יֵשׁ ה' בַּמָּקוֹם הַזֶּה וְאָנֹכִי לֹא יָדָעְתִּי: וַיִּירָא וַיֹּאמַר מַה נּוֹרָא הַמָּקוֹם הַזֶּה אֵין זֶה כִּי אִם בֵּית אֱלֹקִים וְזֶה שַׁעַר הַשָּׁמָיִם:

*And Yaakov awoke from his sleep, and he said, "Surely God is in **this place**; and I did not know." And he was afraid, and said, "How awesome is **this place**! This is none other than the house of the Almighty, and this is the gate of heaven."* (Bereishit 28:16–17)

Yaakov's vision is completely different from anything his father or grandfather saw. He senses God's presence in this place, as did Yitzhak and Avraham before him (see below), but he also senses the grandeur and majesty of the House of God. His vision is specific, detailed, and not the general awareness and understanding of God that his father and grandfather had. He comprehends that the point at which he stands is a gateway to heaven that spans the void between the physical terrain beneath his feet and the heavenly world, the spiritual and transcendent spheres beyond this world. Yaakov's vision is almost unfathomable, for he describes spiritual structures that transcend the physical yet have a physical manifestation.

Only after considering the unique juxtaposition of physical and spiritual that this place embodies, we finally learn that the place does have a name – a name that is abandoned. Yaakov gives this place a new name that reflects his vision and the awesome presence that he senses there:

בראשית כח:יט

וַיִּקְרָא אֶת שֵׁם הַמָּקוֹם הַהוּא בֵּית אֵל וְאוּלָם לוּז שֵׁם הָעִיר לָרִאשֹׁנָה:

*And he called the name of **that place** Beit El [literally, the House of God]; but the name of the city was Luz originally.* (Bereishit 28:19)

Yaakov's sojourn there on his way to Haran seems more than coincidental; the language of the verse may imply that he had set his sights on this spot, and managed to navigate accurately to reach it.[1] Indeed, years later, when he returns from Haran to the land of his fathers, he visits this very particular place once again:

בראשית לה:יג–טו

וַיַּעַל מֵעָלָיו אֱלֹקִים בַּמָּקוֹם אֲשֶׁר דִּבֶּר אִתּוֹ: וַיַּצֵּב יַעֲקֹב מַצֵּבָה בַּמָּקוֹם אֲשֶׁר דִּבֶּר אִתּוֹ מַצֶּבֶת אָבֶן וַיַּסֵּךְ עָלֶיהָ נֶסֶךְ וַיִּצֹק עָלֶיהָ שָׁמֶן: וַיִּקְרָא יַעֲקֹב אֶת שֵׁם הַמָּקוֹם אֲשֶׁר דִּבֶּר אִתּוֹ שָׁם אֱלֹקִים בֵּית אֵל:

*And God went up from him in **the place** where He talked with him. And Yaakov set up a pillar in **the place** where he talked with Him, a pillar of stone; and he poured a drink offering on it, and he poured oil on it. And Yaakov called the name of **the place** where God spoke with him Beit El.* (Bereishit 35:13–15)

While it should come as no surprise that tradition identifies this place with Jerusalem,[2] this is not a pat, easy answer to a geographical word game. The

---

1. The word *va'yifga* is used to describe hitting a target.

2. According to tradition this is where Yitzhak prays as well. See *Akeidat Yitzhak*, chapter 24, where the idea is expressed succinctly.

ספר עקידת יצחק, שער כד

וזש"א אברהם "בהר ד' יראה", וביצחק נאמר "לשוח בשדה" וביעקב "אין זה כי אם בית אלקים", אף כי באמת מקום העקידה, ותפלת יצחק, ומשכב יעקב שלשתם היו לדחז"ל במקום אחד בהר המוריה אשר שם נבנה בהמ"ק.

unique identity of this place, and its central role in our theology, deserve closer examination.

Before turning our attention to the significance of Yaakov's vision, it is important to note that Yaakov is not the first of our forefathers to be granted extraordinary spiritual experiences at this place, nor is he the first to bring offerings there. Although Avraham had built altars to God in various locations in the land of Canaan, and despite the fact that Avraham had prayed to God, had even held conversations with God, in other locations, it was here that Avraham actually brought his very first offering:

בראשית כב:ג–ד, ט, יד

וַיַּשְׁכֵּם אַבְרָהָם בַּבֹּקֶר וַיַּחֲבֹשׁ אֶת חֲמֹרוֹ וַיִּקַּח אֶת שְׁנֵי נְעָרָיו אִתּוֹ וְאֵת יִצְחָק בְּנוֹ
וַיְבַקַּע עֲצֵי עֹלָה וַיָּקָם וַיֵּלֶךְ אֶל הַמָּקוֹם אֲשֶׁר אָמַר לוֹ הָאֱלֹקִים: בַּיּוֹם הַשְּׁלִישִׁי
וַיִּשָּׂא אַבְרָהָם אֶת עֵינָיו וַיַּרְא אֶת הַמָּקוֹם מֵרָחֹק:...

וַיָּבֹאוּ אֶל הַמָּקוֹם אֲשֶׁר אָמַר לוֹ הָאֱלֹקִים וַיִּבֶן שָׁם אַבְרָהָם אֶת הַמִּזְבֵּחַ וַיַּעֲרֹךְ
אֶת הָעֵצִים וַיַּעֲקֹד אֶת יִצְחָק בְּנוֹ וַיָּשֶׂם אֹתוֹ עַל הַמִּזְבֵּחַ מִמַּעַל לָעֵצִים:...

וַיִּקְרָא אַבְרָהָם שֵׁם הַמָּקוֹם הַהוּא ה' יִרְאֶה אֲשֶׁר יֵאָמֵר הַיּוֹם בְּהַר ה' יֵרָאֶה:

And Avraham rose up early in the morning, and saddled his donkey, and took two of his young men with him, and Yitzhak his son, and broke the wood for the burnt offering, and rose up, and went to the place of which God had told him. Then on the third day Avraham lifted up his eyes, and saw the place from afar....
And they came to the place which God had told him; and Avraham built an altar there, and laid the wood in order, and bound Yitzhak his son, and laid him on the altar upon the wood....
And Avraham called the name of that place Adonai Yireh; as it is said to this day, "In the Mount of God He shall be seen." (Bereishit 22: 3–4, 9 ,14)

Avraham and Yitzhak are brought, by divine command, to this specific place, and it is here that Yitzhak is bound up for an offering, and eventually replaced by the ram that is sacrificed in his stead. Here, as in the two later visits by Yaakov, this place is called "*the* place" – above all others, different than all others. This will be the place of the Beit haMikdash, the physical manifestation of God's Presence, the bridge between the physical and spiritual worlds – perhaps the very House of God that Yaakov saw in his prophetic vision.

The word *makom*, which recurs over and over both in the *'akeidah* scene and in our present parashah, appears earlier in the Torah. And while it is often no more than a general description of place, this same word is often used in an even more specific sense than in our present case, referring to God Himself:

ילקוט שמעוני, פרשת ויצא רמז קיז

ויפגע במקום: למה מכנין שמו של הקב"ה וקורין אותו "מקום"? מפני שהוא מקומו של עולם ואין העולם מקומו.

*"And he arrived at **the place**": Why is God called* Makom? *Because He is the place of the world and the world is not His place.* (Yalkut Shimoni Vayeitzei, remez 117)

Let us look back to the very beginning in order to fully understand this far-reaching philosophical usage: the first time the word *makom* is used in the Torah, God gathers all the primordial waters to one place and thus reveals the earth below. This gathering of water is called *mikveh*:[3]

בראשית א:ט

וַיֹּאמֶר אֱלֹקִים יִקָּווּ הַמַּיִם מִתַּחַת הַשָּׁמַיִם אֶל מָקוֹם אֶחָד וְתֵרָאֶה הַיַּבָּשָׁה וַיְהִי כֵן:

And God said, "Let the waters under the heaven be gathered together to one place, and let the dry land appear"; and it was so. (Bereishit 1:9)

The act of gathering the waters that results in dry land being revealed is called *mikveh*, while the place into which the waters are gathered is called *makom*. We know in our own experience that this gathering of water, the *mikveh*, is a place of purity, where people can return to themselves – in the pure, pristine sense of regeneration; it is a place where a person can return to God. In a very real sense, the *mikveh* reconnects us with the very essence of our being, with the foundations of human identity. The Torah describes the creation of man as a hybrid of the spiritual and the physical – a coming together of two worlds:

---

3. Interestingly, Targum Onkelos translates *mikveh* as *beit kenishta* – which would mean *beit kenneset* (or in Latin, synagogue) – a place where people gather for a holy purpose.

תרגום אונקלוס, בראשית א:י

וקרא ה' ליבשתא ארעא ולבית כנישת מיא קרא יממי וחזא ה' ארי טב.

בראשית ב:ז

וַיִּיצֶר ה' אֱלֹקִים אֶת הָאָדָם עָפָר מִן הָאֲדָמָה וַיִּפַּח בְּאַפָּיו נִשְׁמַת חַיִּים וַיְהִי
הָאָדָם לְנֶפֶשׁ חַיָּה:

*And the Almighty God formed man of the dust of the ground, and
breathed into his nostrils the breath of life, and man became a living
soul. (Bereishit 2:7)*

Man is formed out of the dust of the earth, and this very physical stuff
is infused with spirituality. And yet, Rashi explains, even the physical
matter of which man is formed is not devoid of spirituality. Rashi offers
two possibilities for the provenance of this "dust of the earth." According
to the first, God gathered dust from all over the Earth, forming man from
the entirety of the Earth. According to the second interpretation, very
specific earth is used to form man – earth gathered from "*the* place" –
from this very specific *makom* to which Avraham, Yitzhak and Yaakov
were drawn.[4] The Targum Pseudo-Yonatan states clearly that the dust
was gathered from the place where the Beit haMikdash would stand.[5] In
other words, the hybrid creature called man is made of physical stuff –
dust of the earth – and a breath of God – the spiritual "image of God"
with which we are uniquely gifted; but even the physical part of man
originates from the holiest place.

What does this mean for each of us? When we return to Jerusalem, we
return home in a very basic, elemental sense. The very stones of the Temple
Mount are of one piece with our bodies. We are part and parcel of the
holy Altar, and that holiest of places is intertwined with our very essence.
Holiness and purity are not extraneous, external, foreign concepts; they are

---

4. Rashi, Bereishit 2:7.

רש"י, בראשית ב:ז

עפר מן האדמה: צבר עפרו מכל האדמה מארבע רוחות, שכל מקום שימות שם תהא קולטתו לקבורה.
דבר אחר נטל עפרו ממקום שנאמר בו (שמות כ:כא) מזבח אדמה תעשה לי, אמר הלואי תהיה לו כפרה
ויוכל לעמוד.

5. Targum Yonatan, Bereishit 2:7.

כתר יונתן, בראשית ב:ז

ויברא ה' אלקים את אדם בשני יצרים **ויקח עפר ממקום בית המקדש** ומארבעת רוחות העולם ויבלול
מכל מימי העולם ובראו אדום שחור ולבן ויפח בנחיריו נשמת חיים והיתה נשמה בגוף האדם לרוח
מדברת למאור עינים ולשמע אוזנים.

who we are. We are, in the most basic sense, hardwired for holiness, and it is to this state of purity that we strive to return – to our purest selves. It is to this inner, innate purity that the elemental waters of the *mikveh* return us.

Conversely, the ultimate punishment for transgressing against our innate purity, for turning our backs on the image of God within us, is exile. From the very start, sin distanced us from our life source, from the wellspring of our spirituality and vitality. When Adam and Hava sinned, they were exiled; so too, Kayin. In light of what we have learned, exile can now be understood on several levels: Exile is more than replacing the familiar with the unknown, more than a disconnection from the physical environment of one's home. Exile is, above all, a disconnection from the source of our spiritual identity. Exile is distancing of the body as well as the soul from the *makom* of purity; in a certain sense, exile is a sort of quasi-death. Man's physical place is intertwined with his spiritual existence in ways that are often too subtle to discern. The Maharal[6] expressed this idea by pointing out that the word *makom* is related etymologically to *mekayeim*, something that sustains and provides existence. When a person is exiled they lose more than their physical frame of reference; they are denied a part of their very existence. This explains why a person found guilty of negligent or unintentional homicide is forced into exile: In a world of absolute justice, a murderer forfeits his own life. In a case where absolute justice is impossible, a sort of quasi-death is imposed, and the murderer is disconnected from his natural place, from the source of his identity. A person who has taken the life of another is cleansed by the quasi-death experience of exile. Interestingly, this exile comes to an end with the death of the *kohen gadol:*[7] the connection between the *kohen gadol*, custodian of the Beit haMikdash, and the end of this person's wandering presents additional confirmation of the relationship between the *makom haMikdash* and the spiritual source of life.

---

6. See the Maharal's comments in *Hidushei Aggadot* on Tractate Sanhedrin, page 147.

ספר חדושי אגדות, חלק שלישי עמוד קמז – מסכת סנהדרין

הדברים יש להם קיום במקום כמו שאמרו (אבות פ"ד) אין לך דבר שאין לו מקום והמקום נותן קיום לדבר שהוא במקום, ודבר זה יתבאר בסמוך. ולכך נקרא מקום שהוא מקיים הדבר שעומד בו. וכאשר גולה ממקומו וכאלו בטל קיומו, וכמו שהמיתה מכפרת על האדם כך הגלות שהוא בטול דבר שהוא קיומו מכפר.

7. Bamidbar 35:25.

The destruction of the Beit haMikdash was not only the destruction of the symbol of national sovereignty; it was also the dismantling of the bridge that had connected our physical plane with the spiritual realm beyond. The exile that followed in the wake of the destruction of the Beit haMikdash was, above and beyond the physical dispersion of the Jewish people, a spiritual disconnection from the cornerstone of our place of identity and our purest selves.

Careful consideration should be given to the theological ramifications of Yaakov's vision and to the question of "sacred ground." In this very basic yet profound teaching, we may discern the point of divergence between Judaism and pantheism: while Judaism sees Godliness in every element of Creation, pantheism turned every force of nature into a god. In other words, we may say that Judaism is not completely summarized by the concept *monotheism*; Judaism describes God as not only unique and singular, but also transcendent. Thus, according to Jewish theology, God does not exist within the physical world, and no place can confine God.[8] On the other hand, Judaism teaches that while the physical world cannot contain God, and is not itself God, the physical world can be imbued with holiness that emanates from God. Although God is not limited to space, in certain spaces mankind can be more attuned to Godliness. This is the nature of the holiness of the Beit haMikdash: it is not intrinsic; it emanates from God. Before the Temple was built, Yaakov felt God's holiness emanating from the *makom haMikdash*, described by the ladder in his vision. He called the place Beit El, for he envisioned the House of God that would one day give all of his descendants access to God's holiness. Although Yaakov was just beginning his journey and would return to that place only after many painful years in exile, the vision of that place, the knowledge of that

---

8. See the comments of the Maharsha on Brakhot 40a.

מהרש״א חידושי אגדות, מסכת ברכות דף מ עמוד א

...משמוע דלעולם הוא מחזיק לשמוע בריקן דוקא כי הדברים הם דברים גשמיים יש להם גדר במקום שמקום הריק מגשמי מחזיק והמלא מדבר גשמי א״א להחזיק עוד יותר וזו היא מדת ב״ו **אבל מדת הקב״ה** שאין לו גדר במקום כי מלא כל הארץ כבודו כי הוא מקומו של עולם ואין העולם מקומו וע״כ מקום מלא מרוחני אין לו למקומו גדר ויוכל להחזיק עוד יותר להוסיף דבר רוחני אבל הריק **מהרוחני אינו מחזיק דבר רוחני** ולזה בשמיעת המושכלות שהם דברים רוחנים המלא מהם אין לו גדר במקום ומחזיק עוד יותר דהיינו אם שמוע תשמע ואם לאו הרי רוצה בריקן מהרוחני ואינו מחזיק עוד רוחני ודו״ק.

connection to the transcendent, the assurance that the Beit haMikdash would one day be built there, sustained Yaakov throughout his exile, as it sustained his descendants generations later.

God's identity is absolute, yet holiness is often subject to human perception: the method by which God makes Himself manifest in the physical world can be perceived by different people in many different ways. The Talmud relates that one of the most vivid descriptions of the Divine, which was recorded by the prophet Yehezkel, was a subjective vision, limited by the prophet's relatively low prophetic abilities. The far more subdued vision recorded by the prophet Yeshayahu was, in fact, the identical vision, seen through a different human prism:

תלמוד בבלי, מסכת חגיגה דף יג עמוד ב

אמר רבא: כל שראה יחזקאל ראה ישעיה. למה יחזקאל דומה? לבן כפר שראה את המלך. ולמה ישעיהו דומה? לבן כרך שראה את המלך.

Rava said: All that Yehezkel saw, Yeshayahu saw. What does Yehezkel resemble? A villager who saw the king. And what does Yeshayahu resemble? A townsman who saw the king. (Talmud Bavli Hagigah 13b)

Yeshayahu describes God's holiness that fills the world:

ישעיהו ו:א–ג

בִּשְׁנַת מוֹת הַמֶּלֶךְ עֻזִּיָּהוּ וָאֶרְאֶה אֶת אֲדֹנָי יֹשֵׁב עַל כִּסֵּא רָם וְנִשָּׂא וְשׁוּלָיו מְלֵאִים אֶת הַהֵיכָל: שְׂרָפִים עֹמְדִים מִמַּעַל לוֹ שֵׁשׁ כְּנָפַיִם שֵׁשׁ כְּנָפַיִם לְאֶחָד בִּשְׁתַּיִם יְכַסֶּה פָנָיו וּבִשְׁתַּיִם יְכַסֶּה רַגְלָיו וּבִשְׁתַּיִם יְעוֹפֵף: וְקָרָא זֶה אֶל זֶה וְאָמַר קָדוֹשׁ קָדוֹשׁ קָדוֹשׁ ה' צְבָאוֹת מְלֹא כָל הָאָרֶץ כְּבוֹדוֹ:

In the year of King Uzziah's death I saw God sitting upon a throne, high and lifted up, and His train filled the Sanctuary. Above it stood the seraphim; each one had six wings; with two they covered their faces, and with two they covered their feet and with two they did fly. And one cried to another, and said, "Holy, holy, holy, is the Lord of Hosts; the whole earth is full of His Glory." (Yeshayahu 6:1–3)

Yehezkel's vision seems quite different:

יחזקאל ג:י–יב

וַיֹּאמֶר אֵלַי בֶּן אָדָם אֶת כָּל דְּבָרַי אֲשֶׁר אֲדַבֵּר אֵלֶיךָ קַח בִּלְבָבְךָ וּבְאָזְנֶיךָ שְׁמָע: וְלֵךְ בֹּא אֶל הַגּוֹלָה אֶל בְּנֵי עַמֶּךָ וְדִבַּרְתָּ אֲלֵיהֶם וְאָמַרְתָּ אֲלֵיהֶם כֹּה אָמַר אֲדֹנָי ה' אִם יִשְׁמְעוּ וְאִם יֶחְדָּלוּ: וַתִּשָּׂאֵנִי רוּחַ וָאֶשְׁמַע אַחֲרַי קוֹל רַעַשׁ גָּדוֹל בָּרוּךְ כְּבוֹד ה' מִמְּקוֹמוֹ:

And he said to me, "Son of man, all my words that I shall speak to you receive in your heart, and hear with your ears. And go, get you to the exile, to your people, and speak to them, and tell them, 'Thus said the Almighty God'; whether they will hear, or whether they will refuse to hear." Then the spirit took me up, and I heard behind me a voice of a great sound, saying, "Blessed be the Glory of God from His place." (Yehezkel 3:10–12)

While Yeshayahu perceives holiness emanating from God and filling all of Creation, Yehezkel perceives holiness radiating from a specific point, "*the place*," the *makom*. Yeshayahu prophesized in Jerusalem, while the Beit haMikdash yet stood, and he had a very clear vision of how the Glory of God fills all of Creation. Yehezkel prophesized from the exile, as the Temple lay in ruins, and he sensed that the source of blessing, the point from which God's Glory emanates, is that specific place, the *makom HaMikdash*. It seems elementary to our Talmudic sages that the perception of God's manifestation in the physical world will be affected by the different vantage points of each prophet: the vision from exile, seen by a wandering Jew who has been disconnected from his *makom*, will necessarily differ from a vision seen at the epicenter of holiness.

Like Yehezkel, Yaakov calls this place *makom*, yet he renames it Beit El – the "House of God." He sees the angels going up and going down; he understands that this is the gate to heaven, that holiness emanates from this place to the rest of the world. He stands with his feet on the ground of the holiest place on Earth, as did Yeshayahu, yet Yaakov is on his way into exile – like Yehezkel.[9]

---

9. This idea is described by Rav Yitzhak Haver in his Drasha for Parashat Bereishit, section 103.

ספר שיח יצחק חלק א. דרוש לשבת פרשת בראשית, אות קג

והוא מה שראה יעקב אבינו במראה הסולם "והנה סולם מוצב ארצה", רמז כל מ"ש, שהוא קו התפשטות גילוי כבוד מלכותו יתברך וממשלתו והמציאו והשגחתו על נבראיו, שנבראו בסדר השתלשלות המדרגות,

Years later, before Yaakov leaves the Land of Israel for the second time, he seems more reluctant. He is less able to focus on the vision of the future, less willing to exile himself from the place where God's Presence is manifest. And God Himself gives Yaakov assurances:

בראשית מו:א–ד

וַיִּסַּע יִשְׂרָאֵל וְכָל אֲשֶׁר לוֹ וַיָּבֹא בְּאֵרָה שָּׁבַע וַיִּזְבַּח זְבָחִים לֵאלֹקֵי אָבִיו יִצְחָק: וַיֹּאמֶר אֱלֹקִים לְיִשְׂרָאֵל בְּמַרְאֹת הַלַּיְלָה וַיֹּאמֶר יַעֲקֹב יַעֲקֹב וַיֹּאמֶר הִנֵּנִי: וַיֹּאמֶר אָנֹכִי הָקֵל אֱלֹקֵי אָבִיךָ אַל תִּירָא מֵרְדָה מִצְרַיְמָה כִּי לְגוֹי גָּדוֹל אֲשִׂימְךָ שָׁם: אָנֹכִי אֵרֵד עִמְּךָ מִצְרַיְמָה וְאָנֹכִי אַעַלְךָ גַם עָלֹה וְיוֹסֵף יָשִׁית יָדוֹ עַל עֵינֶיךָ:

And Yisrael traveled with all that he had, and came to Be'er Sheva, and offered sacrifices to the God of his father Yitzhak. And God spoke to Yisrael in the visions of the night, and said, "Yaakov, Yaakov." And he said, "Here am I." And he said, "I am the Almighty, the God of your father; fear not to go down to Egypt; for I will there make of you a great nation; I will go down with you to Egypt; and I will also surely bring you up again; and Yosef shall put his hand upon your eyes." (Bereishit 46:1–4)

Once again, Yaakov is forced to leave the Land; once again, he is granted a vision that will comfort and sustain him, but now an important element is added. God says, "I will go down with you." The *Shekhinah*, the Glory of God, will be discernable beyond the borders of Israel, beyond the confines of the Beit haMikdash, beyond the boundaries of that very specific *makom*.[10] God informs Yaakov that He will always be with Yaakov and his descendants – even in Egypt, in the epicenter of darkness and evil. God Himself becomes *haMakom*; the *Shekhinah* that accompanies Yisrael into

---

זה תחת זה, מראשית המשכתו, שהוא מכסא כבודו יתברך, עד מקום המקדש, מקום השראת שכינתו יתברך, אשר שם שכב יעקב אבינו, כמ"ש "ויפגע במקום", והוא מקומו של עולם, וגם מקום הנבחר בהר המוריה, ששם רגלי הסולם, סוף התפשטות הקו הזה, וז"ש "מוצב ארצה וראשו מגיע וכו'", אבל מלאכי אלוהים הם האמצעים, ועלייתם ויֵרידתם בו, ר"ל ע"י יעקב, שהוא כלל האומה הנבחרת לעבודתו יתברך, וכתיב "והנה ה' נצב עליו", ר"ל על הסולם, וכן ר"ל על יעקב, והכל ענין אחד, כי צורת נשמתו מגיע עד ראש הסולם, שהוא התחלת המשכת הקו, ששמו הגדול יתברך הוא עליו וסמוך לו.

10. See Mekhilta Beshallah, Tractate Shirah Parashah 3, and Talmud Bavli Megilah 29a.

מכילתא דרבי ישמעאל בשלח, מס' דשירה פרשה ג ד"ה זה אלי

כך ישראל כשירדו למצרים ירדה שכינה עמהם שנ' אנכי ארד עמך מצרימה (ברא' מו:ד), עלו עלת שכינה עמהם שנ' ואנכי אעלך גם עלה וגו' (בראשית מו:ד)....

exile is the manifestation of that same connection, previously confined to the one awesome space revealed to the forefathers.

In a certain sense, we may think that God's promise to Yaakov was superfluous: God transcends time and space. There is no place devoid of His holiness, and God is not confined to any one place. As Yeshayahu taught, "the entire world is filled with His Glory." And yet, we are not able to be fully attuned to God's Presence at all times, in all of the places we find ourselves. At times we feel alone, ungrounded, restless; we don't feel the *Shekhinah* upon us, and we don't see the ladder. It is not always easy to access the spirituality that transcends the confines of our physical space. For this reason, Yaakov hesitated, and God assured him: "I am with you. I will be with you in exile, and I will return with you from exile."

The words of comfort and reassurance God offers Yaakov/Yisrael remind us of the words we ourselves use to comfort mourners:

הַמָּקוֹם יְנַחֵם אֶתְכֶם בְּתוֹךְ שְׁאָר אֲבֵלֵי צִיּוֹן וִירוּשָׁלָיִם.

May the "Place" [haMakom] *give you solace along with all those who mourn for Zion and Jerusalem.*

Here, God Himself is the *Makom*; when we feel distant, bereft, disconnected from our life source, in need of comfort, it is specifically the aspect of God related to *makom* that comforts us. Moreover, we are consoled by connecting our own personal loss to the comfort that comes from Jerusalem, from that very specific *makom* that is the source of our true identity. Our lives are bound up with the Altar in Jerusalem, with the dust of the earth of the Temple Mount. Every death, then, is a destruction of the Altar and the Temple. When we feel distant, when we feel alienated and exiled, when death strikes and we feel alone, God, *the* Place, the *Makom* and the *Mekayeim* – the Source and Sustainer of all existence – lifts us up by revealing to us, once again, that unique bridge that spans the void and acts as a conduit between our physical and spiritual selves. Like Yeshayahu

---

תלמוד בבלי, מסכת מגילה דף כט עמוד א

תניא, רבי שמעון בן יוחאי אומר: בוא וראה כמה חביבין ישראל לפני הקדוש ברוך הוא, שבכל מקום שגלו – שכינה עמהן.

and Yehezkel, and Yaakov before them, He allows us to see that truly "His Glory fills all existence."

Sulam Yaakov

The parashah begins with Yaakov on the run, at his parents' command, but propelled by fear of his vengeful, bloodthirsty brother. Yaakov's departure is actually recorded at the end of the previous chapter, in Parashat Toldot:

בראשית כח:ה

וַיִּשְׁלַח יִצְחָק אֶת יַעֲקֹב וַיֵּלֶךְ פַּדֶּנָה אֲרָם אֶל לָבָן בֶּן בְּתוּאֵל הָאֲרַמִּי אֲחִי רִבְקָה אֵם יַעֲקֹב וְעֵשָׂו:

And Yitzhak sent Yaakov, and he went to Padan Aram, to Lavan, son of Betuel the Aramaean, brother of Rivkah, mother of Yaakov and Esav. (Bereishit 28:5)

Now, in Parashat Vayeitzei, the Torah returns to this topic in much greater detail:

בראשית כח:י–יא

וַיֵּצֵא יַעֲקֹב מִבְּאֵר שָׁבַע וַיֵּלֶךְ חָרָנָה: וַיִּפְגַּע בַּמָּקוֹם וַיָּלֶן שָׁם כִּי בָא הַשֶּׁמֶשׁ וַיִּקַּח מֵאַבְנֵי הַמָּקוֹם וַיָּשֶׂם מְרַאֲשֹׁתָיו וַיִּשְׁכַּב בַּמָּקוֹם הַהוּא:

And Yaakov left Be'er Sheva, and went toward Haran. And he arrived at the place, and remained there all night, because the sun had set; and he took of the stones of the place, and put them beneath his head, and lay down in that place. (Bereishit 28:10–11)

Somewhere between Be'er Sheva and Haran, Yaakov sleeps in an awe-inspiring place; in a dream, he sees a vision of a ladder with its feet on the ground that stretches up to the heavens. We have already discussed the location of this scene and the significance of the *makom*;[1] let us now consider the content of Yaakov's vision.

---

1. See "The Place – *haMakom*," above.

בראשית כח:יב

וַיַּחֲלֹם וְהִנֵּה סֻלָּם מֻצָּב אַרְצָה וְרֹאשׁוֹ מַגִּיעַ הַשָּׁמָיְמָה וְהִנֵּה מַלְאֲכֵי אֱלֹקִים עֹלִים וְיֹרְדִים בּוֹ:

And he dreamed, and behold, a ladder stood on the earth, and the top of it reached to heaven; and behold the angels of the Almighty ascending and descending on it. (Bereishit 28:12)

The description is reminiscent of the Tower of Bavel, which also had its foundation on the ground and reached toward the heavens.[2] Ironically, it was at that tower that Avraham was thrown into a furnace.[3] Saved by a miracle, he began his journey – away from Ur Kasdim, to the Land of Israel. Now his grandson Yaakov is heading back toward Avraham's homeland because *his* life is in danger in the Promised Land.

Yaakov sees angels ascending and descending, a description that is somewhat counterintuitive: angels should first be described as coming down from heaven and then going back up. This vision leads to an even more profound revelation: Yaakov sees God above him (or above the ladder):

בראשית כח:יג

וְהִנֵּה ה' נִצָּב עָלָיו וַיֹּאמַר אֲנִי ה' אֱלֹקֵי אַבְרָהָם אָבִיךָ וֵאלֹקֵי יִצְחָק הָאָרֶץ אֲשֶׁר אַתָּה שֹׁכֵב עָלֶיהָ לְךָ אֶתְּנֶנָּה וּלְזַרְעֶךָ:

And, behold, God stood above him [or above it], and said, "I am the Almighty, the God of Avraham your father, and the God of Yitzhak. The land on which you lie – to you will I give it, and to your descendants." (Bereishit 28:13)

---

2. See Bereishit 11:4.

   בראשית יא:ד

   וַיֹּאמְרוּ הָבָה | נִבְנֶה-לָּנוּ עִיר וּמִגְדָּל וְרֹאשׁוֹ בַשָּׁמַיִם וְנַעֲשֶׂה-לָּנוּ שֵׁם פֶּן-נָפוּץ עַל-פְּנֵי כָל-הָאָרֶץ:

   "And they said, 'Come, let us build us a city and a tower, whose top may reach to heaven; and let us make us a name, lest we be scattered abroad upon the face of the whole earth.'"

3. See above, "Parashat Vayeira: Elevation."

Yaakov awakens. He now knows that he is on holy ground, and he seems surprised and overwhelmed. Not only is the land holy, this place is the "House of God" and the entrance to heaven:

בראשית כח:טז–יז

וַיִּיקַץ יַעֲקֹב מִשְּׁנָתוֹ וַיֹּאמֶר אָכֵן יֵשׁ ה' בַּמָּקוֹם הַזֶּה וְאָנֹכִי לֹא יָדָעְתִּי: וַיִּירָא וַיֹּאמַר מַה נּוֹרָא הַמָּקוֹם הַזֶּה אֵין זֶה כִּי אִם בֵּית אֱלֹקִים וְזֶה שַׁעַר הַשָּׁמָיִם:

And Yaakov awoke from his sleep, and he said, "Surely God is in this place; and I did not know." And he was afraid, and said, "How awesome is this place! This is none other than the house of God, and this is the gate of heaven." (Bereishit 28:16–17)

This is the first reference in the Torah to a House of God. At this point it exists only in the supernatural sphere, and Yaakov sees it in a vision. But one day a Mishkan (Tabernacle) will be built to travel with the Israelites in the desert, and when the Jews finally return to their homeland the Tabernacle will metamorphose into a permanent physical Temple – the Beit haMikdash. It all begins with Yaakov's dream and his perception of this place as the gate of heaven. The reader, however, still does not know Yaakov's precise location. All that we do know is that he has left Be'er Sheva. He is assured that this is holy land, and that it will one day be his – but where is it?

בראשית כח:יח–יט

וַיַּשְׁכֵּם יַעֲקֹב בַּבֹּקֶר וַיִּקַּח אֶת הָאֶבֶן אֲשֶׁר שָׂם מְרַאֲשֹׁתָיו וַיָּשֶׂם אֹתָהּ מַצֵּבָה וַיִּצֹק שֶׁמֶן עַל רֹאשָׁהּ: וַיִּקְרָא אֶת שֵׁם הַמָּקוֹם הַהוּא בֵּית אֵל וְאוּלָם לוּז שֵׁם הָעִיר לָרִאשֹׁנָה:

And Yaakov rose up early in the morning, and took the stone that he had put for his pillows, and set it up for a pillar, and poured oil upon its top. And he called the name of that place Beit El; *but the name of the city was* Luz *originally. (Bereishit 28:18–19)*

Yaakov calls the place where he has had this vision *Beit El* – literally, the House of God, connecting the entrance to heaven seen in his vision to the House of God he vows to build as a gateway to heaven. The text is devoid of geographical clues; our Oral Tradition supplies much more detail as to the precise location of this holy spot. Rashi draws an image of the ladder on an angle, stretching across all of the Land of Israel, with the base in Be'er Sheva, the top in Beit El, and the middle directly above what would one day be known as Jerusalem.[4]

The Talmud elaborates:

תלמוד בבלי, מסכת פסחים דף פח עמוד א

ואמר רבי אלעזר: מאי דכתיב, (ישעיהו ב) והלכו עמים רבים ואמרו לכו ונעלה אל הר ה' אל בית אלקי יעקב וגו', אלקי יעקב ולא אלקי אברהם ויצחק? אלא: לא כאברהם שכתוב בו הר, שנאמר, (בראשית כב) אשר יאמר היום בהר ה' יראה, ולא כיצחק שכתוב בו שדה, שנאמר, (בראשית כד) ויצא יצחק לשוח בשדה. אלא כיעקב שקראו בית, שנאמר, (בראשית כח) ויקרא את שם המקום ההוא בית אל.

*R. Elazar also said, What is meant by the verse, "And many people shall go and say: 'Come, and let us go up to the mountain of God, to the House of the God of Yaakov'" – the God of Yaakov, but not the God of Avraham and Yitzhak? Not like Avraham, in connection with whom mountain is written, as it is said, "In the **mountain** where God will appear." Nor like Yitzhak, in connection with whom field is written, as it is said, "And Yitzhak went out to meditate in the **field** at eventide." But like Yaakov, who called it [or called Him] **home**, as it is said, "And he called the name of that place **Beit El** [The House of God]." (Talmud Bavli Pesahim 88a)*

פרוש רש"י מדוייק לספר בראשית כח:יט

בית אל: לא זה הוא הסמוך לעי אלא לירושלים ועל שם שהיתה עיר האלקים קראה בית אל והוא הר המוריה שהתתפלל בו אברהם והוא השדה שהתפלל בו יצחק וכן אמרו בסוטה לכו ונעלה וגו' לא כאברהם שקראו הר ולא כיצחק שקראו שדה אלא כיעקב שקראו בית אל.

---

4. Rashi's comments are on the words "this is none other than a house of God" (Bereishit 28:17). Apparently Rashi associates "house of God" with the ultimate House of God – the Temple in Jerusalem.

רש"י, בראשית כח:יז

כי אם בית אלקים: א"ר אלעזר בשם רבי יוסי בן זמרא: הסולם הזה עומד בבאר שבע ואמצע שיפועו מגיע כנגד בית המקדש שבאר שבע עומד בדרומה של יהודה וירושלים בצפונה בגבול שבין יהודה ובית אל היה בצפון של נחלת בנימין בגבול שבין בנימין ובין בני יוסף נמצא סולם שרגליו בבאר שבע וראשו בבית אל אמצע מגיע שיפועו נגד ירושלים.

*Beit El: Not the one that is near the city of Aiy, but [the one adjacent
to] Jerusalem. And because it was the City of the Almighty, [Yaakov]
called it Beit El. This is Har haMoriah,where Avraham prayed, and
it is the field where Yitzhak prayed, Thus, in [the Talmud, Tractate]
Sotah, it states, "Come, let us go up, etc." – not like Avraham who called
it a mountain, nor like Yitzhak who called it a field, but like Yaakov,
who called it the House of God* (Beit El). (Rashi, Bereishit 28:19) [5]

Thus, Rashi solves the question of the exact location of this episode, and,
by identifying Beit El with Har haMoriah, the Talmud connects the other
patriarchs to this same place of prayer. Despite the fact that Avraham lived
in Be'er Sheva and Yitzhak lived in Be'er La'Hai Ro'i, our tradition teaches
us that this spot was a place of prayer for both Avraham and Yitzhak, and
the site of the *'akeidah*. The Talmud compares the prayers of Avraham,
Yitzhak and Yaakov based[6] on a verse in the book of Mikhah regarding the
Messianic Age:

מיכה ד:א–ב

וְהָיָה בְּאַחֲרִית הַיָּמִים יִהְיֶה הַר בֵּית-ה' נָכוֹן בְּרֹאשׁ הֶהָרִים וְנִשָּׂא הוּא מִגְּבָעוֹת
וְנָהֲרוּ עָלָיו עַמִּים: וְהָלְכוּ גּוֹיִם רַבִּים וְאָמְרוּ לְכוּ וְנַעֲלֶה אֶל הַר ה' וְאֶל בֵּית אֱלֹקֵי
יַעֲקֹב וְיוֹרֵנוּ מִדְּרָכָיו וְנֵלְכָה בְּאֹרְחֹתָיו כִּי מִצִּיּוֹן תֵּצֵא תוֹרָה וּדְבַר ה' מִירוּשָׁלָם:

*But in the last days it shall come to pass, that the mountain of the
House of God shall be established in the top of the mountains, and it
shall be exalted above the hills; and people shall flow to it. And many
nations shall come, and say, "Come, and let us go up to the mountain
of God, and to the House of the God of Yaakov; and He will teach us
of His ways, and we will walk in His paths; for Torah shall go forth
from Zion, and the word of God from Jerusalem."* (Mikhah 4:1–2)

Why is it Yaakov whose name is associated with the House of God, more
than the other patriarchs? The verse that the Talmud quotes in reference
to Yaakov is, of course, from our own parashah, when Yaakov sees the

---

5. This comment by Rashi does not appear in all printed texts.

6. The printed text of the Talmud contains a verse in the book of Yeshayahu 2:3, while the
   Ein Yaakov cites the verse from Mikhah.

gateway to heaven and senses the need to build an earthly House of God. All three patriarchs are associated with Har haMoriah, but Yaakov, more than the other patriarchs, is associated with the Beit haMikdash.

The Zohar[7] sharpens this image even further: the first Beit haMikdash is associated with Avraham, the second with Yitzhak, but the third and final Beit haMikdash, which will be established in the end of days and will be everlasting, is related to Yaakov.[8] In the words of the *Shem mi'Shmuel*, this third Beit haMikdash will have as its foundation the first two Temples; it will be the culmination of both previous Temples, just as Yaakov was the spiritual culmination and combination of the first two patriarchs.[9]

The Midrash goes in another direction altogether, associating the ladder of Yaakov's vision with Sinai. The Midrash seems less concerned with the literal, geographic identification of this place and far more interested in the thematic parallel: both Yaakov's ladder and Mount Sinai are conduits to heaven, methods of approaching heaven, of bringing information down from heaven. Perhaps most importantly, both are revelations.

---

7. See Midrash haNe'elam, Parashat Aharei Mot, and Rav Tzadok haKohen, *Kometz haMinhah*, part 2, section 61.

ספר קומץ המנחה, חלק ב אות סא

וכמו שאמרו (פסחים פח.) לא כאברהם שקראו הר. וזהו בית ראשון שאמרו בפרק חלק (סנהדרין קב ע"ב) אילו היית התם וכו' שהיה תוקף היצר הרע על דרך שאמרו (סוכה נ"ב.) צדיקים נדמה להם כהר. ולא כיצחק שקראו שדה, נגדו בית שני שאמרו (יומא סט.) (שביטלו יצרא דעבודה זרה) שזה היה יגיעת אברהם אבינו בכבשן וכן בעקידה להיות כל עבודתו רק לשם ה' אבל יצחק גבור כובש יצרו בתאוה וזה עבודתו כמו שאמרו שם דהניחו שם דעבירה רק נקרינהו לעיניה כמו שנתבאר לעיל (אות מד) על (בראשית כו:א) ותכהינה עיניו וזהו שדה שנרמז בכל מקום למקום התאוות וכמו שנאמר (דברים כ"ב, כ"ז) כי בשדה מצאה. אלא כיעקב שקראו בית המוגדר ומשומר מכל ונגדו בית השלישי שאז יהרג היצר הרע ויהיה קיבוץ גליות מכל האומות רצה לומר כל מיני מדות וכוחות רעות לא יהיה לישראל שום אחיזה בהם.

8. See the Maggid from Kuznitz, *Avodat Yisrael* (Parashat Vayeitzei), who makes this point as well.

ספר עבודת ישראל, פרשת ויצא

והנה ידוע כי בית המקדש הראשון כנגד אברהם ובית שני כנגד יצחק והבית שיבנה ב"ב נגד יעקב שלימו דאבהן ומטתו שלימה ולא יהיה לו הריסה. ואיתא (פסחים פח.) לא כאברהם שקראו הר ויצחק שקרא שדה אלא כיעקב שקראו בית.

9. *Shem mi'Shmuel*, Parashat Matot 5675.

ספר שם משמואל, פרשת מטות, שנת תרע"ה

אבל יעקב קראו בית ע"ש הבית השלישי **שהוא כולל שני המקדשות כאחד** כדברי הזוה"ק מתיחס ליעקב, ולכח הכולל אין לכחות הרע שום אחיזה אחר נקמת מדין כנ"ל.

בראשית רבה, פרשה סח פסקה יב

רבנן פתרין ליה בסיני. "ויחלום והנה סולם" – זה סיני; "מוצב ארצה" –
"ויתיצבו בתחתית ההר" (שמות יט); "וראשו מגיע השמימה" – "וההר בוער
באש עד לב השמים" (דברים ד); "והנה מלאכי אלקים" – זה משה ואהרן;
"עולים" – "ומשה עלה אל האלקים" (שמות יט); "ויורדים" – זה משה: "וירד
משה" (שם); "והנה ה' נצב עליו" – "וירד ה' על הר סיני אל ראש ההר" (שם).

The rabbis related it to Sinai. "And he dreamed, and behold a ladder"
symbolizes Sinai; "set upon the earth" – as it says, "And they stood
at the base of the mount" (Shmot 19:17); "and the top of it reached
to heaven" – "And the mountain burned with fire unto the heart
of heaven" (Devarim 4:11); "and behold the angels of God" alludes
to Moshe and Aharon; "ascending" – "And Moshe went up to God"
(Shmot 19:3); "and descending" – "And Moshe went down from the
mount" (Shmot 19:14); "and, behold, God stood above him" – "And
God came down upon Mount Sinai" (Shmot 19:20). (Bereishit
Rabbah 68:12)

The Midrash[10] goes one step further with this association and reveals that
Sinai and *sulam* (ladder) have the same numerical value (130).[11] This
connection is clarified by a teaching of the Ramban,[12] who states that
the Revelation at Sinai was a singular, "one-time" experience which was
transferred to the Mishkan and eventually to the Beit haMikdash. With
that in mind, the relationship between the ladder and Sinai becomes more

---

10. Bereishit Rabbah 68:12.

בראשית רבה, פרשה סח פסקא יב
והנה סולם זה סיני אותיות דדין הוא אותיות דדין.

11. *Sulam* is spelled in the Torah "defectively" – without a *vav*, rather *samekh* (60) *lamed*
(30) *mem* (40). Sinai is *samekh* (60) *yud* (10) *nun* (50) *yud* (10).

12. See the Ramban's commentary to the Torah, Shmot 40:34.

רמב"ן, שמות מ:לד
ויכס הענן את אהל מועד: אמר כי הענן יכסה את האהל מכל צד והוא מכוסה וטמון בו וכבוד ה' מלא את
המשכן, כי תוכו מלא הכבוד, כי הכבוד שוכן בתוך הענן תוך המשכן, כענין שנאמר בהר סיני (לעיל כ:כא)
אל הערפל אשר שם האלקים ואמר כי לא יכול משה לבא אל אהל מועד אפילו אל הפתח, מפני שהיה הענן
מכסה אותו ולא היה רשאי לבא בתוך הענן ועוד, כי המשכן מלא כבוד ה' ואיך יכנס בו והטעם, שלא יבא
שם בלא רשות, אבל יקרא אותו ויבא בתוך הענן כאשר עשה בהר סיני ויקרא אל משה ביום השביעי מתוך
הענן (לעיל כד:טז), ואמר ויבא משה בתוך הענן (שם יח) ועל דרך הפשט, בעבור שנאמר וידבר ה' אליו מאהל
מועד (ויקרא א:א) לא נכנס משה למשכן, אבל קרא אותו מאהל מועד ועמד פתח אהל מועד וידבר אליו.

clear: emblematic of the merger between the physical and the spiritual, Yaakov's vision of the ladder set the foundation for the Revelation at Sinai, which in turn found more permanent expression in the Beit haMikdash.

One more connection should be noted: the voice of Yaakov may be seen as a type of ladder as well – when used to study Torah, bringing the words of God down to earth, and when raised in prayer, bringing man's praise and supplication up to heaven. The commentaries point out that the word *kol* (voice) has the same numerical value as *sulam* (ladder): 130.[13]

The inherent relationship between Yaakov's vision and Sinai is echoed in the words with which the people are addressed when they are about to receive the Torah:

שמות יט:ג

וּמֹשֶׁה עָלָה אֶל הָאֱלֹקִים וַיִּקְרָא אֵלָיו ה' מִן הָהָר לֵאמֹר כֹּה תֹאמַר לְבֵית יַעֲקֹב וְתַגֵּיד לִבְנֵי יִשְׂרָאֵל:

And Moshe went up to God, and God called to him from the mountain, saying, "Thus shall you say to the House of Yaakov, and tell the people of Israel" (Shmot 19:3)

Appearing at the signifant moment prior to revelation, the term *Beit Yaakov* carries with it a world of meaning that bears on the unique mission

---

13. A number of commentaries also take note that *kol* – as in the voice of Yaakov, which has been connected to Yaakov's learning of Torah – is also equal to 130 and is also written defectively in the Torah. It is more common for *kol* to be written with a *vav* – and then the value is 136 (the same as *sulam* when written with a *vav*). In the verse which speaks of the voice of Yaakov it is written both ways! See Bereishit 27:22:

בראשית כז:כב

וַיִּגַּשׁ יַעֲקֹב אֶל יִצְחָק אָבִיו וַיְמֻשֵּׁהוּ וַיֹּאמֶר הַקֹּל קוֹל יַעֲקֹב וְהַיָּדַיִם יְדֵי עֵשָׂו:

See Baal haTurim, Bereishit 28:12; *Sefer haKaneh.*

בעל הטורים, בראשית כח:יב

חלום בגימטריא זהו בנבואה – סלם. בגימטריא זה כסא הכבוד. סולם. בגימטריא קול...סלם. בגימטריא סיני שהראהו מעמד הר סיני.

ספר הקנה, ד"ה ענין יראת המקום

והוא שאמר הקל קול יעקב וזהו שאמרו משה קבל תורה מסיני וזהו והנה סל"ם מוצב ארצה כי ק"ל סיני"י סלם חשבון אחד להם וכולם רומזין בכנ"י, לכן אתם בני הגלות תנו לב לדעת את אלקיכם ולברכו בכל יום מאה ברכות כדי שתתברכו מהם כי ע"י הברכות הללו אנו קיימים וחיים בגלות לכן שמעו אלי ואל תקלו בם ומה טוב ומה נעים לומר החזן הברכות הקצרות בבה"כ שירגילו בהם אף אותם שאינם יודעים.

with which the Jewish people are about to be entrusted . The word *bayit* (house or home) connotes domesticity, marriage. The Talmud[14] states that the word *bayit* is, in fact used as a synonym for "wife." Rav Tzadok haKohen, cognizant of Yaakov's mission to find a wife in Haran, sees part of the essence of Yaakov linked with this other kind of house as well. Rav Tzadok[15] explains that a home is a place of stability, and a place to build an honest and holy relationship. He contrasts Yaakov's home life with that of Elifaz, son of Esav, who had an illicit relationship with a woman named Timna; the offspring of this relationship was a child named Amalek.

The *Megaleh 'Amukot*[16] explains that when Yaakov describes the place of his epiphany as "awesome" ("How awesome is this place!" Bereishit 28:17), it is the spiritual attributes that he senses. Specifically, he sees that this place can help heal the rift created when Adam and Hava sinned. In the wake of the subsequent expulsion, Adam and Hava's relationship became strained. According to the Talmud they separated for 130 years. When Shet is born the Torah states:

---

14. Talmud Bavli Yoma 2a.

15. *Resisei Laylah*, section 42.

ספר רסיסי לילה, אות מב

וכך הוא בהשתדלות ההכרה דאין עוד מלבדו אינו מצד האמת רק על דרך פשיטת טלפיים. ולא כיעקב שנשא רחל ולאה אשר בנו שתיהם את בית ישראל. שכל אדם זיווגו הוא מה שיסד השם יתברך להוציא כח השתדלותו לפועל וזה נקרא בנין בית ונקרא אשתו ביתו (ריש יומא ב.) שעל ידי זה נבנה ממנו בית קבוע וקיים לעולמי עד. והיא העזר כנגדו להוציא כח הנעלם שבאיש. ותמנע היתה פלגש לאליפז שענין הפלגש הוא שבא עליה במטמוניות כי לא נאה שתהיה אשתו בגלוי. וכן ענין תמנע שהוא עשיית כל הנמנע מצד ההכרה שהכל מה' זהו היפך דאליפז שגדל בחיקו של יצחק שהיינו בענין הרחקת הרע ואין ראויה לשימושו כלל מצד הגילוי שלו. רק באמת במטמוניות ובהעלם היה גם הוא כן דרגא דעשו שנאמר בו (עובדיה א:ו) נבעו מצפוניו. כי במטמוניות הוא באמת שקוע בכל מיני הרע. ולכך היתה לו פלגש שלקח דבר זה של ההכרה בהשם יתברך לפרסם בעולם פעולת כל מיני רע.

16. See *Megaleh 'Amukot*, Parashat Vayeira.

ספר מגלה עמוקות, פרשת וירא

אברהם נקרא ירא אלקים בעקידה יעקב נקרא תם וישר משה הוא רבן של כל הנביאים ועל שלשתן נרמז המכסה אני סלם סיני כלם בזכות ברית ואברהם בזכות היו זה זה הצירף יהיה גם גבי הסולם דרוש הזהר מה נורא המקום הזה על סוד יסוד ברית מילה לתקן ק"ל שנים של אדה"ר שפגם בזה גם במעמד הר סיני אמר בזוהר (שמות יט) ביום הזה באו מדבר סיני שהוא זכות קיימא קדישא דרגא דיסוד לכן אמר ועתה אם תשמעו בקולי ושמרתם את בריתי וכמ"ש שלא נתנה מילה ב' דיברות רק קודם לינכנס בברית מילה ואח"כ קבלו התורה וע"כ אחר שנמולו אתו וירא אליו ד' באה לו מרכבה העליונה וגילה לו הקב"ה כל הסודות.

בראשית ה:ג

וַיְחִי אָדָם שְׁלֹשִׁים וּמְאַת שָׁנָה וַיּוֹלֶד בִּדְמוּתוֹ כְּצַלְמוֹ וַיִּקְרָא אֶת שְׁמוֹ שֵׁת:

And Adam lived one hundred thirty years, and [then] fathered a son in his own likeness, after his image; and he named him Shet. (Bereishit 5:3)

The implication is that prior to the birth of Shet, Adam's offspring were *not* in his image.

תלמוד בבלי, מסכת עירובין דף יח עמוד ב

ואמר רבי ירמיה בן אלעזר: כל אותן השנים שהיה אדם הראשון בנידוי הוליד רוחין ושידין ולילין, שנאמר, (בראשית ה) "ויחי אדם שלשים ומאת שנה ויולד בדמותו כצלמו", מכלל דעד האידנא לאו כצלמו אוליד.

R. Yirmiyah b. Elazar further stated: In all those years during which Adam was under the ban he begot ghosts and male demons and female demons, for it is said: "And Adam lived one hundred thirty years and fathered a son in his own likeness, after his own image" – from which it follows that until that time he did not beget after his own image. (Talmud Bavli Eruvin 18b)

Eviction from Eden had a price. For 130 years Adam and Hava [Eve] were estranged from one another. Once again, the number 130, the numerical value of *sulam* and *Sinai*, is significant: for 130 years, Adam and Hava had no "*bayit*," no stable home life.

Adam and Hava should have had the perfect relationship; after all, God Himself "made the *shiddukh*," and they were, literally, soul mates. But the expulsion from Eden put such heavy pressure on the relationship that instead of a stable home they had a dysfunctional relationship. The Talmud speaks of he- and she-demons created during this time of estrangement, the result of nocturnal emissions.[17] According to Midrashic and kabbalistic

---

17. In kabbalistic language this constitutes a weakness of the *sefirah* of *yesod*, which is related to sexual self-control and fidelity. Yosef, who displays the ability to contain himself despite the seductive overtures of Potifar's wife, is most closely identified with the kabbalistic sphere of *yesod*.

writings, both Adam and Eve[18] failed in this particular area during these 130 years. They lacked fidelity; they lacked stability; they lacked a home.

Now wandering, Yaakov needs stability. He needs a home. He needs a wife. Yaakov understands that this is true on a macro level as well: the Jewish people, his descendants, will also need stability; they will also need a home. But as we have seen, this mystical, connecting thread of 130 goes beyond Yaakov both on the individual level and the House of Yaakov on the national level. Yaakov's vision of the ladder is a personal vision, with national ramifications. Similarly, the voice of Yaakov is a medium through which heaven and earth may be brought closer. Yes – the Revelation at Sinai is the ultimate connection between the Jewish people and their Father in heaven. Similarly, the thematic thread of 130 brings us from the *sulam*, through the *kol* of Yaakov, all the way back to Adam and Eve, asking us to consider the ramifications of Yaakov's epiphany on an even larger scale.

What, then, is the connection between Yaakov and Adam? The Talmud states:

תלמוד בבלי, מסכת בבא מציעא דף פד עמוד א
...שופריה דיעקב אבינו מעין שופריה דאדם הראשון.

... our father Yaakov's beauty was a reflection of Adam's. (Talmud Bavli Bava Metzia 84a)

Yaakov had the same pure, holy countenance as Adam before he ate from the Tree of Knowledge of Good and Evil.[19] In fact, when Yaakov stands on

---

18. The sources view Eve's relationship with the serpent as having sexual overtones.

19. See Ari"zal, *Sefer haLikutim*, Parashat Vayeishev.

ספר הליקוטים, פרשת וישב פרק מח

כבר ידעת, כי יעקב אע"ה היה גלגול אדה"ר, ובעת הציווי שצוה השי"ת לאדה"ר, אמר לו (בראשית ט)
מכל עץ הגן אכל תאכל, ונכלל במכל עץ הגן עץ החיים, ולא אמר ומעץ החיים לא תאכל ממנו, והניח אדה"ר
עץ החיים, ונדבק בעץ הדעת טוב ורע, שהוא מצד אלהים אחרים, סמא"ל ובת זוגו, ופגמו והביא המות
לעולם. והדומם והצומח ובעלי חיים וחי מדבר, ואפילו המלאכים כולם נפגמו בטוב ורע, כי מתים וחיים,
כנרמז במקום אחר, כי בכולם יש טוב ורע. ויש מלאכים שמיתתם בנהר דינור, וראשם נפלו ומתו בארץ,
והם הנפילים היו בארץ, שהם עז"א ועזא"ל. וכוונת הקב"ה היתה, שיהיה ישראל בלבד כלול באדם, ולא
האומות ושבעים שרים שהם הרע, וישב בג"ע לעבדה ולשמרה, כמו שיהיה לעתיד. (קהלת ז:כו) והמה בקשו
חשבונות רבים, שיצאו ממנו שבעים אומות, ולכן (תהלים פב:ז) כאדם תמותון, כולם. ולא היה מצד הטוב
של אדם, כי אם חנוך ואליהו במין האנושי, ולכן לא מתו. וז"ס (בראשית כד) ויתהלך חנוך את האלהים:
ובחטאו הלבישם כתנות עור, במקום שהיו מקודם אור.

that holy ground and sees the ladder, what does he ask for? Bread to eat and clothing to wear (28:20), the two elements affected by the sin in the Garden of Eden. Man's obligation to work and man's need to cover his nakedness originate from this sin. Ironically, the two interactions recorded between Yaakov and Esav also revolve around food and clothing.

Yaakov, then, is connected to the Tree of Life.[20] Yaakov is associated with the tents (of Torah), with Sinai, with the ladder of his vision and with the voice that is in search of the Word of God. All of these point to the Tree of Life, another name for Torah. Esav is connected with the other tree – the tree of death. The personification of evil in the garden was the serpent. His punishment for causing man to be expelled from his home, for causing instability in the intimate relationship between Adam and Eve, is described in the Torah as follows:

בראשית ג:טו

וְאֵיבָה אָשִׁית בֵּינְךָ וּבֵין הָאִשָּׁה וּבֵין זַרְעֲךָ וּבֵין זַרְעָהּ הוּא יְשׁוּפְךָ רֹאשׁ וְאַתָּה תְּשׁוּפֶנּוּ עָקֵב:

And I will put enmity between you and the woman, and between your offspring and her offspring; he [man] shall bruise your head, and you shall bruise his heel. (Bereishit 3:15)

It starts with enmity between Hava and the serpent, and ends with an *'akev*, a heel – the root and source of the name Yaakov! It is Yaakov who is destined to be the ultimate enemy of the serpent. Who is this serpent that he should have such an adversary? The mystical sources identify the serpent with various nefarious characters, but one in particular stands out: Sama'el, the protecting angel of Esav. Variously associated with Esav,[21]

---

20. See *Shlah haKadosh*, Parashat Hayei Sarah.

ספר השל"ה הקדוש, פרשת חיי שרה תורה אור (ב)

שופריה דיעקב מעין שופריה דאדם (ב"מ פד:א), ונתדבק בעץ החיים. כי אדם הראשון קלקל בעץ הדעת, והאבות התחילו לתקן תיקון הקלקול. אברהם שורש עץ הדעת טוב ורע לתקנו, ויצחק הוא עץ הדעת שממנו טוב ורע, ויעקב הוא התוכיות עץ החיים בתוך הגן מטתו שלימה, אשר על אומה ישראלית אמר השם יתברך ואתם הדבקים בה' אלהיכם חיים כולכם, והם מוכנים לחיי עד.

21. The *Megaleh 'Amukot* (Parashat Va'ethanan, section 47) identifies the serpent with Esav.

ספר מגלה עמוקות, פרשת ואתחנן אופן מז

וסוד נחש שהוא עשו.

with the Angel of Death or with the serpent, this demonic angel[22] has an advantage over Yaakov: *Sama'el* has a numerical value of 131.[23]

When Yaakov goes in to see his father, bringing him food, he is wearing the clothing of Esav. This clothing is traced back to Nimrod – and all the way back to Adam. It may actually have been the skin of the serpent.[24] Now Yaakov has merged with the serpent and the Tree of Knowledge of Good and Evil. He has entered a world of confusion.

Yaakov desires stability, clarity, Torah; he seeks life. Yet the Torah testifies that he is destined to be a man of the tents: the ironic vicissitudes of his life have taken Yaakov from the tents of study to his father's tent, dressed up as Esav, and then back out to the road.

Under the open sky, Yaakov seeks stability. He wants a home. He wants happiness. He is an *ish tam* – and he wants an uncomplicated relationship. When it is Esav's turn to marry, he takes two wives at once,[25] inviting

---

22. The Zohar (Bereishit 170a) reveals that this is the identity of the "man" who wrestled with Yaakov.

זוהר, בראשית דף קע עמוד א

ויאבק איש עמו: מאי ויאבק, דאמר רבי יהושע בן לוי, מלמד דסליקו אבק ברגליהון עד כורסי יקרא, כתיב הכא בהאבקו עמו, וכתיב (נחום א:ג) אבק רגליו, וההוא מלאך שרו של עשו היה, ואיהו סמאל.

23. See *Megaleh 'Amukot*, Parashat Va'et'hanan, section 191.

ספר מגלה עמוקות, פרשת ואתחנן אופן קצא

וסוד אף מלא ר"ל לילי"ת וסמא"ל, עולה כמנין ברי"ת, וסמאל רוכב על ק"ל, בסוד והקל נשמע בית פרעה. ואמרו רז"ל שר של נבוכדנאצר קל שמו. ק"ל שנה שפירש אדם הראשון מן האשה, הוליד רוחין. וסוד הקל קול יעקב, קל ראשון חסר, בסוד אם פגם בך מנוול זה, משכהו לבית המדרש. וזה סוד סלם זה סיני, צריך לתקן סמאל, מספר סל"ם, עם סיני.

24. See *Rabbeinu Bahya*, Bereishit 3:21, and the footnotes by Rabbi Chavel in the Mosad Harav Kook edition.

רבינו בחיי, בראשית ג

ויעש ה' אלהים לאדם ולאשתו כתנות עור... ודעת רז"ל שהיו לבושים הללו מצויירין שם כל מיני עופות שבעולם, ואדם הורישם לקין, וכשנהרג קין באו לידו של נמרוד, הוא שכתוב: (בראשית י:ט) הוא היה גבור ציד וג'. וכשהרג עשו לנמרוד נטלן עשו ממנו, והוא שכתוב: (בראשית כז:טו) "את בגדי עשו בנה הגדול החמודות", מאי "החמודות", שחמדן מנמרוד.

כתר יונתן, בראשית כז: טו

ותקח רבקה את בגדי עשו בנה הגדול חמודות שהיו מאדם הראשון וביום ההוא לא לבשם עשו ונשארו אצלה בביתה ותלבש את יעקב בנה הקטן:

25. See Bereishit 26:34–35: "And Esav was forty years old when he married Yehudit the daughter of Be'eri the Hittite, and Bas'mat the daughter of Elon the Hittite. And they made life bitter for Yitzhak and for Rivkah."

disharmony, creating anarchy. Esav's son Elifaz avoids marriage altogether and fathers an illegitimate child, Amalek. The irony of Yaakov's life is that despite his search for stability – he is forced to wander. Despite wanting to marry the one woman that he loves, he is forced into another marriage. Despite wanting simplicity, he receives complexity. His enemy is as old as Creation: Sama'el, the angel who seeks to confuse and ultimately destroy man. But Yaakov is connected to the Tree of Life; thus, in the words of the sages, "*Yaakov Avinu lo meit*" – Yaakov will never die.[26] The secret to his life, his eternal strength, is this: marriage and happiness, holiness and stability, a house for himself and a House for God. As we have seen, the ladder of his vision stretched across all of the Land of Israel, linking Sinai with the Beit haMikdash.

Our rabbi's tell us that the covenant at Sinai was also a marriage.[27] The *kolot* (voices) that the people experienced at Sinai were a joyful celebration of marriage, of the union between the Jewish people and God. So, too, the Revelation at Sinai is described as a healing event.[28] Sinai is where the foundations of stability are laid. Sinai is where happiness is rediscovered. Rabbi Nahman of Breslov taught that the way to defeat the evil inclination is with authentic happiness.[29] The *sulam* and the *kol* are the same: both uplift us when we are down. When the Jewish people were faced with destruction, Yirmiyahu prophesized against despair:

ירמיהו לג:י–יא

כֹּה אָמַר ה' עוֹד יִשָּׁמַע בַּמָּקוֹם הַזֶּה אֲשֶׁר אַתֶּם אֹמְרִים חָרֵב הוּא מֵאֵין אָדָם וּמֵאֵין בְּהֵמָה בְּעָרֵי יְהוּדָה וּבְחֻצוֹת יְרוּשָׁלַם הַנְשַׁמּוֹת מֵאֵין אָדָם וּמֵאֵין יוֹשֵׁב

---

26. Talmud Bavli Taanit 5b.

27. Talmud Bavli Taanit 26b.

28. See Shmot Rabbah 2:4. This is why so many hospitals are named "Mount Sinai" – because of the healing power of that place.

29. *Likutei Halakhot, Hilkhot Birkat Hodaah*, halakhah 6.

ספר ליקוטי הלכות, הלכות ברכת הודאה הלכה ו

וזה מרמז סלם, כי סלם בגימטריא קול כמובא שזה בחינת הקל קול יעקב, שעל-ידי זה כל התגברותו של איש הישראלי נגד כל הסטרא אחרא והיכלי התמורות שכלם כלולים בבחינת עשו, כמו שאמרו רבותינו זכרונם לברכה בזמן שהקול קול יעקב אין הידים ידי עשו, שאין לו שום כח. וזהו הקל קול יעקב שני קולות, כי עקר השלמות הוא בחינת שמחה שעל-ידי זה כל השגת אור האין סוף וכו' כנ"ל, ועקר השמחה הוא בחינת קולות בחינת חמש קולות הנ"ל שהם קול ששון וקול שמחה וכו', בחינת חדות ה' הוא מעזכם שהוא בחינת הן יתן בקלו קול עז וכו' כמו שמובא במקום אחר.

וּמֵאֵין בְּהֵמָה: קוֹל שָׂשׂוֹן וְקוֹל שִׂמְחָה קוֹל חָתָן וְקוֹל כַּלָּה קוֹל אֹמְרִים הוֹדוּ אֶת ה' צְבָאוֹת כִּי טוֹב ה' כִּי לְעוֹלָם חַסְדּוֹ מְבִאִים תּוֹדָה בֵּית ה' כִּי אָשִׁיב אֶת שְׁבוּת הָאָרֶץ כְּבָרִאשֹׁנָה אָמַר ה':

Thus says God: "Again there shall be heard in this place, which you say shall be desolate without man and without beast – in the cities of Yehudah, and in the streets of Jerusalem that are desolate, without man, and without inhabitant, and without beast – the voice of joy and the voice of gladness, the voice of the bridegroom and the voice of the bride, the voice of those who shall say, 'Give thanks to the Lord of Hosts for God is good, for His mercy endures forever'; the praise offering shall be brought in the House of God. For I will cause to return the captivity of the land, as at the first," says God. (Yirmiyahu 33:10–11)

Those words are echoed at every Jewish wedding, and they have redemptive powers; they can bring joy and help rebuild the Temple:

תלמוד בבלי, מסכת ברכות דף ו עמוד ב
ואמר רבי חלבו אמר רב הונא: כל הנהנה מסעודת חתן ואינו משמחו – עובר בחמשה קולות, שנאמר, (ירמיהו לג) "קול ששון וקול שמחה קול חתן וקול כלה קול אומרים הודו את ה' צבאות".
ואם משמחו מה שכרו? אמר רבי יהושע בן לוי: זוכה לתורה שנתנה בחמשה קולות, שנאמר, (שמות יט) "ויהי ביום השלישי בהיות הבקר ויהי קולות וברקים וענן כבד על ההר וקל שפר" וגו' "ויהי קול השפר" וגו' "והאלקים יעננו בקול" וגו'. רבי אבהו אמר: כאילו הקריב תודה, שנאמר, (ירמיהו לג) "מבאים תודה בית ה'". רב נחמן בר יצחק אמר: כאילו בנה אחת מחורבות ירושלים, שנאמר, (ירמיהו לג) "כי אשיב את שבות הארץ כבראשונה אמר ה'".

R. Helbo further said in the name of R. Huna: Whoever enjoys the wedding meal of a bridegroom and does not help him to rejoice transgresses against the five voices mentioned in the verse "The voice of joy and the voice of gladness, the voice of the bridegroom and the voice of the bride, the voice of those who shall say, 'Give thanks to the Lord of Hosts'" (Yirmiyahu 33).
And if he does gladden [the bridegroom], what is his reward? R. Joshua b. Levi said: He is privileged to acquire [the knowledge of] the Torah which was given with five voices. For it is said: "it came to pass on the third day, when it was morning, that there was thunder and lightning and a thick cloud upon the mount, and the voice of a

horn...and when the voice of the horn waxed louder...Moshe spoke and God answered him by a voice." R. Abbahu said: It is as if he sacrificed a thanksgiving offering. For it is said, "Even of those who bring offerings of thanksgiving into the House of God." R. Nahman b. Yitzhak says: It is as if he restored one of the ruins of Jerusalem. For it is said, "For I will cause the captivity of the land to return as at the first, says God" (Yirmiyahu 33). (Talmud Bavli Brakhot 6b)

The voice is a voice of joy, and of commitment; the joy of marriage, of Torah, and of bringing an offering in the Temple of Jerusalem. Those who participate in this joy are actually actively helping rebuild the ruins of Jerusalem, helping to reestablish the cornerstone of covenant with God. This is what Yaakov perceived, lying on the ground someplace between Be'er Sheva and Haran. Despite the fact that he now knew that he was in a holy place – perhaps the holiest place on Earth – and that this place would belong to him and his descendants, he did not abandon his travel plans. He continued his journey to find his bride, while at the same time dedicating himself to building the House of God that he had seen in his dream. He set out to build both homes simultaneously.

Rabbi Nahman offers another perspective on the merger of Sinai and the ladder (*sulam*) which may help us reconcile the divergent interpretations of Yaakov's vision. Rabbi Nahman explains that the angels Yaakov saw "going up and coming down" were, in fact, dancing. The kinetic movement of the dance is the movement of an angel whose feet no longer touch the ground as it reaches toward heaven. Every one of us can imitate this motion as we take part in the greatest of human joys – the building of a new home in which Godliness can dwell. Every wedding is like Sinai; every wedding should connect us with heaven, as if by a ladder that allows us to climb to new spiritual heights.[30] If we are to defeat the evil inclination, the melancholy of self-doubt, we must open our eyes and watch the angels going up and

---

30. *Sihot Moharan*, section 86.

ספר שיחות מוהר"ן, אות פו

החתונה הוא בחינת סיני כמו שכתוב (קעב): "ביום חתונתו" זה מעמד הר סיני (תענית כו:) וסיני גימטריא סולם. וכתוב: "והנה מלאכי אלהים עולים ויורדים בו" (קעג) הינו רקודין שבשעת רקודין עולה ויורד כי כן דרך רקודין שעולה את גופו ויורד את גופו.

coming down, attune ourselves to the possibility of connecting with the spiritual world above and beyond our physical existence. If we do more than just watch, and instead physically join in the dance and song, we will find ourselves that much closer to heaven.

Parashat Vayishlah

Yaakov – or Yisrael?

בראשית לב:כה

וַיִּוָּתֵר יַעֲקֹב לְבַדּוֹ וַיֵּאָבֵק אִישׁ עִמּוֹ עַד עֲלוֹת הַשָּׁחַר:

And Yaakov was left alone; and a man wrestled with him until the break of day. (Bereishit 32:25)

Late one night a nameless, enigmatic adversary meets a man named Yaakov – at least Yaakov thought that was his name.

בראשית לב:כח–כט

וַיֹּאמֶר אֵלָיו מַה שְּׁמֶךָ וַיֹּאמֶר יַעֲקֹב: וַיֹּאמֶר לֹא יַעֲקֹב יֵאָמֵר עוֹד שִׁמְךָ כִּי אִם יִשְׂרָאֵל כִּי שָׂרִיתָ עִם אֱלֹקִים וְעִם אֲנָשִׁים וַתּוּכָל:

And he said to him, "What is your name?" And he said, "Yaakov." And he said, "No longer will you be called Yaakov, but Yisrael; for you have struggled with God[1] and with men, and have prevailed." (Bereishit 32:28–29)

While the identity of this individual is withheld, apparently his statement is accurate, for later God reaffirms the message:

בראשית לה:ט–י

וַיֵּרָא אֱלֹקִים אֶל יַעֲקֹב עוֹד בְּבֹאוֹ מִפַּדַּן אֲרָם וַיְבָרֶךְ אֹתוֹ: וַיֹּאמֶר לוֹ אֱלֹקִים שִׁמְךָ יַעֲקֹב לֹא יִקָּרֵא שִׁמְךָ עוֹד יַעֲקֹב כִּי אִם יִשְׂרָאֵל יִהְיֶה שְׁמֶךָ וַיִּקְרָא אֶת שְׁמוֹ יִשְׂרָאֵל:

---

1. The Hebrew word is *elohim*, and the commentaries disagree whether the word in this instance bears a holy meaning, referring to the Almighty, or a mundane one, referring to a powerful person or being other than God, such as an angel. See *Minhat Shai* on this verse:

מנחת שי, בראשית לב:כט

כי שרית עם אלקים: יש מרז"ל מפרשים אותו קדש ויש מפרשים אותו חול עיין ב"ר וחולין פ' גיד הנשה ועיין מ"ש סוף פ' ויצא.

213

> *And the Almighty appeared to Yaakov again, when he came from Padan Aram, and blessed him. And the Almighty said to him, "Your name is Yaakov; no longer shall you be called Yaakov, but Yisrael shall be your name"; and He called his name Yisrael. (Bereishit 35:9–10)*

While these pronouncements seem straightforward, things may not be as simple as they appear. Although other biblical figures also had name changes, after their new name was bestowed, the old name was never used again. Avraham was born Avram, but after God changed his name, he never again reverted to the previous form of Avram. So, too, Sarai/Sarah. In the case of Yaakov/Yisrael, the name change doesn't seem to stick. One would assume that, as in the other cases that we have noted, from this point onward Yaakov should never again be called Yaakov, but that simply is not the case. God Himself, in subsequent dialogue, addresses him as Yaakov rather than as Yisrael. Perhaps, then, we have not properly understood the "name change."[2]

Avraham's name is changed to reflect his personal, spiritual metamorphosis. The Baalei haTosafot explain that Avraham's new name was given at the juncture at which most Jewish males are given their name – when they are circumcised. Precisely because the new name was part of Avraham's "conversion," the old identity was forfeited or expunged permanently, to the extent that using the old name is halakhically proscribed.[3] Yaakov, unlike Avraham, was born "Jewish"; he was circumcised on the eighth day after his birth and given his name concurrently. The new name he is given later in life must therefore have a different purpose.[4]

---

2. This observation is made by *haKtav v'haKabbalah*, Bereishit 35:10.

הכתב והקבלה, בראשית לה:י

ויהיה א"כ משמעות המאמר כאן שלא יקרא מהיום והלאה בשם יעקב אלא בשם ישראל לבד, וזה א"א לומר שהרי הוא ית' בעצמו קראו בשם יעקב (לקמן מ"ו ויאמר יעקב יעקב).

3. See Talmud Bavli Brakhot 13a: "Whoever calls Avraham *Avram* transgresses a positive precept, since it says, 'Your name shall be Avraham.' R. Eliezer says: He transgresses a negative command, since it says, 'Neither shall your name anymore be called Avram.'"

תלמוד בבלי, מסכת ברכות דף יג עמוד א

תני בר קפרא כל הקורא לאברהם אברם עובר בעשה שנאמר והיה שמך אברהם רבי אליעזר אומר עובר בלאו שנאמר ולא יקרא עוד [את] שמך אברם.

4. Commentary of Baalei haTosafot, Bereishit 35:9.

In fact, Yaakov's name was not changed; rather, he received an additional name,[5] giving us an entirely different set of implications to explore. Suggestions abound regarding the significance of each of these names, and the usage of each, but an overarching explanation into which all the instances fit perfectly and every occurrence is explained still seems lacking. The various approaches are not mutually exclusive, and may complement one another, together giving us a whole picture that is greater than the sum of its parts.

Rashi[6] suggests that the name Yaakov indicates subservience, while the name Yisrael indicates strength and victory; the varying uses reflect different aspects of Yaakov's personality which come to light in different situations. Another view is offered by the *Meshekh Hokhmah*, who sees the different names as expressing the distinction between Yaakov as an individual versus Yisrael as a national identity. Thus, according to the *Meshekh Hokhmah*, God addresses "Yisrael" exclusively when, and only when, there are national issues at hand.[7]

The Netziv[8] proposes that the two names mark a distinction between a supernatural aspect of events or ideas (Yisrael), versus a more mundane

---

פירוש בעלי התוספות, בראשית לה:ט

שאלה מטרוניתא לר' עקיבא שאחר שקראו הקב"ה אברהם שוב לא נקרא אברם. ויעקב נקרא בשמו יעקב אע"פ שקראו הקב"ה ישראל. אמר לה אברהם שהיה לו שם גיות שהרי כשנולד עדיין לא נתגייר אברהם וכיון שקראו הקב"ה שם יהדות אין דין לקרותו שם גיות. אבל יעקב שמתחלה נמי קראו הקב"ה יעקב ולא נשתנה שמו אלא על שם כי שרית עם אלהים ליכא חששא לקרותו בשמו הראשון. והא דכתיב לא יקרא עוד שמך יעקב הכי פירושה כלומר לא יאמר עוד שלקחת הברכות ברמאות אלא ישראל יהיה שמך.

5. Ibn Ezra, Bereishit 35:10.

אבן עזרא, בראשית לה:י

לא יקרא שמך עוד יעקב: לבדו כי גם ישראל.

6. Rashi, Bereishit 35:10. This idea is echoed by Rabbeinu Bahya, 32:29.

רש"י, בראשית לה:י

לא יקרא שמך עוד יעקב: לשון אדם הבא במארב ועקבה אלא לשון שר ונגיד.

7. *Meshekh Hokhmah*, Bereishit 35:10.

משך חכמה, בראשית לה:י

ויקרא את שמו ישראל: הפירוש מפני שלא מצאנו שהשי"ת יאמר בכל התורה על יעקב ישראל רק יעקב וארא אל כו' יעקב בכל מקום שמדבר עליו בעצמו. רק במקום שמדבר בהשתתפותו אל האומה כגון בני ישראל או אלקי ישראל וכי"ב.

8. *Ha'amek Davar*, Bereishit 35:10. See Rabbeinu Bahya (47:29) who sees "Yaakov" as a name indicating physicality, and "Yisrael" as a name indicative of the spiritual.

aspect (Yaakov). Because humans cannot function purely on the spiritual plane, both names are needed.

Each of these suggestions seems to point to an unresolved tension in Yaakov's life that results in a dual identity.

While other patriarchs also experienced tension and conflict, to a great extent their issues were eventually resolved. For example, there is a certain amount of tension in Avraham's life stemming from the battle for status as his "real" wife between Hagar and Sarah. Who is Avraham's "real" son, Yishmael or Yitzhak? The conflicts in Avraham's life are resolved so quickly and efficiently that we are lulled into thinking that they never existed. So, too, with Yitzhak: who is Yitzhak's "real" son, the son who would continue the line and the covenant – Yaakov or Esav? The tension lasts for approximately one chapter and is resolved.

Looking at Yaakov's life, resolutions are scarce. Who is his "real" wife, Rahel or Leah? This is a haunting question; a fair argument could be made for each. Shall we say that the real wife is the woman he first loved? Is it the woman who brought most of Yaakov's children into the world? Or is it perhaps the woman buried beside him in the ancestral burial ground? And who is Yaakov's "primary" son, Yosef or Yehudah? The questions seem more intriguing than the answer could possibly be. And now, what, indeed, is his real name – Yaakov or Yisrael? Yaakov's life is full of unresolved conflicts and tension, but it is within these unresolved conflicts that the depth of Yaakov's identity emerges and his essence is revealed.

Each of the patriarchs has a unique spiritual identity: Avraham is associated with *hesed* (kindness); Yitzhak is identified with *din* (judgment). Yaakov is known as *tiferet* (splendor) or *rahamim* (compassion), the merger of the *hesed* of Avraham and the *din* of Yitzhak.[9] Our first question should

---

העמק דבר, בראשית לה:י

שמך יעקב: ודאי שמך יעקב. **שמורה על הליכות הטבע** כמ"ש בס' תולדת דלהכי אחז בעקב עשו. דאלו לפי הנהגה נסית לא הי' צריך לאחוז בעקב עשו כמו שאמר המלאך ליעקב לעיל ל"ב כ"ט לא יעקב יאמר עוד שמך וגו' וביארנו שאמר שלא הי' צריך לאחוז בעקב עשו כי שרית עם אלהים וגו'. ואמר לו ה' דמכ"מ ודאי שמך יעקב הנך צריך לזה השם שלא הכל ראויים לנס ולהשתרר עם אלהים ועם אנשים.

9. See the comments of the Alshikh on Shmot 17:8.

be, why? Why is Yaakov associated with *rahamim*?[10] Is this identification arbitrary, or is there an intrinsic relationship?

The Vilna Gaon explains that when Yaakov is called *"ish tam"* – a simple or perhaps perfect man – this combination of Avraham and Yitzhak, of *hesed* and *din*, is the nature of his perfection. He is perfect because he is the center, the wonderful balance.[11] But what is *rahamim*? How is it distinguished from *hesed*? The word *rahamim* is etymologically related to *rehem*, womb. Thus, one might render *rahamim* as all-embracing, unconditional love,[12] like that of a mother for her child. Just as a mother has this sort of love for her child despite the inevitable physical pain of childbirth and the unavoidable emotional pain of raising the child, so *rahamim* is love that is acutely aware of the inevitability of pain. Few people experienced the pain of raising children as acutely as Yaakov. Reuven's indiscretion and insubordination, Shimon and Levi's violent adventures, the abuse suffered by Dinah, Yosef's disappearance and apparent death, the potential loss of Binyamin – the story of Yaakov's life was one of parental pain.[13]

ספר תורת משה, שמות יז:ח–יב

עד בא השמש: והגיע זמן יעקב. כי אז רחמים של מדת יעקב יגינו על בניו. וזהו אומרו ויהי לשון יחיד, וידיו לשון רבים. שהוא שייחד מדת יצחק למדת אברהם.

10. See the comments of the *Shlah haKadosh, Shaʿar haOtiot, ot heh*, where he explains that Yaakov asking to bless his children before he dies is a manifestation of *rahamim*.

11. See commentary of the Vilna Gaon to the *Sifra d'Tzniuta*, chapter 3.

פירוש הגר"א לספרא דצניעותא, פרק ג

ולכן יעקב נקרא איש תם שכולל חו"ג כמ"ש בפרשת תרומה דף קס"ט ע"ב דתנינן מאי איש תם כתרגומו שלים כו' עד ואשלים להאי ולהאי ע"ש. וכן אברהם לא נקרא שלם עד שעקד את יצחק שנכלל חסד עם גבורה כידוע וכמ"ש בא"ר דף קל"ח ע"א אברהם אברהם בתרא שלים קדמאה לא שלים כו'.

12. For more on *rahamim* and love, see Maharal, *Netzah Yisrael*, chapter 52.

ספר נצח ישראל, פרק נב

שמדת יעקב מדת רחמים, וזהו עצם החבור. שאינו דומה מדת אברהם, אף על גב שעל ידו יבוא לכלל הדבוק האלקי, אין מדה זאת – שהוא מדת אברהם – עצם החבור. וכן אף על גב שמדת יצחק – שהוא מדת הדין – סבה שעל ידו הדיבוק האלקי לגמרי, אין זה עצם הדיבוק. אבל מדת יעקב – שהוא מדת רחמים – הוא הדבוק בעצם לגמרי. כי זה ענין הרחמים, האהבה והחבור. שכבר בארנו זה כי "אוהב" תרגומו 'מרחמוהו' (בראשית כה:כח), וכן בלשון חכמים (כתובות קה ע"ב) 'לא לדין אינש מאן דמרחם ליה', ודבר זה ידוע. והאהבה היא הדבוק והחבור בעצם, שכאשר דבק נפשו, כמו האב לבן והאם לבנה, מרחם עליו, כמו שהתבאר למעלה דבר זה, עיין שם. ולפיכך מדה זאת בעצמה הוא סבה אל החבור שיש אל השם יתברך לתחתונים, ודבר זה ידוע למבינים.

13. See Talmud Bavli Shabbat 89b, where God acknowledges the pain that Yaakov endured raising his children.

Some commentaries[14] describe *rahamim* as synthesis:[15] *hesed* is thesis, *din*[16] antithesis, and *rahamim* is the resultant synthesis. This is the means Yaakov used to cope with the unresolved conflicts in his life. Other commentaries take a slightly different view: rather than synthesis, the relationship may be more accurately described as symbiosis; *rahamim* combines *din* and *hesed*, but each of the preexisting elements retains its identity as a distinct attribute.[17] This approach is akin to another description of Yaakov: according to the Midrash, Yaakov is associated with the main beam that goes through the width of the Mishkan – the "*beriah hatikhon.*"[18] It was Yaakov who brought this beam to Egypt when he went to see Yosef, effectively beginning the exile.[19] This middle beam holds the edifice together. Yaakov, who has the

---

14. See *Meshekh Hokhmah*, Bereishit 35:1.

משך חכמה, בראשית לה:א

ועשה שם מזבח וכו', ויבן שם מזבח כו' כי שם נגלו אליו האלקים: הענין דמדתו של יעקב אחוזה בתרין דרועין חסד ודין. והוא המתקת הדין הנקרא רחמים.

15. See comments of the *Megaleh 'Amukot*, Parashat Vayehi: when Yaakov is buried in the Cave of the Makhpeilah, the stalemate between *hesed* and *din* is finally resolved.

ספר מגלה עמוקות, פרשת ויחי

והנה מדת יעקב (מיכה ז) תתן אמת ליעקב כמ"ש יעקב ליוסף ועשית עמדי חסד ואמת כשתקברני בשכבות אבותי כי שם אין לב"ד הכרעה לפי שאברהם איש חסד ויצחק בעל דין קשה ואין להם הכרע עד שבא יעקב בעל רחמים והכריע ונמצא כשיהי' הוא קבור שם יהי' חסד ואמת נפגשו (תהלים) שנים מזכין וא' מחייב בטל יחיד במיעוטו והלכה כרבים עז"א המלאך הגואל אותי אות שלי שהוא אמת והוא המלאך הגואל מלא בו'.

16. See comments of *Mevo l'Hokhmat haKabbalah*, part 1, gate 3, chapter 3.

ספר מבוא לחכמת הקבלה, חלק א שער ג פרק ג

וכן יעקב היה מרכבה למדת אמת שהיא תפארת רחמים, כי האמת היא התורה והיא רחמים ממוזג בין חסד לדין.

17. Rabbi Soloveitchik felt that in many instances Judaism has unresolved conflicts, and the desired resolution is not synthesis, which would dull both of the initial elements, but rather in the unresolved dialectic the beauty emerges. Thus, Adam is "created" twice: once as an individual, and once as a part of society. Both aspects are true expressions of self, and neither should be lost in the merger.

18. See Rabbi Moshe de Leon, *Shekel haKodesh*.

ספר שקל הקדש לרבי משה די ליאון ז"ל

והוא יסוד הרוח, אמנם כי סוד הענין הזה הוא היתה התקועה ועיקר האמונה כי היא מדרגה העומדת באמצע מכל צד ומכל עבר ועל כן סוד עיקר המרכבה העליונה בסוד שם של שבעים ושתים שמות של מקום, וזהו מזרח, רוח, הבריח התיכון, יעקב, ישראל סבא, תפארת ישראל, צדקה, שמים העליונים, רחמים, משפט, והרבה אחרים שגם בענין זה שמות הרבה, אמנם נפרש ברמזים עניינים אלה בסוד כל אחד ואחד מהם.

19. See Midrash Tanhuma (Buber edition), Parashat Terumah, section 9.

ability to bring together the attributes he inherited from Avraham and Yitzhak, is uniquely able to hold these two divergent strands together to create the unshakable "middle way," the supporting beam of what will later become our main conduit to spirituality. This is what it means to be the "middle" – to support the structure, to provide tools for redemption at the very start of the inevitable exile.

In fact, Yaakov is the first individual in the Torah to use the word *rahamim*, and the circumstances in which he invokes the attribute could not be more relevant:

בראשית מג:יד

וְקֵל שַׁ-דַּי יִתֵּן לָכֶם רַחֲמִים לִפְנֵי הָאִישׁ וְשִׁלַּח לָכֶם אֶת אֲחִיכֶם אַחֵר וְאֶת בִּנְיָמִין וַאֲנִי כַּאֲשֶׁר שָׁכֹלְתִּי שָׁכָלְתִּי:

And may God Almighty give you mercy before the man, that he may free your other brother and Binyamin. And if I am to be bereaved of my children, then I am bereaved. (Bereishit 43:14)

When Binyamin is brought, ostensibly to satisfy the whimsical request of an Egyptian despot, for the first time all twelve brothers are in Egypt, and the exile, foretold to Avraham, Yitzhak and Yaakov, begins. When the brothers flagged down the band of passing Yishmaelites and sold Yosef into slavery, they did not realize that they were soon to share his plight. It never dawned on them that they were all part of a larger plan that would bring all of the children of Yaakov to Egypt. But Yaakov sends them off with a prayer: "May God give you *rahamim*!"

The *Megaleh 'Amukot* says that when Yaakov prayed for *rahamim*, it was from God, and not from the Egyptian ruler: he prayed that God's attribute of *rahamim* should temper the *din* of the exile. This prayer is the reason that the actual period of slavery lasted only eighty-six years, which is the

---

מדרש תנחומא (בובר), פרשת תרומה פסקה ט

אמרו רבותינו הבריח התיכון ירד ביד יעקב למצרים, שהיה משמש מן הקצה אל הקצה, לא עשה אלא היו הארזים אמרו שירה, הוא שדוד אומר אז ירננו כל עצי היער וגו' (תהלים צו:יב), אין אז אלא שירה שאומר להקב"ה, ואומר אימתי יעשה משכן, וכשאמר הקב"ה [למשה] שיעשה את המשכן, מה אמר לו ועשית את הקרשים למשכן, אותם הקרשים שהתקין להם אביהם.

numerical value of E-lohim.[20] This would be a classic example of *rahamim,* which fuses *hesed* and *din.* The children of Avraham are destined to be slaves, apparently for a period of four hundred years. But tradition tells us that the four hundred years are counted from the birth of Yitzhak and not from the moment the Children of Yaakov begin their sojourn in Egypt.

שיר השירים רבה, פרשה ב פסקה כח

"כי הנה הסתו עבר" – אלו ת' שנה שנגזרו על אבותינו במצרים. "הגשם חלף
הלך לו" – אלו מאתים ועשר שנים. ולא הוא הגשם ולא הוא הסתו? אמר ר'
תנחומא: עיקר טרחותא מיטרא הוא. כך עיקר שעבודן של ישראל במצרים
שמונים ושש שנים היו, משעה שנולדה מרים (פירושה שלכך נקרא שמה מרים
על שום שנאמר, (שמות א) "וימררו את חייהם" כי מרים לשון מירור הוא).

"For lo, the winter is past" – this refers to the 400 years that our ancestors were condemned to be in Egypt. "The rain is over and gone" – this refers to the 210 years [that they were actually there]. Are not rain *and* winter *the same thing? R. Tanhuma said: The real hardship [of winter] is its rain. Similarly the real bondage of Israel in Egypt was 86 years, from the birth of Miriam. She was called Miriam, meaning bitterness, [because it says], "And they made their lives bitter" (Shmot 1:14), because "Miriam" means bitterness. (Shir haShirim Rabbah 2:28)*

The duration of the exile was 210 years, but actual slavery was only for 86 of those years. According to the *Megaleh 'Amukot,* this is a result of the prayers of Yaakov, and reflects his unique spiritual profile:[21] this is a merger of *hesed* and *din.* The exile and enslavement are inevitable, unavoidable. Yaakov prayed, not to cancel these harsh decrees, not to alter the judgment of God's attribute of *din,* but to merge it with God's attribute of *hesed* – 86 years of slavery in place of 400. Indeed, the Talmud teaches

---

20. The numerical value of E-lohim is 86: *alef* (1), *lamed* (30), *heh* (5), *yud* (10), *mem* (40).

21. *Megaleh 'Amukot,* Parashat Va'eira.

ספר מגלה עמוקות, פרשת וארא
והוא סוד גלות מצרים ת' שנה כמנין ב"ד אלו שהסכימו להיות ישראל בגלות. הנה יעקב התפלל אל שדי
יתן לכם רחמים ולא נשארו בגלות רק מנין אלקים ז"ש וידבר אלקים אל משה וארא אל וכו' באל שדי
שיתן רחמים על שם זה ולא יהיו בגלות רק קושי השיעבוד מנין אלקים.

that the enslavement was tempered in another way: Yaakov himself was spared slavery:

תלמוד בבלי, מסכת שבת דף פט עמוד ב

אמר רבי חייא בר אבא אמר רבי יוחנן: ראוי היה יעקב אבינו לירד למצרים בשלשלאות של ברזל אלא שזכותו גרמה לו, דכתיב, (הושע יא) "בחבלי אדם אמשכם בעבותות אהבה ואהיה להם כמרימי עול על לחיהם ואט אליו אוכיל".

R. Hiyya b. Abba said in R. Yohanan's name: It would have been fitting for our father Yaakov to go down into Egypt in iron chains, but his merit spared him, for it is written, "I drew them with the cords of a man, with bands of love; and I was to them as those who take off the yoke from their jaws, and I laid meat before them" (Hoshea 11:4). (Talmud Bavli Shabbat 89b)

Slavery should have begun with Yaakov taken down to Egypt in chains, but he was spared the disgrace. Yaakov arrived in Egypt with a royal escort, and was received by Par'oh himself with full honors. It was the beginning of the slavery, conducted with pomp and circumstance. This combination is *rahamim*. The sale of Yosef[22] and Yosef's ascension to royalty were all part of the greater plan to temper the unavoidable enslavement.[23]

---

22. Midrash Tehillim, Psalm 105.

מדרש תהילים, מזמור קה

ויקרא רעב על הארץ: אמר רבי יהודה בר נחמן בשם רבי שמעון בן לקיש, ראוי היה יעקב לירד למצרים בשלשלאות של ברזל ובקולרין, ועשה לו הקב"ה כמה עלילות וכמה מנגנאות ונמכר יוסף למצרים כדי לירד. ויקרא רעב על הארץ, וכל כך למה, (שם מו:ו) ויבא יעקב מצרימה. אמר ר' פנחס הכהן בר חמא, משל לפרה אחת שהיו רוצין למשוך אותה למקולין שלה ולא היתה נמשכת. מה עשו, משכו בנה תחלה והיתה רצה אחריו. כך עשה הקב"ה מנגנאות, שעשו אחי יוסף כל אותן הדברים כדי שירדו למצרים גם כן כדי שירד גם יעקב, שנאמר (הושע יא:ד) בחבלי אדם אמשכם.

23. See *Eitz haDa'at Tov*, Parashat Vayigash.

ספר עץ הדעת טוב, פרשת ויגש

וישלחני וכו': בתחלה אמר כי מד' היתה זאת למוכרו למצרים מפני מחית הרעב כנו' ועתה חזר והודיע עוד סיבה אחרת יותר נעלמת וביותר תועלת עצום לאין קץ וז"ש וישלחני אלקים לפניכם ובא' עוד לפניכם פעם אחרת רמז אל מש"ז"ל בתנחומא ראוי היה יעקב ובניו לירד בשלשלאות של ברזל למצרים ובעבור כבודו הוריד ליוסף בתחלה וגלגל עליו שיהיה מלך וירד אביו בכבוד גדול למצרים וז"ש לפניכם קודם שאתם תרדו כי אילו לא שלחני לפניכם אלא עמכם היינו יורדים בשלשלאות. וגם לרמוז זה חזר שנית להזכיר שם אלקים וישלחני אלקים הוא מדת הדין שגזר עליו להורידו בגלות ורחם קצת עליו שירד בכבוד כנו'.

Let us return to another unresolved conflict in Yaakov's life: who was his "real" wife? Rahel was the woman Yaakov loved; Leah was the woman who produced the lion's share of *Bnei Yisrael*. According to the Zohar,[24] the real wife of Yaakov was Rahel, and the real wife of Yisrael was Leah. The Midrash articulates the issue as follows: the word *'ikar* ("principal" wife) is related to *'akarah* (childless); when the Torah says Rahel was *'akarah*, the message is that she was the principal wife. Nonetheless, Leah is the mother of the nation.[25]

The complexity of the issue stems from the nature of *rahamim*. Avraham was identified with *hesed*, and his wife Sarah, who insists that Yishmael must be banished, is *din*. It is she who displays clear judgment, is able to isolate the black and the white from amid the grey. Yitzhak, her son, is also identified with *din*; he hears the pronouncement of God and unflinchingly executes the decree. There is no grey area. His wife Rivkah is identified with *hesed*, hence the test employed by Avraham's servant to locate the proper spouse for Yitzhak.

---

24. Zohar, Devarim 281b.

רעיא מהימנא, דברים דף רפא עמוד ב

ועלייהו אתמר לא הביט און ביעקב ולא ראה עמל בישראל כגוונא דאית בישראל ארבע אנפין יעקב ישראל רחל לאה ישראל עם לאה יעקב עם רחל.

25. See Bereishit Rabbah 71:2.

בראשית רבה, פרשה עא פסקה ב

ר' חנין בשם ר' שמואל בר ר' יצחק אמר כיון שראה אבינו יעקב מעשים שרימה לאה באחותה נתן דעתו לגרשה וכיון שפקדה הקב"ה בבנים אמר לאמן של אלו אני מגרש ובסוף הוא מודה על הדבר הה"ד (בראשית מז) וישתחו ישראל על ראש המטה מי היה ראש מטתו של אבינו יעקב לא לאה ורחל עקרה א"ר יצחק רחל היתה עיקרו של בית כמה שנאמר ורחל עקרה עיקרה רחל א"ר אבא בר כהנא רוב מסובין עיקר של לאה היו לפיכך עושים רחל עיקר ורחל עקרה רחל היתה עיקרה של בית.

"R. Yehudah b. R. Shimon and R. Hanan said in the name of R. Shmuel b. R. Yitzhak: When the patriarch Yaakov saw how Leah deceived him by pretending to be her sister, he determined to divorce her. But as soon as the Holy One, blessed be He, visited her with children he exclaimed, 'Shall I divorce the mother of these children!' Eventually he gave thanks for her, as it says, 'And Yisrael bowed down [in thanksgiving] over [at] the head of the bed' (Bereishit 47:31); who was the head of our father Yaakov's bed? Surely Leah.

"'But Rahel was *akarah* (barren)' (Bereishit 29:31): R. Yitzhak said: Rahel was the chief of the house (the main wife), as it says, 'but Rahel was *akarah*,' which means that she was the chief (*'ikar*) of the house. R. Abba b. Kahana said: The majority of those who dined [at Yaakov's table] were Leah's children, therefore Rahel was declared the principal."

Who is Yaakov? A kindly, sensitive tent dweller. A spiritual man. A man of loving-kindness whom one needs no other reason to love. Rahel, too, is kind, generous, giving. Her self-sacrifice for her sister is unparalleled in the annals of *hesed*. Here, at last, is the perfect couple: similar in temperament and inclination, without the stark differences that characterized the home life of the previous two generations. But something went wrong. A different couple, also destined to unite, never materialized – Esav and Leah.

The original plan for the sons of Yitzhak and Rivkah did not include estrangement, rejection or enmity. Had Esav so chosen, he and Yaakov together would have built the Jewish people, a unified *Beit Yaakov* that would have grown from both of their descendants, each of them contributing their own unique strengths to the national identity. In this scenario, each of the two sons of Yitzhak had a perfectly suited mate. Just as Yaakov and Rahel were soul mates, Esav and Leah were meant to be together.[26] Yaakov and Rahel were destined to form a home of complete *hesed*, and Esav and Leah would form a home of total *din*. With these forces joined and working in harmony, the product would become known as *Am Yisrael*. This plan is frustrated when Esav backs out. He scorns his birthright, rejects his responsibility. Esav's powers of judgment are not put to use in the service of God, but rather in the service of self, as part of Esav's rebellion. Esav turns his back on the divine plan. He abdicates.

And when Esav abandons Jewish destiny, a vacuum is created; a replacement for Esav in the pantheon of Jewish leaders must be found. Yaakov steps up. He takes Esav's birthright upon himself, acquires the blessing that was meant for Esav, and sets out to fulfill a dual role: to fulfill the destiny of Yaakov and fulfill God's covenant with Avraham, while at the same time fulfilling the destiny that Esav has abandoned, which will now be filled by Yisrael.[27]

The merger of Yaakov and Yisrael is paralleled by the merger of Rahel and Leah. In fact, we are told that Rahel and Leah were one soul divided between

---

26. See Rashi, Bereishit 29:17.

רש"י, בראשית כט:יז

רכות: (ב"ב קכ"ג) שהיתה סבורה לעלות בגורלו של עשו ובכתה שהיו הכל אומרים שני בנים לרבקה ושתי בנות ללבן הגדולה לגדול והקטנה לקטן.

27. See *Shem mi'Shmuel*, Parashat Vayeitzei 5679.

two bodies.[28] Yaakov had always been the soul mate of Rahel; now, enter Yisrael, the "replacement" spouse for Leah.

Yaakov must now leave the tents. He must reinvent himself. He must live a dual life, and he must marry two women. He must be both Yaakov and Yisrael; he must balance *hesed* and *din*. He must become *rahamim*.

The name Yisrael is given to Yaakov as he is about to enter the Land of Israel, having built his family and his wealth, having brought to fruition the blessings meant for Esav. The name Yisrael is bestowed upon him when he has successfully incorporated into his personality the aspects Esav abandoned. It is bestowed after his confrontation with and victory over Esav. Yaakov has taken on Esav's attribute of *din*, building *Am Yisrael* together with Leah, and this is reflected in his new name. But his previous identity, his natural attribute of *hesed*, coexists with *din*; he has accepted a dual responsibility, and the duality of his name reflects this. He is married to both Rahel and Leah; he is both *hesed and din*, both Yaakov and Yisrael.

Years later, when Yaakov himself finally goes to Egypt, to exile, he has a revelation:

בראשית מו:א–ה

וַיִּסַּע יִשְׂרָאֵל וְכָל אֲשֶׁר לוֹ וַיָּבֹא בְּאֵרָה שָּׁבַע וַיִּזְבַּח זְבָחִים לֵאלֹהֵי אָבִיו יִצְחָק: וַיֹּאמֶר אֱלֹקִים לְיִשְׂרָאֵל בְּמַרְאֹת הַלַּיְלָה וַיֹּאמֶר יַעֲקֹב יַעֲקֹב וַיֹּאמֶר הִנֵּנִי: וַיֹּאמֶר אָנֹכִי הָאֵל אֱלֹהֵי אָבִיךָ אַל תִּירָא מֵרְדָה מִצְרַיְמָה כִּי לְגוֹי גָּדוֹל אֲשִׂימְךָ שָׁם: אָנֹכִי אֵרֵד עִמְּךָ מִצְרַיְמָה וְאָנֹכִי אַעַלְךָ גַם עָלֹה וְיוֹסֵף יָשִׁית יָדוֹ עַל עֵינֶיךָ: וַיָּקָם יַעֲקֹב מִבְּאֵר שָׁבַע וַיִּשְׂאוּ בְנֵי יִשְׂרָאֵל אֶת יַעֲקֹב אֲבִיהֶם וְאֶת טַפָּם וְאֶת נְשֵׁיהֶם בָּעֲגָלוֹת אֲשֶׁר שָׁלַח פַּרְעֹה לָשֵׂאת אֹתוֹ:

ספר שם משמואל, פרשת ויצא, שנת תרע"ט

ויש לומר שזה עצמו הי' ענין רחל ולאה. דבזוה"ק שרחל היא דוגמת עלמא דאתגליא ולאה דוגמת עלמא דאתכסיא. ולפי מה שהגדנו לעיל קל יותר לזכות למעלות הגבוהות ע"י סור מרע, וע"כ י"ל שלאה שהיא דוגמת עלמא דאתכסיא ובודאי הפירוש שיש בה הארות גדולות מעלמא דאתכסיא זכתה בהן ע"י סור מרע, ורחל היו לה הארות מעלמא דאתגליא זכתה בהן ע"י עשה טוב, וא"כ הן מותאמות לעומת תעודת יעקב ועשו, עץ החיים ועץ הדעת ור.

ומעתה לפי הכוונה שהיתה ביצירת יעקב ועשו, שזה יזכה ע"י עשה טוב וזה ע"י סור מרע, הי' זיווגם מתחילת היצירה נאות להם רחל ליעקב ולאה לעשו, ובודאי כך הי' בהכרזת המלאך בת פלוני לפלוני רחל ליעקב ולאה לעשו [כי ההכרזה הוא לעולם לפי מה שהוא מוכן לזה, וכן הוא בזוה"ק שאם אדם קלקל מעשיו מונעים ממנו בת זיווגו, מכלל שהכרזת הזיווג לפי מה שהוא מוכן לעשות ולא לפי מעשיו של אח"כ, וכן בדין שהבחירה חפשית, והדברים עתיקים].

---

28. *Sha'arei Leshem*, part 2, *siman* 2, chapter 3.

And Yisrael traveled with all that he had, and came to Be'er Sheva, and offered sacrifices to the God of his father Yitzhak. And God spoke to Yisrael in the visions of the night, and said, "Yaakov, Yaakov." And he said, "Here am I." And he said, "I am God, the God of your father; fear not to go down to Egypt; for I will there make of you a great nation; I will go down with you to Egypt; and I will also surely bring you up again; and Yosef shall put his hand upon your eyes." And Yaakov rose up from Be'er Sheva; and the sons of Yisrael carried Yaakov their father, and their little ones, and their wives, in the wagons that Par'oh had sent to carry him. (Bereishit 46:1–5)

This passage is confusing, as the text seesaws between Yisrael and Yaakov. "Yisrael" travels, but "Yaakov" is addressed. Then Yaakov travels, and the children of "Yisrael" carry him. Deciphering the names seems a hopeless task, but this passage may be unlocked by referring to the tension between the personal versus the national that pulled Yaakov/Yisrael. The name Yisrael, representing the superior, national, even supernatural identity, is subdued as slavery begins; subservience, embodied in the name Yaakov (from *'akev*, heel), will now be the order of the day. But what of the children of Yisrael and Leah? They, too, march down to Egypt, carrying their father Yisrael. When they sentenced their brother Yosef, son of Yaakov and Rahel, first to death and then to slavery, they turned their backs on the attribute of *hesed* shared by Yaakov and Rahel. They did not understand that the sale of their brother would actually result in their own slavery and subservience, that an exact accounting and judgement would follow. They did not see that *din* untempered by *hesed* would lead to tragedy.[29] This lesson would have to be learned in the long years of exile and enslavement.

---

29. The *Shlah haKadosh* recounts that the brothers actually charged and tried Yosef in a *beit din* they convened, and found him guilty of treason and deserving of death as a *mored b'malhut*. See *Sefer haShlah haKadosh, Torah Ohr* on Vayeishev, section 10.

ספר השל"ה הקדוש פרשת וישב תורה אור (י)

וזה הוא ראובן היה חושב שלפי עומק הדין יוסף הוא בן מות, כי מורד במלכות בית דוד, רק חשב ושפטו העדה והצילו העדה בכל מאי דאפשר להציל, אפילו בזכות קטן ניתן להציל לפנים משורת הדין. אבל לפי האמת לא היה על יוסף שום חיוב, כי לא חפץ במלוכה ולא מרד במלכות בית דוד, ואדרבא ענייני והיה להחזיק מלכות בית דוד כמו שכתבתי. רק הענין היה כמו שכתבתי לעיל, כי שלושה כתרים הן, כתר תורה וכתר כהונה וכתר מלכות, וכהונה ומלכות הוא בשביל תורה. ויוסף הוא כתר תורה, על כן הוצרך לגלגל הזיכוך של ישראל להיותן לעם ראוים למלוכה, היה צריך להיות על ידי יוסף שהוא על ידי כתר תורה. והוא שטנו של עשו

It is possible that when the exile was curtailed to eighty-six years by the merit of Yaakov's prayers, not all things that needed to be accomplished in exile were achieved.[30] Not all the lessons of exile and slavery were learned. Not all the impurities of the collective soul of *Am Yisrael* were cleansed. In God's infinite Mercy and Wisdom, He saw that the Jews needed to leave Egypt sooner than planned: even one more day of exile could have had catastrophic consequences.[31] Redemption came too soon. Consequently, another exile would be necessary to insure that the remaining accomplishments could be achieved. Yaakov/Yisrael would have to continue to vacillate between

---

וכחו למעלה שהוא סמאל הוא השטן הוא היצר הרע, אשר כתר תורה מגרשו, כמו שאמרו רז"ל (סוכה נב,
ב), אם פגע בך מנוול משכהו לבית המדרש. על כן כשהיו ישראל במדבר היו נושאין שני ארונות, ארון שבו
הלוחות והתורה וארונו של יוסף היו נושאין ביחד, לומר קיים זה מה שכתוב בזה. והארון היו נושאין אותו
בכתף, כמו שנאמר (במדבר ז, ט), בכתף ישאו, ועל זה אמר אלו היה יודע ראובן זה אז גם כן בכתף היה נושאו:

30. See comments of the *Beit haLevi* on Shmot 3:11: the premature redemption caused the need for a subsequent exile.

בית הלוי, שמות ג:יא

ארבע מאות שנה: וכתוב אחד אומר (שם) ודור רביעי ישובו הנה, אמר הקב"ה אם הם עושים תשובה אני
גואלם לדורות ואם אין עושים תשובה הריני גואלים לשנים...וידוע פירוש אהיה עמהם בגלות זה אשר
אהיה עמהם בגלות אחר. ויש להבין מדוע אמר לו זה השם דוקא. רק זה דידוע דלפי פעולותיו הוא נקרא,
כשמנהיג העולם ברחמים נקרא רחום ואם בחנינה נקרא חנון וכן בכל המידות, וזהו ששאל משה ואמרו
לי מה שמו, פירוש דישאלוני באיזו בחינה היא הגאולה אם מגיע להם ע"פ הדין מברית בין הבתרים
או בבחינה אחרת. וכן ישאלו באיזו אופן וסדר תהיה הגאולה, דלפי אופן של הגאולה שמו עתה. וזה
לשון הרמב"ן כלומר באיזו מידה הוא שלוח להם. וכיון דהגאולה היא באמצע הזמן על סמך שישלימו
בגלות אחר והגאולה דכעת היא רק הכנה כדי שיוכלו להגאל אח"כ לעתיד וכמו שכתבנו דאם זה היה אז
הגאולה לא היו נגאלים לעולם, א"כ היה נקרא אז אהיה אשר אהיה דפירושו אהיה עמהם בגלות זה אשר
אהיה עמהם בגלות אחר, דעתה הכנה לגאולה השניה, וזהו יודיע דרכיו למשה שהודיע דרך הקץ למשה
שהודיעו באיזו אופן גואלם עתה, ורק לבני ישראל משום דדי לצרה בשעתה לא הודיע להם רק אהיה, וזהו
שאמר לבני ישראל עלילותיו, דלהם לא הודיע רק המעשה והפעולה שפועל להם עתה שיגאלם.

31. This is a teaching cited in the name of the Ari"zal; see *Beit haLevi*, drush 2. Also see Zohar Hadash, Parashat Yitro.

ספר בית הלוי, חלק ג: דרשות – דרוש ב

והגם כי לא ראיתי הדברים כתובים כן על ספר, הנני מסביר לי כן מה שראיתי במחברים הביאו דברי
קדוש ה' האר"י ז"ל שכתב שאם היו עוד במצרים היו נכנסים בשער החמישים של הטומאה ולא היו
נגאלים לעולם, ואין אתנו יודע בנסתרות.

זהר חדש, פרשת יתרו, מאמר למה נזכר נ' פעמים יציאת מצרים

א"ל ת"ח בריך, קב"ה לא אתני עם אברהם, אלא דיפיק ית ישראל מן גלותא דמצרים, ולא מתחות שעבודא
דחלא אחרא. דודאי ישראל כד הוו במצרים, אסתאבו, ואתטנפו גרמיהון בכל זיני מסאבו, עד דהוו
שראן תחות ארבעים ותשע חילי דמסאבותא. וקב"ה, אפיק יתהון מתחות פולחן כל שאר חילין.
ועוד, דאעיל יתהון במ"ט תרעי דסוכלתנו לקבליהון. מה דלא אתני עם אברהם, אלא לאפקותהון
ממצרים, והוא עביד טיבותיה וחסדיה עמהון.

these two identities, between national strength and subservience. But the sages assure us that the second redemption will be the ultimate redemption, making the redemption from Egypt seem a minor episode – like the name Yaakov and the relative powerlessness it connotes as compared to Yisrael, who has struggled with God and men and triumphed:

תלמוד בבלי, מסכת ברכות דף יב עמוד ב–דף יג עמוד א
תניא, אמר להם בן זומא לחכמים: וכי מזכירין יציאת מצרים לימות המשיח?
והלא כבר נאמר: (ירמיהו כג) הנה ימים באים נאם ה' ולא יאמרו עוד חי ה'
אשר העלה את בני ישראל מארץ מצרים, כי אם חי ה' אשר העלה ואשר הביא
את זרע בית ישראל מארץ צפונה ומכל הארצות אשר הדחתים שם! – אמרו
לו: לא שתעקר יציאת מצרים ממקומה, אלא שתהא שעבוד מלכיות עיקר,
ויציאת מצרים טפל לו. כיוצא בו אתה אומר: (בראשית לה) לא יקרא שמך עוד
יעקב כי אם ישראל יהיה שמך. לא שיעקר יעקב ממקומו, אלא ישראל עיקר
ויעקב טפל לו; וכן הוא אומר: (ישעיהו מג) אל תזכרו ראשנות וקדמניות אל
תתבוננו, אל תזכרו ראשנות – זה שעבוד מלכיות, וקדמניות אל תתבוננו – זו
יציאת מצרים.

It has been taught: Ben Zoma said to the sages: Will the Exodus from Egypt be mentioned in the days of Mashiah? Was it not long ago said, "Therefore behold the days come, says God, that they shall no more say: 'As God lives that brought up the Children of Israel out of the land of Egypt'; but 'As God lives that brought up and that led the descendants of the House of Israel out of the north country and from all the countries where I had driven them'"?

They replied: This does not mean that the mention of the Exodus from Egypt shall be obliterated, but that the [deliverance from] subjugation to the other kingdoms shall take the first place and the Exodus from Egypt shall become secondary. Similarly you read: "Your name shall not be called any more Yaakov, but Yisrael shall be your name." This does not mean that the name Yaakov shall be obliterated, but that Yisrael shall be the principal name and Yaakov the secondary one. And so it says, "Remember not the former things, neither consider the things of old": "Remember not the former things" refers to the subjugation to the other nations; "neither consider the things of old" refers to the Exodus from Egypt. (Talmud Bavli Brakhot 12b)

When the final redemption comes, the Exodus from Egypt will be recalled but, placed in perspective, it will pale in comparison. The messianic redemption will be primary. Likewise, in the end of days, the name Yaakov will be secondary, and the name Yisrael will endure forever. And when the time comes to return from exile, it is the tears of Rahel crying for her children – all of her children, all of *Am Yisrael* – that are answered: in the Messianic Age, Rahel will be seen as the mother of all of *Am Yisrael*, finally uniting the divergent attributes and bringing together all of the tribes of Israel:

ירמיהו לא:יד–טז

כֹּה אָמַר ה' קוֹל בְּרָמָה נִשְׁמָע נְהִי בְּכִי תַמְרוּרִים רָחֵל מְבַכָּה עַל בָּנֶיהָ מֵאֲנָה לְהִנָּחֵם עַל בָּנֶיהָ כִּי אֵינֶנּוּ: כֹּה אָמַר ה' מִנְעִי קוֹלֵךְ מִבֶּכִי וְעֵינַיִךְ מִדִּמְעָה כִּי יֵשׁ שָׂכָר לִפְעֻלָּתֵךְ נְאֻם ה' וְשָׁבוּ מֵאֶרֶץ אוֹיֵב: וְיֵשׁ תִּקְוָה לְאַחֲרִיתֵךְ נְאֻם ה' וְשָׁבוּ בָנִים לִגְבוּלָם:

Thus says God: "A voice was heard in Ramah, lamentation, and bitter weeping – Rahel was weeping for her children. She refused to be comforted for her children, because they were not." Thus says God: "Refrain your voice from weeping, and your eyes from tears; for your work shall be rewarded," says God; "and they shall come again from the land of the enemy. And there is hope for your future," says God, "and your children shall come again to their own border." (Yirmiyahu 31:14–16)

Rahel's supreme act of *hesed* will finally be rewarded in the end of days. The children of Leah will finally be able to inherit the attributes of Rahel, to temper *din* with *hesed* and internalize *rahamim*. The children of Yaakov and the children of Yisrael are one and the same. So, too, despite the tension we may sometimes sense between the children of Leah and the children of Rahel, we are one family. Although we live in a still imperfect world, in a world that focuses on differences, in the Messianic Age the truth will be clear, even self-evident: Yisrael and Yaakov are one; Leah and Rahel are one. We are one.

Give Truth to Yaakov

As the parashah opens, Yaakov is once again on the move. This time he is returning home, to the Land of Israel. As has been the case since before his birth, drama and intrigue seem to be Yaakov's constant companions, and this journey is no exception: he fled Israel to escape his brother Esav, who had sworn to kill him, and as he leaves his father-in-law Lavan's home, he is once again being pursued. God Himself intercedes on Yaakov's behalf and warns Lavan against harming Yaakov, clearing the way for Yaakov to finally confront his brother Esav.

This parashah, not unlike the preceding one, is a study in identity. Who is Yaakov – really? From the moment of his birth, his identity is seen through an ever-shifting prism: Yaakov is given a name that reflects his problematic relationship with his twin brother. He is then described as "*ish tam, yosheiv ohalim*"[1] – a pure or innocent man, morally unblemished, a man of home and hearth, a man of the study hall. Yet this is an "editorial" comment on his true character that seems quite different from the way his own parents view him, and it is a description that clashes spectacularly with the trajectory that his life takes. Yaakov, the innocent, makes his brother "an offer he can't refuse," and assumes the role and rights of firstborn. Later, he is forced to take on the identity of his brother Esav. As a result, the "man of the tents" is dispossessed of his home and family, and for years is left to survive by his own cunning and wits in an extremely corrupt environment. Does Yaakov even remember who he is? The simple, introverted, studious man we met just a few chapters ago has become a shrewd businessman, a very wealthy man, a formidable adversary at the negotiating table – a far cry from the *ish tam*, indeed.

In fact, the question of Yaakov's identity comes bubbling to the surface as he stands poised to meet Esav. Yaakov fears this confrontation, and as he

---

1. Bereishit 25:27.

reaches the border of his ancestral land, he prepares for it in various ways. This is a moment of introspection, as well as tactical, practical preparation. Both types of preparation have much to tell us about the nature of Yaakov's fears, and the identity crisis involved.

Yaakov prepares his household for the worst, and sends in a reconnaissance unit with a conciliatory message for Esav, hoping to avert confrontation. The commentaries approach these preparations from different angles. First, Yaakov's message is examined; more precisely, the messengers themselves become an important topic of discussion. Who were these messengers?

בראשית לב:ד

וַיִּשְׁלַח יַעֲקֹב מַלְאָכִים לְפָנָיו אֶל עֵשָׂו אָחִיו אַרְצָה שֵׂעִיר שְׂדֵה אֱדוֹם:

And Yaakov sent emissaries ahead of him to his brother Esav in the Land of Seir, to the fields of Edom. (Bereishit 32:4)

Rashi examines the word *malakhim*, which may be construed as either human or celestial messengers. Were these emissaries men in his employ – household staff, or "angels" – celestial messengers?[2] Rashi says that they were the latter: Yaakov sent angels to his brother Esav. While this may sound like a highly imaginative interpretation to some readers, who would prefer the simple, more mundane interpretation – "messengers," it is wholly in keeping with what we know about Yaakov, and the context in which this episode appears. Yaakov has had interaction with angels before, especially when he travels. When he left Israel, he had a vision of a heavenly ladder upon which angels ascended and descended. This was no simple dream; the vision of these angels changed Yaakov's perspective, changed his life: he understood the holiness of the place on which he stood, and the ability to connect, through it, to God. The angels that he saw were not merely the product of an overactive imagination, part of a strange and disturbing dream. Angels became a very real part of Yaakov's life as he left the Land of Israel, and now, as he is poised to return, his travels are once again accompanied by angels. Note the verses that immediately precede the parashah's opening:

---

2. Rashi, Bereishit 32:4.

רש"י, בראשית לב:ד
וישלח יעקב מלאכים: מלאכים ממש.

בראשית לב:ב–ג

וְיַעֲקֹב הָלַךְ לְדַרְכּוֹ וַיִּפְגְּעוּ בוֹ מַלְאֲכֵי אֱלֹקִים: וַיֹּאמֶר יַעֲקֹב כַּאֲשֶׁר רָאָם מַחֲנֵה אֱלֹקִים זֶה וַיִּקְרָא שֵׁם הַמָּקוֹם הַהוּא מַחֲנָיִם:

And Yaakov went on his way, and the angels of God met him. And when Yaakov saw them, he said, "This is God's encampment"; and he called the name of that place Mahanayim. *(Bereishit 32:2–3)*

Just as Yaakov saw angels in a dream as he prepared to leave Israel, he is met by angels as he prepares to reenter. And as he prepares to confront Esav, in the very next verse, the angels are his emissaries. This being so, we may be even more puzzled than before. If these angels of God are in Yaakov's service, and Yaakov is fulfilling the will of God, why all the angst? Why is Yaakov so fearful of the confrontation with Esav? In the words of the *Shem mi'Shmuel*, if any single angel could have wreaked havoc upon Esav and his camp, why fear the confrontation?[3]

בראשית לב:ח

וַיִּירָא יַעֲקֹב מְאֹד וַיֵּצֶר לוֹ וַיַּחַץ אֶת הָעָם אֲשֶׁר אִתּוֹ וְאֶת הַצֹּאן וְאֶת הַבָּקָר וְהַגְּמַלִּים לִשְׁנֵי מַחֲנוֹת:

Then Yaakov was greatly afraid and distressed; and he divided the people who were with him, and the flocks, and herds, and the camels, in two camps. (Bereishit 32:8)

Yaakov makes a pragmatic military decision, and divides the family into two separate camps. Lest we forget, this happens at the very place Yaakov was met by angels – the place Yaakov names *Mahanayim*. The connection between the preceding parashah and the present parashah, the angels who meet and accompany him and the angels he sends to Esav, is reinforced by the name that reflects both the "encampment of God's angels" and his own household, divided into two camps.

---

3. *Shem mi'Shmuel*, Parashat Vayishlah 5681.

ספר שם משמואל, פרשת וישלח, שנת תרפ"א

והנה הכל תמהה, מאחר שהיו לו כ"כ הרבה מלאכים א"כ מוכח שהוא נרצה להשי"ת, ומה הי' לו עוד להתירא מעשו, הרי מלאך אחד הי' די לכל מחנה סנחריב. ועוד למה צריך למלאכים רבים בשליחות הזאת, ולמה לא סגי לא באחד, עד שנצרך ליטול מאלו ומאלו.

בראשית לב:ט–יא

וַיֹּאמֶר אִם יָבוֹא עֵשָׂו אֶל הַמַּחֲנֶה הָאַחַת וְהִכָּהוּ וְהָיָה הַמַּחֲנֶה הַנִּשְׁאָר לִפְלֵיטָה:
וַיֹּאמֶר יַעֲקֹב אֱלֹקֵי אָבִי אַבְרָהָם וֵאלֹקֵי אָבִי יִצְחָק ה' הָאֹמֵר אֵלַי שׁוּב לְאַרְצְךָ
וּלְמוֹלַדְתְּךָ וְאֵיטִיבָה עִמָּךְ: קָטֹנְתִּי מִכֹּל הַחֲסָדִים וּמִכָּל הָאֱמֶת אֲשֶׁר עָשִׂיתָ אֶת
עַבְדֶּךָ כִּי בְמַקְלִי עָבַרְתִּי אֶת הַיַּרְדֵּן הַזֶּה וְעַתָּה הָיִיתִי לִשְׁנֵי מַחֲנוֹת:

*And Yaakov said, "O God of my father Avraham, and God of my
father Yitzhak, O God who said to me, 'Return to your country, and
to your family, and I will deal well with you' – I am not worthy of the
least of all the mercies and of all the truth that you have shown to
your servant, for with my staff I passed over this Jordan, and now I
have become two camps."* (Bereishit 32:9–11)

Only now, when Yaakov separates his family and makes mention of the two
camps, the full meaning of the name of this place, where he saw angels for
the second time, seems clear. Strangely enough, Yaakov made no mention
of his earlier vision of angels when he first named this place. Only now,
when he divides his family and possessions into two camps, he is given
to introspection and retrospection. He recalls that he was destitute and
alone when he crossed the river in the other direction, and he makes a
comparison with his present status. But how unequivocal is his description
of his good fortune? Is the fact that he has just divided his household into
two separate camps in order to avoid a holocaust a completely positive
statement? And if the reference is somewhat tentative, the overtones are
downright ominous. The Targum Pseudo-Yonatan teaches that the division
itself portended tragedy: Yaakov separated Leah's camp from Rahel's, along
the deep fault line whose negative impact has shaped Jewish history ever
since. Is this, or is this not, one family? Are Yaakov's children united? Do
some enjoy a favored status? Are they all equal, or are some "more equal"
than others?

When the moment to meet Esav arrives Yaakov again divides the camp;
this time the division is precise and specific, the hierarchy clear:

בראשית לג:א–ב

וַיִּשָּׂא יַעֲקֹב עֵינָיו וַיַּרְא וְהִנֵּה עֵשָׂו בָּא וְעִמּוֹ אַרְבַּע מֵאוֹת אִישׁ וַיַּחַץ אֶת הַיְלָדִים
עַל לֵאָה וְעַל רָחֵל וְעַל שְׁתֵּי הַשְּׁפָחוֹת: וַיָּשֶׂם אֶת הַשְּׁפָחוֹת וְאֶת יַלְדֵיהֶן רִאשֹׁנָה
וְאֶת לֵאָה וִילָדֶיהָ אַחֲרֹנִים וְאֶת רָחֵל וְאֶת יוֹסֵף אַחֲרֹנִים:

And Yaakov lifted up his eyes, and looked, and, behold, Esav came, and with him four hundred men. And he divided the children to Leah, and to Rahel, and to the two maidservants. And he put the maidservants and their children foremost, and Leah and her children after, and Rahel and Yosef after. (Bereishit 33:1–2)

What kind of impact would this favoritism have on future generations?[4] The rift that existed from the very start persisted for generations, and eventually caused the disintegration of the United Commonwealth. The prophecy of Hoshea, in whose lifetime this rift burgeoned into a chasm, has much to say about this division, its origins – and its eventual resolution:

הושע א:א; ב:א–ב

דְּבַר ה' אֲשֶׁר הָיָה אֶל הוֹשֵׁעַ בֶּן בְּאֵרִי בִּימֵי עֻזִּיָּה יוֹתָם אָחָז יְחִזְקִיָּה מַלְכֵי יְהוּדָה וּבִימֵי יָרָבְעָם בֶּן יוֹאָשׁ מֶלֶךְ יִשְׂרָאֵל:... וְהָיָה מִסְפַּר בְּנֵי יִשְׂרָאֵל כְּחוֹל הַיָּם אֲשֶׁר לֹא יִמַּד וְלֹא יִסָּפֵר וְהָיָה בִּמְקוֹם אֲשֶׁר יֵאָמֵר לָהֶם לֹא עַמִּי אַתֶּם יֵאָמֵר לָהֶם בְּנֵי אֵל חָי: וְנִקְבְּצוּ בְּנֵי יְהוּדָה וּבְנֵי יִשְׂרָאֵל יַחְדָּו וְשָׂמוּ לָהֶם רֹאשׁ אֶחָד וְעָלוּ מִן הָאָרֶץ כִּי גָדוֹל יוֹם יִזְרְעֶאל:

The word of God that came to Hoshea, the son of Be'eri, in the days of Uzziah, Yotam, Ahaz, and Yehizkiyah, kings of Yehudah, and in the days of Yerov'am the son of Yoash, king of Israel.... "And the number of the people of Israel shall be as the sand of the sea, which cannot be measured nor counted; and it shall come to pass, that instead of saying to one another, 'You are not My people,' they shall say to one another, 'You are the sons of the living God.' Then shall the people of Yehudah and the people of Israel be gathered together, and appoint themselves one head, and they shall come up from the land; for great shall be the day of Yizra'el." (Hoshea 1:1; 2:1–2)

---

4. Rabbeinu Bahya (Bereishit 32:8) says it was future considerations that motivated Yaakov: if one community is ever attacked, another community would still carry on.

רבינו בחיי, בראשית לב:ח

ובמדרש אם יבא עשו אל המחנה האחת והכהו, אלו אחינו שבדרום, והיה המחנה הנשאר לפליטה אלו אחינו שבגולה. כוונתם לומר כי יודע היה יעקב אבינו כי המחנה האחת ישאר לפליטה על כל פנים. והוא רמז לדורות שאין כל זרעו נופל ביד עשו ולא יכלו כלם באורך גלותם, אבל ישארו לפליטה על כרחו של עשו.

וכן דרשו רז"ל והיה המחנה הנשאר לפליטה, על כרחו. והכוונה כי אם יקום מלך ויגזור עלינו גרושין או אבדן גוף וממון באחת הארצות, הנה מלך אחר במקום אחר יקבץ וירחם, ולזה כוונו רז"ל במדרש זה.

Hoshea examines the political and national landscape, and sees before him the just desserts of a corrupt society that has turned its back on truth:

הושע ד:א–ו

שִׁמְעוּ דְבַר ה' בְּנֵי יִשְׂרָאֵל כִּי רִיב לַה' עִם יוֹשְׁבֵי הָאָרֶץ כִּי אֵין אֱמֶת וְאֵין חֶסֶד וְאֵין דַּעַת אֱלֹקִים בָּאָרֶץ: אָלֹה וְכַחֵשׁ וְרָצֹחַ וְגָנֹב וְנָאֹף פָּרָצוּ וְדָמִים בְּדָמִים נָגָעוּ: עַל כֵּן תֶּאֱבַל הָאָרֶץ וְאֻמְלַל כָּל יוֹשֵׁב בָּהּ בְּחַיַּת הַשָּׂדֶה וּבְעוֹף הַשָּׁמָיִם וְגַם דְּגֵי הַיָּם יֵאָסֵפוּ:... נִדְמוּ עַמִּי מִבְּלִי הַדָּעַת כִּי אַתָּה הַדַּעַת מָאַסְתָּ וְאֶמְאָסְךָ מִכַּהֵן לִי וַתִּשְׁכַּח תּוֹרַת אֱלֹהֶיךָ אֶשְׁכַּח בָּנֶיךָ גַּם אָנִי:

Hear the word of God, people of Israel; for God has a controversy with the inhabitants of the land, because there is no truth, no mercy, no knowledge of God in the land. There is swearing, and lying, and killing, and stealing, and adultery; they break all bounds, and blood leads to blood. Therefore shall the land mourn, and everyone who dwells in it shall languish, with the beasts of the field, and with the birds of heaven; the fishes of the sea shall also be taken away.... My people are destroyed for lack of knowledge; because you have rejected knowledge, I will also reject you, that you shall not be a kohen to me; seeing that you have forgotten the Torah of your God, I will also forget your children. (Hoshea 4:1–6)

How can the people of Israel have sunk so low? How can this "kingdom of priests and holy nation" have deteriorated to this degree? Hoshea lays the blame for their decadence at Yaakov's feet; he sees the seeds of their iniquity and disunity in Yaakov's behavior in our parashah:

הושע יב:א–טו

סְבָבֻנִי בְכַחַשׁ אֶפְרַיִם וּבְמִרְמָה בֵּית יִשְׂרָאֵל וִיהוּדָה עֹד רָד עִם אֵל וְעִם קְדוֹשִׁים נֶאֱמָן: אֶפְרַיִם רֹעֶה רוּחַ וְרֹדֵף קָדִים כָּל הַיּוֹם כָּזָב וָשֹׁד יַרְבֶּה וּבְרִית עִם אַשּׁוּר יִכְרֹתוּ וְשֶׁמֶן לְמִצְרַיִם יוּבָל: וְרִיב לַה' עִם יְהוּדָה וְלִפְקֹד עַל יַעֲקֹב כִּדְרָכָיו כְּמַעֲלָלָיו יָשִׁיב לוֹ: בַּבֶּטֶן עָקַב אֶת אָחִיו וּבְאוֹנוֹ שָׂרָה אֶת אֱלֹקִים: וַיָּשַׂר אֶל מַלְאָךְ וַיֻּכָל בָּכָה וַיִּתְחַנֶּן לוֹ בֵּית אֵל יִמְצָאֶנּוּ וְשָׁם יְדַבֵּר עִמָּנוּ: וַה' אֱלֹקֵי הַצְּבָאוֹת ה' זִכְרוֹ: וְאַתָּה בֵּאלֹקֶיךָ תָשׁוּב חֶסֶד וּמִשְׁפָּט שְׁמֹר וְקַוֵּה אֶל אֱלֹקֶיךָ תָּמִיד:... וְאָנֹכִי ה' אֱלֹקֶיךָ מֵאֶרֶץ מִצְרָיִם עֹד אוֹשִׁיבְךָ בָאֳהָלִים כִּימֵי מוֹעֵד...

Efraim surrounded me with lies, and the House of Israel with deceit; but Yehudah still rules with God, and is faithful with the holy ones. Efraim guards the wind, and follows after the east wind; he daily increases lies and desolation; and they make a covenant with the Assyrians, and oil is carried to Egypt. God has also a controversy with Yehudah, and will punish Yaakov according to his ways; according to his doings will he reward him. He took his brother by the heel in the womb, and by his strength he strove with the powerful; And he strove with an angel, and prevailed; he [the angel] wept, and made supplication to [Yaakov]; he found him in Beit El, and there He spoke with us. And the Almighty is the God of Hosts; the Almighty is His name. Therefore turn to your God; keep loving-kindness and judgment, and wait on your God continually.... And I, your Almighty God, will yet redeem you from the land of Egypt, and make you dwell in tents, as in the days of the past. (Hoshea 12:1–15)

Yaakov is criticized for wrestling with his brother in the womb, and the prophet draws a line directly to the wrestling years later, between Yaakov and a mysterious stranger. After dividing the camp for the first time that night, Yaakov busies himself with transporting his family across the river. Once they are all safely across – but before Yaakov faces his brother or divides the camp a second time – he finds himself alone and vulnerable in the dark, and he is accosted:

בראשית לב:כה–ל

וַיִּוָּתֵר יַעֲקֹב לְבַדּוֹ וַיֵּאָבֵק אִישׁ עִמּוֹ עַד עֲלוֹת הַשָּׁחַר: וַיַּרְא כִּי לֹא יָכֹל לוֹ וַיִּגַּע בְּכַף יְרֵכוֹ וַתֵּקַע כַּף יֶרֶךְ יַעֲקֹב בְּהֵאָבְקוֹ עִמּוֹ: וַיֹּאמֶר שַׁלְּחֵנִי כִּי עָלָה הַשָּׁחַר וַיֹּאמֶר לֹא אֲשַׁלֵּחֲךָ כִּי אִם בֵּרַכְתָּנִי: וַיֹּאמֶר אֵלָיו מַה שְּׁמֶךָ וַיֹּאמֶר יַעֲקֹב: וַיֹּאמֶר לֹא יַעֲקֹב יֵאָמֵר עוֹד שִׁמְךָ כִּי אִם יִשְׂרָאֵל כִּי שָׂרִיתָ עִם אֱלֹקִים וְעִם אֲנָשִׁים וַתּוּכָל: וַיִּשְׁאַל יַעֲקֹב וַיֹּאמֶר הַגִּידָה נָּא שְׁמֶךָ וַיֹּאמֶר לָמָּה זֶּה תִּשְׁאַל לִשְׁמִי וַיְבָרֶךְ אֹתוֹ שָׁם:

And Yaakov was left alone; and a man wrestled with him until the break of day. And when he saw that he could not prevail against him, he touched the hollow of his thigh; and the hollow of Yaakov's thigh was out of joint, as he wrestled with him. And he said, "Let me go, for the day breaks." And he said, "I will not let you go, unless you bless me." And he said to him, "What is your name?" And he said, "Yaakov." And he said, "Your name shall be called no more Yaakov, but Yisrael; for you have struggled with the powerful and with men, and have prevailed." And Yaakov asked him, and said, "Tell me, I beg you, your name?" And he said, "Why is it that you ask my name?" And he blessed him there. (Bereishit 32:25–30)

The entire scene circles around the question of identity – shrouded, revealed, mistaken, hidden. While the struggle changes Yaakov's identity, the identity of the mysterious attacker is never revealed. Millennia of Jewish persecution may make us overlook the fact that this unprovoked attack is carried out by a nameless adversary: random attacks, or fear of such attacks, are nothing out of the ordinary in Jewish history. Yaakov himself seeks no explanation or motive; he asks only that his attacker identify himself. Generations later, in the prophecy quoted above, Hoshea reveals the identity of this mysterious adversary: it is yet another angel. "And he strove with an angel, and prevailed."

Why did the angel attack Yaakov? What had he done wrong? The Targum Pseudo-Yonatan[5] seems to weave Hoshea's prophecy into his commentary, suggesting that God sent this angel because Yaakov had not been truthful: before leaving the Land of Israel, Yaakov had vowed to tithe one-tenth of everything God gave him, and that vow had not been fulfilled.[6] Now, as Yaakov took stock of his situation, one of the things he thanked God for was the truth bestowed upon him: "I am not worthy of the least of all the mercies and of all the truth[7] that you have shown to your servant, for with my staff I passed over this Jordan and now I have become two camps." Apparently Yaakov worries that he has not embraced truth, despite the truth that God has showered upon him. This same problem surfaces in

---

5. Midrash Tanhuma (Buber edition), Parashat Vayishlah, section 22, also associates this attack with Yaakov's failure to fulfill his vow.

מדרש תנחומא (בובר), פרשת וישלח פסקה כב

וישר אל מלאך ויוכל וגו' (הושע יב:ה): מה דיבר עמו א"ל לך שלם את נדרך, טוב אשר לא תדור וגו' (קהלת ה:ד).

6. In a fascinating twist, the Targum suggests that the way to fulfill the vow is by giving one of his children to divine service. An accounting is done, and Levi is chosen.

כתר יונתן, בראשית לב:כה

וישאר יעקב לבדו מעבר [לנהר] יובק ויאבק מלאך עמו כדמות איש ויאמר הלא אמרת לעשר לעשר כל שלך והנה יש לך תריסר בנים ובת אחת ולא עשרתם, מיד הפריש ארבע בכורים, לארבעה אמהות, ונשארו שמונה ושנה למנות משמעון, ועלה לוי במעשר, ענה מיכאל ואמר רבונו של עולם, זה הוא חלקך, ועל ענין הדברים האלה השתהה מעבר לנחל עד עלות עמוד השחר.

7. The *Sfat Emet* questions the relevance of the word *emet* (truth) in Yaakov's prayer.

שפת אמת ליקוטים, פרשת וישלח

קטנתי וגו' ומכל האמת אשר עשית את עבדך וגו': וקשה מאי שייך על אמת קטנתי כיון שהוא על פי דין ומשפט אמת....

Hoshea's prophecy, in the form of a dubious legacy passed down from Yaakov to his descendants that eventually leads to their ruin.

Rabbi Eliezer of Germiza, a mystic of the Middle Ages, said that the angel who attacked Yaakov came dressed as Esav, and he had a complaint: He said to Yaakov, "You are a liar! Why did you say [to your father] 'I am Esav your firstborn'?" Yaakov protests: he had purchased the birthright from Esav years earlier. The angel then asks, "What is your name?" and points out that *Yaakov* is a name of deception and chicanery. Your name should be *Yisrael*, a name that implies *yosher* (being straight or upstanding) – you must be *yashar* (straight) with God.[8]

This seems somewhat of a departure from the straightforward meaning of the text. The angel himself explains[9] the name that will replace *Yaakov*; this new identity has to do with struggle, with overpowering invincible adversaries. *Sarita*, the word that lies at the root of *Yisrael*, denotes both struggle and power. The name is pronounced with the letter *sin* (*sarita*), and not the letter *shin* (*yashar*). Apparently, Rabbi Eliezer of Germiza looked beyond the explanation of the word itself, and sought the essential lesson for Yisrael – the individual, and the nation of his namesakes. The identity of the Jew, the essence of what Yisrael and all of the Children of Yisrael should strive to be, is reflected in this name: honest, truthful, upright – *yashar*. In the words of the *Kli Yakar*, the name *Yisrael* comes from the words *Yashar El*, to be straight with God. Although other men will not always perceive the righteousness of Yisrael's ways, God can see to the heart of the matter. The struggle to maintain inner clarity, to pursue God's truth despite obstacles and seeming falsehood, is the struggle that Yaakov/Yisrael faced, and he prevailed. Many of the episodes in his life seemed to lead him off the straight path of truth, but he never lost sight of

---

8. Rabbi Eliezer of Germiza, *Hilkhot haKisei, Hilkhot haMalakhim.*

ספר הלכות הכסא לרבי אלעזר מגרמזיא, הלכות המלאכים

וכך בא המלאך כדמות עשו ליעקב ואמר לו, שקרן אתה, למה אמרת אנכי עשו בכורך. אמר לו, שקניתי בכורתך ואמרתי (בגשתי) [עשיתי] כאשר צויתני הרבה פעמים. אמר לו, ומה שמך. אמר לו, יעקב. אמר, לא יעקב לשון עקבה ומרמה, כי אם ישראל, ישר לאל וראוי לברכה, דכתיב (משלי כח:כ) (ל)איש אמונות רב ברכות, (צפניה ג:יג) שארית ישראל לא ידברו כזב, (במדבר כג:כ–כא) לא הביט און ביעקב וברך ולא אשיבנה. וכשהיו הכהנים מזכירין השם במקדש, היו המלאכים יורדים נ"א רבוא וח' אלפים ות' וממלאים העולם כולו.

9. *Bereishit* 32:29.

God's plan, of God's will.[10] This was his true identity, his eventual identity. He was able to follow his internal moral compass despite the situations into which he was thrust. Although his actions were looked at askance by human eyes, although he struggled with mortal and divine challenges to his inner truth, he emerged victorious. To rephrase Rabbi Eliezer's comments: the name *Yisrael* derives from *sarita*, which means struggle; the meaning of the struggle is to achieve *yosher*.

Yaakov spent the majority of his life dealing with dishonest people, and often played according to their rules. In order to contend with Esav and Lavan, Yaakov acquired survival skills. What lessons are there in Yaakov's behavior for future generations? The prophet Hoshea was unequivocal: "God has also a controversy with Yehudah, and will punish Yaakov according to his ways; according to his doings will he reward him. He took his brother by the heel in the womb…"[11]

While Yaakov's actions may have been justified, Hoshea lays the blame for future generations' immorality at Yaakov's doorstep, implying that many generations of unscrupulous businessmen learned from Yaakov's ways.

Yaakov becomes Yisrael, and the struggle continues. The validity of the moral compass remains, but the path to becoming *yashar* still lies ahead. One more stage is required in the metamorphosis, a stage that links the innocence of Yaakov's youth with the strength and heroic behavior of his

---

10. *Kli Yakar*, Bereishit 32:29.

כלי יקר, בראשית לב:כט

ויאמר לא יעקב יאמר עוד שמך כי אם ישראל: לשון ישר אל כי ישר הוא לשון ראייה, מלשון אשורנו ולא קרוב, והודה לו בזה כי יעקב רואה פני אל ולא עלתה בידו לסמא אותו במציאות האל יתברך, ובאמרו כי שרית עם אלהים עקר שם יעקב ממנו, כי יעקב מורה על עקוב הלב מכל ואנוש הוא (ירמיה יז ט) וישראל לשון מישור כמ"ש לעתיד (ישעיהו מ ד) והיה העקוב למישור, ולא מישור הנראה ישר בעיני הבריות כ"א הנראה ישר בעיני אלהים ואדם, ע"כ אמר כי שרית עם אלהים ואנשים, כי ע"י כושר מפעלך תהיה שר ונגיד עם אלהים ואנשים ותוכל, וזהו ישראל ישר אל, מישור הנראה גם בעיני האל ית'.

11. Rashi (Bereishit 32:29), in describing Yaakov's name change, cites this verse in Hoshea.

רש"י, בראשית לב:כט

לא יעקב: לא יאמר עוד שהברכות באו לך בעקבה וברמיה כי אם בשררה ובגלוי פנים, וסופך שהקב"ה נגלה עליך בבית אל ומחליף את שמך, ושם הוא מברכך, ואני שם אהיה ואודה לך עליהן, וזהו שכתוב (הושע יב:ה) וישר אל מלאך ויוכל בכה ויתחנן לו, בכה המלאך ויתחנן לו, ומה נתחנן לו (שם) בית אל ימצאנו ושם ידבר עמנו, המתן לי עד שידבר עמנו שם, ולא רצה יעקב, ועל כרחו הודה לו עליהן, וזהו (ל) ויברך אותו שם, שהיה מתחנן להמתין לו ולא רצה.

adulthood.[12] A bridge must be created between *Yaakov ish tam yosheiv ohalim*, the "innocent [perfect] man, a dweller in tents," and *Yisrael – sarita im Elokim*[13] *v'im anashim va'tukhal* – the vanquisher of the mighty, the independent man who remains true to God's will.

In the book of Devarim, we find the expression of this identity, the final stage in the development of Yaakov's persona: *Yeshurun*.

דברים לג:ה

וַיְהִי בִישֻׁרוּן מֶלֶךְ בְּהִתְאַסֵּף רָאשֵׁי עָם יַחַד שִׁבְטֵי יִשְׂרָאֵל:

And He was king in Yeshurun, when the heads of the people and the tribes of Israel were gathered together. (Devarim 33:5)[14]

The name *Yeshurun* has the word *yashar*, upright or honest, at its root. Thus, while the name *Yaakov* denotes trickery,[15] and the name *Yisrael*

---

12. See the writings of Rabbi Menahem Mendel of Shklov, *Likutim*, page 405.

כתבי הגרמ"מ משקלוב, ליקוטים, דף תה

כי לא נחש ביעקב ולא קסם בישראל (במדבר כג): כי יעקב איש תם (בראשית כה), וישראל ישר, אשר תם ויישר יצרוני (תהלים כה).

13. Opinions are divided on whether this refers to God or is the more general word *elohim*. See the first footnote of the previous chapter on Parashat Vayishlach, "Yaakov – or Yisrael?"

14. See Targum Onkelos, who translates *Yeshurun* as *Yisrael*.

תרגום אונקלוס, דברים לג:ה

והוה **בישראל** מלכא באתכנשות רישי עמא כחדא שבטיא דישראל.

15. See the Ramban's commentary to Devarim 2:10 and 7:12.

רמב"ן, דברים ב:י

כי השמות ישמרו הטעם ויחליפו המלות, כמו זרח וצחר (בראשית מו:י) מן וצמר צחר (יחזקאל כז:יח), אתונות צחורות (שופטים ה:י). וכן יעשו לשבח, יכנו יעקב שהוא לשון מרמה או לשון עקלקלות ויקראו אותו ישרון, מן תם וישר.

רמב"ן, דברים ז:יב

טעם עקב: כמו בעבור, ...וכן על דעתי, כל לשון עקיבה גלגול וסבוב, עקוב הלב (ירמיה יז:ט), ויעקבני זה פעמים (בראשית כז:לו), ויהוא עשה בעקבה (מ"ב י:יט), ענין גלגולין וסבות. ולכן יקראו יעקב "ישרון", כי היפך העקוב מישר. וכן אחורי הרגל שנקרא עקב, וידו אוחזת בעקב עשו (בראשית כה:כו), יקראנו כן בעבור היותו מעוגל, כאשר יקרא הלשון אמצע היד והרגל "כפות" בעבור היותם כמו כפות הזהב. ומורגל הוא בלשון, כמו שאמרו בספרי (ברכה ב), מימינו אש דת למו (להלן לג:ב), כשהיה יוצא הדבור מפי הקב"ה היה יוצא דרך ימינו של קדש לשמאלן של ישראל, ועוקב את מחנה ישראל שנים עשר מיל על שנים עשר מיל, כלומר מקיף. וכן לשונם (ב"ק קיג א) באים עליו בעקיפין, בסבות וגלגולין, כמו עקיבין, ששתי האותיות האלה שוות להן כאשר פרשתי כבר (ויקרא יט:כ).

indicates strife, the name *Yeshurun* is used here to describe a nation united as one, rallying around the ultimate goal of the Jewish people: to be upright and honest.

In the course of exile the Jews have often been forced to use questionable means to protect themselves. While this behavior may often have been a necessary evil, it was far from ideal. It was not always "straight and honest." Ultimately, our destiny – our identity – is to be a light unto the nations, a beacon of morality, ethics and decency that will show all peoples of the world the beauty of the Word of God. Yeshayahu, the same prophet who spoke of being a "light to the nations," also spoke of comfort for the Jews that will come when we are finally returned to our land and our natural innocence, when what is crooked will be made straight, when Yaakov will be perceived as Yeshurun.

ישעיהו מ:א–ה

נַחֲמוּ נַחֲמוּ עַמִּי יֹאמַר אֱלֹקֵיכֶם: דַּבְּרוּ עַל לֵב יְרוּשָׁלַם וְקִרְאוּ אֵלֶיהָ כִּי מָלְאָה צְבָאָהּ כִּי נִרְצָה עֲוֹנָהּ כִּי לָקְחָה מִיַּד ה' כִּפְלַיִם בְּכָל חַטֹּאתֶיהָ:

קוֹל קוֹרֵא בַּמִּדְבָּר **פַּנּוּ דֶּרֶךְ ה' יַשְּׁרוּ** בָּעֲרָבָה מְסִלָּה לֵאלֹקֵינוּ: כָּל גֶּיא יִנָּשֵׂא וְכָל הַר וְגִבְעָה יִשְׁפָּלוּ **וְהָיָה הֶעָקֹב לְמִישׁוֹר** וְהָרְכָסִים לְבִקְעָה: וְנִגְלָה כְּבוֹד ה' וְרָאוּ כָל בָּשָׂר יַחְדָּו כִּי פִּי ה' דִּבֵּר:

*"Comfort my people, comfort them," says your God. "Speak to Jerusalem's heart, and cry out to her, that her fighting is ended, that her iniquity is pardoned, for she has received from the Almighty's hand double for all her sins." A voice cries in the wilderness, "**Prepare the path of God, make straight** in the desert a highway for our God." Every valley shall be exalted, and every mountain and hill shall be made low; **and the crooked shall be made straight,** and the ridges made into valleys; And the glory of God shall be revealed, and all flesh shall see together that the mouth of God has spoken.* (Yeshayahu 40:1–5)

Similarly, in the same prophecy in which Hoshea rejects Yaakov's behavior, he speaks of the eventual resolution of Yisrael's strife: God's promise to him and his descendants is that they will one day shed the clothes of deceit and return to their true identity, to dwell in the tents of truth, kindness and justice:

הושע יב:י

וְאָנֹכִי ה' אֱלֹקֶיךָ מֵאֶרֶץ מִצְרָיִם עֹד אוֹשִׁיבְךָ בָאֳהָלִים כִּימֵי מוֹעֵד

And I, the Almighty your God, will yet redeem you…, and make you dwell in tents, as in the days of the past. (Hoshea 12:10)

The Jewish people will no longer define their existence through the seemingly endless struggle with falsehood and evil. The transformation from Yaakov to Yisrael will reach its final stage, and both of these names will be left behind as our true identity emerges: Yeshurun, the straight and upstanding servant of God. This identity can only emerge when the rift in the Jewish people, expressed by the division of Yaakov's family into two camps, is finally healed:

דברים לג:ה

וַיְהִי בִישֻׁרוּן מֶלֶךְ בְּהִתְאַסֵּף רָאשֵׁי עָם יַחַד שִׁבְטֵי יִשְׂרָאֵל:

And He was king in Yeshurun, when the heads of the people and the tribes of Israel were gathered together. (Devarim 33:5)

Parashat Vayeishev

Clothes Make the Man

The story of Yosef is one of the saddest and most severe stories in the book of Bereishit. The sons of Yaakov are remembered for their near-fratricide, rather than for displays of love and respect we would have expected. It is this episode – brought on by their hatred of Yosef and consummated in his subsequent sale into slavery – that is the brothers' legacy.

The story itself is well known. The coat of many colors given by Yaakov to his beloved son Yosef became the lightning rod for the brothers' hatred, the symbolic expression of their animosity toward Yosef.

בראשית לז:ג

וְיִשְׂרָאֵל אָהַב אֶת יוֹסֵף מִכָּל בָּנָיו כִּי בֶן זְקֻנִים הוּא לוֹ וְעָשָׂה לוֹ כְּתֹנֶת פַּסִּים:

Now Yisrael loved Yosef more than all his children, because he was the son of his old age; and he made him a striped coat. (Bereishit 37:3)

בראשית לז:כג

וַיְהִי כַּאֲשֶׁר בָּא יוֹסֵף אֶל אֶחָיו וַיַּפְשִׁיטוּ אֶת יוֹסֵף אֶת כֻּתָּנְתּוֹ אֶת כְּתֹנֶת הַפַּסִּים אֲשֶׁר עָלָיו:

And it came to pass, when Yosef came to his brothers, that they stripped Yosef of his coat, his striped coat that was on him. (Bereishit 37:23)

When that same coat was saturated with blood, the effect on the brothers was cathartic: their anger dissipated, their lust for revenge sated.

בראשית לז:לא–לד

וַיִּקְחוּ אֶת כְּתֹנֶת יוֹסֵף וַיִּשְׁחֲטוּ שְׂעִיר עִזִּים וַיִּטְבְּלוּ אֶת הַכֻּתֹּנֶת בַּדָּם: וַיְשַׁלְּחוּ אֶת כְּתֹנֶת הַפַּסִּים וַיָּבִיאוּ אֶל אֲבִיהֶם וַיֹּאמְרוּ זֹאת מָצָאנוּ הַכֶּר נָא הַכְּתֹנֶת בִּנְךָ הִוא אִם לֹא: וַיַּכִּירָהּ וַיֹּאמֶר כְּתֹנֶת בְּנִי חַיָּה רָעָה אֲכָלָתְהוּ טָרֹף טֹרַף יוֹסֵף: וַיִּקְרַע יַעֲקֹב שִׂמְלֹתָיו וַיָּשֶׂם שַׂק בְּמָתְנָיו וַיִּתְאַבֵּל עַל בְּנוֹ יָמִים רַבִּים:

And they took Yosef's coat, and killed a kid of the goats, and dipped the coat in the blood. And they sent the striped coat, and they brought

245

*it to their father, and said, "This have we found; please identify it. Is it
your son's coat or not?" And he recognized [identified] it, and said, "It
is my son's coat; an evil beast has devoured him; Yosef is without doubt
torn to pieces." And Yaakov tore his clothes, and put sackcloth upon
his loins, and mourned for his son many days. (Bereishit 37:31–34)*

Yet this coat is more than a symbol of Yaakov's favoritism. In a much larger
sense, clothing seems to be a major, recurrent theme in this parashah,
providing an intriguing subtext for the narrative: Yosef, Yehudah, Tamar,
and, later in the parashah, Yosef once again, are described in various modes
of dress and undress. There is the familiar theme of rending garments in
mourning, which both Reuven and Yaakov engage in when they believe
Yosef to be dead:

בראשית לז:כט

וַיָּשָׁב רְאוּבֵן אֶל הַבּוֹר וְהִנֵּה אֵין יוֹסֵף בַּבּוֹר וַיִּקְרַע אֶת בְּגָדָיו:

*And Reuven returned to the pit; and, behold, Yosef was not in the pit;
and he tore his clothes. (Bereishit 37:29)*

Moving on from the sale of Yosef, as we continue through the parashah,
references to clothing are no less central to the narrative:

בראשית לח:יד

וַתָּסַר בִּגְדֵי אַלְמְנוּתָהּ מֵעָלֶיהָ וַתְּכַס בַּצָּעִיף וַתִּתְעַלָּף וַתֵּשֶׁב בְּפֶתַח עֵינַיִם אֲשֶׁר
עַל דֶּרֶךְ תִּמְנָתָה....:

*And she took off her widow's garments, and covered herself with a
veil, and wrapped herself, and sat in an open place, which is by the
way to Timnat. (Bereishit 38:14)*

בראשית לח:יח–יט

וַיֹּאמֶר מָה הָעֵרָבוֹן אֲשֶׁר אֶתֶּן לָךְ וַתֹּאמֶר חֹתָמְךָ וּפְתִילֶךָ וּמַטְּךָ אֲשֶׁר בְּיָדֶךָ
וַיִּתֶּן לָהּ וַיָּבֹא אֵלֶיהָ וַתַּהַר לוֹ: וַתָּקָם וַתֵּלֶךְ וַתָּסַר צְעִיפָהּ מֵעָלֶיהָ וַתִּלְבַּשׁ בִּגְדֵי
אַלְמְנוּתָהּ:

*And he said, "What pledge shall I give you?" And she said, "Your
signet, and your cloak, and your staff that is in your hand." And he
gave them to her, and came in to her, and she conceived by him.*

And she arose, and went away, and took off her veil, and put on the garments of her widowhood. (Bereishit 38:18–19)

בראשית לט:יא–יב

וַיְהִי כְּהַיּוֹם הַזֶּה וַיָּבֹא הַבַּיְתָה לַעֲשׂוֹת מְלַאכְתּוֹ וְאֵין אִישׁ מֵאַנְשֵׁי הַבַּיִת שָׁם בַּבָּיִת: וַתִּתְפְּשֵׂהוּ בְּבִגְדוֹ לֵאמֹר שִׁכְבָה עִמִּי וַיַּעֲזֹב בִּגְדוֹ בְּיָדָהּ וַיָּנָס וַיֵּצֵא הַחוּצָה:

And it came to pass about this time, that Yosef went into the house to fulfill his duties; and none of the men of the house were inside. And she caught him by his garment, saying, "Lie with me"; and he left his garment in her hand, and fled, and got out. (Bereishit 39:11–12)

בראשית מא:יד

וַיִּשְׁלַח פַּרְעֹה וַיִּקְרָא אֶת יוֹסֵף וַיְרִיצֻהוּ מִן הַבּוֹר וַיְגַלַּח וַיְחַלֵּף שִׂמְלֹתָיו וַיָּבֹא אֶל פַּרְעֹה:

Then Par'oh sent and called Yosef, and they brought him hastily out of the dungeon; and he shaved himself, and changed his garment, and came in to Par'oh. (Bereishit 41:14)

Clothes are given, clothes are shed, clothes are ripped. They cover and uncover their owners. A variety of terms and descriptions are used for the various types of clothing, indicative of a variety of thematic messages: different words are utilized to describe different garments, indicating distinct motifs.

The word used to describe the gift given to Yosef is *ketonet passim* ("a coat of stripes" or, more commonly, "a coat of many colors"), a term first used at the dawn of history to describe the clothes with which God covered Adam and Hava.

בראשית ג:כא

וַיַּעַשׂ ה' אֱלֹקִים לְאָדָם וּלְאִשְׁתּוֹ כָּתְנוֹת עוֹר וַיַּלְבִּשֵׁם:

And the Almighty God made for Adam and for his wife coats [kotnot] of skin, and clothed them. (Bereishit 3:21)

This clothing supplanted an earlier type of garment that Adam and Hava had fashioned for themselves, in a feeble attempt to cover up in the aftermath of their sin.

בראשית ג:ז

וַתִּפָּקַחְנָה עֵינֵי שְׁנֵיהֶם וַיֵּדְעוּ כִּי עֵירֻמִּם הֵם וַיִּתְפְּרוּ עֲלֵה תְאֵנָה וַיַּעֲשׂוּ לָהֶם
חֲגֹרֹת:

And the eyes of them both were opened, and they knew that they
were naked; and they sewed fig leaves together, and made themselves
belts [possibly loincloths] (Bereishit 3:7)

There is no dearth of terms in biblical Hebrew to describe clothing; why is
it specifically a *ketonet* that Yaakov gives to Yosef?[1] According to tradition,
this is no coincidence: these were the very same clothes fashioned by God
for Adam, handed down from Adam to Nimrod, and then to Esav. Yaakov
wore these clothes to procure the blessings meant for Esav from his father,[2]
and it was this garment that Yaakov gave to Yosef. And yet, while this may
help us understand the resulting enmity between Esav and Yaakov, as well
as the choice of word used to describe the symbol of Yosef's favored status,
we are none the wiser as to Yaakov's motivation in giving these clothes to
Yosef.

In our search for further linguistic clues to unravel this episode, we may look
further on in Tanakh. The unique and seemingly specific combination that
describes this garment *ketonet passim* is used in only one other instance;
there, too, the context involves the relationship between siblings:

שמואל ב יג:י–יח

וַיֹּאמֶר אַמְנוֹן אֶל תָּמָר הָבִיאִי הַבִּרְיָה הַחֶדֶר וְאֶבְרֶה מִיָּדֵךְ וַתִּקַּח תָּמָר אֶת
הַלְּבִבוֹת אֲשֶׁר עָשָׂתָה וַתָּבֵא לְאַמְנוֹן אָחִיהָ הֶחָדְרָה: וַתַּגֵּשׁ אֵלָיו לֶאֱכֹל וַיַּחֲזֶק
בָּהּ וַיֹּאמֶר לָהּ בּוֹאִי שִׁכְבִי עִמִּי אֲחוֹתִי: וַתֹּאמֶר לוֹ אַל אָחִי אַל תְּעַנֵּנִי כִּי לֹא
יֵעָשֶׂה כֵן בְּיִשְׂרָאֵל אַל תַּעֲשֵׂה אֶת הַנְּבָלָה הַזֹּאת: וַאֲנִי אָנָה אוֹלִיךְ אֶת חֶרְפָּתִי
וְאַתָּה תִּהְיֶה כְּאַחַד הַנְּבָלִים בְּיִשְׂרָאֵל וְעַתָּה דַּבֶּר נָא אֶל הַמֶּלֶךְ כִּי לֹא יִמְנָעֵנִי
מִמֶּךָּ: וְלֹא אָבָה לִשְׁמֹעַ בְּקוֹלָהּ וַיֶּחֱזַק מִמֶּנָּה וַיְעַנֶּהָ וַיִּשְׁכַּב אֹתָהּ: וַיִּשְׂנָאֶהָ אַמְנוֹן

---

1. The Midrash is critical of Yaakov for showing favor to one son over the others:
    Bereishit Rabbah 84:8: "'And he made him a *ketonet passim*': Resh Lakish said in the
    name of R. Elazar b. Azaryah: A man must not make a distinction among his children,
    for on account of the coat of many colors that our ancestor Yaakov made for Yosef, 'they
    hated him' (Bereishit 37:4)."

2. Rabbi Menahem M. Kasher cites this unpublished midrash. See *Torah Sheleimah*,
    Parashat Vayeishev, chapter 17, note 50.

שְׂנְאָה גְדוֹלָה מְאֹד כִּי גְדוֹלָה הַשִּׂנְאָה אֲשֶׁר שְׂנֵאָהּ מֵאַהֲבָה אֲשֶׁר אֲהֵבָהּ וַיֹּאמֶר
לָהּ אַמְנוֹן קוּמִי לֵכִי: וַתֹּאמֶר לוֹ אַל אֹדֹת הָרָעָה הַגְּדוֹלָה הַזֹּאת מֵאַחֶרֶת אֲשֶׁר
עָשִׂיתָ עִמִּי לְשַׁלְּחֵנִי וְלֹא אָבָה לִשְׁמֹעַ לָהּ:

וַיִּקְרָא אֶת נַעֲרוֹ מְשָׁרְתוֹ וַיֹּאמֶר שִׁלְחוּ נָא אֶת זֹאת מֵעָלַי הַחוּצָה וּנְעֹל הַדֶּלֶת
אַחֲרֶיהָ: וְעָלֶיהָ כְּתֹנֶת פַּסִּים כִּי כֵן תִּלְבַּשְׁןָ בְנוֹת הַמֶּלֶךְ הַבְּתוּלֹת מְעִילִים וַיֹּצֵא
אוֹתָהּ מְשָׁרְתוֹ הַחוּץ וְנָעַל הַדֶּלֶת אַחֲרֶיהָ:

And Amnon said to Tamar, "Bring the food into the chamber, that
I may eat of your hand." And Tamar took the cakes that she had
made, and brought them into the chamber to Amnon her brother.
And when she had brought them to him to eat, he took hold of her,
and said to her, "Come lie with me, my sister." And she answered him,
"No, my brother, do not force me; for no such thing ought to be done
in Israel; do not do this shameful deed. And I, where shall I carry my
shame? And as for you, you shall be as one of the base men in Israel.
And therefore, I beg you, speak to the king; for he will not withhold
me from you." But he would not listen to her voice; but, being stronger
than she, forced her, and lay with her. Then Amnon hated her very
much, so that the hatred with which he hated her was greater than
the love with which he had loved her. And Amnon said to her, "Get
up, be gone." And she said to him, "Do not add this greater wrong of
sending me away to the other that you did to me." But he would not
listen to her. Then he called his servant who ministered to him, and
said, "Take now this woman away from me, and bolt the door after
her." And she had a ketonet passim upon her; for with such robes
were the king's maiden daughters dressed. Then his servant took her
out, and bolted the door after her. (II Shmuel 13:10–18)

Amnon's shameful, dastardly deed led to his murder, by order of his
brother Avshalom:

שמואל ב יג:יט—כט

וַתִּקַּח תָּמָר אֵפֶר עַל רֹאשָׁהּ וּכְתֹנֶת הַפַּסִּים אֲשֶׁר עָלֶיהָ קָרָעָה וַתָּשֶׂם יָדָהּ עַל
רֹאשָׁהּ וַתֵּלֶךְ הָלוֹךְ וְזָעָקָה: וַיֹּאמֶר אֵלֶיהָ אַבְשָׁלוֹם אָחִיהָ הַאֲמִינוֹן אָחִיךְ הָיָה עִמָּךְ
וְעַתָּה אֲחוֹתִי הַחֲרִישִׁי אָחִיךְ הוּא אַל תָּשִׁיתִי אֶת לִבֵּךְ לַדָּבָר הַזֶּה וַתֵּשֶׁב תָּמָר
וְשֹׁמֵמָה בֵּית אַבְשָׁלוֹם אָחִיהָ: וְהַמֶּלֶךְ דָּוִד שָׁמַע אֶת כָּל הַדְּבָרִים הָאֵלֶּה וַיִּחַר לוֹ
מְאֹד: וְלֹא דִבֶּר אַבְשָׁלוֹם עִם אַמְנוֹן לְמֵרָע וְעַד טוֹב כִּי שָׂנֵא אַבְשָׁלוֹם אֶת אַמְנוֹן
עַל דְּבַר אֲשֶׁר עִנָּה אֵת תָּמָר אֲחֹתוֹ:

וַיְהִי לִשְׁנָתַיִם יָמִים וַיִּהְיוּ גֹזְזִים לְאַבְשָׁלוֹם בְּבַעַל חָצוֹר אֲשֶׁר עִם אֶפְרָיִם וַיִּקְרָא
אַבְשָׁלוֹם לְכָל בְּנֵי הַמֶּלֶךְ... וַיִּפְרָץ בּוֹ אַבְשָׁלוֹם וַיִּשְׁלַח אִתּוֹ אֶת אַמְנוֹן וְאֵת כָּל
בְּנֵי הַמֶּלֶךְ: וַיְצַו אַבְשָׁלוֹם אֶת נְעָרָיו לֵאמֹר רְאוּ נָא כְּטוֹב לֵב אַמְנוֹן בַּיַּיִן וְאָמַרְתִּי
אֲלֵיכֶם הַכּוּ אֶת אַמְנוֹן וַהֲמִתֶּם אֹתוֹ אַל תִּירָאוּ הֲלוֹא כִּי אָנֹכִי צִוִּיתִי אֶתְכֶם חִזְקוּ
וִהְיוּ לִבְנֵי חָיִל: וַיַּעֲשׂוּ נַעֲרֵי אַבְשָׁלוֹם לְאַמְנוֹן כַּאֲשֶׁר צִוָּה אַבְשָׁלוֹם וַיָּקֻמוּ כָּל בְּנֵי
הַמֶּלֶךְ וַיִּרְכְּבוּ אִישׁ עַל פִּרְדּוֹ וַיָּנֻסוּ:

And Tamar put ashes on her head, and tore her ketonet passim that was on her, and laid her hand on her head, crying aloud as she went. And Avshalom her brother said to her, "Has Amnon your brother been with you? But keep silence, my sister; he is your brother; take not this thing to heart." So Tamar remained desolate in her brother Avshalom's house. But when King David heard of all these things, he was very angry. And Avshalom spoke to his brother Amnon neither good nor bad, for Avshalom hated Amnon because he had raped his sister Tamar. And it came to pass after two full years, that Avshalom had sheepshearers in Baal Hazor, which is beside Efraim; and Avshalom invited all the king's sons.... But Avshalom pressed him, that he let Amnon and all the king's sons go with him. And Avshalom had commanded his servants, saying, "Mark now when Amnon's heart is merry with wine, and when I say to you "Strike Amnon," then kill him. Fear not; have I not commanded you? Be courageous, and be brave." And the servants of Avshalom did to Amnon as Avshalom had commanded. Then all the king's sons arose, and every man rode on his mule and fled. (II Shmuel 13:19–29)

Once again, hostile, violent relations between siblings are punctuated by the *ketonet passim*, the coat of many colors.

From this context, it appears that these are royal garments, the trappings of aristocracy.[3] Thus, when Yaakov bestows a *ketonet passim* on Yosef, he indicates that Yosef, rather than Reuven, the rightful heir as firstborn son, would eventually rule. The jealousy and enmity of the sons of the less-favored wives toward Yosef thus seems less capricious or petty.[4]

---

3. Ramban, loc. sit, makes this observation.

4. King Sha'ul's loss of the kingdom is connected to two instances relating to clothing: His clothing is ripped as a sign of his impending loss of the kingdom. Furthermore: "And

There is, however, another usage of the term *ketonet*, without the adjective *passim*, regarding the priestly garments:

שמות כח:מ–מא

וְלִבְנֵי אַהֲרֹן תַּעֲשֶׂה כֻתֳנֹת וְעָשִׂיתָ לָהֶם אַבְנֵטִים וּמִגְבָּעוֹת תַּעֲשֶׂה לָהֶם לְכָבוֹד וּלְתִפְאָרֶת: וְהִלְבַּשְׁתָּ אֹתָם אֶת אַהֲרֹן אָחִיךָ וְאֶת בָּנָיו אִתּוֹ וּמָשַׁחְתָּ אֹתָם וּמִלֵּאתָ אֶת יָדָם וְקִדַּשְׁתָּ אֹתָם וְכִהֲנוּ לִי:

And for Aharon's sons you shall make kutonot *[coats, the plural form of* ketonet*], and you shall make for them girdles, and turbans shall you make for them, for glory and for beauty. And you shall put them upon Aharon your brother, and his sons with him; and [you] shall anoint them, and consecrate them, and sanctify them, that they may minister to Me as* kohanim. *(Shmot 28:40–41)*

While the connection between Yosef and the priestly garb seems obscure, the Midrash draws a line between them:

ויקרא רבה, פרשה י פסקה ו

ואת הבגדים: א"ר סימון: כשם שהקרבנות מכפרים כך הבגדים מכפרים, דתנן: כהן גדול משמש בשמנה בגדים וההדיוט בארבע – בכתונת ובמכנסים במצנפת ובאבנט; מוסיף עליו כהן גדול חשן ואפוד ומעיל וציץ. הכתונת לכפר על לבושי כלאים, כמה דתימא (בראשית לז), "ועשה לו כתונת פסים"; מכנסים לכפר על גילוי עריות כמה דתימר (שמות כח) "ועשה להם מכנסי בד לכסות בשר ערוה"; מצנפת לכפר על גסות הרוח היך כד"א (שמות כט) "ושמת המצנפת על ראשו"; אבנט מאן דאמר על עוקמין שבלב ומאן דאמר על הגנבים....

And the clothes: R. Simon said: Even as the sacrifices have an atoning power, so too have the [priestly] garments atoning power, as we have learned in the Mishnah: The high priest [kohen gadol] officiated in eight garments, and an ordinary priest in four, namely in a ketonet, *breeches, a miter, and a girdle. The kohen gadol wore, in addition, a*

Sha'ul disguised himself, and put on other garments, and went, he and two men with him, and they came to the woman by night; and he said, 'I beg you, divine for me by a spirit, and bring him up for me, whoever I shall name to you'" (I Shmuel 28:8, 18–19). In this episode, in which Sha'ul secretly calls Shmuel up from the dead, Shmuel reveals that Sha'ul is about to meet his death in the upcoming war as a result of not obeying God.

breastplate, an eifod, *a robe, and a head plate. The* ketonet *atoned for those who wore a mixture of wool and linen, as it says, "And he made him a* ketonet passim*" (Bereishit 37); the breeches atoned for unchastity [literally, the uncovering of nakedness], as it says, "And you shall make them linen breeches to cover the flesh of nakedness" (Shmot 28); the miter atoned for arrogance, as it says, "And you shall set the miter on his head" (Shmot 29); the girdle was to atone, some say, for the crooked in heart, and others say for thieves.* (Vayikra Rabbah 10:6)

The *ketonet passim* is understood as being made of *sha'atnez*, the combination of wool and linen that is expressly forbidden by Torah law. Apparently, this is the precise definition of this garment's nature: the *ketonet* – from flax, and the *passim* – of wool. As we know, this is no ordinary, innocuous combination of materials. We are hard pressed to discern any intrinsic connection between Yosef's story and the prohibition of *sha'atnez*, and we are even further challenged when we consider that the Mishnah effectively establishes the story of Yosef and his *ketonet passim* as the prototype for the halakhic prohibition against *sha'atnez*.[5]

The prohibition against *sha'atnez* expresses a deeper mystical concept:[6] The tragic rivalry between the first two brothers in history, Kayin the

---

5. In several instances, the Talmud states that the *ketonet* atones for murder. See Zevahim 88b and Arakhin 17. This would help explain the reference to the *ketonet* in the section of Amnon and Tamar; Amnon was, in fact, murdered. The Midrash in Shir haShirim cites both traditions: Shir haShirim Rabbah 4:8: "...The *ketonet* used to make atonement for bloodshed, as we read, 'And they dipped the *ketonet* in the blood' (Bereishit 37:31). Some say it was for those who wore garments of *sha'atnez*, as we read, 'And he made him a *ketonet passim*' (Bereishit 37:3)."

6. See Midrash Tanhuma Bereishit (Warsaw edition), section 9; Zohar part 3, 87a; Pirkei d'Rebbi Eliezer, chapter 21; Hizkuni and the Baalei haTosafot on Devarim 22:10. Also see the commentary of the Vilna Gaon on the *Sifra d'Tzniuta*, chapter 4. See my discussion in *Explorations*, Parashat Bereishit and Parashat Kedoshim.

מדרש תנחומא (ורשא), פרשת בראשית פסקה ט

ויהי מקץ ימים ויבא קין וגו': יש מקץ שנה ויש שנתים ויש ימים ויש ארבעים שנה אמרו חז"ל בני ארבעים שנה היו קין והבל, ויבא קין מפרי האדמה מהו מן מותר מאכלו, ורבנן אמרו זרע פשתן היה, והבל הביא גם הוא מבכורות צאנו ומחלביהן לפיכך נאסר צמר ופשתים שנא' (דברים כב) לא תלבש שעטנז וגו' ואמר הקב"ה אינו דין שיתערב מנחת החוטא עם מנחת זכאי לפיכך נאסר.

farmer and his brother Hevel the shepherd, ended in fratricide – and the prohibition of *sha'atnez*, the Torah's prescribed remedy for the rift caused by that terrible sin. The fact that the *kohen gadol*, the person entrusted to effectuate spiritual healing, was dressed in a garment that brought together wool and linen is part and parcel of the corrective process.

This being so, we may posit that Yaakov gave Yosef these clothes as an antidote to the divisive jealousies that seethed below the surface of their family life. Perhaps Yaakov hoped to encourage healing, rather than further discord; perhaps, in Yaakov's eyes, Yosef was a prototype of the *kohen gadol*.

We may gain additional perspective by considering the nature of clothing in general, and not only the type of clothing described by the term *ketonet*. As we have already noted, God provided Adam and Eve with the first actual garments:

בראשית ג:כא

וַיַּעַשׂ ה' אֱלֹקִים לְאָדָם וּלְאִשְׁתּוֹ כָּתְנוֹת עוֹר וַיַּלְבִּשֵׁם:

God Almighty made for Adam and for his wife coats (kotnot) *of skin, and clothed them.* (Bereishit 3:21)

The concluding term is *vayalbishem* – "He clothed them." The Talmud takes a careful look at this verb, particularly its etymology:

תלמוד בבלי, מסכת שבת דף עז עמוד ב

לבושה – לא בושה. גלימא – שנעשה בו כגלם.

זוהר, ויקרא דף פז עמוד א

קרבנא דקין הוה פשתים, וקרבנא דהבל הוה צמר, לאו דא כדא ולאו דא כדא, רזא דמלה, קין כלאים הוה, ערבוביא דלא אצטריך, סטרא אחרא דלא זינא דחוה ואדם, וקורבניה מההוא סטרא קא אתיא, הבל מזינא חדא דאדם וחוה, ובמעהא דחוה אתחברו אלין תרין סטרין, ובגין דאתחברו כחדא, לא אתיא מנייהו תועלתא לעלמא, ואתאבידו.

פרקי דרבי אליעזר, פרק כא

ויהי קין איש אוהב לזרוע ויהי הבל איש אוהב לרעות צאן זה נותן ממלאכתו מאכל לזה והגיע לילו ליום טוב בפסח וקרא אדם לבניו ואמר להן עתידין ישראל להקריב קרבנות פסחים הקריבו גם אתם לפני בוראכם והביא קין מותר מאכלו קליות זרע פשתן והביא הבל מבכורות צאנו ומחלביהן כבשים שלא נגזזו לצמר ונתעבה מנחת קין ונתרצה מנחת הבל שנ' וישע ה' אל הבל ואל מנחתו ר' יהושע בן קרחא אומר אמר הקב"ה חס ושלום שלא נתערבו מנחת הבל וקין לעולם אפי' בארג בגד שנ' לא תלבש שעטנז צמר ופשתים יחדו....

Levushah *[means]* lo bushah *(no shame)*. Gelima *(a cloak) [is so called] because one looks in it like a* golem *(a shapeless mass)*. (Talmud Bavli Shabbat 77b)

The purpose of clothing is to hide one's shame. Man, who stood all but naked in the Garden of Eden, was clothed by God in an act of compassion. In a sense, all clothing covers the individual and hides the real person, and must be considered within this context. Many of the terms used to describe various types of clothing have vestiges of the less than positive overtones with which this first set of clothes was created. For instance, the word for coat – *me'il* – has connotations of *me'ilah* – trespass.

Once we understand the association between clothing and sin, the concluding sections of the present parashah become more readily understood. We are told that Yosef is the object of the adulterous advances of the mistress of the house of Potifar, which he heroically withstands:

בראשית לט:ז—יג

וַיְהִי אַחַר הַדְּבָרִים הָאֵלֶּה וַתִּשָּׂא אֵשֶׁת אֲדֹנָיו אֶת עֵינֶיהָ אֶל יוֹסֵף וַתֹּאמֶר שִׁכְבָה עִמִּי:וַיְמָאֵן וַיֹּאמֶר אֶל אֵשֶׁת אֲדֹנָיו הֵן אֲדֹנִי לֹא יָדַע אִתִּי מַה בַּבָּיִת וְכֹל אֲשֶׁר יֶשׁ לוֹ נָתַן בְּיָדִי:אֵינֶנּוּ גָדוֹל בַּבַּיִת הַזֶּה מִמֶּנִּי וְלֹא חָשַׂךְ מִמֶּנִּי מְאוּמָה כִּי אִם אוֹתָךְ בַּאֲשֶׁר אַתְּ אִשְׁתּוֹ וְאֵיךְ אֶעֱשֶׂה הָרָעָה הַגְּדֹלָה הַזֹּאת וְחָטָאתִי לֵאלֹקִים:וַיְהִי כְּדַבְּרָהּ אֶל יוֹסֵף יוֹם יוֹם וְלֹא שָׁמַע אֵלֶיהָ לִשְׁכַּב אֶצְלָהּ לִהְיוֹת עִמָּהּ: וַיְהִי כְּהַיּוֹם הַזֶּה וַיָּבֹא הַבַּיְתָה לַעֲשׂוֹת מְלַאכְתּוֹ וְאֵין אִישׁ מֵאַנְשֵׁי הַבַּיִת שָׁם בַּבָּיִת:וַתִּתְפְּשֵׂהוּ בְּבִגְדוֹ לֵאמֹר שִׁכְבָה עִמִּי וַיַּעֲזֹב בִּגְדוֹ בְּיָדָהּ וַיָּנָס וַיֵּצֵא הַחוּצָה: וַיְהִי כִּרְאוֹתָהּ כִּי עָזַב בִּגְדוֹ בְּיָדָהּ וַיָּנָס הַחוּצָה:

And it came to pass after these things, that his master's wife cast her eyes upon Yosef; and she said, "Lie with me." But he refused, and said to his master's wife, "Behold, my master knows not what is with me in the house, and he has committed all that he has to my hand. There is none greater in this house than I; nor has he kept back any thing from me but you, because you are his wife; how then can I do this great wickedness, and sin against God?" And it came to pass, as she spoke to Yosef day by day, that he listened not to her, to lie by her, or to be with her. And it came to pass about this time, that Yosef went into the house to fulfill his duties; and none of the men of the house were inside. And she caught him by his garment, saying, "Lie with me"; and he left his garment in her hand, and fled, and got out. And

*it came to pass, when she saw that he had left his garment in her
hand, and had fled out...* (Bereishit 39:7–13)

The sages are divided regarding Yosef's intention when he allowed himself
to be secluded with her.

תלמוד בבלי, מסכת סוטה דף לו עמוד ב

א"ר יוחנן: מלמד ששניהם לדבר עבירה נתכוונו. "ויבא הביתה לעשות מלאכתו":
רב ושמואל, חד אמר: לעשות מלאכתו ממש, וחד אמר: לעשות צרכיו נכנס.
"ואין איש מאנשי הבית" וגו': אפשר, בית גדול כביתו של אותו רשע לא היה
בו איש? תנא דבי ר' ישמעאל: אותו היום יום חגם היה, והלכו כולן לבית
עבודת כוכבים שלהם, והיא אמרה להן חולה היא. אמרה: אין לי יום שניזקק
לי יוסף כיום הזה.
"ותתפשהו בבגדו לאמר" וגו': באותה שעה באתה דיוקנו של אביו ונראתה
לו בחלון. אמר לו, "יוסף, עתידין אחיך שיכתבו על אבני אפוד ואתה ביניהם,
רצונך שימחה שמך מביניהם ותקרא רועה זונות?" דכתיב, (משלי כט) "ורועה
זונות יאבד הון".

*R. Yohanan said: This teaches that both [Yosef and Potifar's wife]
had the intention of acting immorally. "He went into the house to
fulfill his duties": Rav and Shmuel [differ in their interpretation].
One said that it really means to do his work; but the other said that
he went to satisfy his desires.*

*"And none of the men of the house...": Is it possible that there was no
man in a huge house like that of this wicked [Potifar]! It was taught
in the school of R. Yishmael: That day was their feast day, and they
had all gone to their idolatrous temple; but she had pretended to be
ill because she thought, "I shall not have another opportunity like
today for Yosef to associate with me."*

*"And she caught him by his garment, saying...": At that moment his
father's image came and appeared to him through the window and
said: "Yosef, your brothers will have their names inscribed upon the
stones of the eifod and yours among theirs; is it your wish to have
your name expunged from among theirs and be called an associate
of harlots?"* (Talmud Bavli Sotah 36b)

Here the term for clothing is *beged*; she grabbed his clothing, *b'vigdo*.
The root of the word is *b-g-d*. This is also the root of the word meaning

"treason" or "rebellion."[7] Clothing bears testimony to the first and perhaps most profound rebellion man staged against God: in the Garden of Eden, when the world was new and man was innocent and pure, man reached beyond his rightful grasp, and the world has never been the same. Clothing is a symbol of the loss of innocence. When Yosef went into the room, he allowed himself to enter a spiritually precarious situation. Sin was only a finger's reach away. Yosef was guilty of rebellion, and Potiphar's wife seized more than just the moment; she grabbed on to Yosef's *beged*, his clothing, seizing his "rebellion."

Nonetheless, Yosef extricates himself, retaining his innocence. He does not forfeit his place on the *eifod*, the breastplate of the *kohen gadol*. He will, once again, wear royal garb, just as his father had envisioned years before.

בראשית מא:יד

וַיִּשְׁלַח פַּרְעֹה וַיִּקְרָא אֶת יוֹסֵף וַיְרִיצֻהוּ מִן הַבּוֹר וַיְגַלַּח וַיְחַלֵּף שִׂמְלֹתָיו וַיָּבֹא אֶל פַּרְעֹה:

Then Par'oh sent and called for Yosef, and they brought him hastily out of the dungeon; and he shaved himself, and changed his attire, and came in to Par'oh. (Bereishit 41:14)

Yosef let go of his rebellion, and he emerged spiritually fortified, a man who was able to withstand temptation. Yosef no longer wore *begadim*. Now

---

7. This association is already implied in the Talmud (Kiddushin 18b): "R. Simeon said: Just as a man cannot sell his daughter for servitude after marriage, so a man cannot sell his daughter for servitude after servitude. Now this enters into the dispute of the following Tannaim. For it was taught: '[To sell her to a strange people he shall have no power], seeing he has dealt deceitfully with her [*b'vigdo bah*]' (Shmot 21:8): once he spread his cloak over her, he can no longer sell her – this is R. Akiva's view. R. Eliezer said: seeing he has dealt deceitfully with her – having dealt deceitfully with her, he may not sell her [again]. Wherein do they differ? R. Eliezer maintains: the traditional text [i.e., letters without vowels] is authoritative; R. Akiva maintains: the text as read is authoritative; whereas R. Shimon holds: both the traditional text and the vocalization are authoritative."

See Rashi's commentary, where he cites the verse referring to Yosef. Also see Baal haTurim and Rabbeinu Bahya on Shmot 21:8. Noteworthy as well is the Ramban on Bereishit 39:9, where he labels Yosef's possible affair as a "*begidah* (rebellion)"; in light of the numerous times the word *beged* is used in this section, I would doubt that the Ramban did not intend this association.

Yosef wore royal clothes, befitting aristocracy. Yosef becomes the person his father knew he would. His clothes now fit.

For a Pair of Shoes

As Yosef approaches his brothers, he does not know that they have been plotting his downfall.[1] Yosef seeks his brothers in earnest,[2] but the sentiment is not reciprocated. When Yosef finally does find his brothers, he is thrown into a pit, where he remains until the opportunity to permanently solve the "Yosef problem" presents itself:

בראשית לז:כה–כז

וַיֵּשְׁבוּ לֶאֱכָל לֶחֶם וַיִּשְׂאוּ עֵינֵיהֶם וַיִּרְאוּ וְהִנֵּה אֹרְחַת יִשְׁמְעֵאלִים בָּאָה מִגִּלְעָד וּגְמַלֵּיהֶם נֹשְׂאִים נְכֹאת וּצְרִי וָלֹט הוֹלְכִים לְהוֹרִיד מִצְרָיְמָה: וַיֹּאמֶר יְהוּדָה אֶל אֶחָיו מַה בֶּצַע כִּי נַהֲרֹג אֶת אָחִינוּ וְכִסִּינוּ אֶת דָּמוֹ: לְכוּ וְנִמְכְּרֶנּוּ לַיִּשְׁמְעֵאלִים וְיָדֵנוּ אַל תְּהִי בוֹ כִּי אָחִינוּ בְשָׂרֵנוּ הוּא וַיִּשְׁמְעוּ אֶחָיו:

And they sat down to eat bread; and they lifted up their eyes and looked, and, behold, a company of Yishmaelites came from Gil'ad with their camels bearing gum, balm and myrrh, going to carry it down to Egypt. And Yehudah said to his brothers, "What profit is it if we slay our brother, and conceal his blood? Come, and let us sell him to the Yishmaelites, and let not our hand be upon him; for he is our brother and our flesh." And his brothers heard. (Bereishit 37:25–27)

---

1. See Bereishit 37:18.

   בראשית לז:יח

   וַיִּרְאוּ אֹתוֹ מֵרָחֹק וּבְטֶרֶם יִקְרַב אֲלֵיהֶם וַיִּתְנַכְּלוּ אֹתוֹ לַהֲמִיתוֹ:

   "And when they saw him from far away, even before he came near to them, they conspired against him to slay him."

2. See Bereishit 37:15–16.

   בראשית לז:טו–טז

   וַיִּמְצָאֵהוּ אִישׁ וְהִנֵּה תֹעֶה בַּשָּׂדֶה וַיִּשְׁאָלֵהוּ הָאִישׁ לֵאמֹר מַה תְּבַקֵּשׁ: וַיֹּאמֶר אֶת אַחַי אָנֹכִי מְבַקֵּשׁ הַגִּידָה נָּא לִי אֵיפֹה הֵם רֹעִים:

   "And a man found him, and, behold, he was wandering in the field; and the man asked him, saying, 'What do you seek?' And he said, 'I seek my brothers; tell me, I beg you, where they feed their flocks.'"

The messy business of murder is avoided, rejected in favor of a more profitable arrangement. Once the decision is formulated to sell Yosef to the Yishmaelites, a second group, the Midianites, is introduced, and the sale forges ahead:

בראשית לז:כח

וַיַּעַבְרוּ אֲנָשִׁים מִדְיָנִים סֹחֲרִים וַיִּמְשְׁכוּ וַיַּעֲלוּ אֶת יוֹסֵף מִן הַבּוֹר וַיִּמְכְּרוּ אֶת יוֹסֵף לַיִּשְׁמְעֵאלִים בְּעֶשְׂרִים כָּסֶף וַיָּבִיאוּ אֶת יוֹסֵף מִצְרָיְמָה:

Then there passed by Midianite merchants; and they drew and lifted up Yosef out of the pit, and sold Yosef to the Yishmaelites for twenty pieces of silver; and they brought Yosef to Egypt. (Bereishit 37:28)

The reference to the Midianites is unclear; Rashi suggests that Yosef was sold more than once,[3] while the Ibn Ezra[4] says that both names refer to the same[5] caravan. There are, however, commentaries who suggest that the brothers did not actually sell Yosef: while the brothers were still discussing the idea, the Midianites rode by, and hearing Yosef's bloodcurdling screams, they "rescued" him from the pit, only to in turn sell him to the band of Yishmaelites the brothers had seen approaching. The Rashbam, who advocates this position, theorizes that the brothers, not wishing to ruin their repast, had positioned themselves at some distance from the pit into which they had thrown Yosef so that they could not hear his cries for help.[6]

---

3. Rashi, Bereishit 37:28.

רש"י, בראשית לז:כח

ויעברו אנשים מדינים: זו היא שיירא אחרת והודיעך הכתוב שנמכר פעמים הרבה.
וימשכו: בני יעקב את יוסף מן הבור ומכרוהו לישמעאלים והישמעאלים למדינים והמדינים למצרים.

4. Ibn Ezra, Bereishit 37:28.

אבן עזרא, בראשית לז:כח

ויעברו: וכאשר עברו עליהם הישמעאלים הסוחרים כי המדינים יקראו ישמעאלים וכן אמר על מלכי מדין כי ישמעאלים הם.

5. This position is also taken by the Bekhor Shor, who first rejects other suggestions:

רבי יוסף בכור שור, בראשית לז:כח

וכל זה איננו שוה לי, אלא אומה אחת היו, כמו שפירשתי, כמו שקוראים אותנו – פעמים "יהודים",
פעמים "עברים", פעמים "ישראלים", פעמים "ישורון".

6. Rashbam, Bereishit 37:28.

רשב"ם, בראשית לז:כח

ויעברו אנשים מדינים: ובתוך שהיו יושבים לאכול לחם ורחוקים היו קצת מן הבור לבלתי אכול על הדם וממתינים היו לישמעאלים שראו וקודם שבאו הישמעאלים עברו אנשים מדינים אחרים דרך שם

The Hizkuni[7] goes even further and suggests that the brothers were unaware that the Midianites had sold Yosef to the Yishmaelites, a theory borne out by Reuven's futile attempt to save Yosef from the pit – *after* he was sold: if, in fact, the brothers had been party to the sale, Reuven's behavior would be inexplicable.[8]

These opinions seem to contradict the brothers' own admission of guilt. When they unknowingly stand before Yosef in Egypt, they admit that they had indeed heard Yosef's cries, and ignored his pleas:

בראשית מב:כא–כב

וַיֹּאמְרוּ אִישׁ אֶל אָחִיו אֲבָל אֲשֵׁמִים אֲנַחְנוּ עַל אָחִינוּ אֲשֶׁר רָאִינוּ צָרַת נַפְשׁוֹ בְּהִתְחַנְנוֹ אֵלֵינוּ וְלֹא שָׁמָעְנוּ עַל כֵּן בָּאָה אֵלֵינוּ הַצָּרָה הַזֹּאת: וַיַּעַן רְאוּבֵן אֹתָם לֵאמֹר הֲלוֹא אָמַרְתִּי אֲלֵיכֶם לֵאמֹר אַל תֶּחֶטְאוּ בַיֶּלֶד וְלֹא שְׁמַעְתֶּם וְגַם דָּמוֹ הִנֵּה נִדְרָשׁ:

וראוהו בבור ומשכוהו ומכרוהו המדינים לישמעאלים וי"ל שהאחים לא ידעו ואע"פ שכתוב אשר מכרתם אותי מצרימה י"ל שהגרמת מעשיהם סייעה במכירתו. זה נראה לי לפי עומק דרך פשוטו של מקרא כי ויעברו אנשים מדינים משמע ע"י מקרה והם מכרוהו לישמעאלים. ואף אם באתה לומר וימכרו את יוסף לישמעאלים כי אחיו מכרוהו אם כן צריך לומר שהם ציוו למדינים סוחרים למושכו מן הבור ואח"כ מכרוהו לישמעאלים.

7. Hizkuni, Bereishit 37:28.

חזקוני, בראשית לז:כח

מן הבור: ואחיו לא ידעו מאומה מכל זאת וכשהלך ראובן אל הבור ולא מצאו חשבו כולם חיה רעה אכלתהו ולא שקרו לאביהם שאם מכרוהו לשום אדם לא היה גוי וממלכה בד' פנות העולם שלא יבקשוהו עד שידעו בירור דבר אם הוא חי או מת. ועוד אם היו מסופקים ממנו אם הוא חי או מת מדוע לא הכירוהו במראה או בדיבור ובבנימין שאמר לו אלקים יחנך בני ובמשאות חמש ידות שלו ובמה שהושיבם לפניו הבכור כבכורתו והצעיר כצעירתו, אלא כן הוא כמו שפי'. ד"א בעוד שהיו מדברים ביניהם לכו ונמכרנו לישמעאלים הבאים עלינו ובטרם הגיעו הישמעאלים אליהם ויעברו אנשים מדינים סחרים ומכרוהו להם בעודו בבור פן יבכה לפניהם ויתבייישו ממנו וימשכו המדינים ויעלו את יוסף מן הבור שהרי קנוהו מיד אחיו ובעודם מושכין אותו מן הבור באו הישמעאלים עליהם ומכרו המדינים את יוסף לישמעאלים והישמעאלים מכרוהו למדינים ומדינים לפוטיפר הרי כאן ד' מכירות. והא דכתיב לקמן ויקנהו פוטיפר מיד הישמעאלים, כך היה המעשה השבטים מכרוהו למדינים וישמעאלים למדינים ומכירה זו לא נכתבה והיל ולא היתה רק לפי שעה ומדינים מכרוהו לישמעאלים ומכירה זו שלישית זו נכתבה לפי שהשלישית הישמעאלים מכרוהו בחפזון ובהצנע כי אמרו שמא יחזרו בהם המדינים מלקנותו ומדינים מכרוהו לפוטיפר כשראה פוטיפר את יוסף שהיה יפה שהיה מראה ביד המדינים שהיו המדינים סוחרים שהרי אחים הם לישמעאלים, תמה בעצמו ואמר גרמני מוכר את הכושי ואין כושי מוכר את הגרמני פי' אדם יפה, אמר פוטיפר ודאי זה אינו עבד תנו לי ערב שלא גנבתם אותו הלכו המדינים והביאו הישמעאלים וערבו שלא גנבוהו והיינו דכתיב ויקנהו פוטיפר מיד הישמעאלים פי' מערבותם כמו אנכי אערבנו מידי תבקשנו.

8. Reuven's part in the entire episode requires further study; he was the only one of the brothers who protested against their plan. Rashi offers different interpretations for Reuven's absence at the moment of the sale.

And they said one to another, we are truly guilty concerning our brother, in that we saw the anguish of his soul, when he besought us, and we would not hear; therefore is this distress come upon us. And Reuven answered them, saying, "Did I not speak to you, saying, 'Do not sin against the child'; and you would not hear? Therefore, behold, also his blood is required." (Bereishit 42:21–22)

Yosef himself would surely have mentioned any mitigating facts or circumstances when he consoled his brothers and attempted to make peace with them years later, but he does not seem to be aware of any such factors. If the Rashbam and the Hizkuni were correct, we would expect Yosef to have said something to them along the lines of, "it wasn't you who sold me" or "you didn't know that I had been sold." Instead, he says "I am Yosef whom you sold…"

בראשית מה:ג–ה

וַיֹּאמֶר יוֹסֵף אֶל אֶחָיו אֲנִי יוֹסֵף הַעוֹד אָבִי חָי וְלֹא יָכְלוּ אֶחָיו לַעֲנוֹת אֹתוֹ כִּי נִבְהֲלוּ מִפָּנָיו: וַיֹּאמֶר יוֹסֵף אֶל אֶחָיו גְּשׁוּ נָא אֵלַי וַיִּגָּשׁוּ וַיֹּאמֶר אֲנִי יוֹסֵף אֲחִיכֶם אֲשֶׁר מְכַרְתֶּם אֹתִי מִצְרָיְמָה: וְעַתָּה אַל תֵּעָצְבוּ וְאַל יִחַר בְּעֵינֵיכֶם כִּי מְכַרְתֶּם אֹתִי הֵנָּה כִּי לְמִחְיָה שְׁלָחַנִי אֱלֹקִים לִפְנֵיכֶם:

And Yosef said to his brothers, "I am Yosef! Does my father still live?" And his brothers could not answer him, for they panicked in his presence. And Yosef said to his brothers, "Come near me, I beg you." And they came near. And he said, "I am Yosef your brother, whom you sold to Egypt. Now therefore be not grieved, nor angry with yourselves, that you sold me here; for God sent me before you to preserve life." (Bereishit 45:3–5)

Indeed, it seems difficult to argue[9] that the brothers were not guilty of this act of perfidy.[10] Jewish tradition refers to the sale of Yosef as a stain on the

---

9. A debate continues in academic circles as to Rashbam's motivation for presenting an exegesis that not only creates textual difficulties, but also goes against rabbinic tradition. There are those who argue that the Rashbam, who insists that his interpretation is *pshat*, and gives an introduction to his methodology specifically here at the outset of chapter 37, was motivated by polemical concerns: The story of the sale of Yosef was a common topic for Christian performances that drew a parallel between the betrayal of Yosef by Yehudah, and the betrayal of the founder of Christianity. By absolving the brothers of guilt in the sale of Yosef, the Rashbam took away a powerful polemical tool, and

collective conscience of the entire nation – a stain that much of Jewish practice and Jewish history is geared toward cleansing. The Rambam notes that a goat is always brought as a sin offering on holidays, and ties this offering directly with the goat's blood with which Yosef's coat of many colors was stained by the brothers. The goat is a symbol of the treachery that continues to haunt the collective, a blot on the integrity and unity of the entire nation. On holidays, when we gather as a family, we bring the sin offering with the blood of the goat in order to attempt to bring about healing for the sale of Yosef at his brothers' hands.[11]

---

may have been saving Jews from persecution. See also Eliezer Touito, "The Rashbam's Exegetical Approach in Perspective of the Historical Situation in His Time," in *Studies in Rabbinic Literature, Bible and Jewish History*, ed. Y.D. Gilat, Ch. Levine and Z.M. Rabinowitz (Ramat Gan: Bar-Ilan University Press, 1982), pages 48–74.

10. See Bekhor Shor, Bereishit 37:28.

רבי יוסף בכור שור, בראשית לז:כח

והאמת כי אחיו מכרוהו, כמו שאמר להם "אשר מכרתם אותי הנה", והשביעוהו כמו שפירשתי, ועשו ממנו סחורה גדולה, כאדם המוכר שדהו מפני רעתה כי היו נותנים משלהם שירחיקוהו מהם, כי תכלית שנאה שנאוהו.

11. *Guide for the Perplexed* 3:46:

ספר מורה נבוכים, חלק ג פרק מו

ולפי זה הענין אשר זכרוהו יראה לי שהטעם בהיות החטאות כולם ליחיד ולציבור שעירים – רצוני לומר, שעירי הרגלים, ושעירי ראשי חדשים, ושעירי יום הכיפורים, ושעירי עבודה זרה – סיבת כל אלו אצלי היות רוב מרים וחטאתם אז בהקריבם לשעירים – כמו שבאר הכתוב, "ולא יזבחו עוד את זבחיהם לשעירים אשר הם זונים אחריהם". אבל החכמים ז"ל שמו טעם היות כפרת צבור לעולם בשעירים – בעבור שחטא עדת ישראל כולה היה בשעיר עיזים – רמז למכירת יוסף הצדיק, שנאמר בענינו, "וישחטו שעיר עיזים וגו'". ולא יהיה זה הטעם חלוש בעיניך, כי כונת כל אלו הפעולות – לישב בנפש כל חוטא וכל איש מרי שצריך לזכור ולהזכיר חטאו תמיד – כמו שאמר, "וחטאתי נגדי תמיד".

"From this argument of our sages I deduce that he-goats were always brought as sin offerings, by individual persons and also by the whole congregation, for example, on the festivals, New-moon, Day of Atonement, and for idolatry, because most of the transgressions and sins of the Israelites were sacrifices to spirits (*se'irim*, lit., goats), as is clearly stated, "They shall no more offer their sacrifices unto spirits" (Vayikra 17:7). Our sages, however, explained the fact that goats were always the sin offerings of the congregation, as an allusion to the sin of the whole congregation of Israel: for in the account of the selling of the pious Yosef we read, 'And they killed a kid of the goats' (Bereishit 37:31). Do not consider this as a weak argument; for it is the object of all these ceremonies to impress on the mind of every sinner and transgressor the necessity of continually remembering and mentioning his sins. Thus the Psalmist says, 'And my sin is ever before me' (Tehillim 51:3)."

In fact, our sages associate one of the most cataclysmic events in Jewish history with our collective guilt for the sale of Yosef: the martyrdom of Judaism's ten greatest scholars, retold in the Yom Kippur liturgy each year, is said to be a *tikkun* for the sale of Yosef. It seems an inescapable conclusion that Jewish theology considers the brothers guilty of the sale, and senses the repercussions of that episode throughout our history.[12]

The haftarah traditionally associated with this parashah leads to an inescapable conclusion of guilt.

עמוס ב:ו

כֹּה אָמַר ה' עַל שְׁלֹשָׁה פִּשְׁעֵי יִשְׂרָאֵל וְעַל אַרְבָּעָה לֹא אֲשִׁיבֶנּוּ עַל מִכְרָם בַּכֶּסֶף צַדִּיק וְאֶבְיוֹן בַּעֲבוּר נַעֲלָיִם:

Thus says the Almighty: "For three transgressions of Israel I will turn away punishment, but for the fourth I will not turn away its punishment; because they sold the righteous one for silver, and the poor man for a pair of shoes." (Amos 2:6)

Yosef, as distinct from all the other patriarchs, is known as "the righteous one," and the words of the prophet Amos supply information that is lacking in the verses of our parashah: tradition teaches that the money they "earned" from the sale of Yosef was used by the brothers to purchase shoes.[13] The

---

12. Mussaf prayer on Yom Kippur, and other sources.

13. See Midrash Tanhuma, Parashat Vayeishev, chapter 2; Pirkei d'Rebbi Eliezer, chapter 37.

מדרש תנחומא, פרשת וישב פרק ב

מה עשה ראובן הלך וישב באחד מן ההרים לירד בלילה להעלות את יוסף ותשעה אחיו יושבין במקום אחד כאיש אחד בעצה אחד להמיתו עברו עליהם ישמעאלים אמרו לכו ונמכרנו לישמעאלים הן מוליכין אותו לקצות המדבר עמדו מכרוהו בעשרים כסף לכל אחד מהם שני כסף לקנות מנעלים לרגליהם וכי תעלה על דעתך שנער יפה כמותו נמכר בעשרים כסף אלא כיון שהושלך לבור מתוך פחד נחשים ועקרבים שבו נשתנה זיו פניו וברח ממנו דמו ונעשו פניו ירוקות לפיכך מכרוהו בעשרים כסף בעבור נעלים אמרו נחרים ביניינו שלא יגיד אחד ממנו ליעקב אבינו אמר להם יהודה ראובן אינו כאן ואין החרם מתקיים אלא בעשרה מה עשו שתפו להקב"ה באותו החרם שלא יגיד לאביהם.

פרקי דרבי אליעזר, פרק לז

ובשעה אחת אחיו היו יושבים במקום אחד ולב אחד ועצה אחת ועברו עליהם ארחת ישמעאלים ואמרו בואו ונמכרנו לישמעאלים ויהיו מוליכין אותו לקצה המדבר ואין יעקב אבינו שומע שמע עוד ומכרו אותו לישמעאלים בעשרים כסף כל אחד ואחד נטל שני כספים לקנות מנעלים ברגליהם שנ' על מכרם בכסף צדיק ואביון בעבור נעלים.

Torah recounts only that twenty pieces of silver[14] changed hands in the exchange;[15] there is not a word to indicate what was done with the money, nor any mention of shoes. This seems altogether fitting: the use made of this "blood money" does not seem relevant to the real issues of the parashah, and to the long-term effects of the brothers' actions. Why, then, do we have a tradition about this? Is the fact that the brothers bought shoes with this money really a salient fact worth recording? The very fact that they sold their brother seems enough of an outrage. What difference does it make what they did with their ill-gotten profit? As we shall see, the seemingly irrelevant information that the prophet preserves and transmits will help reveal other important facets and aspects of the sale.

---

14. In the extracanonical Testament of the Twelve Tribes, Gad "admits" to having taken thirty pieces of gold; in collusion with Yehudah, they only tell the others of twenty! Apparently an attempt was made in this text to be bring the story closer to that of the betrayal of the founder of Christianity, who was supposedly "sold" for thirty pieces of silver:

The Testament of Gad Concerning Hatred:

1. The record of the testament of Gad, what things he spake unto his sons, in the hundred and twenty-seventh year of his life, saying: I was the seventh son born to Yaakov, and I was valiant in keeping the flocks. I guarded at night the flock; and whenever the lion came, or wolf, or leopard, or bear, or any wild beast against the fold, I pursued it, and with my hand seizing its foot, and whirling it round, I stunned it, and hurled it over two furlongs, and so killed it. Now Yosef was feeding the flock with us for about thirty days, and being tender, he fell sick by reason of the heat. And he returned to Hebron to his father, who made him lie down near him, because he loved him....

2. I confess now my sin, my children, that oftentimes I wished to kill him, because I hated him to the death, and there were in no wise in me bowels of mercy towards him. Moreover, I hated him yet more because of his dreams; and I would have devoured him out of the land of the living, even as a calf devours the grass from the earth. Therefore I and Judah sold him to the Yishmaelites for thirty pieces of gold, and ten of them we hid, and showed the twenty to our brethren: and so through my covetousness I was fully bent on his destruction. And the God of my fathers delivered him from my hands, that I should not work iniquity in Israel.

15. Bereishit 37:28.

בראשית לז:כח

וַיַּעַבְרוּ אֲנָשִׁים מִדְיָנִים סֹחֲרִים וַיִּמְשְׁכוּ וַיַּעֲלוּ אֶת יוֹסֵף מִן הַבּוֹר וַיִּמְכְּרוּ אֶת יוֹסֵף לַיִּשְׁמְעֵאלִים **בְּעֶשְׂרִים כָּסֶף**
וַיָּבִיאוּ אֶת יוֹסֵף מִצְרָיְמָה.

"Then there passed by Midianite merchants; and they drew and lifted up Yosef out from the pit, and sold Yosef to the Yishmaelites *for twenty pieces of silver*; and they brought Yosef to Egypt."

Shoes appear in the Torah in several contexts. The first is when Moshe is told to remove his shoes in deference to the holy ground on which he stands:

שמות ג:ג–ה

וַיֹּאמֶר מֹשֶׁה אָסֻרָה נָּא וְאֶרְאֶה אֶת הַמַּרְאֶה הַגָּדֹל הַזֶּה מַדּוּעַ לֹא יִבְעַר הַסְּנֶה: וַיַּרְא ה' כִּי סָר לִרְאוֹת וַיִּקְרָא אֵלָיו אֱלֹקִים מִתּוֹךְ הַסְּנֶה וַיֹּאמֶר מֹשֶׁה מֹשֶׁה וַיֹּאמֶר הִנֵּנִי: וַיֹּאמֶר אַל תִּקְרַב הֲלֹם שַׁל נְעָלֶיךָ מֵעַל רַגְלֶיךָ כִּי הַמָּקוֹם אֲשֶׁר אַתָּה עוֹמֵד עָלָיו אַדְמַת קֹדֶשׁ הוּא:

And Moshe said, "I will now turn aside, and see this great sight, why the bush is not burnt. And when the Almighty saw that he turned aside to see, God called to him out of the midst of the bush, and said, "Moshe, Moshe." And he said, "Here I am." And He said, "Do not come any closer; take your shoes off your feet, for the place on which you stand is holy ground. (Shmot 3:3–5)

In this context, removing one's shoes indicates an awareness of holiness. On the other hand, when the Jews prepared to leave Egypt, they were told to put on their shoes:

שמות יב:יא

וְכָכָה תֹּאכְלוּ אֹתוֹ מָתְנֵיכֶם חֲגֻרִים נַעֲלֵיכֶם בְּרַגְלֵיכֶם וּמַקֶּלְכֶם בְּיֶדְכֶם וַאֲכַלְתֶּם אֹתוֹ בְּחִפָּזוֹן פֶּסַח הוּא לה':

And thus shall you eat it; with your loins girded, your shoes on your feet, and your staff in your hand; and you shall eat it in haste; it is the Pesah for the Almighty. (Shmot 12:11)

While it might seem that the commandment to put on shoes is purely pragmatic, preparing the Jews for the long walk on which they will soon embark, the deeper significance may be learned from the third context in which shoes appear: there is one halakhic section of the Torah, one Torah law, in which a shoe is a significant element. When a man refuses to marry his deceased brother's childless wife, a unique ceremony is carried out:[16]

---

16. The Ramhal, in his commentary to Devarim, links Moshe's removal of his shoes at the Burning Bush with the ritual of *halitzah*; Moshe is commanded to remove his shoes as a symbol of freedom from the constraints of the Israelites' previous relationship with Egypt.

דברים כה:ה–י

כִּי יֵשְׁבוּ אַחִים יַחְדָּו וּמֵת אַחַד מֵהֶם וּבֵן אֵין לוֹ לֹא תִהְיֶה אֵשֶׁת הַמֵּת הַחוּצָה לְאִישׁ זָר יְבָמָהּ יָבֹא עָלֶיהָ וּלְקָחָהּ לוֹ לְאִשָּׁה וְיִבְּמָהּ: וְהָיָה הַבְּכוֹר אֲשֶׁר תֵּלֵד יָקוּם עַל שֵׁם אָחִיו הַמֵּת וְלֹא יִמָּחֶה שְׁמוֹ מִיִּשְׂרָאֵל: וְאִם לֹא יַחְפֹּץ הָאִישׁ לָקַחַת אֶת יְבִמְתּוֹ וְעָלְתָה יְבִמְתּוֹ הַשַּׁעְרָה אֶל הַזְּקֵנִים וְאָמְרָה מֵאֵן יְבָמִי לְהָקִים לְאָחִיו שֵׁם בְּיִשְׂרָאֵל לֹא אָבָה יַבְּמִי: וְקָרְאוּ לוֹ זִקְנֵי עִירוֹ וְדִבְּרוּ אֵלָיו וְעָמַד וְאָמַר לֹא חָפַצְתִּי לְקַחְתָּהּ: וְנִגְּשָׁה יְבִמְתּוֹ אֵלָיו לְעֵינֵי הַזְּקֵנִים וְחָלְצָה נַעֲלוֹ מֵעַל רַגְלוֹ וְיָרְקָה בְּפָנָיו וְעָנְתָה וְאָמְרָה כָּכָה יֵעָשֶׂה לָאִישׁ אֲשֶׁר לֹא יִבְנֶה אֶת בֵּית אָחִיו: וְנִקְרָא שְׁמוֹ בְּיִשְׂרָאֵל בֵּית חֲלוּץ הַנָּעַל:

If brothers live together, and one of them dies, and has no child, the wife of the dead shall not marry outside to a stranger; her husband's brother shall go in to her, and take her to him for a wife, and perform the duty of a husband's brother to her. And it shall be, that the firstborn that she bears shall succeed to the name of his brother who is dead, that his name be not put out of Israel. And if the man does not wish to take his brother's wife, then let his brother's wife go up to the gate to the elders, and say, "My husband's brother refuses to raise to his brother a name in Israel, he will not perform his duty as my husband's brother." Then the elders of his city shall call him and speak to him. And if he persists and says, "I do not wish to take her," then shall his brother's wife come to him in the presence of the elders, and pull his shoe from off his foot, and spit in his face, and shall answer and say, "So shall it be done to that man who will not build up his brother's house." And his name shall be called in Israel "The house of him who has his shoe pulled off." (Devarim 25:5–10)

The ritual performed when a man refuses to marry his brother's widow and carry on his late brother's name and family line is called *halitzah*. One central part of this ritual is the removal of the man's shoe.[17] Alternatively,

---

פירוש הרמח"ל על התורה, ספר דברים

ואז תתקן ויהיה הזיווג "ונקרא שמו בישראל". ובהיות שנוק' עלתה בכח החליצה, בסוד, "של נעלך מעל רגלך", נקראת על שם זה "בית חלוץ הנעל", בית – בסוד ביתו זו אשתו, של מי שהוא חלון הנעל, חלוץ הנעל, חלוץ מצד אחר ודאי.

17. While I found no early or late commentaries who make the suggestion that I put forth here, connecting *halitzah* with the sale of Yosef, there are a number of mystical sources that relate Yosef to Shabbat. See, for example, Zohar Hadash, Parashat Ki Tissa. Also

if the living brother chooses to marry his brother's widow and build the family, the term used to describe the ceremony is *yibum*. In fact, the first appearance of *yibum* in the Torah is found in the verses that immediately follow the sale of Yosef, when Yehudah's surviving sons are responsible for the *yibum* of Tamar. Unfortunately, they were not interested in continuing their brother's legacy and they frustrated the natural *yibum* process.[18]

בראשית לח:ח-י

וַיֹּאמֶר יְהוּדָה לְאוֹנָן בֹּא אֶל אֵשֶׁת אָחִיךָ וְיַבֵּם אֹתָהּ וְהָקֵם זֶרַע לְאָחִיךָ: וַיֵּדַע אוֹנָן כִּי לֹא לוֹ יִהְיֶה הַזָּרַע וְהָיָה אִם בָּא אֶל אֵשֶׁת אָחִיו וְשִׁחֵת אַרְצָה לְבִלְתִּי נְתָן זֶרַע לְאָחִיו: וַיֵּרַע בְּעֵינֵי ה' אֲשֶׁר עָשָׂה וַיָּמֶת גַּם אֹתוֹ:

And Yehudah said to Onan, "Go in to your brother's wife, and marry her, and raise up seed to your brother." And Onan knew that the seed would not be his; and it came to pass, when he went in to his

---

note that on Shabbat we say *retzei v'hahalitzeinu* in our prayers, which according to the Ari"zal is related to *halitzah*. See *Sha'ar haKavanot, Drushei Kiddush Leil Shabbat*, I.

זהר חדש, פרשת כי תשא מאמר עשרת הדברות כנגד ע"ס
זכור את יום השבת, ברזא דברית, דאיהו יסוד, דאחיד ביה יוסף. וע"ד אקרי שבת. דהא יוסף כל אקרי, ושבת נמי איקרי כל. בגין דכל עיגונא ותפנוקא נפיק מניה, לקיימא לעלמין כלהו. ועל דא שבת כלילא מעשה ולא תעשה. בגין דיוסף נמי בוכרא, דנטיל תרין חולקין.

שער הכוונות, דרושי קידוש ליל שבת דרוש א ענין השולחן
ובתוספת ברכת רצה והחליצנו כו' תכוין ענין חליצת הנע"ל דענר מטטרון שהוא היצירה כדי לעלות למע' אל הבריאה שהם בח"י לבושי מלכא ביומא דשבתא וביו"ט כי ברכה זו היא הג' והיא כנגד יצירה הנק' מטטרון ואנו מתפללים שביום שבת לא יתנהג העולם ע"י שליטת מטטרון כמו בחול אבל יהיה חלוץ הנעל כנודע בסוד פ' שלף איש כו' ולא ישלוט עתה בשבת אלא ז"א דאצילות הנקרא איש ע"י הבריאה השולטת בשבת כנודע. ואחר בהמ"ז תחזור לקחת ב' אגודות של הדס בב' ידיך ותחברם יחד בכונה הנ"ל ותאמר זכור ושמור בדבור אחד נאמרו ואח"כ תברך ברכת עצי בשמים ותריח.

18. See *Megaleh 'Amukot* on Parashat Vayeishev, who notes that the portion of *yibum* follows the sale of Yosef, because both sections have a common theme: a sin that requires transmigration of souls in order to achieve perfection.

ספר מגלה עמוקות, פרשת וישב
סמיכת פרשת יהודה לתמר למכירת יוסף כי שם נתברר רזא דיבום שהוא סוד הגלגול (איוב לד) אם ישים אליו לבו רוחו ונשמתו אליו יאסף וכן מכירת יוסף גרמה גלגול הנפשות ולפי המדרשים שנתחלפו ז"ס הנה אחיכם רועים בשכ"ם נרמז סוד (ישעי' מג) נתתי כפרך "מצרים "כוש "ושבא תחתיך ג' אלו נוטריקן שכם למפרע שב"א כוש"מ מ"צרים שרמז ליוסף שיהי' תמורתם בג' אומות אלו ורבי חנינא בן תרדיון שנחלף בליפוס שמלך ו' חדשים (רות ד) וזאת לפנים בישראל על הגאולה ועל התמורה ושלף איש נעלו ונתן לידו ונתן כאן סוד גאולת הנפשות של ו' הרוגי מלכים שהי' בתמורה ונחלפו וכל זה גרמו בעטו דסנדלהון (עמוס ב) על מכרם בכסף צדיק ואביון בעבור מנעלים ושלף איש **נעלו בגי' יוסף** שהי' ברזא דחנוך תופר מנעלים ועל כל תפירה א' ברוך שם כבוד מלכותו דא רזא דיחודא ז"ש יעקב ליוסף לכה ואשלחך אליהם.

brother's wife, that he spilled it on the ground, rather than give seed to his brother. And his behavior was wicked in God's eyes and He put him [Onan] to death as well. (Bereishit 38:8–10)

The tragic story of Yehudah's sons must, necessarily, be seen in light of Yehudah's callous call to sell his brother Yosef in the preceding verses. Yosef is their flesh and blood, and yet he speaks of profit, of personal benefit, of manipulating the law by avoiding murder while capitalizing on the situation for personal gain: "And Yehudah said to his brothers, 'What profit is it if we slay our brother, and conceal his blood? Come, and let us sell him to the Yishmaelites, and let not our hand be upon him; for he is our brother and our flesh.'"

Apparently, Yehudah's children learned a lesson in fraternal relations and responsibilities from their father. They learned that their brother is not their concern; a pair of shoes is preferable to a brother. It is surely no coincidence that when the Torah teaches the law regarding a man who refuses to build his brother's home, the rejected widow is instructed to remove a shoe from the indifferent brother's foot. When he fails to recognize his brother's holiness and the sanctity of the family he is charged to preserve, his shoe is removed as a reminder of that holiness (as it was for Moshe) or as a symbol of his callousness (as when the brothers purchased shoes with "blood money").

The sale of Yosef began as the brothers callously broke bread while Yosef cried out to them from the pit. That meal, the symbol of a family divided, was interrupted by a passing caravan that soon provided shoes for the brothers, and eventually, indirectly, took the brothers themselves to Egypt. They thought they had found a convenient way to dispose of their annoying brother; they thought they were selling him as a slave. Instead, they and their descendants became slaves. And when the time arrives for their descendants to finally leave Egypt and begin their journey back to the Land of Israel, they are commanded to sit and have a meal together – as families, whole and reunited.[19] At that meal, they are finally ready to put shoes back on their feet and begin the long trip back to Israel. This is a

---

19. See Shmot 12:3–4: Each family is encouraged to eat together; a remnant of this is still felt today when families gather to celebrate Passover and have the *seder* together.

healing meal, a celebration in which each recognizes the holiness of the others; finally, they become one family, united.

שמות יב:ג–ז

דַּבְּרוּ אֶל כָּל עֲדַת יִשְׂרָאֵל לֵאמֹר בֶּעָשֹׂר לַחֹדֶשׁ הַזֶּה וְיִקְחוּ לָהֶם אִישׁ שֶׂה לְבֵית אָבֹת שֶׂה לַבָּיִת: וְאִם יִמְעַט הַבַּיִת מִהְיֹת מִשֶּׂה וְלָקַח הוּא וּשְׁכֵנוֹ הַקָּרֹב אֶל בֵּיתוֹ בְּמִכְסַת נְפָשֹׁת אִישׁ לְפִי אָכְלוֹ תָּכֹסּוּ עַל הַשֶּׂה:

"Speak to all the congregation of Israel, saying, 'On the tenth day of this month they shall take every man a lamb, according to the house of their fathers, a lamb for a house; And if the household is too small for the lamb, let him and his neighbor next to his house take it according to the number of the souls; according to every man's eating shall you make your count for the lamb.'"

Keitz Bavel – Zerubavel

The tale of Yaakov's family life unfolds as a dramatic story, replete with jealousy, punctuated by hatred, and nearly culminating in fratricide. Yaakov had many sons, but of all his sons he favored Yosef, the son of his beloved, lamented wife. As the plot unfolds, we find Yosef humiliated, stripped of his royal garb,[1] and taken as chattel. And then the story is put on hold at the end of chapter 37:

בראשית לז:לו

וְהַמְּדָנִים מָכְרוּ אֹתוֹ אֶל מִצְרָיִם לְפוֹטִיפַר סְרִיס פַּרְעֹה שַׂר הַטַּבָּחִים:

And the Midianites sold him to Egypt, to Potifar, one of Par'oh's officers, captain of the guard.[2] (Bereishit 37:36)

In order to follow the story line and find out what happens to Yosef, the reader is forced to wait; throughout chapter 38, our attention is turned to Yehudah. Details of his personal life are shared, and through the recounting of Yehudah's celebration and tragedy, his loves and his lust, we gain insight into his personality. And all this time, Yosef languishes. The Yosef narrative is picked up in chapter 39, almost precisely where it was left:

בראשית לט:א

וְיוֹסֵף הוּרַד מִצְרָיְמָה וַיִּקְנֵהוּ פּוֹטִיפַר סְרִיס פַּרְעֹה שַׂר הַטַּבָּחִים אִישׁ מִצְרִי מִיַּד הַיִּשְׁמְעֵאלִים אֲשֶׁר הוֹרִדֻהוּ שָׁמָּה:

And Yosef was brought down to Egypt; and Potifar, an officer of Par'oh, captain of the guard, an Egyptian man, bought him from the hands of the Yishmaelites, who had brought him down there. (Bereishit 39:1)

---

1. See Ramban, Shmot 28:2.

2. Potifar's precise position and occupation have been the subject of discussion for many rabbinic commentaries. Ramban and others believed him to be the chief executioner, while Rashi and Ibn Ezra believed him to be the chief butcher (of livestock).

As a literary device, the structure of the parashah is understandable: the text is building inexorably to the point at which Yosef and Yehudah meet. These are the two key characters, and the apex of the story is the point at which their two divergent story lines converge. But the Torah is far more than compelling writing; it is more than just "a good read." What lies beneath the surface of the text is far more than character development. The Torah is more than history, more than literature; it is theological truth, which the sensitive reader should seek out and internalize.

Yosef and Yehudah are not merely individuals who lived long ago. They represent leadership, salvation and redemption; they embody the concept known as *Mashiah* (Messiah), and the development of their leadership roles is the key to understanding the structure of the narrative. The Midrash presents us with this key from the very outset, couching it as an answer to its own seemingly brazen question: The Midrash, too, is disturbed by the seemingly disjointed narrative of our parashah, but not only for literary reasons. The problem is one of theology, of theosophy: "Where was God during the sale of Yosef?"[3] The answer is eye opening: God was busy

---

3. Bereishit Rabbah 85:1.

בראשית רבה, פרשה פה פסקה א

ויהי בעת ההיא וירד יהודה מאת אחיו: (מלאכי ב) "בגדה יהודה ותועבה נעשתה וגו'": א"ל כפרת יהודה שקרת יהודה. "ותועבה נעשתה בישראל" – יהודה נעשה חולין. "כי חלל יהודה קדש ה' אשר אהב" – "ויהי בעת ההיא...".

(מיכה א) "עוד היורש אביא לך יושבת מרשה עד עדלם יבוא כבוד ישראל" – יבא מלכן וקדושן של ישראל עד עדולם, יבא כבודן של ישראל עד עדולם. 'יבא' – דכתיב 'ויט עד איש עדולמי'.

ויהי בעת ההיא: רבי שמואל בר נחמן פתח: (ירמיה כט) 'כי אנכי ידעתי את המחשבות" – שבטים היו עסוקין במכירתו של יוסף, ויוסף היה עסוק בשקו ובתעניתו, ראובן היה עסוק בשקו ובתעניתו, ויעקב היה עסוק בשקו ובתעניתו, ויהודה היה עסוק ליקח לו אשה והקב"ה היה עוסק בורא אורו של מלך המשיח. 'ויהי בעת ההיא וירד יהודה': (ישעיהו סו) 'בטרם תחיל ילדה' – קודם שלא נולד משעבד הראשון נולד גואל האחרון.

"'And it came to pass at that time, that Yehudah went down from his brethren, etc.' (Bereishit 38:1): It is written, 'Yehudah has dealt treacherously, etc.' (Malakhi 2:11). He [God] said to him [Yehudah]: 'You have denied, O Yehudah; you have been false, O Yehudah!' 'And an abomination is committed in Israel' – for Yehudah has profaned. 'Yehudah has profaned the holiness of God which He loves....' – as it says, 'And it came to pass at that time [that Yehudah went down, etc.].'

"'I will yet bring unto you, O inhabitant of Mareishah, him that shall possess you; the glory of Israel shall come even unto Adullam' (Mikhah 1:15) – ['The glory of Israel' means] the Holy One of Israel; to Adullam shall come the King of Israel. 'Even unto Adullam shall come' – 'And it came to pass at that time, etc.'

"creating the light of *Mashiah*." In other words, the interlude that delves
into the descent and rise of Yehudah is the tale of Yehudah being primed
for a leadership role. But this is no ordinary leadership role: the Davidic
dynasty, and ultimately *Mashiah ben David*, are Yehudah's offspring.
More importantly, the character traits Yehudah displays are the very same
as those required of the eventual *Mashiah*, and chapter 38 of Bereishit
opens a window through which these character traits can be viewed as they
develop.

This Midrashic teaching regarding God's agenda during the sale of Yosef
goes even further than defining leadership. Through this midrash, we are
given a far-reaching, unifying view of Jewish history: before the Children
of Israel begin the first exile, the light that will guide them home at the
end of the final exile has already been created. The story of Yehudah is no
divergence; it is part and parcel of the larger story of exile and redemption.
But there is even more in this parashah. Parallel to the development of
Mashiah ben David, this parashah and the two that immediately follow it
detail the development of an additional *Mashiah*, one not as well known or
as well publicized: *Mashiah ben Yosef* (the Messiah, son of Yosef). Parashat
Vayeishev is not only the story of Yosef and Yehudah, two dominant
personalities. Knowing that Yosef and Yehudah represent two distinct
elements of redemption, we are forced to reread and reconsider Parashat
Vayeishev on the meta-level, examining both the personal stories and
behavior of the two key characters as well as the implications these have on
the Jewish view of messianic redemption.[4]

Like Yosef, *Mashiah ben Yosef* is a vulnerable Messiah. We don't know
how his mission will work out; like Yosef, his position is precarious, and
at times it appears that he will fall into the traps set by others, and fail.

"R. Shmuel b. Nahman commenced thus: 'For I know the thoughts that I think toward
you, says God' (Yirmiyahu 29:11). The fathers of the tribes were engaged in selling
Yosef, Yaakov was taken up with his sackcloth and fasting, and Yehudah was busy taking
a wife, while the Holy One, blessed be He, was creating the light of Mashiah."

4. The prototype of the two Messiahs resurfaces at various junctures in the Torah: When all
the other spies turn the people against God and the notion of inheriting the Promised
Land, two individuals stand apart from the others. Calev (from the tribe of Yehudah)
and Yehoshua (from the tribe of Yosef) remain strong and do not lose sight of Jewish
destiny.

There were times that Yaakov thought Yosef was dead – but the epic words uttered by Yaakov "'*Od Yosef hai!* Yosef lives on!" reverberate through history, and according to the great mystics, apply equally to *Mashiah ben Yosef.* Just as the rumors of Yosef's demise were greatly exaggerated, so, it is believed, *Mashiah ben Yosef* will ultimately succeed.

תלמוד בבלי, מסכת סוכה דף נב עמוד א

תנו רבנן: משיח בן דוד, שעתיד להגלות במהרה בימינו, אומר לו הקדוש ברוך הוא, "שאל ממני דבר ואתן לך", שנאמר, (תהלים ב) "אספרה אל חוק.... אני היום ילדתיך שאל ממני ואתנה גוים נחלתך". וכיון שראה משיח בן יוסף שנהרג אומר לפניו, "רבונו של עולם! איני מבקש ממך אלא חיים". אומר לו, "חיים, עד שלא אמרת כבר התנבא עליך דוד אביך", שנאמר, (תהלים כא) "חיים שאל ממך נתתה לו [ארך ימים עולם ועד]".

Our rabbis taught: The Holy One, blessed be He, will say to Mashiah ben David *(may he reveal himself speedily in our days!), "Ask of me anything, and I will give it to you," as it is said, "I will tell of the decree.... This day have I begotten you, ask of me and I will give the nations for your inheritance" (Tehilim 2:7). But when he will see that the* Mashiah ben Yosef *is slain, he will say to Him, "Master of the Universe, I ask of You only the gift of life." "As to life," He will answer him, "Your father David has already prophesied this concerning you," as it is said, "He asked life of you, you gave to him [length of days forever and ever]" (Tehilim 21:5).* (Talmud Bavli Succah 52a)

Yosef has two dreams regarding his personal role. The first dream concerns wheat, representing food or economics at the most basic level. The second dream is about the sun, moon and stars; it is about power. Yosef envisions himself as both an economic leader and as the political, popular leader of the people. In the end, however, only the first dream came true. Yosef does collect all the wheat in Egypt; he becomes the "great provider." He feeds his brothers, and insures the physical survival of the Children of Israel. Yet although his brothers eventually bow down to him, they never accept him as their leader, and the repercussions of this non-acceptance resonate and reverberate for the next three thousand years of Jewish history.

What is the essence of the leadership that begins to develop in Parashat Vayeishev? The need for two different Messiahs begins to come into focus, for clearly each has a separate task to accomplish, each has different capabilities. As we will see, when those tasks become confused, when the capabilities do not fit the job at hand, when the battle is fought with the wrong weapon, problems arise. Jewish history is made up of so many confrontations, battles won and lost, exiles of varying nature and duration. These exiles have always been a part of Jewish history – and were foretold to Avraham at the dawn of Jewish history:

בראשית טו:יב–יג

וַיְהִי הַשֶּׁמֶשׁ לָבוֹא וְתַרְדֵּמָה נָפְלָה עַל אַבְרָם וְהִנֵּה אֵימָה חֲשֵׁכָה גְדֹלָה נֹפֶלֶת עָלָיו: וַיֹּאמֶר לְאַבְרָם יָדֹעַ תֵּדַע כִּי גֵר יִהְיֶה זַרְעֲךָ בְּאֶרֶץ לֹא לָהֶם וַעֲבָדוּם וְעִנּוּ אֹתָם אַרְבַּע מֵאוֹת שָׁנָה:

And when the sun was going down, a deep sleep fell upon Avram; and, lo, a fear of great darkness fell upon him. And [God] said to Avram, "Know for a certainty that your offspring shall be a stranger in a land that is not theirs, and shall serve them; and they shall afflict them for four hundred years. (Bereishit 15:12–13)

Rashi[5] explains that the darkness that Avraham feared refers to the exiles his descendants would experience in the future. The Ramban, citing Pirkei d'Rebbi Eliezer, says that Yaakov shared Avraham's dream, and that is the inner meaning of Yaakov's vision of angels ascending and descending the heavenly ladder: the angels represent the various monarchies who ruled over Israel, each rising and eventually falling into the dustbin of history. These exiles are inevitable, inescapable, and an integral part of Jewish destiny. In fact, the future exiles are mentioned in Midrashic comments as early as the second verse of the Torah:

בראשית רבה, פרשה ב פסקה ד

ר"ש בן לקיש פתר קריא בגליות. "והארץ היתה תהו" – זה גלות בבל, שנאמר, (ירמיה ד) "ראיתי את הארץ והנה תהו". "ובהו" – זה גלות מדי, (אסתר ו) "ויבהילו להביא את המן". "וחשך" – זה גלות יון שהחשיכה עיניהם של ישראל בגזירותיהן, שהיתה אומרת להם "כתבו על קרן השור שאין לכם

---

5. See Rashi, Bereishit 15:12; also see comments of the Targum Pseudo-Yonatan, who is
    more specific in identifying these exiles.

רש"י, בראשית טו:יב
והנה אימה וגו': רמז לצרות וחשך של גליות.

חלק באלקי ישראל". "על פני תהום" – זה גלות ממלכת הרשעה שאין להם
חקר כמו התהום. מה התהום הזה אין לו חקר אף הרשעים כן. "ורוח אלקים
מרחפת" – זה רוחו של מלך המשיח. היאך? מה דאת אמר, (ישעיהו יא)
"ונחה עליו רוח ה'".

R. Shimon b. Lakish applied the passage to the various exiles [the
Jewish people endured]. "And the earth was tohu (unformed)"
symbolizes the Babylonian exile, as it is written: "I beheld the earth,
and, lo, it was tohu" (Yirmiyahu 4:23). "And vohu (void)" symbolizes
the Persian exile: "They hastened (vayavhillu) to bring Haman"
(Esther 4:14). "And darkness" symbolizes Greece, which darkened the
eyes of Israel with its decrees, ordering Israel, "Write on the horn of
an ox that you have no portion in the God of Israel." "Upon the face
of the deep" [refers to] this wicked state [the Roman Empire]: just as
the great deep cannot be plumbed, so one cannot plumb [the depths
of iniquity of] this wicked state. "And the Spirit of God hovered" –
this alludes to the spirit of Mashiah, as you read, "And the Spirit of
God shall rest upon him" (Yeshayahu 11:2). (Bereishit Rabbah 2:4)

Not all exiles are created equal. Different exiles present different challenges,
and therefore require different responses. Yaakov himself is exiled twice,
and his varied experiences may be seen as prototypes of the exiles endured
by his descendants. The more prominent exile is clearly the second, when
he goes to Egypt. This sojourn will last hundreds of years, reaching a climax
with the enslavement of Yaakov's descendants. The challenge of this exile
is clear – physical survival.

However, this is not the only exile that Yaakov endures. There was an
earlier episode, which had very different characteristics. Perhaps visiting
one's family might not be seen as an exile; indeed, Yaakov was not really
enslaved by Lavan, he merely had a bad employer. We might say that the
"Lavan experience" was not one of slavery, but it was exile nonetheless.
Much like the Egypt experience, Yaakov enjoys economic success in his
exile, but the success is not to his own benefit: His father-in-law Lavan is the
main beneficiary of Yaakov's good fortune, and the problems only escalate
when Yaakov wants to leave. As opposed to the Children of Israel in Egypt,
Yaakov has a good job and a comfortable life in Lavan's home. Whereas
the hardships of the Egyptian exile began out of physical exigency (a

prolonged famine that threatened the survival of the family) and presented an ever-escalating threat to physical survival (most succinctly expressed by the decree to cast all newborn males into the sea), the challenge Yaakov faced in Lavan's home was one of spiritual survival.

As a nation, our experiences of exile have been equally varied, and have been poetically compared and contrasted with one another throughout our history. The prophet Amos compares these various dark chapters to a series of calamities:

עמוס ה:יח–כב

הוֹי הַמִּתְאַוִּים אֶת יוֹם ה' לָמָּה זֶּה לָכֶם יוֹם ה' הוּא חֹשֶׁךְ וְלֹא אוֹר: כַּאֲשֶׁר יָנוּס אִישׁ מִפְּנֵי הָאֲרִי וּפְגָעוֹ הַדֹּב וּבָא הַבַּיִת וְסָמַךְ יָדוֹ עַל הַקִּיר וּנְשָׁכוֹ הַנָּחָשׁ: הֲלֹא חֹשֶׁךְ יוֹם ה' וְלֹא אוֹר וְאָפֵל וְלֹא נֹגַהּ לוֹ: שָׂנֵאתִי מָאַסְתִּי חַגֵּיכֶם וְלֹא אָרִיחַ בְּעַצְּרֹתֵיכֶם כִּי אִם תַּעֲלוּ לִי עֹלוֹת וּמִנְחֹתֵיכֶם לֹא אֶרְצֶה וְשֶׁלֶם מְרִיאֵיכֶם לֹא אַבִּיט:

Woe to you who desire the day of God! Why would you have the day of God? It is darkness, and not light. It may be likened to a man who fled from a lion, only to be attacked by a bear; [finally,] he enters his house, and leans his hand on the wall, and a serpent bites him. Is not the day of God darkness, and not light? Very dark with no brightness in it? I hate, I despise your feast days, and I will not smell the sacrifices of your solemn assemblies. Though you offer me burnt offerings and meal offerings, I will not accept them; nor will I regard the peace offerings of your fatted beasts. (Amos 5:18–22)

Although the analogy of a person fleeing from one attacker only to fall prey to another is a poignant description of the Jewish condition, Amos's words are interpreted by the sages of the Midrash as referring to specific episodes, specific exiles. Esther Rabbah attempts to decipher Amos's analogy: What is this darkness? Who is the lion? Which bear is he referring to? And what serpent is this?

אסתר רבה, פתיחתות

רבי יודא בר"ס פתח (עמוס ה) כאשר ינוס איש מפני הארי, רבי הונא ור' אחא בשם ר' חמא בר' חנינא: (עמוס ה) "כאשר ינוס איש מפני **הארי**" וגו' – **זו בבל**, על שם קדמיתא כאריה. "ופגעו **הדוב**" – **זו מדי**, על שם (דניאל ז) "וארו חיוה אחרי תנינה דמיה לדוב".

ר' יוחנן אמר: לדב כתיב, דא היא דעתיה דר' יוחנן דאמר ר' יוחנן (ירמיה ה)
"על כן הכם אריה מ**יער**" – **זו בבל.** "זאב ערבות ישדדם" – זו מדי. "נמר שקד
על עריהם" – זו יון. "כל היוצא מהנה יטרף" – זו אדום.

(עמוס ה) "ובא ה**בית**" – **זה יון** שהיה הבית קיים. "ונשכו ה**נחש**" – **זו אדום,**
שנאמר, (ירמיהו מו) "קולה כנחש ילך".

וכה"א "פתחי לי אחותי" – זו בבל, "רעיתי" – זו מדי, "יונתי" – ביון,
"תמתי" – באדום, שכל ימי יון היה בית המקדש קיים, והיו ישראל מקריבין
בו תורים ובני יונה על גבי המזבח.

R. Yehudah b. R. Simon opened with the text: "As if a man did flee
from a lion..." (Amos 5:19): R. Huna and R. Hama in the name of R.
Hanina said: "As if a man did flee from a lion" – this refers to Babylon,
which is designated by the words "The first was like a lion" (Daniel
7:4). "And a bear met him" (Amos 5:19) refers to Media [Persia],
designated in the words "And behold another beast, a second, like a
bear" (Daniel 7:5).

R. Yohanan said: "The word l'dov [like a bear] is written defectively.
This supports the opinion of R. Yohanan given in his dictum:
"Wherefore a lion out of the forest slays them" (Yirmiyahu 5:6) –
this refers to Babylon. "A wolf of the deserts despoils them" refers to
Media [Persia]. "A leopard watches over their cities" refers to Greece.
"Everyone that goes out is torn in pieces" refers to Edom.

"And he went into the house" (Amos 5:19) refers to Greece, during
whose rule the Temple was still standing. "And a serpent bit him"
refers to Edom, of which it says, "The sound thereof shall be like the
serpent's" (Yirmiyahu 46:22).

Similarly it says, "Open to me, my sister" (Shir haShirim 5:2) – this
refers to [Israel under] Babylon. "My love" refers to the Persian
era. "My dove" refers to Greece. "My undefiled" refers to Edom.
"Dove" refers to Greece because throughout the days of the Grecian
domination the Temple stood and Israel used to offer pigeons and
doves on the Altar. (Introduction to Esther Rabbah)

The attack of Yavan (Greece) differs from all the others, because this
one took place "at home." Other than Hanukah, all biblical and rabbinic
holidays commemorate events that took place outside the Land of Israel.
Hanukah is the exception; therefore, in the prophecy of Amos, "he went-

into his house" refers to the Greek period. It is one thing to be attacked on the road, when one is vulnerable, or on your opponent's "home turf." It is quite another thing to be attacked at home. This "exile" of the Greek period took place as the Temple was still standing[6] – a strange exile, indeed.

The Yalkut Shimoni[7] takes the same verse from the book of Amos, and applies it to Yaakov's life: here, Lavan is the lion, Esav the bear and Shekhem the serpent who attacks him at home. This interpretation highlights the parallel between Yaakov's life and the exiles endured by his descendants. Furthermore, it implies that Yaakov endured a third exile. Specifically, a parallel is drawn between the story of Hanukah and the story of Dinah. This is particularly interesting in light of a midrash that credits the Maccabean rebellion to a speech given by one of the Maccabee sisters named Hannah. The Midrash explains that the Jewish uprising was a response to one of the famous Greek laws imposed upon the Jews (and presumably upon other nations that fell under Greek rule), namely the principle of *ius primæ noctis* (also known as *droit du seigneur*) – the authority of the Greek governor to deflower virgin brides on their wedding night. The Midrash relates

---

6. See Midrash Tehillim (Buber edition), Psalm 18:11.

מדרש תהלים (בובר) מזמור יח ד"ה [יא] בצר לי

בצר לי אקרא ה': **בבבל**. ואל אלהי אשוע. **במדי ופרס**. ישמע מהיכלו קולי, **ביון**. ושועתי לפניו תבא באזניו. **באדום**. [ולפי שבטלו את ישראל מן התורה, דכתיב בה והגית (בה) [בו] יומם ולילה (יהושע א:ח), לפיכך אני פורע ממנו באש, שנאמר לעולם יעלה עשנה (ישעיהו לד:י), ולפי ששרפו בית המקדש שהיה עשן יוצא ממנו, שנאמר והבית ימלא עשן (ישעיהו ו:ד), קול (ה') מהיכל (ישעיהו סו:ו), אמר להם אין אתם זכורים מה שעשיתם בהיכלי, קול ה' משלם גמול לאויביו (ישעיהו סו)]. ר' פנחס ורב אחא בשם ר' חמא בר חנינא אמרי למה הזכיר במלכות השלישית היכל ה', שכל ימיה של מלכות יון בית המקדש קיים, ולמה אמר בצר לי במלכות ראשונה, ולא אמר בצרות, לפי שכל הנביאים מייחדין צרותיהן של ישראל וממעטין אותן, שנאמר בצר לך ומצאוך (דברים ד:ל), ראה ה' כי צר לי (איכה א:כ), וירא בצר להם (תהלים קו:מד), אל ה' בצרתה לי (תהלים קכ:א), ר' יהודה אומר מטעם אחר (במלכות יון שלא נחרב הבית בימיו) כאשר ינוס איש מפני הארי (עמוס ה:יט), זו בבל, שנאמר קדמייתא כאריה (דניאל ז:ד). ופגעו הדוב (עמוס ה:יט), זו מדי ופרס, שנאמר וארו (חזווא תנינא דמיא) [חיוה אחרי תנינה דמיה] לדוב (דניאל ז:ה). ובא הבית (עמוס ה:יט), זו מלכות יון, שהיה בית המקדש קיים בימיה, ולא היו מכעיסין על בית המקדש שהיה בנוי, וכשהיו רואין שמעון הצדיק היו עומדין לפניו. וסמך ידו על הקיר ונשכו הנחש (עמוס ה:יט). זו מלכות הרשעה, שנאמר קולה כנחש ילך (ירמיה מו:כב).

7. Yalkut Shimoni, Amos, *remez* 544.

ילקוט שמעוני עמוס, רמז תקמד

וישכב כאשר ינוס איש מפני הארי: זה לבן שרדף אחר יעקב כארי לטרוף נפשו, ופגעו הדוב זה עשו שעמד על הדרך כדוב שכול להמית אם על בנים, ובא הבית וסמך ידו על הקיר ונשכו הנחש, כשבא יעקב אל ארץ כנען לביתו בא עליו שכם בן חמור שנאמר אותה ויענה.

that Hannah, a daughter of Matityahu the *Kohen Gadol*, demonstratively disrobed at her wedding celebration. Her outraged brothers drew their swords to end the outrage and protect the family name in an "honor killing," but Hannah protested: "I disrobed before righteous people, and you are incensed. But this evening I will be taken to the governor, and not to my husband, and you are silent!" She exhorts them to action, and convinces them to take up arms against the true enemy. Thus, according to this midrash, the battle of Hanukah ensued.[8]

There are several parallels between Hannah's story and Dinah's story: As we noted earlier, the Jews are in their homeland, and not on foreign soil. In the story of Dinah, the "saviors" were her brothers Shimon and Levi. Hannah's defenders are her brothers the Maccabees, descendants of Levi. This is more than coincidence; Hannah herself points this out, as quoted by the Midrash: "You should learn from Shimon and Levi brothers of Dinah.… Put your trust in God and He will save you.…"

The larger picture, then, is painted on the backdrop of "home," the Beit haMikdash. The guardians of the home are the tribe of Levi who work in

---

8. *Otzar haMidrashim*, page 189.

אוצר המדרשים (אייזנשטיין) חנוכה עמוד 189

כיון שראו יונים שאין ישראל מרגישין בגזירותיהם עמדו וגזרו עליהם גזירה מרה ועכורה, שלא תכנס כלה בלילה הראשון מחופתה אלא אצל ההגמון שבמקום ההוא. כיון ששמעו ישראל כך רפו ידיהם ותשש כחם ונמנעו מלארס, והיו בנות ישראל בוגרות ומזקינות כשהן בתולות, ונתקיים עליהם בתולותיה נוגות והיא מר לה (איכה א'), והיו יונים מתעללות בבתולות ישראל, ונהגו בדבר הזה שלש שנים ושמונה חדשים, עד שבא מעשה של בת מתתיהו כהן גדול שנשאת לבן חשמונאי ואלעזר היה שמו, כיון שהגיע יום שמחתה הושיבוה באפריון, וכשהגיע זמן הסעודה נתקבצו כל גדולי ישראל לכבוד מתתיהו ובן חשמונאי שלא היו באותו הדור גדולים מהם, וכשישבו לסעוד עמדה חנה בת מתתיהו מעל אפריון וספקה כפיה זו על זו וקרעה פורפירון שלה ועמדה לפני כל ישראל כשהיא מגולה ולפני אביה ואמה וחותנה. כיון שראו אחיה כך נתביישו ונתנו פניהם בקרקע וקרעו בגדיהם, ועמדו עליה להרגה, אמרה להם שמעוני אחיי ודודיי, ומה אם בשביל שעמדתי לפני צדיקים ערומה בלי שום עבירה הרי אתם מתקנאים בי, ואין אתם מתקנאים למסרני ביד ערל להתעולל בי?! הלא יש לכם ללמוד ממשעון ולוי אחי דינה שלא היו אלא שנים וקנאו לאחותם והרגו כרך כשכם ומסרו נפשם על ייחוד של מקום ועזרם ה' ולא הכלימם, ואתם חמשה אחים יהודה יוחנן יונתן שמעון ואלעזר, ופרחי כהונה יותר ממאתים בחור, שימו בטחונכם על המקום והוא יעזור אתכם שנאמר כי אין מעצור לה' להושיע וגו' (שמואל א' יד). ופתחה פיה בבכיה ואמרה רבש"ע אם לא תחוס עלינו חוס על קדושת שמך הגדול שנקרא עלינו ונקום היום נקמתנו. באותה שעה נתקנאו אחיה ואמרו בואו ונטול עצה מה נעשה, נטלו עצה זה מזה ואמרו בואו ונקח אחותינו ונוליכנה אצל המלך הגדול ונאמר לו אחותנו בת כהן גדול ואין בכל ישראל גדול מאבינו, וראינו שלא תלין אחותינו עם ההגמון, אלא עם המלך שהוא גדול כמותינו, ונכנסנו עליו ונהרגהו ונצא, ונתחיל אח"כ בעבדיו ובשריו, והשם יעזרנו וישגבנו, נטלו עצה וכו' ועשה להם הקב"ה תשועה גדולה, ושמעו בת קול מבית קדש הקדשים: כל ישראל נצחו טליא באנטוכיא, כן יעשה המקום ישועה בימינו אלה.

the Beit haMikdash. The savior, in both of these episodes, is not from the tribe of Yehudah, the leader of the brothers, nor is he from the tribe of Yosef, whose leadership was rejected earlier in Bereishit and had not yet been accepted, even in the days of the Maccabean dynasty.

The parallels between the Hanukah story and the stories of Yaakov's children thus highlight the critical role of leadership in the Jewish people's redemption. In the case of Yaakov's family, the sale of Yosef and the story of Dinah are inextricably connected with leadership issues – the brothers refuse to accept Yosef's leadership, and Yehudah has not yet matured into accepting his role. So too, the Greek invasion and the Jews' response to it are bound up with *Leviim* usurping roles not assigned to them.

The very foundations of the Second Temple echo this fractured, unnatural leadership. The prophet Haggai tells us of a man named Zerubavel, governor of Judea, who is chosen to rectify Israel's anomalous situation: God admonishes the Jews, who have attained lives of comfort in the Diaspora, to return to Israel and rebuild the House of God, which lies in ruins:

חגי א:א–ד

בִּשְׁנַת שְׁתַּיִם לְדָרְיָוֶשׁ הַמֶּלֶךְ בַּחֹדֶשׁ הַשִּׁשִּׁי בְּיוֹם אֶחָד לַחֹדֶשׁ הָיָה דְבַר ה' בְּיַד חַגַּי הַנָּבִיא אֶל זְרֻבָּבֶל בֶּן שְׁאַלְתִּיאֵל פַּחַת יְהוּדָה וְאֶל יְהוֹשֻׁעַ בֶּן יְהוֹצָדָק הַכֹּהֵן הַגָּדוֹל לֵאמֹר: כֹּה אָמַר ה' צְבָאוֹת לֵאמֹר הָעָם הַזֶּה אָמְרוּ לֹא עֶת בֹּא עֶת בֵּית ה' לְהִבָּנוֹת: וַיְהִי דְבַר ה' בְּיַד חַגַּי הַנָּבִיא לֵאמֹר: הַעֵת לָכֶם אַתֶּם לָשֶׁבֶת בְּבָתֵּיכֶם סְפוּנִים וְהַבַּיִת הַזֶּה חָרֵב:

In the second year of Daryavesh [Darius] the king, in the sixth month, on the first day of the month, came the Word of God by Haggai the prophet to Zerubavel the son of She'altiel, governor of Yehudah, and to Yehoshua the son of Yehotzadak the Kohen Gadol, *saying, "Thus speaks the God of Hosts, saying, 'This people say that the time has not yet come, the time that God's house should be built.'"*
Then came the word of God through the prophet Haggai, saying, "Is it time for you, yourselves, to dwell in your well-timbered houses, while this house lies in ruins?" (Haggai 1:1–4)

When the foundation stone is laid for the second Beit haMikdash, the prophet exhorts all who hear his words to pay careful attention to the date the building has begun:

חגי ב:יח

שִׂימוּ נָא לְבַבְכֶם מִן הַיּוֹם הַזֶּה וָמָעְלָה מִיּוֹם עֶשְׂרִים וְאַרְבָּעָה לַתְּשִׁיעִי לְמִן הַיּוֹם אֲשֶׁר יֻסַּד הֵיכַל ה' שִׂימוּ לְבַבְכֶם:

Consider well from this day onward, from the twenty-fourth day of the ninth month, from the day when the foundation of God's Sanctuary was laid; pay heed. (Haggai 2:18)

On the twenty-fourth of the ninth month – Kislev – we are ordered to build, and instructed to pay close attention to the date. Perhaps there was something that was missed, an opportunity that was not realized. A second prophecy, received on the very same date, makes the message clearer:

חגי ב:כ–כג

וַיְהִי דְבַר ה' שֵׁנִית אֶל חַגַּי בְּעֶשְׂרִים וְאַרְבָּעָה לַחֹדֶשׁ לֵאמֹר: אֱמֹר אֶל זְרֻבָּבֶל פַּחַת יְהוּדָה לֵאמֹר אֲנִי מַרְעִישׁ אֶת הַשָּׁמַיִם וְאֶת הָאָרֶץ: וְהָפַכְתִּי כִּסֵּא מַמְלָכוֹת וְהִשְׁמַדְתִּי חֹזֶק מַמְלְכוֹת הַגּוֹיִם וְהָפַכְתִּי מֶרְכָּבָה וְרֹכְבֶיהָ וְיָרְדוּ סוּסִים וְרֹכְבֵיהֶם אִישׁ בְּחֶרֶב אָחִיו: בַּיּוֹם הַהוּא נְאֻם ה' צְבָאוֹת אֶקָּחֲךָ זְרֻבָּבֶל בֶּן שְׁאַלְתִּיאֵל עַבְדִּי נְאֻם ה' וְשַׂמְתִּיךָ כַּחוֹתָם כִּי בְךָ בָחַרְתִּי נְאֻם ה' צְבָאוֹת:

And again the Word of God came to Haggai on the twenty-fourth day of the month, saying, "Speak to Zerubavel, governor of Yehudah, saying, 'I will shake the heavens and the earth, and I will overthrow the throne of kingdoms, and I will destroy the strength of the kingdoms of the nations and I will overthrow the chariots and those who ride in them; and the horses and their riders shall come down, each by the sword of his brother. On that day," says the God of Hosts, "I will take you, O Zerubavel my servant, the son of She'altiel," says God, "and I will make you like a signet ring, for I have chosen you," says the God of Hosts. (Haggai 2:20–23)

Both prophecies revolve around the same day – the day that will one day become the eve of Hanukah. God will shake heaven and earth; Zerubavel is the chosen one, a redeemer from the tribe of Yehudah!

When it comes to holiness, Yehudah is at the fore. Nahshon son of Aminadav, from the tribe of Yehudah, is the first to jump into the waters of the Red Sea, the first of the leaders to bring an offering when the Mishkan is consecrated. David and Shlomo build the First Beit haMikdash. Now,

Zerubavel is there to build the Second Beit haMikdash. So, too, the third, final, everlasting Beit haMikdash will be built by *Mashiah ben David*, a descendant of Yehudah.[9]

Zerubavel, however, remains an elusive character. From the prophecies of Haggai, he seems so important and so central: he is the chosen one, sent by God to build the Beit haMikdash – no wonder some commentaries refer to him as "*Mashiah ben David*"![10] Yet he disappears without a trace. What became of him? Why was this nascent messianic movement aborted? How and why did things go wrong?

Let us consider the chronology of events. The story of Purim takes place between the Jews' return to Israel under Zerubavel and the building of the Second Beit haMikdash. The Jews in Shushan, the "heroes" of the book of Esther, were those who chose not to return to Israel and participate in the building of the Second Commonwealth. They stayed in Shushan. Every reference in the book of Esther to "Shushan the capital (*habirah*)" may be

---

9. Midrash Seikhel Tov, Bereishit 49.

מדרש שכל טוב (בובר), בראשית פרק מט ד"ה ורבותינו דרשו ויקרא

לכך נאמר יהודה אתה יודוך אחיך, שכל אחיו מודים שהקב"ה בחר במלכות בית יהודה, וכן בחנוכת המזבח הקריב נחשון בן עמינדב למטה יהודה בראשונה, וכן אחרי מות יהושע כתיב וישאלו בני ישראל בה' מי יעלה לנו (בתחלה) אל הכנעני [בתחלה] להלחם [בו] ויאמר ה' יהודה יעלה (שופטים א:ב), וכן לא בחר הקב"ה באיש שיבנה לו בית אלא בית מבית יהודה, שהרי בית ראשון דוד יסדו, ושלמה שכללו, ובבית שני כתוב ידי זרבבל יסדו (את) הבית הזה וידיו תבצענה (זכרי' ד:ט), ולעתיד אין הקב"ה מושיע את ישראל אלא ע"י גואל מבני יהודה, שנאמר ויצא חוטר מגזע ישי (ישעי' יא:א), ואומר ונשא נס לגוים ואסף נדחי ישראל ונפוצות יהודה יקבץ מארבע כנפות הארץ (שם שם יב), ואומר ודוד עבדי נשיא להם (בתוכם) לעולם (יחזקאל לז כה), ואומר ועבדו את ה' אלהיכם ואת דוד מלכם אשר אקים להם (ירמי' ל:ט), זה מלך המשיח העומד מבית דוד שמזרע יהודה: גור אריה יהודה. זה מלך המשיח.

10. See the comments of Metzudat David, Yehezkel 21:31; also see his comments to Zekharyah 4:6, 9.

מצודת דוד, יחזקאל כא:לא

השפלה: יהויכין שכבר גלה והושפל אותו אגביה כי מזרעו יצא זרובבל מלך המשיח.

מצודת דוד, זכריה ד:ו

זה דבר ה': ר"ל בזה ירמז כאלו אמר ה' על מלך המשיח הבא מזרע זרובבל.

מצודת דוד, זכריה ד:ט

ידי זרובבל יסדו וגומר: זרובבל עצמו הניח היסוד מהבית הזה כן ידיו ישלימו את בנין הבית ר"ל ידי המשיח הבא מזרעו ישלימו להניח אבן היסוד מהבית העתיד ואמר ידיו על ידי המשיח הבא מזרעו כדרך שאמר כי הנה האבן אשר נתתי לפני יהושע (זכריה ג) הנאמר על כ"ג הבא מזרעו אשר יכהן אז ואמר ענין השלמה על כי יהיה הבית האחרון והוא תשלום הבתים ולפי שבית העתיד תעמוד במקום הבית הזה עצמו אמר תבצענה כאלו ישלים הבית הזה וכמ"ש גדול יהיה כבוד הבית הזה האחרון (חגי ב).

seen as veiled criticism; Jerusalem is the *real* capital of the Jewish people. These Jews should have been in Jerusalem, not Shushan. They should have accepted the leadership of Zerubavel and ended their sojourn in the Persian exile; instead, they chose to remain in their comfortable homes and lucrative jobs.

The man who was the instrument of the salvation of these Jews was Mordekhai, together with his cousin Esther. What do we know about them?

אסתר ב:ה–ז

אִישׁ יְהוּדִי הָיָה בְּשׁוּשַׁן הַבִּירָה וּשְׁמוֹ מָרְדֳּכַי בֶּן יָאִיר בֶּן שִׁמְעִי בֶּן קִישׁ אִישׁ יְמִינִי: אֲשֶׁר הָגְלָה מִירוּשָׁלַיִם עִם הַגֹּלָה אֲשֶׁר הָגְלְתָה עִם יְכָנְיָה מֶלֶךְ יְהוּדָה אֲשֶׁר הֶגְלָה נְבוּכַדְנֶאצַּר מֶלֶךְ בָּבֶל: וַיְהִי אֹמֵן אֶת הֲדַסָּה הִיא אֶסְתֵּר בַּת דֹּדוֹ כִּי אֵין לָהּ אָב וָאֵם וְהַנַּעֲרָה יְפַת תֹּאַר וְטוֹבַת מַרְאֶה וּבְמוֹת אָבִיהָ וְאִמָּהּ לְקָחָהּ מָרְדֳּכַי לוֹ לְבַת:

There was a man from Yehudah in Shushan the capital, and his name was Mordekhai, son of Yair, son of Shim'i, son of Kish, a Binyaminite, who had been exiled from Jerusalem with the captivity that had been carried away into exile with Yekhonyah king of Yehudah, whom Nevukhadnetzar the king of Bavel had carried away into exile. And he raised Hadassah, that is, Esther, his uncle's daughter, for she had neither father nor mother; and the girl was fair and beautiful, and when her mother and father died, Mordekhai took her for his own daughter. (Esther 2:5–7)

Mordekhai is described as an *ish Yehudi*, and an *ish Yemini*, a descendant of Yehudah and Binyamin. Mordekhai and Esther mark an important bond, a convergence between the children of Leah and Rahel. This very significant ancestry echoes another significant point at which Yehudah and Binyamin meet: the Beit haMikdash is built straddling the Binyamin-Yehudah border.[11] In this sense, Mordekhai and Esther represent the Temple itself, at a time when many Jews rejected the Temple by choosing to remain in the Persian exile, disobeying God's call to return to their Land under the guidance of Zerubavel and to build the Second Temple.

Arguably, had all Jews returned to Israel with Zerubavel, the Purim story could have been averted.[12] Had the Jews accepted Zerubavel, the Messianic

---

11. See Talmud Bavli Yoma 12a.

12. See Talmud Bavli Yoma 9b.

Age would have begun and the Second Temple could have been the final, everlasting Temple. But when the building actually began – Jews "forgot" to come home. They chose Shushan, arguably the political and economic epicenter of the world, over Jerusalem, the spiritual epicenter, which remained unbuilt. The project began on the twenty-fourth of Kislev but, tragically, stopped. "Pay attention!" said the prophet Haggai: many years later, on the twenty-fifth of Kislev, the process would be completed with the consecration of the Second Temple by the Maccabees. But in an ideal world, the festivals of Purim and Hanukah would not exist!

The sons of Yaakov may have had their reasons for rejecting Yosef's leadership. In fact, they might have argued that this was the wisest course of action. After all, they might have argued, "the man is a dreamer; he has delusions of grandeur, and will surely never amount to anything." Tragically, the story of Hanukah is the story of the rejection of Yehudah's leadership as well. Although Zerubavel, governor of Yehudah, should have been a rallying point for all of the people of Israel, the clear leader and appointed redeemer, he was rejected; his rallying cry fell on deaf ears. Despite the fact that Zerubavel was selected by God Himself, the people largely ignored Haggai's prophecy, failing to seize the opportunity for redemption. Once again, as in the case of Yosef, the repercussions of this nonacceptance were enormous and far-reaching, in both spiritual and historical terms.

God's personally appointed *Mashiah*[13] gathers some of the exiles – but not enough; many stay behind. He starts the building of the Beit haMikdash. He brings people closer to God, and encourages them to leave their non-Jewish spouses.[14] But in the end, he fails to complete the mission. Another candidate will have to be appointed to complete the task, and God's message will be amplified, sharpened to the point that even the most apathetic "post-Zionist" Jews will be unable to ignore it: the Jews who chose to stay in Shushan are brought to the brink of destruction, and Purim celebrates their eventual salvation; all things considered, a bittersweet "victory," a festival that should not have been.

---

13. Haggai 2:23; Zekharyah 4:9.
14. See Haggai 1:14.

Zerubavel is the *Mashiah* the Jews didn't want. He began building the Beit haMikdash[15] they didn't want, and he tried to get people to return to a Land they didn't want. Hanukah actually celebrates the completion of the mission Zerubavel undertook – the building of the Second Beit haMikdash, whose consecration on the twenty-fifth of Kislev completes what was begun on the twenty-fourth of Kislev years earlier. But this Beit haMikdash, when it was finally consecrated by the the Maccabees, had one fatal flaw: the leadership role was never returned to its rightful owner, a descendant of Yehudah. Instead, the Maccabees sinned by retaining the kingship for themselves,[16] once again rejecting the leadership of Yehudah. Inevitably, this led to a whole new exile, a new darkness, with its own struggles and challenges. This is our current reality; these are our own struggles and challenges.

How does this cycle end? The end of days is described by our prophets as the result of accepting the leadership of both Yosef and Yehudah. The Messianic Age will see the fusion of these two paradigms of leadership, a union of Yosef and Yehudah, and the emergence of the *Mashiah*:

יחזקאל לז:יט–כב

דַּבֵּר אֲלֵהֶם כֹּה אָמַר ה' אֱלֹקִים הִנֵּה אֲנִי לֹקֵחַ אֶת עֵץ יוֹסֵף אֲשֶׁר בְּיַד אֶפְרַיִם וְשִׁבְטֵי יִשְׂרָאֵל חֲבֵרָיו וְנָתַתִּי אוֹתָם עָלָיו אֶת עֵץ יְהוּדָה וַעֲשִׂיתִם לְעֵץ אֶחָד וְהָיוּ אֶחָד בְּיָדִי: וְהָיוּ הָעֵצִים אֲשֶׁר תִּכְתֹּב עֲלֵיהֶם בְּיָדְךָ לְעֵינֵיהֶם: וְדַבֵּר אֲלֵיהֶם

---

15. See *Torat ha'Olah*, part 3, chapter 83.

ספר תורת העולה לרמ"א ז"ל, חלק ג פרק פג

אמנם עיקר הקדושה והטהרה הוא בעולם הבא, אמנם מקדש שני הוא נגד ימות המשיח, ולזה נבנה בו שני בתים נגד שני המשיחים המקובלים באומה שהם משיח בן יוסף ומשיח בן דוד, וכן היו עיקרי בוני המקדש זרובבל ועזרא שהם שני משיחים, ונחמיה לא בנה רק חומות ירושלים שהוא דוגמת אליהו ז"ל שיגאלה במהרה בימנו לפני בא יום ה' הגדול.

16. See the comments of Ramban, Bereishit 49:10.

רמב"ן, בראשית מט:י

וזה היה עונש החשמונאים שמלכו בבית שני, כי היו חסידי עליון, ואלמלא הם נשתכחה התורה והמצות מישראל, ואף על פי כן נענשו עונש גדול, כי ארבעת בני חשמונאי הזקן החסידים המולכים זה אחר זה עם כל גבורתם והצלחתם נפלו ביד אויביהם בחרב והגיע העונש בסוף למה שאמרו רז"ל (ב"ב ג:) כל מאן דאמר מבית חשמונאי קאתינא עבדא הוא, שנכרתו כלם בעון זה ואף על פי שהיה בזרע שמעון עונש מן הצדוקים, אבל כל זרע מתתיה חשמונאי הצדיק לא עברו אלא בעבור זה שמלכו ולא היו מזרע יהודה ומבית דוד, והסירו השבט והמחוקק לגמרי, והיה עונשם מדה כנגד מדה, שהמשיל הקדוש ברוך הוא עליהם את עבדיהם והם הכריתום. ואפשר גם כן שהיה עליהם חטא במלכותם מפני שהיו כהנים ונצטוו (במדבר יח:ז) תשמרו את כהונתכם לכל דבר המזבח ולמבית לפרכת ועבדתם עבודת מתנה אתן את כהונתכם, ולא היה להם למלוך רק לעבוד את עבודת ה'.

כֹּה אָמַר ה' אֱלֹקִים הִנֵּה אֲנִי לֹקֵחַ אֶת בְּנֵי יִשְׂרָאֵל מִבֵּין הַגּוֹיִם אֲשֶׁר הָלְכוּ שָׁם
וְקִבַּצְתִּי אֹתָם מִסָּבִיב וְהֵבֵאתִי אוֹתָם אֶל אַדְמָתָם: וְעָשִׂיתִי אֹתָם לְגוֹי אֶחָד
בָּאָרֶץ בְּהָרֵי יִשְׂרָאֵל וּמֶלֶךְ אֶחָד יִהְיֶה לְכֻלָּם לְמֶלֶךְ וְלֹא יִהְיוּ עוֹד לִשְׁנֵי גוֹיִם וְלֹא
יֵחָצוּ עוֹד לִשְׁתֵּי מַמְלָכוֹת עוֹד:

Say to them, "Thus says the Almighty God: 'Behold, I will take the stick of Yosef, which is in the hand of Efraim, and the tribes of Israel his companions, and will put them with him, with the stick of Yehudah, and make them one stick, and they shall be one in my hand."' And the sticks on which you write shall be in your hand before their eyes. And say to them, "Thus says the Almighty God: 'Behold, I will take the people of Israel from among the nations, where they have gone, and will gather them on every side, and bring them into their own land. And I will make them one nation in the land upon the mountains of Israel, and one king shall be king to them all and they shall no more be two nations, nor shall they be divided into two kingdoms anymore at all."' (Yehezkel 37:19–22)

This, then, is essence of the world in its corrected state: one nation, one Temple, one Land, one God – unity.

Postscript for Hanukah

When Hannah's brothers saw her act of defiance at the wedding celebration, they saw only impurity. Only upon further contemplation did they understand that in fact there was a source of purity to her behavior. That essence of purity is akin to the flask of oil found in the Temple. Even though the Temple was defiled, deep in the recesses of the Temple there was a "*pakh katan,*" a small flask containing enough oil for one day. Where did this flask originate? Was it, as the Gemara contends, related to Yaakov searching for "*pakhim ketanim* (little flasks)"[17] on the night before his confrontation with Esav? Was it related to the oil with which Yaakov anointed the monument he built after the episode of Dina?[18] Perhaps the

---

17. See Talmud Bavli Hulin 91a, and Rashi, Bereishit 32:25.

18. See Bereishit 35:14.

lone, pure flask of oil found by the Maccabees was related to both of these events.

Hannah shone a spotlight so that her brothers could see the purity hidden beneath the impurity. She understood that deep inside each of us there is a *pakh katan* that yearns to be uncovered and must be lit. While her brothers saw impurity, she taught them to seek out the inner purity, and to fight for it.

Every Jewish soul is comparable to a small flask of pure oil with the seal of the *kohen gadol*. Sometimes its light is clearly visible, sometimes we must search. But when the Maccabees found the oil and lit the Menorah – the oil didn't last only one day as we would have expected. It didn't even last for seven or eight days. The light of that *pakh katan* of purity, so much like the hidden light within each of us, has lasted for 2,300 years, and still burns strong.

Parashat Mikeitz

Dream, Dream, Dream...Dream

Par'oh has a dream. He is frightened and agitated, yet not one of his advisors can interpret his dream:

בראשית מא:ח

וַיְהִי בַבֹּקֶר וַתִּפָּעֶם רוּחוֹ וַיִּשְׁלַח וַיִּקְרָא אֶת כָּל חַרְטֻמֵּי מִצְרַיִם וְאֶת כָּל חֲכָמֶיהָ
וַיְסַפֵּר פַּרְעֹה לָהֶם אֶת חֲלֹמוֹ וְאֵין פּוֹתֵר אוֹתָם לְפַרְעֹה:

And it came to pass in the morning that his spirit was troubled; and he sent and called for all the magicians of Egypt, and all its wise men; and Par'oh told them his dream, but there was none who could interpret them to Par'oh. (Bereishit 41:8)

Why was this dream so troubling to Par'oh? It seems to speak of produce and agriculture, subjects that would occupy a monarch's mind for a significant part of his working day; it should come as no surprise when these elements bubbled to the surface while he slumbered.

בראשית מא:א–ז

וַיְהִי מִקֵּץ שְׁנָתַיִם יָמִים וּפַרְעֹה חֹלֵם וְהִנֵּה עֹמֵד עַל הַיְאֹר: וְהִנֵּה מִן הַיְאֹר עֹלֹת
שֶׁבַע פָּרוֹת יְפוֹת מַרְאֶה וּבְרִיאֹת בָּשָׂר וַתִּרְעֶינָה בָּאָחוּ: וְהִנֵּה שֶׁבַע פָּרוֹת אֲחֵרוֹת
עֹלוֹת אַחֲרֵיהֶן מִן הַיְאֹר רָעוֹת מַרְאֶה וְדַקּוֹת בָּשָׂר וַתַּעֲמֹדְנָה אֵצֶל הַפָּרוֹת עַל
שְׂפַת הַיְאֹר: וַתֹּאכַלְנָה הַפָּרוֹת רָעוֹת הַמַּרְאֶה וְדַקֹּת הַבָּשָׂר אֵת שֶׁבַע הַפָּרוֹת יְפֹת
הַמַּרְאֶה וְהַבְּרִיאֹת וַיִּיקַץ פַּרְעֹה: וַיִּישָׁן וַיַּחֲלֹם שֵׁנִית וְהִנֵּה שֶׁבַע שִׁבֳּלִים עֹלוֹת
בְּקָנֶה אֶחָד בְּרִיאוֹת וְטֹבוֹת: וְהִנֵּה שֶׁבַע שִׁבֳּלִים דַּקּוֹת וּשְׁדוּפֹת קָדִים צֹמְחוֹת
אַחֲרֵיהֶן: וַתִּבְלַעְנָה הַשִּׁבֳּלִים הַדַּקּוֹת אֵת שֶׁבַע הַשִּׁבֳּלִים הַבְּרִיאוֹת וְהַמְּלֵאוֹת
וַיִּיקַץ פַּרְעֹה וְהִנֵּה חֲלוֹם:

And it came to pass at the end of two full years, that Par'oh dreamed; and, behold, he stood by the river. And, behold, there came up from the river seven cows sleek and fat; and they fed in the reed grass. And, behold, seven other cows came up after them from the river, gaunt and thin; and stood by the other cows upon the brink of the river. And the gaunt and thin cows consumed the seven sleek and fat cows.

And Par'oh awoke. And he slept and dreamed a second time; and,
behold, seven ears of grain came up as one stalk, plump and good.
And, behold, seven thin ears, blasted by the east wind, sprung up after
them. And the seven thin ears devoured the seven plump and full ears.
And Par'oh awoke, and, behold, it was a dream. (Bereishit 41:1–7)

Par'oh's dreams do not seem overly difficult to understand. It seems
strange that all the wise men of Egypt could not muster any suggestion or
interpretation that would satisfy Par'oh. In order to understand the source
of their difficulty, let us consider the dreams through Egyptian eyes.

Par'oh has two dreams that are similar, one focused on cows and the other
on stalks of grain. To the modern reader these seem like innocuous, healthy
symbols of a time and place where man was more connected to the land
and nature: these are the basic symbols of agricultural life, of the farmer
and the shepherd. Yet the Egyptians may have viewed these symbols in
a very different fashion. Yosef actually points out the cultural divergence
when, years later, he prepares his brothers for their meeting with Par'oh:

בראשית מו:לא–לד

וַיֹּאמֶר יוֹסֵף אֶל אֶחָיו וְאֶל בֵּית אָבִיו אֶעֱלֶה וְאַגִּידָה לְפַרְעֹה וְאֹמְרָה אֵלָיו אַחַי
וּבֵית אָבִי אֲשֶׁר בְּאֶרֶץ כְּנַעַן בָּאוּ אֵלָי: וְהָאֲנָשִׁים רֹעֵי צֹאן כִּי אַנְשֵׁי מִקְנֶה הָיוּ
וְצֹאנָם וּבְקָרָם וְכָל אֲשֶׁר לָהֶם הֵבִיאוּ: וְהָיָה כִּי יִקְרָא לָכֶם פַּרְעֹה וְאָמַר מַה
מַּעֲשֵׂיכֶם: וַאֲמַרְתֶּם אַנְשֵׁי מִקְנֶה הָיוּ עֲבָדֶיךָ מִנְּעוּרֵינוּ וְעַד עַתָּה גַּם אֲנַחְנוּ גַּם
אֲבֹתֵינוּ בַּעֲבוּר תֵּשְׁבוּ בְּאֶרֶץ גֹּשֶׁן כִּי תוֹעֲבַת מִצְרַיִם כָּל רֹעֵה צֹאן:

And Yosef said to his brothers, and to his father's house, "I will go up,
and explain to Par'oh, and say to him, 'My brothers and my father's
house, who were in the land of Canaan, have come to me; And the
men are shepherds, for their trade has been to raise cattle; and they
have brought their flocks, and their herds, and all that they have.'
And it shall come to pass, when Par'oh shall call you, and shall say,
'What is your occupation?' you shall say, 'Your servants' trade has
been keeping cattle from our youth until now, both we, and also our
fathers'; that you may live in the land of Goshen; for every shepherd
is an abomination to the Egyptians." (Bereishit 46:31–34)

Rashi explains that because the Egyptians regarded animals as deities, they
considered it an abomination to herd, domesticate or cultivate flocks or herds.

רש"י, בראשית מו:לד

כי תועבת מצרים וגו': לפי שהם להם אלהות.

"Is an abomination to the Egyptians": For they were deities for them.
(Rashi, Bereishit 46:34)

The Ibn Ezra explains that this was not dissimilar to India in his day: these people worshiped cows and would not eat their meat or drink their milk, hence those who raised cows and ate their meat and milk were shunned by the Egyptians.[1] The Riva goes even further, pointing out that practices necessary for tending flocks were abhorrent to the Egyptians, who could not bear the use of force on their deities.[2] The Bekhor Shor interprets Yosef's comment differently, reading it as a condemnation of Egyptian idolatry: the word "abomination" refers to the Egyptian deities, and Yosef is passing a value judgment on Egyptian sensibilities and their worship of four-legged creatures.[3]

The word that Yosef uses to describe the clash between Egyptian and Jewish sensibilities is *to'eivah* (abomination), and this same word appears elsewhere in Yosef's story in another context: When the brothers

---

1. Ibn Ezra, Bereishit 46:34.

    אבן עזרא, בראשית מו:לד

    כי תועבת מצרים כל רועה צאן: לאות כי בימים ההם לא היו המצרים אוכלים בשר. ולא יעזבו אדם שיזבח צאן כאשר יעשו היום אנשי הודו. ומי שהוא רועה צאן תועבה היא שהוא שותה החלב. ואנשי הודו לא יאכלו ולא ישתו כל אשר יצא מחי מרגיש עד היום הזה.

2. Riva, Bereishit 46:34.

    פירוש הריב"א, בראשית מו:לד

    כי תועבת מצרים כל רועה צאן: פרש"י לפי שהם אלהות שלהם, והטעם כ"ח לפי שיראתם היה מזל טלה ובגללו היו עובדין לצאן כי תועבת מצרים כל רועה צאן לפי שדרך רועה צאן לרדות הצאן במקלות וקש' למצרים כשרודים אלהותם, ד"א לפי שהרועים יודעים שאין בצאן כח אלהות והמצרים מאמינים אותם אף כי הם יודעים שאין בהם כח כמו שפ' חזקוני לעיל, ד"א לפי שאי אפשר שלא יהנו הרועים מן החלב ומן הגזה ודבר גנאי ותועבה למצרים שיהנו מאלהותם כ"פ. הרר"א, וי"מ רועה צאן ר"ל אוכל כמו שמצינו רעיה שהיא לשון אכילה כמו ירעו כאן בשן וגלעד וקשה למצרים כשיאכלו אלהותם ואין המקרא משמע כן.

3. Bekhor Shor, Bereishit 46:34.

    רבי יוסף בכור שור, בראשית מו:לד

    כי תועבת מצרים כל רועה צאן: יש לומר מפני שהיא תועבה להם, ירחיקו אתכם מעליהם אל ארץ גושן. ולי נראה שהוא כינוי, כי חשובים בעיני מצרים כל רועי צאן, שמגדל תרפותם. ולפי שכוונתם לע"ז קורא אותם "תועבה", לפי שיאהבו אתכם יושיבו אתכם אל ארץ גושן, שהיא טובה, כי אין נראה שימאיס אחיו בעיניהם.

unknowingly stand before Yosef and are invited to dine with the prince of Egypt, the Torah describes the strange seating arrangements. The brothers are seated by themselves, Yosef by himself, and the other members of the Egyptian court by themselves:

בראשית מג:לא–לב

וַיִּרְחַץ פָּנָיו וַיֵּצֵא וַיִּתְאַפַּק וַיֹּאמֶר שִׂימוּ לָחֶם: וַיָּשִׂימוּ לוֹ לְבַדּוֹ וְלָהֶם לְבַדָּם וְלַמִּצְרִים הָאֹכְלִים אִתּוֹ לְבַדָּם כִּי לֹא יוּכְלוּן הַמִּצְרִים לֶאֱכֹל אֶת הָעִבְרִים לֶחֶם כִּי תוֹעֵבָה הִוא לְמִצְרָיִם:

And he [Yosef] washed his face, and went out, and controlled himself, and said, "Set out bread." And they served him by himself, and for them by themselves, and for the Egyptians who ate with him, by themselves; because the Egyptians would not eat bread with the Hebrews; for that is an abomination to the Egyptians. (Bereishit 43:31–32)

Some commentaries[4] see this as an indication of the arrogance and haughtiness of the Egyptians, who were not willing to eat with "lowly" strangers, yet this would not explain Yosef's exclusion. Other commentaries refer to the Egyptians' disgust at the profession of these guests; again, this would not explain the exclusion of Yosef, a highly respected member of Par'oh's court.[5] It might be possible to apply the same definition of the word *to'eivah* to this passage for a better understanding: one could posit that the word here also indicates a deity. The passage should then be interpreted along the lines suggested by the Bekhor Shor: "for the Egyptians would not eat bread with the Hebrews, for this was (another) *to'eivah*, another idolatrous practice of the Egyptians." Eating bread, certainly publicly, went

---

4. See Hizkuni and Seforno, Bereishit 43:32.

חזקוני, בראשית מג:לב
כי תועבה היא למצרים: בזוי להם לאכול עם אדם נכרי כי אנשי מצרים גסי הרוח כדכתיב לכן קראתי לזאת רהב הם שבת.

ספורנו, בראשית מג:לב
כי לא יוכלון המצרים: לפיכך לא אכל הוא עם אחיו ולא הוא ולא אחיו עם המצרים.

5. See Targum Onkelos, Bereishit 43:32.

תרגום אונקלוס, בראשית מג:לב
ושויאו ליה בלחודוהי ולהון בלחודיהון ולמצראי דאכלין עמיה בלחודיהון ארי לא יכלין מצראי למיכל עם עבראי לחמא **ארי בעירא דמצראי דחלין ליה עבראי אכלין.**

against Egyptian religious sensibilities.[6] This may provide us with a window into the religious world of Pharaonic Egypt: this was a slave-based society, developed not as a result of great affluence but as an outcome of a religious system that rejected all forms of physical labor. Egypt needed slaves – because the Egyptians themselves rejected the concept of physical labor. The production of bread required arduous work, and the Egyptians may have found all types of work and, by extension, those who were engaged in physical labor, an offense to their religious beliefs.

In this context, the two elements of Par'oh's dream are of great symbolic importance inasmuch as they relate to "idolatrous" practices. Two additional elements of the dreams buttress this thesis: the "river" and Par'oh himself. Both of these elements were also perceived as deities – the Nile, seen as the life force of Egypt, and Par'oh, who claimed to be the god of the Nile:

יחזקאל כט:ב–ג

בֶּן אָדָם שִׂים פָּנֶיךָ עַל פַּרְעֹה מֶלֶךְ מִצְרָיִם וְהִנָּבֵא עָלָיו וְעַל מִצְרַיִם כֻּלָּהּ: דַּבֵּר וְאָמַרְתָּ כֹּה אָמַר אֲדֹנָי ה' הִנְנִי עָלֶיךָ פַּרְעֹה מֶלֶךְ מִצְרַיִם הַתַּנִּים הַגָּדוֹל הָרֹבֵץ בְּתוֹךְ יְאֹרָיו אֲשֶׁר אָמַר לִי יְאֹרִי וַאֲנִי עֲשִׂיתִנִי...

Son of man, set your face against Par'oh king of Egypt, and prophesy against him, and against all Egypt. Speak, and say, "Thus says the Almighty God: Behold, I am against you, Par'oh king of Egypt, the great crocodile that lies in the midst of his streams, who has said, 'My river is my own, and I have made it for myself.'" (Yehezkel 29:2–3)

Only when we appreciate that all the elements in the dreams may have been perceived as deities to the Egyptians can we understand the silence of all of

---

6. See Da'at Zekeinim mi'Baalei haTosafot on Bereishit 46:34, who draws the connection between this verse and the word *abomination* found in connection with the Israelites' vocation.

דעת זקנים מבעלי התוספות, בראשית מו:לד

כי תועבת מצרים וכו': מאוסים היו רועי צאן בעיניהם כי הצאן היה דבר מאוס לאכילה כמו שמאוסין העזים לאכילה בהרבה מקומות. וכן לא יוכלון לאכול את העברים לחם כי תועבה היא למצרים מאוסים היו אנשי עבר הנהר בעיניהם ולכן קשה להם לאכול עמהם וכן הן נזבח את תועבת מצרים לעיניהם נזבח בפניהם מה שהוא מאוס להם ולא יסקלונו יהרגונו לא נאמר אלא יסקלונו. ד"א שמעתי כי תועבת מצרים כל רעה וזן עצמו מן הצאן ואוכל אותם כי היא ע"ז שלהם ידועה מלשון הרעה אותי דמתרגמינן דזן יתי.

Par'oh's advisors. They must have perceived in these dreams a foreboding message of a major cataclysm that could shake Egypt to its very core.

These same dreams may be understood in a completely different fashion when viewed within the ideological and religious worldview represented by biblical symbols. In this context, Par'oh's two dreams represent an ancient dichotomy that has persisted from the very first day of man's existence. This may be concisely described as the dichotomy between man's perfect state of existence before the sin and man's post-Eden existence.

Before eating from the Tree of Knowledge of Good and Evil, Adam names the animals. This seems to have been the extent of the "work" with which he is charged:

בראשית ב:טו

וַיִּקַּח ה' אֱלֹקִים אֶת הָאָדָם וַיַּנִּחֵהוּ בְגַן עֵדֶן לְעָבְדָהּ וּלְשָׁמְרָהּ:

And God Almightly took the man, and put him into the Garden of Eden to cultivate it and to keep it. (Bereishit 2:15)

After the sin, Adam is instructed to work the ground. Sustenance, symbolized by bread, will now emerge only when man exerts himself:

בראשית ג:יט

בְּזֵעַת אַפֶּיךָ תֹּאכַל לֶחֶם עַד שׁוּבְךָ אֶל הָאֲדָמָה כִּי מִמֶּנָּה לֻקָּחְתָּ כִּי עָפָר אַתָּה וְאֶל עָפָר תָּשׁוּב:

By the sweat of your brow shall you eat bread, until you return to the ground, for out of it you were taken; for you are dust, and to dust shall you return. (Bereishit 3:19)

This same dichotomy is evident in the different orientations toward work in the next generation:[7]

בראשית ד:ג–ד

וַיְהִי מִקֵּץ יָמִים וַיָּבֵא קַיִן מִפְּרִי הָאֲדָמָה מִנְחָה לַה': וְהֶבֶל הֵבִיא גַם הוּא מִבְּכֹרוֹת צֹאנוֹ וּמֵחֶלְבֵהֶן וַיִּשַׁע ה' אֶל הֶבֶל וְאֶל מִנְחָתוֹ:

---

7. For more on this theme, see *Explorations*, Parashat Bereishit.

And in the process of time it came to pass, that Kayin brought of
the fruit of the ground an offering to the Almighty. And Hevel also
brought of the firstlings and the fattest of his flock. And the Almighty
harkened to Hevel and to his offering. (Bereishit 4:3–4)

Kayin and Hevel take different paths in their pursuit of God's Will, and
these paths are expressed by their vocations. These enduring symbols of
mankind's relationship to nature and to our place in the post-Eden reality
were surely familiar to Yosef. Clearly Par'oh and his advisors did not think
in these terms, and Yosef's interpretation of Par'oh's dreams ignores the
biblical symbolism, while simultaneously steering clear of the minefield of
Egyptian deities. The interpretation Yosef puts forth is firmly embedded in
economics, in pragmatic planning that will enable Egypt to take advantage
of the good years ahead in order to protect itself when the difficult times
follow. This is an interpretation that does not threaten Par'oh or the religious
system of which he is the apex, and Yosef is immediately catapulted to a
position of power that enables him to implement his economic plan.

Yosef's pragmatic interpretation of Par'oh's dreams must be seen as part
and parcel of his interpretation of a previous set of dreams – dreams that
actually laid the foundations for his own liberation. As he languished in an
Egyptian prison, Yosef interpreted the dreams of two fellow inmates:

בראשית מ:ה–ח

וַיַּחַלְמוּ חֲלוֹם שְׁנֵיהֶם אִישׁ חֲלֹמוֹ בְּלַיְלָה אֶחָד אִישׁ כְּפִתְרוֹן חֲלֹמוֹ הַמַּשְׁקֶה
וְהָאֹפֶה אֲשֶׁר לְמֶלֶךְ מִצְרַיִם אֲשֶׁר אֲסוּרִים בְּבֵית הַסֹּהַר: וַיָּבֹא אֲלֵיהֶם יוֹסֵף בַּבֹּקֶר
וַיַּרְא אֹתָם וְהִנָּם זֹעֲפִים: וַיִּשְׁאַל אֶת סְרִיסֵי פַרְעֹה אֲשֶׁר אִתּוֹ בְמִשְׁמַר בֵּית אֲדֹנָיו
לֵאמֹר מַדּוּעַ פְּנֵיכֶם רָעִים הַיּוֹם: וַיֹּאמְרוּ אֵלָיו חֲלוֹם חָלַמְנוּ וּפֹתֵר אֵין אֹתוֹ וַיֹּאמֶר
אֲלֵהֶם יוֹסֵף הֲלוֹא לֵאלֹקִים פִּתְרֹנִים סַפְּרוּ נָא לִי:

And they dreamed a dream both of them, each man his dream, in
one night, each man according to the interpretation of his dream, the
sommelier and the baker of the king of Egypt, who were confined in
the prison. And Yosef came to them in the morning, and saw that
they were sad. And he asked Par'oh's officers who were with him
in the custody of his lord's house, saying, "Why do you look so sad
today?" And they said to him, "We have dreamed a dream, and there
is no interpreter of it." And Yosef said to them, "Do interpretations not
belong to the Almighty? Tell them to me, I beg you." (Bereishit 40:5–8)

וַיְסַפֵּר שַׂר הַמַּשְׁקִים אֶת חֲלֹמוֹ לְיוֹסֵף וַיֹּאמֶר לוֹ בַּחֲלוֹמִי וְהִנֵּה גֶפֶן לְפָנָי: וּבַגֶּפֶן שְׁלֹשָׁה שָׂרִיגִם וְהִיא כְפֹרַחַת עָלְתָה נִצָּהּ הִבְשִׁילוּ אַשְׁכְּלֹתֶיהָ עֲנָבִים: וְכוֹס פַּרְעֹה בְּיָדִי וָאֶקַּח אֶת הָעֲנָבִים וָאֶשְׂחַט אֹתָם אֶל כּוֹס פַּרְעֹה וָאֶתֵּן אֶת הַכּוֹס עַל כַּף פַּרְעֹה: וַיֹּאמֶר לוֹ יוֹסֵף זֶה פִּתְרֹנוֹ שְׁלֹשֶׁת הַשָּׂרִגִים שְׁלֹשֶׁת יָמִים הֵם: בְּעוֹד שְׁלֹשֶׁת יָמִים יִשָּׂא פַרְעֹה אֶת רֹאשֶׁךָ וַהֲשִׁיבְךָ עַל כַּנֶּךָ וְנָתַתָּ כוֹס פַּרְעֹה בְּיָדוֹ כַּמִּשְׁפָּט הָרִאשׁוֹן אֲשֶׁר הָיִיתָ מַשְׁקֵהוּ: כִּי אִם זְכַרְתַּנִי אִתְּךָ כַּאֲשֶׁר יִיטַב לָךְ וְעָשִׂיתָ נָּא עִמָּדִי חָסֶד וְהִזְכַּרְתַּנִי אֶל פַּרְעֹה וְהוֹצֵאתַנִי מִן הַבַּיִת הַזֶּה: כִּי גֻנֹּב גֻּנַּבְתִּי מֵאֶרֶץ הָעִבְרִים וְגַם פֹּה לֹא עָשִׂיתִי מְאוּמָה כִּי שָׂמוּ אֹתִי בַּבּוֹר: וַיַּרְא שַׂר הָאֹפִים כִּי טוֹב פָּתָר וַיֹּאמֶר אֶל יוֹסֵף אַף אֲנִי בַּחֲלוֹמִי וְהִנֵּה שְׁלֹשָׁה סַלֵּי חֹרִי עַל רֹאשִׁי: וּבַסַּל הָעֶלְיוֹן מִכֹּל מַאֲכַל פַּרְעֹה מַעֲשֵׂה אֹפֶה וְהָעוֹף אֹכֵל אֹתָם מִן הַסַּל מֵעַל רֹאשִׁי: וַיַּעַן יוֹסֵף וַיֹּאמֶר זֶה פִּתְרֹנוֹ שְׁלֹשֶׁת הַסַּלִּים שְׁלֹשֶׁת יָמִים הֵם: בְּעוֹד שְׁלֹשֶׁת יָמִים יִשָּׂא פַרְעֹה אֶת רֹאשְׁךָ מֵעָלֶיךָ וְתָלָה אוֹתְךָ עַל עֵץ וְאָכַל הָעוֹף אֶת בְּשָׂרְךָ מֵעָלֶיךָ: וַיְהִי בַּיּוֹם הַשְּׁלִישִׁי יוֹם הֻלֶּדֶת אֶת פַּרְעֹה וַיַּעַשׂ מִשְׁתֶּה לְכָל עֲבָדָיו וַיִּשָּׂא אֶת רֹאשׁ שַׂר הַמַּשְׁקִים וְאֶת רֹאשׁ שַׂר הָאֹפִים בְּתוֹךְ עֲבָדָיו: וַיָּשֶׁב אֶת שַׂר הַמַּשְׁקִים עַל מַשְׁקֵהוּ וַיִּתֵּן הַכּוֹס עַל כַּף פַּרְעֹה: וְאֵת שַׂר הָאֹפִים תָּלָה כַּאֲשֶׁר פָּתַר לָהֶם יוֹסֵף: וְלֹא זָכַר שַׂר הַמַּשְׁקִים אֶת יוֹסֵף וַיִּשְׁכָּחֵהוּ:

And the chief sommelier told his dream to Yosef, and said to him, "In my dream, behold, a vine was before me; And on the vine were three branches, and it was as though it budded, and its blossoms shot forth and its clusters brought forth ripe grapes; And Par'oh's cup was in my hand; and I took the grapes and pressed them into Par'oh's cup, and I placed the cup into Par'oh's hand." And Yosef said to him, "This is the interpretation of it: The three branches are three days, and within three days Par'oh will lift up your head and restore you to your place; and you shall deliver Par'oh's cup into his hand, as you once did when you were in his service. But think of me when it shall be well with you, and show kindness, I beg you, to me, and make mention of me to Par'oh, and bring me out of this house; for indeed I was stolen away from the land of the Hebrews; and here also have I done nothing that they should put me in the dungeon." When the chief baker saw that [Yosef] had interpreted well, he said to Yosef, "I, too, was in my dream, and, behold, I had three white baskets on my head. And in the uppermost basket there were all kinds of baked food for Par'oh, and the birds ate them out of the basket upon my head." And Yosef answered and said, "This is the interpretation: The three baskets are three days, and within three days Par'oh will lift up your head off you and hang you on a tree, and the birds shall eat your flesh off you." And it came to pass on the third day, which was Par'oh's birthday, he made a feast for all his servants; and he lifted up the head of the chief sommelier and of the chief baker among his servants. And he restored the chief sommelier to his stewardship again; and he placed the cup into Par'oh's hand; But he hanged the chief baker, as Yosef had interpreted to them. Yet the chief sommelier did not remember Yosef, and forgot him. (Bereishit 40:9–23)

These dreams contain symbols of the dichotomy we have discussed: the baker is actively involved in the process of making bread. The deeper connection with the post-Eden state of mankind, as well as the thematic connection with Par'oh's dream, should not be overlooked. The wine steward, who is entrusted to discern good wine from bad, represents a major element of the sin committed in the Garden of Eden: according to one tradition, the Tree of Knowledge of Good and Evil was none other than a grape vine, whose fruit causes confusion.[8] The wine steward's job, then, is a delicate one: he must, in his way, unravel the confusion of man's first sin. The baker, on the other hand, performs his task by adhering to the rules of engagement of the post-sin world in which bread is brought forth by the sweat of man's brow. While both wine and bread are the results of a long process of fermentation which produces a finished product that is a vast improvement over the raw materials used to create it, Yosef sees only one of these processes carrying through to a successful finish: the sommelier will be returned to his former glory, which is analogous to a world before sin, before confusion. The baker's death seems to indicate a far weaker commitment to the post-Eden experience: Par'oh has no interest in perpetuating "bread," takes no responsibility for a world of work, of patient toil, and of death. These are left for the Egyptians' slaves to contend with, and it should come as no surprise that the Egyptian economic system eventually becomes completely dependent on slave labor. As a living representation of the human condition after the sin, the baker is doomed. He, his profession –

8. See Talmud Bavli Brakhot 40a.

and what that profession symbolizes – are an abomination to Egyptian theology, just as the Hebrew shepherds would be.

For Yosef, bread was also a troubling symbol. The Torah stresses that his brothers sat down "to eat bread" after they cast him into the pit. Later, "bread" helped land him in prison. When he starts his career in the house of Potifar, we are told that Yosef is entrusted with all of his master's possessions – save one:

בראשית לט:ו

וַיַּעֲזֹב כָּל אֲשֶׁר לוֹ בְּיַד יוֹסֵף וְלֹא יָדַע אִתּוֹ מְאוּמָה כִּי אִם הַלֶּחֶם אֲשֶׁר הוּא אוֹכֵל...

And he left all that he had in Yosef's hand; and he knew not what he had, save for the bread that he ate... (Bereishit 39:6)

Later, this statement is clarified. When his master's wife tries to seduce Yosef, the "bread" is a symbol of something far more personal:

בראשית לט:ח–ט

וַיְמָאֵן וַיֹּאמֶר אֶל אֵשֶׁת אֲדֹנָיו הֵן אֲדֹנִי לֹא יָדַע אִתִּי מַה בַּבָּיִת וְכֹל אֲשֶׁר יֶשׁ לוֹ נָתַן בְּיָדִי: אֵינֶנּוּ גָדוֹל בַּבַּיִת הַזֶּה מִמֶּנִּי וְלֹא חָשַׂךְ מִמֶּנִּי מְאוּמָה כִּי אִם אוֹתָךְ בַּאֲשֶׁר אַתְּ אִשְׁתּוֹ וְאֵיךְ אֶעֱשֶׂה הָרָעָה הַגְּדֹלָה הַזֹּאת וְחָטָאתִי לֵאלֹקִים:

But he refused, and said to his master's wife, "Behold, my master knows not what is with me in the house, and he has committed all that he has to my hand. There is none greater in this house than I, nor has he kept back anything from me but you, because you are his wife; how, then, can I do this great wickedness, and sin against God?" (Bereishit 39:8–9)

The one thing that was off limits to Yosef, earlier described as "bread," was, in fact, Mrs. Potifar. Yosef was accused of "eating another man's 'bread,'" and he was thrown into the pit once again. Once again, Yosef had not, in fact, partaken of the bread. He alone among the brothers did not eat bread when he was in the pit, and he remained a *tzaddik* in the house of Potifar, despite the temptation to partake of the "feast." We may go so far as to say that Yosef is a throwback to man's purest state, to a point before the sin in Eden, to a time before man began to eke out his sustenance by the sweat of his brow, before eating from the Tree of Knowledge – before Adam "knew" his wife, before bread replaced knowledge.[9]

Yosef's vision remains unclouded, unconfused. He correctly interprets the dreams of his fellow prisoners, as well as Par'oh's dreams, while discerning within them a message that transcends the lives and times of the dreamers of these dreams. When the two former ministers reveal their dreams to him, Yosef's interpretation bears similarities to his interpretation of Par'oh's dreams. In both cases, Yosef understands that God is revealing the future. But Yosef also sees much more. Yosef sees the hand of God touching his own life, and he believes that when God speaks to the staff of Par'oh's palace, there is also a message for him in that communication. He hears within the wine steward's dream a harbinger of his own salvation. He understands from Par'oh's dream the reason why he suffered all of the trials and tribulations that brought him to the position of *hamashbir hagadol*, the great sustainer of Egypt and of his own family. Perhaps Yosef connected these two pairs of dreams with yet another pair of dreams: his own dreams, the dreams that caused his brothers to hate him enough to wish him dead.

---

9. Regarding the connection between bread and knowledge, see Talmud Bavli Brakhot 40a, and *Sfat Emet* on Parashat Beha'alotkha 5647.

תלמוד בבלי, מסכת ברכות דף מ עמוד א

דתניא אילן שאכל ממנו אדם הראשון רבי מאיר אומר גפן היה שאין לך דבר שמביא יללה על האדם אלא יין שנאמר וישת מן היין וישכר רבי נחמיה אומר תאנה היתה שבדבר שנתקלקלו בו נתקנו שנאמר ויתפרו עלה תאנה רבי יהודה אומר חטה היתה שאין התינוק יודע לקרות אבא ואמא עד שיטעום טעם דגן.

"For it has been taught: R. Meir holds that the tree of which Adam ate was the vine, since the thing that most causes wailing to a man is wine, as it says, 'And he drank of the wine and became drunk.' R. Nehemiah says it was the fig tree; thus they repaired their misdeed with the instrument of [that sin], as it says, 'And they sewed fig leaves together.' R. Yehudah says it was wheat, since a child does not know how to call father and mother until it has had a taste of wheat."

שפת אמת, פרשת בהעלותך, שנת [תרמ"ז]

והנה כתיב כמתאוננים רע כו'. ביאור הענין כי בודאי לא הי' מחשבותם להרע. רק שרצו בחי' עץ הדעת טוב ורע כמו חטא הראשון. ובאמת עתה אחר החטא שנתערב טוב ורע בעולם אין הנפש יכול להתתקן רק בכח הבירור. וזה רמז ה גם בלא דעת נפש לא טוב. מאי גם. רק להיות כי עיקר הרצון הי' שיתדבק האדם בעץ החיים תורה וחקים ומצות שהוא למעלה מהשגת דעת האדם. אבל עתה אין הנפש בטוב רק ע"י הדעת. ואכילת לחם מן הארץ הוא הדעת המברר בין טוב ורע ובורר אוכל מתוך פסולת כמ"ש בגמ' אין תינוק יודע לקרוא אבא ואמא עד שטועם טעם דגן. וכן אין מרחיקין מצואת קטן עד שאוכל כזית דגן שבלחם מן הארץ מתערב פסולת. וכמו כן בע"ח שהם גדולי קרקע ונזונין ממעשב הארץ.

בראשית לז:ה–יא

וַיַּחֲלֹם יוֹסֵף חֲלוֹם וַיַּגֵּד לְאֶחָיו וַיּוֹסִפוּ עוֹד שְׂנֹא אֹתוֹ: וַיֹּאמֶר אֲלֵיהֶם שִׁמְעוּ נָא
הַחֲלוֹם הַזֶּה אֲשֶׁר חָלָמְתִּי: וְהִנֵּה אֲנַחְנוּ מְאַלְּמִים אֲלֻמִּים בְּתוֹךְ הַשָּׂדֶה וְהִנֵּה
קָמָה אֲלֻמָּתִי וְגַם נִצָּבָה וְהִנֵּה תְסֻבֶּינָה אֲלֻמֹּתֵיכֶם וַתִּשְׁתַּחֲוֶיןָ לַאֲלֻמָּתִי: וַיֹּאמְרוּ לוֹ
אֶחָיו הֲמָלֹךְ תִּמְלֹךְ עָלֵינוּ אִם מָשׁוֹל תִּמְשֹׁל בָּנוּ וַיּוֹסִפוּ עוֹד שְׂנֹא אֹתוֹ עַל חֲלֹמֹתָיו
וְעַל דְּבָרָיו: וַיַּחֲלֹם עוֹד חֲלוֹם אַחֵר וַיְסַפֵּר אֹתוֹ לְאֶחָיו וַיֹּאמֶר הִנֵּה חָלַמְתִּי חֲלוֹם
עוֹד וְהִנֵּה הַשֶּׁמֶשׁ וְהַיָּרֵחַ וְאַחַד עָשָׂר כּוֹכָבִים מִשְׁתַּחֲוִים לִי: וַיְסַפֵּר אֶל אָבִיו וְאֶל
אֶחָיו וַיִּגְעַר בּוֹ אָבִיו וַיֹּאמֶר לוֹ מָה הַחֲלוֹם הַזֶּה אֲשֶׁר חָלָמְתָּ הֲבוֹא נָבוֹא אֲנִי
וְאִמְּךָ וְאַחֶיךָ לְהִשְׁתַּחֲוֹת לְךָ אָרְצָה: וַיְקַנְאוּ בוֹ אֶחָיו וְאָבִיו שָׁמַר אֶת הַדָּבָר:

*And Yosef dreamed a dream, and he told it his brothers; and they
hated him even more. And he said to them, "Hear, I beg you, this
dream that I have dreamed. Behold, we were binding sheaves in
the field, and my sheaf arose, and also stood upright; and, behold,
your sheaves stood around, and made obeisance to my sheaf." And
his brothers said to him, "Shall you indeed reign over us? Or shall
you indeed have dominion over us?" And they hated him even more
for his dreams, and for his words. And he dreamed yet another
dream, and told it to his brothers, and said, "Behold, I have again
dreamed a dream; and, behold, the sun and the moon and the eleven
stars made obeisance to me." And he told it to his father, and to his
brothers; and his father rebuked him, and said to him, "What is this
dream that you have dreamed? Shall I and your mother and your
brothers indeed come to bow down ourselves to you to the earth?"
And his brothers envied him; but his father kept the matter in mind.
(Bereishit 37:5–11)*

Yosef himself has two dreams, and he tells his brothers and his father the
content of the dreams but never offers them *his* interpretation. He is vilified
by his brothers as a self-centered narcissist; they have obviously interpreted
the dreams from their own jaundiced perspective. They understand the
dreams to be an indication that Yosef dreams of ruling over them.

Significantly, there are elements of his dreams that appear to slip by the
brothers, but should not go unnoticed by readers of the text: Yosef's first
dream was of sheaves, a theme that is revisited in the other dreams we
have analyzed, be it the chief baker's handiwork or the sheaves of Par'oh's
dream. In Yosef's dream, the sheaves speak of the larger issue that looms in

the background of all of the dreams: sheaves are a symbol of an agricultural society, but Yosef and his brothers are shepherds. On the one hand, we might interpret this vocation as an expression of their desire to identify with a "pre-sin" world, to identify with Hevel as opposed to Kayin. On the other hand, we may attribute their source of livelihood purely to expediency: although they live in Canaan, they are not masters of that land. Though the family lives in Hevron, the brothers travel a considerable distance to the north, to Shekhem and Dotan, to graze their flocks. This has a distinctly nomadic ring to it: they do not own land, and therefore they cannot engage in farming. They may live in the Promised Land, but it is still just that – promised to them, not yet theirs.

For Yosef's dream of sheaves to be realized, their lives will have to change considerably. Does Yosef see the next stage of their lives as master of the Promised Land, or does his dream reflect a new phase of life in a different land?[10] The brothers never ask; they don't seem to care. As far as they are concerned, Yosef's dream is simply the product of his overactive, self-centered imagination. And as they reject his first dream, they hate him for his second dream. But do they pause to consider its message?

Yosef's second dream deviates from all the dreams that follow; he dreams of celestial bodies, of the stars, the sun and moon. Again, the brothers do not seem interested in the deeper meaning of Yosef's dream. Even his father interprets the dream as an expression of Yosef's self-image. They all overlook the symbolism used in this dream – symbolism that we should not, ourselves, overlook: there was another member of the family who had a vision that involved the stars. His name was Avraham:

בראשית טו:א–ט

אַחַר הַדְּבָרִים הָאֵלֶּה הָיָה דְבַר ה' אֶל אַבְרָם בַּמַּחֲזֶה לֵאמֹר אַל תִּירָא אַבְרָם אָנֹכִי מָגֵן לָךְ שְׂכָרְךָ הַרְבֵּה מְאֹד: וַיֹּאמֶר אַבְרָם אֲדֹנָי ה' מַה תִּתֶּן לִי וְאָנֹכִי הוֹלֵךְ עֲרִירִי וּבֶן מֶשֶׁק בֵּיתִי הוּא דַּמֶּשֶׂק אֱלִיעֶזֶר: וַיֹּאמֶר אַבְרָם הֵן לִי לֹא נָתַתָּה זָרַע וְהִנֵּה בֶן בֵּיתִי יוֹרֵשׁ אֹתִי: וְהִנֵּה דְבַר ה' אֵלָיו לֵאמֹר לֹא יִירָשְׁךָ זֶה כִּי אִם אֲשֶׁר יֵצֵא

---

10. See Rabbi J.B. Soloveitchik, "And Yosef Dreamt a Dream," in *The Rav Speaks: Five Addresses on Israel, History, and the Jewish People* (New York: Judaica Press, 2002), page 27. The Rav notes the fact that Yosef and the brothers are shepherds, yet he dreams of agriculture, and concludes that Yosef's vision was of their impending exile and the lifestyle they would be forced to adopt in Egypt.

מִמֵּעֶיךָ הוּא יִירָשֶׁךָ: וַיּוֹצֵא אֹתוֹ הַחוּצָה וַיֹּאמֶר הַבֶּט נָא הַשָּׁמַיְמָה וּסְפֹר הַכּוֹכָבִים
אִם תּוּכַל לִסְפֹּר אֹתָם וַיֹּאמֶר לוֹ כֹּה יִהְיֶה זַרְעֶךָ: וְהֶאֱמִן בַּה' וַיַּחְשְׁבֶהָ לּוֹ צְדָקָה:
וַיֹּאמֶר אֵלָיו אֲנִי ה' אֲשֶׁר הוֹצֵאתִיךָ מֵאוּר כַּשְׂדִּים לָתֶת לְךָ אֶת הָאָרֶץ הַזֹּאת
לְרִשְׁתָּהּ: וַיֹּאמַר אֲדֹנָי ה' בַּמָּה אֵדַע כִּי אִירָשֶׁנָּה:

After these things the Word of the Almighty came to Avram in a vision, saying, "Fear not, Avram; I am your shield, and your reward will be great." And Avram said, "Almighty God, what will you give me, seeing I go childless, and the steward of my house is this Eliezer of Damascus?" And Avram said, "Behold, to me you have given no seed; and, lo, a member of my household staff is my heir." And, behold, the Word of the Almighty came to him, saying, "This shall not be your heir; but he who shall come forth from your own bowels shall be your heir." And He brought him outside, and said, 'Look now toward heaven, and count the stars, if you are able to count them"; and He said to him, "So shall your seed be." And he believed in the Almighty; and he counted it to him as tzedakah. And He said to him, "I am the Almighty who brought you out of Ur Kasdim, to give you this land to inherit it." And he said, "Almighty God, how shall I know that I shall inherit it?" (Bereishit 15:1–9)

The stars symbolize the number of Avraham's descendants: Avraham, who was childless at this point, receives God's promise that he will be the patriarch of a great nation, with innumerable descendants who will inherit the Land of Canaan. We would have expected the grandchild and great grandchildren of Avraham to have seen the significance of Yosef's dream of stars. We might even have expected them to reinterpret the first dream in light of the second dream, to make a connection with the second part of Avraham's vision that dealt with inheriting the Land. How did they ignore these symbols? Why did they not realize that Yosef's dreams were somehow connected to the future of the Children of Israel, Avraham's descendants, in the Land of Israel? When hearing these two dreams[11] the brothers should have understood that Yosef was describing a situation that did not exist yet,

---

11. Combining the images of Yosef's two dreams – stalks on the ground and the stars and sun and moon in the heavens – creates a vision remarkably similar to his father's dream of a ladder, with its feet on the ground and its top reaching the heavens.

a future time in which they and their descendants would be free to work the Land. They should have remembered Avraham's dreams, especially the dream that immediately follows his vision of the stars:

בראשית טו:יב–כא

וַיְהִי הַשֶּׁמֶשׁ לָבוֹא וְתַרְדֵּמָה נָפְלָה עַל אַבְרָם וְהִנֵּה אֵימָה חֲשֵׁכָה גְדֹלָה נֹפֶלֶת עָלָיו:
וַיֹּאמֶר לְאַבְרָם יָדֹעַ תֵּדַע כִּי גֵר יִהְיֶה זַרְעֲךָ בְּאֶרֶץ לֹא לָהֶם וַעֲבָדוּם וְעִנּוּ אֹתָם
אַרְבַּע מֵאוֹת שָׁנָה: וְגַם אֶת הַגּוֹי אֲשֶׁר יַעֲבֹדוּ דָּן אָנֹכִי וְאַחֲרֵי כֵן יֵצְאוּ בִּרְכֻשׁ גָּדוֹל:
וְאַתָּה תָּבוֹא אֶל אֲבֹתֶיךָ בְּשָׁלוֹם תִּקָּבֵר בְּשֵׂיבָה טוֹבָה: וְדוֹר רְבִיעִי יָשׁוּבוּ הֵנָּה
כִּי לֹא שָׁלֵם עֲוֹן הָאֱמֹרִי עַד הֵנָּה: וַיְהִי הַשֶּׁמֶשׁ בָּאָה וַעֲלָטָה הָיָה וְהִנֵּה תַנּוּר עָשָׁן
וְלַפִּיד אֵשׁ אֲשֶׁר עָבַר בֵּין הַגְּזָרִים הָאֵלֶּה: בַּיּוֹם הַהוּא כָּרַת ה' אֶת אַבְרָם בְּרִית
לֵאמֹר לְזַרְעֲךָ נָתַתִּי אֶת הָאָרֶץ הַזֹּאת מִנְּהַר מִצְרַיִם עַד הַנָּהָר הַגָּדֹל נְהַר פְּרָת:
אֶת הַקֵּינִי וְאֶת הַקְּנִזִּי וְאֵת הַקַּדְמֹנִי: וְאֶת הַחִתִּי וְאֶת הַפְּרִזִּי וְאֶת הָרְפָאִים: וְאֶת
הָאֱמֹרִי וְאֶת הַכְּנַעֲנִי וְאֶת הַגִּרְגָּשִׁי וְאֶת הַיְבוּסִי:

And when the sun was going down, a deep sleep fell upon Avram; and, lo, a fear of great darkness fell upon him. And He said to Avram, "Know for a certainty that your seed shall be a stranger in a land that is not theirs, and shall serve them; and they shall afflict them for four hundred years; And also that nation, whom they shall serve, will I judge; and afterward shall they come out with great wealth. And you shall go to your fathers in peace; you shall be buried in a good old age. But in the fourth generation they shall come here again; for the iniquity of the Amorites is not yet full." And it came to pass, that when the sun went down, and it was dark, behold a smoking furnace, and a burning torch that passed between those pieces. On that same day the Almighty made a covenant with Avram, saying, "To your seed have I given this land, from the river of Egypt to the great river, the river Euphrates; the Kenites, and the Kenazites, and the Kadmonites, and the Hittites, and the Perizzites, and the Refaim, and the Amorites, and the Canaanites, and the Girgashites, and the Yevusites." (Bereishit 15:12–21)

Avraham dreams; he learns that the path to the Land of Israel will not be a short, direct route. The path his descendants will take will be a long, circuitous one that will take them far away from their land. This will be a "descent for the sake of ascent," for when they return, the land will truly be theirs, earned through their labor as slaves. At that time, working the holy land as farmers will be perceived as the greatest blessing.

Yosef, like Avraham, sees the path to Israel. He understands that it will necessarily pass through Egypt. The dreams that he interprets teach him that it is there that he will rise to power, there that his family will become as numerous as the stars.[12] The wine steward's dream foretells his own redemption, and Par'oh's dreams show him the path to the future. Yosef sees God's master plan unfold in the dreams of others; his own dreams speak of the time of their return to the land – not as a nomadic band of brothers but as a nation in possession of their Promised Land. His brothers never ask Yosef to explain his dreams; would they have understood the message had he revealed it to them? Do the brothers share Yosef's ability to see beyond the present, to discern and understand hundreds of years of history in the visions he is granted? It seems not; they see their own personal rivalries and jealousies, and take no responsibility for the future. Yosef is, in more than one sense, a visionary: he sees beyond the present, and teaches others to do the same. For Yosef, all these dreams are of one piece; they are all connected to the glorious dream of Avraham. Yosef understands that his own personal life story is a vehicle for Jewish history. Ultimately, this is his message to his brothers:

בראשית מה:ה, ח

וְעַתָּה אַל תֵּעָצְבוּ וְאַל יִחַר בְּעֵינֵיכֶם כִּי מְכַרְתֶּם אֹתִי הֵנָּה כִּי לְמִחְיָה שְׁלָחַנִי אֱלֹקִים לִפְנֵיכֶם... וְעַתָּה לֹא אַתֶּם שְׁלַחְתֶּם אֹתִי הֵנָּה כִּי הָאֱלֹקִים וַיְשִׂימֵנִי לְאָב לְפַרְעֹה וּלְאָדוֹן לְכָל בֵּיתוֹ וּמֹשֵׁל בְּכָל אֶרֶץ מִצְרָיִם:

Now therefore be not grieved, nor angry with yourselves, that you sold me here; for God sent me before you to preserve life... So now it was not you who sent me here, but God; and he has made me a father to Par'oh, and lord of all his house, and a ruler throughout all the land of Egypt. (Bereishit 45:5, 8)

---

12. When Yosef collects and stores the wheat of Egypt, it is described as "numerous as the grains of sand" (Bereishit 41:49):

בראשית מא:מט

וַיִּצְבֹּר יוֹסֵף בָּר כְּחוֹל הַיָּם הַרְבֵּה מְאֹד עַד כִּי חָדַל לִסְפֹּר כִּי אֵין מִסְפָּר:

Yosef helps them to understand what he has already come to know: his brothers are not the reason he is in Egypt. Their own personal interests are a part of something much greater than themselves. Our lives – all of our lives – are part and parcel of the covenant between God and Avraham: God brought the Children of Israel to Egypt as the final step toward their return, as a great nation, to the Land of Israel. Only then, only there, will the descendants of Avraham, Yitzhak and Yaakov, the Children of Israel, one day live in peace, prosperity and freedom.

Of Spies and Thieves

After a series of strange negotiations and reversals of fortune, Yosef's brothers have procured food, and are finally united and on their way home to their father. The performance of what they had first thought to be a simple task – buying food – turned out to be impossibly difficult. It resulted in threats, arrests, incarceration and at one point, the promise of unimaginable horror and grief. But this is all behind them; they are free, their mission accomplished. Shimon is with them, Binyamin is with them, once again they are united; they are whole. Or are they? There is one more brother who is still unaccounted for, but he is apparently not on their minds.

And then, all too soon, the illusion of a peaceful trip home, with all their trials and tribulations behind them, is shattered – with a vengeance. Yosef sends off a messenger with the following instructions:

בראשית מד:א–ו

וַיְצַו אֶת אֲשֶׁר עַל בֵּיתוֹ לֵאמֹר מַלֵּא אֶת אַמְתְּחֹת הָאֲנָשִׁים אֹכֶל כַּאֲשֶׁר יוּכְלוּן שְׂאֵת וְשִׂים כֶּסֶף אִישׁ בְּפִי אַמְתַּחְתּוֹ: וְאֶת גְּבִיעִי גְּבִיעַ הַכֶּסֶף תָּשִׂים בְּפִי אַמְתַּחַת הַקָּטֹן וְאֵת כֶּסֶף שִׁבְרוֹ וַיַּעַשׂ כִּדְבַר יוֹסֵף אֲשֶׁר דִּבֵּר: הַבֹּקֶר אוֹר וְהָאֲנָשִׁים שֻׁלְּחוּ הֵמָּה וַחֲמֹרֵיהֶם: הֵם יָצְאוּ אֶת הָעִיר לֹא הִרְחִיקוּ וְיוֹסֵף אָמַר לַאֲשֶׁר עַל בֵּיתוֹ קוּם רְדֹף אַחֲרֵי הָאֲנָשִׁים וְהִשַּׂגְתָּם וְאָמַרְתָּ אֲלֵהֶם לָמָּה שִׁלַּמְתֶּם רָעָה תַּחַת טוֹבָה: הֲלוֹא זֶה אֲשֶׁר יִשְׁתֶּה אֲדֹנִי בּוֹ וְהוּא נַחֵשׁ יְנַחֵשׁ בּוֹ הֲרֵעֹתֶם אֲשֶׁר עֲשִׂיתֶם: וַיַּשִּׂגֵם וַיְדַבֵּר אֲלֵהֶם אֶת הַדְּבָרִים הָאֵלֶּה:

And he commanded the steward of his house, saying, "Fill the men's sacks with food, as much as they can carry, and put every man's money in his sack's mouth. And put my cup, the silver cup, in the sack's mouth of the youngest, and his grain money." And he did as Yosef had spoken. As soon as the morning was light, the men were sent away, they and their asses. And when they were gone out of the city, and not yet far off, Yosef said to his steward, "Arise, follow after the men; and when you do overtake them, say to them, 'Why have you repaid evil for good? Is this not the cup from which my lord drinks, and whereby indeed he divines? You have done evil in so doing." *And he overtook them, and he spoke these same words to them.* (Bereishit 44:1–6)

The brothers reply with self-righteous indignation: they are innocent and can prove it from their previous behavior.

בראשית מד:ז–ח

וַיֹּאמְרוּ אֵלָיו לָמָּה יְדַבֵּר אֲדֹנִי כַּדְּבָרִים הָאֵלֶּה חָלִילָה לַעֲבָדֶיךָ מֵעֲשׂוֹת כַּדָּבָר הַזֶּה: הֵן כֶּסֶף אֲשֶׁר מָצָאנוּ בְּפִי אַמְתְּחֹתֵינוּ הֱשִׁיבֹנוּ אֵלֶיךָ מֵאֶרֶץ כְּנָעַן וְאֵיךְ נִגְנֹב מִבֵּית אֲדֹנֶיךָ כֶּסֶף אוֹ זָהָב:

And they said to [the steward], "Why would my lord say such things? God forbid that your servants should do such a thing; Behold, the money that we found in our sacks' mouths we brought back to you from the land of Canaan; how then should we steal from your lord's house silver or gold?" (Bereishit 44:7–8)

Their strategy is strange. Why, in an attempt to prove their innocence, would they dredge up a previous charge of larceny against them? They run the risk of actually reinforcing the suspicions against them: in light of this latest episode, the previous charge could now be reopened and reinterpreted, and their guilt established. They note that they had returned the money that was found in their sacks when they returned home, yet this proves nothing: the fact that they returned the money may have been an act of pragmatism, enabling them to purchase more food despite having earlier left their account in arrears.

The brothers continue to defend themselves, but the next line of reasoning, while noble and dramatic, might easily bear dire consequences.

בראשית מד:ט

אֲשֶׁר יִמָּצֵא אִתּוֹ מֵעֲבָדֶיךָ וָמֵת וְגַם אֲנַחְנוּ נִהְיֶה לַאדֹנִי לַעֲבָדִים:

If any of your servants is found to have it, let him die, and we also will be my lord's slaves. (Bereishit 44:9)

Caution would have been a far wiser path; they knew that on a previous occasion things ended up in their bags without their knowledge. Quite remarkably, they make the most bizarre offer: death to the perpetrator, enslavement for the rest – extreme punishment for the guilty and the innocent alike. The counteroffer is equally strange: While the emissary appears to accept their offer, he actually downgrades the punishments. The death sentence is removed from the table, the innocent will go free, and only the guilty party will be enslaved:

בראשית מד:י–טז

וַיֹּאמֶר גַּם עַתָּה כְדִבְרֵיכֶם כֶּן הוּא אֲשֶׁר יִמָּצֵא אִתּוֹ יִהְיֶה לִּי עָבֶד וְאַתֶּם תִּהְיוּ נְקִיִּם: וַיְמַהֲרוּ וַיּוֹרִדוּ אִישׁ אֶת אַמְתַּחְתּוֹ אָרְצָה וַיִּפְתְּחוּ אִישׁ אַמְתַּחְתּוֹ: וַיְחַפֵּשׂ בַּגָּדוֹל הֵחֵל וּבַקָּטֹן כִּלָּה וַיִּמָּצֵא הַגָּבִיעַ בְּאַמְתַּחַת בִּנְיָמִן: וַיִּקְרְעוּ שִׂמְלֹתָם וַיַּעֲמֹס אִישׁ עַל חֲמֹרוֹ וַיָּשֻׁבוּ הָעִירָה: וַיָּבֹא יְהוּדָה וְאֶחָיו בֵּיתָה יוֹסֵף וְהוּא עוֹדֶנּוּ שָׁם וַיִּפְּלוּ לְפָנָיו אָרְצָה: וַיֹּאמֶר לָהֶם יוֹסֵף מָה הַמַּעֲשֶׂה הַזֶּה אֲשֶׁר עֲשִׂיתֶם הֲלוֹא יְדַעְתֶּם כִּי נַחֵשׁ יְנַחֵשׁ אִישׁ אֲשֶׁר כָּמֹנִי: וַיֹּאמֶר יְהוּדָה מַה נֹּאמַר לַאדֹנִי מַה נְּדַבֵּר וּמַה נִּצְטַדָּק הָאֱלֹקִים מָצָא אֶת עֲוֹן עֲבָדֶיךָ הִנֶּנּוּ עֲבָדִים לַאדֹנִי גַּם אֲנַחְנוּ גַּם אֲשֶׁר נִמְצָא הַגָּבִיעַ בְּיָדוֹ:

And he said, "Now also let it be according to your words; he with whom it is found shall be my servant and you shall be blameless." Then each of them quickly took down his sack to the ground, and each of them opened his sack. And he searched, and began at the oldest, and ended at the youngest; and the cup was found in Binyamin's sack. Then they tore their clothes, and each of them loaded his ass, and returned to the city. And Yehudah and his brothers came to Yosef's house, for he was yet there, and they fell before him on the ground. And Yosef said to them, "What deed is this that you have done? Do you not know that such a man as I can certainly divine?" And Yehudah said, "What shall we say to my lord? What shall we speak, or how shall we clear ourselves? God has found out the iniquity of your servants; behold, we are my lord's servants, both we, and he also with whom the cup is found." (Bereishit 44:10–16)

When the cup is found in Binyamin's sack, again the brothers increase the punishment. Rather than punishment for the "guilty party" alone, as the steward had suggested, the brothers now increase the punishment and suggest that all of them become slaves. They are rebuffed: Yosef gives them a lesson in morality, explaining that only the guilty should suffer. In words that echo his great-grandfather Avraham,[1] he says it is unjust for the innocent to be punished with the wicked.

---

1. See Bereishit 18:25.

בראשית מד:יז

וַיֹּאמֶר חָלִילָה לִּי מֵעֲשׂוֹת זֹאת הָאִישׁ אֲשֶׁר נִמְצָא הַגָּבִיעַ בְּיָדוֹ הוּא יִהְיֶה לִּי עָבֶד
וְאַתֶּם עֲלוּ לְשָׁלוֹם אֶל אֲבִיכֶם:

And he said, God forbid that I should do so; but the man in whose
hand the cup is found, he shall be my servant; and as for you, go up
in peace to your father. (Bereishit 44:17)

Yehudah then delivers a soliloquy, recounting history and finally offering
his own imprisonment in Binyamin's stead. It seems rather obvious that
Yehudah could have arrived at this result with much less fuss had he actually
wanted to: he could have taken the blame for stealing the goblet from the
moment it was discovered, thereby exonerating Binyamin. Yehudah was
surely a more likely culprit, having been present at both episodes, while
Binyamin was only present at the second meeting.

בראשית מד:יח, לב–לד

וַיִּגַּשׁ אֵלָיו יְהוּדָה וַיֹּאמֶר בִּי אֲדֹנִי יְדַבֶּר נָא עַבְדְּךָ דָבָר בְּאָזְנֵי אֲדֹנִי וְאַל יִחַר אַפְּךָ
בְּעַבְדֶּךָ כִּי כָמוֹךָ כְּפַרְעֹה:... כִּי עַבְדְּךָ עָרַב אֶת הַנַּעַר מֵעִם אָבִי לֵאמֹר אִם לֹא
אֲבִיאֶנּוּ אֵלֶיךָ וְחָטָאתִי לְאָבִי כָּל הַיָּמִים: וְעַתָּה יֵשֶׁב נָא עַבְדְּךָ תַּחַת הַנַּעַר עֶבֶד
לַאדֹנִי וְהַנַּעַר יַעַל עִם אֶחָיו: כִּי-אֵיךְ אֶעֱלֶה אֶל-אָבִי וְהַנַּעַר אֵינֶנּוּ אִתִּי פֶּן אֶרְאֶה
בָרָע אֲשֶׁר יִמְצָא אֶת-אָבִי:

Then Yehudah approached him, and said, "Please, your highness, I
beg you to let me, your servant, speak to you personally, and let not
your anger burn against your servant; for you are as Par'oh.... Now
therefore, I beg you, let your servant remain, instead of the lad, a
slave to my lord; and let the lad go up with his brothers. For how
shall I go up to my father if the lad is not with me? I cannot bear
to see the evil misery that my father would suffer." (Bereishit 44:18,
32–34)

The entire episode seems like a wonderful lesson in how *not* to negotiate.
We might better understand the brothers' conduct in this scene if we are
sensitive to their spiritual or religious needs: they are not negotiating, they
are seeking punishment. They are consumed with feelings of guilt for a
crime they committed many years ago – the sale of Yosef. It is this guilt
they express. Ironically, the one brother not involved in any way with that
earlier crime is Binyamin, which makes his entanglement in this episode

confusing. Be that as it may, the brothers have perpetrated a crime and are now seeking punishment. They are prepared to be enslaved.

Yehudah's words lead Yosef to reveal his identity, bringing the story to its bittersweet conclusion. The family is reunited, but in Egypt, where slavery will soon begin. Moreover, their guilt in the sale of Yosef hovers over the brothers for the rest of their days.

This interaction is not the first strange, nearly incomprehensible dialogue between Yosef and his brothers. When they meet after many years of separation, Yosef recognizes them immediately, but they see only an aristocratic Egyptian. The conversation is almost cryptic:

בראשית מב:ז–יב

וַיַּרְא יוֹסֵף אֶת אֶחָיו וַיַּכִּרֵם וַיִּתְנַכֵּר אֲלֵיהֶם וַיְדַבֵּר אִתָּם קָשׁוֹת וַיֹּאמֶר אֲלֵהֶם מֵאַיִן בָּאתֶם וַיֹּאמְרוּ מֵאֶרֶץ כְּנַעַן לִשְׁבָּר אֹכֶל: וַיַּכֵּר יוֹסֵף אֶת אֶחָיו וְהֵם לֹא הִכִּרֻהוּ: וַיִּזְכֹּר יוֹסֵף אֵת הַחֲלֹמוֹת אֲשֶׁר חָלַם לָהֶם וַיֹּאמֶר אֲלֵהֶם מְרַגְּלִים אַתֶּם לִרְאוֹת אֶת עֶרְוַת הָאָרֶץ בָּאתֶם: וַיֹּאמְרוּ אֵלָיו לֹא אֲדֹנִי וַעֲבָדֶיךָ בָּאוּ לִשְׁבָּר אֹכֶל: כֻּלָּנוּ בְּנֵי אִישׁ אֶחָד נָחְנוּ כֵּנִים אֲנַחְנוּ לֹא הָיוּ עֲבָדֶיךָ מְרַגְּלִים: וַיֹּאמֶר אֲלֵהֶם לֹא כִּי עֶרְוַת הָאָרֶץ בָּאתֶם לִרְאוֹת:

And Yosef saw his brothers, and he recognized them, but made himself strange to them, and spoke roughly to them; and he said to them, "From where do you come?" They said, "From the land of Canaan to buy food." And Yosef knew his brothers, but they did not know him. And Yosef remembered the dreams that he dreamed for [or, concerning] them, and said to them, "You are spies; you have come to see the nakedness of the land." And they said to him, "No, my lord, your servants came to buy food. We are all one man's sons; we are honest men, your servants are no spies." And he said to them, "No, you have come to see the nakedness of the land." (Bereishit 42:7–12)

We gather that Yosef was less than overjoyed to see the people who had so mistreated him. He feigns ignorance of their identity and, remembering his dreams, accuses them of being spies. Of course, they deny the charge, yet he repeats it; he insists that the brothers are spies. They interject with what seems like irrelevant information and explain that they are all brothers.

בראשית מב:יג–יד

וַיֹּאמְרוּ שְׁנֵים עָשָׂר עֲבָדֶיךָ אַחִים אֲנַחְנוּ בְּנֵי אִישׁ אֶחָד בְּאֶרֶץ כְּנָעַן וְהִנֵּה הַקָּטֹן אֶת אָבִינוּ הַיּוֹם וְהָאֶחָד אֵינֶנּוּ: וַיֹּאמֶר אֲלֵהֶם יוֹסֵף הוּא אֲשֶׁר דִּבַּרְתִּי אֲלֵכֶם לֵאמֹר מְרַגְּלִים אַתֶּם:

And they said, "Your servants are twelve brothers, the sons of one man in the land of Canaan; and, behold, the youngest is this day with our father, and one is absent." And Yosef said to them, "That is [or, more precisely, he is] [exactly] what I spoke to you about, saying, 'You are spies.'" (Bereishit 42:13–14)

The exchange is unclear: Yosef counters that this is exactly what he meant. What would constitute an appropriate response to charges of this nature? If we succeed in deciphering this passage, we may gain insight into Yosef's thoughts, his motivation, his plan.

The easiest explanation is that in fact none of the dialogue makes sense: Yosef has decided to take revenge, and their attempts to defend or explain themselves are futile. Whatever they would say would be useless in the face of Yosef's power to entrap them. As readers, then, we should not look for deeper meaning in the dialogue.

Yet everything we know from the preceding narrative, everything we have learned about Yosef's personality, indicates that he is neither impetuous nor whimsical. He is a visionary; he considers long-term consequences and implications. When he resists the seductive advances of his master's wife, conquering momentary passion, he displays self-restraint that we might expect to see again in this new scenario. And when he meets Par'oh, he does not merely explain the monarch's dreams, he proceeds to formulate a fourteen-year economic plan, which will rescue the Egyptian economy from drought and recession.

Here, too, when he confronts his brothers, Yosef has a plan. Like a master chess player, he has already thought through all of his moves, their countermoves and his endgame.[2]

---

2. It is unclear whether Yosef succeeded in playing his hand out to the end; when Yosef reveals himself, the text attests that "Yosef could not contain himself any longer." This seems to indicate that he did, in fact, wish to "contain himself" at least a little bit longer. See Bereishit 45:1, and "Plan Interrupted," below.

Accusing the brothers of espionage may have been a preventive strike: Yosef is aware that his rags-to-riches story is well known in Egypt, and he has thought of the only way of preventing his brothers from hearing the details of his miraculous ascent to power. Once he has accused them of being spies, Yosef effectively prevents his brothers from asking the Egyptians, "Who is this *Tzafnat Paneiah*?[3] Where did he come from?" Once they have been charged with spying, such inquiries would effectively prove them guilty, resulting in imprisonment or death. Outflanked, the brothers must now proceed in silence; they cannot ask probing questions about their inquisitioner.

There may be another reason Yosef chooses this particular charge with which to accuse the brothers, and the answer is almost too obvious. When he accuses them of being spies, he inwardly wants them to admit that they are in fact looking for something – or more precisely, for someone: their brother Yosef. Perhaps what Yosef wants more than anything is to hear these words from his brothers: they are searching for him, just as, so many years earlier, when Yosef met an anonymous man in the field who asked him what he was looking for, Yosef responded, "I seek my brothers." The words echo and haunt us. Despite all the enmity, jealousy and hatred, ultimately Yosef is only seeking out his brothers. He hopes that his brothers will ask the anonymous, unfamiliar man who stands before them, "Have you seen our brother?"

How would the story have ended if the brothers had confided in *Tzafnat Panei'ah*: "Yes, long ago we had a twelfth brother, who was last seen when he was taken down to Egypt as a slave. Our elderly father thinks that he is dead. We were young and impetuous, and didn't consider the long-term implications of our actions. We didn't realize that we would break our father's heart. We didn't weigh up the moral and ethical considerations. Now we are indeed searching – not spying. We are looking for something precious, someone whose value we failed to appreciate when he was in our midst. It is our brother we seek."

Had the brothers admitted to being "spies," would the charade have continued? It seems that Yosef leads them precisely to this point:

---

3. Literally, "deciferer of hidden things" – the name Yosef was given by Par'oh upon his successful interpretation of Par'oh's dreams.

בראשית מב:יד

...וְהָאֶחָד אֵינֶנּוּ: וַיֹּאמֶר אֲלֵהֶם יוֹסֵף הוּא אֲשֶׁר דִּבַּרְתִּי אֲלֵכֶם לֵאמֹר מְרַגְּלִים אַתֶּם:

"...and one is absent." And Yosef said to them, "That is [or, more precisely, he is] [exactly] what I spoke to you about, saying, 'You are spies.'" (Bereishit 42:14)

The accusation of being spies is specifically in regard to the one missing brother! He is telling them, perhaps inwardly pleading with them, to admit that they are looking for their lost brother. We can imagine Yosef, his heart racing, hoping, praying, that his brothers have come to Egypt to look for him. But they shatter that sweet illusion and deny any spying. Therefore, Yosef sets an alternative plan in motion: He seeks to jar their memories. He will force them to remember what they have buried away deep in their subconscious. He will remind them that there was once a twelfth brother, that his name was Yosef – and that Yosef is still looking for *his* brothers.

So, the alternative plan begins: they are all arrested and thrown into prison. Yosef forces them to relive his own experience, in an attempt to jolt them into recognition. Interestingly, various words are used to describe both the imprisonment of Yosef and now the brothers. All of these are connected to the "original sin" of the sale of Yosef, who is cast into a pit by his brothers before he is sold. When Yosef tells his life story to a fellow prisoner, he describes his imprisonment "in the pit," referring either to the Egyptian prison in which they are languishing, or perhaps the pit into which his brothers cast him – or both (Bereishit 40:15). When he is released from prison and brought before Par'oh, the narrative describes his release "from the pit" (Bereishit 41:14). Linguistically, thematically, and apparently emotionally, Yosef's prison experience is linked with his initial indignity – when he was thrown into the pit by his brothers. The brothers' prison experience, though engineered by Yosef to hark back to his own trauma, is described in different terms. They are placed under guard, but not in the pit.

A few days in prison brings the brothers to a very raw emotional place. Their guilt rises from the subconscious to the forefront of their consciousness, and the conversation finally turns to Yosef:

בראשית מב:כא

וַיֹּאמְרוּ אִישׁ אֶל אָחִיו אֲבָל אֲשֵׁמִים אֲנַחְנוּ עַל אָחִינוּ אֲשֶׁר רָאִינוּ צָרַת נַפְשׁוֹ
בְּהִתְחַנְנוֹ אֵלֵינוּ וְלֹא שָׁמָעְנוּ עַל כֵּן בָּאָה אֵלֵינוּ הַצָּרָה הַזֹּאת: וַיַּעַן רְאוּבֵן אֹתָם לֵאמֹר
הֲלוֹא אָמַרְתִּי אֲלֵיכֶם לֵאמֹר אַל תֶּחֶטְאוּ בַיֶּלֶד וְלֹא שְׁמַעְתֶּם וְגַם דָּמוֹ הִנֵּה נִדְרָשׁ:

*And they said one to another, "We are truly guilty concerning our
brother, in that we saw the anguish of his soul when he besought us,
and we would not hear; therefore this calamity has come upon us."
And Reuven answered them, saying, "Did I not speak to you, saying,
'Do not sin against the child' and you would not hear? Therefore,
behold, also his blood is required." (Bereishit 42:21)*

They remember, and they acknowledge that punishment is due. They
accept their guilt and believe they should be punished. Yet they take no
action to rectify the situation. Once they are released, they do not make any
inquiries regarding Yosef's fate or whereabouts. They do not admit their
wrongdoing to Yaakov.

When all but Shimon are released and their money is returned to their bags,
they have no inkling that an additional encounter is being engineered.

Eventually, the brothers return to Egypt. The money that they discover
in their sacks is returned, and more provisions are purchased. A joyous
reunion takes place with their brother who has been absent because he
was thrown into prison – Shimon. Yosef watches the brothers rejoice in
their regained unity, as they celebrate their family being "whole" again. Of
course, there is still one brother missing, one brother unaccounted for, one
brother who does not even seem to be missed: Yosef.

They are invited to eat. The last time Yosef saw, or to be more precise, heard
his brothers eating was when he was in the pit: they had callously dined
while Yosef, stripped of his coat, cried out to them from the pit. Now they
eat together, all twelve brothers. Yosef yearns for their companionship, yet
they acknowledge neither his absence – nor his presence. Can they still
hear his cries? Does it haunt them? Late at night when they try to sleep do
they still hear Yosef screaming? Does the image of his being carried away
still fill their minds – or is Yosef forgotten?

As far as the brothers are concerned, they are dining with Egyptian royalty,
and apparently they get carried away, and allow themselves to eat and drink,

and they become inebriated.[4] They have much to celebrate: Their family is whole once again. They are about to go home. They looked forward to putting this entire episode behind them, forgetting all the unpleasantness – just as they forgot Yosef.

Their bags are packed and their money is returned, and Yosef's goblet is surreptitiously placed in Binyamin's bag. Yosef's master plan requires that one more episode be relived.

They are on their way, when they are accosted on the road. Their bags are searched, and they are made to feel vulnerable and humiliated. This happened once before, years earlier, when they were young, when they were still one family:

בראשית לא:כב–כג, לג–לד

וַיֻּגַּד לְלָבָן בַּיּוֹם הַשְּׁלִישִׁי כִּי בָרַח יַעֲקֹב: וַיִּקַּח אֶת אֶחָיו עִמּוֹ וַיִּרְדֹּף אַחֲרָיו דֶּרֶךְ שִׁבְעַת יָמִים וַיַּדְבֵּק אֹתוֹ בְּהַר הַגִּלְעָד:... וַיָּבֹא לָבָן בְּאֹהֶל יַעֲקֹב וּבְאֹהֶל לֵאָה וּבְאֹהֶל שְׁתֵּי הָאֲמָהֹת וְלֹא מָצָא וַיֵּצֵא מֵאֹהֶל לֵאָה וַיָּבֹא בְּאֹהֶל רָחֵל: וְרָחֵל לָקְחָה אֶת הַתְּרָפִים וַתְּשִׂמֵם בְּכַר הַגָּמָל וַתֵּשֶׁב עֲלֵיהֶם וַיְמַשֵּׁשׁ לָבָן אֶת כָּל הָאֹהֶל וְלֹא מָצָא:

And it was told to Lavan on the third day that Yaakov had fled. And he took his brothers with him and pursued him on a seven days' journey, and they overtook him at Mount Gil'ad.... And Lavan went into Yaakov's tent, and into Leah's tent, and into the two maidservants' tents; but he did not find them. Then he went out from Leah's tent, and entered into Rahel's tent. Now Rahel had taken the terafim, *and put them in the camel's saddle, and sat upon them. And Lavan searched the entire tent, but did not find them. (Bereishit 31:22–23, 33–34)*

When Lavan catches up with Yaakov, he has a long litany of complaints, including the accusation that Yaakov has stolen his gods. Accused of a crime of which he knows of he is innocent, Yaakov makes an unfortunate pronouncement: death to the culprit!

בראשית לא:לב

עִם אֲשֶׁר תִּמְצָא אֶת אֱלֹהֶיךָ לֹא יִחְיֶה נֶגֶד אַחֵינוּ הַכֶּר לְךָ מָה עִמָּדִי וְקַח לָךְ וְלֹא יָדַע יַעֲקֹב כִּי רָחֵל גְּנָבָתַם:

---

4. Bereishit 43:34: "...And they drank, and were merry with him."

"With whom you will find your gods, let him not live. Before our brothers, point out what I have of yours, and take it with you." For Yaakov did not know that Rahel had stolen them. (Bereishit 31:32)

Years later, when the brothers recommend a death sentence for the culprit, they are mimicking their father's response to a similar situation: in Yaakov's case, he stood accused of the theft of Lavan's idols,[5] and the cup that they stand accused of stealing is reported to be used for "divination."[6] The brothers are not negotiating. They are under extreme pressure, and they revert back to a time when they were frightened and vulnerable. They recall their father's reaction, and respond likewise.

Later, when Yehudah speaks up, he, too, imitates his father's response to that earlier scene:

בראשית לא:לו

וַיִּחַר לְיַעֲקֹב וַיָּרֶב בְּלָבָן וַיַּעַן יַעֲקֹב וַיֹּאמֶר לְלָבָן מַה פִּשְׁעִי מַה חַטָּאתִי כִּי דָלַקְתָּ אַחֲרָי:

And Yaakov was angry, and argued with Lavan; and Yaakov answered and said to Lavan, "What is my trespass? What is my sin, that you have so hotly pursued me?" (Bereishit 31:36)

Yosef is trying to jar their memories, and he takes them back to the most traumatic episode of their childhood: They are hastily removed from their

---

5. According to the Midrash Tanhuma (Parashat Vayeitzei [Warsaw edition], paragraph 12), Rahel takes the *terafim* to prevent Lavan from divining the location of her family as they escape.

   מדרש תנחומא (ורשא), פרשת ויצא פסקה יב
   ויבא אלקים אל לבן הארמי בחלום הלילה: זה אחד משני מקומות שטמא הטהור כבודו בשביל הצדיקים, כאן, ובמקום אחר ויבא אלהים אל אבימלך בחלום הלילה (בראשית כ) בשביל שרה, התחיל לבן אומר ליעקב ועתה הלך הלכת וגו' למה גנבת את אלהי, השיבו עם אשר תמצא את אלהיך לא יחיה, באותה שעה נגזר על רחל מיתה, וּמִשֵׁשׁ לבן את כל האהל ולא מצא, ורחל לקחה את התרפים, **למה גנבה אותם כדי שלא יהו אומרים ללבן שיעקב בורח עם נשיו ובניו וצאנו, וכי התרפים מדברים הם, כן דכתיב (זכריה י) כי התרפים דברו און.**

6. See Bereishit 44:5: "Is not this it in which my lord drinks, and whereby indeed he divines?"

   בראשית מד:ה
   הֲלוֹא זֶה אֲשֶׁר יִשְׁתֶּה אֲדֹנִי בּוֹ וְהוּא נַחֵשׁ יְנַחֵשׁ בּוֹ הֲרֵעֹתֶם אֲשֶׁר עֲשִׂיתֶם:

grandfather's home, the only home they know. They will soon face the threat of Esav and his henchman. Between these two pressure points, they are chased down on the road, stopped and searched. And they respond exactly as their father did: "Let the thief be put to death!"

Yosef throws it back in their faces. His response seems to shout: "If you identify with your father so completely, so automatically, that you mimic his words, why do you treat him as you do? Why have you let him mourn all these years? If you want to be like your father, why don't you reach out to your estranged brother as he reached out to Esav? Why, in your minds, is Yosef dead and forgotten?"

Time after time, bit by bit, in one subtle act after another, Yosef works on their memory. He replicates harsh experiences in order to achieve catharsis. Like a therapist working with a patient, Yosef forces them to revisit some of the most horrific episodes of their lives, with one goal: to remind them, to wake them up. "Haven't you forgotten something? Aren't you looking for someone? Aren't you really spies?"

Only when Yehudah presses on and finally speaks of his father's pain and loneliness does Yosef abandon his disguise.

בראשית מד:כז-לד

וַיֹּאמֶר עַבְדְּךָ אָבִי אֵלֵינוּ אַתֶּם יְדַעְתֶּם כִּי שְׁנַיִם יָלְדָה לִּי אִשְׁתִּי: וַיֵּצֵא הָאֶחָד מֵאִתִּי וָאֹמַר אַךְ טָרֹף טֹרָף וְלֹא רְאִיתִיו עַד הֵנָּה: וּלְקַחְתֶּם גַּם אֶת זֶה מֵעִם פָּנַי וְקָרָהוּ אָסוֹן וְהוֹרַדְתֶּם אֶת שֵׂיבָתִי בְּרָעָה שְׁאֹלָה: וְעַתָּה כְּבֹאִי אֶל עַבְדְּךָ אָבִי וְהַנַּעַר אֵינֶנּוּ אִתָּנוּ וְנַפְשׁוֹ קְשׁוּרָה בְנַפְשׁוֹ: וְהָיָה כִּרְאוֹתוֹ כִּי אֵין הַנַּעַר וָמֵת וְהוֹרִידוּ עֲבָדֶיךָ אֶת שֵׂיבַת עַבְדְּךָ אָבִינוּ בְּיָגוֹן שְׁאֹלָה: כִּי עַבְדְּךָ עָרַב אֶת הַנַּעַר מֵעִם אָבִי לֵאמֹר אִם לֹא אֲבִיאֶנּוּ אֵלֶיךָ וְחָטָאתִי לְאָבִי כָּל הַיָּמִים: וְעַתָּה יֵשֶׁב נָא עַבְדְּךָ תַּחַת הַנַּעַר עֶבֶד לַאדֹנִי וְהַנַּעַר יַעַל עִם אֶחָיו: כִּי אֵיךְ אֶעֱלֶה אֶל אָבִי וְהַנַּעַר אֵינֶנּוּ אִתִּי פֶּן אֶרְאֶה בָרָע אֲשֶׁר יִמְצָא אֶת אָבִי:

And your servant my father said to us, "You know that my wife bore me two sons. And the one went out from me, and I said, 'Surely he is torn in pieces,' and I have not seen him since. And if you take this [son] from me as well, and harm befalls him, you shall bring down my gray hairs with sorrow to my grave." Now therefore when I come to your servant my father and the lad is not with us – being that his life is bound up in the lad's life, it shall come to pass, when he sees that the lad is not with us, that he will die, and your servants shall bring down the gray hairs of your servant our father with sorrow to his grave. For I, your servant, am collateral for the lad to my father, saying, "If I do not bring him back to you, then I shall bear the blame to my father forever." Now therefore, I beg you, let your servant remain instead of the lad a slave to my lord, and let the lad go up with his brothers. For how shall I go up to my father and the lad be not with me, lest perhaps I see the evil that shall come on my father? (Bereishit 44:27–34)

His father's pain was never Yosef's desire; quite the opposite. It was his father's misery that tormented him. Yosef relents at this juncture, for Yehudah has shown heroism. It would have been easy for Yehudah to reason that Rahel and her sons were all tainted by the same evil: Rahel had stolen the *terafim* years ago, Yosef her son was no better, and now the younger son Binyamin has proved his own mettle – by stealing like his mother and being selfish and self-centered like his brother. In fact, this was the direction in which Yosef was leading him, and would have been the easy way for Yehudah to resolve his own dilemma. But Yehudah displays leadership and responsibility. He is willing to be enslaved so Binyamin can go free. Yehudah is unwilling to cause or endure his father's pain.

To Yehudah's heart-wrenching plea – Yosef has the ultimate response.

בראשית מה:ג

וַיֹּאמֶר יוֹסֵף אֶל אֶחָיו אֲנִי יוֹסֵף הַעוֹד אָבִי חָי וְלֹא יָכְלוּ אֶחָיו לַעֲנוֹת אֹתוֹ כִּי נִבְהֲלוּ מִפָּנָיו:

And Yosef said to his brothers, "I am Yosef! Does my father still live?" And his brothers could not answer him; for they were shocked by him. (Bereishit 45:3)

Yehudah explains that Yaakov's life is intertwined with Binyamin's; he tells this "stranger" that Yaakov had a wife whom he loved and that if this last remaining son were to be wrested from him Yaakov will die. Yosef asks: "*I am Yosef – is my father still alive?* Are you really so concerned about Yaakov's well-being that you claim he will die if his beloved son is taken from him?" He challenges and chastises: "I am Yosef. Could my father be alive? Can he have survived what you have already done, what you did to me?"[7]

To this there is no answer. To this there can be no answer. All of their neat explanations are gone. No justifications will work. The stark truth of Yosef's existence stares them down, shocks them into silence. They have no words, only guilt. The rabbis compared this experience of silence to the Day of Judgment, when God, the All-Knowing, conducts a final reckoning of man's deeds. No finesse, no legalese, no justifications: on that day, only the humiliation of facing the truth remains.[8]

Apparently, what Yosef seeks is not revenge; that could have been easily achieved, given his position of power. Instead, he takes his brothers on a tour – an emotional guilt trip. He does not seek their humiliation; that was never his objective. He wants to remind them of the past, to remind them that there is someone they have forgotten.

בראשית לז:טז
וַיֹּאמֶר אֶת אַחַי אָנֹכִי מְבַקֵּשׁ...

And he said, "It is my brothers whom I seek..." (Bereishit 37:16)

He wants his brothers to be looking for him; all he ever wanted was his brothers.

---

7. See Seforno, Bereishit 45:3.

ספורנו, בראשית מה:ג
העוד אבי חי: אי אפשר שלא מת מדאגתו עלי.

8. Midrash Tanhuma, Parashat Vayigash (Warsaw edition), paragraph 5. Also see *Kli Yakar*, and Rabbeinu Bahya on this verse.

מדרש תנחומא (ורשא), פרשת ויגש פסקה ה
אמר להן יוסף לא כך אמרתם שאחיו של זה מת אני קניתיו אקראנו ויבא אצלכם, התחיל קורא יוסף בן יעקב בא אצלי יוסף ב"י בא אצלי ודבר עם אחיך שמכרוך והיו נושאין עיניהם בארבע פינות הבית א"ל יוסף למה אתם מסתכלין לכאן ולכאן אני יוסף אחיכם, מיד פרחה נשמתן ולא יכלו לענו' אותו אר"י ווי לנו מיו' הדין ווי לנו מיום תוכחה ומה יוסף כשאמר לאחיו אני יוסף פרחה נשמתן כשעומד הקב"ה לדין דכתיב ביה (מלאכי ג) ומי מכלכל את יום בואו ומי העומד בהראותו שכתוב בו כי לא יראני האדם וחי (שמות לג) עאכ"ו.

Parashat Vayigash

Plan Interrupted

Ever since the sale of Yosef, the tension has been building. As the preceding chapters detail Yosef's astounding, meteoric transformation from imprisoned slave to regal viceroy, through the scene in which Yosef and his brothers meet, we know there will have to be a resolution. The "game" of Yosef's hiding will come to an end and he will reveal his identity. What we are less sure of is the atmosphere that will prevail: as we inch toward the moment of resolution, the tension is heightened as we wonder whether Yosef will reveal himself in vengeance, in anger, in violence – or if there will finally be reconciliation. As we reach the crescendo, at the moment the narrative reaches its climax, the verses seem to tell us that the end of the story is somewhat premature.

בראשית מה:א

וְלֹא יָכֹל יוֹסֵף לְהִתְאַפֵּק לְכֹל הַנִּצָּבִים עָלָיו וַיִּקְרָא הוֹצִיאוּ כָל אִישׁ מֵעָלָי וְלֹא עָמַד אִישׁ אִתּוֹ בְּהִתְוַדַּע יוֹסֵף אֶל אֶחָיו:

Then Yosef could not contain himself before all those who stood by him and he cried, "Cause every man to go out from me." And there stood no man with him while Yosef made himself known to his brothers. (Bereishit 45:1)

Yosef, we are told, could contain himself no longer. By implication, we understand that in fact Yosef wanted to continue the charade. He was not completely ready to reveal his identity to his brothers at this point, but was "forced" to do so. What caused Yosef to show himself at this juncture, and what was it that made him want to wait? What did Yosef hope to accomplish by his actions, and what was it that he felt still remained unaccomplished?

Can we say that perhaps Yosef had no master plan, that he was caught up in the charade and did not know how or when to end it? This seems highly uncharacteristic: Yosef is nothing if not a planner. After hearing no more than two of Par'oh's dreams, Yosef created a business plan that would dictate the course of the Egyptian economy for the better part of the next two decades. It seems equally clear that in his dealings with his brothers, Yosef had a very carefully constructed plan, and his behavior was very calculated. All of his words and actions, from the moment his brothers appeared in Egypt, seem to be tactics in the greater strategy. Every step leading up to this moment seems as carefully considered as the moves of a chess grandmaster. While the brothers were unaware that there was a match being played, Yosef seems to have plotted his course many steps in advance. The brothers plod along, oblivious to the fact that they are being watched and tested. Even when Yosef was no longer able to continue his well-conceived and well-executed plan, the reader does not know the goal of his plan, nor what brought Yosef to abruptly abandon it. What caused Yosef to reveal himself to his brothers when he did? What caused Yosef to break down? And what is it that Yosef hoped to accomplish?

This is not the first time Yosef breaks down. Along the way Yosef pauses to regain his composure a number of times. The first such instance occurs when the brothers connect their present dilemma with their guilt in selling Yosef; their admission brings tears to Yosef's eyes:

בראשית מב:כא–כד

וַיֹּאמְרוּ אִישׁ אֶל אָחִיו אֲבָל אֲשֵׁמִים אֲנַחְנוּ עַל אָחִינוּ אֲשֶׁר רָאִינוּ צָרַת נַפְשׁוֹ
בְּהִתְחַנְנוֹ אֵלֵינוּ וְלֹא שָׁמָעְנוּ. עַל כֵּן בָּאָה אֵלֵינוּ הַצָּרָה הַזֹּאת: וַיַּעַן רְאוּבֵן אֹתָם
לֵאמֹר הֲלוֹא אָמַרְתִּי אֲלֵיכֶם לֵאמֹר אַל תֶּחֶטְאוּ בַיֶּלֶד וְלֹא שְׁמַעְתֶּם וְגַם דָּמוֹ הִנֵּה
נִדְרָשׁ: וְהֵם לֹא יָדְעוּ כִּי שֹׁמֵעַ יוֹסֵף כִּי הַמֵּלִיץ בֵּינֹתָם: וַיִּסֹּב מֵעֲלֵיהֶם וַיֵּבְךְּ וַיָּשָׁב
אֲלֵהֶם וַיְדַבֵּר אֲלֵהֶם וַיִּקַּח מֵאִתָּם אֶת שִׁמְעוֹן וַיֶּאֱסֹר אֹתוֹ לְעֵינֵיהֶם:

And they said one to another, "We are truly guilty concerning our brother, in that we saw the anguish of his soul when he besought us, and we would not hear; therefore this calamity has befallen us." And Reuven answered them, saying, "Did I not speak to you, saying, 'Do not sin against the child' and you would not hear? Therefore, behold, also his blood is required." And they did not know that Yosef understood them; for he spoke to them through an interpreter. And he turned himself away from them and wept; and returned to them again and talked with them, and took Shimon from them and bound him before their eyes. (Bereishit 42:21–24)

At a later juncture, Yosef again needs to regain composure:

בראשית מג:ל–לא

וַיְמַהֵר יוֹסֵף כִּי נִכְמְרוּ רַחֲמָיו אֶל אָחִיו וַיְבַקֵּשׁ לִבְכּוֹת וַיָּבֹא הַחַדְרָה וַיֵּבְךְּ שָׁמָּה:
וַיִּרְחַץ פָּנָיו וַיֵּצֵא וַיִּתְאַפַּק וַיֹּאמֶר שִׂימוּ לָחֶם:

*And Yosef made haste; for he was overcome with mercy for his brother,
and he wanted to weep; and he entered into his chamber, and wept
there. And he washed his face, and went out, and controlled himself,
and said, "Set out bread." (Bereishit 43:30–31)*

On more than one occasion, Yosef proceeds despite feelings of compassion,
despite almost being overwhelmed by his brothers' vulnerability. We
should note that when Yosef eventually breaks down and reveals his
identity, the verses supply some seemingly extraneous information: the
text does not simply state that Yosef could not control or contain himself,
but that he could not contain himself "before all those who stood by him."
What does this additional clause mean? To whom does it refer, and what
did these "significant others" have to do with Yosef's discomfort? Perhaps,
as Rashi suggests, Yosef could no longer bear his brothers' humiliation,
and he ordered all of the attending members of court to leave the room.[1]
Perhaps, as the Ramban suggests, Yosef's motives were less compassionate:
he wanted to keep the story of their treachery quiet, either out of concern
for their reputation – or for fear of how their shared history might reflect
upon him.[2] Yet the very next verse seems to contradict these suggestions,
for in what seems to be an outburst of emotion Yosef cries out, and his
cries are heard by all of Egypt.

בראשית מה:ב

וַיִּתֵּן אֶת קֹלוֹ בִּבְכִי וַיִּשְׁמְעוּ מִצְרַיִם וַיִּשְׁמַע בֵּית פַּרְעֹה:

---

1. Rashi, Bereishit 45:1.

רש"י, בראשית מה:א

ולא יכול יוסף להתאפק לכל הנצבים: לא היה יכול לסבול שיהיו מצרים נצבים עליו ושומעין שאחיו
מתביישין בהודעו להם.

2. Ramban, Bereishit 45:1.

רמב"ן, בראשית מה:א

וטעם בהוצאה, שהוציאם משם כדי שלא ישמעו בהזכירו להם המכירה, כי תהיה להם (לחרפה) וגם אליו
למכשול, שיאמרו עבדי פרעה ומצרים עליהם, אלו אנשי בוגדות, לא יגורו בארצנו ולא ידרכו בארמנותינו,
בגדו באחיהם, גם באביהם בגדו, מה יעשו במלך ובעמו, וגם ביוסף לא יאמינו עוד.

And he wept aloud; and the Egyptians heard, and the house of Par'oh heard. (Bereishit 45:2)

The Ramban's suggestion thus seems insufficient, and we are forced to look further.

Rabbi Meir Simha of Dvinsk offers an explanation of Yosef's plan that is both simple and chilling: Yosef had one only thing in mind; he pursued one goal, and that is why he overcame his compassion time after time. His ultimate goal was to bring about the fruition of the dreams of which he spoke to his brothers and his father. This would require that his father be brought before him to pay obeisance to the viceroy of Egypt.[3] This approach paints Yosef as remarkably self-serving, claiming that Yosef was motivated by a single-minded, self-centered desire to bring about the fulfillment of his own dreams.

This approach is not alone in ascribing Yosef's behavior to his dreams: when the brothers admit their guilt, Yosef hides his tears, regains his composure, and throws Shimon into prison. The Ramban reasons that had Yosef been hoping to extract from his brothers an admission of guilt, this should have been the time to end the charade: the brothers' veneer of self-righteousness had been shattered. Clearly, Yosef was seeking something more. The Ramban, too, explains that Yosef's goal was to make the dreams come true:[4] At the point Shimon is seized and incarcerated, Yosef's first dream had been realized nearly completely. Ten of his eleven brothers had bowed to him, and only Binyamin was missing. Yosef sets out to bring

---

3. *Meshekh Hokhmah*, Bereishit 45:1.

משך חכמה, בראשית מה:א

ולא יכול יוסף להתאפק לכל הנצבים: ר"ל כי רצה להתאפק ולהביא את יעקב לקיים לקיים השמש והירח כו' משתחווים לי, ולא היה לו לרחם עליהם כאשר לא שמעו בהתחננו אליהם. אך שלא היה נאות לפני האנשים הנצבים שלא ידעו כל המאורע והיה נראה כאכזר וכלב בליעל בלתי חונן ולא היה יכול להתאפק בסיבת כל הנצבים עליו.

4. Ramban, Bereishit 42:9.

רמב"ן, בראשית מב:ט

ויזכר יוסף את החלומות אשר חלם להם עליהם: וידע שנתקיימו שהרי השתחוו לו, לשון רש"י ולפי דעתי שהדבר בהפך, כי יאמר הכתוב כי בראות יוסף את אחיו משתחוים לו זכר כל החלומות אשר חלם להם וידע שלא נתקיים אחד מהם בפעם הזאת, כי ידע בפתרונם כי כל אחיו ישתחוו לו בתחילה מן החלום הראשון, והנה אנחנו מאלמים אלומים, כי "אנחנו" ירמוז לכל אחיו אחד עשר, ופעם שנית ישתחוו לו השמש והירח ואחד עשר כוכבים מן החלום השני, וכיון שלא ראה בנימן עמהם חשב זאת התחבולה שיעליל עליהם כדי שיביאו גם בנימין אחיו אליו לקיים החלום הראשון תחילה.

Binyamin to Egypt in order to complete his first dream. After Binyamin
is brought before him, Yosef sets out to fulfill the second dream, in which
Yaakov plays a part. The master plan is tailored to the fulfillment of these
dreams, and this is what lies at the bottom of Yosef's "failure" to contact his
father throughout the years that had elapsed: had the brothers or Yaakov
known that he was alive, had they known the true identity of the viceroy
of Egypt before whom they stood, they would not have bowed to him, and
Yosef's dreams would not have come true.[5]

Other commentaries are not comfortable with this approach and take issue
with the Ramban.[6] Still others examine the narrative from the perspective
of the brothers: How did they read the situation? What did they understand,
what motivation did they ascribe to the prince of Egypt who had suddenly
turned their lives upside down? As Yosef manipulates them, step after step,
forcing them in a particular direction, do the brothers discern any master
plan? As the verses clearly tell us, they feel guilt, and seem to sense that this
turn of events is the start of their well-deserved punishment for the way
they treated Yosef.[7] Do they have any other thoughts about the Egyptian
viceroy other than the understanding that he is the vehicle chosen by
Heaven to mete out their punishment?

Yosef is very difficult for them to read. On the one hand, he represents
the Egyptian empire and all it stands for. On the other hand, his words to
them speak of God, and of justice – concepts foreign, if not anathema, to
an Egyptian mind:

בראשית מב:יח

וַיֹּאמֶר אֲלֵהֶם יוֹסֵף בַּיּוֹם הַשְּׁלִישִׁי זֹאת עֲשׂוּ וִחְיוּ אֶת הָאֱלֹקִים אֲנִי יָרֵא:

---

5. The Rosh raises the same question as the Ramban, but states that all the brothers took a
   vow not to reveal anything about the sale of Yosef; Yosef also felt bound by this vow.

פירוש הרא"ש, בראשית מה:א

ולא יכול יוסף להתאפק: תימא יש – איך המתין כל כך יוסף להודיע לאביו שהיה שרוי בצער גדול כי הוא
חי. ויש לומר בשעת החרם שתפו את יוסף עמהם שלא לגלות הדבר ואף כי היה מוכרח כיון שלא מיחה בם
היה נכלל עמהם ולפיכך המתין עד שבאו כולם והתירו את החרם בהסכמת כולם דכל דבר שבמנין צריך
מנין אחר להתירו. ומכאן ראייה שכל אדם שיושב בבית הכנסת ויש בדעתו להוציא עצמו מתקנת הקהל
ומהחרם צריך שיוציא בשפתיו שכל דברים שבלב אינם דברים שא"כ יהיה נאסר בכללם בחרם.

6. I have explored this theme in greater detail in *Explorations*, Parashat Vayigash.

7. The theme of their guilt is explored in "Parashat Mikeitz: Of Spies and Thieves," above.

And Yosef said to them on the third day, "This do, and live; for I fear God." (Bereishit 42:18)

בראשית מג:כג

וַיֹּאמֶר שָׁלוֹם לָכֶם אַל תִּירָאוּ אֱלֹקֵיכֶם וֵאלֹקֵי אֲבִיכֶם נָתַן לָכֶם מַטְמוֹן בְּאַמְתְּחֹתֵיכֶם כַּסְפְּכֶם בָּא אֵלָי וַיּוֹצֵא אֲלֵהֶם אֶת שִׁמְעוֹן:

And he said, "Peace be to you, fear not; your God, and the God of your father, has given you treasure in your sacks; I received your money." And he brought Shimon out to them. (Bereishit 43:23)

בראשית מג:כט

וַיִּשָּׂא עֵינָיו וַיַּרְא אֶת בִּנְיָמִין אָחִיו בֶּן אִמּוֹ וַיֹּאמֶר הֲזֶה אֲחִיכֶם הַקָּטֹן אֲשֶׁר אֲמַרְתֶּם אֵלָי וַיֹּאמַר אֱלֹקִים יָחְנְךָ בְּנִי:

And he lifted up his eyes, and saw his brother Binyamin, his mother's son, and said, "Is this your younger brother, of whom you spoke to me?" And he said, "God be gracious to you, my son." (Bereishit 43:29)

בראשית מד:יז

וַיֹּאמֶר חָלִילָה לִּי מֵעֲשׂוֹת זֹאת הָאִישׁ אֲשֶׁר נִמְצָא הַגָּבִיעַ בְּיָדוֹ הוּא יִהְיֶה לִּי עָבֶד וְאַתֶּם עֲלוּ לְשָׁלוֹם אֶל אֲבִיכֶם:

And he said, "God forbid that I should do so. The man in whose hand the cup is found, he shall be my servant; and as for you, go up in peace to your father." (Bereishit 44:17)

Despite Yosef's repeated references to God, and his invocation of a system of justice that is familiar to them, the brothers seem to interpret Yosef's actions in a completely opposite direction, a far more sordid direction. According to the Midrash, the brothers suspect that this despot has designs on Binyamin. Presumably, Binyamin was very handsome, as the text attests regarding his mother and brother. The brothers are suspicious that Yosef manipulated them to bring their younger brother to Egypt, and, once there, Yosef had the damning evidence planted in Binyamin's pouch in order to take him as his personal slave:

בראשית רבה, פרשה צג פסקה ו

כי כמוך כפרעה: מה פרעה גוזר ואינו מקיים אף את גוזר ואינך מקיים מה פרעה להוט אחר הזכרים אף אתה כן.

"For you are like Par'oh": Just as Par'oh decrees [promises] and does not fulfill his decree, so do you decree and not fulfill. As Par'oh lusts for males, so do you. (Bereishit Rabbah 93:6)

מדרש תנחומא, פרשת ויגש פרק ה

ויגש אליו יהודה: שנגש בתוכחות.... "כי כמוך כפרעה": כשם שפרעה רבך אוהב נשים ומחמדן כך אתה ראית לבנימן שהוא יפה תואר ואתה מחמדו להיות לך לעבד.

"Yehudah approached him": He approached with rebuke... "You are like Par'oh": just as he likes women and lusts after them, likewise when you saw how handsome Binyamin was, you lusted after him and [plotted] to make him your slave." (Midrash Tanhuma, Parashat Vayigash, chapter 5)

Yosef's behavior was suspicious. If, indeed, he wanted a slave, any of the older brothers would have been a better choice than the younger, weaker Binyamin. The brothers were convinced that it was Binyamin's beauty that had attracted Yosef. This is not a new theme regarding Egyptian aristocracy: the Targum Pseudo-Yonatan accuses Potifar of having homosexual designs on Yosef, a fact that exacerbated his wife's forlorn state.[8] Egypt was a hotbed of immorality,[9] infamous for homosexuality and pedophilia.

The brothers' suspicion that Yosef's intentions were less than honorable should come as no surprise; they do not entertain even the faintest notion, even in their wildest dreams, that this inscrutable, immoral monarch is actually their long-lost brother, a man who was not only sold, but was

---

8. Targum Pseudo-Yonatan, Bereishit 39:1.

כתר יונתן, בראשית לט:א

ויוסף הורד למצרים ויקנהו פוטיפר על שראהו יפה בעבור לעשות עמו משכב זכר ומיד נגזר עליו והתייבשו אשכיו ונסתרס והוא שרו של פרעה שר ההורגים איש מצרי, בהתחיבות מהערבים שהורידוהו לשם.

9. From Par'oh's taking of Sarah, to the propositioning of Yosef by Mrs. Potifar, we see a pattern of immorality. Later in the Torah the section of illicit sexual sins is introduced with the general admonition to avoid the "practices of the land of Egypt." See Vayikra 18:3.

ויקרא יח:ג

כְּמַעֲשֵׂה אֶרֶץ מִצְרַיִם אֲשֶׁר יְשַׁבְתֶּם בָּהּ לֹא תַעֲשׂוּ וּכְמַעֲשֵׂה אֶרֶץ כְּנַעַן אֲשֶׁר אֲנִי מֵבִיא אֶתְכֶם שָׁמָּה לֹא תַעֲשׂוּ וּבְחֻקֹּתֵיהֶם לֹא תֵלֵכוּ:

physically excised, cut out of the family. They do not dream that this man is Yosef, and that he has remained chaste – even at the price of being imprisoned. They do not see *Yosef haTzaddik*, nor even do they see Yosef, grown to manhood and power; they see a lustful, powerful pervert. The only master plan they perceive is one engineered to satisfy this Egyptian despot's sexual appetite.

For readers of the text, the brothers' perspective is not helpful, because we know what they do not. We know Yosef's identity – both his familial and personal history, and his moral fiber. What we still do not know is – what was Yosef thinking? His words, and the fact that he aborts his plan, indicate that his motives were not self-serving. He seems to be after more than the satisfaction of bringing his personal dreams to fruition at his family's expense. Yosef is not seeking revenge, nor is he seeking vindication; had either of these been his motivation, the charade would have ended much sooner. We are therefore obliged to see Yosef's words and actions for what they are: no more and no less than educational tools. Everything he says to his brothers and everything he does from the moment they stand before him is geared toward bringing the brothers to recognize him, to see him – and, as a result, to see his dreams – for what they really are. It is toward that end that Yosef pushes them, but they do not seem to understand. They don't understand that it is Yosef that he wants them to seek; they don't understand that it is Yosef he wants them to accept; they don't understand that it is *Yosef haTzaddik* who stands before them.

The brothers' failure to recognize Yosef is more than ironic, more than a personal insult, more than tragic. The fact is that everyone else who came into contact with Yosef throughout his life, including Potifar and his wife, the chief baker and the chief wine steward, the chief officer of Par'oh's prison, and Par'oh himself, immediately saw Yosef's greatness. Yosef rose to the top in every situation – save one: only his brothers could not or would not recognize his leadership qualities, his innate talent, his God-given gifts. This is the essence of *sinat hinam*, the quintessential example of baseless hatred: the brothers' hatred blinded them to Yosef's greatness. Even when Yosef stands before them, having overcome every possible obstacle in his personal rise to power, even when he practically begs them to open their eyes and see the man behind the robes of royalty, they refuse to see. They seem to prefer their jealousy and hatred over acceptance of Yosef as their rightful leader.

It is in this context that many midrashim interpret the exchange between Yosef and Yehudah:

בראשית רבה, פרשה צג פסקה ח

אדוני שאל את עבדיו וגו': אמר לו, "מתחלה באת עלינו בעלילה. כמה מדינות ירדו למצרים לשבר אוכל ולא שאלת אחד מהם! שמא בתך באנו ליקח, או אתה סבור לישא את אחותנו? אף על פי כן לא כסינו ממך". אמר לו, "אני רואה בך שפטיט אתה. יש באחיך פטיט כמותך?" אמר לו, "כל זאת שאתה רואה אני ערבתי אותו". אמר לו, "מפני מה לא עשית כן את אחיך כשמכרת אותו לישמעאלים בעשרים כסף וציערת את אביך הזקן ואמרת לו (בראשית לז) 'טרוף טורף יוסף'?"

כיון ששמע יהודה כך צעק ובכה בקול גדול. אמר, "כי איך אעלה אל אבי...?" אמר יהודה לנפתלי, "לך וראה כמה שווקים במצרים". קפץ וחזר; אמר לו, "שנים עשר". אמר יהודה לאחיו, "אני אחריב מהם שלשה וטלו כל אחד ואחד אחד אחד ולא נשאיר בהם איש". אמרו לו אחיו, "יהודה! מצרים אינה כשכם. אם אתה מחריב את מצרים תחריב את כל העולם".

באותה שעה, "ולא יכול יוסף להתאפק" – כיון שראה יוסף שהסכימה דעתם להחריב את מצרים, אמר יוסף בלבו, "מוטב שאתודע להם ואל יחריבו את מצרים". אמר להם יוסף, "לא כך אמרתם שאחיו של זה מת! אני אקראנו ויבא אצלכם". והיה קורא "יוסף בן יעקב, בוא אצלי! יוסף בן יעקב, בוא אצלי!" והיו מסתכלין בארבע פינות הבית. אמר להם, "מה אתם רואים? אני יוסף אחיכם!" מיד פרחה נשמתן, שנאמר, "ולא יכלו אחיו...", ולא האמינו לו עד שפרע עצמו והראה להם המילה.

"My lord asked": Yehudah said to him, "Behold the proof that you came with a pretext against us. How many countries came down to buy food! Did you ask them questions as you asked us? Did we want to marry your daughter, or did you ask to marry our sister? Nevertheless, we hid nothing from you." "Why so?" "Because I have become surety for him," he replied. "Why didn't you act in that fashion when you sold your brother to the Yishmaelites for twenty pieces of silver and caused your elderly father pain when you said 'Yosef is torn to pieces'?"

When Yehudah heard this he cried and screamed with a great voice and said, "How can I go back to my father?" Yehudah said to Naftali, "Go and see how many market places there are in Egypt." He said, "Twelve." Yehudah said, "I will destroy three; the rest of you destroy one each." They said, "Egypt is not like Shekhem; if you destroy Egypt you will destroy the entire world."

When Yosef saw that they had all agreed to destroy Egypt he said, "It is better that I reveal myself than Egypt be destroyed." Yosef then asked, "Where is your brother whom you said to be dead?" He demanded: "Where is he? Is it certain that he is dead?" "Yes," they replied. "Why do you speak falsely?" he upbraided them. "Did you not sell him to me, and I bought him from your hands? I will call him and he will answer me. Yosef the son of Yaakov, show yourself! Yosef the son of Yaakov, show yourself!" he cried out, while they looked in the four corners of the house. "What do you see?" said he. "I am Yosef your brother!" but they did not believe him until he uncovered himself and showed that he was circumcised. (Bereishit Rabbah 93:8)

The Midrash tells us why Yosef abandoned his plan: When he sees their benevolent, protective behavior directed toward Benyamin, he forces them to think about their behavior in his own case. At that point Yehudah threatens to destroy all of Egypt, and Yosef concludes that he must abort his plan. He tells them that Yosef is in the room, the final clue in his game-plan to open their eyes to his identity. Tragically, the brothers are willing to look everywhere else, anywhere else, rather than look their brother in the eye and see him for who he truly is.

Another midrash questions Yosef's wisdom in asking all others to leave the room, leaving him unprotected.[10] These are, after all, dangerous men;

---

10. See Bereishit Rabbah 93:9.

בראשית רבה, פרשה צג פסקה ט

א"ר חייא בר אבא כל הדברים שאת קורא שדיבר יהודה ליוסף בפני אחיו עד שאת מגיע ולא יכול יוסף להתאפק היה בהם פיוס ליוסף ופיוס לאחיו ופיוס לבנימין פיוס ליוסף לומר ראו היך הוא נותן נפשו על בניה של רחל פיוס לאחיו לומר ראו היאך הוא נותן נפשו על אחיו פיוס לבנימין אמר לו כשם שנתתי נפשי עליך כך אני נותן נפשי על אחיך ולא יכול יוסף להתאפק וגו' רבי חמא בר חנינא אמר לא עשה יוסף כשורה שאלו בעטו בו אחד מהם מיד היה מת רבי שמואל בר נחמן אמר כהוגן וכשורה עשה יודע היה צדקן של אחיו אמר ח"ו אין אחי חשודים על שפיכות דמים.

"Then Yosef could not contain himself…and he cried: 'Cause every man to go out from me' (Bereishit 45:1): R. Hama b. R. Hanina and R. Samuel b. Nahmani discussed this. R. Hama b. R. Hanina said: Yosef did not act prudently, for had one of them kicked him, he would have died on the spot. R. Samuel b. Nahmani said: He acted rightly and prudently. He knew the righteousness of his brethren and reasoned: 'Heaven forfend! My brothers are not to be suspected of bloodshed.'"

the massacre of Shekhem would attest to their violent tendencies (which makes Yosef's "proof" – his circumcision – all the more interesting). Yet Yosef seems to sense – correctly – that the brothers have, indeed, changed. He knows that he can render them speechless, and he does.

Why does Yehudah's threat to destroy Egypt shake Yosef's resolve and cause him to change his plan? Why was it so important to him to save Egypt from his brothers' anger? Was he afraid that he would be out of a job? Perhaps he knows that the survival of Egypt and the storehouses of grain is the only thing that can save the entire region. There may, however, be something else on his mind, something that is discussed by commentaries seeking a more far-reaching understanding of Yosef's behavior and motives: Yosef knows that God's covenant with Avraham, which includes exile and slavery, will lead the Children of Israel to Egypt. It is for this reason that Yosef cannot allow his brothers to destroy Egypt. Yosef's behavior, then, may be attributed to a heightened sense of responsibility for the future.

Yosef was, from a very early stage in his life, able to understand the future through dreams. He understood that the dreams of his youth were a window to the future – not only his own personal fate, but the future of his family and of the entire Jewish people.[11] He understood the other dreams that he came across later in life in similar fashion. Because of this insight, Yosef was uniquely sensitive to the ramifications of the terrible sin the brothers had committed by selling him – ramifications that extended and reverberated throughout Jewish history for millennia:[12] With the sale

---

11. See above, "Parashat Mikeitz: Dream, Dream, Dream…Dream."

12. There are those who connect the terrible *sinat hinam* ("groundless hatred") that caused the destruction of the Second Beit haMikdash, with the sale of Yosef. See Rav Simha Bunim of Pishischa in his *Arugat haBosem*, Parashat Mikeitz.

ספר ערוגות הבושם, פרשת מקץ

איתא בשפת אמת ולא יכול יוסף להתאפק, שיוסף היה צריך להתאפק ועל ידי זה היתה טובה לדורות, אולם הוא לא יכל להתאפק ולכן כתיב ויפול על צוארי בנימין אחיו ויבך, ואיתא בגמרא שבכה על שני מקדשים שעתידין ליחרב, ואיתא ב'קול שמחה' שמה שהיה רצון יוסף כל כך שירד בנימין אליו, הוא לפי שרצה לעשות יחוד השבטים לכן צוה להביא את בנימין שיהיה בזה יחוד יוסף הצדיק עילאה עם בנימין הצדיק תתאה כדאיתא בזוה"ק, זה הוא הענין שבכה על צואריו כי בית המקדש נקרא צואר המחבר עליונים ותחתונים וזה ענין יחודא תתאה. (אמרי אמת גור, ויגש תרצ"ו).

of Yosef, *sinat hinam* was unleashed and the Jewish people has never quite managed to correct this schism.[13]

The sale of Yosef, then, was seen by Yosef on a different plane than it was by the brothers. Yosef saw the sale in terms of Jewish history, and it is on these terms that he attempts to console his brothers when he finally reveals himself to them. From the brothers' perspective, the crime itself, an act of perfidy committed against an individual, was only the superficial level of the sale. Even on this level there is another aspect to the sale. The brothers' underlying attitude is unmasked when they sell him: Yosef is not part of the family. It is surely no coincidence that Yosef is sold to "Yishmaelim" and perhaps Midianites; both of these tribes are descendants of sons of Avraham who had been rejected, dispossessed from the covenant. In some warped way, the brothers, for their part, may have seen the appearance of these tribes on the scene as Divine Providence.

When they first stand before him in Egypt, Yosef accuses them of crimes and has them arrested; the brothers respond with remorse:

---

13. Other traditions connect the sale of Yosef with the tragic and gruesome deaths of the Ten Martyrs. The version of the midrash preserved in the Yom Kippur liturgy makes this connection. See *Shem mi'Shmuel*, Parashat Vayigash 5674.

ספר שם משמואל, פרשת ויגש, שנת תרע"ד

ואפשר עוד דהא כתיב ולא יכול יוסף להתאפק ומשמע דאם הי' יכול הי' עוד מתאפק, ולמה. וכבר דברנו בזה. ויש לומר עוד, דהנה איתא בזוה"ק דעשרה הרוגי מלכות היו גלגול השבטים ונידונו במיתה על חטא מכירת יוסף. ולכאורה הלא אין לך דבר שעומד בפני התשובה ומיתה ממרקת ולמה הי' עליהם עוד דין אחרי שעברו יותר מאלף וחמש מאות שנה.... אבל יהודה הי' דוחק את השעה, ולא הי' יכול יוסף עוד להתאפק עד שיתמרק החטא לגמרי עד התכלית, כי עדיין היתה התקוה נשקפת להם שיהיה בתחנוניו וטענתו ירכך את לבו, ולעומתו נשאר עוד רושם מהחטא שלא היתה התשובה עד התכלית ונשאר עוד שמץ מנהו שהיו צריכין לבוא בגלגול הרוגי מלכות....

כי אותה הי' מבקש לראות שימסור נפשו על בנימין אחיו, כבמדרש כל הדברים שאתה קורא מויגש עד ולא יכול יוסף להתאפק היו פיוס ליוסף ולבנימין וכו'. אך לפי דרכנו יובן, דהנה כ"ק אבי אדומו"ר זצללה"ה הגיד הטעם מה שנתאחר כ"כ הקטרוג על ענין מכירת יוסף עד אחר חורבן בית שני, כי לפי השקפה חיצונית הי' יוסף נוטל נקמה מאחיו במה שציער אותם כ"כ, ואם הי' בעצמו נוטל נקמה מהם שוב לא הי' עליהם דין שמים, אבל באמת ח"ו לא כיון יוסף לנקמה, אדרבה הכל הי' מחמת חמלתו עליהם שלא יהיו עונשין מחמת החטא בזה ובבא, ע"כ רצה שיתמרק החטא, וא"כ לפי האמת לא לקח יוסף נקמה מהם ועדיין נשאר הקטרוג, אך החיצונים אינם יודעים תעלומות לב, ולא ידעו שלא לקח נקמה מהם, ע"כ לא ידעו לקטרג, אך אחר חורבן בית שני שאיתא בזוה"ק שאז נמסרו רזי תורה לחיצונים, נתודעו מסוד זה, ע"כ אז הי' הקטרוג, ודפח"ח.

בראשית מב:יז–כד

וַיֶּאֱסֹף אֹתָם אֶל מִשְׁמָר שְׁלֹשֶׁת יָמִים: וַיֹּאמֶר אֲלֵהֶם יוֹסֵף בַּיּוֹם הַשְּׁלִישִׁי זֹאת
עֲשׂוּ וִחְיוּ אֶת הָאֱלֹקִים אֲנִי יָרֵא: אִם כֵּנִים אַתֶּם אֲחִיכֶם אֶחָד יֵאָסֵר בְּבֵית
מִשְׁמַרְכֶם וְאַתֶּם לְכוּ הָבִיאוּ שֶׁבֶר רַעֲבוֹן בָּתֵּיכֶם: וְאֶת אֲחִיכֶם הַקָּטֹן תָּבִיאוּ
אֵלַי וְיֵאָמְנוּ דִבְרֵיכֶם וְלֹא תָמוּתוּ וַיַּעֲשׂוּ כֵן: וַיֹּאמְרוּ אִישׁ אֶל אָחִיו אֲבָל אֲשֵׁמִים
אֲנַחְנוּ עַל אָחִינוּ אֲשֶׁר רָאִינוּ צָרַת נַפְשׁוֹ בְּהִתְחַנְנוֹ אֵלֵינוּ וְלֹא שָׁמָעְנוּ עַל כֵּן בָּאָה
אֵלֵינוּ הַצָּרָה הַזֹּאת: וַיַּעַן רְאוּבֵן אֹתָם לֵאמֹר הֲלוֹא אָמַרְתִּי אֲלֵיכֶם לֵאמֹר אַל
תֶּחֶטְאוּ בַיֶּלֶד וְלֹא שְׁמַעְתֶּם וְגַם דָּמוֹ הִנֵּה נִדְרָשׁ: וְהֵם לֹא יָדְעוּ כִּי שֹׁמֵעַ יוֹסֵף כִּי
הַמֵּלִיץ בֵּינֹתָם: וַיִּסֹּב מֵעֲלֵיהֶם וַיֵּבְךְּ וַיָּשָׁב אֲלֵהֶם וַיְדַבֵּר אֲלֵהֶם וַיִּקַּח מֵאִתָּם אֶת
שִׁמְעוֹן וַיֶּאֱסֹר אֹתוֹ לְעֵינֵיהֶם:

*And he put them all together under guard for three days. And Yosef
said to them on the third day, "This do, and live; for I fear God. If
you are honest men, let one of your brothers be confined in the house
of your prison; and [the rest of] you go, carry grain to relieve the
famine in your houses. But bring your youngest brother to me; so
shall your words be verified, and you shall not die." And they did so.
And they said one to another, "We are truly guilty concerning our
brother, in that we saw the anguish of his soul when he besought
us, and we would not hear; therefore this calamity has befallen us."
And Reuven answered them, saying, "Did I not speak to you, saying,
'Do not sin against the child' and you would not hear? Therefore,
behold, also his blood is required." And they did not know that Yosef
understood them; for he spoke to them through an interpreter. And
he turned himself away from them and wept; and returned to them
again and talked with them, and took Shimon from them and bound
him before their eyes. (Bereishit 42:17–24)*

As we have already seen, Yosef invoked God, and broke down in tears. He
needed to regain his composure. The brothers admitted their guilt, coming
to realize their personal responsibility for the atrocity they committed
against their younger brother. But this did not satisfy Yosef. He sought
to correct a deeper stratum, a more profound aspect of the sin. Whereas
the brothers had begun to see their guilt on a personal level, they had not
yet come to understand the sin in national terms. They had "gotten rid
of" their annoying brother, and they now regretted it. But they did not yet
understand that they had disrupted the foundations of the Jewish people,
of the twelve tribes of Israel. Yosef's goal was to bring them to this level of

understanding, and his purpose was twofold: not only did Yosef aim to solidify the foundations of the unity of the nation, he hoped to expedite the realization of God's covenant with Avraham.

We may say that Yosef did, indeed, engineer the master plan in order to bring about the fulfillment of his dreams. However, the level at which this is true is not the level of personal satisfaction or vindication: Yosef understood his dreams as visions of the future of the entire nation. He saw his dreams as the continuation of Avraham's vision,[14] and of the covenant with God. Yosef hoped that through his enslavement, the slavery and exile foretold in the covenant with Avraham had begun, but he knew that this could only be so if his own personal suffering was understood by his brothers as their own. Yosef's goal was to open their eyes to the larger picture, to make them aware that they all were a part of something much greater than themselves. If they had been able to identify with Yosef's suffering, if they had made his suffering their own, this would have been the start of the realization of God's words to Avraham. If they did not, they would suffer – and only when they managed to become united in their suffering would the process of redemption begin.[15]

Yosef understood that only when the brothers accepted him as part of the family could the rift be truly healed. Only if the brothers accepted and embraced him, only when they feel his suffering as their own, could the course of Jewish history continue to its culmination. Only through this type of empathy can the years he, and later, they, spent in Egypt be considered part of the fulfillment of the promises made to Avraham. If the brothers reject Yosef, then his slavery is irrelevant, and will need to be repeated; if they accept him, Yosef's personal slavery will be counted toward the preordained national slavery that would soon follow.

---

14. See above, "Parashat Mikeitz: Dream, Dream, Dream…Dream."

15. The Ramban may be hinting at this. See Ramban 42:9, toward the end of the Ramban's comments.

רמב"ן, בראשית מב:ט

אבל היה רואה כי השתחויית אחיו לו וגם אביו וכל זרעו אתו, אי אפשר להיות בארצם, והיה מקוה להיותו שם במצרים בראותו הצלחתו הגדולה שם, וכל שכן אחרי ששמע חלום פרעה שנתברר לו כי יבאו כלם שמה ויתקיימו כל חלומותיו. ויאמר אליהם מרגלים אתם: העלילה הזאת יצטרך להיות בה טעם או אמתלא, כי מה עשו עשו להיות אומר להם כזה, וכל הארץ באו אליו, והם בתוך הבאים, כמו שאמר לשבור בתוך הבאים כי היה הרעב בארץ כנען.

And so, Yosef continues to hide his identity, engineering the arrival of the entire family in Egypt – engineering the beginning of the fruition of Avraham's vision. Each time he sends his brothers away, he sends them with "great wealth"; will they recognize the reference to God's covenant, which promised that Avraham's descendants would leave Egypt in such a manner? If so, they will have begun to see themselves as agents of Jewish history, and they will be able to rise above their petty jealousies. But if they cannot recognize him, if they cannot read the signs and move to a higher level of understanding, Yosef is to remain estranged from the brothers, outside of the family. They may regret what they did to their brother – as they apparently do – but if they do not feel it, identify with it, take responsibility for it, then Yosef alone has taken responsibility for the future of the Jewish people, and his suffering remains his own. The years of his incarceration and isolation will have been for naught, and the Children of Israel will have to endure their own taste of slavery.

As the Midrash (and less explicitly, the verses) indicate, Yosef fails: the brothers cannot recognize him. In their narrative, he is gone – dead, part of their past but not part of their future. His slavery is not the beginning of their slavery; it remains an independent, tragic chapter in Jewish history, whose reverberations are still felt today, every time one Jew mistreats another. Conversely, when we feel mutual responsibility, when we take care of one another, we imbue all of Jewish history, all Jewish suffering, with meaning and purpose, and we bring the redemption[16] that much closer.[17]

---

16. See Rav Tzadok haKohen, *Pri Tzaddik*, Parashat Mikeitz, section 8.

ספר פרי צדיק, פרשת מקץ אות ח

ובזה יובן מה שיפלא לכאורה על יוסף שאמר שאכל ושתה עמהם למה זה ציער אותם אחר כך במעשה הגביע והיה לו להתגלות לפניהם ולשלוח ולהביא את יעקב. אך לפי האמור מתחלה היה סבור שכבר עשה מחיית עמלק וכמו שהוא נתברר בשלימות במדתו כן גם כל השבטים נתבררו ועשו תשובה כשאמרו אבל אשמים אנחנו וגו', והיה סבור שעל ידי שבת יהיו נגאלין מיד ויהיה הוא כמו משיח בן יוסף. אבל אחר כך ראה שהקליפה בתקיפותה והבין מזה שעדיין לא נתבררו כל השבטים תחבולה כדי שיצטערו וישובו בתשובה שלמה ואחר כך יתודע אל אחיו. רק אחר כך ולא יכול יוסף להתאפק וגו', והיינו שמצדו רצה להתאפק עוד עד שישובו באמת ויתקנו שורש הקלקול ויהיה גמר התיקון על ידו שיהיה משיח בן יוסף אך לא יכול להתאפק וגו'. וכמו שכתב הרמב"ן, כי אנשים רבים חילו פניו שימחול לבנימין, כי נכמרו רחמיהם על תחנוני יהודה כו', וזה היה מן השמים כיון שלא היה עוד זמן משיח בן יוסף. ולכן נתן השם יתברך בלבם שיחלו פניו ולא יכול להתאפק ונתודע עליהם אף שעדיין לא תקנו הכל מצדם שיזכו להיות גמר התיקון עד עת בוא דברו ויבא משיח בן יוסף מזרעו.

17. See *Tiferet Shlomo*, Parashat Vayigash.

ספר תפארת שלמה, פרשת ויגש

יש להתבונן בענין טענת הערבות שטען יהודה נגד יוסף מה תועלת יצמח מזה נגד יעקב אביהם. הלא
ערבא צריך. ומה יעשה כי יחזיק את יהודה בעד בנימין ומה יועיל בזה. אולם כבר בארנו במ"א בפי'
הענין יעקב תיקן תפלת ערבית לרמז ענין הערבות אשר בבנ"י התחיל מיעקב אבינו. וז"ש (שה"ש ב:יד)
כי קולך ערב ומראך נאוה. כי בענין התפלה בזאת יעלה לרצון למעלה אם היא בבחי' ערבות להתפלל
כאו"א בעד חבירו. וזה ג"כ מעריב ערבים בחי' הערבות. לכן כאשר בא ראובן לפני אביו בראשונה בטענת
(בראשית מב:לז) את שני בני תמית אם פנה אליו. אך יהודה כאשר בא בטענת הערבות (שם מג:ט) אנכי
אערבנו וגו' כתיב אח"כ (שם יד) ואל שדי יתן לכם רחמים. כי אז בטח לבו כי מהר יצמח להם הישועה
על ענין מכירת יוסף. וז"ש כאן כי עבדך ערב את הנער וכתיב מיד אח"כ ולא יכול יוסף להתאפק כי היה
מיד התיקון נצמח על מכירת יוסף כנ"ל והוא הרמז על הגאולה העתידה ב"ב מה שפגמו בענין הערבות
מה שמכרו את יוסף כמבואר באריכות במ"א. וז"ש (שם מד:לב) אם לא אביאנו אליך וחטאתי לאבי כל
הימים. כי הגאולה העתידה ב"ב יהיה ג"כ ע"י האחדות בבנ"י בחי' הערבות איש את רעהו יעזורו באהבה
ואחוה וריעות אמן.

Wagons

The brothers return from their mission with spectacular, perhaps unbelievable news: Yosef is alive!

וַיַּגִּדוּ לוֹ לֵאמֹר עוֹד יוֹסֵף חַי וְכִי הוּא מֹשֵׁל בְּכָל אֶרֶץ מִצְרָיִם וַיָּפָג לִבּוֹ כִּי לֹא הֶאֱמִין לָהֶם: וַיְדַבְּרוּ אֵלָיו אֵת כָּל דִּבְרֵי יוֹסֵף אֲשֶׁר דִּבֶּר אֲלֵהֶם וַיַּרְא אֶת הָעֲגָלוֹת אֲשֶׁר שָׁלַח יוֹסֵף לָשֵׂאת אֹתוֹ וַתְּחִי רוּחַ יַעֲקֹב אֲבִיהֶם:

And they told him, "Yosef is still alive, and he rules over all of Egypt!" And [Yaakov's] heart skipped a beat, for he did not believe them. They relayed to him the words Yosef had spoken to them, and Yaakov saw the carriages Yosef sent to transport him, and their father Yaakov's spirit came to life. (Bereishit 45:26–27)

Yaakov, who had experienced so much pain in his life, did not wish to be set up for yet another disappointment. How can Yosef be alive? And if he is alive, can he really be the ruler over Egypt? Yaakov dismisses the idea, fights off the news. Only upon seeing the wagons does Yaakov believe his ears and eyes. What changed his perspective? What convinced him? The straightforward meaning of the text would seem to be that Yaakov was convinced only upon seeing the impressive wagons of Par'oh; perhaps seeing a physical indication of the might of the Egyptian empire[1] was what made Yaakov accept the news, for only someone with great power or influence could arrange for the royal fleet to come to this distant land, to his own doorstep, and transport Yaakov and his family to Egypt.

Rashi offers a different explanation of how the wagons convinced Yaakov:

---

1. Perhaps this is the meaning of the passage in "*Moaz Tzur*" that refers to Egypt as *Malkhut 'Eglah*. However, see Yirmiyahu 46:20, and see R. Yissachar Yaacobson, *Netiv Binah* (Tel Aviv: Sinai Publishing, 1978), 2:373, who associates *'eglah* with calf.

341

רש"י, בראשית מה:כז

את כל דברי יוסף: סימן מסר להם. במה היה עוסק כשפירש ממנו? בפרשת עגלה ערופה. זהו שנאמר, "וירא את העגלות אשר שלח יוסף", ולא נאמר, "אשר שלח פרעה".

"All the words of Yosef": By sending the wagons ('agalot), Yosef sent him a sign. What was the [topic] they had studied before [Yosef] left? The topic of the beheaded heifer ('eglah 'arufah). Thus the text states "when he saw the 'agalot that Yosef sent," and not "that Par'oh sent."
(Rashi, Bereishit 45:27)

The visual image of physical *'agalot*, combined with the words of Yosef, send a message, a secret shared by father and son years ago. No one but Yosef and Yaakov could have known the topic of their private conversation. The *'agalot* were a symbol of their intimacy, and this was what convinced Yaakov to believe the incredible.

Rashi's explanation presents several problems of its own: Although Rashi refers to the phrase "all the words of Yosef," the text itself seems to indicate that Yaakov is only convinced when he sees the *'agalot*. Furthermore, Rashi sees the *'agalot* as an allusion to the *'eglah 'arufah*, the beheaded calf – a "secret sign" known only to Yaakov and Yosef. Rashi sets aside the fact that, despite their similarity, the words *'eglah* and *'agalah* do not share a common root; they are in fact two different words.[2] Finally, and perhaps most damaging to Rashi's theory, the idea to send the wagons was Par'oh's, not Yosef's:

בראשית מה:יז–כא

וַיֹּאמֶר פַּרְעֹה אֶל יוֹסֵף אֱמֹר אֶל אַחֶיךָ זֹאת עֲשׂוּ טַעֲנוּ אֶת בְּעִירְכֶם וּלְכוּ בֹאוּ אַרְצָה כְּנָעַן: וּקְחוּ אֶת אֲבִיכֶם וְאֶת בָּתֵּיכֶם וּבֹאוּ אֵלָי וְאֶתְּנָה לָכֶם אֶת טוּב אֶרֶץ מִצְרַיִם וְאִכְלוּ אֶת חֵלֶב הָאָרֶץ: וְאַתָּה צֻוֵּיתָה זֹאת עֲשׂוּ קְחוּ לָכֶם מֵאֶרֶץ מִצְרַיִם עֲגָלוֹת לְטַפְּכֶם וְלִנְשֵׁיכֶם וּנְשָׂאתֶם אֶת אֲבִיכֶם וּבָאתֶם: וְעֵינְכֶם אַל תָּחֹס עַל כְּלֵיכֶם כִּי טוּב כָּל אֶרֶץ מִצְרַיִם לָכֶם הוּא: וַיַּעֲשׂוּ כֵן בְּנֵי יִשְׂרָאֵל וַיִּתֵּן לָהֶם יוֹסֵף עֲגָלוֹת עַל פִּי פַרְעֹה וַיִּתֵּן לָהֶם צֵדָה לַדָּרֶךְ:

---

2. See Da'at Zekeinim mi'Baalei haTosafot, Bereishit 45:27.

דעת זקנים מבעלי התוספות, בראשית מה:כז
וקשה לשני הפירושים לפרש עגלות לשון עגלה....

*And Par'oh said to Yosef, "Say to your brothers, 'Do this: load your
beasts and go to the land of Canaan. And take your father and your
households and come to me, and I will give you the good of the land of
Egypt, and you shall eat the fat of the land. Now you are commanded
to take wagons out of the land of Egypt for your little ones and for
your wives, and bring your father and come. Also give no thought to
your goods, for the good of all the land of Egypt is yours.'" And the
children of Israel did so; and Yosef gave them wagons, according to
the commandment of Par'oh, and gave them provision for the way.*
(Bereishit 45:17–21)

While the text in verse 27 attests that Yaakov had thought the wagons
were sent by Yosef, it was Par'oh's idea – indeed, he commanded Yosef to
send the wagons. Verse 21 stresses that Yosef sent the wagons because of
Par'oh's command.

Why would Rashi seek, in these wagons, the communication of a secret
message? Furthermore, by making the imaginative association between
'agalot and *'eglah*, Rashi introduces an element that is not an organic part
of the discussion; namely a calf – *'eigel*. The very word strikes a problematic
chord, resounding with overtones of the *'Eigel haZahav*, the Golden Calf.
The web of negative associations this element dredges up entangles Yosef
himself,[3] as well as his most infamous descendant, Yerovam.[4] Rashi could
have avoided all these entanglements had the text been left unembellished
by the *'agalot/'eglah* association. In all fairness, we must not lose sight of
Rashi's sources: Rashi's comment in this case, as in most cases, is based

---

3. See Rashi on Shmot 32:4, where the emergence of the Golden Calf from the smelted
   gold is associated with Yosef:

   רש״י, שמות לב:ד

   עגל מסכה: כיון שהשליכו לכור, באו מכשפי ערב רב שעלו עמהם ממצרים ועשאוהו בכשפים ויש אומרים
   מיכה היה שם שיצא מתוך דמוסי בנין שנתמעך בו במצרים, והיה בידו שם, וטס שכתב בו משה עלה שור,
   עלה שור, להעלות ארונו של יוסף מתוך נילוס, והשליכו לתוך הכור ויצא העגל.

4. See I Melakhim 12:28–29, where Yerovam makes not one but two golden calves, in an
   attempt to create a pagan alternative to Jerusalem.

   מלכים א, יב:כח–כט

   וַיִּוָּעַץ הַמֶּלֶךְ וַיַּעַשׂ שְׁנֵי עֶגְלֵי זָהָב וַיֹּאמֶר אֲלֵהֶם רַב לָכֶם מֵעֲלוֹת יְרוּשָׁלַ͏ִם הִנֵּה אֱלֹהֶיךָ יִשְׂרָאֵל אֲשֶׁר הֶעֱלוּךָ
   מֵאֶרֶץ מִצְרָיִם: וַיָּשֶׂם אֶת הָאֶחָד בְּבֵית אֵל וְאֶת הָאֶחָד נָתַן בְּדָן:

on a rabbinic tradition.[5] Our question, then, might be, why did Rashi choose to transmit this particular tradition? And, more pointedly, how can his comments here be reconciled with Rashi's clearly stated mandate, to explain the straightforward, "plain" meaning[6] of the text?[7]

The deeper meaning of these sources becomes accessible only if we understand the elements more fully: What is the *'eglah 'arufah*? When is it used?

דברים כא:א–ט

כִּי יִמָּצֵא חָלָל בָּאֲדָמָה אֲשֶׁר ה' אֱלֹקֶיךָ נֹתֵן לְךָ לְרִשְׁתָּהּ נֹפֵל בַּשָּׂדֶה לֹא נוֹדַע מִי הִכָּהוּ: וְיָצְאוּ זְקֵנֶיךָ וְשֹׁפְטֶיךָ וּמָדְדוּ אֶל הֶעָרִים אֲשֶׁר סְבִיבֹת הֶחָלָל: וְהָיָה הָעִיר הַקְּרֹבָה אֶל הֶחָלָל וְלָקְחוּ זִקְנֵי הָעִיר הַהִוא עֶגְלַת בָּקָר אֲשֶׁר לֹא עֻבַּד בָּהּ אֲשֶׁר לֹא מָשְׁכָה בְּעֹל: וְהוֹרִדוּ זִקְנֵי הָעִיר הַהִוא אֶת הָעֶגְלָה אֶל נַחַל אֵיתָן אֲשֶׁר לֹא יֵעָבֵד בּוֹ וְלֹא יִזָּרֵעַ וְעָרְפוּ שָׁם אֶת הָעֶגְלָה בַּנָּחַל: וְנִגְּשׁוּ הַכֹּהֲנִים בְּנֵי לֵוִי כִּי בָם בָּחַר ה' אֱלֹקֶיךָ לְשָׁרְתוֹ וּלְבָרֵךְ בְּשֵׁם ה' וְעַל פִּיהֶם יִהְיֶה כָּל רִיב וְכָל נָגַע: וְכֹל זִקְנֵי הָעִיר הַהִוא הַקְּרֹבִים אֶל הֶחָלָל יִרְחֲצוּ אֶת יְדֵיהֶם עַל הָעֶגְלָה הָעֲרוּפָה בַנָּחַל: וְעָנוּ וְאָמְרוּ יָדֵינוּ לֹא שָׁפְכֻ[8] אֶת הַדָּם הַזֶּה וְעֵינֵינוּ לֹא רָאוּ: כַּפֵּר לְעַמְּךָ יִשְׂרָאֵל אֲשֶׁר פָּדִיתָ ה' וְאַל תִּתֵּן דָּם נָקִי בְּקֶרֶב עַמְּךָ יִשְׂרָאֵל וְנִכַּפֵּר לָהֶם הַדָּם: וְאַתָּה תְּבַעֵר הַדָּם הַנָּקִי מִקִּרְבֶּךָ כִּי תַעֲשֶׂה הַיָּשָׁר בְּעֵינֵי ה':

If a corpse is found in the land that the Almighty your God gives you to possess, lying in the field, and it is not known who has slain him, then your elders and your judges shall come forth, and they shall measure the distance to the cities that are around the victim. And

---

5. For example see Midrash Seikhel Tov (Buber edition), chapter 37, section 13.

שכל טוב (בובר) בראשית פרק לז (יג), ד"ה ויאמר ישראל

ויאמר ישראל אל יוסף: שנשאר בבית אצלו ועוסק בתורה עמו, ואותו שעה היו עוסקין בענין עגלה ערופה, וכן אנו עתידין לדרוש בוירא את העגלות אשר שלח יוסף (בראשית מה:כז): הלוא. מלא ו', כבר דרשנו: הלא אחיך רועים בשכם לכה ואשלחך אליהם ויאמר לו הנני.

6. See Rashi's commentary to Bereishit 33:20.

רש"י, בראשית לג:כ

ואני ליישב פשוטו של מקרא באתי....

7. See comments of the *Kli Yakar* 45:27, who expresses amazement at Rashi's apparently uncharacteristic commentary to this verse.

כלי יקר, בראשית מה:כז

ופירושו רחוק מאוד וכי דרכו של רש"י להוציא המקרא מפשוטו לגמרי, שהרי הכתוב אומר אשר שלח יוסף לשאת אותו, ועוד עגלות למה לי די בעגלה אחת.

Later in his commentary *Kli Yakar* offers an alternative explanation of this Rashi.

8. The text reads שפכה and tradition instructs us to pronounce שפכו.

it shall be that the city that is closest to the slain man, the elders of that city shall take a heifer that has not been worked and that has not carried a yoke; and the elders of that city shall bring down the heifer to a rough ravine that is neither plowed nor sown, and shall strike off the heifer's neck there in the ravine. And the kohanim, *the sons of Levi, shall come near – for the Almighty your God has chosen them to serve him and to bless in the name of God, and by their word shall every controversy and every assault be tried. And all the elders of that city that is nearest to the victim's body shall wash their hands over the heifer that is beheaded in the valley. And they shall answer and say, "Our hands have not shed this blood, nor have our eyes seen it. Be merciful, O God, to your people Israel, whom you have redeemed, and lay not innocent blood to your people Israel's charge." And the blood shall be forgiven them. Thus shall you expunge the guilt of innocent blood from among you, when you shall do that which is right in the sight of God.* (Devarim 21:1–9)

The law of 'eglah 'arufah was instituted as a ritual of responsibility when a murder was discovered. A lifeless body is found in a field, and the Torah outlines the means of determining halakhic responsibility through a ritualistic measuring of proximity to the scene of the crime. The Talmud stresses that the Torah law has a moral component. Introspection is required. Moral responsibility is what should be measured: "What could our town have done to prevent the murder?" This is what the leadership should be taking stock of. In fact, in Talmudic literature, the 'eglah 'arufah ritual is the point of reference in a dramatic speech regarding a case in which the actual application of the halakhah was precluded, being that the victim was not quite dead yet, and the perpetrator was known:

תלמוד בבלי, מסכת יומא דף כג עמודים א–ב

תנו רבנן: מעשה בשני כהנים שהיו שניהן שוין ורצין ועולין בכבש, קדם אחד מהן לתוך ארבע אמות של חבירו – נטל סכין ותקע לו בלבו. עמד רבי צדוק על מעלות האולם ואמר: "אחינו בית ישראל, שמעו! הרי הוא אומר, (דברים כא) 'כי ימצא חלל באדמה ויצאו זקניך ושפטיך' – אנו על מי להביא עגלה ערופה? על העיר או על העזרות?" געו כל העם בבכיה. בא אביו של תינוק ומצאו כשהוא מפרפר. אמר, "הרי הוא כפרתכם, ועדיין בני מפרפר."

...וירושלים בת אתויי עגלה ערופה היא? והתניא: עשרה דברים נאמרו
בירושלים, וזו אחת מהן: אינה מביאה עגלה ערופה. ועוד: (דברים כא) "לא
נודע מי הכהו" כתיב – והא נודע מי הכהו. אלא כדי להרבות בבכיה.

Our rabbis taught: It once happened that two kohanim *were equal
as they ran to mount the ramp and when one of them came first
within the four cubits of the Altar, the other took a knife and thrust
it into his heart. R. Tzadok stood upon the steps of the hall and called
out: "Our brethren of the House of Israel, hear ye! Behold it says:
'If a corpse is found in the land...' – on whose behalf shall we bring
the* 'eglah 'arufah, *on behalf of the city or of the Temple courts?" The
entire people wept. Then the father of this young* kohen *came and
found him in the throes of death. He said, "Here is your atonement,
and my son is not yet dead."*

...But does [the community of] Jerusalem bring an 'eglah 'arufah?
*Surely it has been taught: Ten things were said concerning Jerusalem
and this is one of them – it does not bring an* 'eglah 'arufah. *Furthermore: "And it is not known who has slain him" (Devarim 21:1) – but
here it is known who has slain him! Rather, [R. Tzadok's question was
rhetorical] to increase the weeping. (Talmud Bavli Yoma 23a–b)*

Given the near-murder almost perpetrated upon Yosef, the reference to
'eglah 'arufah is chilling. Is Yosef calling for a careful measurement of
responsibility; is he blaming his father? Is he blaming his brothers? Or
is Yosef asking all involved to take the necessary steps and bring those
responsible to justice?

While this explanation may be compelling, most commentaries prefer a
more technical approach, associating a particular law derived from 'eglah
'arufah with the case at hand: one of the legal responsibilities that emerges
from this law is the obligation to accompany a guest out of one's home
and send them off with provisions for their journey.[9] Many commentaries
see the allusion to 'eglah 'arufah as Yosef's way of reassuring his father

---

9. See Rashi, Devarim 21:7, based on Talmud Bavli Sotah 45b.

רש"י, דברים כא:ז

ידינו לא שפכה: וכי עלתה על לב שזקני בית דין שופכי דמים הם אלא לא ראינוהו ופטרנוהו בלא מזונות
ובלא לויה. הכהנים אומרים כפר לעמך ישראל.

that he was not to be blamed for what had happened: Yaakov had, indeed, fulfilled his halakhic obligation by accompanying Yosef to the Hevron city limits.[10] When Yosef attempted to persuade his father to turn toward home, Yaakov taught him the law of *'eglah 'arufah*, stressing the importance of accompanying someone at the outset of a journey.

The underpinning of this explanation is a subtle turn of phrase used as Yaakov sends Yosef on his mission:

בראשית לז:יג–יד

וַיֹּאמֶר יִשְׂרָאֵל אֶל יוֹסֵף הֲלוֹא אַחֶיךָ רֹעִים בִּשְׁכֶם לְכָה וְאֶשְׁלָחֲךָ אֲלֵיהֶם וַיֹּאמֶר
לוֹ הִנֵּנִי: וַיֹּאמֶר לוֹ לֶךְ נָא רְאֵה אֶת שְׁלוֹם אַחֶיךָ וְאֶת שְׁלוֹם הַצֹּאן וַהֲשִׁבֵנִי דָּבָר
וַיִּשְׁלָחֵהוּ מֵעֵמֶק חֶבְרוֹן וַיָּבֹא שְׁכֶמָה:

And Yisrael said to Yosef, "Are not your brothers tending [the flock] in Shekhem? Go, and I will send you to them." And he said to him, "Here am I." And he said to him, "Go, I beg you, see whether it is well with your brothers, and well with the flock; and bring me word." So he sent him out from the valley of Hevron, and he came to Shekhem. (Bereishit 47:13–14)

Hevron, the town where Yaakov now lives, is situated up in the hills. Why, then, does the text say that Yaakov sent him from the "valley of Hevron"? This curious phrase is what leads some commentators[11] to understand that

---

10. See comments of Hizkuni, Bereishit 45:27.

חזקוני, בראשית מה:כז

אשר שלח יוסף: אמר יעקב לא היה מוציא בני עלי יציאות על חנם לטרוח ולהביא כמה עגלות אם לא היה
בני. כאן פרש"י סימן מסר להם במה היה עוסק ושפירש ממנו בעגלה ערופה, וא"ת מה סימן הוא זה אלא
אביו ליוהו כדמתרגמין וישלחהו מעמק חברון ואליוה אמר לו יוסף לאביו חזור בך אמר לו בני גדולה
לויה שעתידה פרשת עגלה ערופה שנוספה בתורה, כדכתיב ידנו לא שפכה את הדם וכי תעלה על דעתך
שסנהדרין הורגין אלא לא פטרנוהו בלא מזון ובלא לויה, וסימן בחון הוא שלא היה יודע בו אלא אביו
והוא. וי"ל שבאותן עגלות ששלח היו בהן עגלות למשוך אותם ובכך היה סי' שהלשון נופל על הלשון כמו
ששנינו עגלה המושכת בקרון פסולה לעגלה ערופה, והוכחה יש בדבר דכתיב אשר שלח על פי פרעה וכי
צריך היה יוסף שהיה שליט ליטול רשות לשלוח עגלות לאביו אלא מהעגלות היה צריך ליטול רשות שאין
פרה וחזירה יוצאה משם אלא אם כן ניטלה האם שלה בשביל שלא תלד ועגלות אלו שלח יוסף שלמות
על פי פרעה.

11. See Hizkuni, who cites the Targum as translating "he sent" as "he accompanied." This translation is not in Targum Onkelos 37:14 or Targum Pseudo-Yonatan. See Rabbi Kasher, *Torah Sheleimah*, page 1411, note 107, where he cites others who have the same tradition and a possible source.

Yaakov accompanied Yosef down from the hill area, walking with him out of the city limits, where he taught him the law of *'eglah 'arufah.*

Interestingly, Rashi's comments on this verse take a different approach. "Valley" is understood as a spiritual point of reference, rather than a reference to geography or topographical altitude. In Rashi's comments on this verse, the valley (*'eimek*) relates to something deep (*'amok*) in Hevron: the reference is to the covenant between God and someone who now lays buried deep in Hevron: Avraham. This covenant spelled out the impending exile, slavery and eventual salvation,[12] and at the very moment that Yosef is sent along his way, the elements are in place for the exile to begin. While Yaakov surely thought that Yosef was traveling northward toward Shekhem, little did he know that Yosef was in actuality heading south. The time had arrived for the divine plan to be set in motion, and nothing would hold it back. The covenant would be fulfilled. The exile was beginning, and its seeds lay deep in Hevron.

Yaakov, for his part, was none too keen to see this part of Jewish history come to fruition at this particular juncture. Just prior to Yosef's departure, we are told that Yaakov had finally settled down. Understandably, after a life full of twists and turns and far too much intrigue, Yaakov hoped for some peace and quiet.[13] Commenting on the words, "These are the generations of Yaakov," Rashi tells us that the destinies of Yaakov and Yosef were intertwined. Rashi concludes with an additional comment: Yaakov wished to settle in tranquility, and he was "ambushed" by the anger of the Yosef episode. Yaakov was, at his core, a simple dweller of tents. He wanted peace, but the vicissitudes of his life were enough for many lifetimes. He would have been happy to put the next chapter on hold, to slow the pace of events, to wait a bit. He was well aware that the next chapter was exile, and the Talmud tells us that Yaakov was supposed to be actively involved:

---

12. See Rashi, Bereishit 37:14, based on Talmud Bavli Sotah 11a.

רש"י, בראשית לז:יד

מעמק חברון: והלא חברון בהר, שנאמר (במדבר יג:כב) ויעלו בנגב ויבא עד חברון, אלא מעצה עמוקה של [אותו] צדיק הקבור בחברון, לקיים מה שנאמר לאברהם בין הבתרים (לעיל טו:יג) כי גר יהיה זרעך.

13. See *Explorations*, "Parashat Vayeshev." As I discuss there, Rabbi Soloveitchik held that Yaakov had thought that the details of the covenant with Avraham had already been fulfilled through Yaakov's own exile in the house of Lavan.

תלמוד בבלי, מסכת שבת דף פט עמוד ב

אמר רבי חייא בר אבא אמר רבי יוחנן: ראוי היה יעקב אבינו לירד למצרים
בשלשלאות של ברזל אלא שזכותו גרמה לו, דכתיב, (הושע יא) "בחבלי אדם
אמשכם בעבותות אהבה ואהיה להם כמרימי עול על לחיהם ואט אליו אוכיל".

R. Hiyya b. Abba said in R. Yohanan's name: It would have been
fitting for our father Yaakov to go down into Egypt in iron chains,
but his merit spared him, for it is written, "I drew them with the cords
of a man, with bands of love; and I was to them as those who take off
the yoke from their jaws, and I laid meat before them" (Hoshea 11:4).
(Talmud Bavli Shabbat 89b)

Yaakov was meant to descend to Egypt in iron chains,[14] but instead he
arrived on a royal convoy, with love in his heart, anticipating his reunion
with his beloved son.[15] Unlike Yaakov, Yosef was not spared. Their destinies
were linked; if Yaakov looked away from his historic role at this juncture,
Yosef had to fulfill it instead. It was Yosef who was brought down to Egypt
in *shalshela'ot barzel*, iron chains.[16] The seeds of the covenant, from the

---

14. See *Bat Ayin*, Parashat Vayeishev, who connects Yaakov's desire for tranquility with his
destiny of being dragged off to Egypt in chains.

ספר בת עין, פרשת וישב

ולפרש זה, על פי מאמר חז"ל (ע' בר"ר פו:ב), ראוי היה יעקב אבינו לירד למצרים בשלשלאות של ברזל,
וגלגל הקב"ה את הדבר על ידי יוסף וירד בכבוד גדול למצרים. ולפי"ז נפרש שבוודאי רצון יראיו יעשה,
ויעקב ידע שהוא ראוי לירד למצרים בשלשלאות של ברזל, בבחינת גלות על פי סיבה הידוע להבורא ב"ה,
ולכן ביקש יעקב לישב בשלוה, היינו פירוש שהתפלל מה' שישב בשלוה, וה' ברוב רחמיו עושה רצון יראיו
וגלגל הדבר שתתקפץ עליו רוגזו של יוסף כדי שירד למצרים בכבוד.

15. Midrash Tehillim, Psalm 105, brings the opinion that Yaakov was to come down in
chains, and then adds that this is comparable to the parable: if you want a cow, first
bring the calf – the cow will follow. It is interesting that it uses a calf (*'eglah*) in the
analogy.

מדרש תהילים מזמור קה

ויקרא רעב על הארץ: אמר רבי יהודה בר נחמן בשם רבי שמעון בן לקיש, ראוי היה יעקב לירד למצרים
בשלשלאות של ברזל ובקולרין, ועשה לו הקב"ה כמה עלילות וכמה מנגנאות ונמכר יוסף למצרים כדי
לירד. ויקרא רעב על הארץ, וכל כך למה, (שם מו:ו) ויבא יעקב מצרימה. אמר ר' פנחס הכהן בר חמא,
משל לפרה אחת שהיו רוצין למשוך אותה למקולין שלה ולא היתה נמשכת. מה עשו, משכו בנה תחלה
והיתה רצה אחריו. כך עשה הקב"ה מנגנאות, שעשו אחי יוסף כל אותן הדברים כדי שירדו למצרים גם כן
כדי שירד גם יעקב, שנאמר (הושע יא:ד) בחבלי אדם אמשכם.

16. See comments of the *Siftei Kohen*, Bereishit 37:28.

depths of Hevron, had begun to take root: Yaakov and his entire family were now in Egypt and the exile could begin.

Yaakov's place is taken by Yosef, but this is not without consequences of its own. The Ari"zal teaches that *barzel* (spelled *bet resh zayin lamed*) is an acronym of Bilha – Rahel – Zilpah – Leah, the four matriarchs, the mothers of the twelve tribes of Israel. The implication is that had Yaakov come in chains of *barzel*, his family would have been united, they would have come together as one. Instead they are brought down to Egypt because of the brothers' hatred of Yosef – a family divided.[17]

For the Jewish people, the Egyptian experience is known as the smelting furnace (*kur habarzel*),[18] a place where Jewish character is distilled and refined, where impurities are burned off. It is here that we become a nation, united, and it is here that our destiny is crystallized. The number of times the Torah instructs us to remember that we were slaves in Egypt is almost too many to count.[19] The Egypt experience creates a moral imperative,[20]

שפתי כהן, בראשית לז: כח

עוד יש לומר שנתרצית כדי שירד יעקב בכבוד כמו שאמרו ז"ל (שבת פט ע"ב) עתיד היה יעקב לירד בשלשלאות של ברזל לזה נשתתפה עמהם ולא נתגלה הדבר ליעקב כדי שירד בכבוד.

17. Commenting on Yaakov's blessing to Yosef, the Ari"zal makes reference to Rabbi Akiva, whom the Romans skinned alive with "combs of iron" – *barzel*. According to tradition Akiva is one of those holy souls that makes his way over to Judaism. While the *barzel* is used to kill, Rabbi Akiva accepts his chains and is ready for the next chapter to unfold. He teaches his students the importance of love and ethics, and embraces his role in history. He is Akiva ben Yosef: both a son of Yosef, and Akiva – an alternate form of the name *Yaakov*. He is Akiva the son of Yosef, accepting the role thrust upon Yosef by Yaakov's desire for tranquility. See *Sefer haLikutim*, Parashat Vayeishev, chapter 48.

ספר הליקוטים, פרשת וישב פרק מח

אמר ב"פ פורת, א' על יוסף וא' על ר' עקיבא. ורומז על מיתתו, בפ' וימררוהו ורובו, שסרקו את בשרו במסרקות של ברזל. וזה על כי וישטמוהו בעלי חצים, שנעשו הקליפות בעלים לעשר טיפות שיצאו מעשר אצבעותיו, והם זרועי ידיו. מידי אביר יעקב, נרמז על ר' עקיבא. משם רועה אבן ישראל, שהשיג למעלה מבחינת מרע"ה, והבן.

18. Devarim 4:20, I Melakhim 8:51, Yirmiyahu 11:4.

19. In fact, the exact number is thirty-six times!

20. Aside from building Jewish character, mystical traditions saw the purpose of exile as the liberation of holy souls trapped in non-Jewish bodies. The goal of the exile in Egypt was liberation – of the Jews as well as the souls of some non-Jews. That may be the reason Moshe took out the "mixed multitude," albeit with negative results. See *Pri haAretz*, Parashat Vayigash.

and we are given no choice in the matter.[21] Perhaps this is why it was appropriate that the sojourn in Egypt begin in iron chains.

Had the descent to Egypt taken place in an atmosphere of love, as one united family, perhaps the results would have been different. The exile had indeed been foretold, but the cruelty, the death, the despair were not necessarily preordained. Instead, jealousy and discord led them down to Egypt. One brother was rejected, almost killed. Perhaps this was the hidden allusion of the *'eglah 'arufah*: Had they had enough love for one another, they would have come to Egypt as a galvanized spiritual force. They would have been capable of completing their spiritual mission there without the need for undue suffering. Here, then, is the point of convergence with the *'eglah 'arufah* ceremony: the role of the *kohanim*, the descendants of Levi, is critical.

ספר פרי הארץ, פרשת ויגש

הנה ארז"ל במדרש (ב"ר פו:א) וש"ס (שבת פט ע"ב) ראוי היה יעקב אבינו לירד בשלשלאות של ברזל למצרים אלא וכו' ומשל בהמה שמוליכין אותה למקולין ואינה רוצה לילך מושכין אותה בחבל ע"ש. הנה המשל הוא הוראת ענין ירידת יעקב ובניו למצרים בכדי להעלות נצוצות הקדושות כידוע על (שמות יב:לו) וינצלו את מצרים כתרגומו ורוקינו, ואמרו רז"ל (ברכות ט ע"ב) כמצודה שאין בה דגים.

21. See *Megaleh 'Amukot* on Parashat Vayeishev, who links the furnace of steel, the chains of steel, and Yaakov's desire for tranquility, and the cow following the calf (*'eigel*) to Egypt.

ספר מגלה עמוקות, פרשת וישב

וישב יעקב ראוי היה ר' אבינו יעקב לירד בשלשלאות של ברזל: וקשה התחיל בשלשלאות של ברזל והביא ראי' מ (הושע יא) בחבלי אדם אמשכם היה לו לומר ראוי היה למשוך בחבלים אבל העניין נרמז כאן חטא של גלות מצרים הוא בא מן אדה"ר ולפי שיעקב תיקונו ושופריה של אדה"ר היה לכן היה ראוי לירד להוציא אותם מכור הברזל שהי' מצרים כור של ברזל לכן המשיל במדרש משל לנפח ז"ש בחבלי אד"ם ר"ל החבל ושלשלת קשור מן אדם הראשון וזה קדם הירידה ליעקב דוקא שהוא שופרי' דאדם (משלי ה) ובחבלי חטאתו יתמוך (תהלים קיט) חבלי רשעים עודני הקב"ה עשה (תהלים טז) חבלים נפלו לי בנעימים (דברים לב) יעקב חבל נחלתו (שמואל י) חבל נביאים (תהלים יו) אף נחלת שפרה עלי ר"ל לפי שיונק יוסף מן יצחק ק"ץ ח"י עלמין כשישב יעקב בארץ מגורי אביו קפץ עליו רוגזו של יוסף קפץ באף לא אמר חטאו של יוסף אבל רמז רוגזו של יוסף הוא סוד יניקת יוסף מן רוגזו של יצחק ואף חכמתי עמדה לי דרז"ל חכמתי שלמדתי באף עמדה לי וכן אני אומר שאמר יעקב אף נחלת ר"ל נחלת יוסף שהיא נוטה קצת לאף שפרה עלי כי לטובתו נשברה רגל פרתו ר"ל בן פורת יוסף שראוי הי' יעקב לירד בשלשלאות וגרמה זכות שבא לשם ע"י פרות שחלם לפרעה לכן מדמה במדרש משל לפרה שרוצים לשחוט אותה בבית המטבחיים שלוקחין העגל והיא תבא אחריה וכן (ירמי' מז) עגלה יפיפיה מצרים שירדו למצרים כדמיון עגל ז"ש אף נחלת ראוי' הי' באף רק זכות שפרה עלי קרי בי' פרה. ע"י פרה בא לשם ולפי שמצרים הוא כו"ר הברז"ל שכן מלך מצרים עולה הכי וישלחהו מעמ"ק חברו"ן ג"כ נתאמץ מענין י' פ' אהי"ה שהוא מנין עמ"ק וי"פ הוי"ה מנין חבר"ן שניהם יחד עולים כו"ר הברז"ל והוא סוד וישאו עיניהם והנה נושאים נכא"ת הוא ג"כ שניהם יחד עולים כו"ר הברז"ל עם הכולל שניהם יחד נכא"ת עולה אהי"ה וי"פ הוי"ה במילוי אלפין.

דברים כא:ה

וְנִגְּשׁוּ הַכֹּהֲנִים בְּנֵי לֵוִי כִּי בָם בָּחַר ה' אֱלֹקֶיךָ לְשָׁרְתוֹ וּלְבָרֵךְ בְּשֵׁם ה' וְעַל פִּיהֶם
יִהְיֶה כָּל רִיב וְכָל נָגַע:

And the kohanim, *the sons of Levi, shall come near – for the Almighty
your God has chosen them to serve Him and to bless in the name of
God, and by their word shall every controversy and every assault be
tried.* (Devarim 21:5)

The mandate of the *kohanim* is to create peace; they are described here as
those who bless in the name of God. The essence of the priestly blessing
is peace, and before bestowing this blessing upon the congregation, the
kohanim invoke their mandate to bless the people of Israel "with love."
Ironically, it is the sons of Levi (together with Shimon) who fought against
and annihilated every last inhabitant of the city of Shekhem. Moreover,
they are identified as the instigators of the plan to kill Yosef.[22] What a long
way they come to symbolize brotherly love and responsibility! In the case
of the *'eglah 'arufah* ceremony, God Himself inserts the *kohanim* into the
equation; it is they, specifically, whom the Torah commands to take a role,
to take responsibility. We can only surmise the extent to which Yosef's near-
murder at the hands of his brothers impacts the *'eglah 'arufah* ceremony.

The path to exile was one of hatred, jealousy and deceit. Surely, the path
to redemption is one of mutual responsibility and love. The role of the
kohanim, sons of Levi, serves as a reminder: Change is possible. Growth
is possible. If we learn from the Egypt experience to love one another,
redemption cannot be far off.

---

22. Rashi, Bereishit 49:5.

רש"י, בראשית מט:ה

שמעון ולוי אחים: בעצה אחת על שכם ועל יוסף ויאמרו איש אל אחיו וגו' ועתה לכו ונהרגהו. מי הם א"ת
ראובן או יהודה הרי לא הסכימו בהריגתו א"ת בני השפחות הרי לא היתה שנאתן שלימה שנא' והוא
נער את בני בלהה ואת בני זלפה וגו' יששכר וזבולן לא היו מדברים בפני אחיהם הגדולים מהם על כרחך
שמעון ולוי הם שקראם אביהם אחים.

Parashat Vayehi

Father and Son

The narrative of Parashat Vayehi seems to pose a problem when considered in light of a *halakhah* recorded in the book of Devarim:

דברים כא:טו–יז

כִּי תִהְיֶיןָ לְאִישׁ שְׁתֵּי נָשִׁים הָאַחַת אֲהוּבָה וְהָאַחַת שְׂנוּאָה וְיָלְדוּ לוֹ בָנִים הָאֲהוּבָה וְהַשְּׂנוּאָה וְהָיָה הַבֵּן הַבְּכֹר לַשְּׂנִיאָה: וְהָיָה בְּיוֹם הַנְחִילוֹ אֶת בָּנָיו אֵת אֲשֶׁר יִהְיֶה לוֹ לֹא יוּכַל לְבַכֵּר אֶת בֶּן הָאֲהוּבָה עַל פְּנֵי בֶן הַשְּׂנוּאָה הַבְּכֹר: כִּי אֶת הַבְּכֹר בֶּן הַשְּׂנוּאָה יַכִּיר לָתֶת לוֹ פִּי שְׁנַיִם בְּכֹל אֲשֶׁר יִמָּצֵא לוֹ כִּי הוּא רֵאשִׁית אֹנוֹ לוֹ מִשְׁפַּט הַבְּכֹרָה:

If a man has two wives, one beloved and another hated, and they have borne him children, both the beloved and the hated; and if the firstborn son is hers who was hated; then it shall be that when he makes his sons inherit that which he has, he may not favor the son of the beloved before the son of the hated [wife], who is indeed the firstborn. Rather he shall acknowledge the son of the hated for the firstborn by giving him a double portion of all that he has, for he is the beginning of his strength; the right of the firstborn is his. (Devarim 21:15–17)

Yaakov's complicated home life seems very relevant to this halakhah: Yaakov's first wife, Leah, was wed under duress, and could be called the "hated" wife, at least when compared to Rahel. Leah certainly felt this way, but she was not alone: God Himself assessed the complicated set of interpersonal relationships in similar fashion. Reuven is born as a means of bridging the emotional gaps:

בראשית כט:לא–לב

וַיַּרְא ה' כִּי שְׂנוּאָה לֵאָה וַיִּפְתַּח אֶת רַחְמָהּ וְרָחֵל עֲקָרָה: וַתַּהַר לֵאָה וַתֵּלֶד בֵּן וַתִּקְרָא שְׁמוֹ רְאוּבֵן כִּי אָמְרָה כִּי רָאָה ה' בְּעָנְיִי כִּי עַתָּה יֶאֱהָבַנִי אִישִׁי:

And when God saw that Leah was hated, he opened her womb; but Rahel was barren. And Leah conceived and bore a son, and she called

355

*his name Reuven; for she said, "Surely God has seen my affliction;
now therefore my husband will love me." (Bereishit 29:31–32)*

Yet as Yaakov's sons stand around his deathbed to hear his last wishes,
Reuven is addressed first, and Yaakov leaves no doubt that he is fully aware
of Reuven's rights – and responsibilities – as firstborn:

בראשית מט:ג–ד

רְאוּבֵן בְּכֹרִי אַתָּה כֹּחִי וְרֵאשִׁית אוֹנִי יֶתֶר שְׂאֵת וְיֶתֶר עָז: פַּחַז כַּמַּיִם אַל תּוֹתַר כִּי
עָלִיתָ מִשְׁכְּבֵי אָבִיךָ אָז חִלַּלְתָּ יְצוּעִי עָלָה:

*Reuven, you are my firstborn, my might, and the beginning of my
strength, the excellency of dignity, and the excellency of power.
Unstable as water, you shall not excel; because you went up to your
father's bed; then you defiled it; he went up to my couch. (Bereishit
49:3–4)*

According to tradition, Reuven, as firstborn, should have received three
precious gifts: a double portion of Yaakov's inheritance, kingship, and
priesthood.[1] In fact, Reuven receives none of these: The kingship is
bestowed upon Yehudah, and eventually, the priesthood is given to Levi.
Yosef, who was the firstborn son of the "beloved" wife Rahel, received the
double portion, in seeming contradiction to the law recorded in Devarim.

בראשית מח:ה

וְעַתָּה שְׁנֵי בָנֶיךָ הַנּוֹלָדִים לְךָ בְּאֶרֶץ מִצְרַיִם עַד בֹּאִי אֵלֶיךָ מִצְרַיְמָה לִי הֵם אֶפְרַיִם
וּמְנַשֶּׁה כִּרְאוּבֵן וְשִׁמְעוֹן יִהְיוּ לִי:

*And now your two sons, Efraim and Menashe, who were born to
you in the land of Egypt before I came to you to Egypt, are mine; as
Reuven and Shimon, they shall be mine. (Bereishit 48:5)*

---

1. For example, see Rabbeinu Bahya, Bereishit 49:3.

רבינו בחיי, בראשית מט:ג

ראובן בכורי אתה: היה ראוי ליטול שלש מעלות הבכורה והכהונה והמלכות ובחטאו אבדו ממנו, הבכורה
נתנה ליוסף הכהונה ללוי והמלכות ליהודה. וזהו שאמר פחז כמים והוא מלשון רז"ל עמא פחיזא אכתי
בפחזותיכו קיימיתו. ובאורו על שנמהרת בדרך פחיזות וקלות הדעת כמים הנחפזים והשוטפים. אל תותר
לא יהיה לך אותו יתרון שהיה ראוי לך. והוא הבכורה בכורי אתה. והכהונה יתר שאת מלשון נשיאות כפים
וכתיב (ויקרא י) ואותה נותן לכם לשאת את עון העדה. והמלכות זהו שאמר יתר עז. ויתרון המלכות לשון
(ש"א ב) ויתן עז למלכו. וכתוב (תהלים צט) ועז מלך משפט אהב.

By elevating Efraim and Menashe to the level of Yosef's brothers, Yaakov in effect gives the double portion to Yosef. These two grandsons of Yaakov, sons of Yosef, become tribes in their own right and each one day receives their own portion in the Land of Israel, a clear indication that Yosef – and not Reuven – has received the double portion.[2]

We might say that the contradiction we have raised is a nonissue: the *halakhah* in question was recorded many years after the death of Yaakov, and it is unfair to judge the actions of those who lived before the Revelation at Sinai by Torah-law standards. Nonetheless, the sensitive reader is uncomfortable with this seeming transgression, no matter how theoretical. Yaakov is, after all, one of our patriarchs, a spiritual hero and role model. Is it possible that he was insensitive to the social and spiritual truths that lay at the heart of the *halakhah*?[3] The commandment that protects the rights of the firstborn is not the type of law that is impenetrable by logic; a spiritually sensitive man like Yaakov should have been more judicious. We would like to say that this was an oversight by Yaakov, but the very language he uses rules out that possibility: there is an obvious linguistic connection between the verses that describe the birth of Reuven, the wording of Yaakov's final

---

2. See Rashi and Rabbeinu Bahya, Bereishit 48:5.

רש"י, בראשית מח:ה

לי הם: בחשבון שאר בני הם ליטול חלק בארץ איש כנגדו.

רבינו בחיי, בראשית מח:ה

כראובן ושמעון יהיו לי: בכאן נתן יעקב הבכורה ליוסף, ומה שכתוב (דה"א ה) ובחללו יצועי אביו נתנה בכורתו ליוסף מן הכתוב הזה נאמר כן: והנה דעת רש"י ז"ל כי בכורתו של יוסף לא לענין נחלה רק לענין הכבוד שיקראו בניו שבטים.

והרמב"ן ז"ל דוחה זה כי אי אפשר בשום פנים שיהיה יוסף כשאר השבטים בנחלה ותהיה הבכורה להקרא שני שבטים, אבל בכורתו של יוסף היתה לענין נחלה וזהו שאמר הכתוב בנחלתם. וזהו שתרגם אונקלוס תרין שבטין יפקון מבנוהי יקבלון חולקא ואחסנתא, שחולקא הוא חלק הבכורה, ואחסנתא ירושת הפשוט.

3. See *Eitz haDa'at Tov*, Parashat Vayehi, which records teachings of the Ari"zal. Here he raises the problem; we will return to his solution below.

ספר עץ הדעת טוב, פרשת ויחי

ראובן בכורי אתה וכו': כוונת יעקב עתה כברכתו הראויה לו ואמנם ביקש לתת הבכורה ליוסף והמלכות ליהודה והשומע יאמר על מה זה עבר על ציווי התורה והיה הבכור אשר תלד יקום על שם אביו המת לכל הדברים ובפרט לענין נחלת פי שנים כמ"ש כי את הבכור בן השנואה יכיר לתת לו פי שנים וכן במלכי' מצינו המלוכה והמשפט נתן יהושפט ליהורה כי הוא הבכור וכפי הדין שני הדברים האלה ראויים לראובן. לכן הקדים לתת טעם לדבר ואמר ראובן וכו' יראה מן הדין היו ראויים לך יען כי בכור אתה וכו' אתה יראה הנה ד' בכורות יש לי בקדושת פטר רחם אלא שהם בכורות מן הד' אמהות אבל אתה לבדך בכור מן האב כנודע כי לענין נחלת. פי שנים לא תועיל בכורת האם אלא בכורת האב.

blessing to his firstborn son, and the words of the law dictating that the double portion must be given to the firstborn.

A second, seemingly unrelated question emerges, again, only when we compare this parashah with a later section of text. In the next parashah, the first in the book of Shmot, a textual anomaly arises:

בראשית נ:כו

וַיָּמָת יוֹסֵף בֶּן מֵאָה וָעֶשֶׂר שָׁנִים וַיַּחַנְטוּ אֹתוֹ וַיִּישֶׂם בָּאָרוֹן בְּמִצְרָיִם:

So Yosef died, being one hundred ten years old; and they embalmed him, and he was placed in a coffin in Egypt. (Bereishit 50:26)

The book of Bereishit comes to an end with the death of Yosef, and the book of Shmot begins with Yosef's death, recorded for the second time:

שמות א:ו

וַיָּמָת יוֹסֵף וְכָל אֶחָיו וְכֹל הַדּוֹר הַהוּא:

And Yosef died, and all his brothers, and all that generation. (Shmot 1:6)

While this may seem like a simple literary device, to "catch the readers up" and remind them where we are up to,[4] it should be noted that fundamentally the book of Bereishit is a book of the *avot* and *imahot*, the patriarchs and matriarchs, while the book of Shmot is about the Children of Israel.[5] The

---

4. See *Igra d'Kallah*, page 177a.

ספר אגרא דכלה, דף קעז עמוד א

וימת יוסף וכל וכו' וכל וכו' (שמות א:ו): הנה פטירת יוסף כבר נכתב בסיום הספר. וגם היה לו לומר בקיצור וימת יוסף וכל הדור וכו'. והנראה דמשמיענו גודל רחמנותו ית"ש, איך לאט לאט התחיל ענין השעבוד, ובכל פעם נרגש העניין יותר, דהנה כשמת יוסף היו מכובדים מאד, ואחר כך בפטירת האחים התחילה השעבוד, אבל לא בקושי רק בפה רך, ואחר כך בפטירת הדור התחיל קושי השעבוד בחומר וכו'.

5. See the introduction of the Ramban to the book of Shmot.

רמב"ן, הקדמה לספר שמות

תם ונשלם שבח לבורא עולם חסלת פרשת ויחי פרשת שמות הכתוב השלים ספר בראשית שהוא ספר היצירה בחדוש העולם ויצירת כל נוצר, ובמקרי האבות כולם שהם כעין יצירה לזרעם, מפני שכל מקריהם ציורי דברים לרמוז להודיע כל העתיד לבא להם ואחרי שהשלים היצירה התחיל ספר אחר בענין המעשה הבא מן הרמזים ההם, ונתיחד ספר ואלה שמות בענין הגלות הראשון הנגזר בפירוש (בראשית טו:יג) ובגאולה ממנו, ולכן חזר והתחיל בשמות יורדי מצרים ומספרם אף על פי שכבר נכתב זה (שם מו:ח-כז), בעבור כי ירידתם שם הוא ראשית הגלות, כי מאז הוחל.

והנה הגלות איננו נשלם עד יום שובם אל מקומם ואל מעלת אבותם ישובו – וכשיצאו ממצרים אף על פי שיצאו מבית עבדים עדיין יחשבו גולים, כי היו בארץ לא להם נבוכים במדבר, וכשבאו אל הר סיני ועשו

death of all twelve tribal fathers could have been mentioned in Bereishit, closing the door on that generation, or, alternatively, all twelve sons could have died in the beginning of Shmot. Only Yosef "dies twice." [6]

While this observation about Yosef's death may seem like a question, it actually contains the answer to our first question regarding the wresting of the birthright from Reuven in favor of Yosef. As we shall see, the answer may be understood on many levels, some of which are in the realm of mystical study, while others are accessible to all.

Yosef was fundamentally different from his brothers; he was not truly a part of their generation. Yosef was a "throwback" to a previous generation. The simple, chronological understanding of this phenomenon comes as no radical interpretation: though two people's lives intersect chronologically, one belongs to the previous generation, while the other may be a part of

---

המשכן ושב הקדוש ברוך הוא והשרה שכינתו ביניהם אז שבו אל מעלת אבותם, שהיה סוד אלה עלי אהליהם, והם הם המרכבה (ב"ר מז:ח), ואז נחשבו גאולים ולכן נשלם הספר הזה בהשלימו ענין המשכן ובהיות כבוד ה' מלא אותו תמיד.

6. See Ohr haHayim (Shmot 1:6) who reveals that there is a deep mystical secret in the repetition of Yosef's death. He cites a passage recorded in the spiritual diary of Rav Yosef Karo, *Magid Meisharim*, a document that records mystical revelations shared with him by an angel.

אור החיים, שמות א:ו

וימת יוסף וגו' ובני ישראל וגו': צריך לדעת לאיזה ענין חוזר פעם ב' להודיע מיתת יוסף, וכבר השמיענו (בראשית נ:כו) וימת יוסף בן וגו' עוד צריך לדעת כוונת הודעת הכתוב שמתו האחים וכל הדור עוד מה קשר יש בין מיתת האחים והדור לאומרו ובני ישראל, והנה המגיד של מהרי"ק הגיד לו טעם סמיכות זה, והוא דרך סוד עוד צריך לדעת טעם אומרו כסדר זה ובני ישראל וגו', שאם בא להודיענו פריית ורביית בני ישראל היה לו לומר כסדר זה ויפרו וישרצו וגו' בני ישראל:

אכן שני כתובים הבאים כאחד להודיע השתלשלות התחלת השעבוד וסיבותיו והם במספר ד', הא' מיתת יוסף, שאם היה יוסף קיים יספיק שלא ימשלו בהם המצריים, הא למדת שכל זמן שיוסף היו ישראל בארץ מצרים שקטים ומעונגים.

ספר מגיד מישרים, פרשת שמות

וימת יוסף וכל אחיו, ובני ישראל פרו וישרצו וכו': הכא רמיז רזא דאוליפתך צדיקים מולידים במיתתם יותר מבחייהם, דכד מסתלק צדיק מן עלמא כמה נפשין דאזלין ערטלאין בעלמא ולית להון נייחא אזלין לגבי'. וכד מספידין עליה ואמרין ד"ת עליה נפשיא מתעטפת בהנהו מלין ועי"כ כן היא סלקא בדרגא עילאין, והנך נפשן אוף הכי מתעטפי בהנך מלין קדישין, ועי"כ מתגזר עלייהו דיתגלגלו, וכל חדא וחדא גזרי עלה בההוא שעתא בהי דוכתא יתגלגלו, ומתקנין להו דוכתא דיהון תמן בין כך ובין כך, נמצאו צדיקים מולידים במיתתם יותר מבחייהם, והיינו רזא דהורדת דמעות על אדם כשר רמז להאי שפעא דניחת מלעילא להנגד נפשן, והיינו דלא פרו בני ישראל עד דמית יוסף וכו' ועי' מיתתהון נחתו כל הנך נפשן ואיתגלגלו בישראל, ועי"כ כך פרו וכו' והיו יולדות ששה בכרס אחד רמז לשית ספירין דמשפען במלכות דאיקרי ארץ, והיינו דכתיב ותמלא הארץ אותם.

the next generation. Yosef's case was somewhat more profound: His age placed him firmly in the generation of Yaakov's sons, yet Yosef's essence was related to the previous generation. He was a rare individual who had the ability to transcend his age and transform himself into something else. In fact, most of the people who came into contact with him were struck by this quality. We may summarize this particular attribute in terms of Yosef's place as a "hinge" between two generations. Yosef was not part of a new generation, he was an extension of Yaakov:

בראשית לז:ב

אֵלֶּה תֹּלְדוֹת יַעֲקֹב יוֹסֵף בֶּן שְׁבַע עֶשְׂרֵה שָׁנָה...

These are the generations of Yaakov: Yosef, being seventeen years old... (Bereishit 37:2)

The Torah describes Yosef's unique position in various ways. First, we are told that Yaakov loved Yosef because he was his *ben zekunim*:

בראשית לז:ג

וְיִשְׂרָאֵל אָהַב אֶת יוֹסֵף מִכָּל בָּנָיו כִּי בֶן זְקֻנִים הוּא לוֹ וְעָשָׂה לוֹ כְּתֹנֶת פַּסִּים:

Now Yisrael loved Yosef more than all his children, because he was his ben zekunim; *and he made him a coat of many colors.* (Bereishit 37:3)

This term is often translated as "the child of his old age," though this would be an unlikely explanation on two accounts: A number of Yosef's brothers are very close in age, being that there were four women bearing children during the same time period.[7] Furthermore, Yosef had a much younger brother, Binyamin, who truly was the child of Yaakov's old age. Targum Onkelos translates *zekunim* as wise. Often, age is associated with wisdom;

7.　Ramban, Bereishit 37:3.

רמב"ן, בראשית לז:ג

ואיננו נכון בעיני, כי הכתוב אמר שאהב את יוסף מכל בניו בעבור שהוא בן זקונים, וגם כל בניו נולדו לו בזקוניו, והנה יששכר וזבולון אינם גדולים מיוסף רק כשנה או שנתים.

thus, Yosef is a *"ben zekunim,"*[8] a wise son.[9] The Midrash takes up this theme as well, explaining that all that Yaakov received from his father by tradition was passed on to Yosef. Here there was no generation gap.[10]

Par'oh's estimation of Yosef's unique abilities seems very similar:

בראשית מא:מג

וַיַּרְכֵּב אֹתוֹ בְּמִרְכֶּבֶת הַמִּשְׁנֶה אֲשֶׁר לוֹ וַיִּקְרְאוּ לְפָנָיו אַבְרֵךְ וְנָתוֹן אֹתוֹ עַל כָּל אֶרֶץ מִצְרָיִם.

And he had him ride in his second chariot; and they cried before him, "avreikh!"; and he made him ruler over all the land of Egypt. (Bereishit 41:43)

The term used to describe Par'oh's new right-hand man is somewhat obscure; Onkelos says that the word *avreikh* means "father of the king."[11] Rashi cites this teaching and adds that we have a tradition[12] that the word

---

8. The *Sfat Emet* notices that it says he was a wise child *to him* – that specifically Yaakov saw this quality. The brothers did not see it; they saw Yosef as a *na'ar*, a frivolous child.

   שפת אמת, פרשת וישב, שנת [תרנ"ו]

   וכן הי' בחי' יוסף. ויעקב אבינו הבין זה. ולכן כתיב בן זקונים הוא לו כלומר הם חשבוהו לנער והוא חשבו לזקן. וכן נק' אברך מה"ט אב בחכמה ורך בשנים. ומה שנגלה להם בבחי' נער הי' בעבורם כמ"ש נער את בני בלהה. ומדת הצדיק הוא בפנימיות למעלה מכל. ובחיצוניות הי' נראה קטן מכל השבטים. כמו שקראוהו חכמים יוסף קטנן של שבטים. וזה הי' בחי' חיצוניות שלו.

9. Ramban, Bereishit 37:3.

   רמב"ן, בראשית לז:ג

   ואונקלוס שאמר "בר חכים" ירצה לומר שהיה בן דעת וחכם בעיני אביו, וטעמו כטעם זקנים – ותרגם יליד זקונים, בר סבתין, כי לא אמר הכתוב בכאן "כי בן זקונים היה", אבל אמר "הוא לו", שהיה כן בעיניו וזאת כונתם באמרם (ב"ר פד:ח) כל מה שלמד משם ועבר מסר לו, לומר שמסר לו חכמות וסתרי תורה ומצאו משכיל ובעל סוד בהם כאלו היה זקן ורב ימים.

10. Rashi, based on Bereishit Rabbah 84:8, explains the meaning of the wisdom referred to by Onkelos: Yaakov passed on the traditions of Shem and Ever to Yosef.

    רש"י, בראשית לז:ג

    בן זקונים: שנולד לו לעת זקנתו ואונקלוס תרגם בר חכים הוא ליה כל מה שלמד משם ועבר מסר לו.

11. Targum Onkelos, Bereishit 41:43.

    תרגום אונקלוס, בראשית מא:מג

    וארכיב יתיה ברתכא תנינתא [נ"א, תנינא] די ליה ואכריזו קדמוהי דין **אבא למלכא** ומני יתיה על כל ארעא דמצרים.

12. Sifri Devarim, paragraph 1.

means "a father (*av*) in wisdom, despite being tender (*rakh*[13]) in years" –
one whose wisdom transcends their years.[14]

Yosef himself seems to refer to this quality and this relationship with Par'oh
when he tells his brothers that God sent him to Egypt and placed him as a
"father" to Par'oh.

בראשית מה:ח

וְעַתָּה לֹא אַתֶּם שְׁלַחְתֶּם אֹתִי הֵנָּה כִּי הָאֱלֹקים וַיְשִׂימֵנִי לְאָב לְפַרְעֹה וּלְאָדוֹן לְכָל
בֵּיתוֹ וּמֹשֵׁל בְּכָל אֶרֶץ מִצְרָיִם:

*So now it was not you who sent me here, but God; and he has made
me a father to Par'oh, and lord of all his house, and a ruler throughout
all the land of Egypt.* (Bereishit 45:8)

When it is Yosef's turn to be blessed, Yaakov says:

בראשית מט:כב–כד

בֵּן פֹּרָת יוֹסֵף בֵּן פֹּרָת עֲלֵי עָיִן בָּנוֹת צָעֲדָה עֲלֵי שׁוּר: וַיְמָרֲרֻהוּ וָרֹבּוּ וַיִּשְׂטְמֻהוּ בַּעֲלֵי
חִצִּים: וַתֵּשֶׁב בְּאֵיתָן קַשְׁתּוֹ וַיָּפֹזּוּ זְרֹעֵי יָדָיו מִידֵי אֲבִיר יַעֲקֹב מִשָּׁם רֹעֶה אֶבֶן יִשְׂרָאֵל:

ספרי, פרשת דברים פסקה א

כיוצא בדבר אתה אומר דרש ר' יהודה (בראשית מא) וירכב אותו במרכבת המשנה אשר לו זה יוסף שהיה
אב בחכמה ורך בשנים. אמר לו ר' יוסי בן דורמסקית לר' יהוד' בר' למה אתה מעוות עלינו את הכתובים
מעידני עלי שמים וארץ שאין אברך אלא לברכים שהיו הכל נכנסים ויוצאים תחת ידו כענין שנאמר ונתון
אותו על כל ארץ מצרים.

13. The *Megaleh 'Amukot* says that *rakh* (רך) has a numerical value (*gematria*) of 220,
corresponding to the slavery that will be endured will be for the twenty-two years that
Yosef was separated from his father multiplied by ten brothers.

ספר מגלה עמוקות, פרשת מקץ

ויקראו לפניו אברך: כי הוא אב של גלות מצרים שהי' ראוי להיות ר"ך שנים כדאיתא בזוהר י' אחים כל א'
כ"ב שנה שהי' פירש מאביו. או שהוא אב של עולם היצירה שהוא סוד ר"ך כמבואר באידרא ע"פ ראשך
עליך ככרמל ר"ך עלמין גם ש"ע נהורין שנחלקין על ו' ה' מן השם סוד (תהלים י) הוש"ע עבדך הבוטח
עליך שנחלקין ר"ך לעולם היצירה ו' מן השם ק"ן מטרנותא מקננא באופן וכמו שאברם הוא
אב של ר"ם קבין. וירכ"ב אות"ו בגי' ש"ר העול"ם במרכבת בגי' אכתרי"אל שר הבריאה שהוא סוד רק
הכסא אגדל ממך כי מטטרו"ן הוא עולם היצירה.

14. Rashi, Bereishit 41:43.

רש"י, בראשית מא:מג

אברך: כתרגומו דין אבא למלכא רך בלשון ארמי מלך בהשותפין לא ריכא ולא בר ריכא. ובדברי אגדה
(ספרי פרשת דברים) דרש ר' יהודה אברך זה יוסף שהוא אב בחכמה ורך בשנים אמר לו בן דורמסקית
עד מתי אתה מעוות עלינו את הכתובים אין אברך אלא לשון ברכים שהכל היו נכנסין לפניו ויוצאין תחת
ידו כענין שנאמר ונתון אותו וגו'.

Yosef is a fruitful bough, a fruitful bough by a well, whose branches run over the wall. The archers fiercely attacked him, and shot at him, and hated him. But his bow abode in strength, and the arms of his hands were made strong by the hands of the mighty God of Jacob; from there is the shepherd, the stone of Israel. (Bereishit 49:22–24)

Yosef is referred to as *even yisrael*, which is literally translated as the "stone of Israel." Onkelos[15] understands the word *even* (stone) as an amalgam[16] of *av* and *ben*, father and son: Yosef is not only a son, he is also a father. While this is far from remarkable – many people in the history of the world have been both fathers and sons – Yaakov's comments do much to identify this unique quality Yosef possessed. Yosef was a son and a father; he had the status of one of the twelve tribes, yet he also had the status of one of the patriarchs. He is both an *av* and a *ben*. This is the reason Yosef's death, and none of the other brothers', is recorded in Bereishit together with the other patriarchs; his status was elevated to that of his father Yaakov, his grandfather Yitzhak and his great-grandfather Avraham. Nonetheless, he is also mentioned in Shmot with the other brothers; he is also a son of Yaakov, a member of the collective known as the Children of Yisrael.

When does Yosef achieve this status? When his father bestows upon him a double portion he is thrust above the others of his generation, and his children achieve the same status as the other brothers. That was the blessing of Yaakov, but the message runs much deeper than mere portions and wealth, or even inheritance in the Land of Israel. The Midrash expresses the idea in a teaching in which each of the four species is "matched" with one of the patriarchs. This presents a problem, as there are only three patriarchs. The Midrash brings Yosef to the rescue:

---

15. Targum Onkelos, Bereishit 49:24.

תרגום אונקלוס, בראשית מט:כד

ותבת בהון נביותיה על דקיים אורייתא בסתרא ושוי תוקפא רוחצניה בכן יתרמא דהב על דרעוהי אחסין מלכותא ותקיף דא הות ליה מן קדם אל תקיפא דיעקב דבמימריה זן אבהן ובנין זרעא דישראל.

16. See Rashi, Bereishit 49:24.

רש"י, בראשית מט:כד

אבן ישראל: לשון נוטריקון אב ובן, אבהן ובנין, יעקב ובניו.

ויקרא רבה, פרשה ל פסקה י

ד"א "פרי עץ הדר" – זה אברהם שהדרו הקב"ה בשיבה טובה, שנאמר,
(בראשית כד) "ואברהם זקן בא בימים", וכתיב (ויקרא יט) "והדרת פני
זקן". "כפות תמרים" – זה יצחק שהיה כפות ועקוד על גבי המזבח. "וענף עץ
עבות" – זה יעקב: מה הדס זה רחוש בעלין, כך היה יעקב רחוש בבנים. "וערבי
נחל" – זה יוסף: מה ערבה זו כמושה לפני ג' מינין הללו, כך מת יוסף לפני אחיו.

Another exposition of the text: "The fruit of the hadar *tree": Hadar
symbolizes Avraham, whom the Holy One, blessed be He, honored
(hiddero) with good old age, as it says, "And Avraham was old,
advanced in days" (Bereishit 24:1), and it is written, "And honor
(vehadarta) the face of the elderly" (Vayikra 19:32). "Branches
(kappot) of palm trees" symbolizes Yitzhak who had been tied (kafut)
and bound upon the altar. "And boughs of thick trees" symbolizes
Yaakov: just as the myrtle is crowded with leaves so was Yaakov
crowded with children. "And willows of the brook" symbolizes Yosef:
as the willow wilts before the other three species, so Yosef died before
his brethren. (Vayikra Rabbah 30:10)*

It seems strange to consider Yosef the "fourth wheel," for Yosef was part
of the next generation; nonetheless, this is exactly what this midrash does.
Yosef is added to the three patriarchs, making the trio a quartet.[17]

---

17. This idea that the three *avot* are sometimes seen as three and sometimes seen as four
is represented by the tefilin. The tefilin worn on the head has the Hebrew letter *shin*
engraved on each side, but on one side the *shin* has three arms, while on the other side it
has four. The *Shlah haKadosh* believes that this is two manifestations of the *avot*: alone –
where there are three, or with Yosef, where there would be four.

ספר השל"ה הקדוש, פרשת ויחי תורה אור (ג)

וכן תמצא ביוסף ובניו יהיו בסוד ציון וירושלים, שהם התפשטות יסוד ומלכות. כי נודע כי יוסף הוא
הצדיק יסוד עולם, והנה מייחס תמיד את אפרים ליוסף, כמו שנאמר (במדבר א:לב), לבני יוסף בני
אפרים, מנשה למטה ממנו, הרי יוסף ובניו סוד תפילין של יד, ויעקב בעצמו סוד תפילין של ראש.
וכבר נודע כי סוד שי"ן של שלושה ראשים רומזת נגד שלושה אבות שהן הן המרכבה, כי השי"ן של
ארבעה ראשים רומזת נגד מרכבה שהיא ד', סוד ארגמ"ן ארבע מחנה שכינה, ר-פאל ג-בריאל מ-יכאל
נ-וריאל, וה'א' שהוא הקב"ה רוכב עליהם. והשלושה אבות, ובתוכם נכלל ברא כרעא דאבוה הוא יוסף עם
התפשטותו, כי יוסף הוא יעקב, הם בפנימיות המרכבה ביותר, והבחיר שבאבות הוא יעקב, והוא בסוד
תפילין של ראש. זהו סוד וישתחו ישראל על 'ראש' המטה (בראשית מז:לא), ורומז למטתו של שלמה,
ותפילין של ראש הן ראש המטה. אבל המשכת יוסף וזרעו הם סוד תפילין של יד, והנה תפילין של יד
משך שייכי ביד שמאל, גם בימין, כי צריך לקושרם על יד שמאל, והקשירה היא בימין, וזהו סוד שכל את
ידיו כי מנשה הבכור (בראשית מח:יד).

This teaching has implications regarding a deep mystical teaching known as the Chariot – or *Merkavah*. The *Merkavah* was part of an awesome vision beheld by the prophet Yehezkel. This *Merkavah* is best described as a spiritual vehicle, a means of connecting our physical world and ourselves with the spiritual world that lies beyond our sensory grasp. In a sense, the *Merkavah* is a spiritual elevator that enables man to connect with Heaven. The rabbis teach that the patriarchs are themselves, through their actions and teachings, a *Merkavah*:

בראשית רבה, פרשה פב פסקה ו

"ויעל מעליו אלקים": אמר ר"ל האבות הן הן המרכבה שנא' (בראשית יז) "ויעל אלקים מעל אברהם", (בראשית לה) "ויעל מעליו אלקים", (בראשית כח) "והנה ה' נצב עליו".

"And God went up from him" (Bereishit 35): R. Shimon b. Lakish said: The patriarchs are [God's] Merkavah, for it says, "And God went up from upon Avraham" (Bereishit 17:22), "And God went up from upon him" (Bereishit 35:13), "And, behold, the Almighty stood above him" (Bereishit 28:13). (Bereishit Rabbah 82:6)

A chariot has four wheels; the mystical chariot of Yehezkel is no exception. When aligned with the three *avot*, one wheel is missing; that fourth wheel[18] is Yosef.[19]

---

18. See *Drashot Ri Ibn Shuab* for the first day of Sukkot, who reveals the connection between the four species and the Chariot.

דרשות ר"י אבן שועיב, דרשה ליום ראשון דסוכות

אמרו שם פרי עץ הדר, זה אברהם אבינו שהדרו הקב"ה בשיבה טובה, כמו שנאמר ואברהם זקן, וכתיב והדרת פני זקן. כפות תמרים זה יצחק שהיה כפות על גבי המזבח. וענף עץ עבות זה יעקב, מה הדס זה עבות בעלים אף יעקב עבות בבנים יותר מן האבות. ערבי נחל זה יוסף מה ערבה זאת כמושה ומתייבשת יותר מן שאר המינין, כך מת יוסף קודם אחיו. הנה בכאן רמז ד' מיניו לאבות שהן המרכבה כנגד ד' מחנות שכינה שהעולם מתקיים בהן וכנגדן דגלי השבטים שהן כנגד ד' חיות שראה יחזקאל, ומזה העניין תדע למה ערבה בשמאל והדס בימין ולולב באמצע ואתרוג לבדו. ויש שם מי שהמשיל אתרוג לשרה לולב לרבקה הדס ללאה ערבה לרחל, וכלם מתכוונין לעניין אחד, אלא שכל אחד ואחד נתכוון להסתיר הסודות, כמו שאמר שלמה כבוד אלקים הסתר דבר.

19. See *Megaleh 'Amukot*, Parashat Vayehi.

ספר מגלה עמוקות, פרשת ויחי

מכאן למדו רז"ל שבקש יעקב לגלות קץ הימין העניין כמו שכתבתי אית קץ ואית קץ כמ"ש דוד (תהלים לט) הודיעני י"י קיצי ומדת ימי מה היא על קץ הימים מתי יכלה מן העולם רק שמגיע קיצי שהיא קץ הימין ומאחר שאנו מוצאין בפסוק שיעקב אמר האספו ואגידה לכם מה שיהי' באחרית קץ הימים א"כ

Interestingly, the first biblical character to ride in a chariot is Yosef:

בראשית מא:מג

וַיַּרְכֵּב אֹתוֹ בְּמִרְכֶּבֶת הַמִּשְׁנֶה אֲשֶׁר לוֹ וַיִּקְרְאוּ לְפָנָיו אַבְרֵךְ וְנָתוֹן אֹתוֹ עַל כָּל אֶרֶץ מִצְרָיִם.

And he had him ride in his second chariot; and they cried before him, "avreikh!"; and he made him ruler over all the land of Egypt. (Bereishit 41:43)

There is another, deeper point that connects Yosef to the *Merkavah* of Yehezkel's vision. In describing his vision, Yehezkel recounts the images he saw: on one of the four sides was an elusive image, described in the first chapter as an ox, and in the tenth chapter as a *keruv* – or cherub.

יחזקאל א:י

וּדְמוּת פְּנֵיהֶם פְּנֵי אָדָם וּפְנֵי אַרְיֵה אֶל הַיָּמִין לְאַרְבַּעְתָּם וּפְנֵי שׁוֹר מֵהַשְּׂמֹאל לְאַרְבַּעְתָּן וּפְנֵי נֶשֶׁר לְאַרְבַּעְתָּן:

As for the likeness of their faces, the four had the face of a man, and the face of a lion, on the right side; and the four had the face of an ox on the left side; the four also had the face of an eagle. (Yehezkel 1:10)

Ezekiel 1:10

יחזקאל י:יד–טו

וְאַרְבָּעָה פָנִים לְאֶחָד פְּנֵי הָאֶחָד פְּנֵי הַכְּרוּב וּפְנֵי הַשֵּׁנִי פְּנֵי אָדָם וְהַשְּׁלִישִׁי פְּנֵי אַרְיֵה וְהָרְבִיעִי פְּנֵי נָשֶׁר: וַיֵּרֹמּוּ הַכְּרוּבִים הִיא הַחַיָּה אֲשֶׁר רָאִיתִי בִּנְהַר כְּבָר:

And each one had four faces; the first face was the face of a keruv, and the second face was the face of a man, and the third the face of a lion, and the fourth the face of an eagle. And the keruvim were raised. This is the living creature that I saw by the Kevar River. (Yehezkel 10:14–15)

ממילא רצה להודיע ולגלות לנו קץ הימין שהוא שלנו כי ידו אוחזת בעקב עשו וכשמסיים עשו פותח יעקב נחזור לשמעתין שבמלת אליו המבוארת המרכבה ל' מורה על יוסף שהוא תשלום המרכבה כי בן שלשים הי' יוסף לפי שהוא מגדל הפורח באויר ועלי' נרמז רק הכסא אגדל ממך במלת אגדל יש ד' למדין שבאלף בית רזא עילאה הוא רזא דרתיכא קדישא שאין אנו מוצאין שום ל' בכל אותיות התורה רק ד' אלו שסודם (שם יח) באלק"י אדלג שו' מלשון חומה מגדל עז שם י"י בן ירוץ צדיק שהוא יוסף הצדיק גם רומז על יוסף שהוא בכור שור וכשראה אברהם שלשה אנשים נצבים עליו אל בק"ר רץ אברהם בסוד שור שיהי' ר"ז' וטוב כי הוא א"ב ר"ך שקראו לפניו במצרים (ישעי' ג) ואמרו צדיק כי טו"ב ז"ש ויתן אל הנער לעשותו והוא נער כי תשלום ד' רגלים הי' אז יוסף.

The image of an ox is used elsewhere to describe Yosef:

דברים לג:יג–יז

וּלְיוֹסֵף אָמַר מְבֹרֶכֶת ה' אַרְצוֹ מִמֶּגֶד שָׁמַיִם מִטָּל וּמִתְּהוֹם רֹבֶצֶת תָּחַת: וּמִמֶּגֶד תְּבוּאֹת שָׁמֶשׁ וּמִמֶּגֶד גֶּרֶשׁ יְרָחִים: וּמֵרֹאשׁ הַרְרֵי קֶדֶם וּמִמֶּגֶד גִּבְעוֹת עוֹלָם: וּמִמֶּגֶד אֶרֶץ וּמְלֹאָהּ וּרְצוֹן שֹׁכְנִי סְנֶה תָּבוֹאתָה לְרֹאשׁ יוֹסֵף וּלְקָדְקֹד נְזִיר אֶחָיו: בְּכוֹר שׁוֹרוֹ הָדָר לוֹ וְקַרְנֵי רְאֵם קַרְנָיו בָּהֶם עַמִּים יְנַגַּח יַחְדָּו אַפְסֵי אָרֶץ וְהֵם רִבְבוֹת אֶפְרַיִם וְהֵם אַלְפֵי מְנַשֶּׁה:

And of Yosef he said, "Blessed of God be his land, for the precious things of heaven, for the dew, and for the deep that couches beneath, And for the precious fruits brought forth by the sun, and for the precious things put forth by the moon, and for the peaks of the ancient mountains, and for the precious things of the eternal hills. And for the precious things of the earth and its fullness, and for the good will of him who lived in the bush; let the blessing come upon the head of Yosef, and upon the top of the head of him who was separated from his brothers. As the firstborn of his ox, grandeur is his, and his horns are like the horns of a wild ox; with them he shall push the people together to the ends of the earth; and they are the ten thousands of Efraim, and they are the thousands of Menashe. (Devarim 33:13–17)*

Deuteronomy 33:13-19

Let us look more carefully at Yehezkel's prophecy. The place at which Yehezkel has this vision is the Kevar River. In this vision, one aspect seems to shift between the image of an ox and a *keruv*. So many of the salient points are bound together by the etymology of these Hebrew words that we must stop and take notice.

Ezekiel

The letters *bet kaf resh* (ב-כ-ר) spell *bekhor* (בכר), which means firstborn. Yosef is the fourth side of the *Merkavah*; the root of the word *Merkavah* is *r-kh-b* (ר-כ-ב). The site of Yehezkel's *Merkavah* vision was Kevar (כבר), which is comprised of these same letters. Yosef rode in a chariot, and was called *avreikh*, comprised of these same three letters with the addition of an *alef*. Yosef is represented by the fourth side, which is either an ox or a *keruv*, another word composed of these same three letters.

Earlier we saw various opinions regarding the meaning of the word *avreikh*. The Ibn Ezra is of the opinion that this singular word is extrapolated from the word *berekh* (ברך), which means knee: by Par'oh's order, everyone was commanded to bow on their knees[20] at the sight of Yosef and his chariot.[21] *Berekh* (ברך) is composed of these same three letters.[22] These same three letters seem to have great significance for Yaakov, as well. Throughout Yaakov's life the main issues that motivate and animate his life story were the issues of *bekhorah* (בכורה) – the firstborn status, and *brakhah* (ברכה) – blessings, both of which are composed of these same letters. Yaakov's life story reaches its culmination in Yosef; as an extension of his father, Yosef receives the *bekhorah*, and the choicest *brakhah*.

The nature of these three critical letters, which seem to bind together the narrative of Yaakov and Yosef, encapsulates a very powerful message: These three letters are all "seconds." Hebrew letters have numerical values which are often a key to otherwise unnoticed connections between concepts. The letter *bet* is the second of the single digits (*alef*, *bet*); *kaf* is the second of the tens, and *resh* is the second of the hundreds. The numerical value of these three letters is 222, making the numerical value of all the words that

---

20. See the Ari"zal in *Eitz haDa'at Tov*, Parashat Bereishit.

ספר עץ הדעת טוב, פרשת ויחי

... ולכן ר"ת "ראובן "בכורי "אתה "כחי הוא אברך הנאמר ביוסף ויקראו לפניו אברך דין אבא למלכא אתה היית ראוי לאותה המלוכה וגם לנחלת פי שנים שניתנו ליוסף שהיה בכור פטר רחם מן האם בלבד ומפני חטאתיך ניתנו ליוסף וכמ"ש ויקראו לפניו אבר"ך כי מעלת ראובן בכורי' אתה כחי שהם ר"ת אבר"ך ניתנה ליוסף וכמ"ש בדברי הימים ובחללו יצועי אביו ניתנה בכורתו ליוסף בן ישראל.

21. Ibn Ezra, Bereishit 41:43.

אבן עזרא, בראשית מא:מג

אברך: כל אדם קורא לפניו אכרע ואשתחוה. וזו המלה מבנין הכבד הנוסף. ויברך על ברכיו מהקל וכלם מגזרת **ברכים**. ויאמר רבי יונה המדקדק הספרדי כי אברך שם הפועל והאל"ף תחת ה"א. כמו אשכם ושלוח. ולפי דעתי שאל"ף אשכם לשון המדבר.

22. See *Megaleh 'Amukot*, Parashat Va'ethanan, section 93.

ספר מגלה עמוקות, פרשת ואתחנן אופן צג

כדאיתא בזוהר (פרשת יתרו [ח"ב] עמוד קי"ט [זוהר ח"ב ס"ח ע"א]) משה ויוסף בחדא דרגא אזלא, לכן לקח יוסף בת כהן און (בראשית מא:מה), ומשה לקח אשה בת כהן מדין (שמות ב:כא). אבל לדעתי רזא עילאה הוא רזא דחכמתא, בסוד ויקח משה את עצמות יוסף עמו דייקא (שם שמות יג:יט), וקאי על מרכבה קדושה שסוד און שיוסף הוא ברזא דנער (בראשית לז:ב), דאיתמר גביה בכור שור הדר לו (דברים לג:יז), ל"ו דייקא נאה והדור לתקן פני שור, ולהפך אותו לקרוב שהוא בהיפוך אתוון בכור, וכשבתא במקום שור כרוב, אזי סוד המרכבה הוא בחשבון און. אבל המרכבה שהראה הקב"ה למשה שהיה פני שור מהשמאל, אזי אין הד' שלהם עולים רק למספר מדי"ן בנ' רבתי של אי"ק, שהוא חשבון תשנ"ד. ועל זה בקש משה עתה מאחר שהחלות להראות את עבדך, שהוא יוסף עבד נאמן, או על עצמו כשבא משה לזה העולם היה דיוקנו של יוסף עמו.

are composed of these letters identical. While we might have assumed that the word for firstborn, *bekhor*, should have been composed of the first of each series of numbers (i.e., *alef yud kuf*, totaling 111), we find instead a profound idea: In many societies, firstborn sons wielded unlimited power under the rule of primogeniture. Judaism rejects the philosophical underpinnings of this system, for Judaism teaches that the only creation *ex nihilo* (creation of matter from nothingness) is God's creation of the world. After the creation of Adam and Eve, all living things are extensions of previous generations. Thus, the "firstborn" is not first, he is an extension of the previous generation, hence the numerical value of *bekhor* (רכב) is 222.[23] The firstborn should see himself as an extension of his parents; indeed, the double portion assured the firstborn is a sort of compensation for the tremendous responsibility placed on the shoulders of the eldest son to care for the younger siblings[24] as a quasi-parent.[25]

No one in Tanakh embraces this responsibility as well as Yosef did. Yosef is the quintessential firstborn. Despite his brothers' treatment of him, he provides for all their needs for over seventy years, giving them shelter, food

---

23. See *Be'er Mayim Hayim*, Shmot, chapter 4.

ספר באר מים חיים, פרשת שמות פרק ד

ונראה שעל כן נקרא זה בלשון מרכבה, כי החכמה הוא בסוד כמאמר הכתוב קדש לי כל בכור וידוע אשר הקדש הוא בסוד החכמה שעל כן נקרא השבת קדש שהוא קדש מעצמו שמאיר בו בחינת אבא סוד החכמה מה שאין כן ימים טובים שנקראים מקרא קדש לפי שהם באימא, שהקדש שהוא אבא נעלם בתוכה כידוע מכוונות האר"י ז"ל. וגם כי הבכר נקרא ראשית בסוד (שמות כג:יט) ראשית בכורי אדמתך, וכל בחינת הבכורים כולם הם בבחינה הראשית כמו ראשון לרחם אשה או בהמה או ראשית פרי האדמה הנקרא ביכורים והכל כי הם בסוד החכמה הנקרא ראשית חכמה, וטעם שהחכמה הוא בסוד בכר מפני שהם השניה לאותיות אי"ק המורים על בחינת הכתר והשניים אליהם שהם בכר מורים על בחינת החכמה ועל כן נקרא החכמה בכר והוא עיקר הראשית והראשון להתגלות כי אור הכתר הוא טמיר וגנוז, ובכר הוא אותיות רכב מפני שהוא המרכבה להשראת אור הכתר ועל כן כל מקום השראת קדושתו נקרא מרכבה שהוא שורש רכב אותיות בכר סוד החכמה והיא המרכבה אל אור הכתר והבן. ועל כן אמרו חז"ל (בראשית רבה א:י) למה נברא העולם בב' שהוא לשון ברכה, כי העולם בכללו נקרא מרכבה אליו יתברך כמו שאמר הכתוב (ישעיהו סו:א) השמים כסאי והארץ הדום רגלי וכו' לצד שהוא משרה שכינתו בעולם הזה כמאמר חז"ל (במדבר רבה יג:ו) מן היום שברא הקב"ה את העולם נתאוה לדור עם בריותיו בתחתונים. וזה רכב אותיות ברך ועל כן נברא בב' שהוא מספר השני לאי"ק בחינת בכר שהוא אותיות ברך לשון ברכה כאמור, וזה שאמר הכתוב קדש לי כל בכר כי קדש פירוש זמן לי בחינת הבכר שיהיה קדש ומזומן למעני שאשרה אור קדושתי עליו והוא יעשה מרכבה אלי.

24. See Rav Yitzhak Hutner, *Maamarei Pahad Yitzhak*, Sukkot, chapter 54, especially sections 12 and 14.

25. From an oral lecture by Rabbi Yosef Soloveitchik.

and jobs. Yosef is not just a father for Par'oh, he is a father for all[26] of Egypt and the surrounding territories. He is the *mashbir hagadol*,[27] especially for his brothers.[28]

What, then, of Yaakov's "abandonment" of the Torah law that mandates a double portion for the firstborn? Prior to the Revelation at Sinai, the patriarchs were not bound by commandments *per se*. What set them apart, what made them spiritual giants worthy of fathering God's chosen people, was their ability to discern and live by the deep spiritual meaning of the Torah.[29] Their spiritual sensitivity to the will of God enabled them to live according to the same philosophical principles that would later be codified in the system of Torah law. On that plane, Yosef – not Reuven – was the true firstborn. When Reuven had an opportunity to save his younger brothers from sin, and at the same time save Yosef from death, he was only partially successful.[30]

---

26. The twelve tribes are associated with the twelve months. Significantly, Yosef is associated with the month of Av. See Rav Tzadok haKohen, *Pri Tzaddik*, Parashat Eikev, section 2.

ספר פרי צדיק, פרשת עקב אות ב

וחודש אב נברא באות ט' (כמו שאיתא בספר יצירה) שמורה על אור כי טוב ובזוהר הקדוש (ח"ב קנ"ב א') טית נהירו דחיין בכל אתר והוא כנגד קדושת יוסף הצדיק וכמו שחשב בזוהר הקדוש (שם קל"ה א') ט"ו באב כנגד מדת צדיק יסוד עולם.

27. See Bereishit 42:6.

בראשית מב:ו

וְיוֹסֵף הוּא הַשַּׁלִּיט עַל הָאָרֶץ הוּא **הַמַּשְׁבִּיר** לְכָל עַם הָאָרֶץ וַיָּבֹאוּ אֲחֵי יוֹסֵף וַיִּשְׁתַּחֲווּ לוֹ אַפַּיִם אָרְצָה:

28. See *Noam Elimelekh*, Parashat Shmot.

ספר נועם אלימלך, פרשת שמות

וזהו יש"ר א"ל והיראה נקרא בשם יעקב כמבואר לעיל והצדיק הנקרא בשם יעקב משגיח תמיד על העולם להשפיע להם כמדת יעקב כנ"ל הוא יכול להשפיע לעולם את שלש אלה דהיינו בני חיי ומזוני והמשכת שלשתם הוא על ידי מדרגת הנקרא בשם יוסף כמ"ש ברחל יוסף ה' לי בן אחר דהיינו שהיתה מרמזת למדרגה זו ולהמשיך לאותו מדרגה בני. ויוסף אמר העוד אבי חי רמז להמשיך חי' על ידי מדרגה זו כי למעלה מזו יש מדרגה הנקרא בשם אב והיה ממשיך משם חי'. ונאמר ויכלכל יוסף את אחיו היינו מזוני הוא גם כן על ידי מדרגה זו ושלש אלה הם נשפעים על ידי הצדיק הנקרא בשם יעקב.

29. The Ohr haHayim (Bereishit 49:3) maintains that the patriarchs only kept laws that they found useful, or more precisely, did not observe laws that they found an impediment to them. The *Shem mi'Shmuel* understands that Yaakov fulfilled the commandments – even if he didn't quite perform them. He explains that commandments have bodies and souls, and Avraham was attuned to the souls and therefore didn't need the "body" of the physical performance. The *Noam Elimelekh* (Parashat Devarim), states that Avraham achieved the spiritual perfection of someone who had performed all the commandments. For more on this concept see above, "The Universal and the Particular."

30. See Bereishit 37:21, 22, 29.

Later, in a desperate attempt to convince Yaakov to allow Binyamin to join him on a dangerous mission to Egypt, Reuven assures Yaakov that if any harm befalls Binyamin, Yaakov "can kill two of my sons."[31] This pathetic plea indicates that not only was Reuven not an effective parent for his younger siblings, he was guilty of gross malpractice in terms of his own children.

Yosef, on the other hand, is the true "father." His intelligence, his compassion, his dignity and his unwavering fidelity made him the object of admiration and emulation, trust and dependence for Potifar, Par'oh, and, eventually, for his own family. He was, from a very early age, a *ben zekunim*, a young man far wiser than his tender years, an *avreikh*, and an *even Yisrael*. He was as strong as an ox, and as beautiful and innocent as a *keruv*. His unique combination of attributes made him both father and son. For this reason, his death is included, along with the other patriarchs, in the book of Bereishit, as an extension of Yaakov. And when the book of Shmot begins with the death of all the brothers, Yosef, the brother who was once excluded from the family, is once again counted. He is counted twice, for he was both a son and a father.[32]

---

31. Bereishit 42:37.

32. See Rav Yitzhak Hutner, *Pahad Yitzhak*, Pesach, chapter 49, especially sections 1, 8 and 9.

Salvation

As Yaakov's last days approach, the sense of his own mortality becomes acute. He knows that he will soon depart from this world, and he has an overwhelming desire to impart a message to his children – a message of salvation. He gathers them together to share with them a vision of what will transpire at the end of days.

בראשית מט:א

וַיִּקְרָא יַעֲקֹב אֶל בָּנָיו וַיֹּאמֶר הֵאָסְפוּ וְאַגִּידָה לָכֶם אֵת אֲשֶׁר יִקְרָא אֶתְכֶם בְּאַחֲרִית הַיָּמִים:

And Yaakov called to his sons, and said, "Gather together, and I will tell you what shall befall you in the end of days." (Bereishit 49:1)

Then, instead of a clear picture of nirvana or apocalypse, we receive a series of messages, blessings, and rebukes. In the middle of all this, Yaakov makes a statement that is unclear both in terms of context and relevance:

בראשית מט:יח

לִישׁוּעָתְךָ קִוִּיתִי ה':

I await Your salvation, O God. (Bereishit 49:18)

It is unclear what these words mean, and their placement is even more confusing. Had these words been said in the beginning of the blessings, they would have provided context or background for everything Yaakov says to his sons: Yaakov takes stock of his life as he prepares his parting words to his sons, and he quite naturally reflects upon what might have been. Perhaps we could have read this phrase as an expression of missed opportunity, a prayer that his sons see the redemption he has not merited to see in his own lifetime. But these words are not in the preamble to the blessings.

Alternatively, we might expect these words to have been uttered after Yaakov finishes blessing each of his sons, as a general blessing for redemption – but they are not found at the end. They are found between the blessings of Dan and Gad, making it unclear if this is connected to Dan, or an introduction to the blessing of Gad, or perhaps blurted out in the middle, disconnected from either of the blessings it interrupts.[1]

Perhaps the blessings of Dan and Gad provide internal clues as to the meaning of this strange verse.

בראשית מט:טז–יט

דָּן יָדִין עַמּוֹ כְּאַחַד שִׁבְטֵי יִשְׂרָאֵל: יְהִי דָן נָחָשׁ עֲלֵי דֶרֶךְ שְׁפִיפֹן עֲלֵי אֹרַח הַנֹּשֵׁךְ עִקְּבֵי סוּס וַיִּפֹּל רֹכְבוֹ אָחוֹר: לִישׁוּעָתְךָ קִוִּיתִי ה': גָּד גְּדוּד יְגוּדֶנּוּ וְהוּא יָגֻד עָקֵב:

Dan shall judge his people, as one of the tribes of Israel. Dan shall be a serpent by the way, an adder in the path that bites the horse's heels, so that his rider shall fall backward. I await Your salvation, O God. Gad, a troop shall overcome him; but he shall overcome at the last [literally, heel]. (Bereishit 49:16–19)

Genesis

The tribe of Dan is the seventh to be blessed by Yaakov. First and foremost, Dan will be a judge, which is not surprising – the very name Dan evokes *din*, judgment. It is the second half of the verse, "as one of the tribes of Israel," that is problematic: Why, indeed, is Dan *like* a tribe of Israel? Dan *is* one of the tribes! And which tribe is he like? What follows is even more disturbing: Dan is compared to a serpent, biting the heels of the horse – causing the rider to tumble to the ground. Why the comparison to serpents? Ever since the Garden of Eden, serpents – especially venomous ones – have not enjoyed a wonderful reputation, making this a strange blessing indeed. The combination – judge and serpent – is particularly perplexing. And now that we have been thoroughly confused, Yaakov utters that terse, enigmatic verse: "I await Your salvation, O God."

Rashi[2] helps us decipher these difficult verses by explaining that the "judgment" associated with Dan is connected to vengeance, specifically

---

1. This suggestion is cited and rejected in *haKtav v'haKabbalah*, Bereishit 49:18.

הכתב והקבלה, בראשית מט:יח

וראיתי לי"מ בטעם המקרא, כי אז חזק החולי על יעקב והתפלל שיושיענו השם ויחזק עוד כחו עד שיברך גם שאר בניו: ואין טעם בזה, ומי הרשהו לעשות עצמו כמתנבא לאמר מה שלא ראה.

2. Rashi, Bereishit 49:16.

the vengeance exacted from the Philistines at the hands of a judge born to the tribe of Dan: Shimshon (Samson). Rashi's formulation draws a parallel between Shimshon of the tribe of Dan, and David of the tribe of Yehudah. Although Shimshon may remind us more of Goliath than of David, parallels between David and Shimshon may be found; most notably, both were warriors and both were victorious over the Philistines. Thus, Shimshon will be like David; the tribe of Dan will be "special," like Yehudah: both of these tribes will bring salvation to the Children of Israel.

Rashi stresses that Yaakov's blessing of Dan, and his allusion to Shimshon, is a prophecy. Indeed, the language and imagery of these verses sound as if Yaakov has had a vision. He sees a rider, a horse, and a serpent attacking from below. In this vision, Yaakov – who can no longer see – prophesizes, and it is the image of Shimshon, who in the end of his life also lost his sight, that comes to him. Blinded, humiliated, Shimshon implores God for one more burst of strength so that he can take down the "rider and horse," the Philistines and their cathedral.[3]

רש״י, בראשית מט:טז

דן ידין עמו: ינקום נקמת עמו מפלשתים כמו כי ידין ה' עמו.

כאחד שבטי ישראל: כל ישראל יהיו כאחד עמו ואת כולם ידין ועל שמשון נבא נבואה זו. ועוד יש לפרש כאחד שבטי ישראל כמיוחד שבשבטים הוא דוד שבא מיהודה.

3. See Bereishit Rabbah 98:14:

בראשית רבה, פרשה צח פסקה יד

"יהי דן נחש עלי דרך", מה נחש זה מצוי בין הנשים, כך שמשון בן מנוח מצוי בין הנשים, מה הנחש נאסר בשבועה, כך שמשון בן מנוח נאסר בשבועה, (שופטים טו) ויאמר להם שמשון השבעו לי, מה נחש זה כל כחו אינו אלא בראשו, כך שמשון (שופטים טז) "אם גולחתי וסר ממני כחי", מה הנחש הזה ריסו מחלחל לאחר המיתה, כך (שופטים טז) "ויהיו המתים אשר המית במותו וגו'", "הנושך עקבי סוס", (שופטים טז) "קראו לשמשון וישחק לנו". אמר ר' לוי כתיב (שופטים טז) ועל הגג כשלשת אלפים, אלו מה שהיו על שפת הגג אבל מה שהיו לאחוריהם ולאחורי אחוריהם אין בריה יודעת, ואת אמרת (שופטים טז) "וירדו אחיו וכל בית אביהו וישאו אותו ויעלו ויקברו אותו וגו'" בקבר מנוח אביו, אלא יעקב אבינו בקש רחמים על הדבר, "ויפול רוכבו אחור", יחזרו דברים לאחוריהם.

'"Dan shall be a serpent in the way' (Bereishit 49:17): As the serpent is found among women, so was Shimshon the son of Manoah found among women. As a serpent is bound by an oath, so was Shimshon the son of Manoah bound by an oath: 'And Shimshon said unto them: "Swear unto me"' (Shoftim 15:12). Just as all the serpent's strength resides in his head, so it was with Shimshon: 'If I be shaven, then my strength will go from me' (Shoftim 16:17). As a serpent's eyelid quivers after death, so [we read of Shimshon], 'So the dead that he slew at his death were more than they that he slew in his life' (Shoftim 16:30).

"'That bites the horse's heels': 'Call for Shimshon, that he may make us sport' (Shoftim

שופטים ט:כח–ל

וַיִּקְרָא שִׁמְשׁוֹן אֶל ה' וַיֹּאמַר ה' אֱלֹקִים זָכְרֵנִי נָא וְחַזְּקֵנִי נָא אַךְ הַפַּעַם הַזֶּה
הָאֱלֹקִים וְאִנָּקְמָה נְקַם אַחַת מִשְּׁתֵי עֵינַי מִפְּלִשְׁתִּים: וַיִּלְפֹּת שִׁמְשׁוֹן אֶת שְׁנֵי
עַמּוּדֵי הַתָּוֶךְ אֲשֶׁר הַבַּיִת נָכוֹן עֲלֵיהֶם וַיִּסָּמֵךְ עֲלֵיהֶם אֶחָד בִּימִינוֹ וְאֶחָד בִּשְׂמֹאלוֹ:
וַיֹּאמֶר שִׁמְשׁוֹן תָּמוֹת נַפְשִׁי עִם פְּלִשְׁתִּים וַיֵּט בְּכֹחַ וַיִּפֹּל הַבַּיִת עַל הַסְּרָנִים וְעַל כָּל
הָעָם אֲשֶׁר בּוֹ וַיִּהְיוּ הַמֵּתִים אֲשֶׁר הֵמִית בְּמוֹתוֹ רַבִּים מֵאֲשֶׁר הֵמִית בְּחַיָּיו:

*And Shimshon called to God, and said, "Almighty God, remember
me, I pray you, and strengthen me, I pray you, only this once, O God,
that I may be avenged this one time of the Philistines for my two
eyes." And Shimshon took hold of the two middle pillars upon which
the house stood, and he supported himself on them, on one with his
right hand, and on the other with his left. And Shimshon said, "Let
me die with the Philistines." And he pulled with all his might; and the
house fell upon the lords, and upon all the people who were in there.
So the dead whom he slew at his death were more than those whom
he slew in his life. (Shoftim 16:28–30)*

Judges 16: 28-30

According to Rashi, this is the scene that appears in Yaakov's vision. He
hears Shimshon's prayer to God: "Almighty God, remember me, I pray
you, and strengthen me, I pray you, only this once, O God, that I may be
avenged this one time of the Philistines for my two eyes." According to
Rashi, Yaakov's enigmatic words as he blesses Dan, Shimshon's forebear,
"I await Your salvation, O God," are parallel to Shimshon's prayer, a
paraphrase of what Yaakov saw in his vision of the future.

Although visions are often messages communicated in symbolic fashion,
we would be more comfortable with Rashi's interpretation had Shimshon
uttered the identical words found in the closing line of Yaakov's blessing for
Dan, or vice versa. A slightly different formulation, found in the Ramban's
commentary, avoids this problem.

16:25). R. Levi said: It is written, 'And there were upon the roof about three thousand
men and women' (Shoftim 16:27). These were the number on the edge of the roof, but
no one knows how many were behind them, yet you read, 'Then his brethren and all
the house of his father came down, and took him, and brought him up, and buried
him...in the burying place of Manoah his father' (Shoftim16:31)! This was because our
ancestor Yaakov prayed for mercy: 'So that his rider falls backward' – let all return to
their place."

The Ramban[4] agrees that Yaakov's vision is about Shimshon. Other than Shimshon, there never was a judge who fell into the hands of the enemy. For this reason, Shimshon is compared to a serpent, but to a very specific serpent: Like the serpent in Eden, Shimshon fell from an exalted position. Like the serpent,[5] the fruit of the vine was forbidden to Shimshon. Like the serpent, Shimshon's desire for a forbidden woman[6] caused his downfall.[7] He, too, was humbled, lowered from his previous stature. In the case of the serpent, his physical stature was forever to reflect the lowliness of his spiritual stature. In Shimshon's case, he fell into the hands of the enemy. When Shimshon loses his strength, the causes are clear: Shimshon's transgressions against personal restrictions – the foreign woman, drinking wine and cutting his hair – may be seen as transgressions against the natural state in which he had been commanded to live his life, a state we may identify as an "Eden-like existence." It is these transgrssions that turn him from savior to serpent. Shimshon does not bring authentic salvation. Despite his enormous capabilities, Shimshon does not live up to his potential.

Yaakov saw all of this in his deathbed vision; according to the Ramban, Yaakov sees that Shimshon would fail in his mission as savior. In Yaakov's vision, he sees the *nahash*, the serpent, biting the heel of the horse, a

---

4. Ramban, Bereishit 49:18.

רמב״ן, בראשית מט:יח

לישועתך קויתי ה': לא היה בכל שופטי ישראל מי שנפל ביד אויביו זולתי שמשון שהוא הנחש הזה, כדכתיב (שופטים ב:יח) והיה ה' עם השופט והושיעם מיד אויביהם כל ימי השופט והוא היה האחרון לשופטים, כי שמואל נביא היה ולא נלחם להם, ובימיו מלכו המלכים, וכאשר ראה הנביא תשועת שמשון כי נפסקה אמר לישועתך קויתי ה', לא לישועת נחש ושפיפון, כי בך אושע לא בשופט, כי תשועתך תשועת עולמים.

5. See Zohar, Bereishit 36a: The serpent loses his legs when he seduces Hava to partake of the fruit of the Tree of Knowledge of Good and Evil. According to the Zohar this tree was a vine, and the fruit was grapes – the drink that causes confusion between good and evil.

6. One wonders if, aside from an etymological similarity, Delilah is "related" to Lilit.

7. According to rabbinic teachings, the serpent was motivated by lust for Eve, a woman he could not have. See Rashi, Bereishit 3:1.

רש״י, בראשית ג:א

והנחש היה ערום: מה ענין זה לכאן היה לו לסמוך ויעש לאדם ולאשתו כתנות עור וילבישם אלא ללמדך מאיזו סבה קפץ הנחש עליהם ראה אותם ערומים ועוסקים בתשמיש לעין כל ונתאוה לה.

symbol of pride and power. The horse falls over, crushing and killing the rider – but also killing the serpent. This is a symbolic representation of Shimshon's death,[8] and Yaakov cries out to God: "I await Your salvation, O God:[9] I have not despaired of the final outcome. Shimshon will not be the *Mashiah*, but a true savior will yet come. And even though he may tarry, I (and my descendants) will not lose faith in Your salvation."

For the ultimate redeemer, the Jewish people would have to wait. Shimshon from the tribe of Dan is *like* one of the great tribes; Dan is *like* Yehudah. Shimshon is *like* David, who will eventually have the true *Mashiah* come from his lineage, but Shimshon fails – he proves to be a serpent, not a messiah.[10] The Ari"zal points out the proximity between the Hebrew words

---

8. For this description spelled out fully see the Alshikh, *Torat Moshe* 49:17.

ספר תורת משה, בראשית מט:יז

אמר כי שמשון יהי כנחש עלי דרך, כי תשועתו החילה על ידי היותו נוטר איבה כנחש, שעל שנתנו האשה אשר לו יעדה, למרעהו, הלך במשטמות ושרף בלפידים ועד קמה ועד כרם זית, ואחר כך בלחי החמור הכה אלף איש. ובאחרון היה לו כמשל שפיפון עלי אורח צר, שנושך עקבי סוס מאחוריו. ומכאב עקביו מגביה הסוס ידיו ומפיל רוכבו אחור ונופל הסוס ורוכבו על השפיפון וימות גם הוא. כן קרה לו לשמשון שנדמה לשפיפון שאחז בכח העמודים אשר הבית נכון עליהם, שהם עקבי הבית שידמו לעקבי סוס, ויהי כנושך ואוחז בהם, ויפלו כל הרוכבים ויושבים על הבית עם הבית וימות גם הוא. באופן היתה תשועת ישראל על ידי מה שלא הושיע את עצמו כי מת, ואין זו תשועה אמיתית, כי אם (יז:יז) לישועתך קויתי ה' שהיא הפך זה – והוא ענין מאמרם ז"ל בכמה מקומות (שוחר טוב תהלים צח:א) מציינו שתשועתו של הקב"ה תשועתן של ישראל, זה ה' קוינו לו נגילה ונשמחה בישועתו, ובהושיע את עצמו יושיע אותנו – והוא הפך שמשון שאת עצמו לא הושיע ואנחנו נושענו.

9. Rabbeinu Bahya agrees with the Ramban that Shimshon is a failed leader, and therefore may be referred to as a serpent, yet he allows for Rashi's interpretation – that it may have been Yaakov putting words into Shimshon's mouth and not Yaakov praying upon seeing the failed Shimshon.

רבינו בחיי, בראשית מט:יח

לישועתך קויתי ה': כתב הרמב"ן ז"ל כי הכתוב הזה תפלת יעקב לפי שראה ברוה"ק כי היה שמשון המושיע אחרון לשופטים, ואע"פ שהיה שמואל אחריו נביא היה ולא היה נלחם כמוהו ולפיכך כשראה יעקב כי תשועת שמשון נפסקה עמו ומת בנפילת הרוכב יחדו אמר לישועתך קויתי ה' לא לישועת שמשון הנמשל לנחש ושפיפון.

ויתכן לפרש כי הוא תפלת שמשון כי ראה יעקב אחרית השופט הזה האחרון כי הוא הנושך והמפיל הרוכב אחור, והוא המתפלל לישועתך קויתי ה' שכן התפלל (שופטים טז) זכרני נא וחזקני נא אך הפעם הזה האלהים, ואע"פ שמת בכללם הנה זאת תשועתו שינקם מאויביו וימות עמהם כי בזה היה חפץ כמ"ש (שם) תמות נפשי עם פלשתים.

10. The Midrash says that when Yaakov saw Shimshon, he thought he was the *Mashiah*. See Bereishit Rabbah 98:14. "Our ancestor Yaakov saw him [Shimshon] and thought that he was the *Mashiah*. But when he saw him dead he exclaimed, 'He too is dead! Then I [continue to] wait for Your salvation, O God'" (Bereishit 49:18).

for serpent and savior, נחש and משיח: as he so often does, the Ari"zal points out that the numerical values of these two words are identical. [11]

Rabbeinu Bahya's[12] formulation is in a similar vein: Yaakov utters these enigmatic words when he sees the failure of Dan's descendant and he cries out in a moment of frustration. And then Yaakov looks ahead, to another tribe, for this salvation.

Had Yaakov maintained the age order of the brothers, he should have blessed Naftali after Dan; instead, the next tribe Yaakov blesses is Gad. Therefore, we may infer that Gad somehow is meant to follow Dan in terms of the essence of the prophecy.[13]

Yaakov's blessing for Gad is short but contains at least one word that links it with the blessing bestowed upon Dan:

בראשית מט:יט

גָּד גְּדוּד יְגוּדֶנּוּ וְהוּא יָגֻד עָקֵב:

Gad, a troop shall overcome him; but he shall overcome at the last [literally, heel]. (Bereishit 49:19)

The word *akev* is found in Yaakov's blessing to Dan, as the heel of the horse that the serpent attacks, and in the blessing of Gad, referring to the eventual victory. The word *akev* is relatively unusual in the Torah. The first use of this word is back in the Garden of Eden, and the context is the punishment of the serpent.

בראשית ג:יד

וַיֹּאמֶר ה' אֱלֹקִים אֶל הַנָּחָשׁ...הוּא יְשׁוּפְךָ רֹאשׁ וְאַתָּה תְּשׁוּפֶנּוּ עָקֵב:

---

11. See *Sefer haLikutim*, Shoftim, chapter 5.

ספר הליקוטים, ספר שופטים פרק ה

וכראות יעקב אבינו זה, אמר לישועתך קויתי ה', כי לא בזה שחשבתיו משי"ח, נהפך לנח"ש, כי כן עולה בגימטריא. ונתקטעו רגליו, ונקרא שפיפון, שני פעמים שפי, כי חיגר בשתי רגליו היה, כמ"ש רז"ל.

12. Rabbeinu Bahya, Bereishit 49:19.

רבינו בחיי, בראשית מט:יט

ובמדרש והוא יגוד עקב כיון שראה יעקב לשמשון הבא מדן אמר לישועתך קויתי ה', אין זה מביא את הגאולה אלא מגד, והוא יגוד עקב אותו שבא בעקב שנאמר (מלאכי ג) הנה אנכי שולח לכם את אליה הנביא שהוא מגד, ע"כ בב"ר.

13. This is not the only instance in this chapter that the blessings of the tribes do not adhere to their order of birth. See below.

And the Almighty God said to the serpent...he shall bruise your head, and you shall bruise his heel. (Bereishit 3:14)

The "original serpent" is associated with the heel; Dan is compared to the serpent attacking the heel of the horse. On the other hand, Gad, the next tribe to be blessed, is also associated with a heel. As we shall see, this is no simple literary device; the connection expressed by the recurring word *akev* is part and parcel of Yaakov's vision of the Messianic Age.

Dan, through Shimshon, is like David the Redeemer. Gad, in turn, is like Dan. Whereas Dan (Shimshon) will fail,[14] Gad will eventually bring about redemption. Yet this raises a different question: how do we reconcile these elements of Yaakov's blessing, of Yaakov's prophecy, with the blessing Yaakov bestows on Yehudah:

בראשית מט:י

לֹא יָסוּר שֵׁבֶט מִיהוּדָה וּמְחֹקֵק מִבֵּין רַגְלָיו עַד כִּי יָבֹא שִׁילֹה וְלוֹ יִקְּהַת עַמִּים:

The scepter shall not depart from Yehudah, nor the ruler's staff from between his feet, until Shiloh arrives; and unto him shall the obedience of the peoples be. (Bereishit 49:10)

Redemption comes from Yehudah, through *Mashiah ben David*. What, then, is Gad's role in the messianic process?

The Midrash states that Eliyahu, the precursor of the *Mashiah*, was from the tribe of Gad.

בראשית רבה, פרשה עא פסקה ט

"וַתֹּאמֶר לֵאָה בָּא גָד": אתיא גדא דביתא; אתא גדא דעלמא: בא מי שעתיד לגדד משתיתן של עובדי כוכבים. ומנו? אליהו.

"And Leah said: 'Ba gad (fortune has come)'" (Bereishit 30:11): the fortune of the house has come; the fortune of the world has come; he who will overthrow (gadad) the foundations of the heathen has

---

14. There is another person who is a son of Dan who may be related to our present topic: Hushim, son of Dan, who kills Esav at Yaakov's funeral. It is interesting that while Shimshon has gone blind yet can still hear, Hushim can see but cannot hear. Significantly, Hushim (in Hebrew) is an anagram of *Mashiah*.

come. And who is this person? This is Eliyahu.[15] (Bereishit Rabbah 71:9)

The name of Eliyahu's father[16] is never mentioned in the text; this lacuna makes identification of his tribe quite challenging. We do know that he is

---

15. Despite the unequivocal statement of Eliyahu's lineage, the Midrash does proceed to debate the subject:

בראשית רבה, פרשה עא:ט

אליהו משל מי ר' אליעזר אמר משל בנימין, דכתיב (דברי הימים א ח) ויערשיה ואליה וזכרי בני ירוחם כל אלה בני בנימין, ר' נהוראי אמר משל גד היה, הה"ד (מלכים א יז) ויאמר אליהו התשבי מתושבי גלעד. א"ר פליפי בר נהוראי מאן חזית למימר כן, א"ל דכתיב (יהושע יג) ויהי להם הגבול יעזר וכל ערי הגלעד, מה מקיים ר' אלעזר קרא דר' נהוראי מתושבי גלעד מיושבי לשכת הגזית הוה, ומה מקיים ר' נהוראי קרא דר' אלעזר ויערשיה ואליהו אלא מדרשות הן, בשעה שהיה הקב"ה מרעיש עולמו היה מזכיר זכות אבות בני ירוחם והקב"ה מתמלא רחמים על עולמו. פעם אחת נחלקו רבותינו בדבר אלו אומרים משל גד ואלו אומרים משל בנימין בא ועמד לפניהם, א"ל רבותינו מה אתם נחלקים עלי אני מבני בניה של רחל אני.

"The rabbis debated: To which tribe did Eliyahu belong? R. Eliezer said: To Benjamin, for it is written, 'And Ya'areshiah and Eliyahu and Zikhri were the sons of Yeruham.... All these were the sons of Binyamin' (I Divrei haYamim 8:27, 40). R. Nehorai said: To Gad, for it says, 'And Eliyahu the Tishbite, who was of the settlers of Gil'ad, said...' (I Melakhim 17:1). Said R. Filippi to R. Nehorai: What reason have you for saying so? He replied: Because it is written, 'And their border was Yazer, and all the cities of Gil'ad' (Yehoshua 13:25). How does R. Eliezer interpret the verse quoted by R. Nehorai? 'Of the inhabitants of Gil'ad' means 'of those who sat in the Hall of Hewn Stones.' And how does R. Nehorai interpret the verse quoted by R. Eliezer, 'And Ya'areshiah and Eliyahu'? These names are meant for allegorical interpretation: when He [God] would shake (*mar'ish*) the world [in His wrath], Eliyahu would recall (*mazkir*) the merit of the ancestors, whereupon, lo, 'the sons of Yeruham,' which means that God is filled with compassion (*rahamim*) for His world. On one occasion our rabbis were debating about him [Eliyahu], some maintaining that he belonged to the tribe of Gad, others, to the tribe of Binyamin. Whereupon he came and stood before them and said, 'Sirs, why do you debate about me? I am a descendant of Rahel'" (Bereishit Rabbah 71:9).

16. See Rabbi Moshe Cordovero (*Pardes Rimonim*, gate 24, chapter 14), who cites a mystical teaching in the name of Rabbi Moshe de Leon that Eliyahu's father is never mentioned because Eliyahu was not born; he was an angel and hence returned to heaven when his mission was complete.

ספר פרדס רמונים, שער כד פרק יד

שוב מצאנו בשם ר' משה דליאון ז"ל ועל מה ששאלת בענין אליהו שעלה למרום מה שלא עלה אדם אחר. תדע לך כי בסתרי תורה ראיתי סוד נפלא עד מאד. אליהו לא תמצא לו בכל התורה אב ואם ולא שכתוב בן בן פלוני אלא אליהו התשבי מתושבי גלעד. ואמרו כי קודם לכן ירד מן השמים ושמו ידוע בסתרי החכמה. ועוד שאח"כ נראה אל החכמים_בהרבה מקומות בהרבה דיוקנין ולזמנים בדמות טייעא ולזמנים כפרש לזמנים כא' מגדולי הדור בהרבה עניינים דמותו ותוארו.

from Gil'ad (geographically associating him with the tribe of Gad). Another Midrashic comment on these verses sheds more light:

בראשית רבה, פרשה צט פסקה י

כיון שראה אותו יעקב, אמר "לישועתך קויתי ה'" – אין זה מביא את הגאולה אלא מגד, שנאמר, (בראשית מט) "גד גדוד יגודנו והוא יגוד עקב" – לאותו שהוא בא בעקב: (מלאכי ג) "הנה אנכי שולח לכם את אליה הנביא" שהוא משבט גד. לכך נאמר "והוא יגוד עקב".

When Yaakov saw him [Shimshon] he exclaimed, "I [still] await Your salvation, O God": not he will bring the redemption, but [one descended] from Gad, as it says, "Gad, a troop shall troop upon him, but he shall troop upon their heel (Bereishit 49:18), which alludes to him who will come at the end [literally, heel]: "Behold, I will send you Eliyahu the Prophet before the coming of the great and terrible day of God" (Malakhi 3:23). He was of the tribe of Gad, and for that reason it says, "but he shall troop upon their heel." (Bereishit Rabbah 99:10)

[handwritten margin note: Genesis 49:18 / I wait for thy salvation, O LORD.]

Not *Mashiah*, rather the precursor of *Mashiah*, the harbinger of *Mashiah*, will come from Gad – this is Eliyahu, the herald of *Mashiah*.

Gad and Dan are linked in their messianic roles. Yaakov, who is searching for a vision of *Mashiah*, sees someone with the potential to be *Mashiah*, only to be disappointed: Simshon will be a failed (not a false) *Mashiah*. Then the spotlight turns to Gad, who will give rise to Eliyahu, the herald of *Mashiah*.

This connection may shed light on the blessings given by Moshe to these two tribes. As Moshe takes leave of the nation, he, too, blesses the tribes. Once again, Naftali is skipped; once again, Dan and Gad are mentioned together, but this time the order is inverted, and Gad precedes Dan:

דברים לג:כ–כב

וּלְגָד אָמַר, בָּרוּךְ מַרְחִיב גָּד כְּלָבִיא שָׁכֵן וְטָרַף זְרוֹעַ אַף קָדְקֹד: וַיַּרְא רֵאשִׁית לוֹ כִּי שָׁם חֶלְקַת מְחֹקֵק סָפוּן וַיֵּתֵא רָאשֵׁי עָם צִדְקַת ה' עָשָׂה וּמִשְׁפָּטָיו עִם יִשְׂרָאֵל: וּלְדָן אָמַר דָּן גּוּר אַרְיֵה יְזַנֵּק מִן הַבָּשָׁן:

And of Gad he said, "Blessed be He who enlarges Gad; he lives as a lion, and tears the arm with the crown of the head. And he provided

*the first part for himself, because there, in a portion of the lawgiver,
was he seated; and he came with the heads of the people, he executed
the justice of God, and his judgments with Israel." And of Dan he
said, "Dan is a lion's cub; he shall leap from Bashan." (Devarim
33:20–22)*

Here both Gad and Dan are referred to as lions, evoking traits of royalty, of
courage and leadership. Significantly, Yehudah[17] is referred to as a lion by
Yaakov: royalty will come from Yehudah, the scepter will not depart from
Yehudah. If that is the case, why does Moshe refer to Gad and Dan as lions,
indicating royalty?

The Midrash teaches that the blessings given to each tribe were actually
given to the collective Jewish people, and even though a preponderance of
leadership is found in Yehudah some was spread among the other tribes.

בראשית רבה, פרשה צט פסקה ד

כל אלה שבטי ישראל שנים עשר וגו': כבר כתיב "ויברך אותם" ומה ת"ל "איש
אשר כברכתו ברך אותם"? אלא לפי שבירכן יהודה באריה, דן בנחש, נפתלי
באילה, בנימין בזאב, חזר וכללן כולן כאחד ועשאן אריות ועשאן נחשים. תדע
שהוא כן: "יהי דן נחש", והוא קורא אותו אריה, הה"ד (דברים לג) "דן גור
אריה". לקיים מה שנאמר, (שה"ש ד) "כולך יפה רעיתי ומום אין בך".

*"All these are the twelve tribes of Israel, etc." (Bereishit 49:28): "And
he blessed them" is already written; why add "everyone according
to his blessing he blessed them"? But because he had blessed them,
comparing Yehudah to a lion, Dan to a serpent, Naftali to a hind
and Binyamin to a wolf, he subsequently included them altogether as
one, declaring them all to be lions and serpents. The proof lies in this:
"Dan shall be a serpent" (ibid. 49:17) – yet he [Moshe] calls him a
lion: "Dan is a lion's whelp" (Devarim 33:22). This is in confirmation
of the verse "You are all fair, my love, and there is no blemish in you
(Shir haShirim 4:7). (Bereishit Rabbah 99:4)*

According to this teaching there is something fluid, almost interchangeable,
about the various parts that make up the twelve tribes: Moshe sees the

---

17. Bereishit 49:8–10.

attributes of a lion in both Gad and Dan – even though primarily the lion is associated with Yehudah.

We know that *Mashiah* is a descendant of the tribe of Yehudah; this is one of the messages that Yaakov shares with Yehudah when he blesses him:

בראשית מט:ח–י

יְהוּדָה אַתָּה יוֹדוּךָ אַחֶיךָ יָדְךָ בְּעֹרֶף אֹיְבֶיךָ יִשְׁתַּחֲווּ לְךָ בְּנֵי אָבִיךָ: גּוּר אַרְיֵה יְהוּדָה מִטֶּרֶף בְּנִי עָלִיתָ כָּרַע רָבַץ כְּאַרְיֵה וּכְלָבִיא מִי יְקִימֶנּוּ:לֹא יָסוּר שֵׁבֶט מִיהוּדָה וּמְחֹקֵק מִבֵּין רַגְלָיו עַד כִּי יָבֹא שילה וְלוֹ יִקְּהַת עַמִּים:

Yehudah, your brothers shall praise you; your hand shall be on the neck of your enemies; your father's sons shall bow down before you. Yehudah is a lion's whelp; from the prey, my son, you will rise. He stooped down, he couched as a lion, and as a lioness; who shall rouse him up? The scepter shall not depart from Yehudah, nor the ruler's staff from between his feet, until Shiloh arrives; and unto him shall the obedience of the peoples be. (Bereishit 49:8–10)

Rashi, based on Targum Onkelos, explains the phrase "until Shiloh arrives" as, "until the arrival of the *Mashiah*." The scepter is in the domain of Yehudah forever; *Mashiah* will come from Yehudah. But a potential for salvation existed in Dan, and the precursor is in Gad. In his prophecy, Moshe sees this potential, as did Yaakov, and he refers to both Gad and Dan as lions.

Gad's role in the Messianic Age is manifest in the figure of Eliyahu, but where do we find an active role for Dan? Was there a historical figure from the tribe of Dan who played a role in the redemptive process? Indeed, there was: when the Mishkan was built, the major role was that of the chief architect, Bezalel from the tribe of Yehudah. There was, however, a major auxiliary role performed by Oholiav, the son of Ahisamakh, from the tribe of Dan.

שמות לא:א–ו

וַיְדַבֵּר ה' אֶל מֹשֶׁה לֵּאמֹר: רְאֵה קָרָאתִי בְשֵׁם בְּצַלְאֵל בֶּן אוּרִי בֶן חוּר לְמַטֵּה יְהוּדָה: וָאֲמַלֵּא אֹתוֹ רוּחַ אֱלֹקִים בְּחָכְמָה וּבִתְבוּנָה וּבְדַעַת וּבְכָל מְלָאכָה: לַחְשֹׁב מַחֲשָׁבֹת לַעֲשׂוֹת בַּזָּהָב וּבַכֶּסֶף וּבַנְּחֹשֶׁת: וּבַחֲרֹשֶׁת אֶבֶן לְמַלֹּאת וּבַחֲרֹשֶׁת עֵץ לַעֲשׂוֹת בְּכָל מְלָאכָה: וַאֲנִי הִנֵּה נָתַתִּי אִתּוֹ אֵת אָהֳלִיאָב בֶּן אֲחִיסָמָךְ לְמַטֵּה דָן וּבְלֵב כָּל חֲכַם לֵב נָתַתִּי חָכְמָה וְעָשׂוּ אֵת כָּל אֲשֶׁר צִוִּיתִךָ:

And God spoke to Moshe, saying: "Behold, I have called by name Bezalel son of Uri son of Hur of the tribe of Yehudah. And I will fill him with the Spirit of God, with wisdom and insight and knowledge of every craft, to perform accurate calculations and create in gold and in silver and in brass. And in cutting of stones, to set them, and in carving of timber, to work in all kinds of workmanship. And behold, I have given with him Oholiav, the son of Ahisamakh, of the tribe of Dan; and in the hearts of all who are wise hearted I have put wisdom, that they may make all that I have commanded you." (Shmot 31:1–6)

Exodus 31:1–6

The creation of the Mishkan, the seat of God, is a Yehuda/Dan production. The Pesikta teaches that the same two tribes were responsible for the building of the First Beit haMikdash.[18] Similarly, one of the central roles of the *Mashiah* is the building of the Beit haMikdash. We can now understand that although Dan, via Shimshon, failed to *be* the *Mashiah*, Dan successfully carried out a major supporting role in building the Mishkan and the first Beit haMikdash. Gad, too, succeeds in a supporting role, in the person of Eliyahu. But these are not one-time successes; these roles are paradigms for the future, for the final redemption.

When Yaakov blesses his sons, the tribes of Gad and Dan are not the only ones listed out of order. The first four tribes are blessed in the order of their birth: Reuven, Shimon, Levi, Yehudah. The next son born is Yissakhar, followed by Zevulun, but when Yaakov blesses them Yissakhar and Zevulun are inverted. These two tribes are generally found in close proximity to Yehudah, as in the encampment in the desert they flanked Yehudah on each side. Here, too, the positions are paradigmatic: the shifts

---

18. Pesikta Rabbati, parashah 5.

פסיקתא רבתי פרשה ו

דבר אחר ותשלם כל המלאכה את מוצא כשנעשה המשכן שני שבטים היו שותפין במלאכתן א"ר לוי בשם ר' חמא בי ר' חנינא שבטו של דן ושבטו של יהודה שבטו של דן אהליאב בצלאל שבטו של יהודה בן אחיסמך למטה דן וכן במלאכת המקדש שני השבטים הללו היו שותפין וישלח המלך שלמה [ויקח את חירם וגו'] (מלכים א ז:יג) בן אלמנה הוא ממטה דן ושלמה בן דוד שהיה משבטו של יהודה א"ר לוי בשם ר' חמא בי ר' חנינא מכאן שאין אדם צריך להיות מחליף בצירו והיה שדי בצירך (איוב כב:כה) אתה הוא אלקינו ובצירנו ואנו עמיך אמר דוד כי הוא אלקינו ואנחנו עם מרעיתו וצאן ידו היום אם בקולו תשמעו (תהלים צה:ו).

in the sequence of the tribes all revolve around Yehudah and the concept of *Mashiah*, the major focus of the end of days.

According to the Midrash, the tribes of Yissakhar and Zevulun had an agreement between them: Zevulun embarked on maritime expeditions, while Yissakhar remained behind and was involved in spiritual quests.[19] Yissakhar represents Torah, Zevulun represents business, and these tribes created a symbiosis, dividing responsibility for these two spheres between them and sharing between them the benefits of both pursuits. Yehudah, who represents leadership, kingship, the *Mashiah*, must be flanked by business leaders and Torah sages. Their support is essential for his success. Interestingly, Yaakov inverts the order and places the business leaders before the Torah scholars.

Ultimately, Yaakov's blessings represent his vision of the end of days, of the Messianic Age. Although Yaakov does not tell us clearly what will take place, it is clear that Yaakov had a detailed vision of the elements of the end of days. From our perspective some four thousand years later, we can easily appreciate why the message was cloudy: had the Jewish people known that salvation was so far away, the frustration and despair could have been devastating. And yet, Yaakov himself did not despair: "I await Your salvation, O God!" Yaakov knew with full certainty that the *Mashiah ben David*, from the tribe of Yehudah, will come. Yaakov saw that *Mashiah* will be preceded by Eliyahu from the tribe of Gad, flanked by the scrupulously honest businesspeople of the tribe of Zevulun and empowered by men and women of Torah, descendants of Yissakhar. He will be aided in the

---

19. See Rashi, Bereishit 49:13; also, see Midrash Rabbah Bamidbar 13:16.

רש"י, בראשית מט:יג

זבולן לחוף ימים: על חוף ימים תהיה ארצו. חוף כתרגומו ספר מרק"א בלע"ז (יבמות מח) והוא יהיה מצוי תדיר על חוף אניות במקום הנמל שאניות מביאות שם פרקמטיא שהיה זבולן עוסק בפרקמטיא וממציא מזון לשבט יששכר (תנחומא) והם עוסקים בתורה הוא שאמר משה (דברים לג) שמח זבולן בצאתך ויששכר באהליך זבולן יוצא בפרקמטיא ויששכר עוסק בתורה באהלים.

במדבר רבה, פרשה יג פסקה טז

זבולן לחוף ימים ישכון: מזרק אחד כסף כנגד הארץ שהיא עשויה ככדור שהיתה חלק יששכר שנאמר (שם) וירא מנוחה כי טוב וגו' שלשים ומאה משקלה מזרק אחד וגו' הרי מאתים כנגד מאתים ראשי סנהדראות שהיו בשבט יששכר שנאמר ראשיהם מאתים ולכך תלה חשבון הגדול בזבולן לפי שגדול מעשה יותר מן העושה שלולי זבולן לא היה יששכר יכול לעסוק בתורה שהוא היה מאכילו ונותן לתוך פיו.

building of the Beit haMikdash by spiritual descendants of Dan. And as we wait for that great day, we can only echo Yaakov's conviction:

לִישׁוּעָתְךָ קִוִּיתִי ה'!
I await Your salvation, O God!